D1528187

American Conservatism:
History, Theory, and Practice

American Conservatism:
History, Theory, and Practice

By

Brian Farmer

CAMBRIDGE SCHOLARS PRESS

American Conservatism: History, Theory, and Practice, by Brian Farmer

This book first published 2005 by

Cambridge Scholars Press

15 Angerton Gardens, Newcastle, NE5 2JA, UK

British Library Cataloguing in Publication Data
A catalogue record for this book is available from the British Library

ISBN 1-904303-54-4

Contents

Chapter One

Introduction

The Continued Preeminence of Ideology

At mid-Twentieth Century, noted scholars Henry Aiken (1956), Daniel Bell (1960), and Morton White (1956) were arguing that ideology was no longer as important as it once was. What these scholars and others essentially argued was that rational analysis was taking the place of ideology in politics and that there had been an exhaustion of political ideas in advanced industrial democracies that had culminated in acceptance of welfare-State capitalism. There would still be political conflict for sure, but the basic idea that government intervention into the free market was necessary for steady and more even economic growth and that social action was a proper realm for government at least to some degree, had been accepted by all mainstream political parties. For example, in 1936, Democrat Franklin Roosevelt campaigned on continuation of the New Deal while his opponent, Republican Alfred Landon, essentially campaigned on continuation of the New Deal as well, with the exception that he professed that he could do it more efficiently and without deficits (Roark et al., 2005, 899). For the purposes here, whether the New Deal could be administered more efficiently and without deficits is beside the point. The fact is that both parties were essentially accepting the New Deal programs as within the proper scope of government responsibility, and major ideological divisions over the proper role of government had been minimized.

These ideological differences, however, were perhaps never quite as "minimized" as Aiken, Bell, and White inferred; rather, the public had so greatly accepted the New Deal during the Great Depression that all the Conservatives could do politically was go along with ideas that were fundamental violations of their ideology. The ideological underpinnings of conservatism would continue unreformed among a core minority in the Depression and World War II years only to be released with a vengeance later. Indeed, given the McCarthyism and anti-communist paranoia that gripped the Nation in the early post-war years, it is evident that Aiken, Bell, and White were somehow overlooking the right-wing anti-communist hysteria of the 1950s that immediately preceded their writings. At any rate, it

1

is difficult to consider the Cold War and McCarthyism and conclude that the Nation was experiencing "an end of ideology" in any real sense of the word. Instead, conservatives had acquiesced to the New Deal only due to its popular support, and liberals had jumped on to the anticommunist Cold War bandwagon for similar reasons, thus providing the outward appearance of ideological congruence, when in reality the old conservative/liberal divide was still raging underneath.

In contrast to the superficially closer ideological congruence of the two major Parties at mid-Twentieth Century, the appearance of ideological congruence of the two major Parties in the early Twenty-First Century appears to have greatly eroded. Furthermore, the policies of the Republican Party and conservatives in general in the United States since WWII (as will be demonstrated in the pages that follow) have been driven more by ideologies than by pragmatism and sound analysis, thus destroying the apparent ideological congruence that had developed from the Great Depression until the Vietnam War era. Furthermore, the ideologies that have driven America's more recent "conservative revolution," whether it be the "Reagan Revolution," Newt Gingrich's "Contract with America," or the present "Compassionate Conservatism" of the George W. Bush administration, are ideologies that have been pursued repeatedly throughout American history. Thus, the "new conservatism" lacks little in real qualitative ideological difference from the conservatism of old. In other words, the ideology that recent conservatives have poured forth is merely old wine in new bottles.

For example, the doctrine of laissez-faire, preached so frequently in conservative circles, was the dominant conservative view in the era following the Civil War almost a century and a half ago. Liberals argue that the laissez-faire approach proved only to lead only to worker exploitation, income inequality, monopoly capitalism, unsafe products, and environmental degradation during the Gilded Age of late Nineteenth Century America. Liberals argue that laissez-faire capitalism is the world of company stores and company scrip, the world of Upton Sinclair, the world of Charles Dickens, and the world of great suffering for the masses. Consequently, conservative efforts to eliminate the role of government in the free marketplace are essentially efforts to return America to the Nineteenth Century when 1/3 of the meat packed in Chicago was unfit to eat, when the standard water supply for American factory workers was an open barrel, and when 50% of children died before the age of five (Farmer, 2003, 67). Hence, liberals argue that a return to laissez-faire is not a return to policy by sound analysis as the scholars of the 1950s argued, but instead is a return to a very old and historically discredited ideology.

Similarly, liberals argue that the church-state blend espoused by the Christian Coalition wing of American conservatism has proven itself to be flawed repeatedly throughout human history, whether one is discussing the Taliban in Afghanistan, the Catholic Inquisition of Medieval Europe, or the current views of the Southern Baptist Convention. Liberals argue that to blend Church with State is to return to the time before the American Revolution when colonists in Virginia were whipped for church transgressions and Puritans in Massachusetts were executed for witchcraft. It is a return to the days when scientists were threatened with death if their discoveries conflicted with the teachings of the leaders of religion, and citizens were condemned to death for "heresy," or simply for thinking differently. Essentially, a return to a church-state blend is a return to the Eighteenth Century system that the authors of the Constitution abandoned. Liberals contend that those who espouse and preach these ideologies are essentially ignoring these lessons of history as well as empirical data and theoretical flaws in the ideologies themselves, thus the United States drifts toward ideologically-driven catastrophe. An investigation into the history of this ideological movement, known broadly as conservatism, that contemporary liberals in America so deplore is the subject matter of this book, but it will be left to the reader to determine whether the liberals' criticisms are based on sound analysis of history, or on flawed ideological foundations of their own.

Ideology as a Political Guide

In most American government textbooks there is not a chapter dedicated exclusively to ideology. This omission is somewhat befuddling since Americans obviously are guided politically more by ideology than by facts and knowledge because in order to be guided by facts and knowledge, it is a prerequisite that one must first actually "know something." One need go no further than "Jaywalking" on *The Tonight Show with Jay Leno* to come to the conclusion that most Americans are generally ignorant on political issues and know very little in terms of actual historical and political facts. Night after night, Leno asks some of the most basic questions such as: Who wrote the "Declaration of Independence?" or Who wrote the "Gettysburg Address?," only to get responses such as "Britney Spears" or "Puff Daddy." While it is true that Leno's comedy is unscientific; empirical studies of public political and historical knowledge tend to support the same conclusion one might reach from watching Leno's antics. In other words, when it comes to politics, Americans in general are seriously deficient even in some of the most basic aspects of political knowledge. For example, in a national assessment test in the late 1980s, only a third of American 17-year-olds could correctly locate the Civil War in the period 1850-1900; more than a quarter placed it in the 18th Century. Furthermore, 14% credited Abraham Lincoln with writing the Bill of Rights and 10% credited Lincoln with the Missouri Compromise (which would have been quite an accomplishment for someone who was 11 years old at the time). Finally, 9% named Lincoln to be the author of *Uncle Tom's Cabin*. While this knowledge of history is abysmal, performance on questions concerning current affairs yield equally poor results. In a 1996 public opinion poll, only 10% of Americans could identify William Rehnquist as the Chief Justice of the Supreme Court. During the 1980s, the majority of Americans could not correctly answer whether the Reagan Administration supported the Sandinistas or the Contras in Nicaragua and only a third could place Nicaragua in Central America (Schudson, 2000, 16).

This does not mean, however, that the American public necessarily knows less than their leaders. In 1956, President Eisenhower's nominee as Ambassador to Ceylon was unable to identify either the country's prime minister or capitol during his confirmation hearing. In 1981, President Reagan's nominee for Deputy Secretary of State, William Clark, admitted in his confirmation hearings that he had no idea how America's allies in Western Europe felt about having American nuclear missiles based there (Moore, 2002, 88). For his part, George W. Bush once referred to the Kosovars as "Kosovians," argued that the United States should "keep good relations with the Grecians" and confused a Slovenian foreign minister with the country of Slovakia (Miller, 2002, 198). Perhaps most revealing, however, was Bush's statement in *Glamour* magazine during the 2000 Presidential campaign where he confused the Taliban in Afghanistan, a regime against which he would later launch a war, with "some band" (Quoted in Miller, 2002, 199).

This is not to say, however, that American schools have gotten worse, or that Americans and their leaders are more ignorant than they have been in the past. In 1945, for example, 43% of Americans polled could name neither of their U.S. Senators. In 1952, only 67% could name the Vice President, and in 1945, only 92% knew that the President's term in the United States is set at four years (Schudson, 2000, 16). With this type of ignorance, it is perhaps surprising that Democracy in America has worked as well as it has. If there are so many Americans that are evidently ignorant of even the most basic historical and political knowledge (as the surveys suggest), then they must be making their political decisions based on something other than knowledge. The "something" that tends to serve as a guide in the absence of facts and knowledge is ideology.

Ideology

Ideologies are belief systems through which people view and interpret reality. In the words of Milton Rokeach (1972, 5), "Ideology refers to more or less institutionalized set of beliefs—the views someone picks up." Ideologies are not reality, but instead produce simplified versions of reality for those that view the world through ideological frameworks. Ideology interprets and explains what is wrong with society in simplistic terms and provides simplistic prescriptions purported to solve all societal ills. In general, people are very good at identifying someone else's ideology and noting the flaws in their precepts, but people may not even recognize that they themselves are normally just as ideological as others.

In the United States at present, there are scores of differing ideologies, some mainstream, and some on the political "fringe." The fringe ideologies, such as Nazism, are easily recognizable as ideologies by the masses and generally scorned for their "heretical errors" and deviations from social mores and accepted norms. Consider, for example, the Lilleth character (the wife of Frazier) on the TV situation comedy *Cheers*. The Lilleth character is a satirical portrayal of radical feminist liberation ideology, an ideology that does exist as a political "fringe" ideology in the U.S. The character is humorous to many because the majority of viewers can readily discern the flaws and fallacies of an ideology that is not their own. Similarly, another fringe ideology that the majority of Americans readily recognize as an ideology is the radical black liberation ideology. Pop culture has parodied this ideology in innumerable ways, from Damon Wayans' "Homey the Clown" character on *In Living Color*, to Chris Rock's "Nat X" character on *Saturday Night Live*, the comedians have viciously lampooned an ideology that essentially holds (in the words of Rock), that "the white man did it to me." The routines are humorous to many because the majority of Americans recognize the ideological flaws and they may have recognized approximations of those flaws in the ideologies of a real person with whom they are acquainted.

All ideology, however, is not so benign. If we consider, for example, the racist Nazi ideology of Germany in the 1930s, we will find that the ideology simplistically teaches that, "all of the world's problems" are created by "subversive Jews" and other minorities. The simplistic solution of the Nazis in Germany during WWII therefore included the genocide of Jews and others that the Nazis considered societal "problems," with the disastrous result that ten million people died in the Nazi death camps. Nazism, of course, is only a fringe ideology in the United States and therefore does not appear to be a dangerous force in American politics at the moment. It should be remembered, however, that Nazism was only a fringe ideology in Germany as late as 1928. The fact that the Nazis came from political "nowhere" to assume power in Germany a mere five years later, and then overran virtually all of Europe within a dozen years, is a testimony to the mobilizing power of ideology. If American politics has become more ideological in recent years rather than more practical, then it has also become more dangerous.

Conservative Political Ideology

Samuel Huntington (1957) argues that conservatism is best understood not as an inherent theory, but as a positional ideology. According to Huntington, "When the foundations of society are threatened, the conservative ideology reminds men of the necessity of some institutions and the desirability of the existing ones" (Huntington, 1957, 455). Huntington contends that ideological conservatism arises from an anxiety that develops when people perceive valuable institutions to be endangered by contemporary developments or proposed reforms, and the awareness that perceived useful institutions are under attack then leads conservatives to attempt to provide a defense of those institutions.

Huntington (1957, 456) also explains that conservatism is an extremely situational ideology due to the different societal institutions in different societies at different times that people may desire to conserve. In the words of Huntington, "because the articulation of conservatism is a response to a specific social situation...The manifestation of conservatism at any one time and place has little connection with its manifestation at any other time and place." In other words, conservatism is an extremely situational ideology and conservatives at one time or another have sought to conserve just about every institution ever invented, from monarchies, to aristocracies, to slavery, to tariffs, to free trade, to capitalism, to religion, to the defense of communism in the late 1980s in the Soviet Union.

Conservatism, however, is forced to be selective concerning what traditions and legacies must be retained and which ones may be discarded. In what Edmund Burke referred to as the "choice of inheritance," one may expect disagreement even among conservatives as to which societal institutions are absolutely essential and must be preserved, which ones may be altered and how, and which ones should be abolished completely (Muller, 1997, 31).

In one diverse form or another then, conservative political thought has existed throughout recorded human history as different individuals and groups in different societies have at times desired to conserve selected societal institutions. For example, the Pharisees, Chief Priests, and Teachers of the Law mentioned so disparagingly in the Gospels of the New Testament were by Huntington's definition conservatives bent on retaining long-standing societal institutions against the new teachings of Jesus of Nazareth. Similarly, some of the enemies of Mohammed in the 7th Century that preferred to retain existing traditions instead of the new teachings of Mohammed were certainly also conservatives.

The term "conservative" itself, however, dates to 1818 as the title of a French weekly journal, *Le Conservateur*, that was purposed to "uphold religion, the King, liberty, the Charter and respectable people" (Muller, 1997, 26). If President George W. Bush is inserted for the word "King," and "Constitution" is inserted for the word "Charter," then one may see that the fundamental elements of conservatism in France in 1818 are still present in the U.S. in the 21st Century. Other aspects of conservative thought that have remained constant throughout the centuries are presented below.

Transcendent Moral Order

In spite of the diversity of institutions that conservatives throughout the centuries have sought to defend, a set of assumptions and themes behind conservatism have endured. Among those is the assumption that there exists a transcendent moral order to which humans should attempt to conform society (Kirk, 1982, 17). Conservatism therefore tends to be skeptical of new and abstract theories that attempt to mold society to a new morality because the existing order arose and exists as it does due to its consistency with the transcendent and true morality. Consequently, any theory of a "new" morality represents "immorality" or it would have already emerged through the human experiences of the ages. In the United States of the Twenty-First Century, conservatism has therefore opposed the "abstract theories" of communism and socialism as well as feminism, civil rights, gay rights, "new age religions" and "liberal" welfare programs.

Negative View of Human Nature

Conservative ideologies typically emphasize human imperfections and depravity, especially those of common individuals. Typically, humans are viewed as naturally bad, selfish, uncooperative, untrustworthy, and incapable of honorable behavior unless coerced. Christian religious conservatives in particular tie the negative view of human nature to the doctrine of original sin in the Bible, and argue that human nature has been flawed ever since sin first came into the world in the Garden of Eden. In this perspective, it is impossible for humans to be good without divine assistance (Muller, 1997, 31). It is because of this belief in a flawed human nature that conservatives also view human attempts to create a "just society" through reason, as Plato prescribed in *The Republic,* as unrealizable. Thus, movements such as "secular humanism" are viewed by conservatives as doomed to failure if not immoral as well.

Consistent with their theme of humans as flawed beings, conservatives typically argue that there are limits to human knowledge and this fact should act as a limit on attempts at societal innovation. Consequently, conservatives argue that governments of humans lack the wisdom and knowledge necessary to intervene in the free market in order to remedy poverty or inequalities without producing unintended negative consequences (Quinton, 1978, 17). Similarly, "ideal utopias" prescribed by subsequent philosophers (such as Karl Marx, for instance) are impossible. In the words of conservative political theorist Glen Tinder (1989, 23), "To pursue the ideal of perfect justice is to ignore our fallenness."

Instead, conservatives argue that change, if it is merited, should take place gradually, come from experience, and occur within the bounds of existing customs and institutions. Societal change most certainly should not be derived from abstract theories contained in a prescriptive rule book. As such, conservatives distrust intellectuals, whether sociologists, political scientists, historians, psychologists, or economists, who would reform society based on intellectual arguments (Kirk, 1982, 13-20).

Focus on Order

Conservatives are skeptical of a society without constraints on the "fallen humans" and argue that institutional measures must be taken to ensure order. Conservatives can therefore be expected to clash with liberals over the expansion of rights and the utility of existing institutions (such as Church) that Conservatives view as necessary to control human passions and disorder. In the words of Edmund Burke in *Reflections on the Revolution in France*, "the restraints on men, as well as their liberties, are to be reckoned among their rights." Burke therefore argued for retention of customary moral rules even if those rules had not been subject to rational justification. After all, flawed human reasoning would be unlikely to rationally determine definitively whether customary mores were rationally justified or not. Even if such things could be known, conservatives' low regard for ordinary humans leads them to believe that most people would lack the time, energy, and intellect to reevaluate societal mores anyway. Therefore, conservatives argue that humans have a duty to abide by existing societal rules in most cases (Muller, 1997, 11). Edmund Burke argues that because the dissolution of the social order would also destroy the societal institutions by which human passions are restrained, the individual has no right to opt out of obligation to the State and community (Muller, 1997, 11).

In spite of the low view of common humans and the negative perception of human nature in general, in an apparent contradiction with their view of human nature, conservatives typically argue that there are elites (cultural, political, and economic) who know better than others and should make the decisions for society (Muller, 1997, 18). John Adams, for example, spoke of the existence of a "natural aristocracy" that anyone could join by virtue of merit or ability (Dunn and Woodard, 1991, 62).

Emphasis on History and Existing Institutions

Conservatives place a major emphasis upon history and the history of human institutions. For conservatives, the survival of a human institution throughout history, whether one speaks of religion, marriage, aristocracy, or the free market, proves that the institution itself must serve a human need (Kristol, 1983, 161). The need that is met by the institution, however, may not necessarily be the need for which the institution was created. For example, the practice of the burial of deceased human bodies may have arisen for purposes of sanitation; however, the institution of the funeral and burial serves the purpose of aiding the psychological well-being of the living. The fact that humans at any given time may not recognize the utility of existing institutions is a reflection of the human limitations of the institutions critics rather than the institutions themselves. The ongoing existence of the institutions themselves is sufficient to indicate their superiority in meeting human needs. Conservatives typically point to the family as the most important societal institution, but a major emphasis is also placed on religion. Conservatives typically defend religion under these pretenses and ignore the fact that religion from time to time throughout human history has been the cause of much discord and oppression. For conservatives, it is less important whether religion is true or false, and more important that it offers humans hope and thus helps to diffuse discontent that could disrupt the societal order (Muller, 1997, 13).

Skepticism of Altruistic Efforts

Conservatives typically oppose liberal moral "do-gooders" and scoff at the efforts of those who attempt to improve the lives of those less fortunate. In general, conservatives argue that such efforts only encourage laziness and dependency among the recipients. Furthermore, conservatives argue that such efforts have unintended and unforeseen negative consequences. For instance, a government welfare program that increases aid based on the number of children in a family may be designed to eliminate malnutrition, but would be expected by conservatives to lead to the birth of more welfare-recipient children as people take advantage of the larger government stipend. Conservatives typically view income inequalities as legitimate and natural and therefore attempts at redistribution to the poor are not only "casting one's pearls before swine," but also a violation of the natural order (Muller, 1997, 18). This attitude is reflected in the Majority Opinion of Justice Brown in *Plessy v. Ferguson* in 1896 when Brown stated that "If one race be inferior to the other socially, the Constitution of the United States cannot put them upon the same plane."

Role of the State

The role of the State in conservative thought is for security and the protection of property and the free market. Conservatives therefore emphasize a strong military and favor other coercive measures, such as police, to ensure order, the security of property, and the efficient operation of the free market. The State is also expected to protect and support the important societal institutions of Church and family.

Diversity of Conservative Ideology

As previously discussed, conservatism in general is an extremely diverse area of political thought, and American conservatism is no exception to this rule. While some facets of conservatism (as well as some individual conservatives themselves) are more ideological than others, it is certainly a fact that most American conservatives are driven by ideology rather than analysis, whether it be one coherent ideology or a combination of several. In the words of Winston Churchill concerning conservatism, "It is stirred on almost all occasions by sentiment and instinct rather than by worldly calculations" (Quoted in Manchester, 1983, 3). Similarly, Clinton Rossiter argues that the American conservative "feels more deeply than he thinks about political principles, and what he feels most deeply about them is that they are a gift of great old men" (Rossiter, 1982, 74). Consequently, if conservatism is primarily driven by ideology, then it is important to understand those underlying ideologies within the diverse body politic that make up American conservatism.

There are three dominant ideologies in the United States: Classic Liberalism, Traditional Conservatism, and Reform Liberalism (Contemporary Liberalism). These three ideologies form the core of the two major political parties and the ideologies are generally reflected in the major parties' platforms and prescriptions. Classic Liberals and Traditional Conservatives tend to be Conservative Republicans, while Reform Liberalism is the dominant ideology in the Democratic Party. Conservatism is also home to a pair of important fringe ideologies, Libertarianism and Conservative Extremism, that have become worthy of discussion as well in the post-Oklahoma City Bombing era. These ideologies and their contradictions will be discussed in greater detail in the following chapters.

Chapter Two

American Political Theory, Values, and Beliefs

American Values and Beliefs

The United States is a very pluralistic society with many diverse groups and beliefs. As such, there is perhaps no political issue where Americans display unanimity and there is no coherent set of beliefs that one could indisputably call "American political theory;" however, there are a number of areas where Americans exhibit general trends in opinion surveys and some of those trends are rooted in a long history of relatively consistent American political behavior. Among those consistencies during the period following World War II has been a penchant for conservatism in comparison to the world's other developed democracies. In general, this American penchant for conservatism is often referenced in Europe as "American Exceptionalism."

Roots of American Exceptionalism

The roots of this "American exceptionalism" can be found not only in the conservatism of the seventeenth century Puritans of Massachusetts Bay, but in the traditional conservative principles of Edmund Burke, the eighteenth century British conservative who recoiled at the disorder of the French Revolution and called for the continuation of the traditions and institutions of the past. Burke's English conservatism, which migrated across the waters with the immigrants to the New World, was founded on six basic principles, including a deep suspicion of the power of the state, a preference for individual liberties over equality, a strong sense of patriotism, a belief in established institutions, traditions, and hierarchies, skepticism concerning the ideas of progress, and a preference for rule by elites. Americans in general tend to view all six of Burke's principles more favorable than their European counterparts, thus resulting in Americans being more conservative than their European counterparts and therefore accounting for their "exceptionalism" (Micklethwait and Wooldridge, 2004, 13-14).

Fear of State Power and Tolerance for Inequality

Examples of American "exceptionalism" that conform to Burke's six tenets of conservatism are abundant. For starters, Americans are far more fearful of a strong central government and socialism than Europeans, with lower taxes and lower central government expenditures (in spite of greater military spending) than their European counterparts, reflecting the Burkeian conservative preference for individual liberties. The American Constitution also contains a Bill of Rights, designed to protect individual liberties, that is absent from some European constitutions, including the "uncodified" constitution of the United Kingdom. The purpose of many of the rights granted in the Bill of Rights, such as the Third Amendment ban on the quartering of soldiers in the home and the Fourth Amendment protections against "unreasonable" search and seizure, is to limit the arbitrary use of government power. This fear of central government power in the United States exhibited by the authors of the Bill of Rights reflected an American tradition that has continued through the present in a manner that is truly exceptional by world standards. For instance, although his statement was most likely hyperbole, "Mr. Conservative," Barry Goldwater, once spoke for millions of Americans when he stated, "I fear Washington and centralized government more than I do Moscow" (Quoted in Weisberg, 1996, 42). The European revulsion at the reelection of George W. Bush suggests that Goldwater's perspective, which resonated with American conservatives, is inconsistent with the political views of most Europeans. Meanwhile, in the United States, even Democratic Party politicians in the U.S., such as Bill Clinton, who once proclaimed that "the era of big government is over" (Quoted in Harris, 2005, 221), must run against state power in order to get elected.

Reflecting their fear of state power, love for the free market, and disdain for collectivism beyond that of their European counterparts, the American government spends less as a percentage of GDP than the rest of the world's developed democracies and Americans tolerate higher levels of income inequality, thus conforming to Burke's suspicion of the powers of the state and preference for liberty over economic equality. The result of the American penchant for Burke's conservatism is that the United States is the only developed democracy that does not have a system of fully socialized health care and it is the only Western developed democracy that does not have government-provided child support to all families. Japan and every European advanced democracy also provide paid maternity leave while the U.S. does not (Micklethwait and Wooldridge, 2004, 11-20). Perhaps American President Grover Cleveland best summed up the American attitudes in the 1890s when he stated that "I do not believe that the power and duty of the General Government ought to be extended to the relief of individual suffering" (Quoted in Roark et al., 2005, 630).

President George W. Bush's attitudes toward international institutions have tended to reflect a degree of similar skepticism. For example, as President, Bush has opposed American participation in any International Criminal Court, rejected parts of the Biological Weapons Convention, and opposed the Comprehensive nuclear Test-Ban Treaty and the Ottawa Land Mine Convention. Bush also withdrew the United States from the Kyoto Protocol on global warming and the 1972 Anti-Ballistic Missile Treaty with the Soviet Union. Finally, when Bush was confronted with resistance in the UN to his plan to oust Saddam Hussein from Iraq militarily in 2003, he made it clear that the United States would do the job unilaterally if necessary (Micklethwait and Wooldridge, 2004, 296-298).

Pro-Business and Anti-Union

The United States is exceptional in comparison to Europe in the extent of its decidedly pro-business and anti-union culture. Perhaps President Calvin Coolidge said it best in the 1920s when he declared that "the business of America is business" (Quoted in Nash et al., 1986, 778). Unions in the United States historically have been connected in the minds of the public with "bomb-throwing radicalism" (the Chicago Haymarket riots of 1886), communist infiltration (the series of strikes that accompanied the Red Scare of 1919), and organized crime and violence (the celebrated disappearance of union leader Jimmy Hoffa in 1968) (Nash et al., 1986, 758). As a consequence of the anti-union culture (along with other economic shifts, such as the decline of American manufacturing), union membership in the U.S. was only 12.5% of the workforce in 2004, much lower than in most European countries and days lost to strikes in the U.S. are much lower than the European average (U.S. Department of Labor, 2005).

Individualism

Perhaps as important and salient as any other American trend is the fact that the U.S. is a very individualistic society. Essentially, the role of the individual in American society tends to take precedent over the State. This perspective grew out of the writings of not only of Burke, but of John Locke, from whom the founding fathers' borrowed heavily in writing both the *Declaration of Independence* and the Bill of Rights. The Lockean individualist perspective grew out of the Age of Enlightenment and the struggle of the American Colonists in the 18th Century to release themselves from Monarchical rule. Lockean individualism can be seen in countless facets of American society, from lax laws of incorporation, to expansive criminal rights, to the individualistic icons of pop culture (Bellah et al., 1985).

In general, Americans want to be able to conduct their business and their private lives without governmental interference. In this, Americans are not necessarily exceptional; however, it is the degree to which Americans will go to ensure that they are "let alone" that is indeed exceptional. Robert Bellah et al., (1985, 17) summed up the American individualist perspective by stating that Americans believe that "Anything that would violate our right to think for ourselves, judge for ourselves, make our own decisions, live our lives as we see fit, is not only morally wrong, it is sacrilegious." As a consequence, murderers walk free on the streets in America because policemen violated their due process rights. Similarly, the air in Houston, Texas is the dirtiest in the country because the typically conservative Texas state government is so lax in enforcing environmental laws (viewed as government interference that violates the rights of people to do business) that air pollution in Houston is now worse than in cities much larger, such as Los Angeles (Ivins and Dubose, 2002, 107-110).

Also in Texas, laws requiring individuals to wear motorcycle helmets were repealed because such restrictions are viewed as violations of the right to personal choice. This is in spite of the fact that few would argue that it is safer to ride a motorcycle without a helmet. Instead, it is obvious that the prospect of millions of Texans riding around on motorcycles without helmets has a negative impact on society as a whole. After all, society as a whole will eventually pay indirectly for the medical bills for thousands of motorcycle riders who were injured while riding without helmets. Society will do so through the higher taxes needed to compensate for the increase in bad debts at county hospitals because of the increase in serious head injuries that necessarily follows the repeal of a motorcycle helmet law.

Texas, however, is not alone in its staunch individualism. Individualism is so pervasive in America that many popular heroes, both real and fictional, have strong individualist streaks. Movie and television police dramas, for instance, for decades have been dominated by individualistic police characters that must "do things their own way." From Clint Eastwood's "Dirty Harry," to Peter Falk's "Columbo," to the ever-changing cast of "NYPD Blue," the fictional police hero typically must work outside of standard operating procedures, if not from outside of society as a whole, in order to produce the results necessary for positive reform of society. The celluloid police hero is perpetually in trouble with the well intentioned and intelligent, but "by the book" lieutenant for gross violations of department rules, and it is common for the hero to even be suspended or voluntarily go into temporary "retirement" so that he can continue to chase villains unrestrained by anti-individualistic rules.

As it is in American fiction, so it also is with American non-fiction heroes. Non-fictional individualists in America often enter politics and become Senators (ex-Vietnam-POW John McCain), Governors (ex-Navy Seal and Professional wrestler Jesse Ventura and actor and body builder Arnold Schwarzenegger), and even Presidents (ex-mercenaries and war heroes Theodore Roosevelt and Andrew Jackson). All of the above fit the mold of "Rambo" or "Dirty Harry" in that they tended to march to the beat of a "different drummer" and retained their individualistic attitudes after they moved into the public arena to attempt societal reform.

The American preference for individual liberties has also come to mean that the U.S. has a much more expansive right to bear arms than most other advanced industrial democracies, many of which outlaw handguns. In contrast, the Second Amendment to the American Constitution proclaims that "a well regulated militia being necessary to the security of a free State, the right of the people to keep and bear arms, shall not be infringed." Handguns are therefore legal in some form or fashion in all fifty American states and the Unites States has a significant gun lobby that simply does not exist in many other developed democracies (Micklethwait and Wooldridge, 2004, 176-178).

At any rate, this elevation of the individual at the expense of the common good is very common in the U.S. and certainly more common in the U.S. than in Eastern societies. In Eastern cultures, such as in Japan and the Middle East, greater emphasis is placed on society as a whole rather than on the rights of individuals. These societies are known in political science terms as "holistic" societies where the common good tends to take precedent over the rights of individuals (Nakane, 1986, 1-22). Examples of holistic behavior include the Japanese Kamikaze pilots in WWII and the suicide bombers of al Qaeda. In both cases, it is certainly not the good of the individual suicide bomber that is elevated, since the bomber dies, but theoretically, the death of the suicide bomber benefits the societal common good. In the case of Japan in WWII, the sacrifices of the Kamikazes were intended to prevent an American invasion and thus preserve the whole of Japanese society. In the case of al Qaeda's suicide bombers, the purpose is to please Allah and therefore benefit the common good through Allah's blessings (White, 2001, 47-54). In either case, the suicide bomber is analogous to a honeybee that stings a human that threatens the hive. The bee dies shortly after the sting, but the death of that bee may save the entire hive if the threat is driven away. Americans, in contrast, tend not to have to have such a honeybee mentality, consequently, the Kamikaze attacks of WWII and the suicide-bombers of al Qaeda are very difficult for individualistic-thinking Americans to understand, and the actions of such holistic thinkers in WWII, on 9/11/01, and in Iraq, have left Americans bewildered.

Self-Reliance

Another important facet of American individualism is self-reliance. Alexis De Toqueville (1835, 2001) in his classic work, *Democracy in America*, noted that Americans insist on always relying on their own judgment rather than on "received authority" in forming their own opinions and that Americans tend to stand by their own opinions regardless of the positions of authority figures. In other words, Toqueville argued that Americans tend to be "don't confuse me with the facts, my mind is made up" type of people, or at least they were in 1831. This reliance on self and aversion to "received authority" helps create a situation where common persons can rise to high positions in America; however, it can also create a climate where common Americans distrust their political leaders and refuse to follow those with greater knowledge.

Individualism has another down side as well. Since Americans generally believe that individuals should rely on themselves rather than on society as a whole, among many Americans there is a lack of empathy for societal "losers" and a tendency to view the societal underclass as "those who have failed to take the necessary initiative to take care of themselves." As a consequence, there is a social stigma associated with government aid to the poor or welfare. For example, during the Great Depression of the 1930s, an estimated 50% of Americans that qualified for government relief programs did not apply for relief in order to avoid the social stigma of being "on the dole" (Freidel, 1964, 15-16).

Individualist Conflict with Traditional Structures

A further problem with American individualism is that individualism often conflicts with traditional societal structures, such as church and family, which also have broad support in American society. For example, some American individualists choose to engage in sex outside of marriage, some abuse alcohol, some engage in homosexual relationships, some join nudist colonies, some smoke marijuana, and some pierce their bodies and get tattoos. Which of these activities are legitimate government interests and which are matters that should be left to individual discretion and choice are matters of debate, and exactly where such lines between government interests and individual choice should be drawn, there is no complete consensus.

Utilitarian View of Government

Another very American political belief related to individualism is the belief that politics and government are justifiable and honorable only to the extent that they improve the human condition. In this perspective, governmental institutions may be disobeyed or abolished if they overstep their bounds and disparage people's rights without a clear and present gain in the public good. These principles can be found in the *Declaration of Independence,* where Thomas Jefferson and the founding fathers claimed that the purpose of government is the preservation of rights and that any government that destroys such rights should be abolished. As such, individual liberties are only limited by clear cases of the public good and the rights of others. For example, the Second Amendment guarantees the right to bear arms; however, in the interest of what al Qaeda has proven is a clear case of the public good, the right has been forfeited at airports. Similarly, students may not exercise their rights to bear arms by pointing those guns at the professor because such activity violates the professor's (an individual's) rights to "life, liberty, and pursuit of happiness." In other words, the right of one person to keep and bear arms is curtailed where the rights of another begin.

Crime and Punishment

The U.S. is exceptional from other developed democracies in that it still implements the death penalty while advanced European democracies and even many developing nations do not. In fact, the only other advanced industrialized democracy to sanction the death penalty is Japan. Furthermore, the death penalty is banned (except in extreme cases such as treason) in 110 countries and the only countries that execute people on the same scale as the United States are China, Iran, Saudi Arabia, and the Congo, none of which are generally considered world leaders in the protections of human rights. American "exceptionalism" in crime and punishment, however, is not limited to capital punishment, but extends from the death penalty to other forms of punishment as well. For example, the American incarceration rate is much higher than that in Europe, including five times the incarceration rate of the United Kingdom (Micklethwait and Wooldridge, 300-302).

Values Politics

Reflecting Burkeian conservatism's belief in established institutions, traditions, and hierarchies, as well as skepticism concerning the ideas of progress, the U.S. is unique among industrialized democracies in that "values" politics has supplanted the politics of income distribution and class as the greatest political divide. The U.S. is also decidedly the most religious of advanced industrialized democracies and it is "exceptional" in that religiosity is a better predictor of partisanship than income. There simply is no European parallel with the American Christian right that played such a pivotal role in the election of the Protestant Texan, George W. Bush, to the highest office in the United States (Micklethwait and Wooldridge, 2004, 11-12). What Bush's election and the role of religious conservatives in the 2004 election demonstrate is that American conservatism is decidedly more concerned with Burkeian traditional societal structures, such as church and family, than their European counterparts.

President George W. Bush in particular is known for intermingling his faith with his politics in a way that causes Europeans and secular Americans to shiver, while simultaneously providing comfort to Evangelical Protestant Americans. For example, in 1999 at a debate leading up to Iowa's Republican presidential caucuses, the Texas Governor and presidential candidate Bush named Jesus Christ as the political philosopher or thinker with whom he most identified, adding, "because he changed my heart" (Quoted in Micklethwait and Wooldridge, 2004, 144). While secular Europeans are bewildered at such a statement and secular American liberals may scoff, conservative Americans generally reacted favorably and supported their "favorite son" for the Presidency over Democrat Al Gore, who was connected in the minds of many of America's evangelical Christians with the sexual indiscretions of President Clinton. The election was so close nationally that it took 36 days and U.S. Supreme Court intervention for Bush to emerge as the winner, but among Protestant fundamentalists, he won in a landslide.

Patriotism

The U.S. is also "exceptional" in comparison to other advanced industrialized democracies for its patriotism. Europeans tend to be less patriotic than Americans, not because they do not love their homelands, but because patriotism in Europe has been associated with numerous wars, including WWI and WWII in the last century, that ravaged the continent. Compounding the difference between Europe and the U.S. in patriotism is the fact that more recently, it was the United States, not Europe, that suffered a devastating attack from outsiders. As a consequence, patriotism in the U.S. soared to abnormally high levels after the terror attacks of 9/11/01. Polls after the attacks revealed that 90% of Americans were "proud to be Americans" and conservative Republicans were even prouder than liberal Democrats (Micklethwait and Wooldridge, 2004, 299-300).

While it is true that the polls after the terror attacks may reflect only a short-term spike in patriotic attitudes among Americans, it is unquestionable that patriotism also runs deep in America over the long term, and it is especially acute among conservatives. For example, hyperpatriotism has developed even in traditional bastions of liberalism in the United States, such as the University of California at Berkeley. At Berkeley in 2003, conservative students established a newspaper entitled the *California Patriot* and celebrated the 34th anniversary of the hippie-associated People's Park riots of the 1960s by descending on the park in a noisy display of patriotism, where they waved flags, chanted "U.S.A." and sang the Star-Spangled Banner and other patriotic songs. These conservative students do not, however, represent an extreme deviation from the norm in the United States. Even under normal circumstances (without the effects of terror attacks) eighty percent of Americans respond in surveys that they are "very proud of their country." In no other developed democracy is the flag displayed more obsessively or the national anthem sung more frequently. Furthermore, sixty percent of Americans believe their culture superior to those in other countries as opposed to 30% in France, and 40% in Germany and the UK (Micklethwait and Wooldridge, 2004, 279, 299-300).

Militarism

The United States is also exceptional among developed democracies for its militarism, reflecting Burkeian conservatism's strong sense of patriotism and a conservative distrust of human nature. As a consequence, American military spending is more than all of the other countries of NATO combined and some 45% of the military spending for the entire world. The European Union's total spending on military equipment is approximately half that of the United States, and spending on military research and development in Europe is approximately a fourth that of the United States. As for the "China threat," China's entire military budget has been less than the annual increase in military spending under the conservative President George W. Bush. At the outset, Americans overwhelmingly supported George W. Bush's military invasion of Afghanistan and at the outset, displayed similar support for Bush's invasion of Iraq, while Europeans were generally much more apprehensive and much more favorable toward diplomatic solutions (Micklethwait and Wooldridge, 2004, 211, 245).

Wide-Open Spaces

Finally, the United States differs from its European and Japanese counterparts in its wide-open-spaces geography and the impact that that geography has had on American politics. The great expanse of the United States not only allowed a certain degree of isolation during the early years of the Republic that could not be enjoyed by the Europeans, and thus shaped American politics differently, but the great expanse also allowed escape from the bonds of society into the individualistic frontier where authority was much less imposing. The frontier experience therefore nourished the spirit of conservative individualism and allowed that individualism to grow in the U.S. in a way that it could not in Europe and Japan. America's wide-open-spaces geography may also have had an impact on the development of American labor unions since workers had the option of simply moving to the frontier so as to avoid exploitation by management whereas their European counterparts did not. As a consequence, the American labor movement, and socialist tendencies in general, lagged behind those of their European counterparts.

American Conception of Equality

"Equality" in the American political mindset is a multifaceted concept that is among the most important in American political thought. Nevertheless, "equality" is another political area where Americans are "exceptional" in comparison to other advanced democracies in that Americans are willing to tolerate much greater economic inequality as long as they believe they have provided equality of opportunity.

The roots of the American views of equality arose out of the "age of enlightenment" that influenced American founders such as Thomas Jefferson and Ben Franklin. The American view of equality is reflected and shaped by Jefferson in the *Declaration of Independence* where he asserted, "all men are created equal." Although Jefferson's intention may have been merely go assert that the American people were equal to the English people at the time and therefore entitled to the same status under law, the concept has grown as the Nation has developed in its democratic journey. Obviously, Jefferson's "all men are created equal" was not as inclusive as it might sound, since it did not include blacks, and Jefferson himself was a slave owner, but later generations of Americans would take Jefferson's words at face value rather than limiting them to Jefferson's intentions and actions.

Alexis de Toqueville (1835, 2001) pointed out in his classic work, *Democracy in America*, that equality has a long tradition in America beginning with a great equality that existed among the immigrants that settled the shores of the original American colonies. In the words of Toqueville (speaking of New England), "the germs of aristocracy were never planted in that part of the union." Toqueville goes on to explain how the American laws of inheritance abolished the English tradition of primogeniture and installed a system where all children shared equally in inheritance, thus eliminating the English economic system based on landed gentry and replacing it with a more merit-oriented system. When the experience of settling the American frontier, another great equalizer, is added to that already egalitarian culture, what emerged is a culture that is in some ways greatly egalitarian. One might argue that the very first successful English colony in America (Jamestown) began the trend toward egalitarianism due to an environment where everyone was equally starving and only 60 of 2000 immigrants survived from 1607-1609 (Brinkley, 2003, 35). The experience obviously obliterated some class barriers at Jamestown since 97% of the colonists were equally dead by 1609, and the threat of starvation clearly transcended any other class barriers.

Equality of Opportunity

Among the ways that Americans conceive equality is "equality of opportunity" (Fowler and Orenstein, 1993, 98). Americans generally believe that everyone should have an equal opportunity to succeed, especially in economic life. The concept of equal opportunity takes for granted that results will vary greatly depending on talent, drive, health, inheritance, and of course, just plain luck. The important thing is not that some will achieve more than others, but that all have the opportunity to achieve. It should be stressed that this equality of opportunity is only an ideal and never will be completely achieved in reality. Clearly some have a better chance at becoming millionaires or President than others, for instance, given that they might have a father that was a millionaire or President himself.

Political Equality

Another facet of equality stressed by Americans is "political equality" (Fowler and Orenstein, 1993, 98). The concept of political equality includes the rights of all people to participate in government and the political process. Political equality also includes equal treatment under law. Like equality of opportunity, political equality is an ideal that Americans strive toward; however, complete political equality remains elusive. For example, aggregate statistics reveal that black men typically receive harsher sentences for the same crimes as compared to other groups in society (Siegel, 1989, 488). Some of this inequity is undoubtedly tied to economics (although racism may still be a factor), and African Americans as a group still earn significantly less in income per capita than the general population. A lack of income translates into poorer quality lawyers, which evidently also translates into jail terms.

Equal Value of Each Human Life

A third major facet of equality in American political thought is the concept of the equal value of each individual human life. This concept is embodied in Jefferson's "All men are created equal," but it also has a basis in the Christian value-system that is so pervasive in American society that stresses the concept of "equality before God." Apostle Paul in Galatians 3:28 argued that, "there is neither Jew nor Greek, slave nor free, male nor female, for you are all one in Christ Jesus." The point Paul was trying to make is that everyone is equal in the good Lord's eyes, regardless of gender, ethnicity, or economic status. Americans essentially adopted this Pauline view as evidenced by the current system for the rationing of human organs for transplants whereby organs for those who need transplants are not theoretically awarded to the highest bidder or to one ethnic or gender group over another, but are instead allocated based on who needs them the most. In other words, the heart patient that is closest to death is the one that goes to the top of the list for a transplant, regardless of ethnicity, gender, or economic status.

Equality of Condition

One aspect of equality that Americans in general clearly do not embrace is the concept of equality of condition. This is the essentially Marxist idea that all human beings, regardless of intellect, education, etc., should be equal in terms of their material possessions. Americans reject such an idea as "communist," but the idea itself did not necessarily originate with Marx. Plato, for instance, explained to his pupil Aristotle that within any organization, no one should earn more than five times as much as the lowliest worker. Similarly, early Christians in Jerusalem evidently adhered to equality of condition according to the book of Acts (2:44-45) where it is stated that they "had everything in common, selling their possessions and goods, they gave to anyone as he had need." The parallel with Marx's "from each according to his abilities, to each according to his needs" is perhaps uncanny. For emphasis, the writer of Acts even includes the story of Ananias and Sapphira (5:1-11) who deceitfully kept back a part of their property for themselves rather than donating it to the entire church community. The deceitful couple is then immediately struck dead by the Almighty for their selfish and anti-egalitarian actions.

Americans, in contrast, generally reject such "share the wealth" plans, believe that "life is what you make it," and do not see any problem with CEOs making hundreds of millions of dollars while others make minimum wage, as long as each had the "equal opportunity" to be wealthy. According to a poll published in American Enterprise magazine in 1990, only 29% of Americans thought it was the government's job to reduce income differentials. In contrast, 60-70% of Britons and Germans and 80% of Italians and Austrians indicated that reducing inequalities was part of the government's job (*Economist*, 1994). As a consequence, American society has been measured by the Brookings Institution, Rand Corporation, Lynn Karoly, and World Bank, as the most unequal (in terms of income) of all developed industrialized democracies (*Economist*, 1994).

Americans tolerate these gross inequalities in spite of economic studies, such as that of Torsten Persson and Guido Tabellini in the June 1994 issue of *American Economic Review*, suggesting that income inequality may be harmful to economic growth. In the Persson and Tabellini study of 56 countries, the analysis revealed a strong negative relationship between income inequality and growth in GDP per capita. Similar results have been produced by the Institute for Public Policy Research (*Economist*, 1994).

American Conception of Justice

Justice has been a subject of politics and government from the earliest codifications of law and political science. Plato uttered this "first question" of political science as a simple interrogative offered in *The Republic* when he presented a discussion of "What is justice?" Similarly, if we turn again to the *Bible*, we find that the cry of the prophets (Jeremiah, Micah, and Ezekial) in the ancient Jewish Scriptures was often for "God's justice." The prophets sought justice for the poor, the suffering, the widows and orphans, and for the enemies of the Jews. Americans, of course, have their own conception of the answer to Plato's original question and their own versions of "justice" that they cry for. The American versions, however, again reflect their exceptional conservatism in comparison to other advanced democracies.

Equality as Justice

The American conception of justice includes the multifaceted American conception of equality discussed in the section above. In other words, if people are denied equal opportunity, Americans generally perceive it to be unjust. Similarly, most Americans now tend to view the denial of equal treatment under law or the denial of equal political rights to be anathema to justice. Additionally, if organs needed for human transplants were allocated to the highest bidder rather than based on needs or were reserved for "whites only," most Americans would view the situation as unjust. Justice, however, is not synonymous with "equality" in American thought even though

American conceptions of equality play major roles. Instead, the American conception of justice includes the concept of "just desserts."

Just Desserts

The idea behind the concept of "just desserts" is that each individual receives his or her rewards based on merit. In other words, if an individual works very hard to finish at the top of the class (and also scores in the 98th percentile on the MCAT), then there is a very good chance that person may be accepted to Medical School somewhere prestigious such as Harvard. If that same individual continues to work hard and finishes at the top of the class at Harvard Medical School, then perhaps that person can continue to study and become a top specialist. In American society, the medical specialist in our example is likely to become very wealthy, far wealthier than most fellow citizens. Americans in general, however, do not object to our hypothetical medical specialist's wealth. After all, our specialist worked and studied very hard to achieve success and the wealth is merely the "just dessert" or proper reward for his/her hard work. The basic idea of just desserts in this case is that as long as the opportunity existed for all of Americans, it is fine if those that achieved it become extremely wealthy.

In contrast to our medical specialist example and other examples of Bill Gates-style "meritorious success," there are literally millions of others in America that achieve very little monetary or material success. Consider, for instance, the case of the homeless person that lives in a refrigerator box, does not work, and spends most of every day consuming alcohol. There is a large group of Americans (conservatives in general) that would consider the homeless state of the "alcoholic" to be his "just dessert." Since the "alcoholic" doesn't work and drinks too much, he therefore doesn't deserve any condition better than his homeless state. His activity in life (or lack of it) "merits" no better condition (or at least it does not in this conservative American perspective).

One major impact of the American view of justice as "just desserts" is that it tends to hinder liberals in their efforts to reduce income inequalities. For instance, when the Federal Government filed anti-trust suits against Standard Oil at the beginning of the 20th Century and against Microsoft at the end of that same century, most conservative Americans opposed the government action because John D. Rockefeller and Bill Gates respectively had "earned" their wealth. Conversely, the idea of justice as "just desserts" tends to erode support for "welfare" programs because American individualists tend to believe that the "lazy" poor people are responsible for their own poverty and therefore do not "merit" the government assistance.

American Conception of Freedom

Freedom, like justice and equality in the American conception, is another multifaceted concept; however, there is not complete unanimity in American politics on exactly what are the meanings of "freedom." According to Fowler and Orenstein (1993, 81-86), the American conception of freedom generally includes political freedom, civil liberties, economic freedom, and other particular freedoms listed in the U.S. Constitution. Each of these aspects of freedom will be discussed below.

Political Freedom

The concept of "political freedom" essentially entails the liberty to participate in government and politics. Unfortunately, universal political freedom was not originally guaranteed in the original U.S. Constitution (the subject was left for the States to determine) and the next 180 years of American history following the writing of the Constitution included a protracted struggle of the disenfranchised to gain full participation rights. Landless Americans, women, minorities, and young persons aged 18-21 would eventually all gain full participation rights by 1971, but it certainly was not without a lengthy and difficult struggle. Whether one is discussing participation rights for women, for minorities, or for non-property owners, those with full participation rights tended only grudgingly to give up their exclusive possession of rights to those without who demanded full participation. Once the struggle was won, however, there were typically few sentiments for repeal (with the case of blacks in the American South following the Civil War being a notable exception). Since 1971, when the 26th Amendment extended participation rights to age 18, for instance, there has not been a concerted movement on the American political scene to return to the disenfranchisement of persons 18-20, or for that matter, any of other particular group. Thus, at least for now, the struggle for political freedom in the U.S. appears to be settled on the side of universal participation rights. The struggle to get people to exercise that freedom (if America's comparatively low voter turnout is any indication), however, is another matter.

Civil Liberties

A second facet of the American conception of freedom is the concept of civil liberties (Fowler and Orenstein, 1993, 82). Civil liberties include the right to be treated with respect as a citizen, with equal privileges and equal treatment under the laws. The idea is that there should not be one law in

America for the poor and another for the rich, nor one law for the men and another law for the women, nor should there be one law for whites and another for blacks, but all are treated equally under law regardless of class, gender, ethnicity, etc. Like political freedom, the struggle for civil liberties has permeated American history. Unlike political freedom, however, the struggle over civil liberties is permanent and ongoing. For instance, courts and legislative bodies have been struggling with Affirmative Action for over three decades and the entire concept remains both unevenly applied and controversial. Similarly, political freedom for gay Americans remains unsettled. Gay rights activists argue that gays are "born or naturalized" in the U.S. and therefore receive equal rights or "privileges" under the 14th Amendment; thus, gay rights groups push for the "privilege" or "right" to marriage between same-sex couples. Simultaneously, the Christian Coalition maneuvers to counter the expansion of rights and privileges for gay Americans, claiming that gays may be born in the U.S., but gay sexual activities conflict with the teachings of the *Bible* and therefore their rights and privileges should be limited on the basis of morality.

Civil liberties, however, like the concepts of equality and justice, are only ideals and have not been fully realized in American society. American society is replete with groups and individuals (gays again come to mind) that argue (rightly or wrongly) that they have been denied equal privileges. Furthermore, the recent developments in the War on Terror that have led to the detainment of American citizens on suspicions of terrorism without the granting of the standard rights of due process have led to new questions and disputes concerning American conceptions of civil liberties and the balance between those liberties and security.

Particular Freedoms

A third facet of freedom as it exists in the American conception includes the particular freedoms listed in the Constitution, such as right to remain silent, right to a speedy and public trial, freedom from unreasonable search, and prohibition against excessive bail, etc. Particular freedoms also include liberties that have been constructed by the Supreme Court, such as the right to privacy, that are not specifically enumerated in the Constitution. Most of the disputes over these types of freedoms, such as when speech may be abridged or what constitutes "due process," etc., are eventually settled by those very same Courts, although the public also pushes for legislation to either protect, or take away particular freedoms from certain groups. In other words, the list of particular freedoms in the U.S., like other freedoms, is not forever fixed, but in a state of constant change.

Economic Freedom

The final piece of the American conception of freedom is economic freedom, or the freedom to choose one's own economic course in terms of occupation, and freedom or control over one's own assets. In other words, Americans generally believe that individuals should be able to choose their own occupation (as opposed to being born into it as in the Indian caste system). Furthermore, Americans believe generally that there should be no limits hindering occupational choice based on gender, ethnicity, or religion. In other words, laws limiting blacks to employment only in agriculture or domestic servitude (such laws did once exist in the American South) are viewed as limits on freedom and antithetical to the "American way." Furthermore, parents may encourage their children to choose one occupation over another, but the final decision remains with the individual rather than the parent.

Similarly, there are no legal restrictions on how Americans may spend (or misspend) their assets (although, once again, there were once laws in the South that penalized blacks for "misspending their income"). Complete control over one's own assets may mean that one may live in a low-income neighborhood, yet own a luxury car, a television satellite dish, and expensive jewelry, yet remain completely within the law. While these types of spending patterns may be condemned by some as inappropriate allocations of one's assets, there is no sentiment to curtail them as legal economic choices.

Political Obligation

The concept of political obligation refers to duties and responsibilities that one has in society regardless of personal preference. For instance, in Texas individuals are obligated to "stop and render aid" at the scene of an automobile accident if they are the first on the scene, regardless of one's personal preference for doing so. Americans are also obligated to pay taxes, serve on juries, and generally obey the laws of the land. In spite of these obligations, however, political obligation in general is lightly regarded in the U.S. (as compared to some other developed democracies such as Germany, Japan, and the United Kingdom) and obligation is typically only required upon the consent of the individual. For example, Americans may opt out of obligations to serve their country in combat by claiming conscientious objector status and asserting that their religion precludes such behavior. The famous world champion boxer, Muhammad Ali, is perhaps America's most famous conscientious objector in this regard. Ali opted out of combat duty in Vietnam in the 1960s because he claimed that his peaceful religion, Islam, prevented him from combat duty.

Ali, however, is not alone in his "low view" of political obligation. For instance, only approximately 40% of Americans typically show up for jury duty when summoned, even though Americans say they believe in the right to a trial by a jury "of your peers" in opinion surveys. Similarly, during the Vietnam War thousands of Americans shirked their obligation to serve the military by fleeing to Canada and through other means. The list of leading American political figures that did not serve in Vietnam is long, but includes Presidents Bill Clinton and George W. Bush, former House Speaker Newt Gingrich, frequent Presidential candidate Pat Buchanan, and radio talk show host Rush Limbaugh. According to Ivins and Dubose (2002, 6) and others, President George W. Bush did not even fulfill his obligations in the Air National Guard, yet defeated heavily decorated Vietnam veteran John Kerry for President in 2004. Pat Buchanan, who is evidently now an avid jogger, did not go to Vietnam because of his bad knee (Franken, 2003, 228), and Rush Limbaugh was exempt from service due to his Peridontal Cyst (Franken, 2003, 228). One can surmise from these examples that Americans are evidently not overly rigid concerning political obligations. Perhaps this is why President Carter responded a few years after the Vietnam War by pardoning the "draft dodgers." In any case, failure to seek military service (or to even shirk it) clearly does not mean future political failure for American politicians, and any attempts by politicians to reinstate a military draft are bound to encounter resistance.

Nature v. Nurture Debate

Thus far in this chapter, basic areas where Americans are in some sort of general agreement have been the subjects of discussion. When it comes to the character of human nature, however, there is nothing approximating a consensus, and instead there is a deep divide among Americans related to ideology and partisanship. The "great schism" is essentially over the basic "good" or "bad" character of human nature. There are two dominant views that will be discussed below.

Realism

The first of these two views is the realist "nature" view. Realists believe that nature or genetics plays a dominant role in determining human behavior and argue that humans as a group are naturally "bad" and uncooperative. As such, humans require coercion in order to ensure proper behavior. For example, the posted speed limit on Texas highways is 70mph. Many individuals drive near the speed limit, but perhaps most tend to drive their vehicles a few miles per hour over the speed limit. Obviously, these individuals know that 72mph is over the speed limit because there are "Speed Limit 70" signs in Texas every few miles. The realist perspective can easily explain this deviant behavior. In this perspective, drivers know the speed limit, but being "bad" by nature, they intentionally break the rules and go over the speed limit anyway; however, they do so by miniscule amounts because the Texas Department of Public Safety Officers (State Police) will generally not issue citations for two to three miles per hour over the speed limit, but can be expected to do so for violations in excess of five miles per hour over the posted limit. That being the case, in the realist conception, people can be expected to cheat a little on the speed limit because they are "naturally bad," but may avoid cheating enough to invoke coercion (fines), and therefore drive only a few miles per hour over the posted speed limit.

To reiterate, in the realist conception, people engage in criminal behavior (such as driving 72mph in a 70mph zone) because they are essentially "bad" by nature. Consequently, education, rehabilitation, and counseling are useless as means to correct the deviant behavior. The only thing such "bad people" can be expected to react to is coercion; therefore, criminals should be fined, incarcerated, flogged, and/or executed, depending on the severity of the crime. Realists tend to be politically conservative and their prescriptions tend to be coercive in character (incarceration, corporal punishment, and executions for serious law violators) (Martinson, 1974, 22). In the words of conservative President Ronald Reagan, "right and wrong matter; individuals are responsible for their actions; retribution should be swift and sure for those who prey on the innocent" *(Justice Assistance News*, 1981, 1).

In foreign policy, realism normally translates into diplomacy by force. Statements such as "force is the only thing they understand over there" are consistent with the realist perspective and the idea that the U.S. could work through international organizations, such as the UN, is anathema to realism. In the realist perspective, it would be unwise to "negotiate" with other world leaders such as Saddam Hussein simply because they can't be trusted. In foreign policy as well as domestic, coercion then becomes the chosen policy tool.

Roots of realism can be seen in the American Judeo-Christian heritage. The prophet Jeremiah (17:9) declares that "The heart is deceitful above all things and beyond cure," obviously suggesting that humans are naturally bad. Similarly, Jesus is quoted by Matthew (7:19) as saying "For wide is the gate and broad is the road that leads to destruction, and many enter through it," once again suggesting that the majority of people are more bad than good, and in this case headed to the destruction of their souls.

A quick read of almost any newspaper in America on any given day may act to vindicate the realists. One glance at American crime statistics suggests that there does indeed appear to be a lot of bad present in American society. Furthermore, some deviant behavior, such as that of serial killer Jeffrey Dahmer, who murdered people and ate them, simply cannot be learned from anyone in society and reflects a depraved nature of humans. For a larger historical example, who on earth, with even rudimentary knowledge of the Holocaust, could conclude that human beings are basically good?

Idealism

In contrast to the realist view is the idealist "nurture" view, generally viewed as the "liberal" view of human nature. Idealists believe that human nature is mostly a product of environment. Idealists have a more positive view of human nature, arguing that humans are naturally good, but corrupted by society. Since all behaviors in this perspective (both good and bad) are learned, idealist's prescriptions tend to be education-oriented. For instance, idealists typically favor counseling, rehabilitation, and other educational treatment programs for violators of public law as opposed to incarceration and capital punishment. Idealists defend their positions by noting the innocence of human newborn babies. Perhaps very few individuals can hold a newborn baby in their own arms and declare that the newborn infant is inherently evil and in need of salvation. Society, however, obviously corrupts these wonderful, innocent children and turns them into something much less honorable long before adulthood.

Synthesis of Nature and Nurture

Both realism and idealism are actually simplifications and humans are not as uncomplicated as either perspective might suggest. Instead all people clearly are products of a combination of both genetics and socialization, and both perspectives are therefore lacking. Realists clearly must admit that socialization or learning does impact human behavior, otherwise, there is no reason to listen to the very conservative Dr. James Dobson's "Focus on the Family," because if children are destined to turn out good or bad based entirely on genetics, and it is impossible to fight this human "nature," then all parenting is wasted effort. This is not the positions taken by Dobson and "Focus on the Family," nor is it the position taken by millions of other social conservatives who stress "family values." Furthermore, Dobson's Focus on the Family ministry openly supports conservative politics; hence, it is obvious that American conservatives often mix some idealism with their realism. Similarly, "liberal idealists" in the United States argue for stiffer penalties for hate crimes, suggesting that many liberals do support the same types of coercive measures in some cases as do their conservative counterparts. The real question then is not whether it is nature or nurture that shapes human behavior, but instead which factor is more dominant, since both are significant. In the end, those that view "nature" as more dominant tend to be conservatives and those that view "nurture" as more dominant tend to be liberals, and the debate over which is most important continues unabated.

Chapter Three

Classic Liberalism

Classic Liberalism is one of the dominant ideologies within both conservatism at large and the American Republican Party of the early Twenty-First Century. Classic Liberalism, however, is very different from contemporary liberalism and should not be confused with "liberals" within the contemporary Democratic Party. Classic Liberalism is essentially the "liberalism of 1776" that was espoused by Thomas Paine, Thomas Jefferson, Benjamin Franklin, and many of the other leaders of the American Revolution. In 1776, "liberal" generally meant a belief in representative government, the free market, and greater equality under law. The "equality" component in 1776, however, should not be overstated. Women and minorities, as well as landless white men, were generally prevented from political participation in 1776 by the laws of the States in which they lived. Furthermore, there was no provision in the Articles of Confederation (or later the Constitution of 1789) that provided for universal suffrage. That being the case, the "representative" government that the Classic Liberals espoused in 1776 was largely representative only of land-owning white males. This limiting of political participation to white male property owners is certainly not considered "liberal" by today's standards, but it was very "liberal" in 1776 when the international norm was rule by autocratic monarchy.

The ideas of Classic Liberalism have their roots in the Age of Reason that produced John Locke, Baron Charles de Montesquieu, and Adam Smith, who published *Wealth of Nations* in 1776 during the American Revolution. The ideas of Locke on "natural rights" may have been as influential on the thinking of the American founding fathers as the ideas of any other political theorist. Similarly, Adam Smith is not only considered a major contributor to the ideology of the founding fathers (and Classic Liberalism), but he is also considered perhaps the "godfather" of free market capitalism, which is as essential to Classic Liberalism as limited, republican government.

In *Wealth of Nations*, Smith argued that society should be organized around a limited, representative government and a free marketplace. In this Classic Liberal construct, people pursue their own self-interest within a set of rules that maximizes personal freedom and the free market. The aggregation of all individuals working to secure their own self-interests is what drives economic growth. All society, rich and poor alike, benefits from individual competition in the free market. In Smith's (1776, 1991) conception, great capital accumulation by people seeking wealth is a benefit to society as a whole, and the income inequality that results therefore must be tolerated to a degree. The wealthy capitalist will both consume and invest excess capital, thus creating economic growth and employment for the working classes as well. As a consequence, the natural actions of the wealthy with their capital will end up benefiting not only the wealthy, but all segments of society and the situation of the poor and working classes will improve along with that of the rich. In the words of Adam Smith, "a rising tide lifts all boats."

Leaders in the Classic Liberal framework, both political and economic, arise based on merit and competition. Classic Liberals utilize the "milk vat analogy" arguing that the "cream rises to the top," meaning that the best, hardest working, and brightest will achieve the most economic and political success.

Wages and prices in the Classic Liberal framework will be determined according to Adam Smith's "invisible hand" of supply and demand. The free market also determines which goods will be produced in what quantity, and how and to whom those goods will be distributed. In general, if demand exceeds supply, prices will rise, but if supply exceeds demand, prices will fall. In this construct, labor is treated as just another commodity. If there is an oversupply of workers in any particular sector, wages in that sector can be expected to fall; consequently, workers will abandon that sector for a higher-paying sector of the economy and wages will improve in the sector that has been wage-depressed. Similarly, if there is a sector of the economy that is labor-short, wages will rise in that sector and thus attract workers and eventually place downward pressure on the inflated wages in that economic sector.

Government for Security and Order

The role of government under the Classic Liberal construct is to provide the security and order necessary for the efficient operation of the free market. If the free market does not have sufficient security and order, the entire free market system may collapse or become chaotic (Hoover, 1994, 18-19). The situation in Iraq after the fall of Saddam Hussein may be a case in point. At this writing, the Baghdad airport is still not open for business and some international companies have pulled out of the Iraqi rebuilding efforts in the interest of the safety of their employees. If one is not free to transact business without fear of the loss of life and limb, then the market most certainly cannot be said to be "free" and business cannot transact in a normal manner.

Free Trade Benefits All Countries

Another major tenet of Classic Liberal ideology is a belief that free and unfettered trade benefits all countries (Smith, 1776, 1991). Classic Liberals argue that countries should trade for goods (import) where they hold a comparative disadvantage and export goods where they hold a comparative advantage. Included below is a hypothetical figure to illustrate the Classic Liberals' arguments that trade benefits all countries. In this fictitious construct, each country shifts labor into industries where they hold a "comparative advantage" and shifts labor away from industries where they hold a "comparative disadvantage." The countries then each trade their excess "comparative advantage" goods for the goods they need to meet their shortfall in goods where they hold a "comparative disadvantage." After the trade, both countries are better off economically than they were before trade took place.

In our hypothetical model, the United States has a comparative advantage with Mexico in the computer industry due to a better education system and a better-developed high-tech sector, but Mexico has a comparative advantage with the United States in citrus-growing, due to a climate in some parts of Mexico that is more suited to growing citrus fruits. The United States is comparatively limited in citrus fruit production because there are fewer areas in the United States with subtropical climates where citrus production is stellar and no areas in the continental U.S. with tropical climates at all.

In the case of the production of computer products and citrus fruits, if the United States can shift labor away from citrus-growing, where it is less efficient, to the high-tech sector, where it is comparatively more efficient than Mexico, then the U.S. can produce an excess of computer products that can be traded to Mexico in exchange for the citrus products where it is comparatively inefficient. The shift of labor out of citrus-production to the high-tech sector would obviously produce a citrus shortage in the U.S. if it were not for the fact that Mexico could easily meet America's citrus needs by shifting workers out of their own high-tech sector (where they are less efficient) to the citrus-growing sector (where they are comparatively more efficient). Mexico should then produce a citrus surplus that could be traded to the U.S. in exchange for computer goods to meet the needs of their deficient high-tech sector.

In our fictitious construct, both the U.S. and Mexico increase their wealth by shifting labor to economic sectors where they hold a comparative advantage and engaging in trade for products where they hold a comparative disadvantage. Classic Liberals are quick to focus on the fact that models similar to those in Figure 1 are suggestive of universal economic benefits for free trade. The suggesting from such a construct is that free trade benefits both poor and wealthy nations alike. Although it might be argued that one benefits from the trade more than the other, Classic Liberals focus on the fact that both countries end up in improved positions after trade.

Figure 1: Free Trade Example: U.S./Mexico Citrus for Computers

Hypothetical worker output per hour:

	U.S.	Mexico
Computers	9	4
Citrus	3	2

U.S. Output per 100 Workers		*Mexico Output per 100 Workers*	
Computers	900	400	
Citrus	300	200	

U.S. Shifts 10 Workers to Computers Mexico Shifts 20 Workers to Citrus

	U.S	Mexico
Computers	990	320
Citrus	270	240

Trade

U.S.Exports 80 excess Units of Computers to Mexico->
<-Mexico Exports 30 excess Units of Citrus to the U.S.

After Trade

	U.S.	Mexico
Computers	910	400
Citrus	300	210

Problems with Classic Liberalism

Perhaps the most glaring problem for Classic Liberalism is found in the very nature of the free market "merit system" itself. In other words, by its very nature, the free market creates income inequality because humans are not all endowed with equal talents and abilities. Furthermore, the free market does not provide an equal reward to all talents and abilities. To acknowledge that there is a "last," is also to acknowledge that there is a "first" and therefore to acknowledge inequality. Classic Liberals, therefore, whether knowingly or unknowingly, acknowledge that the free market creates income inequality through their argument that the best and most talented will succeed through competition. It follows that if the societal "cream rises to the top," as Classic Liberals so argue, there must also be a "bottom," and the least talented in society or societal "scum" can be expected to fall to that bottom and stay there. This social "scum" does not necessarily consist of criminals or moral degenerates, but instead includes those that lack the talents monetarily rewarded by society. For example, the janitor may work just as hard today as the physician, and his job may even be more physically demanding, but janitorial services are not the services that are rewarded handsomely in the free market; hence, the janitor earns much less than the physician due to the laws of supply and demand.

Even Adam Smith (1776, 1991), the godfather of free market capitalism, recognized this fact and argued for some luxury taxes and redistribution of wealth to the poor. Although Smith is also famous for arguing that a "rising tide lifts all boats," evidently a rising tide does not lift all boats equally. In fact, it appears that some boats have "holes" and tend to do a good "Titanic" imitation in the "rising tide."

According to Herrnstein and Murray (1996), for instance, the best predictor of individual economic success is ACT scores; hence, those that score very well on standardized tests (supposedly smart people) tend to do very well economically, while those that score poorly on standardized tests (supposedly less-smart people) tend to experience much less economic success. Herrnstein and Murray essentially argue (not without controversy) that the "intelligence" measured on such tests is genetic; therefore, the best and brightest succeed in the free market because they were born with greater talents, while the "dimmer bulbs" tend to fail because they were born with less mental capacity (which is hardly their fault). As a consequence, as the United States became increasingly free-market oriented during the Reagan-Bush years, income inequality in the U.S. also increased and the real buying power of the working class and poor simultaneously declined when adjusted for inflation. Furthermore, since income inequality also has been linked to slower economic growth, the inequality may have the long-term effect of harming even the wealthy in the economic system through slower economic growth (*Economist*, 1994).

Mergers and Monopolistic Capitalism

A further problem with Classic Liberalism is that the free market often leads to merger-mania and monopoly capitalism. Karl Marx argued that capitalism contains the seeds of its own destruction. Marx argued that capitalism contains a constant pressure for expansion driven by the profit motive and capitalists therefore will attempt to increase their market share, in turn creating downward pressure on both wages and prices. Essentially, the capitalists will try to increase sales and market share by cutting prices. Consumers will then purchase more from the capitalistic enterprise with the lower prices, thus increasing the sales and market shares of the merchants with the lower prices. In order to turn a profit at the new lower prices, however, the merchants must cut their costs, meaning that wages will be cut for the laborers within the organization. The low-price merchants' competitors will attempt to regain the lost market share by retaliating with reductions in prices (and therefore lower wages) of their own. In order for the first discounting merchant to regain the market advantage that had been gained from the original price-cutting, prices (and therefore wages) must be slashed again. In turn, the lower wages in the marketplace lead to a diminished buying power of the workers and eventually to a decline in the aggregate demand for goods since the workers earning less must therefore also consume less. The decline in demand then leads merchants to again cut prices to increase sales, and wages again are cut to ensure a profit. In the Marxist framework, the scenario continues in a downward implosive spiral until capitalism collapses.

Obviously, Marx's theory leaves a few items unexplained since capitalism has not imploded in the time since his Nineteenth Century writing; therefore, Classic Liberals delight in concluding that Marx's theory is void of substance. That said, there does appear, however, to be at least a grain of truth in Marx's arguments. One need only look at the American economy in the late Nineteenth Century where John Rockefeller had a monopoly on oil, Andrew Carnegie a monopoly on steel, and the E.C. Knight company enjoyed a monopoly on sugar manufacturing, to see that American capitalism had moved toward monopoly capitalism in numerous sectors and that the economy was beset with tremendous income inequality. The situation was not corrected until the Federal government under Theodore Roosevelt (and later William Howard Taft and Woodrow Wilson) intervened into the free market and broke up the monopolies.

Furthermore, a quick glance at the changes in the American economy since WWII reveals that the Nineteenth Century economic scenario may be repeating itself again. For example, a visit to any antique car museum will reveal the movement in the American automobile industry away from competition toward an oligopolistic, if not monopolistic, market. Whatever happened to Hudson, Packard, Rambler-Nash, Studebaker, Maxwell, and Stanley Steamer of the early 20th Century? In the Twenty-First Century they are all gone, and all that remains are the "Big Three" American automakers. To make matters even worse, it is unclear whether Chrysler (one of the "Big Three") still should be considered an American automaker at all since the corporation is now controlled by the German company, Damler-Benz.

The American retail business is in similar shape. Montgomery Wards, Woolworth's, and Gibson's Discount Centers all seem to have gone the way of the Stanley Steamer. Even Kmart is on the skids in the face of the Wal-Mart retail department store "monopoly." Furthermore, just like Marx predicted, wages in the retail department store industry have dropped precipitously since the 1960s. In the 1960s, workers in American Department Stores were likely to be full time employees with benefits packages, but in 2004, Department Store workers are often part time employees with low wages and minimal benefits packages. It appears that competition in the retail department store industry has driven down wages and prices to the point where few persons in the industry can actually make a living and the industry appears to be moving toward monopoly capitalism (Wal-Mart), just like Marx predicted.

Tyranny of the Majority

Another problem with Classic Liberal ideology is that the free market allows for tyranny of the majority. American history is replete with supporting examples, including, but not limited to, slavery, Jim Crow laws, and the denial of equal opportunity to women. In 1956, 80% of Texans voted for a nonbinding referendum that would have made inter-racial marriage illegal. On that same ballot, 80% of Texans voted for two other measures that were designed to prevent school integration. One might argue that the U.S. has advanced since these times of oppression of minorities, but more recent examples suggest that the majority would still exact its tyranny on the minority if there were no Constitutional protections.

For example, some communities in the United States would perhaps vote to disenfranchise gay Americans were it not for Constitutional protections. A case in point was made in 1998, when a mayoral candidate in Springdale, Arkansas stated as part of his campaign that he favored the placement of a road sign on the outskirts of Springdale with the words "No Fags" printed on it. The campaign stirred a controversy that revealed the willingness of many in the Arkansas community to strip gay Americans of their Constitutional rights. In Fayetteville, the municipality that borders Springdale, the City Council voted 6 to 2 to adopt a resolution that prohibited city officials from discriminating against applicants for city jobs based on their sexual orientation or familial status. Fayetteville Mayor Fred Hanna vetoed the resolution saying it was divisive and "contrary to the public interest of the citizens of Fayetteville." The City Council then voted to override the veto during their May 5, 1998 meeting. This prompted a group opposed to the resolution to begin collecting signatures to bring the matter to a public vote. The measure was put on the November 3, 1998 ballot and the measure was defeated with 7811 (57.7%) voting against and 5731 (42.3%) voting for the resolution to prevent discrimination based on sexual orientation (*Northwest Arkansas Times*, 1998). In short, it appears that a solid majority in Fayetteville, Arkansas favored discrimination against homosexuals in municipal hiring in 1998. It is perhaps unlikely that Fayetteville is completely unique. If there were no Bill of Rights and no powerful national government behind that Bill of Rights protecting gay Americans, there might be nothing preventing the majority from exercising their tyranny over the homosexual minority in Fayetteville. A government with such power is inconsistent with the "limited government" aspect of Classic Liberalism.

Inequality of Opportunity

Similarly, the free market may create, or at the very least allow, inequality of opportunity both in the economic sector and in other social activities. Once again, the examples of Jim Crow laws and the informal system of discrimination in employment against minorities and women prior to the institution of Affirmative Action are testimonies to the inequality of opportunity that often exists in the free market society. Minorities and women were not only denied equal economic opportunities, but also denied equal social opportunities in terms of membership in some societal clubs and organizations. These inequities were only remedied through government intervention into the free market in a manner (Affirmative Action) inconsistent with the "limited government" creed of Classic Liberalism.

Unsafe, Unhealthy, and Immoral Products

The free market also allows for unsafe, unhealthy, and immoral products. For example, prior to the intervention into the free market by Theodore Roosevelt with the Federal Meat Inspection Act, it was estimated that one-third of the meat sold in America was unfit to eat, and any number of contaminants, including animal feces and urine, commonly could be found in meat sold in the U.S. (Carson, 1999, 75). Upton Sinclair (1906) created a political firestorm with his documentation of the unsavory conditions in the Chicago meat packing industry at the turn of the Century in his novel *The Jungle*. Sinclair described spoiled hams treated with formaldehyde and sausages made from rotten meat scraps, rats, and other refuse (Nash et al., 1998). The presentation in Sinclair's work was so graphic that it caused President Roosevelt to push for policy change. Roosevelt's initial reaction to Sinclair's book is well captured by one of his White House servants at the time (quoted in Carson, 1999, 75),

"Tiddy was reading Upton Sinclair's novel, toying with a light breakfast an' idly turnin' over th' pagesiv the'new book with both hands. Suddenly he rose fr'm th' table, an'cryin': I'm pizened,' begun throwin sausages out iv th' window. Th' ninth wan shtruck Sinitor Biv'ridge on the head an' made him a blond. It bounced off, exploded, an' blew a leg off a secret-service agent, an' th' scatthred fragmints desthroyed a handsome row iv ol' oak-trees. Sinitor Biv'ridge rushed in, thinkin' that th' Prisidint was bein'assassynated be his devoted followers in th'Sinit, an discovered Tiddy engaged in a hand-to-hand conflict with a potted ham. Th'Sinitor fr'm Injyanny, with a few well-directed wurruds, put out th'fuse an'rendered th'missile harmless. Since thin th' Prisidint, like th' rest iv us, has become a viggytaryan."

Thousands of other Americans had similar (though less violent) reactions to that of Roosevelt in 1906 upon reading Sinclair's novel; consequently, Sinclair's book created a groundswell of support for government regulation of food products that continues through the present. Meat, of course, is not the only food item that is regulated by the government. Rodent droppings, for instance, most assuredly would be present in breads and cereals without government regulations. The Classic Liberal arguments against "government regulation of business" could essentially allow rodent contamination of grain products to the extent that public health would be seriously endangered.

Tainted food, however, is not the only product problem allowed by an unregulated free market. Child pornography, for example (Included here as an example of an immoral product) would evidently also be present in abundance in an unregulated free market since such materials appear to be still available even in the current "regulated" market. Essentially, the laws of supply and demand that govern the free market mean that for every vice for which there is a societal demand, the market will produce a supply. Consequently, the unregulated market will have prostitutes, mind and body destroying drugs, and pornographic books and films. Obviously, even the regulated market has all of these things, but the problems are likely to be worse without government regulations.

In addition to allowing products that violate public morals, the unregulated free market allows profits to unscrupulous businesses that will sell all manners of products and make all kinds of false claims under the motive of profit. This was the case before government got involved in the business of regulating such things, and it still is. Consider the following article from 1905 (quoted in Nash et al., 1998, 751).

"Gullible Americans will spend this year some seventy-five million dollars in the purchase of patent medicines. In consideration of this sum it will swallow huge quantities of alcohol, an appalling amount of opiates and narcotics, a wide assortment of varied drugs ranging from powerful and dangerous heart depressants to insidious liver stimulants; and, far in excess of all other ingredients, undiluted fraud. For fraud exploited by the skillfullest of advertising bunco men is the basis of the trade."

So it was in 1905 prior to government regulations, but the general trends appear to have continued somewhat even with government regulations. For example, the marketers of a food supplement known as "Enzyte" claim that their product will enlarge penis size up to 41%. Advertisements for Enzyte State that "87% of women secretly revealed they wouldn't mind if their partner had added size. Enzyte can take you there." There are also similar products on the market that are purported to increase the size of women's breasts. Evidently, little has changed since the Pure Food and Drug Act of 1905, and advertisers still make questionable (if not just plain false) claims despite the "big government over-regulation." Clearly, such false claims could be much worse in the absence of government oversight.

Free Market Dislocations

A further problem with Classic Liberalism is that the market produces harsh dislocations and hardships such as unemployment. In truth, all unemployment is not due to the fact that there are some lazy people that do not want to work. Instead, investment in the free market can be expected to produce new technologies that have the negative result of displacing workers. For instance, many a wagon wheel manufacturer was put out of work in the early 20th Century after the introduction of the automobile. Similarly, the ice man that delivered blocks of ice to private residences was quickly put out of work after the invention of electric refrigeration. In either case, the unemployment that resulted had nothing to do with the willingness of people to work, and everything to do with free market-driven changes in technology that displaced workers.

Problems with Free Trade

Another facet of Classic Liberalism that is fraught with problems is the Classic Liberal doctrine of free trade. This is not to say that free trade may be all negative, and indeed it is not; however, it is also far from a panacea. For example, the laws of comparative advantage may shift employment in any given country to low wage industries. In our fictitious free trade example presented earlier, for instance, Mexico would shift labor into citrus farming while the United States would shift labor away from citrus farming and into computers. Obviously, the shift of workers in Mexico from the high tech sector to citrus agriculture would involve a shift from a higher wage industry to a lower wage industry and thus depress wages, consumption, and growth in Mexico as well as technological advancement. In general, empirical studies suggest that more workers in the agricultural sector in any country seems to correlate more with economic underdevelopment, than with development, thus the long term impact of such a shift due to free trade may be negative (Wheeler and Muller, 1986, 314).

A further problem with free trade is that it often leads to dependence on unreliable foreign sources for goods. For example, the OPEC oil embargo of 1973 sent oil prices soaring and contributed to double-digit inflation in the United States. The embargo did not end until Henry Kissinger made a visit to the Middle East to warn the Saudis that the U.S. would not tolerate a continued embargo; hence, the embargo ended thirty days later, but not before significant economic upheaval (Jones, 1996, 637).

Chapter Four

Traditional Conservatism

The second major conservative ideology prevalent in the Republican Party in the late 20th and early 21st Centuries is known as Traditional Conservatism. Traditional Conservatism in American history emerged out of the foundations set by the Pilgrims and Puritans of the 17th Century and has continued as an ideological force in American politics through the Christian Coalition and other social conservatives of the present. Traditional Conservatism has not always dominated American politics, and from time to time it has taken a significant back seat to Classic Liberalism, but its influence always has been noticeably present even when it has not been dominant.

Negative View of Human Nature

Traditional Conservatives tend to espouse the "realist" negative view of human nature and a low view of the average person's intelligence. In other words, Traditional Conservatives tend to view humans as naturally bad, uncooperative, untrustworthy, and in some instances, just plain stupid. As a consequence, Traditional Conservatives tend to view government and politics (both permeated with those corrupt and dull-minded people) with great skepticism (Schumaker, Kiel, and Heilke, 1996, 90). After all, if people are naturally bad, they can be expected to be extra bad when they are entrusted with political power. The popular quote from Lord Acton that "power corrupts, but absolute power corrupts absolutely" is consistent with Traditional Conservative ideology.

Society is in Decay

Traditional Conservatives view the current society as in decay, depraved, and decadent. The government within that society in the here and now is equally flawed, but the government and society of the past are viewed as virtuous, and glorious. As such, Traditional Conservatives have disdain for current politicians such as the "immoral" Bill Clinton, who is a product of the current flawed society, but reverence for the politicians of the past, such as George Washington, Abraham Lincoln, and Thomas Jefferson (Hoover, 1994, 47-51).

Demonization of Enemies

Traditional Conservatives also tend to demonize their enemies. Whether the enemy is Bill Clinton or Saddam Hussein, the enemy is not only despised, but demonized, dehumanized and condemned not only as a political opponent, but as evil by very nature (Berlet, 1998). A very good example of such "demonization" is Osama Bin Laden's ability to portray America as such an evil infidel that God will be happy with his "martyrs" for flying airplanes into buildings and killing thousands of innocent people. Osama Bin Laden and his followers are the Traditional Conservatives of the Islamic world.

A closer look at Traditional Conservatives in the U.S., however, reveals some striking similarities. For example, the web site of Westboro Baptist Church in Topeka, Kansas (www.godhatesfags.com/) denounces homosexuals not only as "workers of iniquity" and "abominable," but also includes a memorial celebration of the number of days that Matthew Shepard (a gay man murdered by exposure in Wyoming) "has been in hell." In such a mindset there is only good and evil, white and black, with us or against us, and no "grey areas" or anything in between. Osama Bin Laden and the Taliban are obviously fabulous examples of this ideology, but then so is the Westboro Baptist Church in Topeka, Kansas.

The views of Westboro Baptist Church, however, are not unique in American society. For example, in a letter to the Editor of the *Amarillo Globe News* on June 28, 2004, a local Traditional Conservative complained that Senator "Teddy" Kennedy should be executed for treason for his statement that "Abu Ghraib prison is still open, all that has changed is the management." Furthermore, the writer goes on to argue that the Iraqi people are a "bunch of animals" and that the torture at Abu Ghraib prison was therefore fitting punishment for them. Obviously, the political enemies according to this Traditional Conservative are so dehumanized that they are not only considered to be "animals," but worse than animals since they should be tortured and executed. When the enemy is thus dehumanized, torture and killing are prescribed with little violation of conscience.

Low Social Trust

The negative view of human nature espoused by Traditional Conservatives also translates into low social trust. As a consequence,

Traditional Conservatives tend to favor rule through coercion and advanced security measures through a strong military, a strong police force, and an emphasis on personal self-defense. For Traditional Conservatives, a strong military is necessary because foreign entities cannot be trusted not to attack. A strong internal police force is also needed because the "naturally bad" humans cannot be trusted and otherwise will not behave. Measures for personal defense, such as the right to bear arms, are required for the same reasons (Hoover, 1994, 60-61).

Policies for dealing with crime are slanted heavily toward retribution and punishment, with incarceration and corporal and capital punishment favored over rehabilitation programs. Essentially, since humans are naturally bad, the only thing they might understand is pain (Territo, Halstead, and Bromley, 1989, 387-388). The Traditional Conservative view on punishment is reflected in numerous passages in both the Koran and the Bible. In the words of Mohammed in the Koran, (5:38) "And the man who steals and the woman who steals, cut off their hands as a punishment for what they have earned." Similarly, Moses writes in Exodus 21:23-24,

> "If there is serious injury, you are to take life for life, eye for eye, tooth for tooth, hand for hand, foot for foot, burn for burn, wound for wound, bruise for bruise."

Reverence for Symbols, Institutions, and History

In spite of the negative view of human nature and the disdain for government and politics of the present, Traditional Conservatives have an extreme reverence for symbols, institutions, and history, both religious and patriotic (Dunn and Woodard, 1991, 31, 48). Traditional Conservatives in the United States generally view the U.S. as the greatest country in the history of mankind, the American form of government the greatest ever invented (if not handed to the founding fathers directly from God himself), and those that criticize the American form of government are not just critics, but an traitorous abominations before God that should be shipped out of the country. Furthermore, the great figures of history, Lincoln, Washington, Jefferson, Franklin, etc., were endowed with brilliance, leadership, wisdom, integrity, and virtue that simply cannot be matched in the present time. Historical figures are placed on a pedestal and the "revisionist" historians that would write things such as the accusation that Jefferson slept with his slaves or that George Washington was not a great general, but also had a mistress, are not only wrong (the DNA evidence on Jefferson and Sally Hemmings being invented by those liberal scientists), but are also just plain evil people that should be silenced. Furthermore, the mere suggestion to the Traditional Conservatives that the First Amendment protects burning the American flag as an exercise of free speech is absolutely preposterous. For the Traditional Conservative in the U.S., America could never be wrong, and those who might say otherwise are not true Americans.

Return to a Better, Vanished Time

A major goal of the Traditional Conservatives is to return society to a mythical, better, vanished time (Eatwell, 1989, 69). To clarify, the "mythical, better, vanished time," is not mythical in the mind of the Traditional Conservative. To the Traditional Conservative, there was indeed once a time of virtue, but today's society has strayed from the original founding principles and what is needed is a return to those original principles and virtues. As a consequence, Traditional Conservatives in the U.S. can be expected to frequently call for a return to "what the founding fathers intended." In religion, Traditional Conservatives tend to hearken back to the original principles supposedly in place when the religion was founded (Dunn and Woodward, 1991, 77). For Traditional Conservatives in fundamentalist Protestantism, this tends to mean a return to "The Bible" or the principles of the "First Century Church." For the Taliban and Osama bin Laden, the call is a return to the Koran and the practices of Mohammed in the Seventh Century.

Rule by the "Good People"

In order to return society to that "better, vanished time," Traditional Conservatives believe that a "good government" resembling that of the past can be reconstructed as long as it is directed by "good people" with the correct set of values and correct ideology. In the Traditional Conservative mindset, there are indeed "those who know best," and it is those people who must be put in place to rule (Hoover, 1994, 49). For the Traditional Conservatives of radical Islam, this means rule by Islamic Clergy. For the Traditional Conservative Christians of the Middle Ages, this meant rule by the Pope and the Catholic Church. For the Traditional Conservatives of the United States in the last several decades, this means that "good Christian leaders" should be elected. As a consequence, the Christian Coalition distributes voter guides that instruct prospective voters as to which politicians are Christians (conspicuously, all conservative Republicans) and which are not.

In this vein, Tim LaHaye, an influential Traditional Conservative due to enormous sales of his fictional *Left Behind* series, also argued for the election of "pro-moral, pro-American, and Christian" politicians in his 1980 book, *The Battle of the Mind*. In this work, LaHaye argued that what America needed was "pro-moral leaders who will return our country to the Biblical base upon which it was founded" (LaHaye, 1980, 36). In other words, LaHaye is calling for a return to the mythical, better, vanished time. LaHaye (1980, 39) further added that the American system of separation of powers and checks and balances was borrowed directly from Biblical scripture. LaHaye then exhorts "Bible-believing pastors" to encourage their congregations to vote. LaHaye is not, however, evidently in favor of voting for all of those who call themselves Christian since he also mentions that there is a "well-known parallel between the social positions of the Methodist Church and the Communist Party" (LaHaye, 1980, 164). In the appendix to his book, LaHaye includes a questionnaire for submission to political candidates that is intended to determine whether they are moral and Christian. Questions include "Do you favor the passage of the Equal Rights Amendment?," "Except in wartime or dire emergency, would you vote for government spending that exceeds revenues?," and "Do you favor a reduction in Government?" (LaHaye, 1980, 164).

Government to Keep Order and Correct Human Weaknesses

The purpose of government in Traditional Conservatism is to keep order and correct human weaknesses (Schumaker, Kiel, and Heilke, 1996, 86, 93). Classic Liberals are congruent with the Traditional Conservatives concerning the "keep order" function, but they are greatly at odds with Traditional Conservatives concerning the "correct human weaknesses" function. Whereas Classic Liberals are generally less concerned with the regulation of homosexual behavior, abortions, alcohol, drugs, pornography, and other "human weaknesses," Traditional Conservatives make these not only areas of government responsibility, but areas of focus. For example, Traditional Conservatives in the United States in the last several decades pushed for laws to end abortions and favored laws against sodomy, pornography, prostitution, alcohol, gay marriage, and other human "weaknesses." Similarly, under more extreme forms of Islam in the Middle East, families may stone to death other family members that have "dishonored" the family. In other words, if an unmarried woman gets pregnant, the family members may stone her to death for this dishonor to the family (*Economist*, 2003). Similarly, Old Testament laws in the Bible call for executions of those who curse their parents, commit adultery, sodomy, or have sex with animals (Leviticus 20:9-15). Furthermore, in the case of sexual relations with animals, not only the human must be put to death, but the animal involved in the sex act must be killed as well (Leviticus 20:15-16).

Moral Absolutism

The use of government to "correct human weaknesses" by Traditional Conservatives is tied to their views of moral absolutes. To Traditional Conservatives, there most definitely *are* moral absolutes and they can most definitely and definitively identify those moral absolutes (Hoover, 1994, 50). As a consequence, it is irresponsible to allow people the freedom to do things that are morally wrong and therefore harm society. Freedoms, including academic freedoms, are therefore limited to these "basic truths" or moral absolutes (Nash, 1979, 40).

Generally, Traditional Conservatives have a source for their moral absolutes, and that source is very likely to be a religious book. In the Middle East, the vast majority of the people are Muslims; hence, the primary source of moral absolutes for most Traditional Conservatives in that region is the Koran. In the United States, the religion of the majority is Christianity; hence, the primary source of moral absolutes for most American Traditional Conservatives is the Bible. In either case, Traditional Conservatives call for governmental enforcement of the moral absolutes found in their Holy books; hence, Osama Bin Laden calls for governments to adopt sharia, the Islamic religious laws, and make those Islamic laws into governmental civil laws as well. Similarly, Traditional Conservatives in the U.S. push for the incorporation of "Bible truths" (such as anti-sodomy laws) into the laws of the U.S. and call for Federal enforcement.

Government to Support Societal Building Blocks

In furtherance of their goal to create a good and moral society, Traditional Conservatives argue that government should reinforce the main societal building blocks of church and family (Freeden, 2003, 88). In Iran, Sudan, and Afghanistan under the Taliban, what this came to mean in practice was Theocracy or rule by religious leaders. In the United States, President George W. Bush has pushed for "faith-based initiatives" or the provision of government goods and services through religious institutions. Traditional Conservatives in the U.S. have also fought to eliminate the "marriage penalty tax" and some States have developed new, more stringent, marriage laws that eliminate incompatibility as a "cause" for divorce (Loconte, 1998). Recent referendums in numerous states purposed to ban gay marriage are also examples of the Traditional Conservative impulse to defend the societal "building block" of the traditional marriage between one man and one woman.

Opposition to Social Change

In general, the adherence to moral absolutes tends to create a resistance to social change among Traditional Conservatives (Freeden, 2003, 88). In the United States at present, gay rights and gay marriages are merely among the latest in a series of social changes opposed by Traditional Conservatives that perhaps date back to the very beginning of human existence. Traditional Conservatives over the centuries also opposed women's rights, the end of slavery, racial integration, the Protestant Reformation, and the teachings of Jesus to name a few (The Pharisees were clearly the Traditional Conservatives of their society, claiming the knowledge of moral absolutes, calling for the application of those moral absolutes to all society, and opposing Jesus of Nazareth, who violated their conception of moral absolutes by healing and picking corn on the Sabbath etc.). In the Middle East, Traditional Conservatives currently oppose equality of the sexes, western dress, western music, western movies, and other "abominations" such as women without veils and men with clean-shaven faces. In short, Traditional Conservatives can be expected to resist most social changes unless those changes (such as those imposed by the Taliban) are a return to a discarded dogma of the past.

Problems with Traditional Conservatism

Problems of Moral Absolutism

One major problem for Traditional Conservatism is that large and complex societies do not have unanimity on what constitutes moral absolutes. No matter what one faction within society may call a moral absolute, there is always another faction in society (sometimes even other Traditional Conservatives) that will argue against such a categorization. For example, Osama Bin Laden opposes the shaving of facial hair, but Saddam Hussein, also a Muslim, did not. Orthodox Jews are careful not to clip the hair on the sides of their heads and do not trim the edges of their beards (as commanded in Leviticus 19:27), but other Jews may trim both. Similarly, Protestant fundamentalists in the U.S. tend to condemn alcohol consumption, but the Catholic Church (not normally noted as a liberal institution) is a bit less condemning on the subject. Conversely, the Catholic Church opposes all forms of birth control, while Protestant fundamentalists do not. Examples of such disagreement are perhaps endless, even when Traditional Conservatives all agree on the same source (such as the Bible) for their moral absolutes.

The validity of the Traditional Conservative view of morality, however, is also challenged by Contemporary Liberals in society. For example,

Traditional Conservatives typically oppose all abortions, yet they also typically oppose welfare programs that address the needs of children after they are born. Liberals argue that it is incongruent for Traditional Conservatives to "care" so much for the "unborn," yet have no compassion for those that are already "born." What purpose is there to save the fetus if its destiny is to starve? How can it be absolutely immoral to abort a fetus, yet it is not absolutely immoral to oppose government support for children that already have been born? What is the basis for such an inconsistent moral judgment?

As previously stated, in American society, the primary source reference for most Traditional Conservatives on moral absolutes is the Bible, and in the Middle East, it is the Koran. Unfortunately, it turns out that it is difficult to pin down some moral absolutes even when these religious books are the primary guides. This is partially because different Muslim and Christian sects differ on interpretation of the same holy books, but also partially because some of the moral precepts and commands presented in the Bible and the Koran are inconsistent with accepted norms and morals of Twenty-First Century Western society.

Consider, for example, the Bible teachings on slavery, an institution generally disparaged in recent decades, which if not outright condoned by the authors of the various books of the Bible, certainly is not condemned. In Ephesians 6:5, for example, Apostle Paul commands, "Slaves, be obedient to those who are your earthly masters, with fear and trembling, in singleness of heart, as to Christ." In contrast with Paul, most Americans in the Twenty-First Century, including most Traditional Conservatives, can be expected to oppose slavery on moral grounds. This is in spite of the fact that many American "founding fathers," such as Thomas Jefferson, were slave owners and the "father" of the American nation, George Washington, owned almost 400 slaves, none of whom were freed during his lifetime.

Furthermore, it is Traditional Conservatives that tend to call for a return to what the "founding fathers intended," the assumption being that the founders were such good "moral Christians" (Murrin, 1990, 19). Since many American founding fathers were slave owners, and slavery is generally condemned in Christendom in the Twenty-First Century, Traditional Conservatives are therefore forced to adopt the position that "we must judge them by their time." To this, liberals can only applaud, since that is exactly what the liberals have been saying all along; namely, that morals are not absolute, and instead are determined by, and change with, society. Traditional Conservatives tend to counter with "back to the Bible" arguments, but the closer one inspects the Bible, the more difficult it is to find a moral absolutist position against many diverse activities, but particularly slavery. For example, in Leviticus 25: 42-46, the God of Israel instructs the Israelites concerning the subject of slavery and condones the enslavement of non-Israelites by the Israelites. There is a bit of a double standard, however, because the Hebrew God specifically commands that the Israelites themselves may not be sold as slaves. Evidently, it is very good to be God's "chosen" people, and not so good for the "unchosen." The entire passage is presented below:

> "Because the Israelites are my servants, whom I brought out of Egypt, they must not be sold as slaves. Do not rule over them ruthlessly, but fear your God. Your male and female slaves are to come from the nations around you; from them you may buy slaves. You may also buy some of the temporary residents living among you and members of their clans born in your country, and they will become your property. You can will them to your children as inherited property and can make them slaves for life, but you must not rule over your fellow Israelites ruthlessly."

That slavery is clearly allowed here by the God of the Israelites is indisputable. That it is allowed for one group and not for another is also indisputable. That God isn't particularly concerned with equal rights is also apparent. That it is all pure and "moral," however, is entirely another issue. Were it found somewhere other than the Bible (such as the Koran, for instance), one suspects that most Bible fundamentalists of the Twenty-First Century might consider its teachings immoral. If, however, slavery was a fine and moral practice in ancient Israel because God allowed it, and if morals are absolute and unchanging, then one can only conclude that slavery in the present is also moral since morality is absolute and does not change (or at least it doesn't according to Traditional Conservatives).

Similarly, Exodus 21: 20-21 allows slave masters to beat their slaves without punishment as long as they don't kill them. This suggests not only that slavery is fine and moral, but it is also moral to physically abuse the slaves as long as one does not go "overboard" and kill them. The entire passage reads,

> "If a man beats his male or female slave with a rod and the slave dies as a direct result, he must be punished, but he is not to be punished if the slave gets up after a day or two, since the slave is his property."

Once again, we can assume that most American Traditional Conservatives would find the above passage morally bankrupt if it were found in the Koran or any other non-Biblical source of moral precepts. One may also assume that most American Traditional Conservatives do not believe these to be moral principles that apply to Christians in the Twenty First Century; thus, in reality, Traditional Conservatives argue for the "moral absolutes" of the Bible, but they are very selective and contradictory concerning which precepts are "moral absolutes."

Some may argue that a presentation of the above passages in Leviticus and Exodus is "misuse" of the Bible. After all, every good Christian knows that Christians are no longer under the "Old Covenant" and can therefore ignore some of the Old Testament commands such as "Remember the Sabbath and Keep it Holy." Somehow, however, Traditional Conservatives never argued that one could ignore the "Thou Shalt Not Commit Adultery" command while Bill Clinton was President. Once again, Traditional Conservatives are selective and inconsistent with their moral absolutes taken from the Bible. Furthermore, the argument that some Old Testament commands can be discarded contains a weakness, because if morals are absolute and unchanging, they should not change from the Old Testament to the New. Because of such arguments, however, included below are statements from the New Testament that appear to be very "uncondemning" of slavery. For example, Apostle Paul States in I Corinthians 7:20-24 that:

> "Every one should remain in the State in which he was called. Were you a slave when called? Never mind. But if you can gain your freedom, avail yourself of the opportunity. For he who was called in the Lord as a slave is a freedman of the Lord. Likewise he who was free when called is a slave of Christ. You were bought with a price; do not become slaves of men. So, brethren, in whatever State each was called, there let him remain with God."

In this passage, Paul is obviously telling his fellow Christians that Christianity does not release individuals from slavery. Instead, if one were a slave at the time of conversion to Christianity, that person should remain a slave. Similarly, that same Apostle in Colossians 4:1 addresses slave owners with the following command: "Masters, treat your slaves justly and fairly, knowing that you also have a Master in heaven." Note that in treating slaves "fairly and justly," Paul doesn't mention anything about freeing the slaves.

As for the slaves themselves, Apostle Paul commands the following in Ephesians 6:5-9:

> "Slaves, be obedient to those who are your earthly masters, with fear and trembling, in singleness of heart, as to Christ; not in the way of eye-service, as men pleasers, but as servants of Christ, doing the will of God from the heart, rendering service with a good will as to the Lord and not to men, knowing that whatever good any one does, he will receive the same again from the Lord, whether he is a slave or free. Masters, do the same to them, and forbear threatening, knowing that he who is both their Master and yours is in heaven and there is no partiality with him."

Clearly, Paul does not advocate freeing the slaves in any of these passages. Instead, whether one is slave or free is immaterial because this world is not the one that matters to Paul. For Paul, the only thing that matters is the "next world" in the "afterlife." For the slave, he is to remain a slave upon his conversion to Christianity and be obedient to his master as to Christ. As for the slave owner, Paul does not tell him to release the slaves, but only to treat the slaves justly and fairly. Exactly what is just and fair about owning someone else remains unclear and these passages raise serious questions concerning slavery and moral absolutes. If slavery is sinful, why does Paul not condemn it? Does sin not matter in this world? Paul certainly does plenty of condemnation of sinful activity elsewhere (Galatians 5:19-21 is a good example). It is difficult to conclude anything from these passages other than that Paul did not view slavery as sinful or morally wrong in itself.

Paul continues with his tacit support for the institution of slavery in the epistle to Philemon, where Paul addresses the problem caused by a runaway slave (Onesimus) who has since converted to Christianity. He tells Philemon (the slave owner) that he is sending the slave back—though he should be received as "no longer a slave but more than a slave, as a beloved brother." In Philemon 12-16, Paul states that,

> "I am sending him back. You therefore receive him, that is, my own heart, whom I wished to keep with me, that on your behalf he might minister to me in my chains for the gospel. But without your consent I wanted to do nothing, that your good deed might not be by compulsion, as it were, but voluntary. For perhaps he departed for a while for this purpose, that you might receive him forever, no longer as a slave but more than a slave, as a beloved brother."

Based on these writings of Paul in Ephesians, Corinthians, and Colossians, it appears inconsistent that Paul's "no longer a slave" statement in Philemon means that Paul is declaring the freedom of the slave. Instead, a logical conclusion is that the slave is returning to his former condition of servitude (the condition he was in when he was called), but he is going to be treated like a "brother" while enduring that servitude. There is no suggestion whatsoever that "owning one's brother" might be morally wrong.

Some may argue that this passage should be interpreted instead to mean that the slave Onesimus has become freed. If this is so, then why is he then being sent back, since it at least infers that returning to Philemon was not Onesimus' choice, but Paul's? Further evidence that Onesimus remains a slave is found in verse 14 where Paul informs Philemon that "without your consent I wanted to do nothing." This suggests Paul recognized that it was the slave owner Philemon who has control over the destiny of Onesimus. The statement "that you might receive him forever" in verse 15 may be Paul's suggestion that because Onesimus is now a Christian brother,

Philemon can now own him "forever," and it was for this purpose that Onesimus was converted! This is far from a condemnation of slavery, and this is not "old covenant" here, but New Testament and Apostle Paul, the most prolific writer of New Testament epistles.

In the final analysis, if one is to hold to the "moral absolutes" of the Bible and argue that morals are constant and unchanging, it is difficult to conclude anything other than that slavery is moral and permissible for Christian believers both then as well as now. If one must hold to moral absolutes, the only other possible conclusion is that Apostle Paul was wrong, and slavery was wrong then as well as now. Accepting this position, however, calls into question the doctrines of Bible literalism and inerrancy, both central to the Traditional Conservatism of the Christian Coalition within the Republican Party.

Slavery, however, is only one example where American Christians of the Twenty-First Century generally differ on a question of morality from that taught in the Bible. Polygamy is another glaring example. In the interest of space, we shall avoid going into as much detail here, but the Old Testament of the Bible is replete with polygamy that goes unpunished and unprohibited either by the Hebrew God or by the Laws of Moses. For instance, in the Book of Genesis, Abraham's grandson Jacob had two wives, the beautiful Rachel and the "sore-eyed" Leah. The story is essentially presented in such a way that one may be caused to feel sympathy for Jacob having to work an extra seven years before he can marry the pretty girl. Instead of being condemned as an immoral polygamist, Jacob is held in high esteem as a "man of God." If "immorality" is *always* condemned in the Bible, one can logically only conclude that polygamy must not be a moral absolute, and Bill Clinton was perhaps not immoral, but merely born in the wrong century.

The polygamy in the Bible, however, does not stop with Jacob. King David, "a man after God's own heart," had 14 wives and 10 "concubines." Not to be outdone, David's son Solomon, "the wisest man that ever lived" had 700 wives and 300 concubines. While, it is true that the Hebrew God in the Bible punished King David for adultery with Bathsheba (not to mention the murder of her husband), there are no condemnations against David for his other sex partners, only for taking his pleasure with the wife of someone else and murdering her husband. In fact, God even helped David's polygamy by striking dead the husband of David's second wife (Abigail) so that David could marry her himself (I Samuel 25:36-44). If morals are absolute and unchanging, one should conclude from the life of King David that polygamy is perfectly moral. The only other possible conclusion (if morals are absolute and unchanging) is that polygamy is morally wrong at present, and that it was also morally wrong for King David circa 1000BC. Once again, Traditional Conservatives might argue that perhaps we must judge King

David by his time, when polygamy was accepted. If so, however, morals are not absolute and are instead determined by society, a position that Contemporary Lliberals espouse and Traditional Conservatives vehemently argue against.

Moral Absolutes Limit Technological Progress.

In spite of the fact that society, including the Traditional Conservatives themselves, cannot agree on moral absolutes, Traditional Conservatives historically have used their moral absolutism to limit academic freedom and therefore hinder technological progress. There is perhaps no greater example than the thousand-year stunting of technological growth in Europe under the auspices of the Catholic Church after the fall of Rome in 410AD. During this time period, the Church monopolized learning and systematically eliminated all ideas that conflicted with the Church's official view of the Bible. The losses in science are incalculable, but one might argue that the destruction of knowledge by the Church set European society back almost 2000 years. Under the oppressive rule of the Church, the aqueducts, plumbing systems, and toilets (yes, toilets) established by the Romans essentially vanished and the road system established by the Romans fell into disrepair and remained so until the Eighteenth Century. The Church taught that all aspects of the flesh should be reviled and therefore the Church discouraged washing of the body. As a consequence, the middle ages were fraught with epidemics, partially due to poor sanitation (Ellerbe, 1995, 43-44).

In contrast to Christian Europe after the Fifth Century, in Pagan and free-thinking Greece in the Sixth Century B.C. (prior to the Catholic Church's monopoly on knowledge), Greek scholars developed thousands of ideas that are now accepted as sound scientific principles, but were later lost after the Catholic Church gained control of knowledge. For example, Pythagoras first developed the theory that the earth was a spinning sphere that revolved around the sun. Related to this discovery, Pythagoras concluded that eclipses were natural phenomena rather than special dispensations of Providence. Pythagoras also argued that the earth's surface hadn't always been just as it was, but that what was then sea, had once been land (and vise-versa); that some islands had once formed parts of continents; that mountains were forever being washed down by rivers and new mountains formed; that volcanoes were outlets for subterranean heat rather than surface entrances into Hell, and that fossils were the buried remains of ancient plants and animals turned into stone (Wheless, 1997, 327). Similarly, Aristarchus (220-143 BC) correctly calculated the inclination of the earth's axis at 23.5 degrees, and thus verified the obliquity of the eliptic and explained the succession of the seasons. Erastosthenes (276-194 BC) knew that the earth was round, invented the imaginary lines of latitude and longitude, and calculated the circumference of the earth at 28,700 miles seventeen centuries prior to Columbus. Democritus developed a theory of atoms, or constituents of matter too small to be cut or divided, in 460 BC. Anaxagoras (500-428 BC) was the first to trace the origin of animals and plants to pre-existing germs in the air and "ether" more than 2200 years before Charles Darwin. Hero of Alexandria (130 BC) discovered the principle of the working power of steam and developed a steam engine 1900 years before steam engines tamed the American West (Wheless, 1997, 327-333).

After the Catholic Church (read here as "Traditional Conservatives) monopolized learning with the fall of Rome, however, the knowledge of the ancients became lost and it would be the Sixteenth Century before Copernicus would reintroduce the theory that the earth revolved around the sun. Galileo later made the same "discovery" as Copernicus (more than 2000 years after Pythagoras), and in 1615, traveled to Rome to defend the Copernican theory that the Earth revolved around the sun. A committee of advisers to the Church Inquisition declared that holding the view that the Sun is the center of the Universe or that the earth moves is absurd and formally heretical. As a consequence, Cardinal Bellarmine warned Galileo not to hold, teach, or defend Copernican theory. In 1633, Galileo was sentenced to prison for an indefinite term for continuing to teach Copernican theory and forced to sign a formal recantation. Galileo was then allowed to serve his term under house arrest.

Galileo also asserted that all objects fall at the same rate, another scientific fact denied by the Catholic Church. Galileo decided to prove his theory and ascended the Leaning Tower of Pisa from which he dropped two iron balls of different weights. When both struck the ground at the same instant, the Christians (again, read as "Traditional Conservatives") refused to accept the results of the demonstration (Galileo must be a witch) and drove him out of the city of Pisa (Wheless, 1997, 329). Two hundred years later in 1835, the Church finally took Galileo's works off of the list of banned books. Finally, in 1992, the Catholic Church formally admitted that Galileo's views on the solar system were correct. Unfortunately, the apology was a few centuries late to do much for Galileo and perhaps a bit too quiet a whisper for the thousand-year constipation of progress.

Traditional Conservatives in the U.S. at present (along with the Catholic Church) now accept the scientific fact that the earth revolves around the sun; however, they tend to argue against Darwin's theory of evolution (which is, in the Twenty-First Century, mainstream science accepted as fact in the scientific community at large and generally rejected only by Protestant Christian fundamentalists). Similarly, Traditional Conservatives in the U.S. at present tend to oppose stem cell research because they believe it violates another moral absolute and may somehow lead to more abortions. While it is certainly possible that the Traditional Conservatives may be right on the stem cell issue, given their track record over the last 2000 years, it is perhaps difficult to expect them to be finally right this time. Moral debates aside, it is impossible to know what medical breakthroughs may be stunted by limits on stem cell research (perhaps none), but it is also possible that future historians will place those against the teaching of evolution and stem cell research in the same bin with the Trial of Galileo and the Flat Earth Society. Time will tell, of course, but the best predictor of future prospects is probably past performance, and the past performances of Traditional Conservatives in the areas of science are consistently sources of later embarrassment.

Limits on Freedoms Misuse Resources

The limits on freedoms imposed by an adherence to moral absolutes also tend to waste (or at least misuse) resources, both human and otherwise. For example, throughout human history, how many great discoveries has the human race not had because half the population (women) was told to stay home, raise babies, and raise no questions? What was lost in Afghanistan under the Taliban as educated women were told to return to their homes and to attend to traditional "wifery"? What was lost in the United States when blacks were reduced to slavery and legally denied education? The answers to these questions, of course, are incalculable, but to argue anything other than that technological advancement was surely hindered by Traditional Conservative ideology in these cases is to ignore thousands of years of evidence.

Sordid History of Traditional Conservatism

The adherence to moral absolutes (and Traditional Conservatism in general) clearly has a sordid history that in retrospect over the centuries appears at best silly, and at worst, just tragic. For example, Traditional Conservatives opposed the Civil Rights movement of the 1960s in the U.S. During this same time period American Traditional Conservative religious leaders (such as Jerry Falwell) preached against integration and civil rights from the pulpit (Conason and Lyons, 2000, 141). Traditional Conservatives also opposed the women's rights movement of the 1960s as well as the women's suffrage movement of the early 20th century. In the case of women's suffrage, protestant fundamentalists argued that God had set a side a traditional place for women in the home as man's "helper" and that place designated by God did not include politics. As a consequence, Traditional

Conservatives argued that women's suffrage would lead to divorce and the destruction of the family (Brinkley, 2003, 586).

Almost as ominous as what Traditional Conservatives opposed over the years are the policies they favored. For instance, Traditional Conservatives typically favored the war in Vietnam and the McCarthy "witch hunts" of the 1950s, as well as the "Red Scare" of 1919 and the KKK of the 1920s. The KKK of the 1920s in particular considered itself a "Christian" organization and membership was open only to White Protestants (Haas, 1963, 52). Traditional Conservatives also favored Prohibition because they viewed alcohol as sinful and drunkenness as condemned in the Bible. This condemnation of alcohol was in spite of the fact that Jesus' first miracle was in making approximately 180 gallons of wine at a wedding feast.

Traditional Conservatives are also typically anti-immigrant since they prefer to conserve American culture as it is, or as it was in the past, and immigrants tend to bring and blend new cultures with the existing ones, thus representing change. In the early Twentieth Century, Traditional Conservatives were able to combine their racist and nativist tendencies with their opposition to alcohol and thus blame alcohol abuse on immigrants and minorities when calling for its prohibition. According to the *Baptist Standard* in 1917, Prohibition was "an issue of Anglo-Saxon culture versus the inferior civilization of niggers in the cities" (Calvert et al., 2002, 307).

Traditional Conservatives also favor prayer in schools and the teaching of "creationism," but opposed flying (if man were meant to fly, he'd have wings) in the early Twentieth Century. Furthermore, Traditional Conservatives opposed the abolition of slavery, favored the Tories in the American Revolution, favored the Salem witch hunts (as well as the rest of the "witch hunts" in both the U.S. and Europe), and, evidently, also favored the crucifixion of Jesus of Nazareth if the Pharisees may be considered (as they should be) the Traditional Conservatives of their time.

Unclear Who are the "Good People"

Another major problem for Traditional Conservatives is that it is unclear just who are the "good people" that should rule. For example, the Taliban in Afghanistan certainly considered themselves to be the "good and Godly people" who were obligated to rule over the people in Afghanistan and correct societal "weaknesses." Meanwhile, most of the rest of the world denounced those same Islamic clerics as "evil tyrants" and a government that "harbored terrorists." Similarly, the Catholic Church killed thousands of people for witchcraft for centuries in Europe, but these actions are now almost universally denounced as morally wrong even by most Catholics.

Furthermore, even the Catholic Church admitted that they were wrong in opposing Galileo's astronomical conclusions.

Closer to home, in 2003, George W. Bush referred to the regime of Saddam Hussein in Iraq as part of an "Axis of Evil" and accused Saddam of "brutality" and of killing his own people. In the 1980s, however, the U.S. had been aiding that same "evil" dictator in his war against Iran. Furthermore, at this writing, there is a ruling entity in Iraq that is still killing Iraqi people on a regular basis, but Traditional Conservatives do not view the American occupying army and their Commander in Chief as "evil." Traditional Conservatives might argue that the U.S. military only kills those "evil" Iraqis that are loyal to the "evil" al Qaeda or Saddam Hussein (who obviously has only really been evil since his invasion of Kuwait in 1990, otherwise he surely would not have been aided by the good and moral Reagan Administration). Regardless, to the families of the dead Iraqis, it probably matters little whether it was "good" Americans or "evil" supporters of Saddam Hussein that killed their family members. In the final analysis, just the fact that there are insurgents against the American occupation may suggest that many Iraqi people are unable to recognize that the American troops are "good and moral." The American actions of torture and humiliation at Abu Ghraib prison most certainly cloud the issue of "good and evil" for many Iraqi citizens. Traditional Conservatives may argue that the insurgents are evil themselves, and the torture and humiliation was therefore justified, but in any case, there certainly is no universal agreement on who is "evil" and who is not.

Finally, Traditional Conservatives themselves do not appear to be consistent in choosing their own "good" leaders. For example, the Christian Coalition argues for the election of "Christian" leaders, but Traditional Conservatives overwhelmingly supported a former Hollywood actor in his second marriage (Ronald Reagan, the only "divorced" American President) over the Southern Baptist Christian, Jimmy Carter, in his first and only marriage, in 1980. Similarly, Newt Gingrich, who led the Republicans back to power in the House in 1994, also had extramarital affairs and announced to his wife that he wanted a divorce while she was in the hospital recovering from surgery (Franken, 1999). Additionally, the wife of frequent Presidential candidate and social conservative Pat Buchanan gave birth to a child two months after they were married, obviously suggesting that the couple had engaged in the Traditional Conservative taboo of premarital sex. Meanwhile, Traditional Conservative Bill Bennet, best-selling author of *The Book of Virtues,* admitted a serious gambling habit, another anathema to Traditional Conservatives, in 2003 (Franken, 2003).

Traditional Conservatives have not even been consistent with their support for their current darling, George W. Bush. Although the Christian

Coalition supported George W. Bush for President in 2000 and have
continued that support ever since, those same Traditional Conservatives
within the Republican Party in Texas just four years earlier prevented some
of George W. Bush's delegates from attending the Republican National
Convention because Bush was too "soft" on abortion (Maxwell and Crain,
2002, 200).

George W. Bush is also representative of the incongruence between what
Traditional Conservatives say they revere in terms of the "self-made man"
and "work ethic." In other words, Traditional Conservatives tend to say that
they support sobriety and hard work and argue that people should be
rewarded based on that hard work; however, their most recent champion,
George W. Bush, actually worked very little in his life before becoming
Governor of Texas in 1995, admittedly focused primarily on alcohol
consumption until the age of 40, and set a record for the number of vacation
days by a President in his first year in office. By April 15, 2004, George W.
Bush had made 33 trips to his ranch at Crawford, TX for recreation and
relaxation. All told, Bush spent almost eight months of his first 38 months in
office at Crawford, Texas (*Economist*, April 17, 2004). The previous record
vacation days was held by the Traditional Conservatives' previous
champion, Ronald Reagan. Conversely, Traditional Conservatives typically
loathed Lyndon Johnson, Jimmy Carter, and Bill Clinton, all three noted
"workaholics" during their time in the White House.

Intolerance and Demonization of Enemies

The adherence to moral absolutes also creates intolerance among
Traditional Conservatives against those that think differently and leads to
demonization of the enemies of Traditional Conservatism. Those that think
differently are considered not only as political opponents, but as "evil"
individuals that may be exterminated. The very meaning of the word
"heresy," for which the Catholic Church executed, tortured, and brutalized
thousands for centuries, is "to think differently." Traditional Conservatives
in the Twenty-First Century that kill others because the others "think
differently" include Osama Bin Laden and the Islamic extremists that carried
out the 9/11 attacks on the U.S. Similarly, in 2005, American Evangelist Pat
Robertson called for the assassination of Venezuelan President Hugo Chavez
on his Christian television program.

On the subject of the Traditional Conservatism that produces religious
terror, Bruce Hoffman (1995) argues that Religious terrorists are different
than other types because they are not constrained by the same factors that
inhibit other types. They see their world as a battlefield between the forces of
light and darkness and winning is not described in terms of political gains.

Instead, the enemy must be totally destroyed. Hoffman argues that Holy terrorists see killing as a sacramental act and the purpose of their operation is to kill. Pointing to Islamic terrorism as an example, Hoffman argues that the purpose of religious terrorism specifically is to kill the enemies of God. In doing so, religious terrorists demonize their enemies, thus making murder much easier because the enemies are no longer people, but are instead equated with the ultimate source of evil. Enemies are devilish and demonic and in league with the forces of darkness. Consequently, it is not enough to simply defeat them. Instead, they must be completely eradicated. Similarly, Chip Berlet (1998) argues that the demonized enemy becomes a scapegoat for all problems and it becomes possible for the group to believe that all evil is the result of some sort of conspiracy involving their scapegoat and the evil entity.

Plot Mentality

The "Plot Mentality" is the ultimate result in this mindset where the Traditional Conservatives view the world as a cosmic struggle between the forces of good and evil (Eatwell, 1989, 71). In this construct, the "evil" forces are always "plotting" to destroy society. The McCarthy hearings and investigations of the 1950s very well fit this type of Traditional Conservative behavior. "Liberals" in the U.S. argue that the Whitewater investigation of Bill Clinton by Kenneth Starr was a similar "witch-hunt." Perhaps George W. Bush's obsession with Saddam Hussein and the other individuals in the famous "deck of cards" should be similarly categorized. In Bush's arguments for invasion, Saddam Hussein was not portrayed merely as a poor leader or a threat, but as an "evil" person plotting to destroy the American way of life with Weapons of Mass Destruction. For Saddam Hussein's now known to be fictitious WMDs to be a threat, one had to assume not only that Saddam was attempting to build them, but that he was also "evil" enough to use them against the United States for the express purpose of killing thousands of innocent Americans without provocation and was secretly plotting to do so.

This "plot mentality," however, is not limited only to George W. Bush or the American side of the "war on terror." In the case of Islamic terrorism, the "Plot Mentality" is a major driving force behind the actions of the terrorists. According to Berlet (1998), fanatic Muslims blame all of the world's problems on a conspiracy between the U.S. and Zionists in Israel. The U.S. is not merely trying to eliminate terrorism or terrorists, but is instead determined to stamp out Islam itself. As a consequence, Religious terrorists are not necessarily seeking a "wider audience," as are other terrorists, but their purpose is the defense of Islam and God himself against evil entities; hence, their play is for God and God alone. Whether or not other humans condemn their actions as immoral is immaterial as long as God is pleased.

Apocalyptic Thinking

Indiscriminate killing by intolerant and demonizing religious traditional conservatives is aided by apocalyptic thinking (Eatwell, 1989, 71). In the Koran, for example, Mohammed speaks of a final judgment against evil, and a similar story is found in the Bible book of Revelation. In this conception, the Islamic terrorists are merely "soldiers of God" aiding him in his judgment, as are the bombers of abortion clinics in the United States. All deterrents to violence are rendered meaningless by the promise of a new age that invites terrorists to fight as holy warriors in a period of fanatic zeal when the deity is about to bring creation to an end. What difference does it make if a mess is made of this world if it is going to end tomorrow anyway? Furthermore, since God rewards the faithful, if innocent people are killed this morning, surely the dead will be in a better place in heaven this afternoon, so what's wrong with that? Finally, if "evil" people are killed, then this world is a better place without those evil people and the sooner that God can be aided in casting them all into hell, the better.

Myth of the "Better, Now Vanished, Time."

If there is any constant in history, it is that basic human nature does not change; consequently, almost every "time" could be categorized as "the best of times, and the worst of times." For example, in the case of the "Godly" Pilgrims and Puritans of the Seventeenth Century, they not only executed people for witchcraft and butchered the Indians, but they also in 1642 put a man to death for "buggery" after he admitted to copulating with "a mare, a cow, two goats, five sheep, two calves and a turkey" (Bradford, 1856, 1981). If one prefers to speak of the "golden age" of the United States in the early years following the American Revolution (an era often spoken of with reverence by Traditional Conservatives), a closer look reveals that here too all things were not quite so perfect. For African Americans at the time, most were in bondage; therefore, it seems reasonable to conclude that most African-Americans at the time would not think of the age of the American Revolution as a "golden age." Nevertheless, all blacks were not slaves in 1776, and manumission, or legal release from servitude was widely practiced during the American Revolution. Manumission, however, was extremely uneven across the states. While 10,000 slaves were voluntarily freed in Virginia during the Revolution, North Carolina passed a law in 1778 to prohibit manumission. The statute assigned "countenance and authority in violently seizing, imprisoning, and selling into slavery such as had been so emancipated" (Andrews, 1995, 35). Once again, though there are undoubtedly positives to be celebrated surrounding the time of the birth of the United States, it hardly could be construed by slaves in North Carolina at the time as a "golden age."

Similarly, the Native Americans of the time of the American Revolution surely could not have thought that things were so "golden" either as they were being forced off of the land they had occupied for centuries. The Cherokee Nation signed a 1791 treaty with the U.S. that recognized and delineated their territory as a sovereign nation within the State of Georgia. A few years later, gold was found within the designated area of the Cherokees and shortly thereafter (1830), Congress passed the Indian Removal Act to move the Cherokees further west and off of the land they had been promised by the 1791 Treaty. The Cherokees appealed to the Federal government to uphold the 1791 treaty (Treaties under the U.S. Constitution could supersede other domestic laws) and the U.S. Supreme Court ruled in favor of the Cherokees, but the tribe was evicted from their homes and marched to Oklahoma along the "Trail of Tears" anyway. The only "gold" in this "golden age" for the Cherokees was found in the land that had been taken away from them and the gold was taken from them along with the land (Perdue and Green, 2005, 1-19,).

Major problems in America's "golden age," however, were not limited to blacks and Native Americans. Since political participation was limited, for the most part, to white male landowners, it stands to reason that all was not viewed as marvelous by the women, nonlanded men, and other disenfranchised minorities of the time. For example, Abigail Adams, the wife of one President and mother of another, wrote a letter to her husband, John Adams, in 1776 asking him to "remember the Ladies" and not to "Put unlimited power into the hands of Husbands." Abigail goes on to declare to John, "that your Sex are Naturally Tyrannical is a Truth so thoroughly established as to admit of no dispute" (Quoted in Andrews, 1995, 33). John, of course, responded by essentially ignoring his wife's pleas and helping forge a country that limited politics to wealthy white men and left the women out of the political processes. Perhaps this "golden age of America" should be viewed as the "better, vanished time" for wealthy white men, sexists, and racists.

Another "better, vanished time" in America that Traditional Conservatives tend to revere is the generation immediately following World War II. It was during these years that the United States had emerged from WWII as the greatest military power in the world and 60% of Americans attended church on a weekly basis, the highest religiosity of any time in American history. A closer inspection of those "golden years" of the 1950s, however, reveals that blacks were relegated to second-class citizenship in a segregated society and women were generally denied equal opportunity in the workplace. Furthermore, greater church attendance did not apparently translate into sexual chastity. Alfred Kinsey (1948) in his revealing study of American culture entitled *Sex and the American Male*, revealed at the time that 67% of college-educated males and 84% of non college-educated males had engaged in sex outside of the bonds of marriage, whether premarital or extra-marital. Furthermore, 37% of American males surveyed revealed that they had experienced some type of homosexual activity (this included mutual masturbation in these numbers) and 18% of rural American males had experienced sex with animals. It appears, therefore, that the postwar period may have been a "golden age" for those engaging in bestiality, hardly the behavior that Traditional Conservatives tend to revere.

Correcting Human Weaknesses Increases Government

Traditional Conservative ideology is essentially in conflict with itself in that it tends to call for "less government," while simultaneously calling for an expansion of government to correct human weaknesses. Prohibition, for example, was an attempt to correct a "human weakness" through government that led to expansion of governmental coercive structures such as the Federal Bureau of Investigation (FBI) and the Bureau of Alcohol, Tobacco, and Firearms. Similarly, if abortions and gay sexual activities were prohibited, as advocated by Traditional Conservatives in the U.S., enforcement would require new divisions within the FBI (if not entirely new bureaucratic entities) charged with ensuring that these "human weaknesses" are curtailed. Such an increase in government power not only conflicts with the Traditional Conservatives' own "less government" mantra, but also conflicts with the Classic Liberals within the Republican Party who do not view the correction of such "human weaknesses" as within the proper scope of government.

There is a further problem in determining exactly what would constitute probable cause to justify a search in such cases? For instance, if homosexuality is illegal, and two men are roommates together and neighbors report to the police that it is suspicious that they have never seen women at the residence, does this constitute the "probable cause" to search or stake out the apartment for evidence of homosexual activity?

Concluding Remarks

Obviously, the problems and contradictions within Traditional Conservatism are legion and therefore the policy prescriptions that can be expected to arise from this ideology can be expected to be fraught with problems and contradictions as well. After all, this is the group in American politics that believes that witchcraft is real (hence the boycotts of Harry

Potter), is seriously concerned about the sexual orientation of Tinky Winky, a fictional puppet character on a television show for small children, and spent the 1970s spinning rock and roll records backwards in a fruitless search for reversed satanic messages. The concern over gay teletubbies (Tinky Winky), though misplaced, is probably largely benign. The same can not be said, however, for the Red Scare of 1919, the McCarthy witch-hunts of the 1950s, the opposition to Civil Rights in the 1960s, the support for the Vietnam War in the 1970s, the Ken Starr investigation, or the invasion of Iraq in 2003. The dangers posed to the world by Traditional Conservatism are what make the study of ideology perhaps as important as any other subject in political science.

Chapter Five

Libertarianism

Libertarianism is a form of Conservatism often considered separate from the more mainstream conservative ideologies, partially because it is a bit more extreme, and partially because Libertarians often separate themselves from other forms of more mainstream Conservatism. In fact, Libertarians, unlike Traditional Conservatives and Classic Liberals, have their own political party in the United States and run their own candidates for office separate from the Republican Party, the party that is generally recognized as the party of mainstream conservatism.

Unlike Classic Liberalism and Traditional Conservatism, Libertarianism is not generally recognized as a dominant ideology in the U.S. and the Libertarian Political Party remains a small, splinter party that can be expected to garner less than two percent of the vote in National elections. This may be a bit misleading, however, since a 2000 Rasmussen Research poll (www.lp.org/organization/history) revealed that up to 16% of Americans might be ideologically Libertarian even if they tend to vote for Republican political candidates instead of those from the Libertarian Party. If these survey data are valid, it suggests that the Libertarians, though much smaller as an organized political Party in the U.S., are nonetheless of significant importance as an ideological force in American politics.

Individualism and Choice

Libertarianism is essentially an offshoot of Classic Liberalism where the basic premises and fundamental centers of attention have been altered from the focus of Classic Liberalism on the free market to a primary focus instead on individual choice. Libertarianism is in many ways similar to Classic Liberalism, but more extreme in its call for limited government, celebration of individual rights, and adherence to the free market. In the Libertarian construct, unlimited consumer choice tends to crowd out or demote other values championed by Classic Liberals and Traditional Conservatives. Essentially, Libertarians are individualist conservatives whose primary political objective is the minimization of government, and through the minimization of government, the maximization of personal freedom and choice (Hoover, 1994, 66-68).

Libertarianism is a hyper-individualist ideology where Libertarians view themselves as the "true believers" in individual freedom and stress the fact that government, by its very nature, limits freedom. Individual freedom is valued above all else and it is assumed that the greater the individual freedoms, the greater the common good.

Focus on Property Rights

A major segment of the Libertarian celebration of individual freedom is the freedom and control over one's own property. For Libertarians, individual property rights are virtually inviolate and the property owners should be free to do whatever they please with their own property regardless of concerns for the common good. In turn, Libertarians tend to view the freedom over one's own property as an encapsulation of the common good in itself.

The Libertarian position on private property is explained in detail by Robert Nozick (1974) in *Anarchy, State, and Utopia*. Nozick argues that individuals are "entitled" to their property and everything in society flows from this property entitlement. For Nozick, individual freedoms and property rights are inextricably intertwined. Consequently, individuals cannot be deprived of their rights to their property without their consent or without just compensation. Furthermore, government cannot make policies that place limitations on individual freedoms or deprive persons of their property because any governmental actions should require the consent of the individuals affected by those actions.

Libertarians also share some similarities with Traditional Conservatives, in that Libertarians tend to hearken back to a "better, vanished time," but for Libertarians, the "better, vanished time" is not necessarily the era of the American "Founding Fathers," but instead the time before the era of "big government" in the U.S. that is generally viewed as beginning with the New Deal of Franklin Roosevelt in the 1930s. Hence, Libertarians view themselves as "conservators" of an earlier political and economic tradition (even though that earlier tradition was really the era of Classic Liberalism and the U.S. has never really had a truly "Libertarian" era) (Hoover, 1994, 70).

Role of Government

The only appropriate role of government in the Libertarian perspective is for security, especially security against threats from "without." In other words, Libertarians may favor a strong military so as to prevent foreign invasion, but that is the extent of their support for governmental activities (Sargent, 1993, 189). In fact, Libertarians are likely to view the military, like other facets of government, as "wasteful" of taxpayer money and a potential danger to individual freedoms; hence, though a strong military may be necessary, it too should be subjugated to the over-riding principle of limited government (Dunn and Woodard, 1991, 42-42). Some Libertarians, however, such as Murray Rothbard (1975) even argue against a large military and instead argue for the privatization of national defense. Similarly, in foreign policy, Libertarians tend to be isolationists and oppose American intervention in the affairs of other nations. Such "globalism," Libertarians argue, can only expand the power and scope of the national government, not to mention possibly lead to "world government" and therefore should be avoided.

In the Libertarian perspective, even security against dangers from "within" should be limited and police protections can be privatized. Optimally, individuals can arrange for their own protection either by defending themselves personally or through the hiring of private security firms (Rothbard, 1975). In other words, every avenue should be pursued to ensure that governmental police protections are kept to a minimum. Similarly, other services that one may normally think of as governmental, such as education, sanitation, public health, etc. would be delivered by private entities and paid for by the users of the services. Those that do not utilize the services available would therefore not have to pay anything. In this construct, for example, the only persons that would be paying to support schools would be the students (or parents/guardians of those students) who attended the schools. Those not using the schools would pay nothing and no one would be coerced to pay anything for the benefit of anyone other than themselves. Ideally, school costs for the indigent would be paid for by voluntary gifts from philanthropists. Persons that do not attend schools nor are responsible for persons attending schools would pay nothing toward the support of education for others unless they chose to do so voluntarily (Muccigrosso, 2001, 103-104).

Premium on the Free Market

Libertarians are generally in agreement with Classic Liberals in seeking free market solutions to societal problems. In the Libertarian vision, wages, prices, employment, and distribution of goods would be properly determined by the invisible hand of supply and demand. Any government intervention into the free market for any purpose is anathema. Libertarians may admit that such a system may produce great inequalities due to inequalities of abilities;

however, they generally argue that incomes that are gained from "just" processes of the free market are moral and proper regardless of any inequality that may result. Furthermore, Libertarians argue that the State has no right to redistribute goods that were "justly" obtained through the free market (Schumaker, Kiel, and Heilke, 1997, 54). In the words of Robert Nozick (1974) in *Anarchy, State, and Utopia*,

> "There is no central distribution; no person or group entitled to control all the resources, jointly deciding how they are to be doled out. What each person gets, he gets from others who give to him in exchange for something, or as a gift. In a free society, diverse persons control different resources, and new holdings arise out of the voluntary exchanges and actions of persons. There is no more a distributing or distribution of shares than there is a distributing of mates in a society in which persons choose whom they shall marry" (Quoted in Schumaker, Kiel, and Heilke, 1997, 54).

Nozick simplifies this theme with a play on Marx's famous dictum, "from each according to his abilities, to each according to his needs," and instead provides his Libertarian version: "From each as they choose, to each as they are chosen." In other words, governmental redistribution programs are viewed as violations of property rights and individual liberties and therefore unacceptable. Furthermore, any governmental solution is assumed to be inherently inefficient as well as a violation of the rights of taxpayers to do what they want with their own property. Taxes in general, necessarily must be kept to an absolute minimum (since government is kept to an absolute minimum) thus; the rights of property owners to control their own assets are maximized. Libertarians argue that the best method for remedying the inequalities produced through the free market is through voluntary action. Libertarians admit that inequalities will remain, but assume that the societal "haves" will be charitable enough to of their own volition prevent starvation among the societal "have-nots." In no case can such charity be coerced by the State.

Libertarians and Human Nature

The Libertarian view of human nature is generally congruent with the negative views of human nature espoused by Traditional Conservatives. Libertarian Albert Nock (1931), for example, in his *Theory of Education in the United States*, argued that the average person was incapable of higher learning and simply uneducable. Consequently, some Libertarians take the realist position that humans are naturally bad, uncooperative, stupid, selfish, and untrustworthy. It follows then that any government led by these "naturally bad" humans is likely to reflect the negative character of human nature. The minimization of government therefore also minimizes the problem of these bad, uncooperative, selfish, and untrustworthy individuals, having oppressive authority over others.

Unlike Traditional Conservatives, however, Libertarians do not favor restrictions on personal behavior or the use of government so as to correct societal weaknesses. In the Libertarian construct, individual behaviors will be regulated by the natural consequences of destructive behaviors. Drug abuse, for example, would not be worse without government restrictions because the drugs themselves are destructive and most people therefore seek to avoid drug addiction so as to improve their lives. Conversely, a minority of persons can be expected to abuse drugs, but since that situation also exists with governmental restrictions and controls, the imposition of such controls only raises taxes and limits freedom and does little to curb drug abuse. Libertarians point out that compliance with laws is for the most part voluntary; hence, coercive measures to restrict personal behavior are of little effect.

Libertarians also have a tendency to disdain written law, including the U.S. Constitution. Albert J. Nock (1936), for instance, argued that the U.S. Constitution betrayed the spirit of individual liberties embodied in the Declaration of Independence by aiding and abetting the rise of State power.

History of Libertarianism

The historical roots of Libertarianism are traced essentially to some of the same roots as Classic Liberalism and Traditional Conservatism. Libertarians, like Classic Liberals, celebrate the writings of Adam Smith and his free-market laissez-faire capitalism. Libertarians are also persuaded by Thomas Paine's (1776) argument in *Common Sense* that oppressive governments are the greatest threat to individual liberties. Libertarians, however, generally apply Herbert Spencer's (1851) essentially "social Darwinist" argument to the free market. Spencer wrote almost a decade before Darwin's *Origin of the Species*, but it was Spencer who coined the term "survival of the fittest." Spencer believed in the evolution of society through free market competition. In this view, the market is essentially a means of "natural selection" among humans and the "fittest" are the brightest, hardest working, and most talented individuals who would achieve success in the free market. The weak, slow-minded, and lazy, would fail in such a system, but this is natural and essentially unavoidable in any competitive system. Spencer also stressed (like Hobbes) that humans are naturally competitive, rather than cooperative, and free market competition is essentially the "state of nature." Spencer argued, however, that the free market competition would produce a better society in the long run, even if the weak and disadvantaged were forced to suffer in the short run. In any case, Spencer eschewed any form of governmental intervention to alleviate the suffering of the less talented.

Taking the Hobbesian negative views of human nature and principles of limited government a step further, Friedrich Von Hayek (1944) argued that the State, even for the purpose of security, could lead to tyranny since reliance on the State would lead to a breakdown in the system of individual self-reliance on which a natural society was based. In Hayek's view, it was this breakdown of individual self-reliance and its replacement with reliance on the State for security that led to the rise of the Nazis and the destruction of liberties in Germany in the 1930s. Hayek's theme that Statism is destructive to self-reliance was also central to the writings of Ayn Rand (1966), Tibor Machan (1974), and Albert J. Nock. Nock (1936, 3), for instance, argued in his book *Our Enemy the State* that,

> "If we look beneath the surface of our public affairs, we can discern one fundamental fact, namely: a great redistribution of power between society and the State."

In Nock's view, Democracy has ceased to function properly because instead of the government being directed by the people, the people were being directed by the government. Nock had been a progressive Democrat and supporter of Woodrow Wilson prior to WWI, but the expansion of government power during the war caused Nock to become disillusioned with progressivism and turn philosophically in the opposite direction. Nock essentially became a Libertarian in the 1920s before there was such a movement, and argued that the blame for the depravity of humans should be laid at the feet of an overgrown and inept government and its laws. Nock published a journal in the early 1920s known as *The Freeman* that championed what would now be termed as Libertarian political positions (Muccigrosso, 2001, 76-78).

Nock and other Libertarians became important as a political force in the 1930s as part of the Conservative backlash against the New Deal. Nock juxtapositioned "social power," defined as the power of individuals and private associations, and State power. Nock and the Libertarians essentially equated capitalism with individual freedom and democracy and argued that the expansion of the State under the New Deal would be destructive to all three. Nock (1936), argued that the State by nature is exploitive, bent on confiscation of property, and exists to further the interests of one class over another. The New Deal, in Nock's conception, was a manifestation of this statism and was "antisocial" in character. As a consequence, Libertarians were part of the partnership of Conservatives in 1934 that formed the American Liberty League, an organization that was formed as a pressure group representing opponents of the New Deal. The American Liberty League condemned both FDR and his policies and compared him to the notorious authoritarian dictators of the time: Hitler, Mussolini, and Stalin (Muccigrosso, 2001, 75-76). Nock (1936) and Ralph Adams Cram (1937), in his work entitled *The End of Democracy,* took the extreme position that the rise of statism would eventually destroy both capitalism and democracy.

In 1943 Libertarian thought received a boost when Ayn Rand published her novel, *The Fountainhead,* a Libertarian work of fiction that essentially defined the human moral purpose as the unfettered quest for one's own betterment and happiness. Rand, like Nock and Cram, argued that freedom and capitalism were inextricably linked, and to further drive the point home, sometimes gave public lectures while wearing a dress covered with dollar signs. Rand was passionately anti-communist and a defender of private property rights, central themes to Libertarianism that have continued through the present (Muccigrosso, 2001, 86-87).

After WWII, Libertarianism received another intellectual boost from what is known as the "Austrian School" or "Chicago School" of economics. Ludwig von Mises, an Austrian economics scholar who immigrated to the U.S. in reaction to the calamity of Nazism in Central Europe, argued against any form of statism, whether Nazi or otherwise. Mises argued that statism, including government economic planning and intervention, were incompatible with capitalism (Muccigrosso, 2001, 86). Mises' younger Austrian colleague, Friedrich A. Hayek, who taught at the University of Chicago, concurred with Mises' analysis of statism, but focused more on the "evils" of socialism. In 1944, Hayek published *Road to Serfdom,* in which he blamed the totalitarianism in Europe on socialist trends from the previous decades. Hayek argued that once the State controls portions of the nation's economy, it begins society down a slippery slope toward the complete control of society by the State. The slide toward State control would be gradual, but nonetheless ruinous to individual freedom and democracy in the end.

In the 1950s, the Libertarian anti-statist theme was continued by Frank Chodorov, an associate of Albert J. Nock. Chodorov railed against statism and taxation in his 1954 work, *The Income Tax: Root of All Evil,* and founded an essentially Libertarian interest group known as the Intercollegiate Society of Individualists, dedicated to ending what he viewed as the dominance of New Deal statism at American Universities. In furtherance of their goals, the Intercollegiate Society of Individualists distributed Libertarian and other Conservative publications on college campuses. Eventually, the organization became the Intercollegiate Studies Institute that distributes Conservative literature and publishes *Campus,* a national conservative newspaper written and edited by students. In addition to

Campus, Libertarianism received another literary boost in the 1950s with the revival of Nock's Libertarian journal, *The Freeman*, which included contributions from Hayek and Mises. As an intellectual movement, Libertarianism was gaining strength (Muccigrosso, 2001, 85).

In the early 1960s, the Chicago School of Economics grew in importance with the ascendancy of Milton Friedman, a student of Friedrich Hayek. In 1962, Friedman published *Capitalism and Freedom*, where he argued that capitalism and freedom were inextricably linked and that both are better served when the role of government is minimized. Furthermore, for what State power is necessary, Friedman argued that it was best placed at the State and local levels, rather than the National level.

Friedman also argued against the Keynesian economics of the New Deal and disputed the claim of contemporary Liberals that the Depression could have been caused by defects in capitalism. Instead, Friedman argued that the Great Depression was the result of government mismanagement through misguided monetary policies of the Federal Reserve. Friedman was elected President of the American Economic Association in 1967 and received the Nobel Prize in Economics for his work in 1976. Friedman, however, did not limit his commentary to the economic realm and also argued for the elimination of military conscription and the implementation of a school voucher system for parents that wanted to use their tax money to send their children to private schools (Muccigrosso, 2001, 101-102).

Libertarian Party

Libertarians largely remained within the Republican Party until the military conscription of Vietnam War of the 1960s that violated the Libertarians' celebration of individual "choice" as the fundamental basis for society (Tucille, 1970). As a consequence, a movement toward the establishment of a Libertarian Party as a viable alternative to the Republicans gained momentum. The American Libertarian Party began in 1971 in Colorado as a group of disillusioned Republicans and others disenchanted with the major Parties set out to provide an alternative. Libertarians were at odds with other Conservatives within the Republican Party over the issues of conscription, personal drug use, and the Vietnam War in general. Libertarians such as Murray Rothbard argued that the Vietnam War and globalist policies promoted statism and thus deprived the individual of liberty. Former Barry Goldwater speech writer Karl Hess argued that,

> "Vietnam should remind all conservatives that whenever you put your faith in big government for any reason, sooner or later you wind up as an apologist for mass murder" (Quoted in Muccigrosso, 2001, 103).

Hess was also appalled by government efforts to coerce its citizens through Federal law enforcement agencies and compared the FBI with the Soviet KGB (Muccigrosso, 2001, 103).

By 1980, the Libertarian Party was on the ballot in all fifty States and Libertarian Presidential Candidate Ed Clark received almost a million votes. Libertarians continued to be appalled at America's globalist foreign policies, the continued expansion of State power, and the continuation of the Cold War under Presidents Carter and Reagan. As a consequence, the Libertarian Party continued to gradually grow in size. Over the next two decades, the Libertarian Party made continued political gains until over 300 Libertarians were serving in elected public offices across the country by 2001. In 2002, the Libertarian Party ran 1642 candidates for public office, the largest slate of candidates for office from any Third Party in American politics since the Second World War (www.lp.org/organization/history).

As the Libertarian movement gained steam, some Libertarians, most notably Karl Hess, advocated not only separation from the Republican Party and the formation of a Third Party, but separation from the community at large. Hess argued that a better society could be forged through self-reliance on the neighborhood-community level and argued that society should become decentralized into self-sufficient neighborhoods. Hess's ideas, as he outlined them in *Community Technology* (1979), spawned a separatist Libertarian community in a Washington, D.C. neighborhood. Though the Libertarian community in the nation's capital was a failure within five years, the idea of neighborhood-level self-help as a strategy for fighting urban decay became adopted by the Reagan Administration in the 1980s. Hess's neighborhood self-help strategy is also reflected in George H.W. Bush's vision of "1000 points of light" and accompanying calls for volunteerism at the end of the decade.

Problems with Libertarian Ideology

Libertarianism suffers from all of the same problems and contradictions stemming from the free market as Classic Liberalism. Essentially, the unregulated free market produces inequalities, unsafe products, environmental degradation, and profits to unscrupulous merchants, to the detriment of the common good. Furthermore, there is no historical example that supports the Libertarian contention that "volunteerism" can adequately solve the problems of poverty and extreme income inequality that tend to result from the free market in a large, industrialized, society. Even the small scale Libertarian neighborhood experiment in Washington D.C. in the 1980s quickly failed.

The Libertarian focus on individual security also appears to be problematic. After all, the very reason that governments are formed in the first place is because humans are unable to provide for their own security on an individual basis, and all too often, a society without sufficient government becomes Thomas Hobbes' savage jungle where life is "nasty, brutish, and short." A case in point may be Iraq after the U.S. invasion when Saddam Hussein's Police State was dismantled and the country quickly devolved into looting, anarchy, and widespread violence as a result. In general, Libertarians are victims of what Jean Jacques Rousseau termed as the "Law-Freedom Paradox." Essentially, while Libertarians are correct in their assertion that law limits freedom, it examples such as Iraq suggest that there is little freedom without law.

Conflict with Traditional Conservatism

Individualism by its very nature also clashes with the restrictive positions on social issues taken by Traditional Conservatives. Libertarian individualism essentially celebrates choice as its highest value; hence, some individuals in such a system can be expected to choose activities such as homosexuality, substance abuse, abortions, and sexual promiscuity, which are abhorrent to Traditional Conservatives. Consequently, the individualism and minimal government positions of Libertarians (much like those of Classic Liberals) also clash with Traditional Conservatives who would use government to rid society of activities they view as human weaknesses such as pornography, prostitution, drug abuse, homosexuality, and abortions. Ayn Rand (1962), for example, criticizes Traditional Conservatives for their failure to wholeheartedly embrace unfettered capitalism. In the words of Rand,

> "The plea to preserve 'tradition' as such, can appeal only to those who have given up or to those who never intended to achieve anything in life. It is a plea that appeals to the worst elements in men and rejects the best: it appeals to fear, sloth, cowardice, conformity, self-doubt—and rejects creativeness, originality, courage, independence, self-reliance" (Quoted in Muccigrosso, 2001, 87).

Similarly, Libertarian pundit Russell Kirk (1982) argues that because of the Libertarians' beliefs in the "moral freedom" for individuals, they oppose restrictions on abortion as restrictions on individual freedoms. Traditional Conservatives respond with criticism of Libertarians for their lack of concern for customs, traditions, history, and societal institutions such as church and family (Dunn and Woodard, 1991, 108-109). Libertarians have also been accused by Traditional Conservatives (and Contemporary Liberals) of following an ideology that is without morality due to their emphasis on individualism that essentially celebrates the "virtues of selfishness." Furthermore, if all persons are selfishly seeking their own good and no one is seeking the common good, it should not be surprising if the common good does not result, since no one is actually seeking it or giving it a priority.

Libertarians counter these charges with the contentions of Ayn Rand in *The Virtue of Selfishness* (1961), where she argued that societal moral decay was not due to selfishness, but due to a tendency to equate morality with altruism. Rand accepts the Hobbesian negative view of human nature and argues that human nature does not allow people to sacrifice for others. As a consequence, altruistic morality is a nice idea, but humans are unable to pursue it in practice. In contrast to what they therefore view as truly futile moralities espoused by Traditional Conservatives, the Libertarian view of a moral person is one that simply respects the rights of others, pursues the best things for their own lives, and does nothing that discourages others from becoming equally self-reliant. The problem with Rand's argument, unfortunately, is that if one accepts the Libertarian premise that humans are naturally bad, then they cannot be expected to live up to the Libertarian view of the "moral person," and instead can be expected to trample on the rights of others when it suits their own selfish motives.

Libertarians have also criticized Traditional Conservatives for what they view as inflexible, archaic, and authoritarian value systems and structures that they view as hindering liberty. H.L. Mencken, a writer for the *Baltimore Sun* during the 1920s and 1930s and a leading Libertarian critic of the New Deal, also criticized Fundamentalist Protestant religions and rural American values. Mencken once declared that the American farmer did not belong to the human race and that the American South was ruled by "Baptist and Methodist barbarism" (Quoted in Contosta and Mucigrosso, 1988, 140). Obviously, such a position places the Libertarians at odds with the core support for the Republican Party at the beginning of the Twenty-First Century.

Finally, in the minds of many, Libertarianism was effectively discredited by the Great Depression and World War II. Contemporary Liberals argue that if there is any lesson to be learned from the Great Depression, it is that sometimes government intervention into the free market is necessary to alleviate free market harshness. While it is true that the free market may have corrected itself in the long run, in the short run, millions might starve to death. Similarly, Contemporary Liberals and Traditional Conservatives alike argue that the World War II experience suggests that security is impossible without collective action in the form of a strong military; hence, Libertarianism is doomed to failure both in the area of security and in the areas of economic and social welfare.

Concluding Remarks

Libertarianism continues to be a growing ideological force in American politics and an important influence within the Republican Party. As the Republican Party under George W. Bush (as well as the Democrats) have continued to violate the Libertarian principles of less government, one might expect Libertarianism to continue to grow in the near future both within and without the Republican Party as a reaction to government expansion. Another severe free market economic downturn where governmental solutions become popular, or another major security threat, however, may again partially discredit the movement; but ideologies tend to be resilient in spite of being exposed as deficient time and time again, so one should not expect such events to spell the demise of Libertarianism. Perhaps just as plausible, Libertarianism may experience greater growth in the coming years in reaction to what many view as the folly of George W. Bush's military globalism. Conservatives who object to the activist foreign policy of George W. Bush, as well as his "big government" conservatism and debt-ridden fiscal policies, may seek alternatives to the Republican Party and find the Libertarians to be a more comfortable and conservative alternative than the Democrats.

Chapter Six

Conservative Extremism

Conservative Extremism is not a dominant ideology in the United States, but that does not mean that it is absent (it is not), or that it is impotent. In fact, the Oklahoma City bombing in 1994 carried out by Conservative Extremist Timothy McVeigh suggests exactly the opposite. Similarly, the rise of the Nazis in Germany from an insignificant splinter party in 1928 to the control of the government in 1933 is a testimony to the power potential of Conservative Extremism as ideology that can mobilize the masses. If such a takeover could happen in Germany in 1933, then it is certainly plausible that it could happen in the exceptionally conservative, rural and religious United States.

The World War II experience, however, largely discredited Conservative Extremist ideologies under the names of Nazism and Fascism; consequently, if Conservative Extremism is to become dominant in the United States, it is perhaps most likely that it will have to resurface under another name, whether it be the "Minutemen" tackling Mexican border violators, the citizen militia movement playing war games on the weekends, or a more militant version of the religious right. In any case, it would be foolish to accept the position that the U.S. or any other advanced industrial democracy is immune to such a movement.

Diversity of Conservative Extremism

Conservative Extremism, like other facets of conservatism, is not monolithic, but diverse. This is perhaps partially due to the possibility that Conservative Extremism, like conservatism in general, tends to be situational in character; however, there is less common agreement among scholars about the use of terms to describe Conservative Extremism as opposed to other ideologies (Eatwell, 1989, 68). For example, McCarthyism in the U.S. in the 1950s is quite different than Nazism in Germany in the 1930s because McCarthyism did not contain the same focus on anti-Semitism. Therefore, should these movements be considered ideologically similar, or different? There is, however, a commonality among Conservative Extremist ideologies in that they tend to be viewed as ideological aberrations from the norm and there is a tendency in society at large to associate a perjorative meaning with the labels attached to the movements themselves (Eatwell, 1989, 68).

Conservative Extremism also differs from other ideologies in that it lacks its own version of a Karl Marx or some other grand theorist to whom all Conservative Extremists turn for guidance. Adolph Hitler's Mein Kampf, most scholars would argue, does not qualify. In the words of Michael Billig (1979, 148),

> "Mein Kampf is better categorized as "a mish-mash of self-serving autobiography, psychopathic hatred and prejudice, should not be considered as an intellectual work of political theory. The mystery is how such nonsense became to be taken seriously by so many people."

If there is any stream of writing to which Conservative Extremists tend to draw their ideas, however, it is the writings in the pseudo-science of eugenicists, who argue that there are genetic differences between peoples and races, with the natural result that some races superior to others (Poliakov, 1974, 14). Writers such as Madison Grant, in the *Passing of the Great Race*, argue that a particular race of people (normally white, anglo-saxons) is superior to all others and that race therefore must be kept pure. In cases of intermarriage between the preferred race and those of the "inferior" races, so argue the Conservative Extremists, the children always go to the "lower case," thus diluting and destroying the "superior race." As a consequence, Conservative Extremists argue for severe immigration restrictions so as to prevent such inter-racial "mixing." Furthermore, segregationist policies and apartheid-style inequalities under law are championed for the same reasons.

Central Tenets of Conservative Extremism

Conservative Extremism, whether termed as fascism, Nazism, or the white supremism of the KKK, is a combination of racism, nationalism, and authoritarianism that has a tendency to center on a belief in the superiority of a specific group of people (Mosse, 1964, 70). Conservative Extremism rests on the fears of foreigners and immigrants among indigenous members of the population. The target of the Conservative Extremists' wrath and fears, however, is not always the same, because as immigration patterns change, it is not always the same "foreigner" that is being denigrated. Furthermore, the form of the Conservative Extremist hatred at differing times is similar, but the content may differ because the ideologies allow "substitutability of targets" (Billig, 1979, 151). The Conservative Extremism of Adolph Hitler in Nazi Germany, for example, had as its basis a belief in the superiority of the

German people, while the Conservative Extremism of Japan during the same time period celebrated the superiority of the people of Japan. Similarly, the Conservative Extremism of the KKK in the U.S. in the 1920s was based on "purer Americanism" and the "God-given right of white protestant males" in addition to the assumed inferiority of African Americans and other non-white, non-protestant individuals (Alexander, 1965, 14). Conservative Extremists in the U.S., however, could easily shift the focus of their wrath from African-Americans to Latin Americans or Asians depending on shifting cultural and immigration patterns and political events. After the terrorist attacks of September 11, 2001, for instance, it would not be surprising if American Conservative Extremists designated Arab Muslims as their new objects of veneration.

Conservative Extremists accept the proposition that different persons have different levels of talents and abilities, a point with which Classic Liberals, Traditional Conservatives, and Libertarians would agree. Conservative Extremists, however, take this principle a step further and generalize it to groups of people based on ethnicity, nationality, religion, or some other societal cleavage. In other words, Conservative Extremists generally argue that different groups of people have differing levels of talents and abilities as groups, in addition to individual differences. Conservative Extremists can be expected to view the talents of their own group as superior to those of all others, and view the world as a hierarchy of groups of peoples with their own group rightfully situated at the top. In the Conservative Extremist construct, race, ethnicity, or nationalism, is normally the motivating and unifying force, and purity of the group is the guiding precept of the community (Cassels, 1968, 23-25).

Conservative extremist ideologies are also typically reactionary in character. The KKK for instance developed as a reaction to the end of slavery and the Southern defeat in the Civil War. Similarly, Nazism in Germany developed as a reaction to the German loss in World War I and as a response to the "threat" of socialism. Fascism in Italy under Mussolini also arose at least partially due to a perceived threat from socialism as did McCarthyism in the U.S. in the 1950s (Cassels, 1968, 23-25).

Priority on Myth

Conservative Extremism generally places a high priority on myth, and like Traditional Conservatives, the Conservative Extremists may hearken back to the symbols and heroes of a better, vanished time as a motivating force. Conservative Extremist ideologies also typically aggrandize selected historical figures to mythical and heroic proportions. The heroes of the past are then connected to an aggressive and romantic vision of nationalism that becomes in the Conservative Extremists' vision, or (to borrow a phrase coined by Rush Limbaugh) "the way things ought to be." In this view, the present is viewed as decadent, often with little or nothing to "conserve." The Conservative Extremism of Osama Bin Laden and al Qaeda, for example, preaches the decadence of the current society, calls for its complete destruction, and hearkens for a return to the 13th Century teachings of ibn Tamiyya (Benjamin and Simon, 2002, 38-52).

Charismatic Leader

Typically, Conservative Extremism includes leadership by a charismatic authoritarian leader who takes on mystic, "messiah-like" characteristics. Osama bin Laden and Adolph Hitler are excellent examples of the "charismatic leader." Without such a strong leader, the movement may not be able to gather momentum. For example, Benito Mussolini, the leader of Fascist Italy in the early twentieth century, once remarked, "What would Facism be, if I had not been." (Quoted in Ingersoll, Matthews, and Davison, 2001, 213). The strong leader is expected to unite the people and return society to the truer version of the past. The charismatic leader in Conservative Extremism typically becomes an authoritarian leader who not only assumes policy leadership, but also assumes a leading role in constructing and perpetuating the myths on which the ideology is based and in identifying and condemning heretics and heresies (Eatwell, 1989, 69-70). Pursuant to these goals, Osama Bin Laden has issued religious fatwas calling for Holy War on the West. Bin Laden has also called for the overthrow of "apostate" Islamic rulers, such as Saddam Hussein and the Saudi Royal family, whom Bin Laden views as straying from the principles of pure Islam (Benjamin and Simon, 2003, 38-42).

Conspiracy Theory

A central component of Conservative Extremism is often conspiracy theory. Senator Joseph McCarthy's assertion in the 1950s that there was a communist conspiracy to undermine the U.S. government and American society and Adolph Hitler's assertion that the German defeat in WWI was because Jewish traitors betrayed Germany, are prime examples. Western culture is perhaps especially susceptible to conspiracy theories since its monotheistic Judeo-Christian beliefs simplify world conflict for people into a struggle between God and Satan, or good and evil. Since in Christianity, there is a general belief in invisible forces of evil plotting against the forces of good, whether those forces are witches, demons, or the Devil himself, it is then very easy to believe that there are invisible human plots as well.

Outsiders to the Conservative Extremists' preferred group (Jews in Nazi Germany, for example) are demonized and cast as societal scapegoats for all of the multiple ills that beset society. Consequently, Conservative Extremists generally argue that these outgroups must be purged, expelled, or at least "controlled," if not completely eradicated in order for society to advance. The most important societal problems are attributed to the scapegoat groups and to those within the preferred group itself that have adopted the ways of the scapegoats. For example, in Nazi Germany, the German defeat in World War I was explained as a result of Jewish officers that betrayed Germany at Versailles and other German officials that collaborated with the Jewish traitors (Bell, 1986, 78-79).

The conspiracy theories of Conservative Extremism help provide a common sense of identity for the Extremists themselves, who view themselves as having true "revelation" as to the dark and evil forces that lurk in the world while others ignorantly ignore their warnings. The Conservative Extremists then view themselves as the last bastion of hope against the hidden, evil, and corrupting forces that are loose on society (Eatwell, 1989).

Conspiracy theories also allow Conservative Extremists to resolve dissonance. In other words, the ideology allows Conservative Extremists to explain away any and all factual evidence that appears to be in conflict with their beliefs. For instance, a Conservative Extremist may be able to believe that the Holocaust never happened because the media and academia are dominated by Jews, liberals, and communists who have forged and perpetuated intricate lies to deceive the people (Eatwell, 1989, 72).

Conspiracy theories in Conservative Extremism, however, do not stop with the enemy scapegoats. Conservative Extremists often see conspiracies among those even within their own organizations. For example, Adolph Hitler purged many a dedicated Nazi out of paranoia and Joseph McCarthy even at one time accused Republican President and hero of WWII, Dwight Eisenhower, of being a communist (Brinkley, 2003, 794-795).

The preferred group itself becomes a central focus in Conservative extremism and the group itself takes on a glorious, mystical, almost religious, character. For the Nazism of Adolph Hitler, the focus was on the "Volk" or German people, and the nature of the group was founded on blood nationalism and sacrifice (Eatwell, 1989, 72). In Fascist Italy, the focus was on the Nation-State itself. In the words of Mussolini (Quoted in Somerville and Santoni eds., 1963, 192),

"The State, as conceived of and as created by Fascism, is a spiritual and moral fact in itself, since its political, juridical, and economic organization of the nation is a concrete thing; and such an organization must be in its origins and development a manifestation of the spirit."

Role of the State

The role of the State in Conservative Extremism includes the provision of security, both internal and external; however, the State is also, in the words of Mussolini (Quoted in Somerville and Sontoni eds., 1963, 194), "the custodian and transmitter of the spirit of the people." In other words, the role of the State in the Conservative Extremist construct includes developing and perpetuating the ideological myths on which the group is predicated. History is interpreted by the State in Conservative Extremist ideological terms and events and symbols of the glorious past are linked with the people of the present. In turn, the group of the present is the manifestation of the glory of the people of the past.

Premium on Order

Conservative Extremists place a premium on order over individual freedoms and argue that unrestrained individualism leads to chaos. Whereas Classic Liberals and Libertarians assert that the State is subservient to the individual, Conservative extremists argue that such individualism leads to conflict, disunity, and disorder. Furthermore, such a society constructed on selfishness and conflict is an affront to progress and morality (Ingersoll, Matthews, and Davison, 2001, 219-220).

Instead, Conservative Extremists argue that there is no freedom without order and it is in a "morally pure" and orderly society that freedom is the greatest. As a consequence, individuals essentially have no rights, but only whatever privileges are granted them by the State or preferred group entity. As a consequence, no parties, interest groups, religions, or other institutions that are deemed to conflict with the good of the preferred group (as defined by the charismatic leader or governing authorities) are allowed. The only societal groups allowed are those so designated by the governing authorities since it is they who determine what is in the interest of the common good (Ingersoll, Matthews, and Davison, 2001, 220-221). The social structure that emerges is one that is termed as "corporatism," where certain societal representative groups are granted monopolies of representation for different segments of society and the representative groups are incorporated into the State itself.

Anti-Communism

Although Conservative Extremism shares a tendency toward authoritarianism with Leninist Communism, and both Leninist Communism and Conservative Extremism have tended to limit individual freedom in practice, Conservative Extremism is in a number of ways antithetical to Communism. First, Leninist Communism constructs a society based on class, regardless of race, ethnicity, religion, or heritage, and theoretically places a premium on equality, including equality of condition, regardless of one's status in terms of race, ethnicity etc. In contrast, in Conservative Extremist ideologies, a pluralist society cannot be classless because ethnic minorities, minority religious groups, and other minority groups designated as substandard by the authorities, cannot be placed on equal footing with the preferred group. Furthermore, class interests could be expected to conflict with group unity and therefore may conflict with the common good. As such, it is not accidental that Mussolini's Fascists came to power in Italy at a time that the middle and upper classes feared the growing political power of Italy's Communists (Ingersoll, Matthews, and Davison, 2001, 220-221).

Militarism

Conservative Extremism has typically contained elements of Spartan machismo and militarism and lent itself toward military adventurism. Typically, the Conservative Extremists view military conflict as inevitable and even desirable and right, since it is only "right" and "natural" that the strong and "better" people should rule over the weak (Woods 1989, 126-127). Essentially, if the preferred group is to be "better" than all others, it follows that the preferred group may prove their superiority on the battlefield. By testing themselves against other groups or Nation-States, the preferred Conservative Extremist group can assess their progress in their quest to become the superior people encompassed in their own mythology. Some Conservative Extremists, however, may become isolationists and anti-internationalists stemming from the lack of trust for outsiders and their reverence for their preferred group (Woods, 1989, 126-127). Why allow the "good people" of the preferred group to be dictated to by a collection of inferiors and barbarians in a body such as the UN?

Anti-Intellectualism

Conservative Extremism also contains a strain of anti-intellectualism due to its preference for emotion over substance. If the charismatic leader is to mobilize the masses, he must move them through emotive symbols rather than sound analysis. After all, sound analysis is unlikely to support the notion of the superiority of the preferred group in the first place. Additionally, the Conservative Extremists typically value action as more important than ideas anyway, consequently, there is little reason to study great questions intently when faster solutions can be achieved through action (Ingersoll, Matthews, and Davison, 2001, 219-221).

The anti-intellectual and "action-based" focus of Conservative extremism is echoed by political theorists Nietzsche and Sorel. Sorel (1969) argued that action was a necessary part of political activity and that "thought" was mere "rationalization." Sorel therefore called for action (including violence), not thought, as a prerequisite for overthrowing what he viewed as the hedonistic, materialistic, liberal democratic State. Similarly, Nietzsche (1969) argued that "rationalism" was bankrupt as a means for political change and that instead, at rare moments an exceptional leader could emerge who could lead the people to correct societal problems.

The action is necessary because Conservative Extremists view the entire existing society as decadent and in need of total abolition and replacement with a newer, better, society (Muller, 1987, 29-30). As a consequence, the typical conservative preference for minimal government is replaced by the urgent need to install the "correct" political program before the forces of darkness (often communism or socialism) completely destroy society. An ideology that has as its basis the need for abolition of an existing order is particularly inclined to stress the "spirit" of a new political order rather than its content; hence, action is placed over substance (Woods, 1989, 127). Consequently, Conservative Extremism typically becomes anti-democratic in character. In this construct, democratic rights and liberties will have to be limited in order to protect the good of the preferred group. After all, democracy allows the possibility that leaders will be elected that do not subscribe to the "true light" as known by the Conservative Extremists. In order to ensure that "right-thinking" individuals of the preferred group are elected, it is therefore necessary to limit political participation to the preferred group itself. Furthermore, rights of those that are not in the preferred group will necessarily have to be limited to ensure that those in the preferred group also occupy the preferred positions in society. As a result, Hitler revoked the rights of the Jews in Nazi Germany and Conservative Extremists imposed segregation and Jim Crow laws on African Americans in the American South following Reconstruction.

Problems with Conservative Extremism

Sordid History

Obviously, the largest problem for Conservative Extremism is its sordid history of intolerance, narrow-mindedness, injustice, brutality, holocausts and witch hunts that have permeated its presence throughout human history. From the Salem witch hunts, to the KKK lynchings, to the bombing of abortion clinics, to the death of Matthew Shepherd, to the Oklahoma City Bombing, to the attacks of 9/11, Conservative Extremists have repeatedly proven their danger to their fellow human beings. In the early Twentieth Century, Conservative Extremist ideologies came to power in a number of countries with disastrous results. Most notably, Conservative Extremism led to the military expansionist policies of Nazi Germany, Imperial Japan, and Fascist Italy in the 1930s and the oppressive regime of the Taliban in Afghanistan at the end of the century. Rights were trampled everywhere the Conservative Extremists took over, nations and peoples were conquered against their will by the Conservative Extremist regimes, and enemies of the regimes were massacred by the millions. With the Holocaust in Europe, the Bataan Death March in the Pacific, and the great calamity in general that was World War II largely blamed on Conservative Extremists by the rest of the world, Conservative Extremism was effectively discredited as of 1945. After the photographs of the Nazi concentration camps became public knowledge, the idea of the great State built on racial supremacy could no longer be innocently supported (Billig, 1989, 157-158). As a consequence, Conservative Extremist groups have been relegated to the fringes of the American political spectrum with very limited support, and their Parties and ideas are typically shunned by more mainstream conservatives (Billig, 1989, 152-153). Furthermore, no Conservative Extremist party has risen to power in any developed industrial Democracy in the six decades following World War II. The closest that any have come is Jean Marie LePen's second place showing in France in 2003, but Le Pen was trounced in the National Election for President against Jaques Chirac, gaining only 18% of the vote. Although LePen's second place showing is certainly significant, it is difficult to say that he was near winning an election when he lost five votes out of six.

Conflict with Classic Liberalism and Libertarianism

Although the legacy of the past is undoubtedly the biggest problem for Conservative Extremism, Conservative Extremism also has another impediment to its success in that it very much conflicts with the individualism of Libertarianism and Classic Liberalism. In Conservative Extremism, the good of the preferred group takes precedent over any individual rights. In the words of Mussolini (Quoted in Somerville and Sontoni eds., 1963, 426),

> "The Fascist conception of life stresses the importance of the State and accepts the individual only insofar as his interests coincide with those of the State."

As a consequence, Conservative Extremist ideas can be expected to be shunned as anathema by the more "mainstream" Classic Liberals in the Republican Party as well as Libertarians who place a premium on the individual.

Conservative Extremism also created very large, powerful, and coercive States in Germany, Italy, and Japan in the 1930s. The idea of a large, powerful, and coercive State is completely at odds with the "limited government" ideals of Classic Liberals and Libertarians. Similarly, the coercive States in Germany, Italy, and Japan of the 1930s created corporatist structures, command economies, and tremendous governmental intervention into the social order to the degree that the ideology became so penetrating into human activity that even individual thought was a concern of the State. The space between public and private spheres became blurred or destroyed with the result that the State was entitled to regulate all aspects of economic, political and social life (Freeden, 2003, 91). All of these State intrusions, whether social, economic, or political, are abhorrent to Classic Liberals and Libertarians.

Conservative Extremism also tends to break down rule of law and replace it with rule by the whim of the charismatic leader. The distinctions between legality and illegality become blurred so that ordinary citizens (especially those that do not belong to the preferred group) are unable to discern which side of the law they are on and whether or not the State is their friend or foe. This break down of rule of law is in direct conflict with the rule of law premises of Classic Liberalism and therefore hinders the ability of Conservative Extremists to expand their appeal in contemporary "Liberal" democracies.

Inaccurate Views of History and Reality

Conservative Extremism has also often been criticized for championing inaccurate portrayals of reality and history. For instance, Jean Marie Le Pen in 1987 all but denied the Holocaust during WWII. In the words of Le Pen,

"I ask myself a certain number of questions. I'm not saying that gas chambers did not exist. I have not been able to see any myself. I have not specially studied the question. But I consider it a matter of detail in the history of the Second World War…I say that some historians are debating these questions" (*Observer*, 1987).

If Le Pen's perspective were unique, then one could discount it as a function of Le Pen's individual personal ignorance and psychology. Instead, however, Holocaust denial has become prevalent in Conservative Extremist literature. For example Richard Harwood (1974) wrote a pamphlet in the

1970s denying the Holocaust, entitled, *Did Six Million Really Die?* The pamphlet became widely circulated among Conservative Extremists all over the world and led to the publication of more similar works (Billig, 1989, 157). Soon, Holocaust denial began to even spread marginally over into mainstream conservative American Politics. For instance, Pat Buchanan, a former speech writer for President Richard Nixon and frequent American candidate for the Presidency, essentially denied some aspects of the Holocaust in an article he wrote in the *New York Post* in 1990. In this article, Buchanan discusses what he termed as a "Holocaust Survivor Syndrome" that involved what he labeled as "group fantasies of martyrdom and heroics." Buchanan went on to deny that people were killed in Nazi death camps from toxic fumes produced by diesel engines and pumped into sealed rooms, thus essentially denying known historical facts while simultaneously displaying an ignorance of diesel engines. More recently, the "tradition" of Holocaust denial among Conservative Extremists continued with the publication of Arthur R. Butz (2003) book entitled *The Hoax of the Twentieth Century: The Case Against the Presumed Extermination of European Jewry*. The title itself perhaps tells the reader all one needs to know.

The denial of the Holocaust, as incredible as it may seem, is not merely an attempt to rewrite or deny one isolated event in history, but is part of the "plot-mentality" paranoia that tends to afflict Conservative Extremists. The Holocaust-denying extremists are essentially arguing that recorded history is a lie and a myth that has been fed to the people as part of a global plot, in this case by the Jews and Liberals who control the media, the Universities, and, in their view, just about everything and everyone else. The Conservative Extremists in this case view the whole world as hopelessly duped, while they alone possess the wisdom and understanding to see through the plot for what it is (Billig, 1989, 158). To the rest of the world, however, the plot-mentality Conservative Extremists merely appear to be either stupid, ignorant, mentally unstable, or all three.

Concluding Remarks

Whether it be African-American Jesse Owens winning a sprint, African-American Joe Louis winning a boxing match, or Soviet tanks rolling into Berlin, Adolph Hitler was faced with constant reminders that his myth of Aryan supremacy was in reality just that: nothing but myth. Obviously, the inglorious deaths of both Hitler and Mussolini did little to perpetuate the myths of their superior leadership. In essence, all racial superiority myths and leader-cult myths are doomed to failure because all groups of humans and all human leaders suffer from human flaws and imperfections, not to mention their own mortality. Those flaws and imperfections are easily exposed when challenged, thus eventually exposing the Conservative Extremist myths for what they are. The only real question is how many people can be deceived by the myths and for how long. Unfortunately, in the cases of Germany, Italy, and Japan in the 1930s, it was too many people for too long, and the result was the death of millions.

No such charismatic leader has yet arisen in the United States with a legitimate chance at taking power, but if it were possible for Conservative Extremists to take over in Japan, Germany, and Italy in the 1930s, it is certainly possible for them to take over in the United States of the early Twenty-First Century, a nation that is exceptionally predisposed to conservatism in comparison to other developed democracies. In fact, many American Liberals draw numerous parallels between President George W. Bush and the most notorious Conservative Extremist of the last century, Adolph Hitler. Columnist David Lindorff (2004), for instance, in *This Can't Be Happening!*, compares Bush's War on terror to Hitler's rampage across Europe, equates propaganda from the Bush administration to the Hitler/Goebbels propaganda of the 1930s, and compares John Aschcroft's Justice Department to the former East German police state of "citizen spies." Similarly, Bush's popularity in Europe is the lowest of any American President in recent memory. Nevertheless, Bush achieved reelection in 2004 with a majority of the popular vote, suggesting that majority of Americans are exceptionally conservative in comparison to their European counterparts and the liberal critics of the Bush administration in the U.S. This exceptional American predisposition to conservatism is clearly related to the people and traditions that have permeated its unique history that will be discussed in the following chapters.

Chapter Seven

Colonial Conservatism

The years between the settlement of Jamestown and the American Revolution were a period of enormous changes in the North American colonial political landscape, replete with the arrival of hordes of European immigrants and thousands of unwilling immigrants from Africa. Amid this period of immigration, settlement, rapid change, and upheaval in the New World, conservative ideologies were present, inherited from the mother countries of the immigrants themselves, planted in the New World by the immigrants themselves, and taking root in the Colonial culture.

In spite of the clamor of the brave new world, complete with all of the change it represented that is in part antithetical with conservatism, and in spite of the not-so-conservative impulse that impelled people to leave their homes in Europe to begin with, the spirit of conservatism remained constantly with the early colonists. Though the early immigrants to the New World in some respects must be considered optimistic pioneers, they were also still people of their age, circumscribed by its points of view, limited by its traditions, and trained in its habits of mind. While it is certainly true that many were ready and able to move into new directions of thought and action as they left one world for another, there were others, the conservatives of the time, often among the most prominent and influential, who clung to the old and the accustomed and did what they could do to resist the forces of change.

Conservatism in the English New World was present throughout the colonial period in the attitudes of a number of specific societal groups. Certainly, conservatism dominated the thought processes and social structures of the landed gentry of the North American South, where colonial planters forged a society that essentially attempted to conserve the aristocratic social structures of mother England. The beginning of this strand of conservatism in the colonies was present even at the original settlement at Jamestown, where Captain John Smith lamented that one third of his immigrant group were gentlemen who were "averse to work," work being in their view the exclusive domain of the "lower" classes (Quoted in Kupperman, 1988, 42). Conservatism was also prevalent in the attitudes of the Northern urban merchants, who opposed any notion of political participation by the non-propertied classes. Other conservative forces in the colonial period included the forces that made up the royal government, especially the royal governors and councils, the Anglican clergy, academia as it was at the time, and Puritan religious and social orthodoxy in New England. All of these groups and institutions in colonial society typically favored a hierarchical social structure, opposed social disorder, and generally favored tradition and the maintenance of the status quo as opposed to social and political change (Muccigrosso, 2001, 3). The conservatism of these groups in colonial society will be discussed in greater detail below.

Ruling Classes

Conservatism typically is a political ideology of the ruling class in any society since it is the ruling class that has a vested interest in resisting changes to the system that has allowed them to attain their elevated positions. In the pre-revolutionary period in North America, there was essentially a small, elite ruling class in virtually every colony, and that ruling class typically dominated the political machinery and public offices in each colony. As a consequence, the ruling classes in the American colonies tended to oppose any changes that would lead to the development of a more democratic system that might erode or more equally disperse their power. The ruling classes typically provided a voice on public matters for their own benefit, but also at least made pretense of speaking on public matters for the benefit of all citizens so as to ensure their continuing support from the common masses. In reality, the ruling classes characteristically used their political power largely for the benefit of themselves at the expense of the less privileged, even though they might couch their actions in language that made it appear beneficial for the common classes as well (Labaree, 1948, 2).

The ruling classes in each colony naturally included the men of the greatest wealth, whether they were Northern merchants or Southern planters. An exception to this was Puritan New England where wealth was more evenly distributed throughout the early colonial period due to the more democratic and communal Puritan political/economic system and the fact that status in Puritan New England often owed more to religious zeal than to wealth (Labaree, 1948, 4).

Colonial Councils

Economic elites typically dominated the Colonial Councils, perhaps the most important agency of colonial government prior to the American Revolution. The Councils essentially served as the upper houses of legislatures, as supreme courts of the colonies, and as the colonial governors' advisory bodies in executive matters. Colonial governors appointed the members of the Councils, and their instructions for choosing appointees from the King reflected elitism and the traditional conservative preference for rule by the "good people." The governors' royal appointment instructions directed them to,

"take care that they be men of good life and well affected to our government, and of good estates and abilities, and not necessitous persons or in much debt" (Quoted in Labaree, 1935, 55-56).

In 1728, however, in what was a reflection of the nature of the Southern planter class, the King's instructions were altered to delete the last clause concerning debts because it was determined that this was too idealistic a qualification for a Southern planter (Labaree, 1935, 56).

Nevertheless, the Councils, both North and South, came to be dominated by a very few families of wealth and status, and since their families were typically all intermarried, the Councils became family bodies that effectively governed the colonies in the interest of the privileged classes. For example, in Virginia, only 57 family names appeared on the twelve-member council from 1680 to the American Revolution, and nine of those names account for a third of the Council membership (Stanard and Stanard, 1902, 55). Similar situations existed in the rest of the colonies as well. In New York, for example, a fourth of its Council membership for the entire colonial period was accounted for by 13 families (Becker, 1909, 35).

Planters

The positions on the Councils, as political positions often do, carried with them tremendous economic advantages. Most conspicuously, from the early settlement until well into the eighteenth century, colonial governors often granted large tracts of land to their supporters on the Councils. As a result, a class of great landowners arose who would tend to dominate politics in the colonies (Mark, 1940, 62). In the case of the Southern planters, the Councils left them with tremendous autonomy on their own land, with the result that the planters each essentially grew accustomed to being "sovereign" on his own plantation. As such, the planters became conservative in their politics in that they resisted any attempts by the non-propertied classes to exercise influence on the political system in which the planters had been propelled to dominance. In the words of Durand of Dauphine, a Frenchman exiled from France who toured Virginia in the 1780s,

"among them (the planters) they had always divided the great offices and they controlled the political life of their colonies against influence from without or

from within in the interest of their class and section as a whole. For a long
time they were able to forestall any serious challenge to their leadership,
partly at least, by denying to the newer settlements legislative representation
in just proportion to their growing population" (Quoted in Chinard, 1934, 10).

What the Southern planters constructed would eventually come to
resemble a system of "taxation without representation" against the non-
propertied classes. Ironically, the planters themselves would revolt against
such a system in 1776 when the same principles were applied to them by the
English government. In their own colonial system prior to the revolution,
however, the planters would maintain the status quo against the wishes of the
non-propertied classes by force if necessary. In 1768, for example, when
small farmers in North Carolina revolted against the taxation without
representation system imposed by the planters, the planters utilized the
military force of the colonial government to put down the insolent rebellion.
In that instance, small farmers took up arms and attacked the North Carolina
Courts over what they viewed as unfair taxation without fair representation.
The planters reacted with their support of the colonial governor in calling out
the militia to quell the rebellion. The planter class even provided the military
leadership for the governor's militia of 1300 with a total of twelve colonels,
two major generals, and six lieutenant generals. In May of 1771, the planter-
led militia finally defeated the insurgent small farmers, and leaders of the
rebellion were executed or forced into exile (Saunders, 1999, 889).

Academia

Academia in the American colonial period also reflected the influence of
conservatism. Of the nine colleges established during the colonial era,
Harvard, William and Mary, Yale, Princeton, Columbia, Penn, Brown,
Rutgers, and Dartmouth, only Penn was begun as a secular institution. All of
the others, beginning with Harvard in 1636, were essentially begun as
theological seminaries, typically institutions of conservationist thought. Yale
in particular was founded in 1701 essentially as a conservative
Congregationalist theological seminary in reaction to the perception of
Congregationalist conservatives in Connecticut that the seminary at Harvard
had strayed too far from its conservative Puritan roots (Labaree, 1948, 98).
This was in spite of the fact that the authorities at Harvard could hardly be
categorized as anything but conservatives at the time since it was just nine
years earlier that they were involved in providing opinions concerning
witches for the Salem witch trials (Mather, 1999, 95). Curriculum in the
colonial institutions reflected the conservatism of the academics themselves

in that it essentially remained unchanged from medieval Europe with a focus on wrote memorization rather than critical thinking.

Merchants

In the eighteenth century, the largest American enterprise was the international shipping business; consequently, some of the men of the greatest wealth in America were the international shipping merchants. The wealthy colonial merchants constituted a strongly conservative force, especially opposing the "radicalism" of the frontier regions, such as that which spawned the North Carolina farmers' rebellion of 1768 and Bacon's Rebellion in Virginia in 1675. Like the planters, they opposed the "radicalism" of the frontier primarily because of the threat that it posed to their preferred position in society. Like the elite planters, the wealthy merchants tended to support the status quo so as to retain the system in which they had risen to the top. The merchants were also in more frequent contact with England and perhaps more than any other group understood the benefits of the British Empire. The British navy protected their overseas cargo and their sales often depended on the British market. Unlike the small farmers and frontiersmen to whom England was a foreign and distant place, the coastal shipping merchants experienced contact with England as part of their daily lives and were therefore more inclined to favor an American society modeled after the ways of the older country (Schlesinger, 1993, 31).

Merchants also tended to be conservative due to the fact that a certain degree of stability and order is necessary for the efficient operation of the free market. Merchants, therefore, could be expected to oppose significant changes in taxation or measures that could significantly and suddenly alter the value of currency to the detriment of the free market. Conversely, merchants typically could be expected to exert their political influence on the side of measures that perpetuated market stability and maintenance of the accustomed order of affairs (Schlesinger, 1993, 32).

The issue of the currency was the public question that most consistently epitomized the conflict between the elite merchant class and other economic groups in society during the colonial era. In a precursor to the currency disputes at the time of the Revolution, the banking and monetary disputes of the Jacksonian era, and the greenback and silver coinage disputes of the gilded age, the merchants generally favored hard money and non-inflationary policies, while farmers and debtors favored looser monetary policies and rising prices. The colonial situation was further complicated by the fact that all thirteen colonies issued paper money. Since the quantities of paper issued, the terms of redemption, and the credit of the issuing governments, varied greatly from time to time, and colony to colony, the result was monetary confusion that complicated business transactions, especially across colonial boundaries. British merchants in particular felt the adverse effects of depreciated colonial currencies, but experienced none of the inflationary benefits enjoyed by the colonial debtors and farmers. As a consequence, the British government, and therefore colonial governors and Councils, almost always supported hard-money policies in the colonies (Labaree, 1948, 49-51).

Wealthy conservative creditors disliked inflationary policies because the currency depreciation caused by the emission of large sums of paper money made it possible for debtors to pay off their debts at rates that creditors felt cheated them out of their just dues. (Labaree, 1948, 52). Some conservatives in the colonial period viewed paper money not only as bad policy, but as an evil. Judge Samuel Sewall of Boston, for instance, argued that a medium of exchange should have an intrinsic worth. In the words of Sewall,

> "If money be wanting, twere a better expedient to oblige creditors to take wheat, Indian corn, salt, iron, wool at a moderate valuation, as twas of old: then there would be quid pro quo; whereas now private creditors are forced to take the public faith for payment for their commodity" (Quoted in Yazawa, 1998, 166).

Wealthy conservatives essentially argued that loose money policies relaxed industry, promoted idleness, encouraged debt, and opened the door to excesses of every kind by the undisciplined lower classes. For these persons, who exhibited the conservative attitudes of paternalism toward the lower classes, frugality, not libertine monetary policies, was the solution to economic problems (Kemmerer, 1940, 303-304).

Merchants, Planters, and the Revolution

It is true that the liberal American Revolution was generally supported by the conservative merchant and planter classes in violation of their history of typically supporting the status quo. The Revolution, obviously, represented a change from the status quo, and in that sense it is inconsistent with conservatism; however, certain facets of planter and merchant support for the revolution can be viewed as consistent with conservatism.

In essence, the new taxes and economic controls imposed on the colonies by the British after the conclusion of the Seven Years War represented a break with the status quo. The changes in the status quo imposed by the British had adverse effects on the economic interests of the planters and merchants; consequently, the support of the planters and merchants for the revolution partially can be explained as protecting their economic interests and opposing the abrupt changes in the status quo imposed by the British.

Thus, the revolutionary leanings of the merchant and planter classes are at least partially rooted in a reactionary objection to changes in the status quo and therefore have their bases in conservatism.

In opposing the British authority, the merchants and planters opened the way for the lower classes to also oppose some of the authority and privileges that the colonial leaders had long maintained in the colonies. Such concessions by the upper colonial classes to the lower can be viewed as a necessary ploy by the upper classes in order to gain the support of the masses for their revolt, the purpose of which was to reinstall the economic status quo. Consequently, the elites purported to speak for the common people and lead them in an attack upon the entrenched privilege that they themselves had every intention of retaining (Labaree, 1948, 57).

Some elites, such as Landon Carter of Virginia, supported the opposition to England at first, but then backed off out of fear of a decline in the power of the ruling classes in the colonies. In the words of Carter,

"we might fall into a worse situation from internal oppression and commotions than might have been obtained by a serious as well as cautious reconciliation." (Carter, 1965, 178)

Carter's fears were essentially realized during the revolutionary period as economic instability visited the ruling classes in the form of runaway inflation, currency devaluations, and the lack of a uniform tariff. The disruptions brought disarray to the international shipping industry and eventually forced the elites to reconvene for the Constitutional Convention of 1787, the purpose of which was to create a new set of rules for the orderly conduct of international trade (Breckinridge, 2002, 7). A second impetus for the writing of the American Constitution was also based in conservatism in that elites reacted negatively to the disorder of Shays' Rebellion, which proved to the conservative elites that the system under the Articles of Confederation allowed for too much disorder and threatened the position of the ruling classes (Brinkley, 2003, 154-155).

Of course, not all merchants and planters supported the American Revolution at all. Instead, many were loyalists and favored the continuation of British rule, not only for the order and security that accompanied that rule, but out of admiration for the British traditions and the British form of "balanced government" with its division into institutions representing the monarchy, aristocracy, and commoners. Among the loyalist elites that favored the British system were the noteworthy lawyer Jared Ingersoll, the statesman Joseph Galloway, and the well-known minister Jonathan Boucher (Muccigrosso, 2001, 4).

To these Burkeian-style conservatives, the Colonial break with England would not only lead to chaos, disorder, and economic calamity, but could also create a breech in security and result in mob rule, essentially giving too much power to the uneducated masses. In the words of Elbridge Gerry of Massachusetts at the Constitutional Convention, "The evils we experience flow from the excesses of Democracy" (Muccigrosso, 2001, 4). Consequently, Gerry favored removing government from the masses as much as possible and retaining an elite-led system.

Colonial Religion and Conservatism

Organized religion very often represents a conservative, even reactionary, force in society that places emphasis on traditions and resists change. Such attitudes are well exemplified by words of the writer of Proverbs (24:21) in the Old Testament when he stated, "My son, fear thou the Lord and the king: and meddle not with them that are given to change." The Christian religions of the American colonial period very often well-conformed to the conservative religious pattern exemplified by the writer of Proverbs and tended to resist change. Especially in the areas where churches were established, the dominant churches typically resisted changes, both political and religious. Consequently, the most conservative religious institutions of the colonial period were the Anglican and Puritan churches due to their preferred position as state-established churches in their various locations (Cousins, 1958, 116).

Jamestown

Most of the colonists of Jamestown were nominally Anglican and attendance at Sunday services and conformity to Anglican doctrines were required of all Virginia colonists. The Anglicans officially did not allow religious dissent, and Baptists, Presbyterians, Catholics, Quakers, and other "heretics" were persecuted, whipped, fined, imprisoned, and forced to financially support the Anglican Church through the Church tax imposed by the Virginia colony. Anglican Church Courts punished fornicators, blasphemers, and served notice on those who spent Sundays "goeing a fishing." Fines were imposed for fornication, and in 1662, a law was passed making the fine double if one were caught fornicating with a negro (Cousins, 1958, 116).

Pilgrims and Puritans

The Pilgrims of the Mayflower that arrived at Plymouth Rock in 1620 were decidedly conservative in their religious and social ideology, as has been so well chronicled in American folklore, complete with religious fundamentalism and "puritan" social mores. The Pilgrims arose from a group of Puritans at Scrooby, England, at the turn of the seventeenth century, but the Pilgrims themselves differed somewhat in outlook from ordinary Puritans. The Puritans in England at the time generally called for reform or "purification" of the Anglican Church that they viewed as corrupt. The group at Scrooby agreed with other Puritans that the Anglican Church had become corrupt, but differed with the other English Puritans in that they viewed the Anglican Church as too corrupt for reform, thus requiring the devout Christian to separate from the corruption of the mother Church in order to properly follow God's will. Consequently, in 1608, fearing persecution, the Pilgrims or "Separatists" (as they called themselves) thus fled the corruption of England for the Netherlands (Murphy, 1981, xii).

After settling in the Netherlands, the Separatists found it also to be corrupt, and fearing possible persecution that could arise as a truce between the Netherlands and Catholic Spain came to an end (thus potentially elevating Catholicism at the Separatist's expense), the Separatists secured the Mayflower and headed across the Atlantic Ocean to the New World (Murphy, 1981, xii-xiii).

Once in the New World, the Separatists elected William Bradford their governor in 1621, and began construction of their Separatist conservative utopia, free from the corruption of England and Europe. Bradford's powers as governor in the new settlement were near dictatorial in character, as Bradford served as the principal judge and treasurer of the colony, chief business manager, and secretary of state. He assigned all disputes to either the church or to the civil court, and all strangers to Plymouth had to receive his permission to travel within the colony (Murphy, 1981, xiii).

The Pilgrims adhered to Traditional Conservative ideological viewpoints in that they were fundamentalist in terms of their religion and very fatalistic in their outlook, viewing all events as happening according to God's will. For example, eight days after landing at Plymouth, the hungry Pilgrims sent an expedition of men to explore the surrounding area. In the course of doing so, the exploration party ended up stealing corn and beans from the natives' dwellings while the native homeowners were away about their daily activities. Bradford then reflected his fatalistic worldview where he interpreted everything that happened to the Pilgrims as part of a Divine plan and praised God for allowing the Pilgrims to steal the natives' food (Bradford, 1981, 75). Similarly, almost two decades later in 1637, Bradford credits God for giving the Pilgrims a victory over the Indians in the Pequot war, recounting how the Pilgrims massacred 400 Indians in a raid on the natives' village, with most of the Indians dying in a fire set by the Pilgrims that burned the Indians out of their homes. In the words of Bradford,

> "It was a fearful sight to see them thus frying in the fire and the streams of blood quenching the same, and horrible was the stink and scent thereof; but the victory seemed a sweet sacrifice, and they gave the praise thereof to God, who had wrought so wonderfully for them, thus to enclose their enemies in their hands and give them so speedy a victory over so proud and insulting an enemy" (Bradford, 1856, 1981, 331).

By the time Bradford wrote this account of Pilgrim fatalistic conservatism, the Pilgrims essentially had been overwhelmed by the arrival of the Puritans in Massachusetts Bay, who had arrived 1100 strong in 1630. The Puritans, like the Pilgrims, were a fundamentalist reaction to what they viewed as the corruption of the Anglican Church. While Bradford and the Mayflower Pilgrims viewed the Anglican Church as so corrupt that they had to separate themselves from it, the Puritans, in contrast, essentially viewed the Anglican Church as something that was corrupt, but could be reformed from within (Gaer and Siegel, 1964, 74-76).

The Puritans grew as a movement in the early seventeenth century and subsequently gained power in the English Parliament with the goal of using it to reform the Anglican Church. King Charles I, an Anglican, reacted by closing Parliament and charging Anglican Bishop William Land with harrying the Puritans out of the land. Consequently, the Puritans began immigration to the New World in order to escape the persecution by the English government (Gaer and Siegel, 1964, 74-76).

Puritan Conservatism

Puritanism was a textbook example of Traditional Conservative ideology and so well conformed to the ideology that the word "Puritanism" has become virtually interchangeable with Traditional Conservatism in common usage. Puritanism is representative of a Traditional Conservative attempt to return to a "better, vanished time," in this case, the time of the Christian Church in the days of the Acts of the Apostles. The Puritans viewed the First Century as an uncorrupted golden age of Christianity that had become corrupted over the centuries, first by the Catholic Church, and then the Anglican Church, complete with defiling and unnecessary traditions, rules, and decorations. Human history, in the Puritan view, was a history of religious (and therefore human) decline and increasing human depravity (Gaer and Siegel, 1964, 118).

The Puritans were heavily influenced by John Calvin and believed Calvin's doctrine of predestination, which holds that before the creation of the world, God exercised his divine grace and chose a few human beings to receive eternal life. Only God, however, could know who the elect are, and nothing could change God's choice; however, if one were among the elect, one would be expected to act like it and the saintly behavior would be visible to all.

An obvious problem with the Puritan predestination doctrine, however, is that if one is predestined to eternal bliss, and nothing could change God's mind, why worry about sin? In another apparent contradiction with Calvin's predestination doctrine, the Puritans stressed the conversion of "those who could not find God's truth in their hearts" (Mitchell, 1979, 44-45). Once again, if the decision predestined by God before the beginning of the world and has nothing to do with humans, why evangelize?

The Puritans, being typical religious ideologues, rarely saw the contradictions in their logic, and even when they were forced to do so, they continued to believe that their position was sound because it came from God, and the Puritans were confident that they knew the truth from God in its entirety; consequently, their logic was necessarily infallible regardless of any problems that seemed to be obvious contradictions on the surface. Puritan logic was not a method of discovery or of learning the truths in science and nature. Instead, Puritan logic was a rhetorical means of communicating the logic received from God to others. Since the Puritans already knew the truth, there was little need for inductive reasoning (Mitchell, 1979, 45).

Nevertheless, the Puritans viewed the salvation of themselves as well as the salvation of others within the Congregation as the concern of everyone in the Puritan community and each Puritan was responsible for helping others achieve their spiritual goals. To further this purpose, the Puritans engaged in "Holy Watching," or moral surveillance of each other to ensure that they did not sin. Puritan houses were built in close proximity so that one could hear his or her neighbors and know what they were doing. Curtains on the windows were forbidden so that one could see inside of the house of one's neighbor and ensure that no one inside was engaging in sin. The physical layout of the towns was such that houses faced inward toward their neighbors so as to allow Puritans to keep better watch on one another and guard against ungodly behavior (Gaer and Siegel, 1964, 87).

Puritans and Human Nature

Puritans, like other Traditional Conservatives, espoused the negative view of human nature, believing that humans are naturally bad and untrustworthy. Consequently, single men and women were prevented from living alone because left to their own devices, it was expected that people would sin. In the words of Thomas Hooker, "Every natural man and woman is born as full of sin as a toad is of poison" (Quoted in Mitchell, 1979, 118). In order to compensate for the depravity of human nature, Puritans believed that coercion was necessary to ensure proper behavior and civil and religious transgressions therefore were severely punished. Puritans also believed that people were naturally slothful, but work was Godly, and therefore stressed work as the primary method of serving God. To ensure that Puritans served God faithfully through work, the Puritans meted out punishment for slothfulness (Mitchell, 1979, 118).

Puritan View of the Bible

The Puritans viewed the Bible as a complete guide to societal organization, and much like the present-day conservative Muslims of Iran and Saudi Arabia, they believed that "God's laws," as outlined in their Holy book, also should be civil laws. In the Puritan mindset, everything that occurred in their world was somehow analogous to some event in the Bible and therefore a reproduction of divine will. The fact that the Bible was "complete" meant that anything that could not be justified by a passage found somewhere in the Bible was forbidden. In the minds of the Puritans, they spoke when the Bible spoke and were silent when the Bible was silent. The Puritans were extremely legalistic in their approach to the Bible and paid great attention to Biblical details, so much so that they were often open to the criticism that they were paying more attention to the Biblical "trees" than to the forest. In the words of Kai Erikson, (1966, 47),

> "The Scriptures not only supplied rules for the broader issues of church polity but for the tiniest details of everyday life as well, and many Puritans were fully capable of demanding that a clergyman remove some emblem from his vestments unless he could justify the extravagance by producing a warrant for it from the pages of the Bible."

Puritans and Free Thought

Like the Anglicans and the Catholics, and with unrestrained zeal, the Puritans refused to tolerate those that thought differently than themselves in religious matters and such heretics were therefore vigorously persecuted. The Puritans not only believed in the literal interpretation of the inerrant Bible, but believed that the teachings of the Bible were moral absolutes that transcended time and place. Furthermore, they believed that they had possessed the correct interpretation of the Bible to the exclusion of all other groups with whom they disagreed. As a consequence, if anyone offered a persuasive argument that shook the Puritan's certainty, or if someone developed a clever line of reasoning that could confuse the Puritan or cause him to question his beliefs, the Puritans suspected that Satan must somehow be involved. In order to prevent such confusion, settlement grants in the Puritan colony were granted only to groups of Puritans that signed a compact signifying the unity of their purpose. The compact stated that,

> "we shall live by all means, labor to keep off from us such as are contrary minded, and receive only such unto us as may be probably of one heart with us" (Gaer and Siegel, 1964, 31).

Hutchinson Heresy

In 1636, the Puritan Community of Boston became divided between the male clergy and the theological teachings of Anne Hutchinson. Hutchinson considered herself a devout Puritan, but she challenged the Puritan view of women as subservient. In I Timothy 2:10-11, the writer states that women should be submissive to men, silent in Church, and not teach men. Hutchinson essentially violated all three, teaching her own version of the gospel, and built up a major following at her home after church services. Hutchinson had no official church training or standing, but gained a wide respect from converts within the community with her teachings. Hutchinson preached that salvation was through grace, which she viewed as more important than works, thus violating the premium placed on works in orthodox Puritan theology. Hutchinson also stated that the "Holy Spirit was absent in the Preaching of some Ministers," thus challenging the spirituality, and legitimacy of the Puritan leadership (Erikson, 1966, 91).

Hutchinson was therefore placed on trial by male clergy and judges in 1637, convicted of sedition and contempt, and banished as a "woman not fit for our society, cast out and delivered to Satan to become a heathen and a leper" (Erikson, 1966, 91-92). Hutchinson was also convicted of the heresy of prophecy, the "erroneous" claim that God revealed his will directly to a believer instead of exclusively through the Bible. On the stand in her trial, Hutchinson claimed that "the Lord hath let me see which was the clear ministry and which was wrong by the Voice of God's own Spirit into my Soul" (Quoted in Erikson, 1966, 92). In claiming that God had spoken to her directly, Hutchinson committed heresy before the Puritans' very eyes. In all, Hutchinson was convicted of preaching 82 heresies and banished from the Massachusetts colony, only to help found a colony of dissenters in Rhode Island (Erikson, 1966, 91-105). In establishing Rhode Island, however, the Puritan dissidents did not prove to be any more open minded. The Rhode Island Constitution of 1644 persecuted Catholics and Quakers for "Belching out fire from Hell" (Erikson, 1966, 79-105).

Puritans and Quaker Persecution

In furtherance of their goal of unity, the Puritans persecuted Quakers for blasphemy when members of the competing sect began arriving in Massachusetts in the 1650s. The General Court ordered that any Quaker literature found in the colony should be publicly burned, and the first Quakers that arrived in Boston (a pair of housewives) were arrested before they had even disembarked from their ship (Bishop, 2003, 11).

The Puritan interpretation of "contrary minded" was essentially broadened to include those that not only thought differently, but acted differently or looked differently. For instance, Puritans identified the Quakers among them as "persons who wore hats in the presence of magistrates" (a violation of Puritan customs), and used outdated terms such as "thee" and "thou" in conversation. In fact, the first two Quakers arrested in the Massachusetts Bay Colony in the seventeenth century were actually identified, arrested, and committed to jail after one of them was heard using the word "thee" in conversation (Bishop, 2003, 11.)

In this instance, the two Quaker women were jailed, stripped naked and body-searched for marks of the devil, the Puritan belief being that the Devil's children (witches) had a mark on their body where the Devil had physically touched them when he made them his own. The windows of the jail were boarded so that the women could not infect the rest of the community with their heresies, after which the women were deported to Barbados, in spite of the fact that there was no law per se against Quakerism at the time. The Quaker books that were in the possession of the women were then burned in a ceremony in the public marketplace (Erikson, 1966, 116).

Puritans did nothing, however, without finding justification for what they were doing in the Bible; hence, in order to charge the Quakers with blasphemy, the Puritans searched the Bible for a Biblical basis on which the charge could rest. The failure of Quakers to "put off their hats" in the presence of the magistrates was a practice that was particularly galling to the Puritans. The Quakers had their own Biblical reason for refusing to do so in that they believed that all were equal in the eyes of God and the custom of tipping the hat violated God's natural equality. Puritans, however, searched the scriptures until they found what they interpreted as a command from God against the practice in the Ten Commandments themselves. Specifically, the Puritans ruled that failure to "put off the hat" violated the commandment to "Honor thy mother and father." The following conversation between a Puritan magistrate and Quaker Edward Wharton illustrates this point (Quoted in Bishop, 2003, 198-199).

Wharton: "Friends, what is the cause and wherefore have I been fetched from my habitation, where I was following my honest calling, and here laid up as an evil-doer?"

Magistrate: "Your hair is too long and you are disobedient to that commandment which saith, 'Honor thy mother and father.'"

Wharton: "Wherein?"

Magistrate: "In that you will not put off your hat before the magistrates."

Obviously, the Quakers' real crime was the failure to show any respect for Puritan customs, rather than disrespect to their parents, but for the Puritans, the Biblical connection between command and violation was certain enough. The Quakers were also condemned for a number of other practices foreign to the Puritans that most Protestant Christians in later generations would view as well within Biblically imposed limits on Christian behavior. In particular, the Quakers were known to sometimes gather together in private for religious services rather than appear as a group at the "Lord's Barn." In doing so, the Quakers' religious separateness was interpreted as blasphemy (Erikson, 1966, 130-136). Consequently, in October 1656, the Puritans passed a law against "that cursed sect of heretics lately risen up in the world," providing fines for ship captains who brought Quakers to Massachusetts and larger fines for Puritans who sheltered Quakers. Finally, it was decreed that,

> "what person or persons soever shall revile the office or persons of magistrates or ministers, as is usual with the Quakers, such persons shall be severely whipped or pay the sum of five pounds" (Erikson, 1966, 116).

The Quakers reacted to the persecution by choosing martyrdom, and Quaker efforts to infiltrate the Puritan community actually increased, rather than decreased, as a result. Not learning from their heavy-handed mistake that had only created a religious "cause" for Quakers, the Puritans reacted the next year by passing the following harsher law, including the extremes of corporal punishment and amputations, against Quakerism.

> "And it is further ordered, that if any Quaker or Quakers shall presume, after they have once suffered what the law requireth, to come into this jurisdiction, every such male Quaker shall for the first offense have one of his ears cut off, and be kept at work in the house of correction till he can be sent away at his own charge, and for the second offense shall have his other ear cut off, and kept in the house of correction, as aforesaid; and every woman Quaker that hath suffered the law here and shall presume to come into this jurisdiction shall be severely whipped, and kept at the house of correction at work till she be sent away at their own charge, and so for her coming again she shall be alike used as aforesaid; and for every Quaker, he or she, that shall

a third time herein again offend, they shall have their tongues bored through with a hot iron, and kept at the house of correction, close to work, till they be sent away at their own charge" (Quoted in Erikson, 1966, 117).

Three persons lost an ear for violating the law, but there were numerous beatings, imprisonment, and other tortures. One man was beaten with 117 blows from a corded whip and left for dead. A witness to the event stated that,

> "his flesh was beaten black and as into jelly, and under his arms the bruised flesh and blood hung down, clotted as it were into bags; and it was so beaten into one mass, that the signs of one particular blow could not be seen" (Bishop, 2003, 57).

Evidently, however, the severe punishment was not enough. In October 1658, the General Court passed another new law that required that anyone guilty of Quaker disorders would be banished from the territory "upon pain of death." In other words, Quakers were not only to be banished, but if Quakers failed to honor the conditions of their banishment, they would be executed (Erikson, 1966, 115). The law was quickly implemented, with the result that in May 1659, the General Court banished six persons from Salem, Massachusetts for Quakerism, and two young Quaker children were promptly sold into slavery in order to satisfy claims against their parents (Bishop, 2003, 89).

More banishments of Quakers followed in the summer of 1659, with the result that several Quakers, prepared to die as martyrs, defied the law by returning to Boston in protest during a meeting of the General Court. A group of Puritans from Salem who sympathized with the Quakers came to the Court with them, one person bringing linen "wherein to wrap the dead bodies of those who were to suffer" (Bishop, 2003, 99). The General Court proceeded to arrest all of the protesters, over 20 people in total, and incarcerate them in the Boston jail. The Court then selected three persons from those incarcerated, William Robinson, Marmaduke Stevenson, and Mary Dyer (who formerly had been a follower of Anne Hutchinson) and sentenced them to death (Bishop, 2003, 99-100). The two men were hanged, but Mary Dyer was given a reprieve and taken down from the scaffold at the execution due to unrest among the Puritan audience attending the public execution. Dyer would continue to defy the Puritan Courts, however, and was hanged for her defiance the next year in 1660 (Bishop, 2003, 102-103).

Following the executions, local constables conducted a purge of their community in the months that followed, complete with household raids, confiscations of property, and public floggings. The executions and increased persecution, however, had the opposite effect than that intended by the Puritan magistrates. Instead of being cowed by the Puritans' display of savagery, the Quakers, in the words of Bishop (2003, 99), "came together in the moving and power of the Lord, to look your bloody laws in the face, and to accompany those who should suffer by them." In other words, the Quakers rebelled in demonstrative open defiance of the laws and offered themselves as martyrs, forcing the Puritans to either relent or play the role of mass slaughterers.

Noteworthy of the Quaker demonstrations the Puritans found impossible to ignore was that of John Burton, who accused the Puritan Court of being "robbers and destroyers of the widows and the fatherless," and argued that the "Puritan worship was not the worship of God," in front of the magistrates in the Puritan Court itself. Other Quakers engaged in equally bold and bizarre types of "impossible-to-ignore" behavior. For example, Thomas Hutchinson, governor of Massachusetts at the time before the American Revolution, later wrote that,

> "At Boston one George Wilson, and at Cambridge one Elizabeth Horton, went crying through the streets that the Lord was coming with fire and sword to plead with them. Thomas Newhouse went into the meeting house at Boston with a couple of glass bottles and broke them before the congregation, and threatened, 'Thus will the Lord break you in pieces.' Another time M. Brewster came in with her face smeared and black as coal...One Faubord, of Grindleton, carried his enthusiasm still higher and was sacrificing his son in imitation of Abraham, but the neighbors hearing the lad cry, broke open the house and happily prevented it" (Quoted in Erikson, 1966, 123).

Two Quaker women performed the outrageous act of parading naked in public as a protest of their unjust treatment by the Puritans. The demonstrations, of course, were merely further proof to the Puritans of Quaker wickedness, and the naked-parading women were punished. The sentences from the Essex County Court were as follows,

> "The wife of Robert Wilson, for her barbarous and inhuman going naked through the town, is sentenced to be tied at a cart's tail with her body naked downward to her waist, and whipped from Mr. Gidney's gate till she come to her own house, not exceeding thirty stripes" (Erickson, 1966, 122).

Similarly, Quaker woman Lydia Wardell was ordered by the Court to be, "severely whipped and to pay costs to the Marshall of Hampton upon her presentment for going naked into Newbury meeting house" (Quoted in Erikson, 1966, 122).

Each of the Puritans' escalating stern actions, however, only caused the Quakers to be even more defiant, with the result that the number of Quakers awaiting execution overflowed the jails, and the waiting list for Quaker trials grew to an unmanageable length that overwhelmed the Puritan Courts. It soon became clear that either the Puritans would have to develop new tactics in order to deter the Quakers or they would have to engage in a bloodbath of unprecedented proportions, even for the Puritans. In late 1661, however, the insanity was laid to rest when the Massachusetts General Court received a letter from King Charles II prohibiting the use of either corporal or capital punishment in cases involving Quakers (Bishop, 2003, 214).

Puritans and Witches

The Puritan witch trials in general and those at Salem in particular are replete with numerous incredible examples of the Puritans' inability to think critically due to their fundamentalist religious beliefs that often limited their capacity for rational thought. Concerning witches, the Puritan capacity for rational thought was compromised by Exodus 22:18, which states "Thou shalt not allow a witch to live," obviously meaning to the Puritans that there were such things as witches and that it was the duty of God's children not only to seek them out, but to kill them when they were found. The Bible itself, however, does not contain a complete and concise discussion of how to identify and apprehend witches, so the Puritans were forced to rely on traditions that had developed over the prior centuries. Many of the Puritans' ideas concerning witches had been shaped by the Catholic Church in Medieval Europe prior to the Protestant Reformation and the Puritans were merely the beneficiaries of ideas developed and handed down over the centuries. The official Catholic Church position on witches was spelled out in detail in the *Malleus Maleficarum* of 1484, written by Heinrich Kramer and James Sprenger, and the ideas contained therein remained ideas concerning witches that were prevalent in society among Protestants and Catholics alike in the Seventeenth Century.

Kramer and Sprenger in the *Malleus Maleficarum* explained for the Catholic Church the concept of witches, their power, and how they should be dealt with by the authorities. The *Malleus Maleficarum,* was approved by the Catholic Church as valid in 1487, and its prescriptions and procedures became the official policies of the Inquisition in the late fifteenth and sixteenth centuries. In this truly incredible work, Kramer and Sprenger argue such absurdities as that "devils" can "truly and actually remove men's members" as well as "work some prestidigitatory illusion so that the male organ appears to be entirely removed and separate from the body" (Kramer and Sprenger, 1971, 58). Furthermore, Kramer and Sprenger (1971, 121) explain that witches are able to, "collect male organs in great numbers, as many as twenty or thirty members together, and put them in a bird's nest, or shut them up in a box, where they move themselves like living members, and eat oats and corn, as has been seen by many and is a matter of common report?"

Exactly how a detached penis eats oats and corn is not explained, but Kramer and Sprenger (1971, 121) do provide the story of a "certain man," who explained that,

"when he had lost his member, he approached a known witch to ask her to restore it to him. She told the afflicted man to climb a certain tree, and that he might take which he liked out of a nest in which there were several members. And when he tried to take a big one, the witch said: You must not take that one; adding, because it belonged to a parish priest."

Kramer and Sprenger (1971, 65) also explain how men can be turned into "werewolves," both voluntarily and involuntarily, and how one such "werewolf" was condemned by the court of Dole, Lyons, in 1573 and burned alive. Other nonsensical creatures explained by Kramer and Sprenger include Fauns, Trolls, and Incubus devils (with penises of ice) and Succubus devils, both of which are known to have sex with humans.

In an atmosphere of such scientific ignorance and religion-dominated superstitious stupidity, almost anything supernatural becomes possible in the minds of the believers and critical thinking becomes virtually nonexistent. Such was obviously the case not only with the Catholic Church and its Malleus Maleficarum of the Middle Ages, but with the Puritans of the Seventeenth Century, who constructed their society on the groundwork that had been laid before them by their pre-scientific, religious fundamentalist predecessors. In the interest of space, one such vivid example of the Puritans' limited reasoning capabilities will suffice for the discussion here.

In the cases of witches, the Puritan court accepted without question the idea that Satan could take the "shape" of persons and use that shape to terrorize innocent Christians (as had been argued by Kramer and Sprenger two centuries before). The Puritans also contended that the Devil could not assume the "shape" of an innocent person; thus, if someone testified that they were visited by a "specter" that came to them in the "shape" of a particular person, it was a foregone conclusion that the person whose shape the Devil assumed was therefore guilty of "signing the Devil's book" that had allowed him to thus use that person's "shape" (Erikson, 1966, 151).

During an early hearing in the Salem witch proceedings, a young girl had been named as one whose "shape" had terrorized the other young girls in Salem. When the Puritan authorities inquired of the girl "How comes your appearance to hurt these (girls)?" the girl replied, "How do I know, he that appeared in the shape of Samuel, a glorified saint, may appear in anyone's shape," a reference by the girl to I Samuel 28: 7-17, where the Witch at Endor conjures the shape of the prophet Samuel at the behest of Israel's King Saul. Obviously, by any rule of logic, the girl had just proven through the very Bible itself that if the Devil can take the "shape" of humans, then he must be able to take the shape of innocent humans, since he took the shape of Samuel, whom Puritans all knew to be prophet and an "innocent" man of God. The Puritans, however, their ability to reason destroyed by their religious ideology, were not persuaded by the testimony and continued to condemn persons to death based on "spectral evidence" (Erikson, 1966, 151).

As if this were not enough, the Puritans also altered the rules of evidence in witch trials; much like conservatives of future generations would alter the rules of trials for suspected terrorists. Puritans normally followed the rule that two eye-witnesses were necessary for conviction in capital cases. In witch trials, however, they abandoned this standard and ruled that any two witnesses, even if they were not necessarily eye-witnesses to the events in question and even if they were testifying about different events at different times, would be sufficient to gain convictions in witch proceedings (Erikson, 1966, 150). Regardless of how they stacked their cards, however, the Puritans' efforts to squelch heresy and witchcraft would inevitably end in failure due to the massive immigration and accompanying religious diversity that would eventually rend the narrow Puritan experience untenable.

Established Religions and 18th Century Sectarianism

As immigration increased in the early 18th Century, and with it increasing religious diversity, the more established Puritans and Anglicans both opposed the new religious diversity and sectarianism as heresy, violations of God's will, and contrary to Apostle Paul's (I Corinthians 14:40) admonition, "Let all things be done decently and in order." Puritans and Anglicans viewed the new sects as not only erroneous and heretical, but also exceedingly unruly and therefore unpleasing to God. In the words of Isaac Stiles, a Puritan clergyman, members of other religious sects were:

> "subversive of peace, discipline, and government, lay open the sluices, and make a gap to let in a flood of confusion and disorder, and very awfully portend the ruin of these churches. If sectarianism increased, Connecticut would soon be an habitation of dragons and a court for owls" (Quoted in Labaree, 1948, 62).

Anglicans, like the Puritans, tended to believe that their Church was the only one among English-speaking Protestant Churches founded on the principle of Apostolic succession; therefore the Anglican church was the only one that was valid. To the Anglicans, ministers in other sects were not truly ordained and other sects were a perversion of sound church doctrine, organization, and discipline that undermined civil society. For example, Lieutenant Governor Colden of New York essentially blamed land riots in the 1760s on trouble caused by "religious dissenters from the diverse sects" (Colden, 1973, 208).

Similarly, Anglican minister Jonathan Boucher described the sectarians as those referenced by Apostle Paul as "persons having itching ears and unstable in all their ways," who are "easily tossed about with every wind of doctrine." Boucher declared (in an uncanny parallel with George W. Bush and terrorism) that "those who are not for the (Anglican) Church are against it," and viewed the dissenting sects as representative of revolts not only against the Church, but also against the state and society. Boucher argued for rigid enforcement of regulations and laws against dissenting sects and warned of the ultimate destruction of society if the sects were allowed to go unpunished (Boucher, 1967, 77-88).

Anglicans and Puritans, however, were also disdainful of each other, as well as the sects. Anglicans were particularly appalled by the democratic leanings within the Puritan community that they viewed as an affront to the hierarchical structure of the Anglican Church. In the words of Anglican rector of Stratford in 1760, Samuel Johnson,

"All the disadvantages it (Puritan Connecticut) labors under are owing to its wretched constitution, being little more than a mere democracy, and most of them upon a level, and each man thinking himself an able divine and politician; hence the prevalence of rigid enthusiasms and conceited notions and practices in religion, and republican and mobbish principles and practices, next door to anarchy, in polity" (Quoted in Labaree, 1948, 66).

Johnson's sentiments were most certainly the dominant views of the Anglican Church hierarchy throughout the early colonial period; however, by the time of the American Revolution and the subsequent writing of the American Constitution, the Anglicans had come to recognize that suppression of dissent, no matter how distasteful, was no longer possible. Nevertheless, during the reign of King James II, the governors of all royal provinces had instructions,

"to permit a liberty of conscience to all persons except Papists, so they be contented with a quiet and peaceable enjoyment of the same, not giving offense or scandal to the government" (Labaree, 1935, 494-502).

Eventually, the diversity of the population produced from massive immigration would mean that laws punishing heretics and dissenters would be overturned and eliminated on a state by state basis between the end of the Seven Years War and the Jacksonian era. Thomas Jefferson's famous Virginia Statute on Religious Liberty of 1786 declaring that "no one shall be compelled to contribute to any opinion with which he disagrees" became a model for other states to follow and its ideas gradually supplanted official intolerance as the norm (Labaree, 1935, 502).

The Anglican Church in particular had a special proclivity to oppose the movement toward freedom of conscience in the colonial period given that it was the established Church, not only in a number of the colonies, but in the mother country as well. Thus, for political reasons, specifically, the motivation to retain their preferred positions both in England and in the colonies, as well as reasons theological and ideological, the Anglicans could be expected to resist religious tolerance.

In Maryland, for example, which recognized religious tolerance upon its founding in 1632, the Anglicans overthrew the religiously tolerant political authorities in 1689 following the overthrow of a Catholic King in England the previous year. The Catholic family of the Maryland Governor, Lord Calvert, had begun the colony as a planned refuge for Catholics during a time of Anglican religious intolerance in England. The religious tolerance imposed by the Calverts, however, meant that Protestants were as free to come to the Maryland colony as were Catholics, with the result that Maryland's population was majority Protestant throughout the colonial period. In 1689, the Catholic Lord Calvert was accused of not swearing allegiance to the new Protestant English King, William of Orange, and subsequently deposed by intolerant Anglicans. The Puritans in Maryland at the time, fearing Catholic reprisals, did not join the Anglicans in revolt. As a result, when the Anglicans took power after deposing Lord Calvert, they imprisoned the Puritan leaders for not taking part in the revolt. The Anglicans then made the Church of England the official state Church of the colony of Maryland in 1692. In 1704, the Anglicans padlocked the Catholic Church in Maryland, and then demolished it a few years later. "Papists" could no longer hold office in Maryland and Catholics would not be able to legally worship publicly again in Maryland until after the American Revolution (Ives, 1969, 129-135).

Anglican Ministers and Conservatism

In addition to their motivation to retain their preferred status in the English political system, Anglican ministers had a further motivation toward conservatism in that there were none ordained in the colonies, but instead, all were ordained in England and then shipped to America. Their salaries were not paid by the home congregations, but by the mother church in England; thus, the Anglican clergy had extraordinary incentive to be loyal to the British crown and the British system of government that were responsible for their personal livelihood (Finke and Stark, 1993, 36). Hence, when the American Revolution came, the Anglican clergy could be expected to denounce the Revolution as a rebellion against God since it was also a rebellion against the authorities that had supplied them with their positions. Such was the position of the Anglican Reverend George Micklejohn in 1768 who argued that,

"Resistance to the lawful authority God has set over us could never possibly be productive of anything but the wildest uproar and most universal confusion...every such wicked and desperate attempt (was) not only treason against an earthly sovereign, but rebellion against the most high God" (Quoted in Labaree, 1948, 75).

It is difficult not to see the Traditional Conservative spirit of Edmund Burke in the words of Micklejohn even if Micklejohn's primary motivation might actually have been his own personal livelihood. Micklejohn's position was generally representative of the position of the majority of the Anglican clergy and the Anglican Church as a whole during time of the American Revolution. Though it is true that both Puritans and Anglican conservatives did often give lip service to the principle of religious liberty, there was also a strong tendency to then add contingencies to the supposed religious freedoms consistent with the interests of their established churches and the requirements of their religious beliefs. Their basic positions, though purportedly to be in favor of freedom of conscience, were typically in opposition to religious freedom in practice and their tolerance of religious diversity after the Revolution was reflective primarily of the changing political realities stemming from ethnic and religious diversity that they lacked the power to do anything about (Labaree, 1948, 75-80).

On the eve of the American Revolution, for example, Jonathan Boucher preached in Maryland against the "toleration of Papists" and argued that "many great evils would arise from a state's giving equal countenance to all religions indiscriminately." Boucher even argued that such an idea could lead to the demise of civil society itself. In the words of Boucher,

"Equally fatal to the religion and the morals of the people would be the introduction of that visionary project of some rash theorists in whose ideal states no preference should be shown to any particular system of religion. Such a scheme would inevitably bring a relaxation of principle and give countenance to systems unfavorable to good morals and sometimes to

systems hostile to the very state by which they are supported and destructive
of all civil authority" (Quoted in Boucher, 1967, 259-261).

Similarly, Puritan leaders argued that civil law must be subordinate to
religious law and that God does not permit men to be free to follow their
consciences. In the words of William Worthington in 1744,

> "Some were disposed to deny the magistrate any right to make laws about, or
> take cognizance of, religious affairs, as if every man had a good right to
> follow his conscience how dreadfully soever it errs, a valuable privilege he
> ought not to suffer an encroachment upon in the least. But, as the Old
> Testament makes clear, God gave laws circumscribing conscience and
> forbidding the Jews to worship idols, and modern society should follow this
> divine example" (Quoted in Labaree, 1948, 70).

Worthington's words reflect the Traditional Conservative position that there
are moral absolutes, and that there is a class of men who know what those
absolutes are, consequently, it is that class of men that must rule. In this, the
Puritans' ideology is strikingly similar both to that of the Catholic Church
that Protestants had broken away from two centuries earlier, and the
Christian Coalition of the American political right three centuries later.

Conservatives and the Great Awakening

During the Great Awakening of the mid-18th century, a time in which an
evangelistic fervor exploded throughout the colonies, conservatives of all
denominations opposed the new religious excitement, denouncing it as not
the work of God, but of the Devil. Conservatives argued that even when the
new untrained exhorters had honest intentions, in their ignorance, they might
unwittingly serve as the mouthpiece of Satan while intending to preach
God's Holy Word (Miller and Johnson, 1968, 25).

The established Churches generally looked on the Awakening as false
religion based on emotional experiences and believed that the evils that
would arise from the endeavor would far outweigh any good that could be
accomplished. According to the Philadelphia Presbyterian Synod, the
"enthusiasts" preached,

> "the terrors of the Law in such manner and dialect as has no precedent in the
> Word of God. They so worked on the passions and affections of weak minds
> as to cause them to cry out in a hideous manner and fall down in convulsion-
> like fits, to the marring of the profiting both of themselves and others, who
> are so taken up in seeing and hearing these odd symptoms that they cannot
> attend to or hear what the preacher says" (Quoted in Tracy, 1997, 71-72).

In fact, the very words "enthusiasm" and "enthusiast" became terms of reproach and suspicion much in the same way that "Communism" and "Communist" became so negatively regarded by conservatives in the twentieth century and "liberal" and liberals became so repugnant the hard right in the late Twentieth and early Twenty-First Centuries. For example, one conservative referred to evangelist George Whitefield, regarded by many as the among the most important of the evangelists of the Awakening, as a "rant" and a "novice," while others referred to him as a "fanatic" and a "deceiver," and still others referred to him as an "imposter," and "incendiary," or simply, "that wild enthusiast" (Tracy, 1997, 71-72).

Ironically, the same "enthusiasms" and displays of emotion that were exhibited by the New Light preachers and their congregations during the Great Awakening that were so disparaged by the conservatives of the time would also be prevalent among the leaders and followers within the conservative religious right in the United States in the Twentieth and Twenty-First Centuries. "Raving expressions founded on sudden impulses," such as those of the "enthusiasts," posed threats to the conservatives' preference for order, and in the view of the conservatives of the time, were a direct contradiction with Apostle Paul's command that things of the Church should be commenced "decently" with "order." In the words of eighteenth century Reverend Charles Chauncy,

> "Discipline is necessary in all societies whatever; and where this is neglected, if there is the appearance of confusion, what is it more than may justly be expected" (Quoted in Lippy, 1981, 86).

Particularly galling to the professionally trained ministers of the Anglicans and Congregationalists was the fact that many of the "New Light" preachers had little or no religious training at all. In contrast to the Anglicans, who required that their clergy first study at an English theological seminary, Baptists and Methodists allowed anyone who felt the call of God in their hearts, regardless of their religious training, to preach the gospel of Christ. Furthermore, many of the new evangelists were young, and some, in what constituted perhaps the greatest of insults in the minds of the conservative ministers, were even black or female. In the words of Eighteenth Century conservative clergyman Charles Chauncy of Boston,

> "These exhorters are men of all occupations, who are vain enough to think themselves fit to be teachers of others; men who, though they have no learning and but small capacities, yet imagine they are able, and without study, too, to speak to the spiritual profit of such as are willing to hear them. Nay there are among these exhorters, babes in age as well as understanding. They are chiefly, indeed, young persons, sometimes lads, or rather boys; nay,

women and girls; yea, Negroes, have taken upon them to do the business of
preachers" (Quoted in Lippy, 1981, 226).

New Light preachers and their congregations were also criticized by the
conservatives of their day for their tolerance, an attitude rarely characteristic
of conservatism. George Whitefield in particular, though an Anglican,
preached in churches of other denominations and accepted other ministers
who had not received Anglican ordination, thus opening himself to
conservative criticism. In 1740, Whitefield was denounced in a pamphlet in
Philadelphia known as *The Querists* for "displaying too tolerant a spirit." If
Whitefield, an Anglican, was willing to join with Antinomians, Arminians,
Calvinists, and Lutherans in religious work, why not even the Papists? In
essence, orthodox Anglicans viewed such tolerance as an assault upon the
true faith (Labaree, 1948, 85).

Conservative ministers also argued that the New Light preachers and their
revivals were not to God's glory because they kept people from their daily
labor. This was particularly heinous to the Puritans, who viewed work as a
primary method of serving God that should not be shirked. For the common
people to neglect the "religion of labor" was to shirk their duties as
Christians, fall into sin, and undermine the moral foundation of society
(Labaree, 1948, 86).

In this atmosphere, the conservatives used all of the powers at their
disposal in efforts to squelch the New Light preachers and silence the Great
Awakening. For instance, when James Davenport, a Whitefield disciple,
arrived in Boston in 1742, all Boston Churches closed their doors to
Davenport, thus forcing him to do his preaching in the streets where, as fate
would have it, his message was actually more effective. When closing the
churches to him did not have the desired effect, Davenport was brought
before the Connecticut Assembly in 1742 and charged with "disturbance of
the religious peace." After reviewing his case, the Assembly concluded that
Davenport was insane and ordered him deported to his home parish on Long
Island. The next year, Connecticut passed an Act that withdrew much of their
tolerance for nonconformists. After that, "New Lights" were fined and a few
imprisoned for failure to pay church taxes.

Academia in Connecticut at the time, dominated by the mainline
Congregationalist Church, was no more forward thinking. In one incident,
for example, two Yale students were expelled by Yale authorities for having
attended a New Light church with their parents during their summer
vacations (Tracy, 1997, 86).

In Anglican Virginia, the General Court took over the licensing of
preachers in an unsuccessful attempt to limit the number of evangelists and
the places where they could hold their meetings. When this did not produce

the desired results, the Royal governor banned all traveling preachers in 1750. The revivalists continued undaunted, however, the persecution (much as Christ was persecuted) being proof enough to the evangelists themselves that they were indeed doing God's work (Tracy, 1997, 86). After all, in II Timothy 3:12, the writer proclaims that "all who desire to live godly in Christ Jesus will suffer persecution."

In the end, much of the conservative reaction to the Awakening ended up unsuccessful, but that does not mean that the conservatives were not energetic and dedicated to their causes. Instead, the failure exemplifies the fact that conservatism so often fails to accomplish its goal of preventing change and is often unable to even do much in the way of slowing the pace, even when the conservatives control the political, economic, and religious structures of society.

Conservatism and Colonial Education

The Reverend Jonathan Boucher (1967, 63) perhaps best summed up the conservative attitude toward education in the colonial period when he declared that "the relinquishment of old opinions, or the adoption of new ones, without sufficient examination and evidence, are equally proofs of weak minds, and equally criminal." During the colonial period, Boucher's attitude was also the dominant attitude of the times. Whether new ideas were forged in the realm of scientific inquiry, in social relationships, or even in the trivial matters such as the wearing of a periwig, the colonial conservatives tended to cling tenaciously to the old, the tried, and the traditional, and looked with suspicion on the new and unfamiliar. As a consequence, education essentially made few advances in the more than century-and-a-half between Jamestown and the American Revolution, whether one is concerned with basic philosophy, method, or content (Cremin, 1970, 95).

Massachusetts led the way in the construction of what eventually became the American system of education with the Massachusetts school laws of 1642 and 1647. The Massachusetts laws called for universal compulsory education on the primary level and specified that the responsibility for providing that education rested with the local communities. Connecticut followed Massachusetts with similar legislation, as did several other colonies in the Seventeenth Century (Cremin, 1970, 95-96).

In the Seventeenth Century, however, the education system reflected the conservative preference for free market, rather than socialistic solutions. As such, education was generally viewed as a commodity to be paid for like any other, and the idea that education should be funded with tax money and free to the students did not make an effective appearance until after the American Revolution. While there were a few free schools, and some were supported by tax money, most were regarded as charity organizations that existed only for the children of the poor (Cremin, 1970, 102-105).

Curriculum was largely unchanging, clinging to rote memorization, studies in classic writings, and Latin language. Conservatives resisted changes in textbooks and pretty much everything else. For example, Robert Carter, a wealthy Virginia planter, once ordered that his son be removed from the school he was attending if the school did not adopt a fifty-year-old book that he himself had studied in school as a child (Wright, 1970, 251-252). While it is possible that the book Carter was so concerned about may have been a wonderful text, his insistence was part of a general pattern where conservatives attempted to ensure that their children would be exposed in school only to the "right" sort of ideas and taught only by the "right" sort of people. The same attitude has carried forth to the present as conservative religious fundamentalist parents fight to ensure that students learn about creationism and abstinence regardless, of other theories, social changes, and scientific evidence that may have been developed.

Eighteenth Century conservatives also attempted to ensure that their children were taught patriotism and loyalty to the political system in the schools. As such, conservatives favored loyalty oaths for teachers, much like those imposed on teachers in the Twentieth Century during communist scares. For example, just prior to the American Revolution, Reverend Jonathan Boucher was asked by governmental leaders of Maryland to prepare a sermon on education for a meeting in 1773 concerning consolidation of schools. Boucher argued that the schoolmaster must have "zeal for the Christian religion; diligence in his calling; affection to the present government; and conformity to the doctrine of the disciple of the Church of England." Boucher then prescribed a loyalty oath where schoolmasters would acknowledge the exclusive sovereignty of the King, their obedience to the government, and adherence to the laws of the land (Boucher, 1967, 195-196).

Conservatism and Colonial Higher Education

In higher education in the colonial period, conservatism was also dominant. From the founding of Harvard in 1636, to the American Revolution, the curriculum of the American Universities essentially remained unchanged and conformed to the pattern of the Universities of Medieval Europe. Nevertheless, conservatives often condemned the Universities for departing from the old ways, and demanded returns to the traditions of their fathers. In this vein, Yale University was founded in 1701 by conservative Puritans who believed that Harvard had become too radical. This was in spite of the fact that Harvard's administration had acquiesced in the Salem witch trials less than a decade earlier, hardly an indicator that Harvard had become overly progressive. Similarly, King's College (Columbia) was founded in New York by Anglicans in 1754 partly in reaction to the perceived radicalism of the Puritan universities at Harvard and Yale (Labaree, 1948, 98). In the words of New York conservative Cadwallader Colden, it was

"highly requisite that a seminary on the principles of the Church of England be distinguished in America by particular privileges, not only on account of religion, but of good policy, to prevent the farther growth of republican principles, which already too much prevail in the colonies" (Colden, 1973, 355).

Obviously, it was the intention of Colden to construct an educational institution that would exert a conservative influence on the community, reinforce loyalty to God and the crown, and support the conservative notion that elites, rather than common men, should rule. American conservatives essentially have been attempting to shape education along these principles ever since.

Colonial Conservatism and Social Theory

Society and social practices, mores, and folkways, have been in a state of constant change throughout American history, and conservatives have been a consistent force against those changes. In general, conservatives have also tended to view themselves as the defenders of public morality; thus, many new societal innovations have been resisted by conservatives on moral grounds. The colonial period was no exception to these trends.

For example, when plays began to become common in the colonies in the mid-eighteenth century, conservatives typically denounced them for "collecting crowds, obstructing traffic, and disturbing the peace." The heaviest charges, however, were that the playhouses were "propagators of vice and immorality" that would lead their youth into wickedness and immorality. In the words of one Pennsylvania conservative, speaking of theaters,

" vice and immorality are there exhibited in such pleasing colors as to induce many giddy and unwary youth to realize and reduce to practice what they see displayed there under fictitious characters. The playhouse without exaggeration may be called the school of vice and debauchery" (Quoted in Labaree, 1948, 103).

Colonial conservatives were also resistant to changes in clothing fashions, preferring their traditional garb instead of the new and different. Puritans and Quakers, as might be expected, were especially conservative in their dress and even made an issue of the introduction of periwigs in the late Seventeenth Century. Conservatives condemned periwigs as "against nature" and even suggested that those that violated such a law were in danger of falling out of God's Grace. In the words of the Reverend Samuel Sewall concerning periwigs, "He that contemns the Law of Nature is not fit to be a publisher of the Law of Grace" (Quoted in Yazawa, 1998, 49). In another instance, Sewall eulogizes a revered schoolmaster who died in 1708 thusly, "A rare instance of piety, health, strength, serviceableness. The welfare of the province was much upon his spirit. He abominated periwigs" (Quoted in Yazawa, 1998, 231).

Puritans in particular purged themselves of the latest in clothing fashions as part of their avoidance of all "luxuries" so as to better focus on God's work. Physical beauty and other aesthetics in general were disparaged in the Puritan community. For example, in 1634, the Massachusetts General Court forbade "garments with any lace, silver or gold thread, all cutworks, embroidered or needlework caps, bands and rails, all gold and silver girdles, hatbands, belts, ruffs, and beaver hats." Clothing whereby the "nakedness of the arm may be discovered" were also forbidden, as was the wearing of long hair (Gaer and Siegel, 1964, 87-88).

The Puritans were also particularly concerned that no one should enjoy themselves when they could be otherwise better employed in work for the Lord. As a consequence, in Puritan society of the Seventeenth Century, laws were passed ensuring that one was not entertained. Prohibited entertainment in the Puritan community included sledding, swimming, music, and dancing. In the words of Puritan leader Increase Mather,

> "Mixt or Promiscuous Dancing of Men and Women could not be tolerated since the unchaste Touches and Gesticulations used by Dancers have a palpable tendency to that which is evil" (Quoted in Miller and Johnson, 1968, 110).

Other prohibited activities included playing cards, dice, shuffleboard, other games of chance, enjoyment on the Sabbath, Sunday walks, visits to the harbor, and "enjoyment when one might be better employed" (Gaer and Siegel, 1964, 87-88)

To demonstrate how serious the Puritans were concerning their ban on "enjoyment," in 1670, John Lewis and Sarah Chapman were convicted of the heinous crime of "engaging in things tending much to the dishonor of God, the reproach of religion, and the prophanation of the holy Sabbath."

Specifically, Lewis and Chapman committed the despicable act of "sitting together on the Lord's Day, under an apple tree in Goodman Chapman's orchard" (Gaer and Siegel, 1964, 87-88).

Colonial Conservatives and Inequality

Colonial conservative elites typically viewed social and income inequality as naturally right and inherent in mankind. To most colonial merchants and southern planters, it was inequality among men that made the entire concept of a "gentleman" possible in the first place, and it was therefore "just" that certain men should lead and others should follow. Furthermore, it was "just" that the "inferior" classes should defer to their "betters" (Miller and Johnson, 1968, 16-19).

As a consequence, the conservatives of the colonial period tended to oppose democratization, viewing the upper classes as not only wealthier, but also superior in education, wisdom, and morality, and therefore worthy of ruling. Since Democracy could possibly replace elite rule with rule by commoners, it was viewed as fundamentally unsound. For elite rulers to be replaced by commoners would be to replace sound and wise rule with rule from the gutter. In general, elite conservatives thought of the poorer classes in the American backcountry as lazy, ignorant, irreligious, and stupid (Wright, 1970, 16-19).

For example, a South Carolina clergyman in 1774, on the eve of the American Revolution, declared from the pulpit that "Mechanics and country clowns had no right to dispute about politics, or what kings, lords, and commons had done" (Quoted in Schlesinger, 1993, 433). Similarly, Jonathan Boucher argued that "to be very popular it is, I believe, necessary to be very like the bulk of the people, that is, wrongheaded, ignorant, and prone to resist authority." Boucher added that "whenever it happens that a really sensible man becomes the idol of the people, it must be owing to his possessing a talent of letting himself down to their level" (Boucher, 1967, 309-310). To that, John Randolph, the Loyalist attorney general of Virginia added the following concerning those who were, "running the race of popularity,"

"Whilst they are the greatest sticklers for the liberty of others, are themselves the most abject slaves in politics. They have no opinion of their own, but are the echo of the people. Propriety and wisdom are often abandoned, in order to pursue the wills of their noisy constituents" (Quoted in Labaree, 1948, 115).

It was clear to the elites that the lower classes had their "place" in the scheme of things and they should remain in their place and not trespass in the areas reserved for their "betters." Among the sharpest class divisions with unwritten lines that were not to be crossed was marriage between the classes. William Byrd, for instance, writes his comments concerning a story of a planter's daughter who married a common overseer. In the words of Byrd,

> "Had she run away with a gentleman or a pretty fellow, there might have been some excuse for her, though he were of inferior fortune; but to stoop to a dirty plebeian, without any kind of merit, is the lowest prostitution" (Quoted in Basset, 1989, 338).

Elite conservatives of colonial America often translated these attitudes into law, with the result that there were often different sets of laws for gentry and commoners. In 1674 Virginia, for example, a lowly tailor was fined one hundred pounds of tobacco for arranging a horse race between his mare and a horse belonging to a member of the privileged class. It was the opinion of the court that it was "contrary to law for a laborer to make a race, being a sport only for gentlemen" (Quoted in Labaree, 1948, 111).

The conservatives that championed such laws would cling to these mechanisms that justified their unequal status and therefore resist the democratizing changes that accompanied the American Revolution. Though there are numerous reasons that thousands of conservatives opposed the American Revolution, it is obvious that in many cases, a primary reason is that support for the British meant support for the continuation of a system that had provided them with privileged positions in American society. In such cases, Toryism was driven not by high-mindedness, a sense of right, or a conservative vision of morality, but by the fact that it was to the personal economic or legal advantage of many conservatives to remain loyal to England.

Conservatives and the American Revolution

As of 1762, it is generally accurate to say that the citizens in the North American English colonies were content to remain English colonies and were not planning a massive revolt of independence against the English Crown. After the end of the Seven Years War in 1763, however, the English Government was saddled with an unprecedented debt and the new Prime Minister, Lord Greenville, sought new sources of revenue to address the growing problem. Compounding Greenville's colonial troubles was the fact that the British also suddenly controlled French Canada and had therefore inherited an unruly population that did not so happily accept English rule. As if the new French subjects of the English Crown did not present enough challenges by themselves, Greenville was also of the opinion that the English colonies of North America were exceedingly unruly and in need of tighter

British control; hence, Greenville determined that it was necessary to leave 10,000 British troops on the North American continent to ensure order. In turn, the forward placement of troops created another problem of its own in that was very expensive, further exacerbating the English fiscal problems and inducing Greenville to search elsewhere for sources of revenue. Greenville therefore moved to impose a series of taxes and controls on colonial trade in the effort to raise needed revenue (Brinkley, 2003, 107).

Again, at the end of the Seven Years War in 1763, the Political philosophy of the American colonists was decidedly British and most Americans still had a deep appreciation for the British system and traditions. In general, it was the conservatives, more than any others, who had been responsible for the perpetuation of British traditions and cultural heritage in the colonies since their founding at Jamestown and it was the conservatives who therefore could be expected to hold most tightly to their cultural heritage. It was also the conservative planters and international shipping merchants who remained in the closest contact with the British nation, government, and people, and were therefore most connected to the mother country (Labaree, 1948, 134).

During the first century and a half of British colonization of North America, there had been little controversy over questions of political philosophy. In each colony, the elites that drove politics were essentially guided by the British traditions, and there was little question as to their "correctness." Colonial government had been essentially a series of compacts between the aristocrats and the commoners whereby the colonists agreed to settle in the new land, often receiving land as compensation, in return for submission to elite rule (Labaree, 1948, 135).

Balanced Government

The guiding political principle of the colonies was essentially the English idea of "balanced government." The governmental structures were created to reflect the effort to strike a balance between the three segments of society, the crown, the gentry, and the commoners. This balance was satisfied through the creation of the colonial governors, who represented the crown, the colonial councils (essentially upper houses) that represented the gentry, and the colonial assemblies that represented the commoners. The intention was to replicate the British system of King, Lords, and Commons in the colonies. As long as this "balance" was maintained, conservatives would oppose any attempt by commoners to seriously alter the system (Labaree, 1948, 136).

American Revolutionaries, however, were influenced by John Locke's "Social Contract" and Locke's arguments that the people had a right to overthrow despotic government. Locke asserted that society was founded on natural law and that government was based upon the consent of the governed. Locke further argued that when men in a state of nature (with no government) agree among themselves to submit to a common authority (in this case the King) for their mutual good, they had made a compact, binding on both sides, under which the ruler was to govern according to the principles of justice and in the interest of the people and the people were therefore to submit to the governing authority. If, however, the ruler overstepped the bounds of authority agreed upon, the compact was violated and no longer valid and the people were therefore released from any obligations of submission.

The problem with Locke's theory, of course, is that whether or not the ruling authorities have violated the compact is to a large degree subjective. In the eyes of the American Revolutionaries, the English king had clearly violated the compact and therefore the colonists were released from their obligations of submission and rebellion was justified. Conservatives, however, tended to view the situation much differently (Labaree, 1948, 137).

Conservatives generally stressed the virtues of the British system of governance and the proper balance that its institutions exemplified. In this, the conservatives and the liberals that led the American Revolution were congruent, however, conservatives differed with the Revolutionaries over which segment of society was the greatest threat to liberty. While the liberal Revolutionaries feared encroachments by the Crown, the elite conservatives were most concerned with the threats to what they viewed as the proper balance from commoners, who encroached on the proper authority of the King and the aristocracy. Conservatives also denounced what they viewed as the lawless radicalism of the revolutionaries, but their basic position was preservationist in character and called for continuation of the system and principles that had guided the colonists for the duration of their existence in the New World. To the conservatives, it was the revolutionaries, not the British Crown, that were violating the social contract (Labaree, 1948, 138).

For example, conservative gentleman Cadwallader Colden argued that between the Crown, aristocracy, and commoners, the greatest danger to the proper balance actually came from the commoners because "People are always jealous of the monarch, but fond of everything that increases the democracy" (Colden, 1973, 252-254). Similarly, James Duane, a New York gentleman, agreed with Colden and argued that the real problem with the "balance" was not enough strength for the gentry. Consequently, Duane argued that the strength of the councils should be increased through the granting of life tenure to the councilors themselves. Duane also argued that the development of an American peerage, mirroring the peerage of England, should be developed so as to "serve as a shock absorber between prince and people" (Quoted in Alexander, 1938, 97). Joseph Galloway of Pennsylvania concurred with Duane, arguing that proper balanced government required "an independent, aristocratical authority" positioned between the king and the people, "able to throw its weight in either scale as the other should preponderate" (Quoted in Labaree, 1948, 136). In Galloway's view, the absence of a strong aristocratic element in Massachusetts had upset the balance of government and produced the crisis. Concurring with Galloway, Anglican Samuel Johnson, the first President of King's College, declared that the government of Connecticut was "much too popular" and that it was under a "Junto rule." (Schneider and Schneider, 2002, 149-150).

In general, conservatives tended to consider "republican" or "democratical" as disparaging terms of reproach that equated with mob rule or rule from the gutter. Boucher (1967, lvii) argued that popular governments were weak governments, and Colden (1973, 355) argued against any system in which important questions of governance rested with men of "little credit or reputation."

Some conservatives argued essentially that the colonists lacked the right to rebel as asserted by Locke and therefore acted lawlessly. Jonathan Boucher, for example, argued that humans were unequal in their abilities to discern right from wrong and wisdom from folly; consequently, Boucher denounced the revolution as leading to anarchy. Boucher also argued that the same Lockeian principles that would justify one revolution might justify further revolutions in the future, thus leading to chaos (Boucher, 1967, 495-560).

Boucher essentially rejected Locke's right to rebel completely, arguing that governmental authority must be absolute and irresistible. In the words of Boucher, it was a "damnable doctrine and position that any government lawfully established may be denounced or resisted by any self-commissioned persons invested with no authority by law, on any pretense whatsoever" (Boucher, 1967, 483). Boucher argued that government could not be limited even by itself or it would lose the essential quality of supremacy and thus destroy itself. Boucher argued that everyone who is a subject must owe to the government under which he lives an obedience which is neither active nor passive. When political duty does not conflict with conscience, obedience must be active. In cases where obedience might be forbidden by the laws of God, Boucher argued that obedience should be passive. In other words, the subject should not perform the acts required by the government, but should patiently "submit to the penalties annexed to disobedience" (Boucher, 1967, 294-324). Anglican clergymen generally adopted Boucher's views that obedience should be passive and nonresistant and devoted themselves to furthering that view in their churches.

In line with the arguments of Boucher were the Quakers of Pennsylvania. In Philadelphia in 1774 when the Boston Port Act went into effect closing Boston Harbor, a group of Philadelphians called for the closing of all businesses that day in protest. The Quaker leaders of Philadelphia, however, protested the business closings, even for one day. The Quakers essentially argued that the colonists had no right to show such disobedience to authority (Lincoln, 1968, 168). In the Quaker mindset, the King had been put on the throne at the pleasure of God (Romans 13:1-6), and it was therefore not the prerogative of the people to unseat he whom God had placed on the throne. To do so was essentially not only to oppose the authority of the king, but to usurp the authority of God himself (Lincoln, 1968, 238-239). Thus, when the Revolution came, the conservatives became known as the Tories or Loyalists, the substantial minority who eventually sided with the British against their fellow colonists in the conflict.

As previously discussed, although Revolution by nature is typically antithetical to conservatism in that it generally seeks to throw off existing institutions rather than preserve them, the American reaction to Greenville's efforts (revolt) can be viewed at least partially as motivated by conservative impulses in that American merchants and farmers were essentially rejecting what they viewed as changes in the status quo as imposed by Lord Greenville. In this sense, the American Revolution is one that is conservative in character. In a similar vein, the great English conservative, Edmund Burke, simultaneously led a movement for the repeal of the Stamp Act in the English Parliament because he believed that tradition must be upheld, and that the rights and liberties traditionally granted to the colonists should not be abruptly abrogated (Nagle, 1989, 25). The American Revolution therefore should be viewed at least partially through the conservative lenses of Edmund Burke, as the American Revolutionaries were largely in revolt in an effort to restore traditional rights and privileges they believed they had lost. Such was the nature of John Adams' legal briefs he filed in reaction to the Stamp Act and other English changes in colonial policies (Nagle, 1989, 30). The guiding principle for Adams and the American Revolutionaries was not whether or not they were morally right, but whether or not they were in the legal right. In this sense, the Revolution reflects that fact that it was not a revolt of the proletariat, but a revolt of the colonial societal elites who sought to maintain their status.

While many conservatives actually opposed the new Parliamentary taxation, they generally supported the right of Parliament to impose the taxes, feared "mob rule," and denied the colonists the right to revolt. For example, New York merchant John Watts argued that although he objected to the Stamp Act, he believed it imprudent to meddle with the question of parliamentary taxation, except among friends and then only as a matter of speculation (Watts, 1928, 400).

Another famous conservative loyalist important in the Revolution was John Dickinson of Pennsylvania. Dickinson is most famous for his "Letters from a Pennsylvania Farmer to the Inhabitants of the British Colonies" that contained pleas to the British government to reach reconciliation with the colonies. For his efforts, Dickinson became known as the "Penman of the Revolution," but Dickinson showed his conservative side in 1776 when he opposed the resolution against England and refused to sign the *Declaration of Independence*. Dickinson remained committed to the repeal of what he viewed as changes in the status quo imposed by England, however, and eventually wrote the first draft of what would become the Articles of Confederation, which reflected his conservative nature in its distrust of concentrated power and preference for states' rights (Flower, 1983, 76-90).

In many cases, however, as previously stated, it was not for any high-minded principle or revulsion to disorder at all that the Tories remained loyal, but for personal gain, as many individuals saw it to be to their own personal economic advantage to preserve the system currently in place. Among these, the Anglican clergy and Royal government officials were obviously prominent. It is also estimated that one half to two-thirds of the councilors supported the British cause. Finally, many of the landed gentry and international shipping merchants also opposed the Revolution since it threatened to undermine a system in which they had risen to the top. In this, their loyalty to England is perhaps best explained as the inclination of the upper classes to ensure that they continued to hold on to their high positions and that their property rights were protected (Labaree, 1948, 147).

Persons with elite positions within the Royal government, for example, could be expected to lean toward loyalism out of vested interests. For example, William Franklin, the son of Ben Franklin, was the Royal Governor of New Jersey at the time of the Revolution and was imprisoned for two years by the New Jersey legislature for his efforts in enforcing the English Stamp Act (essentially, his responsibility as the Royal Governor of New Jersey). William Franklin's loyalist actions in the Revolution caused a rift with his father that was never mended, and the younger Franklin was forced to flee the country and died in exile in England in 1813 (Farquhar, 2003, 3-6). The demonization of one's political opponents, even when they are blood relatives as in this case, reflects the influence of Traditional Conservative ideology even in the "enlightened" Ben Franklin.

In the case of the Anglican clergy, they, like the Quakers, argued essentially that resistance to established authority was morally wrong and Christians had a duty to support the King. In 1771, the Anglican ministers of

New York and New Jersey issued a declaration of support for the British Government. In the declaration, they stated,

> "the members of the National Church are from principle and inclination firmly attached to the [British] Constitution. From them it must ever derive its surest support" (Quoted in Labaree, 1948, 153).

Loyalists and Property Rights

A further inducement to Toryism was the fact that the actions of the Revolutionaries were often threats to the property rights of the upper classes, the Boston Tea Party being a prime example. Although many merchants objected to the English restrictions on trade that led to the Boston Tea Party, propertied classes were also horrified by the destruction of property in Boston harbor by the Revolutionaries (Labaree, 1948, 148-149). Fearful of the chaos that they believed would result from such mob action, averse to "rule from the gutter," and undoubtedly in some cases in fear for their own lives, 30,000 loyalists left the colonies for England with the British army in the fall of 1783, their hopes to preserve the system as it had existed in America destroyed by the Revolution that was not conservative enough for their liking (Roark et al., 2005, 242).

Chapter Eight

Conservatism from the Revolution to the Civil War

Conservatism and the Constitution

The elite conservatism of the political leaders of the Revolutionary period is reflected both in the Articles of Confederation in 1776 and the American Constitution that followed the 1787. Power in the national government in both documents was limited, there were no direct taxes on wealth, neither document provided for universal suffrage, women remained disenfranchised, slavery continued, the Senate and the President under the Constitution were indirectly elected (thus removing the positions from the direct control of commoners), and no process was designed for the input of the common people in the Presidential nomination process. In short, the Constitution of 1787 was very democratic for its time, but was constructed to ensure that elites would continue to rule.

The impetus to the 1787 constitutional convention itself was also based on conservative impulses. Essentially, two problems spurred the political elites of the time to call for a constitutional convention; a lack of security and economic chaos under the Articles of Confederation. Both problems were heavily intertwined in the conservatism of the time. In the case of security, the founding fathers had not provided for a standing national army under the Articles of Confederation, instead preferring to rely on state militias. The British established military posts along the American frontier, however, and did not remove them after the American Revolution. Reflecting their new status as a sovereign nation, the Americans did not desire a hostile foreign army on their soil, but without a national army, Congress was in essence militarily unable to do anything about the situation. Similarly, the Spanish controlled the lower Mississippi River and closed the River to American trade. Once again, the U.S. was too weak militarily to do anything about the situation, thus providing impetus to the calls from conservatives for a national standing army to ensure the preservation of their property and the protection of business enterprise (Starkey, 1955, 75-79).

Preference for Order and Preservation of Property

A third security impetus to change was provided by Massachusetts farmers under Daniel Shays, who gathered an army of followers and stormed the Massachusetts Courts in an attempt to prevent farm foreclosures by those same Courts. The Massachusetts government asked Congress for help, but Congress had neither the authority nor the means to do anything about the situation. Elite conservatives were aghast at what they viewed as "liberty run mad" in Massachusetts and became convinced that the current form of government under the Articles of Confederation was insufficient for the protection of their property and interests. George Washington, for example, proclaimed that, "We are fast verging to anarchy and confusion!" To elite conservatives, Shays' rebellion was proof that the national government had to be granted more military authority so as to ensure security and protect property from mob violence (Starkey, 1955, 79).

Economically, the former colonies after the Revolution were beset with a number of problems, among the most glaring of which was a problem with the currency. During the Revolution, the American government had borrowed heavily, both from the American citizens through bond issues and from foreign governments, in order to finance their war needs, partly due to the inability of the new American government to raise revenue from its citizens. Under the Articles of Confederation, Congress was not granted the power to tax, but could requisition money from the states. This system proved untenable since states sent Congress only 10% of the amount requisitioned, thus leaving the fledgling national government in fiscal crisis during wartime. The conservative anti-tax ideology that had led to the revolution in the first place had also effectively hamstrung the new government (Ferguson, 1961, 163).

The short-term solution by Congress was to issue $240 million in paper currency. Meanwhile, the States, also bound by conservative anti-tax ideology, issued $200 million in paper money of their own, with the predictable result that inflation reached 12,000 percent in some areas of the country. In the end, Americans essentially paid for the Revolution through the depletion of their personal savings due to the massive inflation (Ferguson, 1961, 165).

Finally, there was the problem of the lack of a uniform tariff, as each state sought to increase its own volume of trade in competition with the others. In 1786, twelve of the thirteen states agreed on a uniform tariff, but New York, with the busiest harbor and water access to the American interior via the Hudson river system, failed to reach agreement with the other twelve states, surmising that a lower tariff in New York would further increase New York trade at the expense of their competition (Ferguson, 1961, 167).

In order to correct such calamity, the political and economic elites sought to create a government with a national standing army so as to secure their economic interests against military threats, both foreign and domestic. They also sought to increase the National government's economic powers to correct the currency, tariff, and debt problems that beset the nation. As a result, the greatest new powers that were granted to the national government were the powers to raise and maintain armies, suppress insurrections, coin money and regulate its value, and regulate interstate commerce. The motivation behind the granting of these new powers to the national government was clearly the conservative penchant for order and preservation of property (Ferguson, 1961, 164-170).

Anti-Democratic Sentiments

The Constitution reflects the conservatism of the men who forged it in numerous and diverse ways, but among the most glaring is its anti-democratic character. Although the constitution was the most democratic document of its kind in 1787, neither the document nor those that forged it would be considered to be excessively democratic in character if judged by twenty-first century standards. For example, the Constitution has no guidelines concerning voting rights, and the issue of the suffrage was left to the States to determine for themselves, with the result that women, minorities, and non-landed white men generally could not vote.

A decade earlier during the writing of the Articles of confederation, John Adams' wife, Abigail, wrote him a letter imploring him not to "leave the women out," but John and his colleagues obviously ignored her advice. Adams even went so far as to counsel the Massachusetts legislature against even discussing the property issue as a voter qualification under the pretense that if non-landed men could vote, then women would also want to vote. Similarly, Roger Sherman opposed giving the vote to the common people because they are "ignorant and easily misled." In concert with Sherman, John Dickinson argued that the "people lack the principles necessary to govern themselves" and therefore opposed the franchise for the non-propertied Americans (Dahl, 2003, 76).

The Constitution further reflected conservatism in that it removed the common Americans, distrusted by conservative elites, from the government through the creation of the Electoral College system for electing the President. Essentially, the founders did not envision a two-party system producing two candidates with nationwide recognition and appeal. Instead, in the horse-and-buggy-age, when distances were magnified by the difficulty of travel, it was easy for them to envision a system where multiple candidates (perhaps as many as thirteen total, representing the thirteen

different States) would most likely compete for the Presidency. In such a
system, it would be somewhat unlikely that any candidate would win half of
the electoral votes. In such cases where no candidate achieved a majority in
the Electoral College, under the Constitution, the House of Representatives
would be obligated to elect the President. In other words, the framers of the
Constitution constructed a system where it appeared very likely that
members of the House of Representatives might actually be choosing the
President in *every* election due to the unlikelihood that any candidate would
receive half of the electoral vote in a multi-candidate system. Consequently,
it was reasonable to assume that elites in the House of Representatives,
rather than the people directly, would in the final analysis be the ones
electing Presidents rather than the people (Dahl, 2003, 81). Similarly, the
constitution also provided for indirect election of the U.S. Senate, a clear
attempt by elite conservatives to remove the government from the people and
place it in the hands of an insulated elite class.

The Constitution did not provide any instructions into the nomination
process; consequently, Presidential nominees were chosen in the early years
through Congressional caucus, thus putting the real Presidential candidate
nomination decision in the hands of elites. The voting public was therefore
given the choice between two candidates presented to them by the elites who
had selected them without their input.

The Constitution also reflected the conservative fear of arbitrary
government power with the inclusion of the Bill of Rights and the limits that
those rights place on government, including free speech, press, religion, and
assembly, but also all manner of criminal due process rights designed to limit
the power to take life, liberty, or property without the restrictions of due
process.

The conservative retributive attitude toward crime and punishment is also
reflected in the Bill of Rights in the Fifth Amendment guarantee of the right
to grand jury in all capital crimes, thus inferring the constitutionality of the
death penalty itself, a form of punishment championed by conservatives,
otherwise there would be no need for the right to grand jury in *capital* cases.

For many conservatives, however, the Constitution was not quite
conservative enough. Support for ratification of the Constitution was
generally weakest in the rural areas (the rural areas being typically the most
conservative). Additionally, some prominent figures of the American
Revolution, including Patrick Henry, who termed the Constitution as
"frightful" and a "squint toward monarchy" opposed the Constitution,
arguing that the national government would grow too powerful and destroy
State sovereignty (Rutland, 1983, 200). This preference for State and local
dominance in political affairs remains a major segment of conservative
rhetoric through the present.

Conservatism and the First President

Once the Constitution was ratified and George Washington was elected President, the first President and his administration quickly proved to have some firm grounding in conservative ideology. Washington's goal in being President was to be a "disinterested gentleman," the point being that Washington was so wealthy, in fact the wealthiest man in Virginia by virtue of marrying the wealthiest woman in Virginia, that it mattered not to him which side won in politics since either way, the point being that he was a wealthy enough gentleman to remain above the political fray. Instead of applying himself to policymaking, Washington focused on ceremony and appearances in his administration, with a carriage drawn by six horses, a saddle of leopard skin edged in gold, and 21 servants (7 of whom were slaves) to attend to his needs at the Presidential Mansion (Freeman, 1996, 204).

Washington also exhibited conservative attitudes toward education, viewing education in general as an "object of veneration" and "not desirable for a gentleman." John Adams once described Washington's ignorance by stating, "that Washington is too unread for his station is beyond dispute." Similarly, Jefferson said of Washington that "His colloquial talents are not above mediocracy. He has neither copiousness of ideas nor fluency of words" (Ellis, 2004, 149).

Instead of guiding himself by intensive education, Washington guided his life by a book of "gentility" containing 110 maxims for proper gentlemanly behavior known as the *Rules of Civility and Decent Behavior in Company and Conversation.* In this book, which Washington copied and carried at age 15 so as to have a guide for his life, one is instructed, "do not puff up the cheeks," "do not loll out the tongue," "do not thrust out the lips," and "in speaking to men of quality, do not lean or look them in the face" (Brookhiser, 2003).

Washington took these instructions to heart, but also took further steps to ensure that he distanced himself from those below him on the social scale. Washington's elitist conservatism is evident in virtually all that he did. For example, Washington refused invitations to France as President because he could not speak French, and viewed speaking through an interpreter as "humiliating" for a person of his stature. As for his title, rather than the fairly humble "Mr. President" of the contemporary era, Washington favored, "his high mightiness, the President" (Freeman, 1996, 205). Washington bowed when meeting with other gentlemen, but never shook hands, being that he considered himself to be equal with no one. Washington was notoriously aloof, and especially made efforts to distance himself from commoners. In one such instance, a painter named Gilbert Stuart attempted to get the uptight general to relax so that he could paint a portrait. Stuart then said to the general, "You must forget that you are General Washington and I am Stuart the Painter." Washington's telling reply was that "Mr. Stuart need never feel the need of forgetting who he is or who General Washington is" (Freeman, 1996, 207).

Washington also displayed his conservative side in his attitudes toward slavery. Washington viewed blacks as inferior and owned 390 slaves, freeing none until after his death. While he was alive, he instituted whippings on his plantation and demanded that the slaves work from "can, until can't" (in other words, can see, to can't see, or sunup to sundown) and "be diligent all the while." In his younger years, Washington bought and sold slaves without scruple, and even raffled off children in order to settle debts. In Washington's will, he stated that all the slaves would be free upon Martha's death; consequently, Martha immediately freed the slaves so that she would not have to live with the ominous fact that 390 people would be immediately free if she should suffer a fatal misfortune (Wiencek, 2003, 11).

Finally, Washington displayed his conservatism and his preference for authority and order in his heavy-handed approach to the Whiskey rebellion, where he and Alexander Hamilton saddled up their ponies to lead 13,000 troops into Western Pennsylvania in order to enforce collection of a federal tax that had been opposed on Pennsylvania farmers. For Washington, the failure of the farmers to pay the taxes was not only threats to his authority, but a disorderly slippery-slope toward anarchy. Ironically, a revolt against taxation from afar was precisely the precipitant to the American Revolution during which Washington had commanded a rebel army in revolt (Freeman, 1996, 261).

Federalists

During the presidency of George Washington, the beginnings of the American two-party system began to emerge. The Federalist Party, led by Alexander Hamilton, essentially represented the ideas and interests of the elite conservatives of the time. The Federalists in many ways mirrored the conservatism of Edmund Burke, and favored a stronger national government so as to best protect their economic interests. In the words of Hamilton, "As too much power leads to despotism, too little leads to anarchy, and both, eventually to the ruin of the people" (Quoted in Muccigrosso, 2003, 8). Like Burke, a preference for order was the root of Federalist conservatism. As such, Hamilton and the Federalists were staunch opponents of the French Revolution and the chaos that it spawned, with Hamilton terming the French Revolution as a "great monster," and a "disgusting spectacle" brought about by "unprincipled reformers" (Muccigrosso, 2003, 8).

Hamilton's conservative preference for elitism is also reflected in his support for high tariffs, which was partially motivated by the goal of nation-building and promoting Amercan nationalism, but also by the desire to help enrich the wealthy men of commerce and industry of the time. Hamilton was endowed with the basic conservative distrust of common people and the low regard for the average intelligence and morality of humans in general that typifies Traditional Conservatism. Hamilton also believed that the national government should generally foster religion so as to provide order and morality in society, a strain of Traditional Conservatism that continues in the Twenty-First century through the religious right (Chernow, 2004).

America's second president and first vice president, John Adams, was also a Federalist who exhibited some strong conservative tendencies. Adams' political ideology was influenced by his Puritan religious roots, giving him a worldview that was often consistent with Traditional Conservatism. Adams shared Hamilton's negative view of human nature and elitist attitudes, consequently, Adams joined Hamilton in preferring property ownership as a qualification for the franchise. Adams also viewed blacks as inferior and opposed the inclusion of women in the political process in spite of the persuasive intellect of his own wife, Abigail. Finally, Adams essentially shared Jefferson's romantic conservative notion that the United States should remain a nation of small property owners, businessmen, and farmers, and had disdain for a society of densely packed cities full of factories (McCullough, 2001).

Consistent with the tenets of Traditional Conservatism, Adams regarded the national government as a restraining force against disorder; however, Adams also believed that the national government should serve to advance the well-being of the people. For Adams, given his Puritan background, this not only meant that government should promote education, but (like Hamilton) Adams also believed that government should also foster religion; consequently, Adams condemned the French Revolution for its attacks against religion and denounced the French Revolutionary regime as a "republic of thirty million atheists." (Muccigrosso, 2003, 11).

Much like conservatives Richard Nixon and George W. Bush, who would ascend to the Presidency in the late Twentieth and early Twenty-first century, Adams was thin-skinned and did not react well to criticism. Consequently, when Adams was vehemently criticized in the press for his handling of relations with France following what was known as the XYZ affair, Adams and the Federalist Congress took action with the passage of the Alien and Sedition Acts that limited criticism of his government, and therefore limited First Amendment freedoms. In an action eerily similar to the PATRIOT Act of 2002, the Alien Enemies Act gave Adams the power to arrest or expel aliens in time of war. The Alien Act went even further, authorizing the president to expel all aliens whom he thought were "dangerous to the peace and safety of the United States." Finally, the Sedition Act made it a crime to "impede the operation of any law" or to attempt to "instigate a riot or insurrection, or to publish or utter any false, scandalous and malicious criticism of high government officials" (Smith, 1966, 176). James Madison, one of Adams' political opponents at the time, criticized the Acts for their anti-democratic elitism. In the words of Madison, the Acts rested on the discredited doctrine that "the government officials are the masters and not the servants of the people" (Quoted in Smith, 1966, 178). Adams' administration went further than mere theory, however, and implemented the Acts, leading to the prosecution of 25 persons and the conviction of ten, (mostly newspaper editors) for criticisms of the Adams administration. Criticisms of Adams' political opponents, however, did not fall under the Acts.

Another important conservative Federalist opponent of Jefferson from Jefferson's very own state of Virginia was John Randolph, who took Patrick Henry's Congressional seat and then went on to election in the Senate. Randolph was an ardent supporter of states' rights and an admirer of Edmund Burke. In the words of Randolph, "to ask any State to surrender part of her sovereignty, is like asking a lady to surrender part of her chastity" (Quoted in Miner, 1996, 199). As such, Randolph argued for greater limits on the national government and argued that democracy, if defined as absolute majoritarianism, was anathema to liberty. In the words of Randolph, "I am an aristocrat; I love liberty, I hate equality" (Quoted in Miner, 196, 200). Randolph was also a man of contradictions, however. In spite of his love for states' rights, he opposed the "nullification" of federal laws by the States. Randolph was also a bit of a racist who viewed the English-speaking peoples as superior, yet personally claimed to be a descendent of Pocahontas. Randolph also condemned the manners of the common people, yet he himself drank excessively and developed an addiction to opium (Miner, 1996, 20).

Conservatives and the Thomas Paine Controversy

Thomas Paine, a hero of the American Revolution, whose words in *Common Sense* had spurned Americans toward revolt against England, became the object of conservative wrath in the 1790s after his publication of *The Rights of Man*, where he defended the French Revolution and condemned hereditary privilege. Paine wrote the book in England, but his condemnation of the monarchy made him a target of the English Crown, and Paine was forced to flee to Revolutionary France. The English tried Paine for sedition in abstentia, burned his books, and permanently banished him from England (Jacoby, 2004, 40).

In the United States, conservatives (primarily Federalists) objected to Paine's linkage of the American and French Revolutions, given that the French version was so violent and disorderly as well as challenging to established conservative institutions. Thus, Federalists feared that the influential Paine could infect American commoners with French chaos and the notion that American elites should be deposed (Jacoby, 2004, 40).

Paine followed his publication of *The Rights of Man*, however, with his even more objectionable *Age of Reason*, where he offered a scathing condemnation of literal and inerrant interpretations of the Bible, thus outraging fundamentalist religious conservatives. William Cobbett, a conservative Englishman who came to the United States in 1792, wrote a disparaging biography of Paine in 1797, exemplifying the Traditional Conservative sentiments toward Paine. Cobbett denounced Paine as a "devil's spawn" and concluded of Paine that,

"Like Judas, he will be remembered by posterity; men will learn to express all that is base, malignant, treacherous, unnatural, and blasphemous by the single monosyllable of Paine" (Quoted in Jacoby, 2004, 36).

Cobbett's denunciation of Paine is perhaps a perfect example of Traditional Conservative demonization of political enemies.

Conservatives went even further, however, and essentially blamed Paine and his heretical ideas for all that was wrong in the world and suggested that his "atheism" led to social disorder. Lyman Beecher, for instance, blamed what he viewed as a most "ungodly state" at Yale, complete with "rowdies," and "intemperance, profanity, gambling, and licentiousness" on the heretical ideas of Paine and the deists. In the words of Beecher,

"Boys that dressed flax in the barn, as I used to, read Tom Paine and believed him; I read, and fought him all the way. Never had any propensity to infidelity. But most of the class before me were infidels, and called each other Voltaire, Rousseau, D'Alembert, etc." (Quoted in Cross, 1961, 43).

The next President of Yale, conservative Congregationalist Timothy Dwight, evidently agreed with Beecher since he delivered more than 200 sermons to Yale undergraduates on the dangers of deism and religious heresy. Dwight could hardly be accused of being forward-thinking, however, since he also proclaimed smallpox vaccinations, introduced in 1796, to be immoral. In Dwight's thinking, since God had predetermined that an individual's destiny was death by smallpox, it was sinful to interfere with God's plan (Jacoby, 2004, 49). The similarities between Dwight's arguments and those of the twenty-first century Christian Coalition concerning homosexuality and stem-cell research are striking.

Conservatives also connected the sin of heresy with the death from yellow fever of the wife of the free-thinker, Elihu Palmer in Philadelphia. A few years earlier, Palmer had attempted to preach a sermon in Philadelphia challenging the divinity of Jesus. A mob assembled outside the church where Palmer was to speak and prevented the sermon, after which the mob proceeded to effectively run Palmer out of town. Palmer then abandoned the ministry for the practice of law and returned to Philadelphia in 1793. A few months later, Philadelphia was gripped by a yellow fever epidemic that cost Palmer his eyesight and took the life of his wife. Religious conservatives viewed the epidemic, Palmer's blindness, and his wife's death as God's punishment for his heresy (Jacoby, 2004, 53).

Meanwhile, Thomas Paine found himself in even further trouble in France after his exile from England when he condemned the execution of the deposed French king, Louis XVI. Paine was subsequently arrested on the orders of the French Revolutionary leader, Maximilien Robespierre, and cast into a French prison. Gouvernor Morris, the conservative American minister to France, could have secured Paine's release, but Morris detested Paine for his views on both politics and the Bible and therefore proceeded to lie to both George Washington and the French so that Paine would remain in Prison. Morris erroneously informed the French that the U.S. did not recognize Paine's claim to American citizenship (Paine was English by birth), while he simultaneously assured George Washington that he was doing all that could be done to secure Paine's release. Washington, of course, had ordered the reading of Paine's words to his troops before crossing the Delaware River in 1776 to mount his famous surprise attack on Hessian mercenaries at Trenton. Nevertheless, due to Morris' obstruction, Paine would not be released from prison in France until Morris was replaced as minister to France by James Monroe. In the mean time, Paine almost died of a suppurating ulcer. (Jacoby, 2004, 40-42).

Upon Paine's return to the U.S. in 1802, he found the reception much less hospitable than it had been to his Revolutionary words in 1776, at least partially due to a resurgence of religious conservatism in the late 1790s and early 1800s. Paine, just a generation earlier a hero of the American revolution, was therefore an object of veneration in Federalist newspapers for his "atheism," and his association with Jefferson caused Federalists and religious fundamentalists to denounce not only Paine, but Jefferson as well, as an atheist and an infidel. The following passage from a Federalist publication, the *Philadelphia Port Folio*, epitomized the nature of the Federalist discourse.

"If, during the present season of national abasement, infatuation, folly, and vice, any portent could surprise, sober men would be utterly confounded by an article current in all our newspapers, that the loathsome Thomas Paine, a drunken atheist and the scavenger of faction, is invited to return in a national ship to America by the first magistrate of a free people. A measure so enormously preposterous we cannot yet believe has been adopted and it would demand firmer nerves than those possessed by Mr. Jefferson to hazard such an insult to the moral sense of the nation. If that rebel rascal should come to preach from his Bible to our populace, it would be time for every honest and insulted man of dignity to flee to some Zoar as from another Sodom, to shake off the very dust of his feet and to abandon America" (Quoted in Jacoby, 2004, 61).

Some took the "shake off the dust" advice to heart. Upon Paine's return to the U.S., in Trenton, NJ, the sight of the reading of his great words during the Revolution, Paine was refused a seat on a stagecoach by the coach driver. In New York, a Paine admirer was expelled from his Church for shaking Paine's hand. In New Rochelle on Christmas Eve, 1802, the anniversary of Washington's crossing of the Delaware, an assassin fired a bullet into Paine's home and narrowly missed his head (Jacoby, 2004, 61). For Paine personally, perhaps the statement, "These are the times that try men's souls" was more applicable to 1802 than to 1776.

Federalists and Separation of Church and State

By 1802, the Federalist Party had become associated with religious fundamentalism and resistance to the separation of Church and State espoused by the Jeffersonians. In the words of Susan Jacoby (2004, 44), "not all Federalists were religious conservatives, but nearly all religious conservatives were Federalists." Obviously, the same could be said for the conservative Party of the Twenty-First Century, the Republicans, in 2005.

The link between religious conservatism and political conservatism has been fairly consistent throughout American history. In the 1790s, for example, John Mason, a New York minister, led the charge against Jefferson and his deistic religious views. Mason condemned Jefferson's deism as the,

"morality of devils, which would break in an instant every link in the chain of human friendship, and transform the globe into one scene of desolation and horror, where fiend would prowl with fiend for plunder and blood—yet atheism neither picks my pocket nor breaks my leg. I will not abuse you by asking, whether the author of such an opinion can be a Christian" (Quoted in Koch, 1933, 270).

Mason's words are yet another clear example of the ability of religious conservatives to demonize their political opponents and view their society as in decay. Boston Congregationalist minister Jedidiah Morse took the argument a step further to add conspiracy theory, arguing that there was an anti-religion conspiracy of deists, Federalists, Freemasons, dissatisfied farmers (read as Jeffersonians), and debtors attempting to avoid paying their debts and conspiring "against all religions and governments" (Quoted in Nye, 1960, 213). The atheistic anti-Christian conspiracy theory, in an altered form, still resonates well with American religious conservatives over 200 years later.

Democratic-Republican Conservatism

The opponents of the Federalists, the Jeffersonians or Democratic-Republicans, however, also exhibited some conservative leanings in the early years of the Republic. Specifically, Jefferson and the Democratic-Republicans supported states' rights and more limited powers for the national government, two staples of conservatism in the Twenty-First Century. Consequently, Jefferson objected to the Congressional Alien and Sedition Acts as violations of the First Amendment guarantees of free speech and press, but Jefferson supported the right of states to pass their own sedition laws. As a consequence, Jefferson and Madison drew up resolutions to be introduced in State legislatures arguing that the Alien and Sedition Acts were unconstitutional. The resolutions were subsequently passed in Virginia and Kentucky.

In effect, the resolutions of Virginia and Kentucky allowed those states to nullify the Alien and Sedition Acts within their states, thus placing state power over federal power and essentially destroying the federal structure established by the Constitution (Smith, 1966, 37). Though Jefferson and Madison instructed the States not to implement their resolutions and Virginia and Kentucky did not attempt to interfere with enforcement of the Alien and Sedition Acts, the States' rights argument championed by Jefferson and Madison would become a central rallying cry for conservatives throughout the antebellum South in the decades leading up to the Civil War. The conservative preference for States' rights as opposed to national power is explained at least partially because States' rights was viewed as a means through which southerners could perpetuate slavery if it became an object of veneration among the people of the more populous northern states. The States' rights position was also, however, consistent with the conservative preference for limited government power.

This was not the only area, however, where Jefferson and his followers exhibited conservatism. Jefferson favored an agrarian society, and opposed the building of cities, sentiments that would be espoused by conservatives in America's rural areas through the present. Jefferson, a slaveholder, also viewed blacks as inferior and favored (at least in rhetoric) the repatriation of blacks to Africa so that they would not "mix" with whites and thus dilute the white race (Bernstein, 2003, 156). Jefferson was also famous for his echo of Thomas Hobbes' "That government which governs least governs best" (Quoted in Miner, 1996, 122). Finally, Jefferson argued for a "strict constructionist" approach to the constitution that is still favored by America's conservative politicians and judges (at least in rhetoric), although Jefferson himself was forced to abandon this position in his purchase of Louisiana since the Constitution does not specifically grant the President the authority to purchase territory, yet Jefferson did it anyway.

James Madison

Jefferson's chief political ally, James Madison, also exhibited some conservative leanings in his preference for fragmentation of power in government. Madison's fear of the concentration of power was rooted in his conservative negative view of human nature. As Madison (1987, 337) explains in *Federalist #51*,

> "If men were angels, no government would be necessary. If angels were to govern men, neither external nor internal controls on government would be necessary. In framing a government which is to be administered by men over men, the great difficulty lies in this: you must first enable the government to control the governed: and in the next place oblige it to control itself."

Obviously, Madison (like Burke) emphasized social stability and placed an emphasis on governing institutions and their mechanisms for bringing social order. As a consequence, Madison's own proposals at the Constitutional convention were more elitist in character and centralizing than the Constitution that eventually emerged (McDonald, 1985, 205). Madison also reacted negatively to Shays' Rebellion as a dangerous threat to order; consequently, Madison sought to limit the role of the unruly masses in political decision-making and create a federal government insulated from the popular passions. Madison also believed that the federal government needed to be endowed with enough power to attract the elite classes to its service (Muller, 1997, 149). Madison's foreign policy too exhibited some decidedly conservative elements, specifically in his military conquest of West Florida during the War of 1812 and his adamant position against international encroachment on American sovereignty rights that caused him to lead the nation into the War of 1812 in the first place.

Federalist Views of Jeffersoninans

In spite of these conservative tendencies among the Jeffersonians, however, the more conservative Federalists viewed the election of Jefferson as a complete disaster for the country and feared that the country might be destroyed due to Jefferson's radical policies and mob rule. For example, Fisher Ames, a Federalist from Massachusetts, argued in Burkeian conservative style that the nation was imperiled and could degenerate into anarchy followed by military despotism since the "mob" had replaced the rule by the "wise and good and opulent" (Quoted in Muccigroso, 2003, 12). Ames was essentially anti-egalitarian and an advocate of public order and the protection of private property above all else; consequently, he viewed democracy as dangerous to what was most important in society. In the words of Ames, "Democracy is a volcano, which conceals the fiery materials of its own destruction. These will produce an eruption, and carry desolation in their wake" (Quoted in Muccigrosso, 2003, 12). Ames was typical among federalists in his disdain for the French Revolution and the havoc that it had wrought. In the words of Ames,

> "Ought we not then to be convinced, that something more is necessary to preserve liberty than to love it? Ought we not to see that when the people have destroyed all power but their own, they are the nearest possible to a despotism, the more uncontrolled for being new, and tenfold the more cruel for its hypocrisy?" (Quoted in Miner, 1996, 15).

The Federalists thus reacted to the changes around them as part of an evil and conspiratorial plot led by politically illegitimate men. As a consequence, any means was justified to ensure that the "right" people were in charge of the controls of government, and the American experiment could be prevented from falling into the disorder of the French revolution and its "radical" democracy.

Illuminati Conspiracy

It was at this time that a conspiracy theory developed among conservatives concerned with a group known as the Illuminati. The Illuminati were a secret Masonic society formed in Germany in 1776 in opposition to the Jesuits. The Illuminati never had more than a few thousand members in Germany, but the German Jesuits developed the reactionary theory that the Illuminati were behind the effort to spread the French Revolution and its secular anti-Catholicism across Europe. The plot theory concerning the Illuminati quickly made its way across the waters to America in a book by Scottish scientist John Robison in 1797 entitled, *Proofs of a*

Conspiracy Against All the Religions and Governments of Europe, carried on in the Secret Meetings of Free Masons, Illuminati and Reading Societies. Robison argued that the Illuminati were tools of both the Pope and atheism and that the Illuminati sought the return of absolutism or the rise of radical democracy as in France (Lipset and Raab, 1970, 35).

In 1798, Jedidiah Morse, who had read Robison's book, began preaching against an Illuminati conspiracy in the United States. Morse argued that the United States and the entire civilized world were in the midst of a secret Illuminati revolutionary conspiracy. Furthermore, the political clubs in the United States that had been started five years prior by French envoy Edmund Charles Genet (who had been in the U.S. seeking American support for the French Revolutionary effort to prevent the restoration of the monarch) were actually part of the Illuminati plot. Morse argued that Jefferson's Democratic Republicans were both dupes and accomplices in the Illuminati plot and that the Illuminati were conspiring to overthrow all government and all religion in the world (Palmer, 1964, 542-543).

Two months after Morse's sermons, the president of Yale University, Timothy Dwight, gave a speech in which he asked, "Shall our sons become the disciples of Voltaire, and the dragoons of Marat; or our daughters the concubines of the Illuminati" (Quoted in Hofstadter, 1965, 13). Clearly Dwight agreed with Morse's conspiracy theory and the idea that the Jeffersonians were on the verge of pushing America into anti-religious French Revolutionary chaos.

Other Federalists went even further, denouncing Jefferson as "the real Jacobin, the very child of modern illumination, the foe of man, and the enemy of his country" (Quoted in Lipset and Raab, 1970, 37). Another Federalist conservative argued that,

> "the zeal of the Democrats for office was to be treated as a part of the scheme of Illuminatism in America to worm its votaries into all offices of trust, and importance, that the weapon of government, upon signal given, may be turned against itself" (Quoted in Lipset and Raab, 1970, 37).

Still another argued that "the one concern of the Democrats of Connecticut was to dispense to the people of this state the precious doctrines of the Illuminati" (Quoted in Lipset and Raab, 1970, 37). For these Federalist conservatives, Jefferson and his followers were not just political opponents, but part of a global sinister evil with plots to destroy America. The contention or belief that political opponents are a "sinister evil" involved in a massive plot would become continuing themes among American conservatives throughout American history, whether the evil entities were

Illuminati, Freemasons, communists, liberals, secular humanists, or the witches of Salem Village.

In 1799 in an event similar to the antics of Joseph McCarthy some 150 years later, evangelist Jedidiah Morse contended that,

> "I have now in my possession complete and indubitable proof that such societies do exist, and have for many years existed, in the United States. I have, my brethren, an official, authenticated list of the names, ages, places of nativity, professions, etc. of the officers and members of a Society of Illuminati…consisting of one hundred members, instituted in Virginia, by the Grand Orient of France" (Quoted in Lipset and Raab, 1970, 36-37).

Morse went on to discuss how the secret Illuminati societies, under the influence and direction of France, were working undercover in America to subvert and destroy both "holy religion" and "free government." Morse then blamed the Illuminati conspiracy for every ill in the land, including disregard for the rule of law, the Whiskey Rebellion, "baneful and corrupting books," and "the spread of infidelity, impiety, and immorality" (Lipset and Raab, 1970, 37). Federalists, whether or not they actually believed in the Illuminati plot, used the threat of the insidious foreign plot to justify the passage of the Alien and Sedition Acts. After all, if there were a foreign threat to the American government and a society hell-bent on subversion working within American government and society at large, then the Federalists were justified in taking bold action against them. The PATRIOT Act of the early Twenty-First Century would have similar motivation.

Eventually, the Illuminati conspiracy dissipated because no Illuminati actually surfaced and so subversive illuminati were ever caught in their efforts to undermine the government, religion, or society in general. Furthermore, the failure of President Adams to expel any dangerous "alien enemies" essentially suggested that there were no dangerous alien enemies to begin with, but were instead figments of the conservatives' imaginations. That being the case, conservatives sought new subjects of conspiracy, and settled on the Society of United Irishmen, a group founded in the United States in 1797. A year later, rebels across the Atlantic in Ireland itself, aided by Revolutionary France, revolted against British rule. The Federalist conservatives viewed the Irish rebellion as proof of an international French Revolutionary conspiracy, and the presence of the Society of United Irishmen in the United States was therefore proof that the French and Irish were conspiring together to undermine American society. John Fenno, the editor of the Federalist paper, the *Gazette of the United States*, argued that the Irish revolt proved the existence of plots motivated by the "secret spirit of the Illuminati" and that the Irish in America were now conspiring with French Jacobins to undermine American society. Fenno argued that the

United Irishmen were a "group of assassins" and implored others to keep a close watch on the United Irishmen's activities (Lipset and Raab, 1970, 38).

In spite of the failure of the conservatives' conspiracy theories, as evidenced by their electoral defeat of 1800, the Federalists turned to the use of the same ploy of playing to conservative fears and popular prejudices as means of regaining mass support, a tactic that would become a staple of conservative politics during the Twentieth Century. In the early Nineteenth Century version, the Federalists railed against new immigrants, especially the Irish, whom they argued were different in race and religion, but also were "uncouth, unclean, ignorant, unskilled, and immoral." Given that most of the newly arriving immigrants supported the Democratic Republicans, Federalist newspapers began touting their party as the "American ticket" (Fox, 1965, 78).

Federalists and the War of 1812

As a group, Federalists were generally less receptive to the War of 1812 than the Democratic Republicans, the generally more progressive political party that held the Presidency at the time under James Madison. At least part of the Federalist disdain for the War can be accounted for as the normal role of political opposition. The most important factor in producing Federalist opposition to the War, however, was clearly economic in character as Federalist economic elites opposed the disruptions of trade that occurred due to embargoes prior to the war and during the conflict. Opposition to the War was also sectional, with the most vociferous war opposition occurring in New England, with its robust international shipping-based economy.

One particular group of New England Federalists, led by Thomas Pickering, a former Secretary of State under John Adams, formed a group known as the Essex Junto for the purpose of leading a secessionist movement in New England in opposition to the War and its accompanying commercial disruptions. New Englanders in particular had experienced severe economic hardships during the War of 1812 due to the economic embargoes prior to the war that had disrupted the New England-based international shipping trade. Consequently, the Massachusetts General Court denounced the War as "impolitic, improper, and unjust." Federalist State administrations acted in manners consistent with the sentiments of the Massachusetts Court and refused to provide militia for the War and discouraged lenders from aiding the national government. Furthermore, a healthy smuggling business developed overland from New England to Canada where goods were then shipped to England via the St. Lawrence Seaway in violation of federally imposed embargoes on trade with England. (Fischer, 1975, 70).

Hartford Convention

Federalists met at a convention in Hartford in 1814 and 1815 and passed a number of resolutions denouncing the War of 1812. The delegates resolved that in case of "deliberate, dangerous and palpable infractions of the Constitution," States had the right to "interpose their authority." Obviously, the "interposition" strategy was similar to the Virginia and Kentucky Resolutions that had been passed by the Jeffersonians in the 1790s, and in effect, the resolutions would destroy national supremacy and the federal system if implemented. "Interposition" as an idea would later be used by conservatives in the American South in early Nineteenth Century to block federal tariffs and again in the Twentieth Century in their efforts to block federally-mandated school integration (Fischer, 1975, 91).

At the Hartford Convention, the delegates also passed a number of proposed constitutional Amendments that would have limited national power and shifted power away from the Southern states. The proposals included a proposed repeal of the 3/5 compromise in the U.S. Constitution, which the delegates viewed (with good reason) as a flaw in the Constitution that granted to the South disproportionate representation in Congress by counting persons with no voice in the political system.

Another provision was passed that would have required a two-thirds vote in Congress for the admission of new States to the union, and for declaring war, thus theoretically reducing the ability of the national government to wage a war that would be unpopular in large segments of the country. A third proposal would have reduced the power of Congress to restrict trade by measures such as embargoes. After all, a primary reason for the American Revolution in the first place had been the British restriction of colonial trade. Another proposal would have limited Presidents to a single term. The term limits idea would resurface among conservatives in the twentieth century, and the Constitutional Amendment limiting Presidents to two terms would finally be adopted in 1951 following the four terms won by conservative anathema Franklin Roosevelt. Finally, the delegates at the Hartford Convention revealed their conservative, nativist roots with a proposal that would have made it illegal for "naturalized" citizens, as opposed to those that were citizens by birth, to hold office (Fischer, 1975, 99). In this, the Hartford Convention was only a foreshadowing of some of the battles that conservatives would wage for the rest of the Nineteenth and Twentieth Centuries against their demonized domestic enemies. At least temporarily, however, the end of the War of 1812 at the end of 1814 resulted in the elimination of the international threats and restrictions on trade that had fueled the secessionist fires of conservatives in New England.

Decline of the Federalists

After Andrew Jackson's victory at the Battle of New Orleans in 1815, the Democratic Republicans received political vindication in the form of support from the American people. The young Republic had stood firm against the most powerful nation in the world and people erroneously convinced themselves that it was Andrew Jackson's battlefield victory at New Orleans that had cowed the British into a negotiated peace. It was Madison and the Democratic Republicans that had steered the ship of state during the conflict, and they would reap the rewards to such an extent that the Federalists would essentially disintegrate as political opposition. The Federalists had argued against the war and argued that the British could not be defeated, thus making the Party the object of ridicule and scorn after the war that Americans at the time viewed themselves as winning (Garraty and McCaughey, 1987, 221).

Though the Federalists would never again be a force, their ideas continued to live and would be adopted not only by the Whig Party that would essentially replace them, but in some instances by the Democratic Republicans who fought so heartily against them. For example, in 1816, Madison's Congress passed, and Madison signed, an Act creating the Second Bank of the U.S. (an old Federalist idea of Alexander Hamilton) in an effort to help steady the economy. Furthermore, Madison's Congress also adopted protective tariffs and federal aid to transportation and infrastructure projects that Hamilton and wealthy industrialists had favored in the decades previous (Garraty and McCaughey, 1987, 227).

Daniel Webster

As the Federalists abated, some of their banners were taken up by New Hampshire lawyer Daniel Webster, who made a name for himself in Congress during the War of 1812 in opposition to the Embargo Act. Webster almost always reflected the positions of the dominant business elites in his native New England and therefore reflected the conservatism of those New England elites. Webster opposed high tariffs because New England shipping merchants viewed them as depressing trade and therefore detrimental to their economic well-being. Webster also represented a departure from Hamiltonian Federalist conservatism, however, in that he opposed the National Bank (until the bank hired him as its lawyer) and opposed federal infrastructure spending, though he typically favored national power over states' rights. The primary argument against the National Bank was that it was unconstitutional since the power to create a bank was not specifically granted to Congress in the Constitution. This "strict constructionist" approach to the Constitution eventually would be the mantra of conservative judges in the late Twentieth and early Twenty-First Centuries. Similarly, the opposition to federal infrastructure spending would become standard fare of conservatives as a violation of Hobbesian "limited government" from the Civil War Reconstruction era through the present (Current, 1955, 76).

In 1819, Webster helped develop the conservative doctrine of the sacrosanct character of contracts as he argued the case for Dartmouth College in *Dartmouth College v. Woodward*. In this case, the Democratic Republicans had attempted to revise the Dartmouth College charter that had been granted by King George III in 1769 to convert the private college into a State university. Webster argued that the college's charter was a contract, and that the contract clause of the U.S. constitution precluded the government from violating its sanctity. The Court agreed with Webster, ruling that corporate charters such as the one granted the college by the colonial legislature were contracts and thus inviolable. The decision therefore restricted the ability of State governments to regulate corporations, consistent with the anti-regulatory/limited government position of conservatives from the time of Reconstruction through the present (Current, 1955, 28-32).

In 1829, during Webster's second stint in public service in Congress, Webster engaged in a heated debate over the tariff, infrastructure spending, and States' rights with Southern conservative and States' rights advocate Robert Y. Hayne of South Carolina. For two days, the Webster-Hayne debate gained the center stage of the nation's political arena as Webster defended the interests of New England elites by painting the States' rights position as disunionist, if not treasonous. Webster argued that the nation was a compact of the American people rather than merely a compact of the States, and indissoluble. Though inconsistent with the arguments of Southern conservatives at the time and Conservatives in general in the next Century, Webster's arguments would be mainstays of conservative Northern unionists throughout the antebellum period (Current, 1955, 185-186).

Anti-Masonry

With the international threat abated, conservatives after the War of 1812 turned their attention to threats from within, both real and imaginary. The time of the early Nineteenth Century was a time of the second Great Awakening, where the country again erupted in religious revival. It was also a time when the center of religious fundamentalist intolerance shifted from Puritan New England to the evangelical South. Within this environment, the anti-masonic movement emerged as a preservationist, anti-elitist, mass movement based on provincial and traditional elements in society. The geographic areas of KKK influence, McCarthyist support, and Christian Coalition strength in the Twentieth Century would mirror the Nineteenth Century areas of anti-masonry strength (Lipset and Raab, 1970, 40).

The Orders of the Masons were easy targets for conservative conspiracy theorists since they kept their teachings and rituals secret from non-members. This secrecy easily lent itself to suspicion in the minds of religious conservatives, but also prevented the Masons from effectively defending themselves without sacrificing their vows of secrecy. The anti-Masonry movement was precipitated by the 1826 murder of an ex-mason, William Morgan, who attempted to publish a book exposing the Mason's secrets. The Masons burned the press that was setting up the book and then (evidence suggests) abducted and murdered Morgan to prevent the book's publication. Committees were established to investigate Morgan's disappearance, and soon books and articles appeared crediting the Masons with the murder of Morgan and other crimes. An anti-Masonry convention was held in Leroy, New York in 1828, and the conventioneers resolved that the press throughout the U.S. had been subjugated to the control of Free Masonry and they proposed the establishment of free presses that would expose the Masonic conspiracy. The movement snowballed, and by 1830, 124 anti-Masonry newspapers had been started, mainly (of course) in rural areas (Lipset and Raab, 1970, 41). As a consequence, religious conservatives mounted unrelenting scurrilous attacks on the Masons and accused the Masons of association with "secret, infidel orders of Revolutionary France: with deism, radicalism, and terrorism." A number of churches declared that their members could not also be members of Masonic lodges (Cross, 1950, 123). Lipset and Raab (1970, 41) explain the anti-Masonry movement thusly,

> "Basically, the Masons were seen as a conspiratorial order of evil, immoral men who sought to control politics and community life. Church groups passed resolutions denouncing the order as not only anti-Christian but also engaged in profanity and sinful revelry."

Similarly, Lee Benson (1961, 42) explains that Masonry was portrayed "as a secret, sinister monster with powerful tentacles which reached everywhere and threatened everybody." The Masons were also attacked as anti-Christian groups hell-bent on the destruction of Christianity. Since the Masons admitted Muslims, Jews, and deists, by the fundamentalists' logic, they had to be anti-Christian because Jesus had stated that whoever is not with him, is against him and "no one comes to the father but by me," thus certainly removing Muslims, Jews, and deists from Christian salvation (Benson, 1961, 193).

Given that anti-Masonry was a distinctly Protestant movement, the anti-Masonry movement quickly associated Catholicism with Masonry and tied Masonic "plots" to sinister scheming by the Pope to destroy America. In spite of the fact that Masonry had been in existence for centuries, anti-Masons argued that Masonry was a new movement shaped by Jews, Catholics, and French atheists as a means of spreading infidelity to Christ and destroying democracy (Benson, 1961, 475, 544).

As the anti-Masonry movement moved into full swing in the late 1820s and 1830s, the movement became connected by conservative conspiracy theorists to the Illuminati conspiracy of decades past. The Massachusetts anti-Masonry state conventions in 1828 and 1830 resolved that there was a direct connection between "French Illuminism" and Masonry. A similar anti-Masonry convention in Vermont in 1830 drew the same conclusion (Hofstadter, 1965, 14).

With such grand conspiracy theories raging in the newspapers and in the churches, the anti-Masonry movement quickly assumed the status as a major political movement. After the disintegration of the Federalists in 1920, conservatives had no viable Party to represent them in opposition to the Democratic Republicans. Consequently, into this void in 1828 in Massachusetts, the anti-Masonry movement formed its own political Party and held a state convention. In September, 1830, the anti-Masonic movement then held a national convention in Philadelphia. The Party quickly achieved electoral success on the State and local levels. In Massachusetts, 150 of the 490 elected to the Massachusetts House were anti-Masons, and in Rhode Island, an anti-Mason became speaker of the House (Lipset and Raab, 1970, 41). In 1834, the Massachusetts anti-Masonry convention went a step further and connected anti-Masonry to nativism and the anti-immigrant movement, resolving in favor of altering naturalization laws to exclude members of "secret societies" from American citizenship (Lipset and Raab, 1970, 41).

National Republicans and Whigs

After Andrew Jackson defeated John Quincy Adams for the Presidency in 1828, his conservative opposition rallied together to form the National Republicans, a Party that was essentially conservative in the elite Federalist tradition, but they also adopted the causes of fundamentalist Christianity, favoring Sunday closings and government support of Protestant fundamentalist Christianity. Though the National Republicans were essentially elitist in character, while anti-Masonry was generally more provincial, less affluent, and uneducated, the convergence of National Republicans with anti-Masonry on religious issues helped them coalesce with anti-Masonry to eventually form the Whig Party (Howe, 1979, 30).

The Whigs objected to the unrestrained passions and anarchic freedom of Jacksonian Democracy and instead emphasized the need for institutional direction of political passions. The Whigs were not necessarily nativist in character, but believed in the superiority and civilizing nature of Anglo-Saxon institutions. The Whigs were essentially Burkeian conservatives in that they also valued self-control, and viewed the Jacksonians as undisciplined rabble who disdained the institutional controls of societal institutions, but lacked the self-control to construct an orderly society without the institutional order. The Whigs viewed society hierarchically, and favored deferential politics, essentially contending that those without education and affluence should defer to the wisdom of the elites. The Whigs were instilled with a reverence for American institutions, the Constitution, and the law, all of which occupied a pedestal in their thinking of almost divine proportions. In short, the Whigs were a near perfect study in Traditional Conservative ideology (Howe, 1979, 30-40).

Among the more distinguished of the Whig conservatives in the antebellum period was Rufus Choate of Massachusetts, who served as a U.S. Congressman and Senator in the 1840s. Choate stressed the role of the Constitution as an institutional limitation on democratic passions and argued (similar to Burke) that government played a necessary role as a keeper of law and order. Choate emphasized the need to develop reverence for institutions and that the U.S. needed no further revolutions because it was grounded upon solid institutional foundations. As a consequence, any alterations to the political system should be restricted to change through the institutional channels provided by the Constitution (Muller, 1997, 154-155).

The elite/provincial coalition that emerged as the Whig Party in the 1830s bears a striking resemblance to the elite/provincial coalition that has emerged as the Republican Party in 2005. The blending of elite and provincial politics in the Whig Party, like the Republicans of 2005, allowed the elites to build a mass base for their elite policies and lure voters that might otherwise have economically favored Andrew Jackson, but instead favored the Whigs due to their program of cultural preservationism (Lipset and Raab, 1970, 46).

Andrew Jackson

Andrew Jackson's political rise was decidedly populist in character and his support would in many ways resemble the populist support base of George W. Bush in the Twenty-First Century. Like Bush, Jackson was a Southerner, not particularly well-read, endowed with few intellectual interests, and prone to abuse of the English language with improper grammar and poor syntax. Also similar to Bush, Jackson was sometimes simplistic in his thinking and logic, prone to strong opinions in issues about which he was ignorant (such as banking), and impetuous and militaristic in his actions. Jackson also was endowed with a violent temper and a significant vindictive streak, fighting multiple duels and pressing over 100 lawsuits against individuals that owed him money (Garraty and McCaughey, 1987, 264-265).

Jackson became an American hero and set himself on the path to the Presidency with his victory over the British in the Battle of New Orleans at the conclusion of the War of 1812. Jackson also gained fame as an Indian-fighter, but invoked strong divisions among Americans with his actions in 1818 when he led an armed invasion of Florida, apparently without authorization from President Monroe. Jackson claimed to have received a letter authorizing the invasion, but when asked to produce it, he incredulously said that he had burned the letter (Jones, 1996, 96-97).

Jackson was a believer in the "Southern Code of honor" that he claimed to have received from his mother, who told him to "never lie, cheat, steal, or sue anyone at law for insults to your honor. Handle insults to your honor yourself." As a consequence, Jackson became involved in the dubious institution of dueling. In one of these contests, Jackson was wounded when he purposefully allowed his opponent to fire first, but was saved only because the bullet struck a rib (Farquhar, 2003, 59).

Jackson was a wealthy land speculator and Tennessee planter as well as slave owner, but his humble birth in a North Carolina log cabin and intense patriotism (along with military heroism and common language) gave him great appeal to the American common folk. Jackson, however, was often shunned by the refined upper classes in spite of his wealth due to his crude mannerisms. For example, the educated and aristocratic John Quincy Adams once referred to Jackson as a "barbarian" (Garraty, 1987 250). Jackson also believed that common people could know what was right by instinct and therefore needed no formal education to make sound political choices. This attitude would be echoed in the Twenty-First Century by President George W. Bush, who told his first Secretary of the Treasury, Paul O'Neill that he had not read much, but he had "good instincts" (Quoted in Suskind, 2004, 165). At any rate, Jackson's ability to extol mediocrity and commonality as virtuous, along with contempt for expert knowledge, would become staples of populist-style conservatism through the present.

Also similar to George W. Bush in the Twenty-First Century, Jackson took office with a determination to reward his faithful followers and punish his political opponents. Those who were disloyal to Jackson would be turned out of the government offices and those that were loyal were rewarded with government positions irregardless of their technical competence for the jobs. Consequently, Jackson ushered in the institutionalization of the "spoils" system in American politics, where government jobs and contracts became based on patronage. Jackson also eschewed his cabinet in favor of an informal group of advisers and friends (again like George W. Bush in the Twenty-First Century). Nevertheless, Jackson did not completely practice what he preached in that most of his political appointees were actually social and economic elites rather than the common men he extolled in rhetoric (Garraty, 1987, 269). Unlike George W. Bush, however, Jackson took a true conservative approach to the federal budget and ensured that the national debt was paid off during his tenure in office, the first President to accomplish such a feat, although the accomplishment was made much easier by a period of rapid inflation (Nagle, 1988, 79). Adherence to a balanced budget and "hard money" (which Jackson also favored) would become staples of conservatism after Reconstruction until the supply-side economics of Ronald Reagan in the 1980s shattered the conservative focus on "fiscal responsibility."

Anti-Catholicism

The ante-bellum period of American politics witnessed a shift in immigration from overwhelming Protestant dominance to a much larger influx of Catholicism. Predictably, conservative political groups then reacted with political movements in opposition to the unfamiliar, non-Protestant, and "un-American" values in the form of Catholic immigrants. As the newest immigrant group, the Catholic immigrants (many from Ireland) typically occupied the lower social strata in the coastal urban centers. Consequently, anti-Catholicism was not only nativist and religious in character, but was also class-based as the middle and upper classes reacted negatively to the poor, uneducated, immigrants in the urban slums. The conservative literature of the times repeatedly described the new immigrants as lazy, indolent, willing to accept charity, averse to work, and predisposed to criminal behavior (Billington, 1938, 194-195).

Like most societal myths, however, there were some underlying truths to the nativists' allegations. In 1850, immigrants accounted for 11% of the population, but the majority of those convicted of crimes were foreign born. Furthermore, immigrants were ten times as likely to be receiving some sort of charity as were native-born Americans. Half the Irish in New York City and two thirds of those in Boston were unskilled workers, thus ensuring that the immigrants would occupy a low place in the economic social strata (Billington, 1938, 324). Such facts were well-publicized by nativists, and these facts helped them fan the flames of nativist hatred.

Protestant fundamentalists in particular, always socially conservative in their outlook, viewed the influx of Catholicism to be a threat to their religious and moral values and everything they viewed as "American." In the words of Davis (1960, 215),

"Nativists identified themselves repeatedly with a strange incoherent tradition in which images of Pilgrims, Minute Men, Founding Fathers, and true Christians appeared in a confusing montage. Opposed to this heritage of stability and perfect integrity, to this society founded on the highest principles of divine and natural law, were organizations formed by the grossest frauds and impostures, and based on the wickedest impulses of human nature...Moreover, the finest values of an enlightened nation stood out in bold relief when contrasted with the corrupting tendencies of subversive groups. Perversion of the sexual instinct seemed inevitably to accompany religious error."

Thus, the nativists viewed their own interests as Godly, legitimate, and American, while their Catholic immigrant opponents were associated with an immoral, ungodly, un-American conspiracy. The resemblance to the McCarthyists of the 1950s and the Christian Coalition of the present is striking. In fact, the anti-Catholic movement of antebellum America differed from McCarthyism, the Christian Coalition, and anti-Masonry, primarily only in that anti-Catholicism included the urban working class in addition to the religious rural population, because it was the urban working class that lived with the immigrants and competed with them for jobs (Lipset and Raab, 1970, 49).

In 1843, nativists in New York established the American Republican Party, which won 23% of the vote in New York City that year. In 1844, the Whigs made an alliance with the nativists, supporting their local candidates in return for American Republican support of Whig Presidential candidate Henry Clay. Though the Whigs were unsuccessful in the Presidential race, they won six Congressional races in New York City and Philadelphia and won the mayor's offices in New York and Boston (Lipset and Raab, 1970, 50).

While achieving some limited electoral success through the Democratic process, the nativists proved that they were not above stooping to nondemocratic means to eradicate their enemies when necessary. For example, in an anti-immigrant inspired riot in Philadelphia in 1844, a Catholic church was burned, thirteen people were killed, and the militia had to be called in to restore order. The Philadelphia riot, however, was also instrumental in losing conservative middle and upper class support for the nativists' cause since such action threatened property and replaced order with mob rule (Billington, 1961, 233-234).

The Whig/nativist alliance would crumble eight years later in 1852 when Southerners and Northern Catholic urban workers voted overwhelmingly for Democratic Candidate Franklin Pierce. Simultaneously, the slavery issue began to overwhelm other issues in politics and force Party realignment.

Southern Whigs demanded that the Party take a pro-slavery stance, while Northern Whigs demanded abolition. The result was dissolution of the Whigs, the rise of the Republicans as the abolitionist, Northern Party, and the rise of the American Party or "Know-Nothings" to take up the nativist cause. Like the other nativist groups that had come before them, the "Know-Nothings" focused on anti-Catholicism, Americanism, and Protestantism, and appealed to the native-born Protestant urban working class. The rise of slavery as the most important issue, however, would mean that the Know-Nothings would never be able to dominate American politics, even though at their peak in the 1850s, they dominated politics in Massachusetts and achieved 34% of the vote in New York. In 1856, the Know-Nothings would cooperate with the Republicans, the beginning of an eventual collapse into the sectionalism of the Republican Party (Lipset and Raab, 1970, 53-60).

Southern Conservatism

Southern conservatism in the antebellum period rested on the pillars of fundamentalist Protestantism, States' rights, individualism, and the sanctity of the rights to property. As for slavery, it was justified on the basis of Calvinist Protestant fundamentalism. The idea was that God had set every man in his place and the blacks were in bondage because God had ordained that they would be there. To overturn slavery therefore would be to fight against nature and the divine order created by God himself (Cash, 1941, 81). To Southerners, the abolitionists in the North were not only political opposition, but haters of God, unnatural, and un-American. In the words of Presbyterian minister and president of the college of South Carolina, J.H. Thornwell, in 1850,

> "the parties in this conflict are not merely abolitionists and slaveholders—they are atheists, socialists, communists, red republicans, Jacobins on the one side, and the friends of order and regulated freedom on the other" (Quoted in Cash, 1941, 80).

When the Civil War did finally come, it was naturally viewed by Southern conservatives in religious terms. Southern preachers compared the Civil War to the final battle in Revelation, with the Union playing the role of the Anti-Christ. In this view, the Civil War was no ordinary War, but the Biblical battle of Armageddon, with the South serving as God's chosen people defending the covenant of justice. In the end, God would condemn those who bore false witness against the South and reward the Southerners in their fight for their righteousness (Cash, 1954, 91-93).

John C. Calhoun

Perhaps no figure better exemplifies the attitudes of Southern conservatism in the antebellum period than John C. Calhoun of South Carolina. Born in 1782, Calhoun was elected to the House of Representatives in 1809 and spent more than 40 years in public service. Calhoun was essentially the "mouth of the South" during the antebellum period, beginning with his position as a leading war hawk urging armed resistance to the British in 1812. Subsequently, Calhoun became almost everything but President in his political career, serving as Secretary of War under Monroe, Vice President under both John Quincy Adams and Andrew Jackson, U.S. Senator from South Carolina for two terms, Secretary of State under John Tyler, and finally U.S. Senator again at the time of his death.

During the 1820s, Calhoun articulated South Carolina's opposition to the tariff of 1828, and in doing so, revived the old idea of State nullification of national legislation that met with their displeasure. As sectional conflict intensified in the 1840s, Calhoun thus became the leading spokesperson for States' rights. In Calhoun's final days, he wrote *Disquisition on Government*, in which he developed the idea of concurrent majorities, whereby intensely held interests, like those in the South, could be protected against majority "tyranny" by requiring that on such questions, majority support must be obtained in each major group or section concurrently. In other words, Calhoun was essentially proposing that the Southern Congressional delegation be given veto power in Congress so as to prevent eventual free-soil dominance in Congress from legislating the abolition of slavery (Lence, 1995, 100-114).

Southern Conservatives and the Tariff

The tariff issue was another issue that pitted Southern conservatives against their Northern counterparts due to the agricultural raw material export economy of the South as opposed to the manufacturing-based economy of the North. Southerners believed that lower tariffs would induce Europeans to also lower tariffs and thus boost Southern agricultural exports, the life blood of the Southern economy. Furthermore, the high tariffs, favored by the North to prop up American manufacturing, merely created higher prices for imported goods in the South where there was little manufacturing that could benefit from protective tariffs. After the raising of tariffs in 1828, John C. Calhoun articulated the position of Southerners in his *South Carolina Exposition and Protest*. Drawing on Jefferson's Kentucky Resolutions of 1798, Calhoun argued that the U.S. Constitution was a compact of sovereign States, which as sovereigns could therefore refuse to obey federal laws that were "unconstitutional." Though Congress is granted the exclusive power to impose tariffs in Article I of the Constitution, Calhoun reasoned that the 1828 tariff law was unconstitutional since Congress was granted the tariff power for the purpose of raising revenue rather than for the protection of industry (Muccigrosso, 2003, 29-30).

Four years after Calhoun penned his arguments, Congress lowered tariffs in an attempt to placate Southerners, but the tariffs were not reduced far enough to satisfy Southern demands. South Carolina's legislature reacted to the tariffs by calling a convention where they voted to nullify the tariff and secede from the Union if the federal government attempted to enforce it. The Ordinance of Nullification further authorized the raising of an army and appropriated money to supply the South Carolina Army with weapons (Freehling, 1992, 79-90).

Calhoun resigned as Andrew Jackson's Vice President, and by prearrangement, was appointed to replace South Carolina Senator Robert Hayne in the Senate, where Calhoun then spearheaded a Congressional quest for a peaceful solution to the crisis. Henry Clay, who had lost in his bid for the Presidency against Andrew Jackson in 1824, became a political ally. President Andrew Jackson, a Southerner who actually favored lower tariffs, but opposed challenges to his federal authority, threatened to hang Calhoun for Treason and to send 200,000 federal troops to South Carolina to enforce the tariff. Jackson almost certainly was not bluffing since he sent armed ships to Charleston Harbor in a show of force. On December 10, 1832, Jackson delivered a "Proclamation to the People of South Carolina" whereby he warned that nullification could only lead to the destruction of the Union. Jackson further argued that as chief executive, he lacked the discretion to choose not to execute federal law, (a reversal of his position following the Supreme Court decision in *Worcester v. Georgia* in the Indian removal case). Jackson further warned the South Carolinians that "Disunion by armed force is treason," suggesting that South Carolina's nullification of federal law would invoke a civil war between South Carolina and the U.S. Jackson also pushed through Congress a Force Bill that defined the South Carolina position as treason and authorized military action to collect the federal tariffs (Freehling, 1992, 96-105).

While assuming his belligerent position, Jackson simultaneously pushed Congress to further lower tariffs and defuse the situation. Meanwhile, South Carolina appealed to other Southern States to join with them in rejecting the tariff, but all other States declined. Finding themselves alone in a potential struggle with the United States, and facing internal pressure from South Carolinians that opposed nullification, the South Carolina legislature postponed their nullification law pending the outcome of the tariff debates raging in Congress. In March, 1833, a lower, compromise tariff was pushed through Congress dropping tariffs by half, essentially to the level that had existed in 1816, and thus defusing the crisis (Freehling, 1992, 316). The States' rights issue, however, would resurface again at mid-century in the debates over slavery.

Indian Removal

President Andrew Jackson generally viewed Indians as "savages," if not subhuman, and displayed his capability for cruelty toward them during the War of 1812 when he commanded the American troops that massacred over 500 Indians at Horseshoe Bend (Jones, 1996, 88). Jackson also viewed the Indians as incapable of self-government, as well as impediments to progress; hence, he favored their eradication, and moved swiftly to accomplish this goal.

Jackson's election as President encouraged the State of Georgia to extend State jurisdiction over the Cherokee nation within their borders. Jackson refused to use the federal government to intervene, arguing that Georgia had a sovereign right to govern all the territory within its borders (Perdue and Green, 195, 18). This States' rights argument reflected Jackson's Southern conservatism, consistent with the States' rights perspective of John C. Calhoun, but it would be in conflict with his stance on States' rights in the Nullification crisis in subsequent years (discussed above). In his first message to Congress in 1829, Jackson declared that the Indians could not remain independent nations within the U.S. and retain control over their tribal lands, thus paving the way for their removal. Congress was controlled at the time by Jacksonian Democrats and therefore quickly responded with the Removal Act of 1830 appropriating $500,000 to relocate tribes west of the Mississippi (Perdue and Green, 1995).

Jackson argued that the Indian nations were not sovereign and that negotiating treaties with them was therefore "absurd." Instead, Jackson argued that Congress should treat the Indians as "subjects" and "legislate their Boundaries" (Perdue and Green, 1995, 14). Jackson's contention that the Indians could not be "civilized" was essentially a racist assertion that the Indians lacked the capacity to change when confronted with new situations or knowledge due to their supposed racial inferiority.

In this racist view of the Indians, Jackson was not unique. For example, Senator John Forsyth of Georgia characterized the Indians as,

"a race not admitted to be equal to the rest of the community; not governed as completely dependent; treated somewhat like human beings, but not admitted to be freemen; not yet entitled, and probably never will be entitled to equal civil and political rights" (Quoted in Perdue and Green, 1995, 15).

Forsyth's argument was undermined, however, by the Cherokees of Georgia, who had adopted a written constitution modeled on that of the U.S. Specifically, the Cherokee Constitution provided for a bicameral legislature and a separation of powers system similar to the structures created in the American Constitution. Furthermore, over 200 of the 17,000 Cherokees in the Southeast had intermarried with whites, and the Cherokees had adopted housing, clothing, religion, and the cotton agriculture of the white south, even to the point of owning 1,000 slaves. The Cherokees also had their own written language, newspapers, and even Christian prayer books (Perdue and Green, 1995).

In 1830, the State of Georgia imprisoned two missionaries for violating a Georgia law that prohibited missionary aid to Indians without State permission. The Cherokees sued in federal court, and in *Worcester v. Georgia*, the U.S. Supreme Court under John Marshall ruled that the Cherokees were a "distinct community, occupying its own territory, in which the laws of Georgia can have no force." Andrew Jackson ignored enforcement of the Supreme Court's decision since his position was that the Indians were not a sovereign nation and that Georgia had exclusive sovereignty within its borders, even to the exclusion of the U.S. government. Once again, Jackson's position on State sovereignty in the Georgia case was essentially the opposite of the position he took in the Nullification Crisis in South Carolina the next year when he argued that the President was obligated to execute federal laws within the State of South Carolina. Such duplicity on the States' rights argument among conservatives has continued through the present with conservatives typically favoring States' rights, but also favoring Constitutional Amendments banning gay marriages and abortions in all of the States.

In 1835, some unauthorized members of the Cherokee tribe signed a treaty ceding all the tribal lands to the State of Georgia and the State rapidly sold their land to whites. In exchange for their land, the Indians were to get $5 million and equal acreage in present-day Oklahoma. Most of the Cherokees refused to move, and in May of 1938, Jackson's successor, Martin Van Buren, carried out Jackson's Indian removal plan by sending federal troops to force the Cherokees to Indian Territory, where they joined over 30,000 Creek, Choctaw, and Chickasaw Indians that had been removed under Jackson's administration. In his Farewell Address in 1937, Jackson argued that the removal was necessary in order to save the Indians from "degradation and destruction to which they were rapidly hastening while they remained in the States." In other words, Jackson incredulously argued that the removal was for the Indians' own protection and preservation (Perdue and Green, 1995, 127-128).

Jackson, the National Bank, and the Panic of 1837

Though Jackson had no problem using federal power to remove Indians from their property or putting down a State that challenged his authority as in the nullification crisis, when it came to the Bank of the U.S., Jackson suddenly became a strict constructionist proponent of laissez faire and limited federal power. By the early 1830s, the Bank of the U.S. had grown to become a major economic influence, with twenty-nine branches throughout the U.S., performing not only general banking functions, but also issuing bank notes, which served as a medium of exchange. The bank was opposed by other banks, both because of the competition with the federal government and because it restrained them from freely issuing bank notes. Those that favored expansion of the currency and inflationary policies therefore opposed the bank for its restraining influence on the money supply. Conversely, hardmoney advocates opposed all bank notes, including those issued by the bank of the U.S., because they naively believed that gold and silver were the only sound basis for money (Brinkley, 2003, 248-249).

The ignorant Jackson was a hard-money advocate, evidently not understanding the role that expansion of the money supply could play in economic development. Jackson had become involved in land speculations based on paper credit in the 1790s and had suffered economic hardship and fallen deeply into debt after the Panic of 1797. In the case of the bank, Jackson's conservatism can then be explained not only due to his ignorance of banking and economics, but also due to his harsh personal experience (Brinkley, 2003, 248-249).

The president of the Bank of the U.S., Nicholas Biddle, began courting men of power and influence so as to preserve the Bank when its charter came up for renewal in 1836, while Jackson simultaneously made it clear that he would not renew the charter. Biddle named Daniel Webster the Bank's legal counsel and Webster became a frequent borrower from the Bank. Through Webster, Biddle also gained the support of Henry Clay, who along with Webster and others, persuaded Biddle to apply to Congress for a renewal of the Bank's charter in 1832, four years ahead of schedule. Clay and Webster desired to make the Bank renewal an issue in the election of 1832. Clay was nominated as the Presidential candidate for the National Republican Party and his intention was to use the Bank issue to defeat Jackson for the Presidency (Brinkley, 2003, 249).

As expected, Congress passed a bill renewing the Bank's charter, but Jackson vetoed the bill and Congress was unable to over-ride the veto. Jackson's veto contained hyperbolic language intended to stir his populist support and condemning the privileges of the moneyed elites who "oppress the liberties of the Democratic masses in order to concentrate wealth in their own hands." Jackson also contended that "Many of our rich men have not been content with equal protection and equal benefits, but have sought us to make them richer by act of Congress" (Quoted in Roark et al., 2002, 353).

Biddle and Clay thought that Jackson's invocation of class warfare would stir the men of money and power into massive political revolt, so they distributed thousands of copies of the bank veto as campaign material. Biddle and Clay had miscalculated, however, because there were many more uneducated masses that opposed the men of wealth and power than there were men of wealth and power who would be outraged at Jackson's words. As a consequence, Jackson rode his bank veto and class warfare to 55% of the vote in 1832 (Brinkley, 2003, 249).

Jackson then moved to "destroy the monster" (as he called it), removed federal deposits from the Bank of the U.S., and deposited them in private institutions. This, along with an influx of silver from Mexican mines, gave private bankers the reserves to support the issuance of ever more bank notes, thus inflating the money supply. Prices rose 50% from 1834-1837 and interest rates hit 30%. The high inflation spurned a rush to invest in land, and Jackson was concerned that wealthy land speculators would buy up all the land and deny it to yeoman farmers. In fact, from 1835-1837, the federal government sold 40 million acres of land, three-fourths of which was purchased by speculators, who intended to resell the land at a profit. The land sales along with the inflation helped Jackson to pay off the national debt and the federal government had a surplus by 1836. Jackson's Congress then determined that the surplus money should be returned to the States as interest-free unsecured loans. The States immediately spent the money on infrastructure projects, further inflating the money supply and overheating the economy (Brinkley, 2003, 252-253).

Jackson then followed his conservative hardmoney leanings and had the Treasury Department issue the Specie Circular, an order stating that public land could be purchased only with specie. In other words, Jackson had killed the Bank in the interest of laissez faire, but then contradicted the principles of laissez faire with this federal limitation on the free market. Jackson's ignorant actions initiated an economic chain reaction that led to the Panic of 1837 (a severe economic recession) a month after he left office. Bankers realized that Jackson's hardmoney policies would lead to a general contraction of the economy; hence, they reduced the volume of loans, thus further depressing the money supply. Land sales ground to a halt and land prices plummeted, followed by bank failures, business failures, unemployment, and bread riots. It was the worst economic depression in American history to that point, lasting five years and destroying the political fortunes of the Jacksonian Democrats and Jackson's successor, Martin Van Buren (Brinkley, 2003, 252-253). It was also perhps the only economic depression in American history precipitated single-handedly by the ideologically-driven actions of an ignorant President.

Conservatism, Slavery and the Sectional Dispute

John C. Calhoun exemplified the attitudes of Southern conservatives in 1837 when he informed his fellow members of the Senate that slavery was, "instead of an evil, a good—a positive good" (Quoted in Muccigrosso, 2003, 31). In reaction to a flood of abolitionist petitions to Congress, Calhoun urged an alliance between elite northern capitalists and southern planters. Calhoun urged northern elites, the force of conservative preservationism in the north, to restrain the impulses that sought the destruction of slavery, while southern planters would work diligently to avoid inciting northern workers by drawing attention to their shabby pay and poor working conditions in the north. Tirades against the abuses of northern factory workers were the standard southern planter response to abolitionist denunciations of slavery at the time (Muccigrosso, 2003, 31).

Calhoun's appeal to elite conservatives in both sections of the country to preserve the status quo is ironic in that the impulses that laid underneath the sectional dispute in favor of changes in the status quo, were themselves at least partially rooted in conservatism. In essence, northern abolitionists viewed slavery as an affront to both fundamentalist Christianity and Jefferson's ideals in the Declaration of Independence. In the minds of the abolitionists, Jefferson's assertion that "all men are created equal" and endowed with "unalienable rights" were moral absolutes that were being violated by the institution of slavery, which was therefore not only anti-American, but anti-Christian.

The leadership of the abolitionist movement arose almost entirely out of New England and was composed largely of Transcendentalist intellectuals who provided the theoretical justifications for abolition as well as the impetus for its growth. The actual leaders of the abolitionist organizations were typically drawn from upper middle-class, formerly Federalist families from Congregationalist, Presbyterian, Quaker, and Methodist denominations. Most were persons from rural areas or small towns rather than the urban centers. In other words, the leaders of the abolitionist movement tended to be the elites of the northern fundamentalist provincial society, essentially the Northern conservative counterparts of the Southern pro-slavery conservatives (Lipset and Raab, 1970, 63). Avery Craven (1942, 125) described the individuals in the Northern abolitionist movement thusly,

"Descended from old and socially dominant Northeastern families, reared in a faith of aggressive piety and moral endeavor, educated for conservative leadership, these young men and women who reached maturity in the 1830s faced a strange and hostile world...Expecting to lead, these young people found no followers...In these plebian days they could not be successful in politics; family tradition and education prohibited idleness; and agitation allowed the only chance for personal and social self-fulfillment...With all of its dangers and all its sacrifices, membership in a movement like abolitionism offered these young people a chance for reassertion of their traditional values, an opportunity for association with others of their kind, and a possibility of achieving that self-fulfillment which should traditionally have been theirs as social leaders. Reform gave meaning to the lives of this displaced social elite."

Craven's analysis reflects the fact that the position of New England as an economic and social leader in the United States had eroded with the commercial rise of New York, Philadelphia, and the cotton exports of the South. As a consequence, abolitionism can be explained at least partially as a product of the New England elites who were experiencing frustration at the downgrading of their social and economic position within the U.S. (Lipset and Raab, 1970, 62). In the words of Roy F. Nichols (1962, 43),

"Numerous New Englanders developed a political self-consciousness born of frustration; it manifested itself in a particular type of tactics well adopted to the Protestant attitude. This peculiar political behavior was dominated by ways of thought inherited directly from the Puritans. The unhappiness and frustration which New England suffered must be due to sin, and, urged on by conscience, the dissatisfied soon found that the sin was the sin of slavery."

This pattern repeated itself in Northern States outside New England as well in that abolitionism was strongest in areas that had once been economically dominant, but had lost status in a relative sense to other areas (Donald, 1961, 28). Abolition, consequently, reflected the combination of fundamentalist Protestantism with socially displaced conservative elites manifested as a political movement bent on moral political action against the "immorality" of the society that no longer perched them at the top.

As Lipset and Raab (1970, 64-65) point out, nonfundamentalist Protestants, such as Episcopalians and Lutherans, in addition to Catholics, typically did not join the abolitionist movement because only fundamentalism was able to paint the issue in such black and white terms that slavery could be defined as evil, requiring the Godly therefore to eliminate it. Instead, the abolitionist movement was led by the fundamentalist Methodists and Baptists, the same groups in the South that would justify slavery by the Bible itself. In the end, support for abolition in the North was essentially strongest among the same types of provincial fundamentalist groups that supported George W. Bush in 2004.

The impact of the slavery issue on religion in the mid-nineteenth century was that Baptists, Presbyterians, and Methodists divided into Northern and Southern wings in the 1840s and remain divided along the slavery lines through the present. Furthermore, the church leaders at the time tended to define the source of the religious conflict, as well as the Civil War itself, as centered on slavery, as opposed to States rights and other disputes. For example, the Assembly of the Southern Presbyterian Church stated "that it is the peculiar mission of the Southern church to conserve the institution of slavery" (Niebuhr, 1957, 194). Similarly, Cash (1941) argues that Southerners were certain that theirs was the true Christianity and that God had placed the slaves under their control for his own purpose. Consequently, in the minds of the Southerners, to fight to free the slaves would be to fight against God. In the words of Cash (1941, 91),

> "From pulpit and hustings ran the dark suggestion that the God of the Yankee was not God at all but Antichrist loosed at last from the pit. The coming war would be no mere secular contest but Armageddon, with the South standing in the role of the defender of the ark, its people as the Chosen people...Every man was in his place because he had set him there. Everything was as it was because he had ordained it so. Hence, slavery, and indeed everything that was, was his responsibility, not the South's. So far from being evil, it was the very essence of Right. Wrong would consist only in rebellion against it."

Thus, on both sides of the slavery divide, the question was both religious and moral, the position was ordained by God, justified by the Bible, and therefore impossible to compromise. It should be noted, however, that some Northerners disliked slavery not on religious or moral grounds, but because they feared that the spread of slavery North and West would have a depressing effect on wages due to the cheap labor competition from slaves. Other Northerners, motivated by racism, opposed slavery simply because they opposed the presence of blacks in the country in the first place and favored the return of all blacks to Africa (Gould, 2003, 8).

Similarly, in the South, some defenders of slavery rested their arguments not on the Bible, but upon what they viewed as the irrefutable scientific truth of black inferiority. For instance, Thomas Jefferson in his "Notes on Virginia" describes black inferiority at length in everything from what Jefferson viewed as deficiencies in reasoning capacity to the suggestion that blacks sweat and stink more than white people. University of Louisiana Professors Josiah Nott and George R. Gliddon (1856) argued that blacks were naturally inferior and therefore suited to nothing more than slave status (Quoted in Muccigrosso, 2003, 32). Additionally, historians, such as Thomas R. Dew, President of William and Mary in the 1830s, pointed out that slavery had abounded throughout human history and was a vital element in constructing human civilization. Dew even argued that slavery had helped alleviate the sufferings of wars, helped societies advance from hunting and gathering to agriculture, and even advanced the positions of women. Dew also argued that true liberty for whites was not possible without slavery and it was slavery that allowed all whites in the South to achieve equality among themselves (Muccigrosso, 2003, 32).

Southern Romantic Nationalism

Slavery and the "Southern" way of life were also spurned on by a conservative impulse in the South that emerged in the form of romantic nationalism. Southerners were essentially dwarfed by their northern neighbors in terms of both population and economic development; hence, the notion developed that Southern society was both separate and superior to its northern counterpart in terms of character and culture. In the words of Muccigrosso (2003, 33), Southern romantic nationalism was,

> "forged in the crucible of defensiveness, it sought inspiration, guidance, and justification from examples drawn eclectically from the ancient, medieval, and modern worlds. And from the crucible emerged a highly positive if distorted image of a singular society superior to its northern rival...Sometimes consciously, sometimes not, Southerners managed to incorporate (Sir Walter) Scott's values of chivalry, bravery, honor, and a sense of noblesse oblige into their own nexus of cultural values and to compare them invidiously with what they considered the crass materialistic culture of northern society...This was the conflict...between Cavalier and Yankee."

The Party System at Mid-Century

The Southern Democratic Party by the 1850s had evolved to become a conservative party of limited government and slavery. The Southern Democrats opposed the Whig's penchant for using federal power for infrastructure building and economic regulation; hence, the Democrats applauded Andrew Jackson's attacks on the National Bank and other efforts to limit the scope of the federal government. The Southern Democrats were also suspicious of executive power in spite of Jackson's expansion of the same in numerous instances. Furthermore, the association of the Whig Party with big business elites of the Northeast caused Southern Democrats to condemn the Whigs as the party of the rich (Porter and Johnson, 1972, 16-17).

Southern Democrats also differed with their Northern counterparts over the meaning of the Missouri Compromise of 1820 that specified that slavery would be prohibited north of Missouri's Southern border in all of the territories west of Missouri. Southerners viewed the Compromise as an improper limit on the right to take one's property (human or otherwise) wherever one desired. In contrast, Northerners generally favored the Compromise, viewing it as containing slavery in the South and preventing its spread (Gould, 2003, 12-13).

In 1854, a firestorm was ignited by Stephen Douglas and his Kansas-Nebraska Act that organized the Kansas and Nebraska territories with the concept of "popular sovereignty" determining the status of slavery within the territories themselves. In other words, Douglas proposed that the people in the territories should be able to vote for themselves in order to settle whether slavery should be legal or illegal in their territories. Northerners opposed the Act because they viewed it as the "reintroduction" of slavery in territories north of the Missouri Compromise line where slavery had been prohibited for over three decades. Outraged at Douglas' proposal, citizens from both Democratic and Whig Parties in Michigan and Wisconsin quickly began to organize and shape what would become the Republican Party. The Republicans held a convention in Michigan in July, 1854, and the Republican Party was essentially born out of opposition to the possibility of the introduction of slavery in the territories (Gould, 2003, 16).

The emergence of the Republican Party, however, meant that the North was divided between the Whigs, the Northern Democrats, the Know-Nothings, and the Republicans, thus giving all of the Northern Parties a disadvantage against the Southern Democrats due to the Northern Party fragmentation. In order to compete, the Republicans needed to consolidate support from the other Parties, and at that they were quickly successful.

The Republicans initially had difficulties attracting Know-Nothings, however, because the Know-Nothings viewed Catholicism as a greater threat than slavery. In the words of one Massachusetts Republican in 1855, who in exasperation at the failure of Massachusetts Republicans to focus on the slavery issue, exclaimed that anti-Irish and anti-Catholic voters "want a Paddy hunt and on a Paddy hunt they will go" (Quoted in Holt, 1978, 159). That problem was solved, however, when the Republicans were able to elect Nathaniel Banks, a former Know-Nothing, as Speaker of the House in 1856. In May that year, Northerners were outraged when South Carolina Congressman Preston Brooks took out his cane and beat elderly Massachusetts Senator Charles Sumner on the floor of the Senate after Sumner had mocked Brook's uncle, Senator Andrew Butler, on the floor of the Senate for drooling. The attack by a Democratic Southerner against a Northerner helped to solidify Republican support in the North as Northerners abandoned the "barbaric" Democratic Party. Brooks was Censured by the House and resigned his seat, but Brooks' action was popular in the South and he was re-elected in South Carolina that November, thus providing even more proof to those in the North of Southern barbarism (Garraty, 1987, 407). With the Nation in a severe economic recession in 1857 and the ruling in the *Dred Scott* case the same year intensifying fears in the North of nationwide slavery, the more anti-slavery Republicans gained strength at the expense of the other Parties in the North. Furthermore, the Democrats became split between Southern conservatives, who favored President Buchanan and slavery, and Northern "free soil" Democrats, that opposed slavery in Kansas and the territories. In 1860, the Republican Platform opposed slavery in the territories, but also opposed the complete abolition of slavery (Gould, 2003, 25-27).

Secession

The Southerners perhaps over-reacted to the 1860 Republican Platform, viewing themselves and their "way of life" as under attack. In spite of the fact that Republican Presidential nominee Abraham Lincoln himself had stated that he expected slavery to last another hundred years and he viewed blacks as inherently inferior, Southerners became convinced that a Republican victory by Abraham Lincoln would be a prelude to the abolition of slavery. As a consequence, the impetus to the Southern secession was decidedly preservationist and conservative in character as Southerners attempted to hold on to the traditions of the past. Similarly, many of those that preferred the continuation of the Union also did so based on conservative preservationism. The remnants of the Whigs, Know-Nothings, and some Unionist Democrats fused to form the Constitutional Union Party and promoted John Bell for President on a patriotic platform that exalted the history of the United States and the preservation of the Constitution and the Union (Calvert, DeLeon and Cantrell, 2002, 137).

Southern legislatures began to pass laws limiting speech and some made the voluntary manumission of slaves illegal. In February, 1860, Alabama's legislature formally resolved that the State should secede if a Republican were elected President. After Lincoln was elected in November, the South Carolina legislature met on December 20 and announced its secession from the Union. Six other Southern States would follow South Carolina out of the Union before the first shots were fired at Fort Sumter the following April. Each State listed its causes of secession, and opposition to the Republican platform that opposed slavery in the territories and the preservation of slavery were mentioned prominently. For example, in Texas' "Declaration of Causes," the Lone Star State proclaimed that it was in part in opposition to the Republican Party's platform that opposed slavery in the territories, in part because of the Republican Party's platform of racial equality, and in part to "preserve a southern way of life that made racial distinctions, in part, by maintaining blacks in a condition of servitude" (Calvert, DeLeon, and Cantrell, 2002, 138).

Although "States rights" clearly played a role, it was not specifically mentioned, only inferred, in Texas' "Declaration of Causes." Instead, the Declaration contained three main reasons (above), all directly linked to the issue of slavery, and all decidedly preservationist and therefore conservative in character. In essence, it was conservatives that led the secession from the Union, and largely, it would be a conservative impulse, "preservationism," that would provide the Northern impetus to fight a war to bring them back.

Chapter Nine

Conservatism in the Laissez-Faire Era

Both Sides Claim "God" in the Civil War

Perhaps as soon as the first shots were fired to begin the Civil War, the belief began in earnest in both North and South that "God" was on their side. As Southerners were certain (due to Biblical teachings) that God had sanctioned slavery, Northerners were just as certain (based on Biblical teachings) that God was using the Union army as his instrument for slavery's destruction. In the case of the Union, nowhere was this belief more evident than in the Battle Hymn of the Republic, the signature song of the Union during the Civil War, which could hardly be more religious. Consider, for instance, the opening and closing lines to the first verse and the chorus, which read,

"Mine eyes have seen the glory of the coming of the Lord, he has trampled down the vineyard where the grapes of wrath are stored...his truth is marching on...glory, glory hallelujah."

As if the message were not clear enough, the final verse of the hymn is not only religious, but proclaims the war itself to be an act of religious martyrdom for the abolition of slavery.

"In the beauty of the lilies Christ was born across the sea; with a glory in his bosom that transfigures you and me; as he died to make men holy, let us die to make men free, while God is marching on."

While these may be merely song lyrics and they therefore capture the sentiments only of the songwriter rather than the singers, the fact that the song was adopted so prevalently at the time is reflective of a general turn toward religion in the North during the war. This turn to religion in the North is at least partially measurable by a significant upturn in Bible sales in the North during the War. For instance, the American Bible Society published 370,000 more Bibles in 1861 than it did in 1860, and by the end of the war, over 5.2 million Bibles were printed, reflecting a trend toward a return to religion in the North that could be expected to accompany any calamity of the magnitude of the Civil War (Jacoby, 2004, 104).

The general mood of religious conservatives in the North was not only that they believed that God was on their side, but they believed, as so often happens during times of social and economic upheaval, that inattention to God was what had led to the conflict in the first place. Specifically, religious conservatives argued that the seeds of disunion were sewn when "God" was left out of the Constitution at the Constitutional Convention in 1787. It is perhaps noteworthy that the religious conservatives at the time of the Civil War recognized the Constitution as secular in character and viewed that secular Constitution as a problem, while religious conservatives of the next two centuries would instead claim that the Constitution was grounded in Christian principles, a position that at the very least suggests that Nineteenth Century religious conservatives were the better historians, if not more honest. In any case, the remedy to the nation's problems in the minds of the religious conservatives of the 1860s would have been to amend the Constitution so as to put "God" in his "rightful" place in the document. Consequently, in 1863, the National Reform Association was formed by religious conservatives in order to pressure Congress to achieve that purpose. The "God" that the National Reform Association favored putting in the Constitution, however, was decidedly Christian with an evangelical Protestant flavor, since their proposal to reword the preamble included the phrase, (Quoted in Jacoby, 2004, 105),

> "Recognizing Almighty God as the source of all authority and power in civil government, and acknowledging the Lord Jesus Christ as the Governor among the nations, His revealed will as the supreme law of the land, in order to constitute a Christian government."

Neither Congress nor President Lincoln took up the National Reform Association's cause, but Lincoln, though himself a religious skeptic who was opposed by 20 of 23 Springfield, IL ministers in his bid for the Presidency in 1860 due to his irreligion, did issue an order in 1862 requiring his military commanders to observe Sunday as a day of rest in deference to the religion of his Christian soldiers. Lincoln also pandered to religious conservatives when he ended his Emancipation Proclamation by invoking the "gracious favor of Almighty God" and included the phrase, "this nation, under God," in the Gettysburg Address (Thomas, 1952, 359). Not to be outdone, Congress also got into the act, adding "In God we trust" to Union coins in 1864 to suggest that the faith of the Union was superior to that of the godless South (Thomas, 1952, 359).

Conservative Preference for Order and the Civil War

Outside of religion, other Northern conservatives also supported the Union cause based on the Burkeian conservative preference for order. For instance, George Templeton Strong, a New York lawyer, and Henry W. Bellows, a New York Unitarian minister, supported the War as a means to quiet the unruly democratic passions that they credited with causing the conflict, and to restore order from above. Similarly, Orestes Brownson argued that the war was not for emancipation, but to *preserve* the nation and the Constitution. Although Brownson believed that slavery should be ended, he argued that in the end, the North should adopt the Southern aristocratic society, a position that could hardly be considered as liberal progressive (Muccigrosso, 2003, 38).

Republicans, Racism, and Civil War Government Expansion

There is a general tendency toward the expansion of national government powers during wartime, whether it is conservatives or their opponents that control the mechanisms of government. In this, the Civil War is no exception as the Republicans in the north established a national banking system, imposed an income tax, created a system for dispersing public land in the West, began a transcontinental railroad, expanded the military, imposed a draft, imposed some press censorship, and suspended habeas corpus. These factors, coupled with the Republican association with emancipation, allowed the Democratic Party in the North to attract white supremacists and those that opposed the expansion of federal power. Consequently, the Northern Democrats, reflecting their conservative racism, opposed the passage of the 13th Amendment in Congress in 1864. The Democrats were therefore able to label the Republicans as the Party not only of blacks, but of high taxes and "big government," both during the Civil War and in the decades immediately following (Gould, 2003, 32-39).

In 1864, the Northern Democrats ran General George B. McClellan for President on a peace platform. McClellan's candidacy showed promise early in the war-weary nation, but its popularity was derailed when General Sherman took Atlanta in September, thus suggesting to voters in the North that the war was almost over and the Union had won. In addition to his pacifist stance, McClellan condemned Lincoln and the Republicans as the champions of black equality, thus playing to the racism of whites in the North. The racist strategy struck enough of a chord with Northern conservatives that the Democrats won 45% of the vote in 1864 in spite of the Union battlefield victories under Lincoln's leadership (Gould, 2003, 32-39).

Conservatism after the Civil War

After the Civil War, the Republican Party came under the control of the "Radicals" who favored improving conditions for blacks. This, combined with the fact that Southerners viewed the Republicans as the Party of a stronger national government, a principle that Southerners had fought against in the Civil War, meant that the Republicans were going to make little headway in the South in the decades following the War regardless of how they handled Reconstruction. Furthermore, Southern Conservatives linked the Republican Party with Northern big business corruption and blamed the Republicans for the Civil War in the first place. As if that were not enough, those same "Radicals" were in control of Congress during Reconstruction and could therefore be blamed for any and all abuses in the chaotic Reconstruction South (Gould, 2003, 32-35).

The Republicans, however, had their own conservative elements within their Party in the North. Those Republicans that had favored winning the Civil War to preserve the Union, but did not want the government to play a proactive role in assisting the freed blacks, became known as "conservatives" (Gould, 2003, 35). Abraham Lincoln's successor in the White House, Andrew Johnson, was one of those conservatives as a Southerner who viewed blacks to be inferior and incapable of governing themselves. Johnson favored a non-punitive reconstruction and took measures to return control of the South as quickly as possible to the same white Southerners that had enslaved blacks and seceded from the Union. When the Radical Republican Congress in 1866 renewed the Freedmen's Bureau to assist blacks, Johnson vetoed the bill. Similarly, Johnson vetoed a bill intended to safeguard the rights of the freed slaves on the grounds that it eroded States rights. The Radicals, however, overrode Johnson's Veto and made the Civil Rights Act of 1866 law over his objections. Johnson also opposed the 14th Amendment, which was intended to ensure equal rights for blacks, and urged states to oppose ratification (Gould, 2003, 45-49).

Johnson's prejudices against blacks were shared by a large segment of the Northern population as witnessed by the negative reaction of Northerners to the Emancipation Proclamation and the widespread fears that hordes of blacks would move north if they were emancipated. As a consequence, the official Union policy after the Emancipation Proclamation became "containment" or policies designed to keep the blacks in the South (Garraty and McCaughey, 1987, 439). Further evidence of conservative racist sentiments in the North emerged after the Civil War with the rejection by Voters in three Northern States of Amendments that would have given blacks the right to vote. In five Northern states in 1867, the Democrats won the state elections after Republicans had campaigned in favor of black voting (Gould, 2003, 54-55).

Simultaneously, racists in both the North and South turned to extra-legal means to ensure that blacks did not achieve full equality. The Ku Klux Klan, which was started in 1866 as a secret fraternal order, quickly became an organization that terrorized blacks who attempted to exercise full citizenship rights and the Klan attempted to enforce the social order that kept blacks on the bottom of the social structure (Haas, 1963, 10-22).

With anti-black momentum building, Conservative Democrats made race a focus in the national elections of 1868. The Democratic Platform of 1868 called for the abolition of the freedmen's bureau and "all political instrumentalities designed to secure negro supremacy." The Democrats claimed that they were following in the tradition of Stephen Douglas, who had proclaimed in 1858 that he favored a government "by white men, of white men, for white men." Furthermore, the Democrats accused the Republicans of attempting to subject the South to "military despotism" and "negro supremacy." Fearing Democratic gains with the race issue, the Republicans sacrificed their moral principles of equality and endorsed a platform of "States' rights" concerning the suffrage (Silbey, 1977, 199). Even with this backtracking on the race issue, Union war hero Ulysses S. Grant and the Republicans would only defeat New York Governor Horatio Seymour and the race-card Democrats by a margin of 53 to 47 percent (Gould, 2003, 59).

Liberal Republicans

The biggest challenge facing the Grant administration was, of course, the Reconstruction of the South. Conservative Southern Democrats favored the immediate end to Reconstruction, but they were joined by a group in the North who called themselves "Liberal Republicans" who also favored the end of federal interference in State affairs in the South. The word "liberal" in this context was essentially Adam Smith-style Classic Liberalism that referred to a preference for smaller government, free trade, and States' rights; in other words, a similar platform to that of Republican Conservatives under Ronald Reagan over a century later. The "Liberal Republicans" of the 1870s, however, differed from the Conservative Republicans of the late Twentieth Century in that they opposed any semblance of Black rights and black participation in politics (Porter and Johnson, 1972, 44). Liberal Republicans also opposed President Grant because of the increases in federal power during his tenure in office and due to his interference in State affairs in the South (Gould, 2003, 65).

With the racist themes dominating the South and also receiving much support in the North, the Democrats picked up 41 seats in the House in the election of 1870 and six seats in the Senate. With these results, the Republicans realized that they would have to abandon their moral position on the race issue in favor of a more pragmatic approach if they were to retain their hold on power. The economic issues of the currency, government regulation of business, and the tariff would subsequently replace the preoccupation with black rights and reconstructing the South (Gould, 2003, 63).

In 1872, the Liberal Republicans held their own convention and nominated New York newspaper editor Horace Greeley, who endorsed prohibition, vegetarianism, spiritualism, and the use of human manure in agriculture. The Democrats joined with the Liberal Republicans in nominating Greeley, viewing the nomination of Greeley as their best chance for unseating Grant (Porter and Johnson, 1972, 41, 44).

The Republican Congress lowered tariffs and extended amnesty to former Confederates so as to diffuse the Southern Democrat and Liberal Republican coalition. As a result, the Republican Grant won 56% of the vote and a second term as President. The Liberal Republicans would essentially dissolve and the Republicans would become the Party of high tariffs and big business for the remainder of the century. As such, the Republicans under Grant opposed public works programs as outside the proper scope of government and favored the gold standard. The preference for the gold standard was a monetary position that favored creditors, who tended to be elite conservative Republicans, rather than debtors (Keller, 1977, 189).

Ku Klux Klan

The most notorious of the conservative extremist groups to arise after the Civil War was begun on Christmas Eve, 1865 in Pulaski, Tennessee by six Confederate army veterans who were simply bored and restless after the end of the Civil War and sought something for their own amusement. The name "Ku Klux Klan" was derived from the Greek word "Kuklos," the root of the English word "circle." Since the six founding members were of Scotch-Irish ancestry, they added the word "Klan" and then added the word "Klux" to add "mystery and baffle" as well as something "secret-sounding" and "nonsensically inscrutable" (Haas, 1963, 12).

With nothing sinister in mind, Jon C. Lester reportedly said to his other listless five founding members, "Boys, let's start something to break the monotony and cheer up our mothers and girls. Let's start a club of some kind." Evidently, the original goals of the six men were merely to play practical jokes and serenade women and had nothing to do with racism or terror. (Haas, 1963, 11-12).

In furtherance of their playful goals, the men dawned white regalia and rode through the Tennessee countryside in search of mischief. Accidentally, the men discovered that their midnight marauding frightened the black freedmen who were aimlessly wondering the Tennessee countryside at the time in large numbers. Accident then turned to purpose, and the Klansmen began a campaign of scare tactics against wondering blacks, originally intended primarily as practical jokes rather than terror. An unforeseen consequence was that blacks quickly tended to avoid the roadways in the area where the Klansmen were playing their games. Word of the KKK fun and games spread rapidly and others in the surrounding area contacted the Klan wanting to know how they could set up Dens of their own for the express purpose of scaring vagrant blacks away from the roadways. By the end of 1866, the Klan's activities spread into several states and Klan tactics escalated from practical jokes to violence, contrary to the original intensions of the Klan's founders. By 1868, the Klan claimed to have 500,000 members and their expressed purpose had grown from playful mischief, to overt resistance to the Congressional Reconstruction Act of 1867 (Haas, 1963, 19-25).

Klan members were sworn to secrecy and had to swear that they were opposed to Negro equality and in favor of a white man's government, including the "restoration of civil rights to Southern White men." The Klan stated in its bylaws a reverence for the "majesty and supremacy of the Divine Being" and recognized the supremacy of the U.S. Constitution. The Klan claimed that it was an institution of Chivalry, Humanity, Mercy, and Patriotism that existed to protect the weak, defend the Constitution, and execute all Constitutional laws (Haas, 1963, 27).

In 1870, KKK violence had grown sufficient that it drew the attention of radical Republicans in Congress, who passed "An Act to Enforce the Provisions of the 14th Amendment to the Constitution of the United States, and for Other Purposes," more generally known as the First Ku Klux Klan Act. The Act imposed heavy penalties for violations of the Fourteenth and Fifteenth Amendments and gave the State governments, then still under the control of the radical Republicans, the authority to take whatever action they deemed necessary against the Ku Klux Klan. In furtherance of the execution of the Act, Union troops or state militia arrested Klansmen and tried them for their crimes, sending many to prison. Under this pressure from both the federal and State governments, the KKK was no longer a force by the end of 1872, but it would be destined to return with even greater force some half-century later (Haas, 1963, 42).

End of Reconstruction

After a series of scandals had rocked the Grant administration, the Republicans in 1876 nominated Ohio governor Rutherford B. Hayes to represent their Party against Democrat Samuel Tilden. The Republican platform called for the protection of "all citizens in the South," and endorsed civil service reform, viewed as a necessary measure for more honest government after the Grant administration scandals that were viewed at least partially as a result of the "corrupt" patronage system. The Republicans also painted themselves as the true American patriots (a consistent theme of the Republican conservatives later in the Twentieth Century) as opposed to the Democratic Southerners who still harbored ideas of rebellion (Porter and Johnson, 1972, 53, 55).

Nevertheless, Democrat Samuel Tilden won the popular vote, but the electoral votes of three states, South Carolina, Louisiana, and Florida, were in dispute. Tilden had won the popular vote in these states, but blacks generally had been prevented from voting by racist Southerners. Republicans argued that if the blacks really had been able to exercise their Constitutional rights, Hayes would have won. A special electoral commission was established composed of eight Republicans and seven Democrats to determine the status of the disputed electoral votes. Predictably, the commission voted 8-7 along strict Party lines to give all of the electoral votes in dispute to Hayes, thus giving Hayes the election. Southerners threatened a filibuster, therefore forcing Republican leaders to work out what became known as the "Compromise of 1877" with their Democratic opposition. Under this compromise, Southerners would accept Hayes as President and Hayes would withdraw federal troops from the South, in addition to providing federal infrastructure spending in the South and appointing a Southerner to his cabinet (Brinkley, 2003, 423-424).

With Hayes' election, a re-alignment in American politics was complete. For the next five decades, Republicans and Democrats both would exhibit strong conservative tendencies. Democrats tended to favor States' rights, limited government, limited taxation, and balanced budgets. Republicans would generally be the Party of big business and elitism, but the Republicans viewed the federal government as a cooperative entity with business that would help promote economic development and growth (Croly, 1997, 87). In furtherance of their goals of promoting American industry, the Republicans also became the party of high tariffs. In an argument that would be echoed by conservative "trickle-down" economists of the late Twentieth Century, Republicans argued that the tariff did not just favor the wealthy business elites, but instead its benefits were shared by all levels of society since tariffs enabled manufacturers to provide jobs for all Americans (Weisman, 2002, 82).

Half Breeds and Stalwarts

The Republican Party became divided in the late Nineteenth Century between two factions led respectively by James G. Blaine of Maine and Roscoe Conkling of New York. Blaine and his faction, known as the "Half-Breeds," favored high tariffs, federal revenue sharing with the States, and federal assistance for the education of blacks in the South. Blaine and his followers also at least gave lip-service to civil service reform in an effort to curb corruption. Roscoe Conkling and his followers, known as "Stalwarts," favored Party-controlled patronage and favored the continuation of the politics of Union patriotism that heightened sectional tensions and alienated Southerners (Gould, 2003, 93-100).

Blaine and the half-breeds received a boost in 1881 when the assassination of President James Garfield by a deranged political office-seeker shifted public opinion in favor of civil service. Garfield's successor, Chester Arthur, was in ill health by 1884 and chose not to run, for re-election, thus paving the way for Blaine to receive the Republican nomination in 1884. Blaine was opposed within his own Party, however, by a faction known as the "Mugwumps," who favored not only civil service, but honesty in government, and Blaine had been connected to an earlier Arkansas railroad scandal that tainted his credibility. To make matters worse, Blaine and his wife had been married only three months when their first child was born, thus alienating conservative moralists (Gould, 2003, 101). Due to Blaine's scandalous reputation, a large contingent of Republican voters in 1884 were appalled at Blaine's nomination and broke with the party to vote for conservative Democratic candidate Grover Cleveland.

Moralist Conservatism: The Comstock Laws

In 1865, Congress passed a law that gave the Postal Service the power to confiscate obscene publications (but authorized no criminal penalties). The law was a response to complaints about Union soldiers during the Civil War collecting and exchanging "French" postcards with pictures of nude women. A decade later, a young retail store clerk named Anthony Comstock would goad Congress into passing a more stringent law that he could use as a springboard for a crusade to purify America against "smut." Comstock's crusade against what he viewed as obscenity would be similar in character to the crusade of Joseph McCarthy against communists in the 1950s. Like McCarthy and "McCarthyism," Comstock would become immortalized by the term "Comstockery," that would eventually enter the English language as a common noun (Jacoby, 2004, 208).

Anthony Comstock was in many ways an unlikely crusader since in 1868 he was a lowly 24 year-old shipping clerk in a dry-goods store in New York City. As of this time, Comstock's main claim to fame evidently was merely his tendency to annoy his coworkers by expressing his disapproval of their off-color jokes. From this position and young age, Comstock mounted an improbable but effective campaign against public immorality that would forever immortalize his name as synonymous with censorship. Somewhat similar to Jerry Falwell of the late Twentieth Century, Comstock was a self-appointed censor who saw obscenity everywhere, including many places that the majority did not, and embarked on a personal crusade toward its eradication. For example, Comstock once described George Bernard Shaw as an "Irish smut dealer," and chastised young boys for lying on the beach and looking up women's bathing suits (Jacoby, 2004, 209).

Due to his personal zeal and energy, Comstock eventually became head of the YMCA Society for the Suppression of Vice, and drafted an anti-obscenity statute that was passed by the New York legislature. Comstock's success caught the eyes of noteworthy wealthy and self-righteous conservatives who provided funding for his cause. Fresh from his New York success, Comstock received significant financial support for his endeavors from both financier J.P.Morgan and toiletries magnate Samuel Colgate, and then set his sights on Congress, where he would achieve remarkable success due not only to the financial support of the rich and powerful, but also due to his own obstinacy. According to Comstock's own diary, some Congressmen may have voted in favor of his obscenity statute for the sole purpose of getting rid of the persistent pest (Comstock) from their offices (Broun and Leech, 1927, 15-17).

Nevertheless, in 1873, Congress passed what became known as the "Comstock Law," which was similar to the 1865 law against sending obscene materials through the mail, but the Comstock Law went a step further in that it established federal criminal penalties in addition to allowing the government to confiscate "obscene" materials. Unfortunately, the definition of "obscenity" in the law was left vague and open to interpretation. As if to add insult to injury, Comstock himself was then appointed as a special postal agent with the discretion to determine what exactly did or did not violate the law. As a result, information concerning contraception, anatomical drawings, freethinking criticisms of the Bible, medical terms, and any book or writing that any local postal "Comstock" considered obscene, were subject to prosecution. Under these rules, Samuel Colgate himself could have been prosecuted for advertising the benefits of Vaseline, which he erroneously touted as a contraceptive (Jacoby, 2004, 208).

Comstock's modus operandi was to write a letter to a publisher that Comstock had already determined to be a "smut peddler," order a publication that Comstock had already deemed to be "obscene," and subsequently arrest the publisher for sending obscene materials through the mail after the requested publication arrived. Comstock used this method to arrest and imprison D.M. Bennett, the editor of the free-thought magazine, *Truth Seeker*. For his crime, Bennett served thirteen months hard labor. Similarly, Charles C. Moore, the publisher of the *Blue Grass Blade*, was sentenced to two years in jail for *Cupid's Yokes*, where he advocated looser divorce laws that would allow women to sue for divorce on the basis of drunkenness or physical abuse rather than adultery only. Ezra H. Heywood, the President of the New England Free Love League, received six months for distributing *Cupid's Yokes* and sending anatomical drawings through the mail (Jacoby, 2004, 210-221). Other publications that Comstock and his allies attempted to ban as obscene included works from Theodore Dreiser, Walt Whitman, and Mark Twain (Jacoby, 2004, 207-213).

Obviously, Comstock was guilty of over-reach and would become a public laughingstock for targeting Egyptian belly dancers and circus trapeze artists as obscene, but in the mean time, Walt Whitman's publisher withdrew *Leaves of Grass* from publication in 1882 and Emma Goldman was imprisoned for urging the unemployed to "ask the rich for work, then for bread, and if they received neither, to just take the bread" (Jacoby, 2004, 221-222). Although "Comstockery" would fade due to over-reach at the end of the nineteenth century, the spirit of "Comstockery" would ebb and flow with religious conservatism throughout the Twentieth Century and into the next millennium.

Anti-Catholicism Revisited

In addition to their essentially racist sentiments and elitism, the conservatism of the Republican Party in the North during the Gilded Age contained decidedly nativist, anti-immigrant and anti-Catholic elements (Lipset and Raab, 1970, 73). The anti-Catholic Know-Nothings that had existed before the Civil War had essentially been absorbed by the Republican Party in the North, and their ideological leanings and policy preferences remained fairly constant. While the Know-Nothing Party itself no longer existed as a major political force, a number of new anti-Catholic and anti-immigrant organizations arose in the North, including the Order of United American Mechanics, the Patriotic Order of the Sons of America, the American Alliance, and the American Protective Association. These groups opposed the election of Catholics to public office and generally argued that "Americans should rule America" as their primary platform (Lipset and

Raab, 1970, 77). Reflecting the anti-Catholic element within their midst, Northern Republican conservatives blamed Catholics for slavery and the Civil War. There was a very small amount of truth in these allegations in that the Catholic clergy had not supported abolition, preferring instead gradual emancipation, and most Catholic publications in the U.S. had opposed fighting the war to preserve the Union. As a consequence, conservatives were able to take their "grain of truth" and build it into a much more substantial smear campaign (Lipset and Raab, 1970, 72-73).

In an 1872 article in *Harper's Weekly*, which served as an organ of anti-Catholicism after the War, it was argued that,

> "The unpatriotic conduct of the Romanish population in our chief cities during the late rebellion is well known. They formed a constant menace and terror to the loyal citizens; they thronged the peace meetings, they strove to divide the Union; and when the war was over they placed in office their corrupt leaders and plundered the impoverished community" (Quoted in Lipset and Raab, 1970, 73).

From this launching pad, Northern Republican conservatives recklessly argued that the Catholics were involved in the Lincoln assassination and a widespread treasonous plot to destroy the republic. Conservative Republicans further argued that Catholics could not be trusted in positions of political authority because they owed their allegiance to the Pope rather than to the United States, and would therefore obey Papal orders in cases of conflict between the directions of the Catholic Church and the government of the United States. The Indiana Republican convention in 1875 took the argument a step further, issuing the statement that it was "incompatible with American citizenship to pay allegiance to any foreign power, civil or ecclesiastical," a statement that was essentially a glossy version of the argument that Catholics had no right to American citizenship since their loyalties lay elsewhere (Lipset and Raab, 1970, 74).

Perhaps the most prominent names among the staunch anti-Catholics were Republican Presidents Ulysses S. Grant and Rutherford B. Hayes, and Republican Half-Breed leader James G. Blaine. Grant had briefly belonged to the Know-Nothings prior to the Civil War, and his two Vice-Presidents had also been Know-Nothings. Grant went so far as to predict an eventual religious war between Protestants and Catholics and left no doubt as to which side he would be on, stating that such a war would be between "patriotism and intelligence on one side" (meaning Protestants) and "superstition, ambition and ignorance on the other" (meaning Catholics) (Lipset and Raab, 1970, 74).

Rutherford B. Hayes, the first American President after Reconstruction, also subscribed to anti-Catholic dogma. Hayes campaigned against

Catholicism while running for Governor of Ohio in 1875 and again during his campaign for the Presidency in 1876. Simultaneously, the Republican Congressional Campaign Committee proved that Hayes did not stand alone in his anti-Catholicism by publishing a document entitled "Vaticanism in Germany and the United States" where they argued that the Catholic Church was secretly working through the Democratic Party to undermine the U.S. government and society. Hayes appointed the anti-Catholic Richard Wiggington Thompson, who wrote the anti-Catholic work, *The Papacy and Civil Power*, as Secretary of the Navy. In his work, Thompson argued that there was an "irreconcilable conflict between papal theory and popular government" (Quoted in Kinzer, 1964, 10).

In Congress, Republican House leader James G. Blaine introduced a Constitutional Amendment that specified that no governmental authority could allow any public property or revenue to be used for the support of religious schools (a measure that would clearly be opposed by religious conservatives a century later). Blaine's Amendment, however, allowed Bible reading in schools, a measure opposed by Catholics because they surmised that a Protestant version of the Bible would be used (Butts, 1950, 142).

Blaine's Amendment failed as Democrats voted against it, largely along strict Party lines, but the issue would continue to be raised well into the Twentieth Century (Butts, 1950, 142). Blaine's anti-Catholic Amendment became part of the Republican Party platform in 1880 and Blaine himself would be nominated by the Republicans for President in 1884. Some historians contend that Blaine lost the election of 1884 when Dr. Samuel Burchard, a Protestant minister campaigning for Blaine in the very Catholic New York City, reportedly referred to the Democratic Party as the Party of "Rum, Romanism, and Rebellion." The statement was viewed by Catholics as a slur against their religion and may have cost Blaine enough votes in the City to cost him New York State and therefore the entire national election, since the swing of New York to the Republican column would have given him enough electoral votes to win the close election (Brinkley, 2003, 534).

The American Protective Association

The American Protective Association (APA), formed in 1887, was the largest anti-Catholic organization of the late Nineteenth Century with up to 2.5 million members by the mid-1890s. Like the original Know Nothings and the KKK, the APA was a secret organization which engaged in elaborate rituals and dawned elaborate costumes at its meetings. Also similar to the KKK of the early Twentieth Century, the APA claimed to be defending "true Americanism" against an "un-American ecclesiastical institution." Consequently, the APA fought against immigration, but also against the system of Catholic parochial schools. APA members took oaths never to vote for a Catholic, never to employ one, and never to go on strike with Catholics. The APA also subscribed to a well-developed conspiracy theory that the Pope and the Catholic Church were trying to subvert American government and society and place it under the subordination of the Pope (Higham, 1955, 62-85).

The APA relied on fabricated documents and fraudulent lectures by bogus ex-nuns and priests who testified of their escapes from Catholic captivity to expose their plots. The APA also circulated a bogus Catholic encyclical addressed to American Catholics by Pope Leo XIII that absolved American Catholics from any oaths of loyalty to the United States and instructed them to exterminate all heretics. In response to this threat, the mayor of Toledo had the Ohio National Guard on duty for a week in September 1893 to protect Protestants against the expected Catholic murder rampage. No murder rampage ensued, but the myth continued unabated nonetheless (Desmond, 1912, 52-54).

The APA also made a legion of outlandish and false claims against Catholicism based on fabricated statistics. At one time or another, the APA claimed that half of all public office-holders in the U.S. were Catholics (when Catholics were one eighth of the population), that Catholics were favored in Civil Service Examinations, and that all civil servants were forced to contribute to Catholic charities (Higham, 1955, 85). The APA also blamed the Panic of 1893 on a Catholic plot in conjunction with Terrence Powderley and the Knights of Labor, who were purportedly working with the Catholic Church in formenting strikes and labor unrest as part of a grand scheme to overthrow the United States (Higham, 1955, 62).

The APA largely worked within the Republican Party and its influence was taken seriously by the Party (Desmond, 1912, 33). Though the APA obviously alienated any Catholics who could potentially vote Republican, the APA was useful to the Republican Party in that it appealed to working class Protestants that might otherwise have found a kindred spirit with the more pro-labor Democrats, but felt threatened by cheap labor competition from immigrants. In fact, the APA first emerged in conjunction with anti-immigrant railroad workers, but the leftist elements among the railroad workers staunchly opposed the APA. In spite of this urban worker connection, the APA's appeal, however, was greatest not in the urban centers, but in the Western states, such as California, that were experiencing great influxes of immigrants (Lipset and Raab, 1970, 84, 89). The APA would subside as an organization after the turn of the century, but anti-Catholicism would remain a significant factor in conservative politics as late as the Presidential election of 1960 involving the Irish-Catholic John F. Kennedy.

Anti-Masonry Revisited

The years following the Civil War also experienced a revival of the antebellum Anti-Masonry conspiracy theory. In May 1868, the Anti-Masonic movement held a national convention in Pittsburgh where they constructed a platform based on the belief that Masons held the majority of government offices, were working to undermine America, and were maneuvering to ensure that Masons were acquitted when charged with crimes. Masonry was supposedly linked to Satan and the ongoing activities of the Evil one to undermine human society and the Church. The Anti-Masonry movement printed a monthly magazine, the Christian Cynosure, where the antebellum charges against the Masons were repeated and the conspiracy between the Masons and Illuminati was resurrected, but Mormons and the KKK were also added to the mix of supposed conspirators (Levington, 1870, 304-305).

The Anti-Masonic movement after the Civil War, like the antebellum version, was again driven by Protestant Fundamentalism. For example, the 1876 Platform of the American Party (the preeminent anti-Masonry Party) stated that "Ours is a Christian nation and not a heathen nation," and that "the God of the Christian Scriptures is the author of civil government" and "That God requires and man needs a Sabbath" (McKee, 2004, 103).

The Anti-Masonic Party was also strongly in favor of Prohibition of alcohol, and as a consequence dissolved into the American Prohibition National Party in 1884. The American Prohibition National Party, in turn, was based in Protestant fundamentalism and argued that the Bible must be used as the basis of scientific and cultural education in the schools. In addition to their anti-alcohol and anti-Masonry stance, the American Prohibition National Party also displayed the fairly consistent conservative position against immigration, arguing that immigration should be halted to the U.S. from all foreign countries (Porter and Johnson, 1972, 63).

Grover Cleveland

Between 1884 and 1892 Democrat Grover Cleveland won the Presidency of the United States twice and the popular vote in Presidential elections three times, giving him perhaps the greatest popular support of any President during the Gilded Age. Cleveland garnered this public support by exhibiting perhaps as much conservative spirit as most Republicans of the age. Like the Republicans, Cleveland favored hard money policies, and pursuant to his goal of creating a more sound currency based on gold, he was supported by Republicans in Congress in his repeal of the Sherman Silver Purchase Act in 1893, which he blamed for the reduction in federal gold reserves during the economic Panic of 1893 (Morgan, 1969, 445-447).

Cleveland also exhibited staunch conservatism on the subject of government intervention to alleviate the plight of the poor during the same economic Panic of 1893. In this instance, Cleveland proved to be even more conservative than his Republican opposition. While former Republican President Benjamin Harrison stated his position in favor of federal government intervention to aid the poor, arguing that,

> "The Republican theory has been all along that it was right to so legislate as to provide work, employment, comfort to the American workingman" (Quoted in Morgan, 1969, 445).

Cleveland stated what would become the position of the conservative Republicans in the Twentieth Century and beyond when he argued that "while the people should patriotically and cheerfully support their government, its functions do not include support of the people" (Quoted in Morgan, 1969, 447).

Cleveland's laissez-faire "do nothing" approach to the Panic of 1893, however, would cost his Party dearly as the Republicans would gain 113 seats in the House in 1894, the largest shift in American history, and then hold the House for 28 of the next 34 years (Gould, 2003, 119). Unfortunately for the Republicans, who would clearly emerge as the "conservative" Party by 1920, the conservatives would not learn a lesson from Cleveland's experience and the conservative Republican Herbert Hoover's lack of aggressiveness in confronting the next great economic downturn from 1929-1932 would propel the Democrats back to dominance 40 years later.

William McKinley

The person that would inherit the reins of government after the Panic of 1893 led to the downfall of Grover Cleveland and the Democrats was William McKinley of Ohio. McKinley was not a dynamic speaker, but he defeated the "silver-tongued" populist Democrat William Jennings Bryan with a choreographed front-porch campaign in 1896 that would later serve as a model for the candidacy of George W. Bush, another limited orator, 104 years later. This would be the first of numerous of similarities between conservative Republicans Bush and McKinley, separated by a century. The idea behind the McKinley campaign was to keep him out of the public eye as much as possible and carefully choreograph what appearances he did make so as not to expose his weaknesses. Karl Rove and the Republican Party of 2000 would successfully follow a similar strategy for success in the election of 2000 (Gould, 2003).

In addition to winning the Presidency with McKinley in 1896, the Republican Party also won the mid-term elections of 1898 and thus controlled the Presidency and both Houses of Congress. Consequently, the policies that would emerge during the McKinley administration can be squarely credited with the Republican Party, and the direction of those policies under the Republicans and McKinley would prove to be decidedly conservative.

In foreign policy, McKinley led the nation into a new era with the Spanish-American War and thus ushered in the age of American "imperialism" that would often characterize conservative policies in the century to follow. Furthermore, McKinley's decision to go to war in Cuba in 1898 would be based on evidence and arguments that were flimsy and flawed due to yellow journalism and the corrupting influences of American business interests abroad. McKinley created military governments in Cuba and the Philippines after the Spanish-American War without Congressional oversight, and the United States not only occupied the countries militarily, but became involved in a large scale military effort to put down a local insurgency against American rule in the Philippines (Jones, 1996, 252).

McKinley also evidently came to his decision to support the annexation of the Philippines following the Spanish-American War after getting on his knees and praying about the matter to God, whom McKinley claimed told him to annex the Philippines so that it could be "Christianized" (Jones, 1996, 252). This message from God is somewhat curious, however, since the Philippines, as a Spanish possession, had been forced to adopt Catholic Christianity by the Spanish (Jones, 1996, 252).

On the issue of black rights, McKinley essentially chose the typical conservative path of neglect that had been in place since 1877. McKinley followed this laissez-faire approach toward race relations in spite of the presence of an upsurge in racial violence in the 1890s. When a riot in Wilmington, North Carolina resulted in the death of eleven blacks, McKinley had little to say about the matter and did even less. Black leader T. Thomas Fortune described McKinley as "a man of jelly, who would turn us loose to the mob and not say a word" (Quoted in Gould, 2003, 131).

Concerning government intervention in the economy under McKinley, the approach remained decidedly laissez-faire. The Republicans reconfirmed the gold standard, which actually boosted the American economy only due to new gold finds in Alaska, and the big business trusts were allowed to operate unchecked as McKinley did not authorize the use of the Sherman Antitrust Act against trusts or monopolies. In general, the Gilded Age position of the Republican Party as the Party of high tariffs and American big business continued unabated. The general attitude was perhaps well-summed by Republican Senator and McKinley campaign manager Marc Hanna who stated that "a man had a right to do what he pleased with his own" (Gould, 2003, 131-132).

Junior Order of the United American Mechanics

While McKinley led the more mainstream conservatives into the Twentieth Century, conservative extremists were reinventing themselves under the name of the Junior Order of the United American Mechanics (JOUAM). The APA had essentially disintegrated after 1896, but the ideas that had spawned the group, anti-Catholicism and anti-immigration, remained powerful forces in a time of massive immigration from predominantly Catholic areas of Europe. The JOUAM had been in existence since the mid 1880s, but grew from 15,000 members in 1885 to 224,000 by 1914 (Higham, 1955, 173-174). Anti-Catholic sentiments in the U.S. in the first two decades of the Twentieth Century, however, were much more prevalent than the JOUAM's membership roll might suggest. A weekly anti-Catholic periodical entitled *Menace*, in which it was consistently argued that the Catholic Church was trying to take over the country through immigration, enjoyed a circulation of over one million by 1914 (Williams, 1932, 97).

Although the JOUAM was anti-Union, anti-communist, and anti-anarchist in conformity with more mainstream conservative thought, they also directed their wrath against the monopolies and the "selfishness of plutocratic capitalists" and thus differed from the McKinley big-business conservatives (Higham, 1955, 58). This essentially populist element in the JOUAM had been absent in its predecessor, the APA. In fact, the populists of the 1890s had actually condemned the APA, and the APA, likewise, was decidedly anti-populist.

This antagonism between populism and nativism, however, began to change around the turn of the century as former populists, such as 1896 populist candidate for Vice President, Tom Watson, increasingly aligned themselves with anti-Catholic and anti-immigrant extremists. Watson in particular opposed blacks, Catholics, and Jews, while simultaneously condemning the "evil" of big business and Wall Street. In 1910, Watson denounced the Catholic hierarchy as "the deadliest menace to our liberties and our civilization" (Quoted in Woodward, 1963, 419). Watson also wrote a book entitled *Maria Monk and Her Revelation of Convent Crimes,* where he argued that there were murders of infants in Catholic convents. Finally, Watson argued that the Pope had secretly organized and armed the Knights of Columbus for a takeover of the United States (Woodward, 1963, 438-445).

Anti-Semitism and the Leo Frank Case

In 1914, Watson became involved in an anti-Semitic propaganda campaign against Leo Frank, a Jewish man in Georgia accused of murdering a fourteen year-old girl, Mary Phagen. Phagan's body had been found in the cellar of a pencil factory at Marietta, Georgia. She had been raped and strangled, but before dying she had managed to scribble on a pad a note accusing an unnamed black man of the crime. In spite of the note, the twenty-nine-year-old Leo Frank, a Jewish Northerner, was charged with the crime and convicted based on the testimony of a black man who, like Frank, had been in the factory at the time the murder occurred. Prominent lawyers throughout the country analyzed the testimony and pointed out the obvious that it was most likely the black man who had testified against Frank who was the real culprit. Nevertheless, the anti-Semitic conservative ire of the Georgia citizens had been piqued and threatening mobs gathered about the courthouse during the trial demanding that the Court "hang the Jew" (Dinnerstein, 1968, 149).

Frank was sentenced to death by a Georgia Court, but his sentence was later commuted, causing outrage among Georgia nativists. Watson helped found the Knights of Mary Phagen, a group whose purpose was to make sure that Leo Frank died for Mary Phagen's murder (Dinnerstein, 1968, 149-150). Frank was eventually lynched in 1915 by a Georgia mob, an action Watson defended as just. Watson further argued that the demands of the Frank affair suggested that it would be prudent to reorganize the Ku Klux Klan (Woodward, 1963, 438-445). Later that same year, the men that would come together in Georgia to reform the Klan would all be former members of the Knights of Mary Phagen (Dinnerstein, 1968, 149-150).

Watson also published his own magazine (*Watson's Magazine*) that he used after the Frank lynching to rail against the Jews. Watson equated the Jews with the excesses of monopoly capitalism due to their prevalence in the banking industry, a subject that was a long time component of populist conspiracy theory. Watson even took his anti-Semitism to the extreme and absurd allegation that the Jews and Catholics were working together in a grand scheme to undermine American society. Watson viewed the Catholics as behind every "evil" in the U.S., and when the United States entered World War I, a decision Watson opposed, Watson condemned the American decision as subservient to Catholics. In spite of his outlandish conspiracy theories, Watson was elected to the U.S. Senate in 1920 on his anti-Catholic platform, but he would be unable to use Congress for his anti-Catholic and anti-Semitic crusade because he died shortly after taking office in 1922. At his funeral, however, was a cross of roses eight feet high sent by the Ku Klux Klan (Woodward, 1963, 486).

Theodore Roosevelt and Conservatism

Upon William McKinley's untimely death in 1901, Theodore Roosevelt, who was viewed as a dangerous loose cannon by most conservatives, suddenly occupied the White House. Roosevelt would take conservatism in new directions, and in the end, his activism would stretch conservatism so far that conservatives would eventually reject his leadership. From the outset, Roosevelt and conservative Republicans would be on an inevitable collision course. Roosevelt did not adhere to the conservatives' traditional position in favor of protective tariffs, nor did he oppose regulation of big business in the public interest. In the words of Roosevelt,

> "The great corporations which we have grown to speak of rather loosely as trusts are the creatures of the State, and the State not only has the right to control them, but it is in duty bound to control them whenever the need of such control is shown" (Quoted in Roosevelt, 1904, 15).

Roosevelt's position obviously conflicts greatly with the staunch conservative view of property rights as impervious to governmental intrusions. As if Roosevelt's property views were not bad enough (as far as big business conservatives were concerned), Roosevelt abandoned the conservatives' traditional pro-business position on labor disputes when he intervened in the United Mine workers' strike in 1902. Instead of sending in federal troops to protect scab workers and mine owner interests as conservative Presidents had done repeatedly in the past, Roosevelt offered his services both to the labor unions and the mine owners as an arbitrator. The labor unions, unaccustomed to even-handed federal intervention in such affairs, quickly accepted Roosevelt's offer while the mine owners rejected it. Roosevelt was incensed at the obstinacy of the mine owners and threatened a Federal takeover of the mines by U.S. troops. Faced with such an ominous threat and pressure from J.P. Morgan on the financial end, the mine owners agreed to arbitration, but the incident displayed vividly that Roosevelt was not the same type of conservative Republican as his Gilded Age predecessors had been (Morris, 2001, 156-167).

Roosevelt generally opposed the power of concentrated wealth, a basic breech with traditional conservative ideology, and favored an inheritance tax as well as income redistribution to the poor. Roosevelt's reasoning for doing so, however, was conservative in character in that he believed that if the major social inequities were not addressed, it would lead to political unrest and even greater reforms (Gould, 2003, 158-160).

These "anti-business" polices of Roosevelt were in direct opposition to the conservatives' traditional position of resistance to change. For example,

Republican Senator and former McKinley campaign manager Marc Hanna argued against Roosevelt's reforms, contending that the best policy was to "let well enough alone" or "stand pat" (Gould, 2003, 156). Similarly, Republican House Speaker Joseph Cannon, (known as "Czar Cannon" due to the power he wielded in the House) enunciated the standard conservative position concerning Roosevelt's reforms when he bluntly stated, "I am god-damned tired of listening to all this babble for reform" (Bolles, 1951, 5-6, 11).

Roosevelt's use of the federal government as a means to reform and regulation of business caused conservative Republicans to shift toward a States' Rights position consistent with that of the conservative Democrats in the South (Gould, 2003, 162). This too, however, turned out to be a bone of contention between the President and conservative Republicans since Roosevelt also eschewed the States' Rights arguments of both the northern conservative Republicans and the conservative Democrats in the South in favor of a more activist federal government and an expansion of national power in both foreign and domestic policy realms.

On the race issue, Roosevelt greatly differed from Southern conservatives as evidenced by the fact that he entertained Booker T. Washington at the White House, even dining with the African-American leader, and thus enraging Southern conservatives at this violation of their social mores. Roosevelt was accused of "mingling and mongrelization" of the white race, and Newspaper headlines proclaimed such things as "Roosevelt Dines a Darkey," and "Our Coon-Flavored President" (Morris, 2001, 53-55).

In foreign policy, Roosevelt was an internationalist, but also an America-first conservative. Although Roosevelt talked of "speaking softly and carrying a big stick," in reality, he mostly yelled loudly while wielding his big stick since his path was a militaristic, America-first, and heavy-handed approach to foreign policy problems. Roosevelt continually expressed his disdain for foreign leaders and Latin Americans in particular, referring to the Colombians in general as "dagoes," and Colombian leader Cipriano Castro as an "unspeakable, villainous little monkey" (Jones, 2001, 40). Roosevelt essentially viewed the Latin Americans as in an immature stage of Darwinian evolution and advised German diplomat Speck von Sternburg, "If any South American country misbehaves toward any European country, let the European country spank it" (Quoted in Morris, 2001, 178). Roosevelt did not limit his disdain to Latin Americans, however, as he also referred to Russian Tsar Nicholas II as "a preposterous little creature" (Jones, 2001, 46).

In action, Roosevelt displayed his globalist/imperialist conservatism when he essentially helped create the nation of Panama, aiding a Panamanian revolt against Colombia and then signing a canal treaty with the Panamanians when the Colombian Senate had rejected his first offer. The sovereignty rights of foreign powers obviously were not his major concerns. In fact, the famous Roosevelt Corollary to the Monroe Doctrine that states that,

> "in cases of chronic wrongdoing in Latin America, since the Monroe Doctrine prevents European intervention in Latin America, the U.S. must intervene and exercise international police power" (Quoted in Jones, 2001, 284-285),

is probably about as close to the policies of George W. Bush one hundred years later as it is to any other American leader. Similarly, Roosevelt's intervention in the Venezuelan crisis of 1902 and his takeover of the Dominican Customs Houses in 1904 have more than a few parallels with Bush's takeover of Iraq to correct "chronic wrongdoing" as Roosevelt would say. Similarly, the Platt Amendment to the Cuban Constitution of 1902 allowed the U.S. to control Cuban foreign relations and intervene militarily in Cuba at any time. Furthermore, the Platt Amendment granted the United States a permanent base at Guantanamo Bay, Cuba, a violation of Cuban sovereignty that continues through the present in spite of the fact that the Cuban government under the Constitution of 1902 has not been in existence since 1959 (Jones, 1996, 269-274).

In spite of his America-first conservatism in foreign policy, by 1908, a substantial segment of the Republican Party had decided that Roosevelt was too much of a reformer and an anti-business socialist; hence, they planned to withdraw their support from Roosevelt for the Republican nomination. These sentiments intensified when a severe financial Panic occurred in late 1907. Conservatives viewed the stock crashes and bank failures as the predictable result of Roosevelt's overzealous meddling in the economy with the powers of the federal government (Gould, 2003, 163). Fortunately for conservatives, the popular but inconsistent (with conservatism) and unpredictable Roosevelt had promised in 1904 that he would not run again in 1908, and Roosevelt's hand-picked successor, the more conservatively reliable William Howard Taft, would succeed Roosevelt in the White House.

William Howard Taft

Taft attempted to bridge the gap in the Republican Party between conservatives and progressives, but in the end he would satisfy neither. In his campaign of 1908, Taft alienated conservatives when he endorsed the legitimate role played by labor unions, pledged to support lower tariffs, and promised continued regulation of the trusts in the tradition of Theodore Roosevelt (*American Monthly Review of Reviews*, 1908, 517).

Taft was constrained, however, by his much more strict interpretation of the constitution than that held by Theodore Roosevelt. Roosevelt essentially believed that the President had the authority to do anything he pleased unless it was specifically prohibited by the Constitution. In contrast, Taft viewed any power exercised by the President that was not specifically granted in the Constitution to be illegitimate. As a consequence, Taft viewed many actions of the Roosevelt administration as unconstitutional and arbitrary abuses of power that could lead to misuse of Presidential power and political crises (Taft, 1916, 144).

Taft would alienate conservatives, however, with his vigorous trust-busting that would exceed that of the generally more progressive Roosevelt. While Roosevelt merely wanted to regulate the trusts, Taft viewed the trust arrangements themselves as illegal combinations in restraint of trade and therefore felt that the President was obligated to enforce the law of the land by eliminating the trusts completely. While this stance did please reformers, Taft's trust-busting would be insufficient to satisfy the progressive faction within the Republican Party entirely since they tended to be more reformist than Taft on most other issues. When progressives in the House attempted to oust Conservative Republican Joseph Cannon as Speaker in March, 1909, Taft declined to become involved and thus lost the confidence of the progressives. To make matters worse, that fall Taft supported the conservative-backed Payne-Aldrich tariff, thus providing further proof to progressives (who favored lower tariffs) that Taft was on the side of conservatives (Taft, 1916, 222).

Taft also alienated Progressives in a controversy over public lands. Taft's Interior Secretary, Richard Ballinger, removed approximately one million acres of forests from public land reserves created during the administration of Theodore Roosevelt. Interior Department investigator Lewis Glavis uncovered evidence suggesting that Ballinger had engaged in a plan to turn over public coal reserves in Alaska to private investors for profit. Glavis took what he believed was condemning evidence to former Roosevelt ally Gifford Pinchot, who was still head of the Forest Service. Pinchot presented the evidence to Taft, who also heard Ballinger's rebuttal and announced that the charges were groundless. Pinchot then leaked the story to the press and to Congress, and an enraged Taft dismissed Pinchot for insubordination. In firing Pinchot, Taft alienated Progressives and Roosevelt supporters who viewed Pinchot as a defender of the public interest against greedy industrialists (Brinkley, 2003, 608-609).

Roosevelt had been on a tour of Europe and on hunting expeditions in Africa at the time of the Ballinger-Pinchot affair. In the Spring of 1910 Roosevelt returned to the U.S., and within a week announced a speaking tour where he denounced Taft for his "archaic" anti-trust policy and "maudlin folly" (Quoted in Roark et al., 2005, 772). In September, Roosevelt re-entered the political arena with a program that was certain to alienate conservatives. Roosevelt's program included a graduated income tax, lower tariffs, worker's compensation insurance, more federal government regulation of business, federal government health insurance, and regulation of child and female labor (Roark et al., 2005, 772).

Meanwhile, the Congressional elections of 1910 saw Democrats gain control of the House for the 1st time since 1894. Additionally, Progressive Republican Candidates ousted Conservatives in 40 seats, creating not only a majority Republican House, but a majority Progressive House (many Democrats in the South were very conservative, anti-black, opposed to women's rights, and certainly not Progressive). The shift in Congress suggests that the mood of the country had clearly shifted in favor of progressivism. Then in October 1911, Taft engaged in an anti-trust action that normally would have delighted progressives, but in this case, it would end up further alienating the Roosevelt faction of the Republican Party. Consistent with his belief that trusts were illegal, Taft filed an anti-Trust suit against U.S. Steel, alleging that the 1907 U.S. Steel acquisition of Tennessee Coal and Iron violated the Sherman Act. Roosevelt was incensed since the suit essentially inferred that his approval of the corporate acquisition in 1907 during the economic Panic of that year was improper. Roosevelt used the incident as a pretense for announcing his candidacy for President in February 1912 (Roark et al., 2005, 772).

Election of 1912 and Realignment

Roosevelt was aware that he had the backing of what had become a progressive majority and called for primary elections to determine the Republican nominee. Six states held primaries and Roosevelt won all six, suggesting that the Republican voters in the aggregate were leaning progressive and strongly favored Roosevelt. Conservatives at the Republican Convention, however, assigned approximately ninety percent of unassigned delegates at the Convention to Taft, thus causing Roosevelt and his supporters to withdraw from the Republican Convention in protest. Roosevelt then ran as a Third Party candidate against Taft and Democratic nominee Woodrow Wilson. With the Republicans divided between Taft and Roosevelt, Woodrow Wilson would win a plurality of the vote and become the first Democrat to occupy the White House since Grover Cleveland. The departure of Roosevelt and his supporters from the Republican Party left the Republicans less progressive and more laissez-faire, a position they would occupy for the rest of the Twentieth Century. Simultaneously, the Democrats, who had been the Party of reactionary Southern sectionalism, racism, and States' rights, would become the progressive and constructive Party for the same time period (Gould, 2003, 193-195).

The 1912 defeat left the Republican Party in disarray and conservatives in particular out of power for perhaps the first time since the Civil War. Joe Cannon wrote that,

"the party landed in Purgatory, from which place according to orthodox teaching there is an escape. We have to be thankful we didn't land in that other place from which it is said there is no escape" (Quoted in Gould, 2003, 195).

President Wilson almost immediately began to play out the conservatives' worst fears as he pushed for his "New Freedom" that included the creation of the Federal Reserve System, a lower tariff, the creation of the Federal Trade Commission, and the enactment of an income tax under the Sixteenth Amendment to the U.S. Constitution. Republicans opposed all of these measures as expansions of government power and intrusions into private business. In the case of the tariff, Republicans argued that the lower tariffs would lead to economic disaster. The passage of the income tax, however, provided the government with another source of revenue, thus rendering the tariff less important for the purpose of balancing federal budgets, and the tariff would therefore diminish in importance to conservatives as a political issue (Porter and Johnson, 1972, 205).

Woodrow Wilson, however, was not completely captured by progressivism and displayed some conservative stripes of his own. Wilson reversed Roosevelt's integration policies in the U.S. armed forces, opposed women's suffrage, was slow to act on child labor, and proved to be just as imperialistic in foreign policy as Roosevelt, with his invasions of Mexico during the Mexican Revolution and invasions of Haiti and the Dominican Republic in 1915 and 1916 to protect American business interests (Jones, 2001, 58-63).

Conservatism and World War I

When war broke out in Europe in 1914 and Wilson took a more progressive stance in favor of peace, conservatives were placed in the unfamiliar position of being painted as unpatriotic if they did not support their President during wartime, even if the President's policy preference was for peace instead of war (Gould, 2003, 199). While Democrats campaigned in 1916 on the peace slogan, "He kept us out of the war," Republicans were placed in the unenviable position of needing to avoid the "unpatriotic" label while simultaneously appearing to take a strong stand. The result in 1916 was a vague platform that called for a "firm, consistent and courageous foreign policy" as well as "a strict and honest neutrality," seemingly calling for both war and peace simultaneously depending on how one might want to interpret the vagaries. Republicans also called for a return to high tariffs, but capitulated to progressives with a call for regulation of railroads, child labor, and large corporations (Porter and Johnson, 1972, 204-206).

Republican candidate Charles Evans Hughes avoided the big issue of the War and instead attacked Wilson on his mediocre appointments to office and mixed record on civil service. Unfortunately, his campaign was tantamount to touring the country "telling the people small, petty things which amount to nothing" (Gould, 2003, 205). Hughes' message became further muddled, however, as Teddy Roosevelt toured the country arguing for intervention into the War while ostensibly campaigning for Hughes. Though Hughes had not taken an identical position, Roosevelt's campaigning made it appear that Hughes could be influenced by Roosevelt to lead the United States to War in Europe. Given the choice between war and peace at the polls, the American people chose Wilson and peace (Gould, 2003, 205).

While campaigning that he was "too proud to fight," however, Wilson simultaneously pushed Congress to increase American war readiness. Republicans then (perhaps correctly) denounced Wilson's swift position change in favor of war in 1917 as disingenuous. Republican Henry Cabot Lodge argued that Wilson had "lowered the American spirit and confused the popular mind" by coming out in favor of a war after he had sought "Peace without victory" during the electoral campaign (Widenor, 1980, 264).

Wilson and the Government Economic Takeover

At the time of the U.S. entrance into World War I, the nation was ill-prepared for war and Wilson engineered a federal takeover of the economy that was essentially unprecedented. Wilson created War Boards with the authority to allocate or ration resources, standardize production, fix prices, coordinate the manufacture and government purchase of military goods, suspend anti-trust laws, and dictate to corporations which ones would convert to production of war materials. The War Railroad Board coordinated all of the nation's railroads into a single transportation system, the War Fuel Administration rationed coal and other fuels, and the War Food Administration encouraged conservation of food commodities through "Wheatless Monday" and "Meatless Tuesday" campaigns. The War Food Administration also purchased grain at above-market values in an effort to stimulate food production. The War Labor Board pressured corporations to agree to eight hour days, collective bargaining, and government-set wages, in return for Union pledges not to strike. Conservatives objected to the wholesale economic intervention, but since prices were typically set artificially high to encourage production, big business complaints were minimized. Furthermore, vehement condemnation of Wilson's policies again risked the possibility of being labeled unpatriotic (Nash et al., 2005, 767-768, Roark et al., 2005, 801-802).

Wilson and the Wartime Conservative Backlash

World War I whipped the American public into a frenzy of hyperpatriotism that was perhaps unparalleled in American history. Fanning the flames of this pro-war frenzy, President Wilson again displayed his conservative side and created the Committee on Public Information (CPI), essentially a federal war propaganda agency, and endowed it with the responsibility for selling the war to the American public. The CPI painted the war as a crusade for freedom and democracy and the German enemies were portrayed as cruel, savage, anti-democratic thugs bent on destroying the American way and dominating the world. The CPI placed ads in magazines and newspapers asking Americans to keep watch on their neighbors and report evidence of disloyalty, pessimism, or yearning for peace. Under such an atmosphere, free speech and truth and accuracy in the news media became seriously compromised as the news media essentially published the CPI's accounts of the war without question or criticism (Bernays, 1928, 2004).

With the urging from the CPI, persons against Wilson's war policies became subject to public ridicule and attack. School boards outlawed the teaching of the German language. The German department at the University of Texas was closed so as to promote "purer Americanism" (Calvert et al., 2002, 308). Wisconsin progressive Senator Robert LaFollette was censured by the University of Wisconsin for his anti-war views. The director of the Boston Symphony was fired simply for being German. German books and music were removed from library and retail store shelves, and German-Americans changed their names so as to conceal their ethnicity and avoid ridicule and attack (Nash et al., 2004, 757).

Conservative Vigilantes

Conservative vigilante organizations quickly developed to enforce American Patriotism. The most important of these was the American Protective League, a group whose purpose was to "mobilize respectable members of the community to root out disloyal members." The American Protective League claimed over 250,000 members at its peak in 1918. Other similar organizations including the National Security League, American Defense Society, and Boy Spies of America, collectively claimed another

250,000 members. The organizations opened mail, tapped telephones, subjected targeted citizens to shakedowns, and engaged in lynchings and violence against suspected disloyals. In Cincinnati, a pacifist clergyman was pulled from his bed, dragged to a nearby hillside, and whipped "in the name of the women and children of Belgium." In Indiana, a man was acquitted of murdering an alien who had yelled, "to hell with the United States." In Montana, one member of the Industrial Workers of the World (IWW) (a left-leaning labor organization that conservatives viewed as communist and un-American) was hanged and another was dragged to death behind a truck. IWW leader Big Bill Haywood fled to the Soviet Union rather than face potential lynching at the hands of vigilantes (Nash et al., 2004, 757-758).

Espionage and Sedition Acts

To make matters worse, Congress fanned the flames of hysteria with two Acts that essentially criminalized political dissent. The Espionage Act of 1917 made it a crime to "aid the enemy" or "obstruct the U.S. war effort." On the surface, these items do not appear to be out of the ordinary, but in practice, they became launching pads for oppression and the erosion of freedom. In May 1918, however, Congress took things a step further with the passage of the Sedtion Act, that declared that it was illegal to utter, print, write, or publish, any disloyal, profane, scurrilous, or abusive language about the government, constitution, or armed forces. Furthermore, "saying anything" to discourage the purchase of war bonds was declared to be criminal activity (Nash et al., 2004, 757).

The similarities between the Alien and Sedition Acts of 1798 and the Congressional actions of WWI are uncanny, and the results of the Twentieth Century Acts were just as oppressive as those in the Eighteenth Century if not more so. Under the Sedition Act of 1918, communist and socialist parties (who criticized the U.S. government effort in the War) were effectively silenced and over 500 communists were deported. The Justice Department initiated over 2,000 prosecutions under the Acts resulting in the incarceration of 900 persons during the nineteen months of American involvement in WWI.

The conservative oppressive rampage was not limited to the socialists and communists, however. Anarchist Ricardo Flores Magon was sentenced to twenty years in prison for publishing a statement criticizing Wilson's policies in Mexico (where there was much to criticize, but space limits us from elaborating here) that were completely separate from the issue of U.S. involvement in the Great War. One woman, Sarah Parker, received a five year prison sentence for writing, "I am for the people, and the government is for the profiteers" (Nash et al., 2004, 758). Movie producer Robert

Goldstein, who had made a film about the American Revolution entitled *Spirit of 76,* was sentenced to ten years in prison because his film's depiction of atrocities committed by the British during the American Revolution was deemed by a judge to be a violation of the Espionage Act under the pretense that it might lead the public to "question the good faith of our ally, Great Britain" (Irons, 2000, 268).

Red Scare

The Great War ended on November 11, 1918 with an Armistice, but the reactionary conservative backlash spawned by the War experience continued for several years afterward through a time of political mass paranoia that has since become known as the "Red Scare." The Red Scare was essentially a continuation of the wartime hysteria fanned by the Wilson administration, but was also related to a small amount of real communist activity, a large amount of strike activity, a few actual bombings by left-wing radicals, and a personal reactionary anti-communist campaign by the conservative Attorney General of the United States, A. Mitchell Palmer (Nash et al., 2004, 781-782).

While it is true that there were some left-wing and radical elements in American Labor Unions at the time, and some 20% of the workforce was estimated to be on strike at one time or another in 1919, the strikes were much less due to left wing ideological radicalism than they were due to the fact that the American cost of living doubled between 1913 and 1921 and wages had not kept up with inflation (Nash et al., 2004, 781). Under such economic upheaval, labor unrest perhaps should be expected even when no communists are involved at all.

The political violence that precipitated the conservative reactionary backlash began during an international shipping strike in 1919 when a bomb was sent to the home of the Mayor of Seattle, who had opposed the labor union activity in Seattle shipyards. Although the Seattle bomb did not detonate, it provided more evidence for the American people that the labor unions were dominated by dangerous left-wing radicals. Labor Unions had been connected with bombs, political radicalism, communism, and anarchism in the minds of American conservatives ever since the Chicago Haymarket riot of 1886, where four anarchist labor leaders were executed for a bomb that killed seven policemen at a labor rally. Although there was no direct evidence that the labor leaders in the Haymarket affair had anything to do with the bomb, they were actually indicted and convicted of "inciting the person who threw the bomb into doing it" (Nash et al., 2004, 638). The Haymarket affair combined with other violence-filled strikes, such as the American Railway Union sympathetic strike against the Pullman Palace Car

Copany and the Homestead Steel strike (both in 1892), to indelibly etch the connection between labor unions and left-wing political violence into the minds of American conservatives. The strike against Pullman was ended only after federal troops were sent in by President Grover Cleveland to end the strike, and the Homestead Steel strike ended after intervention by the Pennsylvania National Guard. Both strikes left a trail of death and property damage that American conservatives were determined not to repeat (Nash et al., 1986, 619-620).

In 1919, the conservative perception of labor unions as organizations of communist and anarchist "bomb throwing radicals" was greatly reinforced not only by the Seattle bomb, but by the discovery by the U.S. Post Office of 16 bombs that were not delivered due to insufficient postage. A subsequent examination revealed that each was addressed to prominent persons such as John D. Rockefeller, Oliver Wendell Holmes, and Attorney General A. Mitchell Palmer (Farquhar, 2003, 197). In April, 1919, a bomb was delivered and detonated that blew the hands off of the maid of a former Georgia senator, Thomas Hardwick, who was known to be anti-union. In June, a bomb destroyed the front of the home of U.S. Attorney General, A. Mitchell Palmer. The damage to Palmer's home could have been much worse, but the bomber's plan went awry when he apparently tripped on Palmer's porch, dropped the bomb, and blew himself to pieces. The bombing of Palmer's house was followed by several other bombings, suggesting to many that the terror activity was widespread. In all, seven bombs were detonated in five states (Farquhar, 2003, 197).

Congress and the American public demanded that something be done about the terror and the U.S. Senate passed a motion of Censure against Attorney General Palmer for his inaction (Farquhar, 2003, 199). After the bombing of his home, however, Palmer launched an unparalleled crusade against the terrorists and organized an anti-radical division within the Justice Department. Palmer then put the ultraconservative J. Edgar Hoover in charge of coordinating the anti-radical division's activities and ensuring that safeguarding the Constitutional rights of the terror suspects received a low priority. In November, 1919, the Justice Department rounded up and detained 250 members of the Union of Russian Workers. Thirty-three of the Russian workers were severely beaten by Justice Department officers, suggesting gross rights violations, but the raids were popular with the public. The next month, 249 aliens were deported for being "threats to the government," including the famed left-wing feminist, Emma Goldman. Palmer's raids were a tremendous success with the American people and the decidedly conservative American press who applauded Palmer's actions. In the words of the *Washington Post*, "There is no time to waste on hairsplitting over infringement of liberty" (Quoted in Murray, 1955, 217).

On January 2, 1920, Palmer ordered hundreds of federal agents to 33 American cities to destroy the imagined Bolshevik conspiracy. In all, Palmer and Hoover's agents arrested 6,000 individuals on charges of conspiracy to overthrow the U.S. government. In furtherance of his crusade, Palmer attempted to alter basic criminal rights protections, a clear sacrifice of principles in the service of a desired end. Specifically, Palmer attempted to persuade Secretary of Labor William B. Wilson to amend a portion of the deportation law that allowed suspects to secure counsel. He also requested a blanket deportation warrant to cover any aliens discovered once a raid had commenced. Wilson refused, but while he was on sick leave, one of Wilson's underlings, John W. Abercrombie, provided the changes that Palmer requested. Rights to Counsel and Habeas Corpus, along with the rule that suspects had to be informed of the charges against them were suspended for those arrested by Palmer's men (Farquhar, 2003, 200).

Armed with the blanket suspensions of civil liberties, Palmer's abuses were legion. In Detroit, armed with 3,000 blank mimeographed warrants (with the names to be filled in later), Palmer's men arrested and jailed 800 people. It is certain that the experience was at least uncomfortable for those arrested since 800 detainees were allowed access to only one toilet for the entire group (Murray, 1955, 215). In Boston, similar raids jailed another 800 people. In New Jersey, one man was arrested simply because he "looked like an alien" (Farquhar, 2003, 201-202). The practice of arresting people simply because of how they looked was essentially encouraged by the Attorney General himself. In the words of Palmer,

"Out of the sly and crafty eyes of many of them leap cupidity, cruelty, insanity, and crime; from their lopsided faces, sloping brows, and misshapen features may be recognized the unmistakable criminal type" (Quoted in Roark et al., 2005, 817).

In all, 6,000 people were arrested and 556 were deported by the end of 1920 and Palmer had lists with over two hundred thousand names as suspects. In spite of his gross abuses, Palmer briefly became a national hero for "ferreting out communists" (Murray, 1955, 212-217).

All of this activity from the Justice Department, however, was carried out without any supporting or enabling legislation from Congress. Palmer appeared before a Congressional committee and asked for legislation authorizing the suppression of sedition during peacetime, and seventy bills were pending in Congress within five months of his request, but none of the measures passed (Cummings and McFarland, 1937, 429). Palmer's paranoid zeal, however, would eventually become his own undoing as his overreactive brutal raids began to stir the public conscience. In the words of William Preston (1963, 221),

> "the net was so wide and bureau detectives were so careless that some ten thousand persons were arrested including many citizens and many individuals not members of either party. Abuse of due process characterized the early stages of the drive. This ill-treatment proceeded from the official decision to protect undercover informers. Indiscriminate arrests of the innocent with the guilty, unlawful searches and seizures by federal detectives, intimidating preliminary interrogation of aliens held incommunicado, high-handed levying of excessive bail, and denial of counsel were the government's response to stiffening alien radical resistance to deportation."

Additionally, less than ten percent of arrests led to deportation, suggesting that the threat was overblown. Palmer's raids uncovered no explosives and confiscated only three pistols in 6,000 arrests (Nash et al., 2004, 782).

Finally, Palmer discredited himself by making the mistake of playing the role of false profit in predicting the day of the apocalypse. Palmer announced in April, 1920, that the communists were going to launch a major revolt on May Day (May 1) 1920. In New York and other major U.S. cities, the police were put on round-the-clock alert and National Guards were called out to head off the crisis. May Day passed without a single incident, however, and Palmer's actions made him appear paranoid and ridiculous. As a consequence, public support for his reactionary tactics evaporated and the Red Scare dissipated as the economy adjusted to the end of the War and the American public came to realize that the communist threat had been greatly overstated (Murray, 1955, 240-242).

Return of the KKK

With the defeat of the "evil" Huns secured sooner than anticipated, the end of WWI found the American people essentially whipped into an emotional patriotic and moral fervor that was suddenly without direction. In the words of *Life* Magazine Editor Robert Coughlan, the American political mindset was essentially in a state of "Coitus Interruptus" (Quoted in Haas, 1963, 50). The general emotion among the American people at the time was one of continued chauvinistic patriotism and hatred for the devil they had been fighting, but the evil entity had essentially cheated them by surrendering before it could be obliterated. Into this void would step the KKK to provide substitute devils to slay in place of the old ones, and provide different means by which to slay them.

The KKK was reorganized on Thanksgiving night, 1915, by William J. Simmons, a Methodist minister from Georgia, and fifteen like-minded followers. At first, Simmons experienced difficulties in recruiting members, although he claimed over 1500 recruits by the end of WWI, but in 1920 he enlisted the help of wealthy Atlanta widow Elizabeth Tyler and former newspaperman and solicitor for the Woodmen of the World, Edward Young Clarke, and the KKK fortunes would abruptly change (Haas, 1963, 46-52).

With Simmons as the front man, Clarke as the organizer, and Tyler as the financier, the KKK quickly rose to prominence, playing on conservative American moralism, nativism, religion, patriotism, greed, and the social energy and inertia that followed WWI. Simmons and Clarke developed what they termed as the "four major tenets of the Klan philosophy" or "character" of the Klan as a white man's organization, a gentile organization, an American organization, and a Protestant organization. Anything that the Klansmen did not view as "white gentile" and American Protestant in character would become a Klan target (Haas, 1963, 52).

The Klan was modeled loosely after religious organizations and much attention was given to titles, symbolism, and ceremony. Any room could serve as a Klan meeting place, but all meetings would have an altar, upon which there would be an American flag, a Bible open at Romans chapter twelve, an unsheathed sword, and a container of initiation water that was sprinkled over new members to ceremonially cleanse them of any "alien" defilement (Haas, 1963, 54).

The suggestion and symbolism of the twelfth chapter of Romans is that service in the KKK is service to God and sacrifices made for the KKK are sacrifices to God. In Romans chapter twelve, Apostle Paul "beseeches" his brethren to "present your bodies a living sacrifice, holy, acceptable to God, which is your reasonable service. And do not be conformed to this world..." The parallels between the KKK symbolism in this case and that of the martyrs of al Qaeda in the Twenty-First century are uncanny. Interestingly, however, Romans chapter twelve also contains the commands, "Beloved, do not avenge yourselves, but rather give place to wrath; for it is written, 'Vengeance is Mine, I will repay,' says the Lord," and "Do not be overcome by evil, but overcome evil with good." Exactly how the KKK reconciled these verses with the rest of their activities can only be considered curious at best.

KKK Growth and Recruitment

The Klan's rapid growth as a 1920s is at least partially explained by its financial aspects in that it was essentially an early Twentieth Century version of a multi-level marketing scheme. New members were required to pay a $10 initiation fee, of which $4 went to the Klansman that recruited the new member. The Cyclops (local leader) of the Klavern (local group) joined by the new member received $.50. The Imperial Kleagle, Edward Clarke, received $3 and the remaining $1.50 went to the Imperial Wizard, William J. Simmons. Klansmen also had to purchase the official robes for $6.50, a figure that included a minimum profit of $3.50 for the Klan. Initiation water had to be purchased at $10 per quart from the Imperial Wizard, who drew the water straight from the Chattahoochee River in Georgia. Other Klan profits were made from the robes for the Klansmen's horses, carrying cases for the costumes, pocketknives, and other "official" Klan paraphernalia (Haas, 1963, 55). Given that the Klan estimated its membership before a Congressional investigation in 1921 at 700,000, it is not difficult to determine that Simmons and Clarke reaped tremendous windfalls. A postal inspector testified before Congress that Clarke's department alone received $860,393.50 from June 1920 to September 1921 (Haas, 1963, 55).

This, however, was only the beginning. Publicity in 1921 caused by an undercover investigation of the Klan by the *New York World* and a Congressional investigation that followed the *New York World* piece provided a boost to Klan membership as conservatives who had not known about the organization prior to the publicity rushed to join. The Klan was essentially swamped with 1.2 million applications for membership in the year following the Congressional investigations. In 1922, Simmons boasted that the Klan's membership increased daily by 3500 new members and the Klan's average daily income was $45,000 at a time when GNP per capita was under $1000. The Klan also claimed membership in all 48 states, Alaska, and the Panama Canal Zone (Haas, 1963, 59-63).

KKK Goals and Beliefs

The stated goals of the Klan were to "return America to its Godly heritage and purge America of un-American and un-Godly influences." The Klan also claimed that it existed "to enforce law at a time of lawlessness." Hence, the Klan's appeal had as much to do with conservative reactions to the "immorality" of the roaring twenties, with excesses of alcohol, uptempo dancing, shorter skirts, and shorter hair for women, along with perceived greater sexual promiscuity (Alexander, 1965, 23). Similar to other conservative extremist groups, the KKK integrated elements of conspiracy theory into their teachings. In the words of Emerson Loucks (1936, 38),

"The belief in the minds of the nativists that there was a serious plot against American ideals and institutions, the success of which only immediate organization and united action could prevent, was as important for the growth of the Ku Klux Klan as the belief in the Devil and his angels was for the growth of the medieval Christian Church. It was the sine qua non of its existence."

For example, D.C. Stephenson, a prominent northern Klan leader argued that WWI was the result of a conspiracy by Jewish bankers and part of a systematic plan designed to limit Christianity. Other Klan arguments included the contention that Jews had organized the Bolshevik Revolution in Russia and were the driving force behind international communism. The KKK also espoused conspiracy theories concerning the death of Warren G. Harding and the assassinations of Presidents Garfield and McKinley, essentially arguing that Harding's death was actually a Catholic assassination plot, as were the assassinations of Lincoln, Garfield, and McKinley. In *Searchlight*, the national publication of the Klan, it was proposed that a secret Catholic army of a million Knights of Columbus were secretly arming themselves for a takeover of the country (Lipset and Raab, 1970, 138-139).

Another consistent Klan theme that conforms to the conservative extremist pattern was anti-intellectualism. In particular, College professors were accused of encouraging communism. In the words of one Klan leader (Quoted in Loucks, 1936, 36),

> "In a nation toleration becomes a vice when fundamentals are in danger...The American liberals...have extended their liberality til they are willing to help the aliens tear at the foundations of the nation. They have become one of the chief menaces of the country, instead of the sane intellectual leaders they should be...They give an almost joyous welcome to alien criticism of everything American. The unopposed attack on the Puritan conscience is only one illustration; our liberals today seem ashamed of having any conscience at all. Tolerance is more prized by them than conviction."

This Klan leader's message contains one further theme that is consistent among conservative extremists, and that is that it is they that are being somehow persecuted. In the words of Lipset and Raab (1970, 140),

> "Most successful spokesmen found that the best way to appeal to prospective followers was by casting 'the native white Protestant—not as belonging to the predominant and controlling group...but as the oppressed poor, oppressed sufferer, plundered by foreigners, tricked by Jesuits, and robbed of his birthright by scheming descendants of Abraham.'"

In doing so, the Klan appealed to the sympathy that the American masses tend to have for the "underdog;" hence, the Klan was able to link itself to anti-elitist and egalitarian populist traditions while simultaneously fostering bigotry and hate (Lipset and Raab, 1970, 140).

Selling bigotry and hate is much easier if it is cloaked in morality and patriotism. As a consequence, the KKK advocated specific curriculum for school children that would include the Golden Rule, the Ten

Commandments, opposition to Charles Darwin's theory of evolution, and opposition to the evils of alcohol, as part of their stated goal of fostering "morality" (Mecklin, 1924, 13, 28). The Klan was not the first, nor would they be the last conservative group to cloak their bigotry under the guise of "morality," but in the 1920s, they were perhaps the most successful. It is worthy of not, however, that in these Klan positions, as well as in their persecution syndrome and anti-intellectualism, the Klan's views, goals, and platform of the 1920s are almost indistinguishable from that of the Christian Coalition of the early Twenty-First century, with the exception that the Christian Coalition is much less noteworthy for racial bigotry.

KKK Targets and Strategy

The targets of KKK activities in the 1920s were not exclusively racial, and certainly included blacks, but also included everything and everyone else that conservative extremists at the time viewed as unchristian, un-American, or immoral. The list of targets therefore also included Catholics, Jews, Mexicans, immigration in general, short skirts, abortions, all forms of sexual immorality, adultery, divorce, "demon rum," dance halls, movie theaters, businessmen charged with corrupting young women, husbands who abandoned their wives, divorcees who set "immoral" examples, pimps, prostitutes, gamblers, thieves, bootleggers, and doctors who performed abortions. The KKK also identified paintings and books that they considered to be immoral and argued for their censorship. Among other things, the Klan opposed beauty contests, carnivals, and jazz clubs as activities that led to immorality (Alexander, 1965).

The KKK (along with other Protestant fundamentalist groups) also led the fight for State laws that required the closing of businesses on Sundays. Muncipal Laws were passed against "public flirting," women smoking in public, and the playing of jazz after midnight. Other municipal laws imposed restrictions on the brevity of bathing suits. In Texas, A bill was introduced in the legislature banning women's heels to no more than one inch (Alexander, 1965, 29).

The fact that the KKK and Protestant fundamentalism were intertwined in the 1920s is testified to by the fact that two-thirds of the national Klan lecturers were Protestant ministers (Hull, 1932, 317). The Klan's tirades against evolution and immorality were attractive to fundamentalist Protestant ministers, who regularly filled their sermons with similar messages. One of the Klan's most effective tactics to enlist the support of Protestant ministers was to have its members appear unannounced at Sunday Church services in full regalia. Klansmen would march solemnly and silently down the aisles, hand the minister envelopes full of cash, and then silently march out of the

Church as quickly as they had arrived (Haas, 1963, 75). The tactics were evidently effective. In Knoxville, Tennessee for example, Klan files of membership applications showed that 71.2% were Baptist and 24.4% were Methodist (Jackson, 1967, 26).

The Klan's solicitation of ministers was part of an overall effort to recruit members from the "top" of society down. The strategy was to recruit the leaders of communities, including political and religious leaders, as well as the prominent businessmen of the communities, and then enlist their help in getting others to fall in line. As a result, Klan leadership in any town often mirrored the leadership of the community. The Klan also recruited the police in every town, an obvious advantage for a group that engages in illegal activities. It is estimated that ten percent of the policemen in California, including the police chiefs in Los Angeles and Bakersfield, and the sheriff of Los Angeles County, belonged to the Klan in the 1920s (Jackson, 1967, 118). The rank and file of the Klan, however, were predominantly the blue collar, uneducated, working class (Lipset and Raab, 1970, 127). Hiram Evans, the Grand Wizard in 1926 described the Klan thusly,

> "We are a movement of the plain people, very weak in the matter of culture, intellectual support, and trained leadership. We are demanding, and we expect to win, a return of power into the hands of everyday, not highly cultured, not overly intellectualized, but unspoiled and not de-Americanized, average citizen of the old stock…This is undoubtedly a weakness. It lays us open to the charge of being hicks and rubes and drivers of second hand Fords. We admit it" (Quoted in Randel, 1965, 201-202).

Whether "hicks and rubes" or not, with money and numbers comes political influence, and by the 1920s, the Klan had accumulated its fair share. Retail merchants were told to display a TWK (Trade With Klansmen) sticker in their window or expect to suffer a boycott by the Klan, and Klansmen were instructed to frequent businesses owned by other Klansmen. By economic boycott, the Klan could (and did) bankrupt merchants that opposed it. The Klan became so economically powerful at one point that it purchased its own college, Lanier University in Atlanta, and attempted to purchase Valparaiso University in Indiana as well, for the purpose of providing a place where one could receive a "proper" education (Haas, 1963, 69-70).

The Klan also used its economic might to provide political backing for electoral candidates, and numerous Klansmen were elected to political office throughout the South. In Georgia, U.S. Senator William J. Harris won a bid for re-election after his opponent produced a letter signed by Elizabeth Tyler to Harris in which she addressed him as "Hon. W. J. Harris, A.K.I.A." (A Klansman Am I). Clifford Walker, the governor of Georgia in 1924, admitted that he was a Klansman and addressed the Second Imperial

Klonvokation of the Klan in 1924. In Alabama in 1926, a U.S. Senate seat was won by future U.S. Supreme Court Justice Hugo Black, who had resigned from the Klan just prior to the election. The other Alabama Senator was another Klansman, the rabidly anti-Catholic Tom Heflin. In Texas in 1922, Earle Mayfield, an admitted Klansman, won a U.S. Senate seat (Haas, 1963, 71-72). Two years later, Klan candidate Felix Robertson, who claimed he stood for the "God-given right and supremacy of white Christian men" almost won the governorship of Texas, but on the day of the primary election, a white-sheeted crowd threw rocks at the home of his female gubernatorial opponent (Ma Ferguson). Unfortunately for Robertson, the attack backfired since conservatives in Texas viewed the attack as an unmanly attack on a woman. Robertson garnered more votes than Ferguson in the primary that day, but the KKK rock-throwing incident helped Ferguson gain enough votes to force a runoff and defeat Robertson in November, 1924 by 98,000 votes (Sizer, 2002, 32-33).

Perhaps the apex of Klan political strength was at the 1924 Democratic Convention, where it is estimated that 300 Klan members were present as delegates. The Klan proved that it essentially controlled the Convention when William H. Pattengall of Maine introduced an anti-Klan plank in the Party platform. Chaos ensued following Pattengall's proposal and Madison Square Garden was filled with the hissing and booing of Klansmen along with fist fights, chair tossing, and destruction of Convention decorations. Among the notables that came out opposed to the anti-Klan plank was the old populist warrior from Nebraska, William Jennings Bryan. The anti-Klan plank was defeated along with the Presidential nomination bid of Al Smith of New York, whom the Klan opposed due to his Roman Catholicism and anti-prohibition stance. Smith would win the Democratic nomination four years later only after the Klan had begun to subside (Haas, 1963, 73-74).

In August, 1925, the Klan further demonstrated its political strength when it held a national parade in Washington, D.C. where over 50,000 Klansmen participated in a four-hour march down Pennsylvania Avenue. Although the march was peaceful, the sight of 50,000 robed Klansmen filing past the White House provided an ominous symbol less than a decade before the National Socialists of Adolph Hitler took power in Germany (Haas, 1963, 73-74).

Decline and Failure of the KKK

After 1925, however, the KKK began to decline, with the result that the organization would become a shadow of its former self by World War II. There are numerous reasons why the Klan in the U.S., in spite of its comparatively superior strength in 1925, was unable to take over power completely like their German Nazi counterparts in Europe. The fact that the U.S. was on the winning, rather than losing side in WWI (WWI being the primary precipitant for the right-wing backlash in both the U.S. and Europe) was certainly one reason that the Klan failed in the U.S. while Hitler's Nazis succeeded, but Klan violence also clearly violated the sensibilities of millions of Americans who clamored for their government to act against Klan threats to stability. In response, States began ushering "Anti-Mask" bills through their legislatures that prevented Klan members from wearing their hoods in public, with the result that the "undedicated" members of the KKK quickly abandoned the organization in an overt sense. The Klan was also certainly guilty of over-reach. Put simply, if all of the people and all of the activities that the Klan were supposedly against were combined, (All minorities, immigrants, all non-protestants, consumers of alcohol, anyone who had sex outside of marriage, etc.), it clearly represented the majority of Americans. It should be a fairly safe assumption that persons who were potential Klan targets would be less inclined to support the Klan.

Some of the decline of the Klan, however, is perhaps best explained by the fact that the Klan did experience some successes and achieve some of its goals. In fact, many of the issues which concerned the Klan were essentially taken up by the major Parties and other groups (religious fundamentalists in general, for instance) as part of their platforms. In 1924, for example, the passage of strict immigration restrictions limiting immigration to a total number of 150,000 persons should be considered a Klan victory, but it also in part diffused the anti-immigration elements that were drawn to the Klan (Gould, 2003, 231). Similarly, numerous Southern states passed laws outlawing the teaching of evolution, and prohibition was firmly embedded. In these instances, the Klan's demise falls into the pattern of other interest groups, such as the anti-nuclear protesters of the 1980s, whose demise is at least partially due to their own success. Finally, as the decade of the 1920s came to a close, the passage of time allowed the nation to distance itself from the hyperpatriotism and "100% pure Americanism" that had accompanied WWI. As they had before, however, these patterns of nativism, moralism, and bigotry, would resurface again during the next political crisis.

1920s Religious Fundamentalism

Coterminous with (and intertwined with) the rise of the KKK, and rooted in a similar Traditional Conservative ideological worldview, was the rise of the Protestant fundamentalist influence in politics in the early Twentieth Century. In the minds of many, the publication of Charles Darwin's *Origin of the Species* in 1859 and his theory of evolution called into question the literal creation story contained in the Bible book of Genesis. This combined with growing scholarly historical criticism of the Bible in the late Nineteenth Century to present challenges to the literalist interpretations of the Bible espoused by religious fundamentalists. These "attacks" on fundamentalism then combined with the anti-communism, nativism, and hyperpatriotism of Red Scare era to form the foundation of a Protestant fundamentalist political movement that would continue in ebbs and flows through the rest of the Twentieth Century.

At the turn of the century, most American biology texts supported the concepts of organic evolution and Darwin's theory of natural selection. One botany text in 1912 even went so far as to infer the rejection of the Bible creation story by stating that,

"evolution has been accepted because it appeals to the mind of man as being more reasonable that species should be created according to natural laws rather than by an arbitrary and special creation" (Quoted in Webb, 1994, 63).

The inclusion of these types of statements in textbooks did not create much of a furor prior to WWI at least in part because so many rural Protestant fundamentalists received so little formal education prior to WWI. In the first three decades of the Twentieth Century, however, States required an ever growing number of students to attend public schools, with the result that rural fundamentalists were suddenly exposed in far greater numbers to ideas apparently in contradiction with their literal interpretations of the creation story in Genesis (Webb, 1994, 63-75).

William Jennings Bryan perhaps well-captured the sentiments of the Protestant fundamentalists in 1924 (a year before the Scopes trial) when he argued that,

"a scientific soviet is attempting to dictate what shall be taught in our schools, and, in doing so, is attempting to mold the religion of the nation" (Quoted in Levine, 1965, 279).

Bryan's statement obviously infers a connection between Darwin's scientific theory and Bolshevism. Throughout the remainder of the Twentieth Century, religious fundamentalists would repeatedly charge the scientific community with being influenced by the radical political left. In the minds of the fundamentalists, the science itself had to be false because it conflicted with "God's Word," and the false doctrines must therefore be the work of the Godless political left, who had somehow taken over the scientific community and were using it to further their atheistic "soviet" political agenda. Many religious fundamentalists agreed with William Jennings Bryan, who not only believed that evolution was a false doctrine, in conflict with "God's Word," and therefore evil, but also believed that Christians had a right, if not a duty, to suppress that evil if they were able. Bryan argued that when science and religion come into conflict, the issue should be decided by the will of the "common people" rather than by scientific scholars. Bryan echoed the sentiments of thousands of fundamentalists when he declared that he could not understand "why should the Bible, which the centuries have been unable to shake, be discarded for scientific works that have to be corrected and revised every few years" (Quoted in Hofstadter, 1962, 128). Bryan further declared that,

"all the ills from which America suffers can be traced back to the teaching of evolution. It would be better to destroy every other book ever written, and save just the first three verses of Genesis" (Quoted in Hofstadter, 1962, 125).

Similar to Bryan in his analysis of the evolution question, popular evangelist of the 1920s, Billy Sunday, summed up his attitudes toward the scientific revolution by stating, "When the Word of God says one thing and scholarship says another, scholarship can go to hell" (Quoted in McLoughlin, 1955, 121).

All Americans, however, did not sympathize with William Jennings Bryan and the fundamentalists, and the nation became somewhat divided between the secular and scientific left and the fundamentalist Protestant right. Columnist Walter Lippman perhaps well summed up the rebuttal of the scientific community when he stated that

"the religious doctrine that all men will at last stand equal before the throne of God was somehow transmuted in Bryan's mind into the idea that all men were equally good biologists before the ballot box" (Quoted in Hofstadter, 1962, 128).

In addition to their disdain for science and evolution, Protestant fundamentalists in general, like the KKK, were decidedly patriotic and blended their patriotism with their religion. Billy Sunday epitomized this direction of Protestant fundamentalism in his assertion that "there can be no religion that does not express itself in patriotism." As a consequence, during WWI, Reverend Sunday taught children to hiss at the German flag, advocated incarceration for those who criticized Wilson's War policies, and encouraged men to volunteer for the army (although Sunday himself, who was only 26 at the time of the American entry into the war, did not). Concerning economics, Sunday espoused laissez-faire pro-business capitalism. Sunday denounced the use of government to help alleviate social ills, such as poverty, as "godless social service nonsense" (Quoted in Martin, 1996, 10).

Consistent with the views of other Traditional Conservatives throughout American history, Protestant fundamentalists of the 1920s viewed the "once-moral" America as in decay and adrift from its founding principles and addicted to alcohol and sin. Consequently, the Protestant fundamentalists were staunch proponents of prohibition. When prohibition became enforced on January 16, 1920, Billy Sunday celebrated by holding a mock funeral for John Barleycorn (Martin, 1996, 10-11).

Religious conservatives reacted to what they viewed as an attack on their religious beliefs and American society at large by proposing laws outlawing the teaching of evolution in the public schools. Such bills were introduced into the legislatures in half of the States and enacted a number of States in the South, including Mississippi, Arkansas, Florida, Oklahoma, and Tennessee (Martin, 1996, 14). Several bills banning evolution failed in the Texas legislature, so Texas Governor Ma Ferguson directed the State textbook commission to adopt a policy of selecting textbooks that did not mention evolution (Calvert et al., 2002, 314). In issuing the directive, Ferguson proclaimed, "I am a Christian mother... and I am not going to let that kind of rot go into Texas textbooks" (Quoted in Webb, 1994, 101). The stupidity surrounding these and other laws extolling the Bible as a science book can hardly be overstated. For instance, in Kentucky in 1922, a teacher was brought to trial for teaching that the earth was round. The teacher was fired when his opponents were able to prove in court through the use of Bible scriptures that the earth was indeed flat (Martin, 1996, 14).

Scopes Monkey Trials

The fundamentalists were dealt a major blow in 1925 in the famous "Scopes Monkey Trial" where 25 year-old biology teacher John Scopes defied Tennessee law by teaching evolution. In this celebrated case that received national media attention, the American Civil Liberties Union (ACLU) provided free legal defense for Scopes in the persons of Maynard Shipley and renowned agnostic defense lawyer Clarence Darrow. The old Protestant fundamentalist, William Jennings Bryan, volunteered his services to aid the prosecution.

The national media descended on Dayton, Tennessee and covered the trial in a manner that made the religious fundamentalists appear backward and foolish. Bryan ended up taking the stand as a Bible expert and subsequently embarrassed himself by declaring that the earth was only 5,000 years old, the earth was created in six days, and then revealing some confusion over how "Cain took a wife." Bryan was forced to concede, however, that the earth moved around the sun, which led to his admission that the Bible is filled with metaphors that need not be interpreted literally.

Bryan also conceded that each of the "six days" of creation might actually stand for millions of years (Jacoby, 2004, 248). Scopes was convicted and fined $100, but the fundamentalists were thoroughly embarrassed in the national press and there were no additional anti-evolution laws passed in any states (Furniss, 1963, 90-91).

Nevertheless, the Scopes trial did not result in a complete defeat for the anti-evolutionists. Allyn and Bacon publishing of Boston admitted to the *New York Times* that their books were "tactfully" written so as to prevent disturbing the sensibilities of the religious fundamentalists. Other publishers followed a similar strategy so that the very word "evolution" vanished from most textbooks written after 1925. Generally, the word "development" was inserted into texts anywhere that the word "evolution" might have been used (Jacoby, 2004, 250). In short, publishers made economic decisions not to lose the book sales in the South that might be lost from the inclusion of the word "evolution." In the end, the mighty dollar would accomplish for the fundamentalists what their political efforts in State legislatures could not.

Isolationism

Though they had favored the U.S. entry into WWI, conservatives reacted negatively to Woodrow Wilson's global internationalism after the War and effectively prevented American involvement in the League of Nations and the International Court, both of which they viewed as threats to American sovereignty. Nevertheless, the Republican Secretary of State under Presidents Harding and Coolidge, Charles Evans Hughes, signed, and the Republican Senate confirmed, the Five Power Treaty limiting American naval construction, a limitation that conservatives viewed as a threat to American sovereignty, and the Nine Power Treaty, which called for the Open Door in China, which was hardly isolationist in principal (Jones, 2001, 120-122). Later in the decade, Republican Secretary of State Frank Kellogg signed, and the Republican Senate confirmed, the Kellogg-Briand Pact of 1928, where the U.S. agreed with 63 countries that war would be illegal under international law. The treaty was obviously unenforceable (if not completely nonsensical), but it reflects at least partially the isolationist attitudes that pervaded conservatism throughout the decades of the 1920s and 1930s (Jones, 2001, 128).

Election of 1920

Woodrow Wilson's failing health following a stroke in 1919 prevented him from serving a 3rd term, so in his place, the Democrats nominated Ohio Governor James M. Cox and Assistant Secretary of the Navy Franklin D.

Roosevelt. The Democrats campaigned essentially on a continuation of Wilson's Progressive Idealism. Republicans nominated Ohio Senator Warrren G. Harding and his running mate Calvin Coolidge, the Governor of Massachusetts who had gained fame during the Boston Police strike of 1919 by declaring that there was no right of public employees to strike, "any time, anywhere," and thus capturing the hearts of anti-union conservatives. Harding was nobody's first choice for President, but essentially received the Republican nomination when the Republican Convention became gridlocked between warring factions and Harding seemed an inoffensive "second choice." Harding himself perhaps best summed up the situation when he exclaimed, "we drew a pair of deuces and filled" (Gould, 2003, 222).

In 1920, Harding's nomination made sense to the Republicans because his candidacy seemed to offend no one and he was, in the words of Ohio boss Harry Daugherty, "a handsome devil...and women could vote" (Farquhar, 2003, 204). In other words, Harding received the Republican nomination at least partially because he "looked like a President," rather than because of immense talent. Harding and his successor Calvin Coolidge would essentially be a return to the precedent set by conservatives in the Gilded Age of choosing mediocre Presidents of average talent, but who possessed the correct conservative ideological leanings (Gould, 2003, 222).

Harding's campaign promised what Harding referred to as a "return to normalcy." The "normalcy" campaign resonated with Americans in the upheaval following WWI, complete with economic and labor unrest along with the excesses of the Red Scare. Furthermore, Americans had experienced twenty years of progressivism that had brought prohibition, women's suffrage, and government economic and social regulation. By 1920, perhaps progressivism had merely run its course and Americans were ready to return to conservatism. In the words of progressive journalist William Allen White, Americans in 1920 were "tired of issues, sick at heart of ideals, and weary of being noble" (Quoted in Tindall and Shi, 2000, 919). At any rate, the election of Harding would signal that the progressive era was over.

Harding took a non-controversial approach to the 1920 campaign and straddled the fence on divisive issues so as not to alienate progressives. For example, Harding avoided the issue of segregation and neither attacked nor endorsed the KKK. Harding's non-controversial "normalcy" campaign worked to perfection as he carried every state outside of the South and won by a landslide with 61% of the popular vote (Gould, 2003, 229-230).

Warren G. Harding

Warren Harding as President would be an abrupt change from his predecessor Woodrow Wilson. Unlike Wilson, Harding had few strong convictions, was open to compromise, and could be easily persuaded to change his position on most issues. Harding was also non-confrontational and indecisive by nature, and therefore did not enjoy the Presidency, an office that epitomizes confrontation and decision-making.

Harding is perhaps unique among Presidents in that he possessed an overwhelming awareness of his own incompetence. For example, Harding once stated, "I am not fit for this office and never should have been here." Similarly, to Judge John Barton Payne, Harding once exclaimed, I don't think I'm big enough for the Presidency." In a similar vein, to Calvin Coolidge, Harding once offered, "I am a man of limited talents from a small town....I don't seem to grasp that I am President" (Quoted in Farquhar, 2003, 204). Harding was generally ignorant of policy issues and realized the situation as such. For instance, he once stated his frustration on a tax issue by proclaiming, "I don't know what to do or where to turn on this taxation matter" (Quoted in Farquhar, 2003, 204). Although generally ignorant in most policy areas, Harding was particularly ignorant on foreign affairs. When asked once by a reporter about European affairs at the time, Harding replied: "I don't know anything about this European Stuff" (Jones, 2001, 113).

Harding's doubts about his own abilities were widely shared by intellectuals and astute politicians. Harding frequently butchered the English language in his speech and made frequent mis-statements. Republican Senator Bose Penrose of Philadelphia perhaps best summed up the Republican Party's position on Harding when argued that the Republicans should,

"Keep Warren at home. Don't let him make any speeches. If he goes out on a tour, somebody's sure to ask him questions, and Warren's just the sort of damn fool to try to answer them" (Jones, 2001, 113).

Due to these shortcomings, Harding did not enjoy being President. In the words of Harding, "The White House is a Prison and I cannot get away from the men who dog my footsteps" (Quoted in Farquhar, 2003, 203). As a consequence, Harding focused on the positive input from the public in the way of letters he received from his adoring fans and spent much of his time writing letters to citizens and greeting ordinary people at the White House. When one White House aide questioned the amount of time Harding spent in his letter-writing and small-talking with the public, Harding responded with,

> "I love to meet people. It's the most pleasant thing I do; it is really the only fun I have. It does not tax me, and it seems to be a very great pleasure to them" (Quoted in Farquhar, 2003, 204).

In his preference for ceremony and glad-handling over policy, Harding was a foreshadowing of the conservative champion of the 1980s, Ronald Reagan.

Harding's Policies

In terms of economic policy, Harding was essentially a standard laissez-faire and pro-business conservative. In the words of Harding, "What we need is less government in business and more business in Government" (Quoted in Farquhar, 2003, 204). In 1921, Harding exhibited his conservative pro-business and anti-labor stripes when he called in the National Guard to put down a United Mine Workers' Strike in West Virginia and Pennsylvania. As a result of the federal government's tilt back toward management, Union membership dropped from 5 million in 1921 to 3 million in 1929 (Gould, 2003, 229).

Harding proved to be a "compassionate conservative," however, in that he pardoned radical dissidents imprisoned during the Wilson years, including Eugene V. Debs, the Socialist Party leader imprisoned for his anti-war stance against WWI. Harding also denounced lynching in a message to Congress in 1921, but did not follow up with initiative for an anti-lynching bill (Gould, 2003, 229). In most cases, however, Harding personally was able to provide little in the way of policy direction, with the result that leadership flowed to Congress and Harding's Executive appointees.

Harding concentrated on appointing what he believed were capable aides and cabinet members and delegating most of his authority. Harding rewarded Party leaders who had helped him gain the nomination with important positions, however, and Harding's trust in what eventually came to be known as the "Ohio Gang" turned out to be partially misguided as Harding's appointees plundered the government for personal gain. Harry Daugherty, an Ohio Republican Party leader, was appointed Attorney General. Albert B.

Fall, another leading Ohio Republican, was made Secretary of the Interior. Both would become involved in embarrassing scandals prior to the time of Harding's death in 1923.

Among Harding's most important appointees was Treasury Secretary Andrew Mellon, whose economic policies became those that guided the nation. Mellon moved quickly to push for lower taxes for the wealthy, arguing that such tax relief would allow the rich to invest and therefore create jobs for ordinary people (essentially the same argument as Ronald Reagan's "trickle-down economics of the 1980s). Mellon opposed, however, tax breaks for persons making under $66,000, apparently not understanding that economic expansion requires the expansion of consumption. In this, Mellon's tax cuts would suffer the same criticism as those of future Republican President George W. Bush, whose tax cuts in the first decade of the Twenty-First Century would be criticized for disproportionately benefiting the upper classes. At Mellon's urging, Congress reduced the highest income tax rates from 73% to 40% by 1924. Congress offset the tax cuts by keeping tariffs high, and therefore unlike the free-trading administrations of Reagan and George W. Bush several decades into the future, Mellon's tax cuts did not lead to deficits (Garraty, 1991, 744-745).

Harding and the Ohio Gang

While Harding enjoyed the public support from Protestant fundamentalists and the KKK, a few blocks from the White House at the "House on K Street," Harding and the "Ohio Gang" drank mass quantities of bootleg liquor during Prohibition while they gambled, entertained women, sold government favors, and bribed Congressmen. Alice Roosevelt (Theodore's daughter) once came into the White House study and found the air "heavy with tobacco smoke, its tables cluttered with bottles containing every imaginable brand of whiskey and cards and poker chips at hand" (Quoted in Murrin et al., 1996, 770). The Ohio Gang plundered the government, private business and taxpayers in almost every way imaginable. Jesse Smith, a top aide to Daugherty in the Attorney General's office, used his office to sell pardons, government contracts, and government access. Smith was accused of influence peddling and committed suicide in 1923 (Gould, 2003, 229). After the incident, Harding is reported to have stated,

> "My God, this is a hell of a job. I have no trouble with my enemies. I can take care of my enemies all right. But my damn friends, my God-damn friends, they're the ones that keep me walking the floor nights" (Quoted in Farquhar, 2003, 203).

Similarly, Charles R. Forbes, head of the Veterans Bureau, pocketed millions of dollars appropriated for construction of Veterans hospitals. Forbes fled to Europe, later returned, and was sentenced to two years in prison. Forbes' assistant, Charles F. Cramer, committed suicide. Thomas W. Miller, the Alien Property Custodian, who was in charge of seized German assets from World War I, was sentenced to prison for accepting bribes in exchange for the release of assets to their original owners. Attorney General Harry Daugherty was implicated in the scandals, but took the 5th Amendment on the stand and was not convicted (Murrin et al., 1996, 770).

The most celebrated of the Scandals during the Harding Administration, however, was the Teapot Dome Scandal involving Secretary of the Interior Albert Fall. Fall arranged with Navy Secretary Edwin Denby for the transfer to the Department of the Interior of Navy oil reserves in Elk Hills, California, and Teapot Dome, Wyoming. Fall then leased the reserves to Edward L. Doheny's Pan-American Petroleum and Harry F. Sinclair's Mammoth Oil Company. Doheny "loaned" Fall $100,000.00 in cash (handed over in a "little black bag") while Sinclair gave Fall $300,000 in cash and securities. Sinclair was given 9 months in jail for tampering with a jury, but acquitted of defrauding the U. S. Government. Fall was fined $100,000 and given one year in prison for accepting a bribe, while Doheny went unpunished. President Harding evidently knew nothing of the scandal and it did not become public until after his death; hence, the scandal did not harm Harding's reputation during his lifetime (Noggle, 1962, 71-95).

Also in 1927 (some four years after Harding's death) it became publicly known that Harding had had an extramarital affair with Nan Britton, a young woman thirty years his younger, who began seeing Harding in 1917 after she wrote him from her home in Harding's hometown of Marion, Ohio and asked him for a job. Harding was able to secure employment for Britton in a clerical position at U.S. Steel in Washington and they then commenced with their affair, which continued until Harding's death. Britton gave birth to Harding's daughter, Elizabeth Ann, in 1919 and Harding made child support payments to Britton from the White House that were hand-delivered by the Secret Service. After his death, Britton sued Harding's estate to gain a trust fund for her daughter. Britton then wrote a book entitled *The President's Daughter* which she dedicated to "all unwed mothers and to their innocent children whose fathers are usually not known to the world." Britton recounted details of the affair in the book, including trysts with Harding in the Oval Office and a closet of the White House (Adams, 1970, 165).

Harding also had a fifteen year relationship with Carrie Phillips, the wife of his longtime friend, James Phillips. The affair began in Marion, Ohio in 1905 and continued until Harding was running for President of the United States. This is in spite of the fact that in 1917 Phillips, a German sympathizer who had lived in Berlin, tried to blackmail then Senator Harding into voting against a Declaration of War on Germany. In 1920, the Republican National Committee removed Ms. Phillips from the picture so as to avoid any possible embarrassment of their Presidential candidate, by paying Mr. and Mrs. Phillips $20,000 in cash and providing them with a free, slow, trip to Japan, along with monthly hush money (Adams, 1970, 173).

Calvin Coolidge

Harding was never seriously damaged by the sexual affairs and scandals, since he died of a heart attack on August 2, 1923, while in San Francisco on a speaking tour. Harding's successor, Calvin Coolidge, was a standard conservative clone of Harding in regard to economic and social policy, but a great contrast on a personal level. Coolidge's conservative laissez-faire ideology was perhaps best summed up by Coolidge himself when he stated, "The Chief Business of the American People is Business The man who builds a factory, builds a temple. The man who works there, worships there" (Quoted in Nash et al., 2004, 805).

On the personal level, however, Coolidge differed greatly with Harding in that he was quiet, detached, sober, endowed with a puritan moral ethic, and honest beyond reproach. In these things, unlike Harding, Coolidge was at least consistent with the ideals of his conservative Protestant fundamentalist supporters. Coolidge's ethical standards proved to be much more than window dressing; consequently, he quickly forced the resignation of Attorney General Daugherty and others tainted by scandal during the Harding administration (Gould, 2003, 240).

Coolidge would be less quick to action in other areas, however, since his stated goal was "to become the least President that the country ever had." Coolidge's statement is a reference to his Hobbesian conservative laissez-faire philosophy of government, but he may have achieved his goal in more ways than one. Coolidge was non-energetic, both in policy and in his personal life, and generally chose to confront crises by taking long naps in the White House. Those around Coolidge described his disposition as "eternally tired." Coolidge's "Silent Cal" nickname was earned by keeping appointments and meetings to a minimum, and engaging in as little conversation as possible (McCoy, 1990, 1-10). Coolidge himself acknowledged his own preference for "silence" and once remarked to reporters that "I don't recall any candidate for President that ever injured himself very much by not talking" (Quoted in Gould, 2003, 241). Comedian and political commentator Will Rogers perhaps summed it up best when he observed of Coolidge, "Silent Cal. He don't say much, but when he does say something, he don't say much" (Quoted in Sterling, 1997, 5).

When Coolidge did choose to speak, he sometimes revealed that he was actually better off remaining silent. A good example of this is Coolidge's assessment of the economy in 1928 prior to the onset of the Depression when he stated, "The future may be better or worse....I am certain of one thing, however, when people are thrown out of work, unemployment results." On another occasion, Coolidge astutely observed that "The final solution for unemployment is work" (Quoted in Ferrell, 1998, 201).

Election of 1924

In spite of his poor communications skills, Coolidge won re-election in 1924 with 54% of the popular vote over divided opposition. Wisconsin Senator Robert LaFollette did the conservatives a favor by running on the Progressive Party ticket and thus dividing the votes on the left between Democrats and Progressives. LaFollette won his home state of Wisconsin and 16% of the popular vote, which most likely would have been enough to swing the election to the Republicans even if the Democrats had produced a strong candidate. The Republicans were able to successfully paint La Follette as a "dangerous radical" and characterized the decision as "Coolidge or Chaos" (Gould, 2003, 241). In a reversal of the general trend of the late Twentieth and early Twenty-First Centuries, Hollywood movies stars provided support for the conservative Republican Party (Gould, 2003, 241). Meanwhile, Democratic Candidate John Davis did not prove to be a serious challenger to Coolidge and won only 30% of the popular vote. Comedian Will Rogers summed up the disarray of the left with his assertion that "I am not a member of any organized political party, I'm a Democrat" (Quoted in Sterling, 1997, 5).

Coolidge Policies

Coolidge's policies, like those of Harding, were mostly the work of his appointees, among the most important of which was Treasury Secretary Andrew Mellon. Under Mellon's urging, Congress continued the conservatives' anti-tax crusade and lowered both individual and corporate taxes. As a result, taxes for both individuals and corporations were cut over 50%, and persons making less than $3,500.00 paid no tax at all (Nash et al., 2004, 805). Simultaneously, Mellon and Coolidge successfully cut the Federal Budget and accomplished their tax cuts without running huge federal deficits (Ferrell, 1998, 218-220).

A second Coolidge appointee that became prominent was Commerce Secretary Herbert Hoover. Hoover, in contrast to Coolidge and Mellon, favored an active role for government in both the economy and in social areas. Hoover's goals included using government to remedy poverty, a violation of standard conservative social Darwinist ideology. Coolidge, however, exhibited the stereotypical conservative aversion to government income redistribution programs. For instance, the 1920's brought falling prices and economic hardship to American farmers. The development of the farm tractor increased American production at the same time that European demand for farm products dropped due to the end of World War I. Farmers organized and pushed for government farm subsidies and Congress passed the McNary-Haugen Farm Relief bill that provided for government payments to farmers for products at a set price and government marketing of the products at the local market price on the world market. Coolidge displayed his conservative laissez-faire ideological leanings when he vetoed the Act as outside the proper scope of government. Undaunted, Congress passed the Act passed again in 1928, only to have Coolidge dutifully veto it again (Ferrell, 1998, 202-203).

Coolidge also exhibited his conservatism on the subject of the war debts from World War I. European nations owed the U.S. over $10 billion in 1925, with France and England accounting for 75% of the unpaid balance. France and England pushed the U.S. to forgive the debts, arguing that they had paid with their lives, given that fifty percent of the men between 20 and 32 years of age died in France during WWI. Coolidge refused, however, reportedly exclaiming, "They hired the money didn't they" (Quoted in Nash et al., 2004). Further exacerbating the problem, Coolidge's high tariff policies made repayment of the debt more difficult for European countries since they depressed European exports to the U.S. and therefore hindered a major source of capital for European countries (Nash et al., 2004, 805).

Herbert Hoover

On August 2, 1927, Coolidge announced simply, "I do not choose to run for President in 1928." With this announcement, the energetic Herbert Hoover became the obvious Republican choice for President. Hoover won the Republican nomination at the Republican National Convention on the first ballot despite a stinging rebuke from Coolidge, who labeled the more progressive Hoover as a "spendthrift," with "bad ideas." Coolidge further exclaimed that, "That man has offered me unsolicited advice for six years, all of it bad" (Quoted in Nash et al., 1998, 809).

Hoover was supported both by big business and by conservative moralists, who favored his "dry" position on Prohibition. Democratic nominee Al Smith of New York was a "wet" and an Irish Catholic who therefore had little support outside the South. The campaign contained anti-Catholic mud-slinging by conservatives against Smith as State and local

Republican Party organizations distributed anti-Catholic literature condemning Smith. Hoover appealed to white Democrats in the South, not only by championing prohibition, but by eliminating language from the Republican platform that favored enforcement of the Fourteenth and Fifteenth Amendments. Republicans also alleged that Smith encouraged inter-racial marriage, and circulated photographs of mixed couples in New York so as to drive home their point (Gould, 2003, 252). Hoover won five Southern States and Smith won only one State outside the South, Irish Catholic Massachusetts, even losing his home State of New York. Hoover won the electoral vote by a 444 to 87 landslide (Gould, 2003, 253). Unfortunately for Hoover and the Republicans, they would have only a few months to implement Hoover's activist version of conservatism before the stock market crash sent the nation and the world into the Great Depression and destroyed both Hoover's Presidency as well as the era of Republican dominance.

Chapter Ten

Conservatism in the New Deal Era

The stock market crash of 1929 and the Great Depression that followed ushered in a new age in American politics that effectively ended the era of conservative dominance and the accompanying laissez-faire approach to politics and the economy. The failure of the Republican administration under Herbert Hoover to effectively deal with the Depression elevated Democrat Franklin Delano Roosevelt (FDR) to the Presidency and initiated an era of Democratic dominance in Congress that would not completely crumble until the Newt Gingrich Revolution of 1994, some sixty years later.

Conservative policymakers in the Hoover administration at first attempted to remedy the Great Depression through optimism and laissez-faire Classic Liberal free market principles. Treasury Secretary Andrew Mellon in particular echoed this optimism. Mellon favored a conservative approach and argued for allowing the free market to correct itself. In the words of Mellon in November, 1929,

> "I see nothing in the present situation that is either menacing or warranting pessimism. All evidence indicates that the worst effects of the crash on unemployment will have passed within the next 60 days" (Quoted in Garraty and McCaughey, 1987, 756).

Mellon believed that the economy should be allowed to slide unchecked until it hit bottom in what he viewed as a normal business cycle occurrence. In the words of Mellon,

> "let the slump liquidate itself, liquidate labor, liquidate stocks, liquidate farmers. People will work harder, live a more moral life, values will be adjusted, and enterprising people will pick up the wrecks from less competent people" (Quoted in Garraty and McCaughey, 1987, 756).

Republican President Herbert Hoover initially concurred with Mellon's optimism and laissez faire approach due to his own ideological belief in the free market and a patriotic confidence in America itself. Hoover regarded individualism as the most important element in the development of American economic and social life and tenaciously believed in the power of voluntarism. In general, Hoover was ideologically opposed to federal involvement in welfare programs out of the belief that they would erode individual and community responsibility and encourage a "dole mentality" (Burner, 1979, 141). As late as April, 1931, Hoover argued in his memoirs that the country was recovering from a "normal recession due to domestic causes" (Quoted in Burner, 1979, 146). Hoover's ideological leanings are reflected in his statement of November 15, 1929, (after two devastating months of stock market crash) when Hoover argued that "any lack of confidence in the economic future or basic strength of business in the United States is foolish" (Quoted in O'Sullivan and Keuchel, 1989, 170). As a consequence, Hoover's initial response to the Depression was to call on businesses to voluntarily maintain prices and wages and wait for the free market to correct itself. Unfortunately, the magnitude of the economic crisis quickly made such voluntary efforts untenable and Hoover was soon forced to abandon the conservative principles of laissez faire and Classic Liberalism in favor of government economic intervention.

Hoover's Active Conservatism

First, Hoover moved to attempt to jump-start the economy with a tax cut, but the volume of dollars returned to consumers for consumption through a tax cut was insufficient to remedy the cash shortage in the economy (Gordon, 1974, 188). In June 1930, Hoover attempted to attack the Depression from another traditionally conservative direction and reverted to the Nineteenth Century Republican Party posture of economic prosperity through tariffs. Despite a petition signed by a thousand economists warning Hoover against increasing tariffs, Hoover signed the Smoot-Hawley bill increasing tariffs on imports to the U.S. The tariff, of course, led to retaliatory tariffs by European nations and contributed to a precipitous decline in international trade. The Smoot-Hawley tariff would later become notorious among most free market economists as a factor that contributed further to the economic malaise by depressing trade and therefore hindering international debt repayment (Friedman and Schwarz, 1965, 133).

Hoover also adhered to the Nineteenth Century conservative monetary position of remaining on the gold standard, thus putting the United States at a trade disadvantage with the Europeans, who abandoned the gold standard in late 1931. When the Bank of England defaulted on gold payments in September, 1931, the American Federal Reserve Board responded by raising interest rates in an effort to prevent a drain on American gold reserves. The raising of interest rates in turn further hindered the American economy by discouraging borrowing and thus further reducing the money supply (Friedman and Schwarz, 1965). Hoover exacerbated the capital shortage even more by stressing the traditional conservative belief in the importance of a balanced federal budget, his reasoning being that since citizens had to live within their means, the government should lead through the example of fiscal responsibility (Burner, 1979, 162). Hoover also vetoed the Bonus Act of 1931 that was slated to give almost $1 billion to veterans, but Congress passed the measure over his veto. In Hoover's conception, economic crisis was not reason enough to abandon the conservative economic principle of the balanced budget and fiscal responsibility (Nagle, 1988, 190).

Hoover did not, however, strictly adhere to all conservative economic budgetary principles. By June 1931, Hoover's Federal budget was $500 million in the red since the economic decline had also produced declining federal revenue. Hoover also supported increased public works programs, favored federal loans to banks, businesses, farmers, and homeowners, and called for expansion of State and local relief programs (hardly Conservative positions), though he continued to oppose federal involvement in direct relief. Hoover also created the Federal Farm Board (created under the Agricultural Marketing Act of 1929) to establish semipublic stabilizing corporations with the authority to purchase excess farm products and thus prop up prices. Such a program was hardly inconsistent with the principles of the Agricultural Adjustment Act of 1933, a major part of Franklin Roosevelt's New Deal, championed by the liberal Democrats and opposed by conservative Republicans after Hoover was voted out of office. The Federal Farm Board efforts, however, failed to stop the collapse of agricultural prices because farmers continued to overproduce (Friedman and Schwarz, 1965, 191).

Hoover justified Federal loan programs on the premise that such loans eventually would be repaid; hence, to Hoover, loans were not the same thing as the government dole. Direct grants or relief, however, were anathema to Hoover (Burner, 1979, 167). By 1932, Hoover's federal government was spending was a very "New Dealish" $500 million per year on public works, but because of the coincident decline in State and local spending on public works, total public outlays on public works in 1932 were almost $1 billion below the levels of 1929. Hoover also refused to allow the Federal government to become involved in local relief efforts due to his individualist ideology and his belief that welfare was a State, rather than Federal, responsibility under the U.S. Constitution (Burner, 1979, 169). Hoover's refusal to initiate direct federal relief programs was viewed by many Americans as evidence that Hoover neither understood nor cared about the plight of the common person. Furthermore, Hoover's offhand remarks that "no one is actually starving" and that "the Hoboes are better fed now than they've ever been" were proof enough to many that Hoover lacked compassion; consequently, many Americans came to identify the calamities of the Great Depression personally with Hoover. Makeshift shantytowns outside of cities became known as "Hoovervilles" and an empty pocket turned inside out became known as a "Hoover Flag" (Nash et al., 2004, 818).

The incident that most discredited Hoover, however, was his decision to order the U.S. army under Generals Douglas MacArthur and George Patton to remove 20,000 WWI veterans from Washington who had marched to the capitol to petition the government for early payment of a bonus that was due veterans in 1945 (O'Sullivan and Keuchel, 1989, 171). Hoover and MacArthur had viewed what was known as the "Bonus March" as part of a communist conspiracy (in spite of Army intelligence reports to the contrary) and thus viewed the military expulsion of the unemployed veterans as a necessary measure to prevent communist revolution in the United States (MacArthur, 1964, 97).

In the final analysis, historians John Garraty and Robert McCaughey (1987, 758) argue that Hoover's policies to combat the Depression failed due to the limitations of his conservative ideology. In the words of Garraty and McCaughey,

> "Hoover was too rigidly wedded to a particular theory of government to cope effectively with the problems of the day…flexibility and a willingness to experiment were essential to any program aimed at restoring prosperity. Hoover lacked these qualities."

In other words, Hoover's adherence to conservative (Classic Liberal) ideological, rather than practical, approaches to the problems posed by the Great Depression contributed to his own downfall, and with it, the demise of the Republican Party and Conservatism as the ruling force in the United States.

The Interruption of Conservative Dominance

Given the State of the economy in 1932, it is likely that American voters, who rarely could be accused of being given to too much complex analysis, were poised to unseat the ruling party regardless of the policies pursued, thus obviously placing the Democrats in an enviable political position. The Democrats perhaps helped their own fortunes even more when they nominated for President the progressive New York Governor, Franklin Delano Roosevelt (FDR). Roosevelt did not have a concrete plan for ending the Depression, but argued for a "re-appraisal of values," and a "new deal." In the words of Roosevelt,

> "The country needs bold, persistent experimentation. It is common sense to take a method and try it. If it fails, admit it frankly and try another. But above all, try something" (Quoted in Garraty and McCaughey, 1987, 762).

Instead of adhering to Hoover's conservative ideological limits on federal power, Roosevelt took a more practical approach and argued that the federal government should do whatever was necessary to protect the unfortunate, and to advance the public good (Garraty and McCaughey, 1987, 762). Roosevelt's "try something" approach obviously was not well defined, but it was also not subject to the same ideological constraints as Hoover's conservatism; hence, Roosevelt's ill-defined "try-something" approach at least offered greater flexibility. For the American voters who had suffered through over three years of economic Depression, "try something" was an easy winner over the continuation of Hoover's failed policies. Franklin Roosevelt's margin of victory, 22.8 million votes to 15.8 million, signaled the end of the "Republican system" of 1896.

With the election of 1932, the Democratic Party was no longer merely a sectional party with some urban strongholds, but it became a national party that dominated the cities, blacks, recent immigrants, labor unions and blue collar workers, as well as the South. Armed with national popular support, Franklin Roosevelt and the Democrats began a propaganda campaign against laissez faire and what Roosevelt termed as "economic royalists." Using populist-style rhetoric, Roosevelt argued that a small group of Americans had concentrated wealth into their own few hands, thus leading to the collapse of 1929. Against such tyranny, Roosevelt argued that American citizens could appeal only to the organized power of government (Rosenman, 1938, 232).

Conservative Objections to the New Deal

Conservatives objected to what they viewed as Roosevelt's assault on the "Republican system," the "American way," and capitalism, and accused Roosevelt of initiating "class warfare." For certain, the electorate became more divided along class lines and remained that way in the decades after Roosevelt's death. In 1948, for example, when Harry Truman ran for reelection based on a continuation of the New Deal, it is estimated that he won almost 80% of the blue collar vote, while the white collar vote went overwhelmingly Republican (Campbell et al., 1960, 189).

To the Conservatives, not only was Roosevelt engaging in Bolshevik-style class war, but his policies were viewed as socialistic, anti-capitalist, and sometimes even fascist by conservatives. Federal relief and public works programs were obviously socialistic in character, but some Republicans saw something equally sinister in Roosevelt's National Recovery Administration (NRA) that worked with business groups and trade associations to establish "Codes of Fair Business Practices" that controlled prices and production in their industries. Not only did this violate free market competitive principles, but in effect, the government had sponsored cartels, resembling the Fascism of Mussolini's Italy or Hitler's Germany. To make matters worse, Roosevelt introduced reforms into banking and the stock market, removed the nation from the gold standard, and thus altered the monetary system in ways that appeared to Conservatives to be violations of all traditional, sound, tried and true, free market economic principles. Adding insult to injury, in the "Second New Deal" beginning in 1935, Roosevelt confirmed the worst fears of conservatives with the introduction of Social Security, collective bargaining, and progressive tax reforms.

To more extreme conservatives, the New Deal was not just bad policy, but part of a global plot by international socialist and communist forces to destroy America. In the words of Conservative critic of the Roosevelt administration John T. Flynn (1955, 93),

> "What had gone before was a confused hodgepodge of measures—some socialist, some fascist, most of them mere devices for keeping people on the dole…The crackpot schemes had failed; most were liquidated. And recovery remained aloof. The socialist cabal, now well schooled in the stratagems of a socialist Europe—in Germany, France, Italy and England—saw its opportunity here. They now appeared in Washington to confront a triumphant but frustrated and planless President with a workable plan. This was the hour of fate for America. We can see now and understand clearly the overall program of the socialist revolutionaries to make a socialist America—without making any lawful change in our great charter of freedom, the Constitution of the United States."

Flynn's apocalyptic language and "plot mentality" were extreme, but they were undoubtedly sentiments shared in varying degrees by the conservative mainstream. Those sentiments, however, were muted somewhat during the 1930s due to the fact that the New Deal was simply too popular for most conservative politicians to publicly oppose. Republican leaders with state-wide constituencies, such as Governors and U.S. Senators, normally had to take a more moderate approach toward the New Deal so as to ensure their own popular support. Urban Eastern Republicans, with much larger constituencies of urban blue-collar workers than their Southern and Western colleagues, were generally willing to concede some of the social reforms of the New Deal in an attempt to appeal to the working class urban voters.

Roosevelt further divided and conquered the Republicans by making overtures to the more progressive wing of the Republican Party that generally accepted the New Deal. Roosevelt even appointed Progressive Republicans Henry Wallace and Harold Ickes to his Cabinet as Secretary of Agriculture and Secretary of the Interior. (Gould, 2003, 267-268).

Conservatives as Opposition

Conservative Congressmen from rural areas that did not have to attract a broader vote held hard and fast to traditional conservative laissez-faire Republican Party principles. Representatives Harold Knutson of Minnesota, Leo Allen of Illinois, and Bartel Jonkman and Clare Hoffman of Michigan led the rhetorical attack on the New Deal in Congress with the support of Republican leaders Joseph Martin of Massachusetts and Charles Hallek of Indiana (Mayer, 1967, 469-470). Former President Herbert Hoover joined with the anti-New Deal rural Republicans to select Henry P. Fletcher, a staunch opponent of the New Deal, as the Republican National Committee chairman in 1934. The RNC then launched a Party propaganda campaign against the New Deal only to find that the New Deal-minded public gave the Democrats nineteen seats in the House and ten in the Senate in the off-year elections of 1934, thus paving the way for a more moderate Republican strategy in 1936 (Mayer, 1973, 2268).

Conservatives in opposition to the New Deal also had the support of major segments of the American media. William Randolph Hearst, who controlled twenty-eight newspapers, thirteen magazines, and eight radio stations, concentrated his media empire against Roosevelt and the New Deal in 1936 after supporting Roosevelt in 1932. Similarly, Robert R. McCormick, who published the *Chicago Tribune, New York Daily News*, and *Washington Herald,* openly opposed Roosevelt and the New Deal. Together, the Hearst and McCormick media empires controlled 36% of the Sunday Newspaper circulation in the U.S. McCormick's *Chicago Tribune* also helped to organize the Mutual Broadcasting System radio network which employed conservative radio commentator Fulton Lewis Jr. Lewis was essentially the "Limbaugh" of the 1930s, with the largest political radio audience in the country at over 16 million listeners (Emery, 1999, 461).

Wealthy Conservative industrialists also worked outside the parties and media through interest groups to push their agenda. Among the most important of these conservative political interest groups was the American Liberty League, founded in 1934 by some of the elite families of the American corporate establishment. Members of the League included prominent members of the DuPont family, J. Howard Pew of Sun Oil, Alfred P. Sloan and John Jacob Raskob of General Motors, and Ernest T. Weir of National Steel. The League mounted an anti-New Deal propaganda campaign that attacked Roosevelt's programs as violations of the Constitution, individual liberties, and free market capitalism. The league complimented these arguments with comparisons between Roosevelt and the authoritarian dictators of the 1930s, Hitler, Mussolini, and Stalin (Wolfskill, 1974, 116).

Literary Opposition to the New Deal

Academically, there were several notable challenges to the New Deal, including the writings of Albert Jay Nock, who in *Our Enemy the State* (1935, 22), protested the centralized planning strategies of the Roosevelt administration in particular and statism in general. According to Nock (1936, 47), there is a difference between government and "the state." In Nock's conception, government provides for defense against foreign enemies and maintains justice domestically, but "the state," in contrast, is exploitive, born out of conquest and confiscation, and exists only to further the economic interests of one class over another. Nock argued that the New Deal was proof of the dangers of the state and also proved that the state is by nature anti-social. Nock further argued that the American Constitution itself violated the Declaration of Independence by creating governmental structures that aided and abetted state power, which reached new heights of oppressiveness under the New Deal.

Concurring with Nock, journalist Walter Lippman, who had earlier embraced socialism and progressivism, argued against the dangers of increasing federal government power in *The Good Society* (1937). Lippman argued that it was illusionary to believe that a planned economy in times of peace could be achieved without creating an oppressive state and despotism. Similarly, American author, architect, and devout Roman Catholic, Ralph Adams Cram (1937) in *The End of Democracy* argued that the income redistribution plans of the New Deal could only lead to despotism. In the words of Cram (1937, 69),

> "The first law in the Book of Man is inequality. Individuals vary in intelligence, character, capacity for doing one thing or another, and well or ill, far more than they do in their physical characteristics...Any society that does not recognize this and attempts to liquidate this disparity can last but a short time and is boud to quick dissolution after a sad and unsavoury record...Where status is eliminated, caste takes its place and democracy is no longer attainable."

Similar to Nock, Lippman, and Cram, but posing the most important academic challenge to the New Deal in terms of its long term impact, was the work of Austrian economist Friedrich A. Hayek (1944) in *Road to Serfdom*. Hayek argued that central planning of the economy leads directly, albeit not inevitably, to totalitarianism. According to Hayek, once the state controls a certain portion of the nation's economic resources, its effects on the remaining portion balloon so that in an indirect manner its control is nearly total. At that point, argued Hayek, it is simple to discern the ruinous consequences for individual freedom and Democracy. Hayek further argued that the economy is a host of individuals making choices in markets of uncertainty and the multiplicity and complexity of their actions are too much for any centralized government bureaucracy to have sufficient knowledge in order to regulated it properly. Hayek would be a founding member of the so-called "Chicago School" of free market economics that would remain influential into the Twenty-First Century.

Father Coughlin

Father Charles E. Coughlin, a Catholic clergyman from Michigan, had been broadcasting on the radio since 1926 with a format that focused on religious matters. Beginning in 1930, however, Coughlin began broadcasting his views on politics, which were decidedly fascist in character. Coughlin's message was an odd mix that denounced communism, exploitation by big business, and unregulated capitalism. Coughlin also strongly opposed the League of Nations and supported the fascist regime in Italy under Benito Mussolini, in addition to supporting the policies of Adolph Hitler in Germany, and denouncing Winston Churchill in Great Britain (Tull, 1965, 52-64).

Coughlin supported the New Deal at first, and then turned against it with a vengeance, viewing it as part of an international communist conspiracy. Coughlin contended that Adam Weishaupt, the founder of the Illuminati, was the inspirer of Karl Marx, essentially tying the global communist threat to an Illuminati conspiracy. Also in cahoots with the communists were international bankers, Jews, and Masons, but especially Jewish Masons. Coughlin was decidedly anti-Semitic and generally denounced those with whom he disagreed politically as Jews. Coughlin even went so far as to argue that Alexander Hamilton, who favored national government economic intervention, was actually Jewish and his original name was Alexander Levine (Tull, 1965, 52-64). Coughlin also published a newspaper, *Social Justice*, where he denounced FDR as "stupid," referred to him as "Franklin Double-crossing Roosevelt," and called for his impeachment (Martin, 1996, 19).

Coughlin wielded tremendous influence with conservatives in the 1930s and used his radio show to organize a political lobby of five million members. In 1934, his lobby group was responsible for sending 200,000 letters to Congress protesting the establishment of the World Court. In 1934, Coughlin received more mail than any person in the world and took in over $500,000 in donations at the height of the Great Depression (Martin, 1996, 19).

After the outbreak of WWII, the Roosevelt administration decided to fight back and threatened to charge Coughlin with Treason. Coughlin's

Bishop offered him the choice of silence on political and social issues or leaving the priesthood. Coughlin decided to retire from politics so as to retain his position as a priest, thus ending the political career of one of the New Deal's harshest and most effective critics (Martin, 1996, 19).

Defenders of the Christian Faith

The Defenders of the Christian Faith were formed by Protestant fundamentalist Gerald Winrod in 1925 as an organization for pushing fundamentalist political issues. Winrod began a periodical known as *Defender* as an outlet for his views and toured the West with a group of pilots known as "Flying Defenders" in a campaign to ban evolution from the schools. Winrod was a dispensationalist who interpreted current events as the fulfillment of the prophecies of Revelation. Like Coughlin, he denounced Roosevelt for being duped by an international conspiracy of Jewish bankers, whom he blamed for conspiring to cause the Depression. Winrod denounced the New Deal as a "Red program," and praised Hitler's efforts to combat Jewish "occultism, communism, and finance" (Martin, 1996, 20).

Winrod was also anti-black and anti-Catholic and believed that there was a plot between Catholics, Jews, and the Illuminati, to produce the Great Depression. Winrod even published a book, *Adam Weishaupt, A Human Devil*, where he exposed the international Illuminati conspiracy. In spite of his outlandish claims, Winrod's periodical had 100,000 subscribers in 1936 (Roy, 1953, 28).

Like Coughlin, however, Winrod eventually found himself the subject of the Roosevelt Administration's wrath after the beginning of WWII. Winrod and twenty-eight members of the German American Bund were charged with "conspiracy to cause insubordination in the armed forces" for endorsing the policies of Nazi Germany. The case ended in a mistrial, but Winrod's sympathy for Nazi Germany at a time when the U.S. was at war with the same destroyed his popularity (Martin, 1996, 20).

Gerald L.K. Smith

A third major conservative religious figure that arose in opposition to the Roosevelt administration was Gerald L.K. Smith, a Protestant Fundamentalist from Wisconsin. In 1937 Smith began radio broadcasts over the network Father Coughlin had constructed, assailing the Roosevelt administration, international Jewry, and communism. Smith also began a periodical named *Cross and the Flag* where he spewed his blend of right-wing fundamentalist politics. Unlike Coughlin and Winrod, however, Smith would continue his tirades unabated into the 1960s (Martin, 1996, 20-21).

Right-Wing Paramilitary Groups

Another right-wing fundamentalist extremist group that arose at the end of the 1920s was the Black Legion. The Black Legion was formed by former Klansmen in the industrial Midwest where the Klan had been strong. The secret oath required by members to join the organization plainly stated the purpose of the group as to

"keep the secrets of the order to support God, the United States Constitution, and the Balck Legion in its holy war against Catholics, Jews, Communists, Negroes, and aliens" (Lipset and Raab, 1970, 157).

The Legion blended its KKK fundamentalist-style nativism with European fascist-style militarism and organized itself into a military hierarchy where all members were trained in the use of firearms. By 1936, there were an estimated 40,000 members of the Black Legion, most of who resided in Michigan. (Janowitz, 1951, 306-310).

A second similar right wing group with European fascist leanings and KKK ties was the Silver Shirts, organized in 1943. William Dudley Pelley, the leader of the Silver Shirts, was a Protestant fundamentalist whose father had been a Methodist minister. Like Winrod, Pelley was avowedly anti-Semitic and blamed the Great Depression on an immoral global Jewish-backed communist conspiracy. Pelley also denounced blacks, Native Americans, and immigrants, and proposed that these "improvident and shiftless" people be made wards of the government. Pelley advocated the use of extra-legal violence to suppress trade unions and called on the captains of industry to back him in stopping the communist threat and establishing a fascist dictatorship in America (Janowitz, 1951, 318-319).

Erosion of Support for the New Deal

The Conservative literary, ideological, and organizational assault on the New Deal had an impact, but several other factors combined with these assaults to erode support for Roosevelt and the New Deal in the late 1930s. First, the recession of 1937-38 cast doubts in the minds of the voting public on the New Deal, and the timing of the recession was too far into the Democratic President's tenure of office to be blamed on Hoover. That the recession might have been caused by Roosevelt's capitulation to conservatism, where he attempted to balance the budget by cutting government spending and thus removing capital from the capital-short economy, apparently was too complicated for most of the public to grasp.

FDR feared the mounting deficits in the late 1930s, the economy had rebounded somewhat, and conservative economists were suddenly more concerned about inflation than with unemployment (which was still over 10%) by 1937. FDR therefore pushed the Federal Reserve to increase interest rates so as to curb inflation. In doing so, the money supply diminished and the economy slowed. FDR also attempted to balance the budget by instituting sweeping budget cuts in New Deal Public Works and Relief programs. As a result of Roosevelt's lapse into conservatism, the index of industrial production was 117 in August 1937, but dropped to 76 by May 1938 and four million more Americans were added to the lists of unemployed (Brinkley, 2003, 718).

Simultaneously, Union workers staged a series of sit-down strikes, most notably against General Motors in Flint, Michigan in 1937 that most Americans opposed and viewed as radical and dangerous. Two-thirds of the American public favored legislation and the use of force against the striking workers, but Roosevelt opposed such measures. The very idea that workers would go on strike in a time of such high unemployment was anathema to conservatives in particular and most Americans in general; consequently, the New Deal became associated with strikes and radicalism, thus eroding public support (Mayer, 1965, 480).

Finally, Roosevelt presented Congress with a plan to increase the number of justices on the Supreme Court from nine to fifteen. In eight of ten major New Deal cases in the previous four years, the Supreme Court had ruled against the constitutionality of Roosevelt's New Deal programs and it was rumored that FDR could expect the Court to strike down the Social Security Act of 1935 as unconstitutional as well. Roosevelt became exasperated at what he termed as the "nine old men" on the Court and attempted to remedy the problem through the addition of six more justices (FDR's New Deal had been losing by votes of 6-3 on a divided Court).

The majority of the American public, however, opposed Roosevelt's plan as radical and irresponsible changes to the structure of the American system that they did not view as flawed (Goodwin, 1995, 214). Due to these factors, along with perhaps a fatigue factor that impacts public opinion of Presidents entering their sixth year in office, the Republicans gained six seats in the Senate and eighty in the House in the 1938 mid-term elections. Robert Taft, the son of former President and Supreme Court Chief Justice William Howard Taft, was elected to the U.S. Senate from Ohio and quickly became a leader in the conservative anti-New Deal wing of the Republican Party. Taft and the new conservative wing of the Republican Party were staunchly opposed to the New Deal, but also vehemently anti-communist and opposed to internationalism in foreign affairs.

Anti-Communism and the New Deal

With Roosevelt and the New Deal on the defensive in 1937, Martin Dies, a conservative Democrat from Texas, introduced a House resolution calling for an investigation of the automobile industry sit-down strikes. The resolution did not pass, but Dies followed it with another resolution to create a Special Committee on Un-American Activities, which passed in 1938. The Committee then devoted itself primarily to attacks on the New Deal, its allies, and the Roosevelt Administration, with the intention of showing a connection between the New Deal and Communism. The House Un-American Activities Committee (HUAC) then quickly launched investigations of the American Communist Party and communist infiltration of the Unions. As a result of these investigations, Communist Party leader Earl Browder was convicted of traveling on false passports. Boosted by this "victory," HUAC in the following years investigated the Works Progress Administration, the Tennessee Valley Authority, and the wartime Board of Economic Warfare. HUAC also supported the Smith Act of 1940 that made teaching or advocating the overthrow of the U.S. government illegal and led to the imprisonment of leaders of the American Communist Party. HUAC investigations also led to the passage of the Hatch Act, which prohibited partisan political activity by Federal employees. Conservatives then used the Hatch Act to remove left-wing members of the National Labor Relations Board (Goodman, 1969, 87).

Unfortunately for the conservatives and in spite of their attacks, Roosevelt abandoned his conservative fiscal and monetary policies that had coincided with the recession of 1937 and embarked on a renewed deficit-spending binge in 1938. In April 1938, Roosevelt asked Congress for an additional $5 billion for public works and relief and the Democratic Congress complied. Not uncoincidentally, by 1940, unemployment returned to the level of 1937 and GNP returned to the level of 1937 by 1939. In spite of this success, opposition to the New Deal in Congress was such by 1939 that FDR would have difficulty enacting any major new programs. In effect, conservatives had rebounded sufficiently that Roosevelt's "New Dealing" had largely come to an end (Brinkley, 2003, 718).

Conservatism and World War II

In 1938, Nazi Germany annexed Austria and the Sudetenland of Western Czechoslovakia; the latter acquiesced to by Britain and France in the much-maligned Munich accords, where the French and the British agreed to the Nazi annexation of the disputed territory as long as Hitler agreed to no further expansion. Winston Churchill at the time, and American

Conservatives after WWII, would refer to the Munich Accords as the policy of "Appeasement" and argue that tyrants, such as Hitler, cannot be "appeased," but should be thwarted at the outset (Jones, 1996, 390). Hitler, of course, proved Churchill to be correct by over-running the rest of Czechoslovakia six months later and invading Poland the following September.

At the time of the Munich Accords, however, the Republican Party was divided over what should be the proper American role. For the Conservative "Nationalist" wing of the party, sound foreign policy was based on isolationism with regard to European affairs, unilateralism, protectionism, anti-communism, and the Monroe Doctrine in the Western Hemisphere. In furtherance of these foreign policy guides, Republicans had generally opposed Roosevelt's recognition of the Soviet Union in 1933, regardless of whatever benefits trade with the Soviets might bring to the American economy. While conservatives typically supported the free market, it did not extend to doing business with communists. Rural Republicans in particular tended to support isolationism and opposed alliances and any encroachments on sovereignty embodied in international organizations such as the League of Nations. In 1935, Republicans had thwarted Roosevelt's effort to secure American participation in the World Court under the premise that it would erode American Sovereignty. Similarly, rural Republicans tended to view foreign aid and loans to foreign countries as idealistic utopian fantasies outside the parameters of American National interests. Conservatives also supported neutrality amid the heightening of the tensions in Europe surrounding the rise of Nazi Germany. In the words of Lewis Gould (2003, 279),

> "Disillusion with the outcome of World War I, antipathy toward Great Britain, some degree of anti-Semitism, and sympathy for Germany moved together in various degrees to feed the argument on behalf of continued isolation. Senators such as William Borah of Idaho and Gerald Nye of North Dakota led the block of Republicans in the upper house who wanted to stay out of European disputes."

Beginning with Germany's invasion of Poland September 1, 1939, the political debate over intervention into the war in Europe dominated foreign policy discussions. American public opinion quickly shifted in favor of support for Britain and France short of war, thus leaving conservative isolationism at odds with the opinion of the majority. Congress quickly voted to repeal the arms embargo portion of the Neutrality Acts and allowed belligerents to purchase military goods from the U.S., but the "cash and carry" limitation that had been imposed under the Neutrality Acts remained. The U.S. would not extend credit to the warring nations and belligerents would have to pick up the military goods in U.S. ports using their own ships (Brinkley, 2003, 740). Republicans opposed the end of the arms embargo and other subsequent aid to the Allies by an average of 85% on the key votes in Congress. Conservative Southern Democrats, however, broke with the isolationist conservative Republicans and favored war intervention, thus helping to shore up support for Roosevelt in 1940 for his record third term (Mayer, 1967, 280).

Nationalist Isolationism

The Nationalist/isolationist faction of the Republican Party led by Robert Taft, however, continued to oppose intervention in the European war even after the fall of France in June 1940. Nationalist Republicans argued that U.S. intervention in the war would increase the power and scope of the national government as it did in World War I, and thus institute a form of "national socialism" in the United States and destroy American freedom, the supposed purpose for intervention in the war in the first place. Furthermore, the Nationalist Republicans argued that the expansion of Nazi Germany posed no threat to the security or economic well-being of the United States (Mayer, 1967, 282-283). Nationalist Conservatives also argued that Britain and France had made a mistake in Declaring War on Germany after the Nazi invasion of Poland. The argument was that the Allies should have allowed Hitler to take Eastern Europe, with the result that the totalitarian dictators, Hitler and Stalin, would eventually come to blows and slug out between themselves to the benefit of the free world. Hitler's army then would have bogged down in the Soviet Union, thus preventing an invasion of Western Europe and eliminating any necessity of another war between Germany and the powers of Western Europe. Furthermore, intervention in the European war would be unlikely to advance the causes of freedom and democracy any more than did WWI. Instead, WWI had created the chaos and destruction that led to the germination and growth of communism and fascism, the current scourges of international politics. Why would another war be expected to do anything different (Chamberlin, 1950, 1962, 51)?

Robert Taft echoed the sentiments of leftist war protestors in the conflicts of later decades in Southeast Asia (1960s) and Iraq (2000s) when he argued that the Republican Party,

"should be opposed to risking the lives of five million American boys in an imperialistic war for the domination of Europe, Asia, and Africa, and the supposed 'manifest destiny' of America" (Taft, 1941, 612).

Taft argued that it was the Eastern Wall Street wing of the Republican Party
that favored intervention, while the farmers, working men, and small
businessmen opposed the war. In Taft's words,

"The war party is made up of the business community of the cities, the
newspaper and magazine writers, the radio and movie commentators, the
Communists, and the University intelligentsia" (Taft, 1941, 612).

America First Committee

In the summer of 1940, Nationalist Republicans organized the America
First Committee to lobby and produce propaganda against war intervention.
Backed by the financing of Robert E. Wood, chairman of the board of Sears,
and William H. Regnery, President of the Western Shade Cloth Company,
the America First Committee had over 800,000 members by the end of 1941,
including Charles Lindbergh, a bonafide American hero and the first man to
fly nonstop across the Atlantic in 1927. Lindbergh himself was an
isolationist, who viewed the interventionists' position as part of a grand
conspiracy, the primary forces behind which were "the British, the Jewish,
and the Roosevelt Administration" (Cole, 1953, 1971, 15).
      It is clear from the arguments of the America First Committee and others
that conservatives generally preferred Nazi Germany to the communist
Soviet Union and were essentially comfortable with, and unthreatened by,
the Nazi presence. Nationalist Conservatives argued that the entry of the
Soviet Union in the war against Germany in 1941 took the pressure off of
Britain and eliminated the need for U.S. intervention. Furthermore, entrance
in the war on the side of Britain would now aid the communists in Russia;
hence, the war could not be a war to end totalitarianism (Cole, 1953, 1971,
85). In essence, the policy that the Nationalist/isolationist conservatives
pursued is the policy that would later be condemned by conservatives as
"appeasement." It was the "Liberal" Democratic President Roosevelt, not the
conservatives, who led the push for intervention.
      Conservatives did, however, typically support the British in principle
against Nazi Germany and believed that there was a need for military
preparedness. The America First Committee argued that military
preparedness would prevent war because with an impregnable defense, no
foreign power could dare attack the United States (Cole, 1953, 1971, 85).
Similarly, Herbert Hoover in 1940 argued, "we are determined to be armed
to the teeth to defend ourselves and the Western Hemisphere" (Hoover,
1941, 35). Military preparedness, in turn, did not necessitate aid to the
British, and it most certainly did not necessitate aid to the Soviet Union. The
America First Committee argued that "aid short of war" weakened military

preparedness at home by siphoning off resources. Furthermore, "aid short of war" was likely to cause the United States to cross paths with Nazi Germany and thus drag the United States into the war. Aid to the communist Soviet Union, on the other hand, was complete anathema. On August 5, 1941, a group of Republican leaders, including Herbert Hoover, 1936 Presidential nominee Alf Landon, former Vice President Charles Dawes, and former RNC Chairman Henry P. Fletcher, issued a statement criticizing what they viewed as "unauthorized aid to Russia" and arguing that American aid should be "utilized only to protect the independence of 'democracies'" (*New York Times*, August 6, 1941).

Conservatives and Pacific Policy

Concerning Japan and the Pacific, the Nationalist Republicans were generally in favor of Roosevelt's policies toward Japan in the Pacific and did not oppose the freezing of Japanese assets in July, 1941. As a consequence, the conservatives' hard-line policy against Japan, intended to be consistent with America's Open Door approach to China of the past, actually reinforced Roosevelt's policies that unwittingly led the U.S. on a collision course with Japan and entry into World War II. After Pearl Harbor, some conservatives claimed that FDR had conspired to get the United States into the war "though the back door" in the Pacific while conservatives were focused on preventing entry into the European theater. The argument was that Roosevelt had purposefully provoked Japan through his inflexibility in negotiations and then baited the Japanese by placing the Pacific fleet at Pearl Harbor within Japan's striking distance. A joint Congressional Committee was established to investigate the issue and the Committee issued their report in 1946 exonerating Roosevelt. Conservative Republicans Owen Brewster and Homer Ferguson dissented from the final report, however, and placed the blame for the Pearl Harbor defeat on the Roosevelt administration rather than on military commanders in Hawaii (Morgenstern, 1947, 1987, 192).

Internationalist Republicans

A group of Internationalist Republicans led by Wendell Wilkie, however, had advocated American aid to Britain and France from the beginning in the face of German aggression. Internationalist Republicans were active in the Committee to Defend America by Aiding the Allies, which followed the internationalists' position of all aid to the Allies short of war. In spite of his own internationalism, in the months leading up to the election of 1940, Willkie, the Republican candidate for the Presidency, criticized Roosevelt for being overly zealous in his support of the Allies and argued that

Roosevelt's policies would lead to war, which was opposed by the majority of Americans until the attack on Pearl Harbor. The internationalism of the Willkie faction of the Republican Party, however, was very different from the internationalism of Woodrow Wilson in WWI in that it was based on Realism rather than Idealism. Internationalism was for the purpose of preventing military or economic dominance by a foreign power, not for some altruistic goal of spreading freedom and democracy worldwide (Mayer, 1967, 290).

Conservative Majority and WWII

The Pearl Harbor attack in December of 1941 settled the war issue in favor of intervention, and political attention turned to prosecution of the war. The first six months of the war went very poorly for the United States in the Pacific, as the U.S. lost Guam and the Philippines and the Japanese over-ran French Indochina. This combined with low voter turnout for the Democrats among their working class and poor constituents, many of whom had joined the military, to allow the Republicans to gain seats in Congress in the mid-term elections in 1942. The Republicans combined with conservative Southern Democrats to form a conservative majority in Congress and the conservatives then used their new position of strength to eliminate New Deal programs such as the WPA, the Civilian Conservation Corps, the National Youth Administration, and the National Resources Planning Board. Over FDR's veto, Congress also passed the Smith-Connally Act, which restricted the right of wartime workers to strike and prohibited political contributions to labor unions (Mayer, 1967, 293).

Conservatives partially adopted a "politics ends at the water's edge" strategy on foreign policy during the war and generally supported the war effort; however, conservative Republicans opposed Roosevelt's "Europe First" strategy and instead favored a "Pacific First" strategy based on the premise that America's real long-term interests were in China and the Pacific. Given that the Soviet Union was not involved in the Pacific theater, this position had the added advantage of avoiding collaboration with the communists. Conservatives also sided with General Douglas MacArthur, who argued that the sound military strategy would be to defeat the weaker opponent (Japan) first (James, 1975, 52).

Douglas MacArthur

Douglas MacArthur was a Conservative individualist and nativist who had spent much of his military career in Asia, recognized the Asian long-term potential, and thus viewed Asia as most important interest to the United

States. To conservatives, MacArthur was a symbol of America's imperial duty in the Pacific and Roosevelt's ineptitude in handling the war effort. MacArthur blamed Washington for his losses in the Pacific in 1942 for not providing him the necessary materials for defense. When American fortunes in the Pacific theater reversed after the battle of Midway, MacArthur's popularity soared. Consequently, Republican Nationalists led by Senator Arthur Vandenberg and Sears chairman George Wood began to organize a MacArthur candidacy for President in 1943. The "draft MacArthur" movement gained steam with the endorsement from the Hearst media empire and McCormick's *Chicago Tribune*. In April 1944, however, MacArthur's candidacy was derailed when Republican Representative A.L. Miller of Nebraska published his personal correspondence with MacArthur without authorization from MacArthur. In a letter of MacArthur's to Miller, MacArthur stated that "unless this New Deal can be stopped our American way of life is forever doomed" (James, 1975, 435). The New Deal still had a great deal of popular support in 1944, so MacArthur's opposition to it was a political loser, but the publication of the letter also revealed that MacArthur was not at all above the political fray, thus destroying his political advantage. Shortly thereafter, MacArthur issued a statement removing himself from consideration as a candidate (James, 1975, 436).

Post-War Struggle Over Internationalism

In 1943, Republican Party leaders met at Mackinac Island, Michigan to work out a new Party platform. The idea of an international organization for peace was popular with the American public at the time, thus giving the internationalist wing of the Republican Party the upper hand at Mackinac. Consequently, the "Mackinac Charter" that was forged at the meeting declared the Republican Party to be in favor of American participation in a post-war international cooperative organization for peace. Shortly thereafter, the Republican Party almost unanimously supported the United Nations Participation Act in Congress, but seven Republican Senators voted against the Act, led by the chief Republican Nationalist, Robert Taft (Westerfield, 1955, 153-155). The Republicans did not, however, support the Democrats' liberal position on Free Trade, and Republicans in the House stuck to their Nineteenth Century McKinley roots and voted 140-33 against the extension of the Reciprocal Trade Agreements Act of 1934 (Mayer, 1967, 298). The high tariff position of the Republicans immediately after World War II would later be repudiated by conservative economists such as Friedrich Hayek and Milton Friedman, as well as by the political leader of the conservative resurgence in the 1980s, Ronald Reagan.

Conservatives were also skeptical of the new system of international currency and banking that arose from the Bretton Woods Agreement of 1944. Republicans in the Senate actually voted for the Bretton Woods Agreement 19 to 14, but Republican Nationalists led by Robert Taft denounced the Agreement as irresponsible and pointed to the European defaults on loans after WWI as proof of the danger the agreement posed to American assets. Taft also rejected the argument that increased trade and investment among nations would promote peace. Instead, Taft and the Republican Nationalists viewed the Bretton Woods Agreement and post war programs as a form of "international welfare" and "World New Dealism." The UN in particular was viewed by the Nationalists as a socialist threat to American sovereignty (Westerfield, 1955, 160).

An ideological problem for the Nationalists, however, existed over the conflict between their vehement anti-communism and their staunch isolationism. The only way that they could ensure that Soviet influence in Europe would be kept at to minimum would be to support American commitments to Europe. Anticommunism therefore prevented the Republicans from uniting against Truman's internationalism and thus reduced the ability of the Republicans to seize political control after the death of Roosevelt. The Republicans gained 56 seats in the House and 13 in the Senate in the off-year elections of 1946 and thus gained control of Congress for the first time since 1932, but the moderate wing of the Party supported the Truman Administration's internationalist policies in Europe, thus partially negating the Republican advantage. Republican Senator Arthur Vandenberg, the new Chair of the Senate Foreign Relations Committee, supported the Truman Doctrine, the Marshall Plan, and the North Atlantic Treaty Organization, and was even appointed by Truman as an American Representative to United Nations and Council of Foreign Ministers Conferences. Among those that were supporters of Vandenberg's (and therefore Truman's) internationalism was a young Senator named Joseph McCarthy of Wisconsin (Mayer, 1967, 303).

Republican opposition to Truman's internationalism was led by Robert Taft, Senator Kenneth Wherry of Nebraska, and Senator John Bricker of Ohio. In 1946, the Nationalists led a fight against a $3.75 million loan to Britain on the premise that the British were now ruled by a Labour government and had become too socialistic. Truman then sold the loan as a measure against communism and the measure passed, although Republicans voted against it 2-1 in the House and 18-17 in the Senate (Mayer, 1967, 306). From this point forward, Truman was able to successfully sell his aid to Europe plans in Congress based on the anticommunist angle. The majority of Republicans in both Houses voted for aid to Greece in 1947, when the Greek Monarchy was threatened by communist insurgents, and the majority of

Republicans in both houses supported the massive aid to Europe package known as the Marshall Plan in 1948. Robert Taft and the Nationalists denounced the Marshall Plan as "European TVA," but only 13 voted against the measure in the Senate and 61 in the House (Mayer, 1967, 307-308).

Part of the reason that conservatives were congruent with the Truman Administration on so many post-war foreign policy issues is that the Truman Administration had essentially adopted conservative positions in numerous foreign policy issues. Truman's policies reconstructing, and to a degree rearming, Japan and Germany were consistent with conservative "balance of power" politics aimed at using German and Japanese power as a check on the Soviet Union. Congruent with this strategy, even Robert Taft supported a measure in 1950 to include fascist Spain as part of the Marshall plan as a check on the Soviet Union (Miles, 1980, 88).

In general, conservatives favored military aid over economic aid and supported economic aid only if it could be shown that it was a check on communism (Miles, 1980, 89). Robert Taft perhaps best exemplified this position when he argued,

> "We do have an interest, of course, in the economic welfare of other nations
> and in the military strength of other nations, but only to the extent to which
> our assistance may reduce the probability of an attack on the freedom of our
> own people" (Quoted in Muccigrosso, 2001, 83).

Consequently, Truman's package of technical assistance to lesser developed countries in 1950 was opposed by Congressional Republicans 25-8 in the Senate and 118-29 in the House because it was unconnected to fighting communism and therefore viewed by conservatives as merely a global "welfare" program (Miles, 1980, 89).

Miracle of 48

On the surface, it appeared that Harry Truman had little chance of reelection in 1948 since the Democratic Party was split three ways. The mainstream of the Democratic Party supported Truman and his policies, which were essentially a continuation of the New Deal in domestic policy and anti-communist internationalism in foreign policy. The Southern conservative Democrats, however, broke off from the mainstream Democratic Party to form the States Rights Party or "Dixiecrats." The Dixiecrats were opposed to Truman's proposed integration of the U.S. military and his proposals for federal anti-lynching legislation. Consequently, the Dixiecrats nominated Strom Thurmond of South Carolina for President on a segregationist, "States' rights" platform.

Liberals in the Democratic Party, however, were also at odds with Truman over his hard line against the Soviet Union. Liberals therefore also broke off from the mainline Democratic Party to form the Progressive Party, and nominated Henry Wallace on a platform of conciliation with the Soviet Union (Mayer, 1967, 312).

Republican Party candidate Thomas Dewey supported both the United Nations and the Marshall Plan and failed to repudiate the New Deal, therefore offering no real change from Truman's policies, but Dewey preferred to play it safe and make no voter-alienating mistakes. Truman deflected charges from the right that he was soft on communism with the creation of the Loyalty Review Board that investigated and fired federal employees for supposed communist ties. Truman's anti-communist credentials were also boosted with the Berlin Air Lift as a response to Stalin's blockade of West Berlin. The Berlin crisis created a "rally around the flag" effect that was beneficial to Truman and his administration. Truman's continuation of the New Deal was also a political winner among both agricultural interests and the urban working class. As a consequence, Truman won the election in a major upset and the Democratic Party won a major electoral victory in Congress for the first time since 1936, gaining 9 seats in the Senate and 75 seats in the House (Mayer, 1967, 315).

China, the Bomb, and the New Conservative Offensive

The Conservative reaction to the elections of 1948 was to move even further to the right and to become even more anti-Truman. Robert Taft and the most conservative Republicans believed that the Republicans' bipartisan approach in foreign policy had been the real source of the Republicans' defeat, tying their hands and giving the Democrats an edge as policy leaders while the Republicans could only react. Consequently, conservative Republicans argued that what was needed was for conservatives to seize the initiative at the earliest possible opportunity (White, 1954, 85).

In September 1949, Truman announced that the Soviets had developed the atomic bomb. The development created a perceived American vulnerability to the Soviets since the U.S. had greatly reduced its conventional forces and relied on the atomic bomb to maintain strategic superiority in what had become the Cold War with the Soviet Union. This fact, combined with the revelation shortly thereafter that the Soviets had gained the bomb through espionage by Western scientists, created vulnerability for Truman and the Democrats, in spite of the fact that Republicans had worked shoulder-to-shoulder with them to forge the atomic weapon-based American foreign policy (Westerfield, 1955, 166).

Conservatism and Communist China

A third factor that provided Republicans with an opportunity to launch an offensive against the Truman administration in 1949 was the successful overthrow of the Nationalist Chinese government of Chiang Kai Shek by communist revolutionaries led by Mao Ze Dong. During World War II, the Roosevelt Administration did not take a hard line against Mao's communists because those same communists were vehemently anti-Japanese. In a memorandum entitled "How Red Are the Communists?" John Paton Davies, a Foreign Service adviser to General Joseph Stilwell in China, referred to the communists as "backsliders" and compared them to the British Labour Party (Mayer, 1967, 203). When in July 1949, however, Mao announced a foreign policy he termed as "leaning to one side," (the side of the Soviet Union), the conservatives grabbed the opportunity to paint the Democrats as fools, dupes, or even worse--sympathetic to the communists (Miles, 1980, 102).

In support of their argument that the Democrats had "lost" China to the communists through short-sided policies too congenial to communism, the conservatives pointed to the Yalta Agreements. At Yalta, the Soviets had agreed to enter the war against Japan after the defeat of Germany on the stipulation that the Soviet Union would have the rights to operate railroads in Manchuria in a joint operation with the Chinese government. Furthermore, the Soviet Union was to conclude a "pact of friendship" with the Nationalist Chinese government of Chiang Kai-Shek. In signing such an agreement, conservatives argued that FDR had compromised the long-standing American principle of the Open Door in China and instead provided the communist Soviet Union with a foothold in China. As if things could not have been more unsavory, the terms of the Yalta agreements on China were not disclosed for over a year, thus suggesting to conservatives that there was a secret subversive plot involved by FDR and the Democrats to hide their pro-communist policies (Miles, 1980, 103-104).

To make matters worse, in February 1945, (six months before the fall of Japan) George Atcheson forwarded a policy recommendation to Washington from China where he recommended that military necessity required that the U.S. militarily arm and supply the Chinese communist forces. U.S. Ambassador to China, Patrick J. Hurley, opposed this approach and perpetuated the theory that other Diplomats in the Truman Administration favored the communists as opposed to the Nationalists and were therefore undermining the Nationalist Chinese government. In reaction, Republican Representative Clare Boothe Luce of Connecticut sent a letter to Secretary of State James Byrnes on July 25, 1946, arguing against aid to the Chinese Communists and further arguing against any U.S. support of negotiations between the Nationalist Chinese government and the communists (Miles, 1980, 105, 110).

Conspiracy Theories

In 1944 Alfred Kohlberg, a Conservative businessman and importer of Chinese textiles, became convinced that the Institute of Pacific Relations (IPR), an international research organization, had been infiltrated by communists. IPR was funded by the Rockefeller and Carnegie Foundations, as well as by large American corporations, and was hardly "communist," but an IPR staff member, Frederick Vanderbilt Field, had left his position at IPR in 1940 to become director of the American Peace Mobilization, a left-wing anti-war organization. Field also helped to found *Amerasia*, a left-wing publication focused on Asia. In June 1945, the editors of *Amerasia* were arrested by the FBI along with two U.S. Foreign Service Officers and a Navy intelligence officer, and classified documents were confiscated. The group was charged with conspiracy to violate the Espionage Act, but because the FBI had conducted illegal searches, the defendants plea-bargained for small fines. Conservatives believed that a government conspiracy to cover up espionage was involved, however, and pointed to the affair as proof that American diplomats in the State Department were secretly working to further communism in China. Conservatives launched an investigation in Congress led by conservative Alabama Democrat Samuel F. Hobbs. The Hobbs Committee found no evidence of a government conspiracy, but the belief among conservatives that the *Amerasia* case proved the existence of a conspiracy within the Roosevelt Administration to foster Communist takeover in China continued. Among those who subscribed to this position was Alfred Kohlberg, who then became one of the organizers of the conservative "China Lobby" that argued for unbending support for the Nationalist Chinese government (Westerfield, 1955, 180).

Kohlberg and other like-minded conservatives published and perpetuated their views in *The China Monthly*, a conservative Catholic American journal. In September of 1948, Mark Tsai argued in *China Monthly* that "Red Second Fronters" were responsible for the low priority of China in U.S. foreign policy and that journalists who criticized the Nationalist government were either misled followers of communism or traitors (Tsai, 1948, 55). Alfred Kohlberg continued with a similar theme in *China Monthly* in 1948 when he argued that a small group in the State Department including Alger Hiss, Owen Lattimore, Lauchlin Currie, Edgar Snow, John Carter Vincent, Assistant Secretary of State Dean Acheson and Vice President Henry Wallace, planned to slowly "choke to death" the Nationalist government of

China and build up the communists for a takeover of the country after the war (Kohlberg, 1948, 286).

Conservatives and China Aid

Republicans pushed for aid to the Nationalist government in China in a vain attempt to prevent the fall of the country to communism. In an article in *Life* magazine, former Ambassador to the Soviet Union William Bullit argued for $1.35 billion in economic and military aid to China. Due to popular support for such a measure, the Truman administration submitted a 15 month $570 million aid program to Congress for the Nationalist Chinese government, although insiders within the Truman administration had already given up on China as "lost" to the communists (Westerfield, 1955, 210).

In 1948, General George Marshall argued before the House and Senate foreign relations committees that the U.S. would probably be unable to reduce the influence of Mao's communists in China without an American takeover of the Chinese government and its military affairs, including the introduction of American ground troops into China. Marshall argued that such a policy was untenable because the U.S. lacked both the human resources and the financial resources to undertake such an endeavor. Furthermore, any such large commitment in China would most certainly undermine American efforts in Europe by diverting resources from Europe to China. Marshall viewed China as less strategically important in the short term due to its vast economic problems; hence, Marshall concluded that China was unworthy of such a U.S. commitment at European expense (Miles, 1980, 107-108).

Marshall's arguments held sway in the Truman Administration, but conservatives were not so convinced. In February of 1949, 51 conservative Congressmen sent a letter to President Truman proposing the creation of a Commission to reassess China. Additionally, conservative Democrat Patrick McCarran of Nevada submitted a bill for a $1.5 million loan to China regardless of whether such a Commission was created. Later that spring, the Nationalist government in China fell to the Communists of Mao Ze Dong and twenty-one conservative Senators wrote a letter to Truman arguing against recognition of the new Communist Chinese government. Mao's announcement in July, 1949, that he was leaning to the Soviet side merely confirmed the conservatives' beliefs that the Communist takeover in China was orchestrated as part of a global plot by the Soviet Union (Miles, 1980, 117). The "loss of China" provided the groundwork for Joseph McCarthy and the anti-communist hard liners to embark on their anti-communist witch-hunts of the next decade.

Chapter Eleven

Conservatism in the Age of McCarthy

The failure of Thomas Dewey's centrism to defeat Harry Truman in the election of 1948, combined with the "loss of China" to communism, the 1950 communist invasion of South Korea, the discovery of real and validated cases of espionage and treason, and the subsequent Soviet development of the atomic bomb, caused right-wing Republicans and hard-right Democrats to view the developments as the result of the lack of resolve by conservatives in the face of the liberal/socialist/communist onslaught. These beliefs worked in concert with the Cold War and Traditional Conservative ideological paranoia to create a political atmosphere conducive to McCarthy's witch-hunts and the anticommunist hysteria that gripped the nation in the post-war era.

For the hard line conservatives, the enemies were not just the communists abroad in Russia and China, but the perceived communist/socialist infiltration of American society and the American government itself, beginning with, but not limited to, the State Department within the Truman administration. The issue of Communist infiltration in the government that dominated what became known as the "McCarthy Era" had its beginnings in the perception of conservatives that the Democratic Party was in reality a Trojan Horse of Socialism and Communism; therefore, the issue for Republicans became less the about actual Communist Party in the United States, and more about the Democratic Party, which came to be viewed by right-wing conservatives as almost an equal evil with Communism itself. In essence, McCarthyism and the McCarthy attacks on the Democratic Party were merely the practical application of the Traditional Conservative "plot mentality," and in that sense differ very little from the Puritan witch hunts of the Seventeenth Century.

At the Republican National Convention in 1948, Carroll Reece, the Chairman of the Republican National Committee, exemplified the conservative viewpoint when he put the Conservatives' struggle against communism in Traditional Conservative apocalyptic "good versus evil" terms. In his address to the Convention, Reese stated,

"In the world today, there are two powerful forces. They are exponents of two systems of government diametrically opposed to one another. One of these forces is the Republican Party of the United States—the traditional and undeviating defender of the principles of our representative Republic...The other force is the Communist Party, which may aptly be described as an international conspiracy—a conspiracy to destroy free government. Its headquarters are in Moscow, but its cells of adherents are in almost every nation on earth, including, unfortunately, our own where Fellow-travelers— the typhoid Marys of Communism—have insinuated themselves into so many important positions, in and out of Government, during the New Deal regime" (Quoted in Miles, 1980, 129).

Reece's view of the struggle between the Republican Party and their political opponents as "good versus evil" casts the Democratic Party not as a mere political opponent, but as an evil entity involved with Moscow in some dark plot to take over the world, and only the good and righteous Republican Party, which had the wisdom to see the truth, stood in their way.

Similarly, in February 1950, Republicans in both Houses and the Republican National Committee issued a "Statement of Principles" criticizing the Truman administration for what they viewed as a,

"planned economy modeled on the Socialist governments of Europe, including price and wage controls, rationing, socialized medicine, regional authorities, and the Brannan Plan with its controls, penalties, fines, and jail sentences. This program is dictated by a small but powerful group of persons who believe in socialism, who have no concept of the true foundation of American progress and whose proposals are wholly out of accord with the true interests and real wishes of the workers, farmers, and businessmen" (Quoted in Miles, 1980, 124).

Obviously, the Republicans blatantly and openly contended that Truman and his policies constituted a "Trojan Horse" for State socialism.

Although Truman had won the election of 1948 in the face of such ideological demonization, he had done so by essentially adopting some of the same tactics as his opponents so as to deflect the charge that he was "soft on communism." Consequently, Truman's actions only contributed to the anti-communist hysteria and the entities he created provided much more than just lip-service. The Loyalty Review Board that Truman created went quickly and zealously to work. By the time the decade of the 1950s was over, 2700 government workers had been discharged for supposed disloyalty, the vast majority for illegitimate reasons. A much larger number simply resigned rather than be subjected to the indignities of the investigations (Garraty and McCaughey, 1987, 833). Employees that were investigated were prevented from knowing the identity of their accusers, thus denying them their Sixth

Amendment rights to confront witnesses against them. Rather than being innocent until proven guilty, the burden of proof was on the accused to prove his or her innocence. Hearings and prosecution before the Loyalty Review Board could drag on for years and even those who were exonerated might be told that they were now considered security risks, a status that was also grounds for dismissal (Nash et al., 2004, 931).

Infiltration and Epionage

Still, the anti-communist hysteria of the 1950s, like the Red Scare of 1919, might not have had the same energy if there were not a certain real amount of communist or subversive activity which conservatives could claim as a case in point. The real incidents of subersion would be provided for the conservatives in 1948, when during the hearings of the House Un-American Activities Committee (HUAC), Elizabeth Bentley, a former courier for Soviet espionage, testified that Lauchlin Currie, a White House assistant during the Roosevelt Administration and former Lend Lease Administrator for China, and Harry Dexter White, formerly Assistant Secretary of the Treasury and architect of the World Bank and IMF, had been involved in the transfer of government documents to Soviet Agents. In the same hearings, Whittaker Chambers, editor of *Time* magazine and a former communist, testified that he knew former State Department employee and President of the Carnegie Endowment for International Peace, Alger Hiss, to be a communist. While in the State Department, Hiss had played a role in organizing the United Nations, was in attendance at Yalta, and was a friend of Secretary of State Dean Acheson, whom Conservatives vilified for "losing China." In essence, Hiss perfectly fit the profile for the right-wing's fantasy that the U.S. government, especially the State Department, had been infiltrated by communists in some sort of grand plot against America (Miles, 1980, 127-128).

In spite of these "discoveries" of "communist infiltration, Truman won the election of 1948, partially by beating his own anti-communist drum. After the election was over, the anti-communist machinery set in place continued its onslaught against the imagined demons. In October 1949, the Department of Justice obtained the conviction of the leaders of the American Communist Party under the Smith Act of 1940 that had made teaching or advocating overthrow of the U.S. government illegal. In 1950, the Congress of Industrial Organizations expelled Communist-led Unions from its organization. In essence, the Communist Party in the United States, which had never been a major force in American politics, even during the worst years of the Great Depression, was at low ebb.

In 1949, however, Whittaker Chambers launched new fears by introducing new evidence to HUAC that Alger Hiss had actually passed State Department documents to him back in the 1930s. Chambers produced his so-called "pumpkin papers" (so named because he had supposedly kept them buried in his pumpkin patch) that included some State Department documents copied in Hiss' handwriting and some typed on Hiss' typewriter. Hiss could not be indicted for espionage due to the statute of limitations, but he was charged with perjury and after one mistrial resulting from a hung jury, was convicted and given a five-year jail sentence in January, 1950 (Garraty and McCaughey, 1987, 833).

In February 1950, more "proof" emerged that the Nation had been infiltrated by Communists when British physicist Klaus Fuchs, who had worked at Los Alamos, was arrested in Britain on charges of giving nuclear secrets to the Soviets. The apprehension of Fuchs then led to the arrest of Americans Harry Gold and Julius and Ethel Rosenberg on the charge of conspiracy to commit espionage. Although the information transferred to the Soviets was not the information that led to the Soviet development of the atomic bomb, the Rosenbergs were executed. For conservatives, the discovery of espionage by nuclear scientists not only proved once again that there was communist infiltration, but that it was also gravely dangerous (Garraty and McCaughey, 1987, 833-834).

Joseph McCarthy

On February 9, 1950, at a speech to the Women's Republican Club of Wheeling, West Virginia, Senator Joseph McCarthy of Wisconsin stated,

"The reason we find ourselves in a position of impotency…is not because our only potential enemy has sent men to invade our shores, but rather because of the traitorous actions of those who have been treated so well by this nation…The State Department is infested with communists…I have here in my hand a list of 205—a list of names that were known to the Secretary of State as being members of the Communist Party and who nevertheless are still working and shaping…public policy" (Quoted in Garraty and McCaughey, 1987, 834).

The Associated Press picked up McCarthy's speech and suddenly his reckless charges became a real political issue. On February 20, McCarthy followed up his Wheeling performance with a speech in the Senate where he presented what he said were some eighty cases drawn from the loyalty files of the State Department compiled by Robert E. Lee, an investigator for HUAC. McCarthy ignored the fact that 40 of the cases already had been cleared by the FBI and not all of the "loyalty" files had anything to do with

Communism in the first place. Republican minority leader Kenneth Wherry demanded a Senate investigation of McCarthy's charges, and a subcommittee of the Senate Foreign Relations Committee under Democratic Senator Millard Tydings of Maryland was given authority over the investigations. Tydings' lack of zeal for McCarthy's witch-hunt would give McCarthy reason to later target Tydings himself (Griffith, 1970, 1987, 96).

The Republican right, however, rallied to McCarthy's aid. Reporters for the Hearst and McCormick media empires provided McCarthy with information and gave him favorable coverage. McCarthy did not bring forth any new information, but instead unearthed the names of 22,000 presumed communist sympathizers from a report that had been compiled by the Dies Committee staff in 1944, but withdrawn by the full Committee. McCarthy also used material from previous investigations by HUAC that had gone nowhere (Griffith, 1970, 1987, 98).

In March 1950, McCarthy recklessly named Owen Lattimore, a Johns Hopkins professor, as the "top Russian espionage agent" in the United States, and Louis Budenz, the former managing editor of *The Daily Worker* (the newspaper of the Communist Party), stepped forward to identify Lattimore as a Communist. Lattimore was anathema to Republicans because he was associated with the Institute of Pacific Relations, had been an adviser to Chiang Kai-shek, and had accompanied Henry Wallace on a trip to China in 1944. Unfortunately for McCarthy, Budenz' testimony directly contradicted statements he had given to the State Department in 1947 that he knew nothing to implicate Lattimore with the Communist Party (Griffith, 1970, 1987, 101).

The Tydings subcommittee also again investigated the *Amerasia* incident. Former Office of Strategic Services (OSS) employee Frank Bielaski testified that he had noticed a document in the *Amerasia* office that was marked "A-bomb," but none of the other OSS officers who had accompanied him on the raid could remember such a document, and the term "A-bomb" had not come into use yet at the time of the OSS raid of the *Amerasia* offices. In the end, the Tydings subcommittee found McCarthy's charges to be groundless and therefore refused to conduct an independent investigation of the State Department as McCarthy wished. In July, the subcommittee issued a majority report, which described McCarthy's claims as "a fraud and a hoax" (Griffith, 1970, 1987, 106).

In June 1950, Communist North Korea invaded South Korea and President Truman committed American troops to prevent the spread of Communism. Approximately two-thirds of Americans supported the Korean intervention and the War briefly put an end to the McCarthy hysteria. In spite of the "rally-around-the-flag" effect, however, the Republicans won five seats in the Senate in the mid-term elections and 28 seats in the House.

Outside the South, the Democrats elected only 126 members of the House and 9 Senators (Mayer, 1967, 315).

Importantly for the McCarthyists, Senator McCarthy "invaded Maryland" during the campaign and campaigned for John Marshall Butler against his nemesis Millard Tydings. Butler was also aided by the McCormick publishing empire that provided Butler with the *Chicago Times-Herald's* printing services at cut-rate prices. McCarthy's staff worked with *Times-Herald* employees to produce a faked photograph of Tydings conversing with Communist Party leader Earl Browder, with the result that Tydings was defeated in his Senate re-election bid. Tydings filed a complaint with the Senate's Subcommittee on Privileges and Elections, but the damage had been done and McCarthy had been vindicated (Griffith, 1970, 1987, 110).

McCarthyists and General George Marshall

The McCarthyists exhibited no limits in their attacks on those friendly to the Democrats. In 1950, President Truman appointed General George Marshall as Secretary of Defense to replace Louis Johnson, who had sided with Douglas MacArthur and the Republican Internationalists in favoring a military commitment to the defense of Taiwan. The appointment of Marshall was in part an attempt by Truman to install an individual who could place some controls on MacArthur, the irrepressible American hero, who differed with Truman on the subject of a neutral Formosa Strait and publicly argued in *U.S. News and World Report* for an American military defense of Formosa if it were attacked by Communist China (Miles, 1980, 154).

Republicans opposed Marshall's nomination as Secretary of Defense and opposed a bill that would exempt Marshall from a requirement that the Secretary of Defense be a civilian. Republicans also attacked Marshall, however, for his supposed links to Communist traitors. Republican Senator William E. Jenner of Indiana exemplified the McCarthyist position when he referred to Marshall specifically as a "front man for traitors." Jenner denounced Marshall in apocalyptic language, arguing that,

> "The day of reckoning had arrived concerning how the Democratic Party has been captured from within and used to hasten our destruction, both from within and without, during these tragic years" (Quoted in Miles, 1980, 156).

Jenner then denounced and blamed Marshall for the Pearl Harbor defeat and for his role in helping FDR "trick America into a war," the extension of lend-lease to the Communist Soviet Union, the "selling out" of Eastern Europe at Yalta, the loss of China, and the inclusion of an offer of aid to the Soviet Union under the Marshall Plan (Miles, 1980, 157).

Joseph McCarthy emerged in June 1950 to also denounce Marshall on the floor of the Senate. McCarthy claimed that since WWII, the free world had been losing 100 million people per year to international communism. Though this might technically have been true since it had been only five years since WWII, and the communist People's Republic of China had a population of 500 million, if China and Eastern Europe were removed from the picture, the "advance" of Communism appeared much less bleak (Miles, 1980, 178).

McCarthy denounced the Communist advance in apocalyptic language and viewed the world situation in typical Traditional Conservative black and white, "with us or against us" terms. McCarthy argued that the West was in decline and that that decline was due in part to the traitorous Communist conspiracy led by Marshall and Dean Acheson. For McCarthy, the fall of China to Communism had nothing to do with deficiencies of the Nationalist China regime or the status of Mao's movement to the Chinese people as true patriots for their valor against the Japanese invaders in WWII, but instead had to be due to the efforts of communist conspirators in high places in the American government (Miles, 1980, 178-179).

Republican Nationalist leader Robert Taft also condemned the appointment of Marshall as "encouraging Chinese Communism" and further denounced Marshall for attempting to force the Nationalists in China to accept Communists into their cabinet in a coalition government. In the words of Taft,

> "If I voted for General Marshall, I should feel that I was confirming and approving the sympathetic attitude toward Communism in the Far East which has dominated the Far Eastern Division of the State Department" (Quoted in White, 1954, 214).

Following Taft's lead, the Republicans voted 20-10 against the bill (passed by the Democrats) permitting Marshall to be exempted from the requirement that a civilian be Secretary of Defense. Republicans also cast all eleven votes in opposition to Marshall's eventual nomination as Secretary of Defense (Mayer, 1967, 320).

Attack on Dean Acheson

George Marshall was certainly not the only scapegoat for the conservatives, who at mid-century continually claimed that the federal government, especially the State Department, was infiltrated with disloyal communists. It is perhaps only natural then that Secretary of State Dean Acheson would become a focal point for the conservative anti-communist witch hunts. The conservatives' loathing of Acheson is well-exemplified by Republican Senator Hugh Butler of Nebraska, who stated of Acheson,

> "I watch his smart-aleck manner and his British clothes and that New Dealism, everlasting New Dealism in everything he says and does, and I want to shout, Get out, Get out. You stand for everything that has been wrong with the United States for years" (Quoted in Hoover, 1941, 1972, 208-209).

Fuel to the fires against Acheson was provided by Adolf A. Berle, a former Assistant Secretary of State, who testified before HUAC that he had been fired from the State Department in 1944 for advocating a hard line against the Soviets in opposition to a pro-Soviet view taken by Acheson. Conservatives then connected Acheson to Alger Hiss and described Acheson's policies as Secretary of State as "Acheson-Hiss" policies (Griffith, 1975, 119). Joseph McCarthy, in a speech on the Senate floor, directly accused Acheson of Treason. In the words of McCarthy,

> "I have studied Acheson's public utterances sidewise, slantwise, hindwise, and frontwise; I have watched the demeanor of this glib, supercilious, and guilty man on the witness stand; I have reflected upon his career, and I come to only one conclusion: his primary loyalty in international affairs runs to the British labor government, his secondary allegiance is to the Kremlin, with none left over for the country of his birth" (Quoted in Miles, 1980, 180).

Conservatives followed up McCarthy's tirade by accusing Acheson of "inviting" the North Korean invasion by excluding South Korea from the U.S. defense perimeter. Conservatives further suggested that the State Department was being manipulated by communist spies who had infiltrated the government under the direction of Moscow. Senator Styles Bridges argued that there was a Soviet "Master Spy" in the State Department and demanded that Acheson be thoroughly questioned by the Tydings subcommittee (Lipset and Raab, 1975). In December 1950, The Republicans passed a resolution at the Republican Conference in Congress demanding Acheson's resignation, but any such move was blocked by the Democrats (Miles, 1980, 183).

MacArthur and Korea

When communist North Korea, armed with Soviet Weapons, attacked capitalist South Korea in June, 1950, both conservatives and the Truman Administration viewed the attack as "Soviet Aggression" and viewed the events in Korea as requiring American intervention. The Truman Administration responded through the UN, which unanimously denounced

North Korea as the aggressor and passed a resolution to militarily aid South Korea. The USSR could have vetoed the measure on the UN Security Council had their representative been present, but the Soviet minister was absent that day in protest of the failure of the UN to admit Communist China to the UN. Americans at the time simply thought that they had been lucky that the Soviets had been absent the day of the vote, but the fact that the Soviets were absent at the UN actually suggested that North Korea was acting on its own. If the Soviets had been behind the attack, or had known of the attack in advance, surely the Soviet Representative in the UN would have ended the Soviet boycott of the UN and registered a veto of the resolution to aid South Korea (Jones, 1996, 501).

The North Korean troops using Soviet Tanks rolled through South Korea with ease because the South Koreans had no weapons that could penetrate the armor on the Soviet Tanks. Seoul fell on June 28th and Truman responded with U.S. air strikes against targets in North Korea. General Douglas MacArthur recommended that the U.S. send an invasion force, blockade the coast, and launch air strikes wherever militarily necessary (Jones, 1996, 503). Truman did not ask for a Declaration of War because he described the situation as a "police action," beginning a change in the nomenclature of war for the United States that has continued into the Twenty-First Century. Truman recognized that Korea had no strategic importance, but had great symbolic importance in showing the Soviets that the U.S. would not allow the spread of communism (Jones, 1996, 502).

By September 1950, North Korea had driven the South Koreans into a tiny 60 square mile area around Pusan at the Southeast tip of the Korean Peninsula. MacArthur counterattacked with an amphibious invasion at Inchon on the Western side of Korea, hundreds of miles North of the communist advance. MacArthur's subordinates argued against the Inchon landing due to high tides and rocky cliffs, but MacArthur believed that those same conditions gained him the element of surprise. When U.S. troops arrived in sufficient numbers, the communists were quickly driven back across the 38th Parallel and MacArthur's stature once again grew among conservatives (Jones, 1996, 502-503).

Truman then altered his war strategy from "containment" to "liberation" and began what was known as "Operation Rollback," and the military purpose suddenly became to liberate all of Korea from communism. Truman consequently approved the advance of MacArthur's troops north of the 38th parallel into North Korean territory. Ambassador to the Soviet Union George Kennan warned that the Soviets would resist such a move, and the People's Republic of China warned the U.S. that they would intervene if the U.S. approached the Chinese border. Truman and his advisers, however, believed that China was too weak to intervene. Dean Acheson in particular argued that Chinese intervention would be "sheer madness." MacArthur in this case concurred with the conservative whipping-post, Acheson, believing that the Chinese would not intervene because they had no air force and would therefore be completely vulnerable to the advanced U.S. air power. Therefore, on September 29th, Secretary of Defense Marshall gave MacArthur the authority to cross the 38th parallel. October 9th, the U.N. General Assembly passed a resolution calling for a unified democratic Korea, thus providing international authorization for MacArthur to invade North Korea and begin "Operation Rollback" (Jones, 1996, 503).

MacArthur requested permission from Truman to attack strategic spots in China itself, but Truman rejected MacArthur's request, preferring not to provoke the Chinese any further so as to ensure the limiting of the conflict to Korea. In Furtherance of his "limited war" objective, Truman even authorized UN forces to bomb only the Southern half of bridges on the Yalu River (the North Korean border with China). MacArthur famously replied to this absurd request of the President's that he did "not know how to bomb half a bridge" (Jones, 1996, 504).

MacArthur's invasion forces quickly pushed the North Koreans across the 38th Parallel and into North Korea. Chairman Mao of the People's Republic of China then retaliated against the invasion by sending a group of "Chinese Volunteers" to attack the UN forces on October 26, 1950. The attack by Mao's "Volunteers" was a warning from Mao that he would not tolerate the UN takeover of communist North Korea (Jones, 1996, 504).

MacArthur called for an all-out offensive in North Korea on November 24th, and declared that his men would drive the communists out by Christmas. Two days later on November 26th 1950, Chairman Mao responded to MacArthur's offensive by sending 600,000 Chinese troops, some without weapons, over the border into North Korea. In temperatures of 30 degrees below zero, the American forces of only 20,000 troops were pushed back across the 38th Parallel by December 10th. In January of 1951, the Chinese invasion force pushed all the way to Seoul and retook the South Korean capitol (Jones, 1996, 504).

The UN denounced the Chinese invasion and called for their withdrawal, but the Chinese responded with their own demands, calling for the withdrawal of UN troops, the cessation of U.S. aid to Taiwan, and admission of the PRC to the UN. MacArthur, determined to settle the issue on the battlefield rather than the negotiating table, regrouped his forces and launched a counter-offensive that pushed the Chinese back to the 38th Parallel in March, 1951.

The schism that existed between President Truman and his General widened as Truman favored a negotiated peace while MacArthur favored a military victory. MacArthur was not only a warrior, but a staunch conservative anti-communist who believed that the Korean War should be used as a vehicle for stamping out communism in Korea completely. MacArthur also viewed himself as at war with China (a fact that is difficult to dispute given the presence of 600,000 Chinese troops in Korea); consequently, MacArthur called for a blockade of the Chinese coast, bombings of Manchuria and China's major industrial Center, a Nationalist/American invasion of the Chinese mainland from Taiwan, and the dropping of a field of radioactive cobalt along the Chinese-North Korean border. MacArthur also favored the use of atomic bombs on the North Koreans (Jones, 1996, 505). MacArthur did emphasize in his address to Congress, however, that "no man in his right mind would advocate sending our ground forces into continental China" and therefore MacArthur was also, like Truman, actually advocating a limited war, but with a victory over communism in Korea (Miles, 1980, 173).

Truman/MacArthur Schism

Truman feared that MacArthur's strategies would lead to Soviet intervention and possibly WWIII. Furthermore, the U.S. allies were not in favor of expansion of the war, the Nationalists in Taiwan had already proven incapable of defeating the communists on the Mainland, and MacArthur's proposed bombings would surely not stop the continued Chinese intervention in North Korea (Jones, 1996, 505).

MacArthur, in contrast, believed that America's long-term interests were in Asia, rather than Europe, and believed that Truman was sacrificing America's true long-term interests (Asia) in favor of the interests of the past (Miles, 1980, 170-172). MacArthur also viewed Truman's "limited war" as "prolonged indecision" and tacit acceptance of a long, bloody, stalemate where the only military objective was to kill as many of the enemy as possible. MacArthur denounced the strategy, stating that, "the very concept shocks me, old soldier that I am" (Quoted in MacArthur, 1964, 349).

Following MacArthur's lead, a group of Republican Senators issued a Statement on the floor of the Senate condemning Truman's policies as immoral (Miles, 1980, 175). MacArthur then wrote a letter to Republican leader Joseph Martin in the House of Representatives in an attempt to get Congressional support for his plan. In doing so, Truman felt that MacArthur had undermined his authority and broken the chain of command; hence, Truman believed that he had no choice but to relieve MacArthur of his command in Korea for his insubordination, which he then promptly did. MacArthur returned to the United States to a hero's welcome and his name received some discussion again for the Presidency, but sentiments within the

Republican Party were already shifting toward MacArthur's former clerk,
General Dwight Eisenhower (Miles, 1980, 176).

Eisenhower

Eisenhower had been courted by both Republicans and Democrats,
including President Truman, but Eisenhower was favored by the wealthy
Eastern wing of the Republican Party and friendly with New York Herald
Tribune publisher, William Robinson. Eisenhower was also a proponent of
"Europe first" internationalism in foreign policy and therefore was in conflict
with the isolationist foreign policy positions of Robert Taft. When Senator
Henry Cabot Lodge visited Eisenhower as a possible candidate for the
purpose of blocking Taft's Presidential ambitions, Eisenhower became
interested (Mayer, 1967, 332). The Republican Party then adopted a platform
of repudiation of the Yalta agreements and in favor of "Liberation" of
Eastern Europe in foreign policy. Eisenhower, however, realized the dangers
of such a policy and called for a "Peaceful restoration of the freedom of the
captive nations, both of Europe and Asia" (Ambrose, 1984, 177).

By 1952, Truman's popularity had plummeted to 23% and the
Democratic Party nominee, Adlai Stevenson, had little chance against the
popular General from World War II. Stevenson campaigned on a platform of
continuation of the New Deal and honesty, while the Republicans focused on
communism, the corruption of the New Deal, and Korea. Republicans
labeled the Democrats as "soft on communism" and argued that General
Eisenhower would take a more aggressive approach against the Communists.
Not surprisingly, the popular war hero Dwight Eisenhower was elected
President in 1952 with 55% of the vote and a plurality in 41 States.
Furthermore, Eisenhower took office with a Republican Congress, thus
setting the stage for a Conservative Revolution (Ambrose, 1984, 177-182).

Eisenhower also assumed office in 1953 with an "inherited" bloody war
in Korea in its third year. Although the American "Kill ratio" against the
Communists approximated 20-1, the war essentially stalemated near the 38th
Parallel by mid 1951 and little progress was made on the battlefield. Peace
talks began between the U.S. and the communists in the summer of 1951, but
the talks went nowhere over the issue of repatriation of prisoners. The
communists demanded that all prisoners be returned to their host countries,
but the UN refused to repatriate those who did not want to go home, and
80,000 of the UN's 170,000 North Korean prisoners opposed their own
repatriation (Jones, 1996, 514).

Eisenhower opposed the repatriation of prisoners, as did the Republican
Party in General, but something had to be done to break the impasse at the
negotiating table. The new President therefore secretly offered the

communists a cease-fire, but simultaneously threatened the use of nuclear weapons to win the war if necessary. The communists then agreed to an Armistice that returned the border to the status quo ante bellum. The cost of containment of communism in Korea had been great, with 54,000 American deaths and 2 million Korean and Chinese (one million on each side), but the objective of preventing the spread of communism into South Korea had been achieved (Jones, 1996, 516). The goal of "Liberation" as espoused by both Eisenhower and the Republican Party in 1952, however, had not been served since communists remained in control of North Korea. Conservatives would continue to talk about "who lost China" for the remainder of the decade, but would generally ignore discussion about "who lost North Korea."

Culture Wars and Anti-Communism

The McCarthy era produced a struggle over American core values and the institutions of culture that has continued in altered forms through the present. Social changes, such as equal rights for blacks, women's rights, the sexual revolution, and gay rights, had been dealt a setback by the Great Depression and WWII, but were due for resurgence as the nation resettled in the post-war era. The urbanization that followed WWII would only exacerbate the coming trends as the more traditional ties in society were eroded through the dislocating structures and processes of the urban centers. In such a situation, a conservative reaction against the changes and threats to traditional societal structures was perhaps certain to occur. As a consequence, conservatives began an attack against schools, universities, publishers, theater, the media and the entertainment industry that they viewed as perpetuating nontraditional values and permissiveness (Miles, 1980, 180).

In 1952, Republicans Robert Taft and Clarence Brown of Ohio supported a measure introduced by Eugene Cox, a conservative Democrat from Georgia, to investigate major "foundations" with leftist leanings, including the Carnegie Endowment and the Ford Foundation. A Committee was put together under Representative Carroll Reece of Tennessee and the Committee issued a report in 1953 condemning the Foundations. According to the Reece Committee, the foundations formed an "intellectual cartel that dispensed various forms of patronage which carry with them the elements of thought control." The Reece Committee specifically named the Rockefeller foundations, Ford foundation, and Russell Sage as leading the cartel (Griffith, 1970, 135).

In a tirade that would resemble the complaints of the Moral Majority and the Christian Coalition of future generations, the Reece Committee denounced the foundations for sponsoring "moral relativity, social engineering, and scientism," and for their "tendency to induce educators to

become agents for social change and collectivism." In the area of foreign
policy, the Committee argued,

"The net result of these combined efforts has been to promote
internationalism in a particular sense—a form directed toward world
government and a derogation of American nationalism. Foundations have
supported a conscious distortion of history, propagandized blindly for the
United Nations as the hope of the world, supported that organization's
agencies to an extent beyond general public acceptance, and leaned toward a
generally leftist approach to international problems" (Quoted in Miles, 1980,
229).

The conservatives' attacks on the institutions of culture were at least
partially off-base since major segments of the media supported conservative
politics in general and McCarthy in particular. The Hearst and McCormick
publishing empires were ardent supporters of conservatism as were the
Saturday Evening Post and *Reader's Digest*. Additionally, small town
newspapers across America, small towns being overwhelmingly
conservative, typically supported McCarthy. In the 1930s and 1940s, two-
thirds of the nation's newspapers had opposed the Presidential candidacies of
Roosevelt and Truman, and the print-media support for the Republicans
continued unabated throughout the 1950s with the candidacies of the popular
war-hero, Dwight Eisenhower and his Vice President, Richard Nixon
(Emery, 1999, 198).

Nevertheless, the right-wing attack on the media commenced in 1947with
the formation of American Business Consultants Inc. (ABCI), a reactionary
propaganda mill that published *Counterattack: The Newsletter of Facts on
Communism*. In 1950 ABCI also published *Red Channels, the Report of
Communist Influence in Radio and Television*, which listed 151 people and
associations the ABCI considered to be communist. Among those listed were
conductor Leonard Bernstein, singer Lena Horne, stripper Gypsy Rose Lee,
actors Burl Ives, Zero Mostel, and Edward G. Robinson, broadcasters
Alexander Kendrick, William L. Shirer, and Howard K. Smith, and Federal
Communications Commissioner Clifford J. Durr. The President of the Screen
Actors' Guild, Ronald Reagan, believed that the Communist Party was trying
to take over Hollywood, and consequently led a campaign to blacklist left-
leaning actors, writers, directors, and other workers in the movie industry
(Davis, 1992, 32-33).

The anti-communist paranoia spread to seemingly all areas of American
life in all corners of the country. In New York City, school children were
given dog tags so that they could be recognized if the City were destroyed in
a communist nuclear attack. Meanwhile, New York City subway workers
were fired for holding "communist beliefs." Similarly, in Seattle, a fireman

was fired 40 days before his 25 year pension because he had once applied for, and been denied, Communist Party membership. Navajos in New Mexico were denied government relief due to their "un-American" communal lifestyles that they had been practicing before the landing of Columbus (Nash et al., 2004, 960). Teachers in Texas were investigated for their political leanings, three were fired for being Communists, and loyalty oaths for teachers were imposed. The Texas Legislature also passed a law making Communist Party membership a felony punishable by a $20,000 fine and up to twenty years in prison (Campbell, 2003, 418). Over one million private bomb shelters were constructed nationwide and Architectural Digest reported that the bomb shelter would become as much a part of the American home as the garage (Miles, 1980, 204).

Democratic Response

The Democrats, led by Senator William Benton of Connecticut, fought back against the McCarthy assault. Benton had served as Assistant Secretary of State in the early years of the Truman administration and was a supporter of Acheson, thus bringing him into direct confrontation with McCarthy and the far right. In the summer of 1951, Benton introduced a resolution calling for McCarthy's expulsion from the Senate. When it appeared that the resolution did not have the necessary support, Benton altered the resolution to a call for Censure. Benton's Resolution was timed to coincide with a denunciation of McCarthy by President Truman (Griffith, 1970, 139).

The Benton Resolution was referred to the Senate Subcommittee on Privileges and Elections which eventually issued the Hennings Report in 1953 that focused on McCarthy's finances. The Hennings report detailed the possible diversion of contributions to from McCarthy's election campaign to McCarthy's anti-communist crusade; technically, in other words, funds were diverted for McCarthy's own personal use. The Hennings Report also raised the possibility that McCarthy had violated both tax laws and political campaign laws; consequently, the Report was referred to the Justice Department, the Internal Revenue Service, and the Federal Deposit Insurance Corporation, but none of these agencies in the new Republican Eisenhower administration found any basis in the Hennings Report for subsequent legal action against McCarthy (Griffith, 1970, 141).

McCarthy Leadership

In 1953, Robert Taft died and General Douglas MacArthur retired to private life after being fired by Truman, thus leaving McCarthy as the flag bearer for the far right. McCarthy became chair of the Senate Government hapter Eleven

Operations Committee (GOC) and used the Permanent Investigations Subcommittee of the GOC to further his attacks against the imagined "Communist infiltration." As chief counsel to the subcommittee, McCarthy hired Roy Cohn, one of the government's attack-dog prosecutors in the Rosenberg case, and McCarthy's machinery quickly went to work investigating trade with the Communist bloc, subversion in the State Department, Voice of America, and Communist infiltration of the Army, defense industries, and the United Nations (Griffith, 1970, 327-328).

McCarthy's concentration on investigations of Communist infiltration represented a clear shift in focus for Congress. During the 79th Congress, from 1945-1947, there were only four Congressional hearings on the subject of Communist infiltration. When the Republicans took over control of Congress in 1947, the number of investigations of Communist infiltration increased over the next two years to twenty-two. During the 83rd Congress, however, when McCarthy was the head of the Government Operations Committee, the number of investigations rose to fifty-one from 1953-1955. After McCarthy's departure, the number of investigations dropped back to the levels of the 79th Congress (Griffith, 1970, 328). The conservative penchant for investigation would return as a chief political strategy of the Republicans in the 1990s during the years of the Clinton administration.

Although President Eisenhower himself was not directly supportive of McCarthy's activities, he did not condemn them either; consequently, Eisenhower's inaction and silence on the matter had the impact of legitimizing McCarthy. Polls in the early summer of 1953 showed that the majority of Americans approved of both McCarthy and his activities (Miles, 1980, 211). Nevertheless, some Republicans were apprehensive about McCarthy and Vice President-Elect Richard Nixon was dispatched from the White House to the McCarthyists to discuss the directions of McCarthy's attacks. At a meeting at Key Biscayne, Florida, on December 30, 1952, Nixon pressed McCarthy to agree that he would direct his venom only at the Democrats (Miles, 1980, 213).

In spite of McCarthy's assurances to Nixon, McCarthy pressed forward in an effort to obtain the loyalty/security files of the U.S. Army. The military is typically a conservative institution, but in this instance, McCarthy and the Republican Right viewed the military under Secretary of Defense George Marshall and Chairman of the Joint Chiefs of Staff Omar Bradley (who had been an open supporter of Truman's foreign policies) as a manifestation of New Deal internationalism (Miles, 1980, 213).

McCarthy's primary attack Dog, Roy Cohn, however, had his own personal reasons for going after the army. Cohn's assistant and homosexual lover, G. David Schine, had been drafted by the U.S. Army. Cohn pressed the army for special release privileges for Schine, but the Army refused to grant his requests. In retaliation, Cohn launched his ill-fated crusade against the U.S. Army (Von Hoffman, 1988, 262).

The Downfall of McCarthy

In taking on the army, however, Cohn and McCarthy had taken on a formidable foe with near unlimited resources and legions of Allies. President Eisenhower, obviously, could be expected to have sympathies with the Army due to his lifetime of military service and role as Supreme Allied Commander during WWII. By taking on the Army, McCarthy essentially risked taking on the Eisenhower Presidency, which had much more in terms of popularity, resources, and political allies than McCarthy. Furthermore, more than forty percent of the Army's officer corps was of Southern or border state origin, and although the South was predominantly conservative, it was also overwhelmingly loyal to the Democratic Party (*New York Times*, August 6, 1953). As a consequence, McCarthy's attack on the Army could be expected to alienate Southerners, many of who were already somewhat uncomfortable with McCarthy's unrelenting attacks on Democrats (Griffith, 1970, 334).

In January, 1954, Assistant to the President Sherman Adams, Army Counsel John G. Adams, Henry Cabot Lodge, and Attorney General Herbert Brownell asked the Army counsel to prepare a chronology of the efforts of McCarthy and Cohn to secure special treatment from the Army for G. David Schine. In February, the Eisenhower Administration released the "chronology." The release of the chronology prepared the way for an investigation both of the Army's charge against McCarthy, and McCarthy's contention that the Army was using Schine as a means to forestall his investigation of communist infiltration of the Army. Vice President Richard Nixon, endowed with a solid reputation as a staunch anti-communist himself, publicly criticized McCarthy's "reckless talk and questionable methods" (Griffith, 1970, 335).

McCarthy's hearings on the Army dragged on for two months and were televised to the nation, but there was little doubt as to who won the encounter. At the end of the hearings, McCarthy's approval rating had dropped to 35%. While Cohn ranted and raved, Army counsel Joseph Welch calmly revealed how McCarthy had introduced altered photographs as evidence in an attempt to smear Army personnel (Von Hoffman, 1988, 266). Cohn resigned as McCarthy's chief counsel and the Senate Select Committee recommended Censure of McCarthy on two counts of contempt of the Senate. Specifically, the Select Committee cited McCarthy's refusal to appear before the Subcommittee on Privileges and Elections in 1952 and the abuse of Brigadier General Zwicker before the Permanent Investigations

Subcommittee. The Democrats voted unanimously for Censure, 45-0, with only Senator John F. Kennedy of Massachusetts abstaining, and the Republicans were split evenly, 22 for and against (Griffith, 1970, 340).

The Democrats won the off-year elections in 1954 and McCarthy died three years later of cirrhosis of the liver, thus ending the most reactionary wave that followed WWII. Within the Right, however, the attitudes toward the New Deal, socialism and communism did not change. Furthermore, the idea that the global rise of communism was somehow linked to decline and decay in the United States continued unabated, as did the view of the world as a zero-sum game between communism and democratic capitalism. The conservatives were forced, however, into using tactics that were somewhat less brazen due to the defeat of McCarthy. Furthermore, their attacks on the New Deal had to be somewhat more subdued due to the fact that Eisenhower essentially legitimized and gave tacit approval to the New Deal through his inaction and unwillingness to dismantle New Deal programs (Mayer, 1964, 313).

William F. Buckley

The heir apparent to McCarthy as the voice of the conservative attack-dogs in the late 1950s became the young conservative writer, William F. Buckley, Jr. Buckley had been a student at Yale in the 1940s where he was influenced by the staunch anti-communist professor Willmoore Kendall. Kendall's conservative views were so radical and he so aggravated the other faculty members and Administration at Yale that they bought out his tenure. Buckley, however, agreed with Kendall's views and viewed most of the rest of the faculty at Yale as engaging in what he termed as "miseducation." Shortly after his graduation from Yale, Buckley published his first book, *God and Man at Yale*, with the help of Kendall and Frank Chodorov in 1951. In his book, Buckley accused Yale of neglecting its mission to foster Christianity and capitalism. Moreover, Buckley argued that Yale had permitted its faculty to express views that violated widely accepted American religious, political, and economic values under the guise of academic freedom (Muccigrosso, 2001, 92). Buckley further argued that left-leaning professors should be fired for inculcating values that were "against the public welfare" (Buckley, 1951, 86). Included among those that Buckley believed should be fired for their "collectivist" values was Paul Samuelson, a New Deal Keynesian economist and author of a standard text, *Economics: An Introductory Analysis* (Miles, 1980, 244).

In foreign policy, Buckley was an admirer of the isolationism of Albert J. Nock, as well as a Nationalist and an Anglophobe, and therefore opposed American intervention in World War II. Buckley was also vehemently anti-communist and therefore supported a hard line against the Soviet Union and Communist China. Buckley's conservatism, however, was a philosophy of radical conservative dissent rather than accommodation of the status quo; consequently, Democratic Party positions and policies (such as the anti-communism of Truman and John F. Kennedy) could be opposed even when they were consistent with his own conservatism (Miles, 1980, 255).

In 1954, Buckley published his second book, *McCarthy and His Enemies,* with his brother-in-law L. Brent Bozell. Buckley was critical of McCarthy's methods, but defended McCarthyism by arguing that communist infiltration of the government had occurred, and was a real threat to the nation. Furthermore, the government in general and the State Department in particular had failed to seek out and eradicate the communist penetration (Miles, 1980, 255).

National Review

In 1955, Buckley founded perhaps the most important periodical of the conservative movement with the creation of *National Review.* National Review was dedicated to the conservative traditions of the free market, laissez-faire capitalism, individualism, Christianity, and hyper-Americanism. *National Review* provided a forum for conservative writers of all stripes, including William Rusher, Robert Morris, and Whittaker Chambers, as well as libertarians Frank Chodorov, Max Eastman, Frank Meyer, and Russell Kirk. *National Review* only tacitly supported the Eisenhower administration and chose Eisenhower over Adlai Stevenson in 1956 only as the lesser of two evils. In 1960, *National Review* did not even endorse the Republican candidate and vehement anti-communist, Richard Nixon, instead choosing to endorse no one (Miles, 1980, 255-256).

In spite of Buckley's extreme conservative positions, circulation of *National Review* grew to 95,000 by 1960 and the magazine could be credited with increasing the intellectual vitality and respectability of conservatism (Muccigrosso, 2002, 93). Willam F. Buckley's newspaper column, "On the Right," was syndicated to more than 300 newspapers across the country and Buckley would eventually parlay his publishing success into the control of Starr Broadcasting, which owned a number of radio stations, and a starring role on the interview program on public television, "Firing Line." The renewed intellectual "vitality," however, did not necessarily translate itself into political power, even though the Republicans held the Presidency for eight years under Dwight Eisenhower. Eisenhower considered himself a moderate, and therefore essentially left the legacy of the New Deal intact throughout the 1950s, much to the chagrin of the Buckley conservatives (Miles, 1980, 256-257).

National Review and the Hungarian Uprising

In 1956, the Soviet Union brutally suppressed a Democracy uprising in Hungary and an estimated 30,000 Hungarians died in the fighting. Although the Nationalist wing of the Republican Party had been calling for "liberation" of Eastern Europe from communism, Buckley's *National Review* did not call for American military intervention in Hungary at the risk of World War III. Instead, a more subdued James Burnham asked, "Liberation, What Next?" in the January 19, 1957 issue of the magazine, abandoning the hard-line anti-communist belligerence that the *National Review* had championed throughout the decade. When faced with harsh realities, "rolling back" communism proved to be little more than rhetoric, even for the hard-line conservatives at *National Review* (Miles, 1980, 257).

Racial Integration

In 1954, the Supreme Court under Republican Chief Justice and Eisenhower appointee Earl Warren issued its landmark decision in *Brown v. Board of Education,* mandating the racial integration of public schools. Eisenhower, however, shared the Southern segregationist view on race and did little to enforce the Court's decision in his first term. Eisenhower would later refer to Earl Warren's appointment to the position of Chief Justice as his "greatest mistake." Eisenhower's passive resistance of school integration helped his standing among white Southern voters in the election of 1956 (Gould, 2003, 338).

Southern Conservatives, both Republican and Democrat, were aghast at the integration ruling and worked to do everything they could do to undermine the Court's decision. Segregationists launched a campaign across the South known as "massive resistance," which involved total rejection and active opposition to integration. Southern conservatives also reformulated and supported John C. Calhoun's old ante-bellum idea known as "interposition," or using the powers of the States to prevent integration. The idea was premised on the view of the Constitution as a compact among the States. The argument was that States could "interpose their own sovereignty" between the federal government and the people when the federal government exercised unconstitutional power (Miles, 1980, 275).

Southern conservative Democrats in Congress, including 19 Senators and 81 members of the House, banded together and signed the "Southern Manifesto" that commended the "motives of those states which have declared the intention to resist forced integration by any lawful means" (www.cviog.uga.edu/Projects/gainfo/manifesto.htm). The Southern Manifesto then essentially accused the U.S. Supreme Court of acting unconstitutionally by "substituting "naked power for established law." Furthermore, the Manifesto contended that Congress had no power to be involved in education, thus ignoring the Constitutional provision in Article I that granted Congress the power to "promote the progress of science and useful arts." Finally, the Southerners argued in the Manifesto that the Court did not have the authority to decide what was "established law," a power it had certainly held ever since the landmark case of *Marbury v. Madison* in 1803 (*Congressional Record*, 1956).

The Southern conservative point of view quickly became translated into what was essentially unconstitutional action by conservative-led State governments in the South and the result was a virtual repeat of the "nullification crisis" of the 1830s, though the issue had shifted from tariffs to school integration. Conservative Democratic Senator Harry F. Byrd took the lead in pushing for the interposition strategy in Virginia. Senator Byrd argued for "massive resistance" to school integration in Virginia, and the Virginia General Assembly passed "enabling legislation" in the summer of 1956 that compelled the Governor to close any school that came under a court order to integrate. If a second court order were issued requiring the school to reopen, the Virginia Governor would then be required to cut off State funding for the school (Miles, 1980, 274-275).

Interposition in Texas

In Texas, conservative Democratic Governor Allan Shivers and Attorney General John Ben Shepperd quickly adopted interposition. Governor Shivers announced his personal opposition to integration, stating, "I am the kind of Texan who believes colored people do not want to go to school with whites" (Campbell, 2003, 425). Shivers also played on Southern conservative racist sentiments and made racism and integration the centerpiece of his gubernatorial campaign of 1954. Shivers announced a platform "against organized labor, northern liberal Democrats, communists, and the NAACP." Shivers purposely played up racial fears in claiming that his opponent in the Democratic primaries, liberal Democrat Ralph Yarborough, was tied to the NAACP and that the goal of the NAACP was to "end segregation in social activities and in residential neighborhoods" (Cox, 2002, 267).

Shivers' supporters then launched an underhanded campaign to play to the worst demons among conservatives' fears of integration. As part of their efforts, Shivers' supporters paid a black man to drive a Cadillac through East Texas plastered with Yarborough stickers. As part of the stunt, their black employee stopped at gas stations manned by white attendants, rudely demanded fast service, insulted employees, and claimed that he was "in a hurry to return to work for Mr. Yarborough" (Cox 2002, 270). Shivers' ads declared that Yarborough was a "negro lover" controlled by "labor bosses and the NAACP" and the Shivers literature pointed out that every "colored" precinct went for Yarborough by 10-1 to 20-1 margins (Cox, 2002, 270).

Shivers' campaign created a pamphlet and a television program that became known as the "Port Arthur Story." In a 12 minute black and white film produced for TV, the "Port Arthur Story" depicted the Texas coastal city as crippled and destitute due to a labor union strike precipitated by northerners and negroes. In the film, the narrator explained how the once-thriving city of Port Arthur was now literally deserted and a community where no one smiled. As the camera panned empty streets and businesses, the narrator explained that the city was closed by communist-inspired negroes and organized labor as part of a larger plot to take over all Texas Cities. Port Arthur was merely the first beachhead for this negro-communist-based program of internal subversion and the entire city was under the control of the union-dominated negro strikers. White businessmen and women in the film complained that their livelihood and community was destroyed by "outside organizers and communist-dominated labor unions." Governor Shivers, of course, had discovered this plot and was fighting the invasion. Ralph Yarborough, in contrast, was on the side of this negro-communist plot (Cox, 2002, 271-272).

In the "Port Arthur Story" brochure, photos of Port Arthur showed white women and black men together, where they "mix daily on these picket lines. They drink from the same bottles and smoke the same cigarettes." One photo pictured a black woman in her car with her arm around a white woman and another showed a black man and a white woman together. Jake Pickle, later a Texas Congressman and head of the agency that produced the film and brochure. stated after the fact that "of course it was deserted, it was 6:00AM on a Sunday" (Cox, 2002, 272).

Another group, known as the "Citizens Protective Committee," issued a pamphlet with a "warning" to voters that if Yarborough wins, blacks "will flock to the white schools and demand their children be enrolled." Yarborough attempted to deflect the damage inflicted on him by the campaign and issued a statement that he was "against the mingling of our white and colored children in our public schools against the will of either race." Despite Yarborough's denials, Shivers' attack was successful and Shivers defeated Yarborough by a vote of 775,088 to 683,132 (Cox, 2002, 273).

In the fall of 1956 Mansfield High school became the first school in Texas to attempt to comply with Federaly mandated integration. Local conservatives in Mansfield threatened to physically prevent the integration and Governor Shivers sent the Texas Rangers to Mansfield to prevent the black students from attending. Local conservatives hung an effigy of a black man by the neck over the school's main entry way, where it remained for the first week of school, as a warning to any blacks that dared challenge the social order (Campbell, 2003, 427).

Texas' Governor Shivers also attempted to confront integration through the use of the mechanisms of democracy. With Shivers' support, the July 1956 Texas Democratic primary ballot included 3 nonbinding referendums. Voters were asked to respond yes or no to whether or not they opposed compulsory attendance at integrated schools, would favor legislation that outlawed inter-racial marriages, and supported state "interposition." Texans approved of all three measures by 80%. Shivers then created an Advisery Committee on Segregation in the Public Schools that was instructed to find ways to prevent integration. The Committee produced 21 recommendations in 1956, two of which passed the legislature in 1957. In the first measure, Texas State funds would be denied to local school districts that integrated without local voter approval. The second measure declared that "morality, space, and transportation" became legally recognized as justification for not complying with federal integration orders. The Texas legislature passed a third bill after federal troops forced integration in Little Rock, Arkansas, that authorized the closing of public schools if federal troops were used to integrate them. Furthermore, mandatory attendance was suspended for the parents of children that were exposed to integration (Campbell, 2003, 427).

Other conservative Democrat-dominated Southern States passed similar laws suspending mandatory attendance and allowing schools to close if they were forced to integrate. Laws were also passed at the State level making school integration illegal if the decision were not supported by a majority of the voters in any given school district, an unlikely occurrence in any white-dominated Southern school district (Cox, 2002, 280).

Election of 1956

The 1956 Presidential race was not to be much of a contest with the popular Eisenhower running for reelection against the same man he had defeated four years earlier, Adlai Stevenson. The Republicans moved somewhat to the left in forging their Party platform in an effort to pick up swing voters. The Republican Platform included a commitment to Social Security and a proposed Equal Rights Amendment for women, along with the more traditional conservative positions in favor of a balanced budget and the elimination of the National Debt. Eisenhower would win the right, the middle, and some of the left from the political spectrum in 1956 and defeat Stevenson by 9.5 million popular votes and 457-79 in the Electoral College (Gould, 2003, 339).

Republican Divisions under Eisenhower

In spite of Eisenhower's landslide victory, however, he was unable to control the hard-right grass-roots movement that was growing within conservatism. Eisenhower favored an active role for the United States abroad, a position staunchly opposed by conservative nationalists, and his commitment to the continuation of some New Deal programs, such as Social Security, were anathema to anti-statist conservative ideologues. Eisenhower also favored a scaling down of the U.S. military budget, but anti-communist conservatives instead favored a strong military and cuts in social spending instead (Pach and Richardson, 1991, 168-169). Other conservatives, such as Barry Goldwater, simply wanted smaller government and opposed the President's fiscal policy in his second term for its continuation of New Deal spending. Eisenhower's 1957 budget proposal increased spending 3.9%, causing Eisenhower's own Treasury Secretary George M. Humphrey to urge Congress to make substantial cuts in Eisenhower's proposal. Goldwater commented after looking at Eisenhower's budget that the President had been "beguiled by the siren song of socialism." The final result was a Congressional trimming of the President's budget led by members of Eisenhower's own Party (Edwards, 1995, 158).

Eisenhower further alienated Southern Traditional Conservatives later in September 1957 when he used National Guard troops to enforce school integration against the wishes of the defiant Arkansas Governor, Orval Faubus. When the Soviets announced the successful launch of Sputnik later that fall, conservatives viewed it as proof that Eisenhower had dangerously allowed the U.S. to fall behind the Soviets in space and military technology. The development allowed the Democrats the opportunity to paint Eisenhower as a poor steward of American security. Further injuring their own cause, the Republicans then launched an anti-labor campaign for the Congressional elections of 1958 stressing "right to work" laws that prevented closed union shops. The anti-labor campaign alienated urban workers in America's manufacturing based economy; consequently, the Republicans suffered defeat in the 1958 Congressional elections (Gould, 2003, 342-343).

John Birch Society

The late 1950s also spawned a more extreme group known as the John Birch Society (JBS) that was a combination of McCarthyism and Libertarian individualism. The John Birch Society was founded in 1958 in Indianapolis by Robert Welch, a Southern Baptist from North Carolina and an avid supporter of both Robert Taft and Joseph McCarthy. John Birch himself was a Baptist missionary to China who was killed in China by the communists shortly after World War II; hence, to Welch, Birch was a martyr for the greater causes of American-style freedom, democracy, and Christianity. Welch argued for a return to Nineteenth Century free enterprise with tariffs, and denounced both Woodrow Wilson's New Freedom, especially the income tax, and the New Deal (Broyles, 1964, 62).

Like so many conservative extremists before him, Welch constructed his organization on the twin pillars of conservatism and conspiracy theory. Welch himself was a communist conspiracy theorist and argued that 60 to 80 percent of Americans were pro-communist. Welch also believed that President Eisenhower, Secretary of State John Foster Dulles, and Chief Justice Earl Warren, were conscious agents of an international communist conspiracy. In furtherance of combating the international communist conspiracy, Welch mounted a billboard campaign across the country to "Impeach Earl Warren," the "Communist" propagator of school integration (Miner, 1996, 123).

Welch was a hyper-Americanist and opposed international organizations such as the UN and NATO as useless and costly encroachments on American sovereignty, but Welch also opposed large defense budgets and foreign interventionism as connected to the international communist conspiracy (Broyles, 1964, 249).

The John Birch Society (JBS) found fertile ground among rural conservatives and grew to an organization of 75,000 members by the end of 1964. The Society had a national network of reading rooms and book stores, a publishing house, Western Islands, and a periodical, *American Opinion* (Broyles, 1964, 252).

The JBS received a boost in the late in 1950s when President Eisenhower sponsored a program to spread right-wing propaganda against communism among the American military. In furtherance of Eisenhower's anti-communist goal, the U.S. military sponsored "Project Alert," a program that involved bringing together representatives of local community groups with those from the armed services to "alert" the population to the communist menace. Seminars were conducted involving leaders of the JBS, who were invited to give speeches to Project Alert. The military worked in concert with the religious fundamentalist Harding College in Arkansas, a place so conservative that even instrumental music in daily Chapel was disallowed, to produce programs that explained that the primary American enemy was the communist menace within (Lipset and Raab, 1970, 313-314).

Defense Secretary Robert McNamara ordered Project Alert shut down in 1961 and relieved Major General Edwin Walker of duty for continuing to circulate right-wing propaganda among his troops. Senator Strom Thurmond of South Carolina subsequently demanded an investigation of "Defense Department censorship of speeches of officers" and of the firing of Walker.

The JBS then followed up Thurmond's tirade with a Bulletin in September, 1961, urging JBS members to "Support Senator Thurmond's demand for the investigation of the military gag rule" (Lipset and Raab, 1970, 314-315).

All conservatives, however, were not necessarily in sync with the JBS. In 1962, the *National Review* repudiated the JBS, as did Richard Nixon in his California gubernatorial campaign. At a meeting in 1962, Russell Kirk encouraged Senator Barry Goldwater of Arizona to renounce the JBS. In Kirk's words to Goldwater, "Eisenhower isn't a communist, he's a golfer." Kirk and Nixon, not the JBS, embodied the sentiments of the conservative mainstream (Miner, 1996, 123). Later, the JBS would oppose the internationalism of the Vietnam War and thus provoke a deluge of criticism from numerous prominent Republicans, including former National Republican Party chairman Senator Everett Dirksen, Representative and future President Gerald Ford, and 1964 Republican Presidential candidate and Arizona Senator, Barry Goldwater. In 1965, even William F. Buckley's *National Review* condemned the JBS for what was termed as its "psychosis of conspiracy" (Quoted in Miner, 1996, 123). Other conservatives, however, especially those in the rural South (including a young Congressman named George H.W. Bush), refused to repudiate the Birch faction, and the JBS would remain important on the fringes of conservatism through the present.

Chapter Twelve

Conservatism from Goldwater to Nixon

Not since the Civil War had any decade in the United States brought as much political and social turmoil as did the 1960s. Within this turmoil, conservatives, like others, had varying responses, but the fundamental conservative revulsion at the changes in American society that took place in the 1960s laid the groundwork for the construction of a conservative majority that arose in the decades that followed. Foremost among those building the conservative foundations in the 1960s was the man who eventually became known as "Mr. Conservative," Arizona Senator Barry Goldwater.

Barry Goldwater

Barry Goldwater had been a friend and supporter of Joseph McCarthy in the 1950s and McCarthy himself had campaigned for Goldwater when the latter ran for the U.S. Senate in Arizona in 1952. As a consequence, Goldwater's conservative anti-communist credentials were impeccable. Furthermore, Goldwater was one of McCarthy's defenders when McCarthy was under attack in the U.S. Senate and facing censure in 1954. Goldwater describes his position on the movement against McCarthy as follows,

> "The news columns and the airwaves have been filled with their pious talk about civil liberties, ethical codes, and protection of the innocent, while at the same time these people have dipped in the smut pot to discredit Senator McCarthy and his work against communism" (*Congressional Record*, 1954).

Goldwater remained a loyal supporter of McCarthy until the end, stating upon McCarthy's death that "because Joe McCarthy lived, we are a safer, freer, more vigilant nation" (Goldwater, 1990, 34).

Commitment to the battle against communism, however, was only one facet of Goldwater's conservatism. Goldwater combined his rabid anti-communism with what was essentially Classic Liberal ideology, coalescing laissez-faire free-market economics and a premium on States' rights. Goldwater was essentially anti-union, and thus opposed to collective bargaining and instead favoring a prohibition on political activity by labor unions (Goldwater, 1990, 38). By advocating a prohibition against labor unions, Goldwater obviously violated his own laissez-faire ideology that supposedly called for an end to government regulation. What this demonstrates is that in actuality Goldwater only favored a reduction in the regulation of entities he supported and not those he opposed, an approach that has been a consistent facet of conservatism in the four decades since Goldwater's failed Presidential bid.

Goldwater also argued for the end of graduated taxes and the withdrawal of the federal government from a whole host of other areas, including social welfare programs, education, public power, agriculture, public housing, and urban renewal. Goldwater argued that these activities were either better suited to State and local government or should be the domain of private institutions and private enterprise. In particular, Goldwater applied his preference for State and local control to the subject of school integration. Goldwater argued,

> "I am firmly convinced—not only that integrated schools are not required— but that the Constitution does not permit any interference whatsoever by the federal government in the field of education" (Goldwater, 1990, 34).

Goldwater, however, was not a typical KKK-style racist. Goldwater employed minorities at his department store in Arizona and contributed financially to minority-advocate organizations including the Urban League and the NAACP. In Congress, he broke with Southern conservatives and voted in favor of the Civil Rights Acts of 1957 and 1960. Furthermore, Goldwater actually argued in favor of the basic idea of school integration in theory, arguing,

> "it is both wise and just for negro children to attend the same schools as whites, and that to deny them this opportunity carries with it strong implications of inferiority. I am not prepared, however, to impose that judgment of mine on the people of Mississippi or South Carolina, or to tell them what methods should be adopted and what pace should be kept in striving toward that goal" (Goldwater, 1990, 37).

In other words, Goldwater's opposition to *Brown v. Board of Education* was ostensibly all about "States' rights," rather than racism. In this and in his stated preference for integration in general, Goldwater was actually out of step with typical Southern white conservatives in the late 1950s and early 1960s. Virtually all of the rest of positions taken by Goldwater in the late 1950s and early 1960s, however, would remain solid platforms for conservatives throughout the rest of the Twentieth Century and into the next millennium.

Goldwater burst into national prominence and inspired conservatives to support him when he won his Senate seat in Arizona in 1958 based on the above conservative ideological program. Goldwater's victory was particularly impressive because it came at a time when conservatives nationwide were suffering defeat in the mid-term elections while espousing similar views. Consequently, Goldwater would quickly become recognized, along with Vice President Richard Nixon, as a leader of the Republicans' most conservative faction.

Rockefeller and the Moderate Republicans

Goldwater and Nixon, however, faced a challenge for Party leadership from Nelson Rockefeller, a moderate Republican from New York with obvious name recognition and financial connections. As Vice President, Nixon considered himself to be the heir apparent to Eisenhower's Presidency, but Rockefeller had ambitions of his own and won the New York governorship in 1958. Rockefeller then sought to use his New York victory as a springboard for the Presidential race in 1960 (Perlstein, 2001, 13).

Rockefeller would develop marital problems that would destroy his candidacy, but his money and popularity in the nation's largest state still made him a force to be reckoned with. Rockefeller sought to guide the Party in a more moderate direction while Vice President Richard Nixon and Barry Goldwater favored a more traditional conservative stance. Realizing that a divided party would surely lose to the Democrats in 1960, Nixon and Rockefeller met in New York City in July, 1960 to reconcile their differences. Their meeting in New York produced a compromise joint declaration that became known as the "Compact of Fifth Avenue." In this agreement, Nixon favored an increase in defense spending to counter the Soviet Union, thus satisfying conservatives, but essentially contradicting the policies of President Eisenhower, who favored downsizing the military at the time. Nixon also announced his support for civil rights in an effort to placate Rockefeller and the Republican moderates (Perlstein, 2001, 14).

Barry Goldwater viewed the agreement as a sellout of conservative principles and referred to the "Compact" as the "Munich of the Republican Party" (Perlstein, 2001, 14). Consequently, Goldwater gained respect from the Republican conservative faction for his unwillingness to compromise on his conservative principles. At the Republican Convention where Nixon received the Party's nomination, Goldwater made a speech where he argued that conservatives needed to "take this Party back." In making this statement,

Goldwater was arguing that the conservatives should wrestle control of the Party from Nixon and Rockefeller and move it to a direction that was more conservative (Edwards, 1995, 138-139).

1960 Election

The Republicans faced a stiff challenge for the Presidency in 1960 from John F. Kennedy, an articulate young WWII veteran and son of the wealthy Boston magnate, Joseph Kennedy. The Republicans' cause was not helped in 1960 by President Eisenhower's lukewarm support of the candidacy of his Vice President. When asked for an example of a major Nixon idea that his administration had adopted, Eisenhower replied, "If you give me a week, I might think of one" (Nixon, 1978, 219).

John F. Kennedy, for his part, stole some of the conservatives' thunder by campaigning on a Cold War platform and arguing that the Eisenhower administration had allowed a "missile gap" to develop between the U.S. and the Soviet Union. Kennedy argued that the U.S. was behind the USSR both in missile technology (as proven by Sputnik) and in terms of numbers of missiles. The American "inferiority" in these areas that Kennedy spoke of was primarily fiction, but Sputnik provided all of the political ammunition Kennedy needed in order to make his point. After all, many conservatives had voiced the same criticisms of the Eisenhower administration for years, so the casting of America as "behind" the Soviet Union in missile technology was an easy sell (Jones, 1996, 544). Kennedy also fared well in his televised debates against Nixon, partially due to Kennedy's youthful good looks and use of Hollywood makeup in contrast to Nixon's 5:00 shadow, lack of makeup, and profuse sweating (Jones, 1996, 544).

As an Irish-Catholic from Massachusetts, Kennedy had little appeal in the South; consequently, Kennedy invited the Senate majority leader, Lyndon Baines Johnson of Texas, to be his running mate so that he could have a chance in Texas and the Southern states. Kennedy won the electoral vote in Texas (and therefore the nation) at least partially due to this choice. Kennedy outpolled Nixon by only 118,000 votes, and the Democrats actually lost seats to the Republicans in Congress, so the Kennedy victory was not a complete Republican defeat. The conservative coalition that would rise to dominance in 1980 was beginning to take shape (Gould, 2003, 348).

The Rise of the Goldwater Faction

With the country almost evenly divided between Republicans and Democrats, the conservative Goldwater faction used Nixon's defeat as an opportunity to realize Goldwater's goal of "taking back" the Republican

Party. Unfortunately for the Goldwater conservatives, as of early 1963, Republican Party members preferred Nelson Rockefeller to Goldwater by almost a 3-1 margin. In the spring of 1963, however, Rockefeller followed his divorce with remarriage to Margaretta Fitler Murphy, a divorcee with four children. Conservative moralists were scandalized, and Rockefeller's stock within the Party plummeted (Miles, 1980, 289).

To add to Rockefeller's woes, in April and May 1963, civil rights protests led by Martin Luther King against segregated lunch counters erupted all over the South. Rockefeller was a known supporter of civil rights through the Rockefeller philanthropic organizations, and the racial unrest further discredited Rockefeller in the eyes of conservatives. By the end of May, 1963, more Republicans favored Goldwater than Rockefeller (Miles, 1980, 290).

In June 1963, President Kennedy did the Goldwater conservatives a favor by proposing a sweeping Civil Rights Act that would end segregation in public accommodations and eradicate racial discrimination in employment. Shortly thereafter, several hundred thousand African-Americans descended on Washington to press the federal government for civil rights (Branch, 1989, 847-992). Conservative Republicans viewed the development as an "opportunity" since civil rights were greatly unpopular among the conservative majority in the South, and there was therefore very good reason to believe that any candidate pushing for civil rights would be swept in the South. Furthermore, Kennedy was almost swept in the West in 1960, and a conservative Westerner that espoused "States' rights," such as Goldwater, had a chance to sweep the South and West (a strategy that would be employed successfully 40 years later by George W. Bush) and thus win the election.

The Southern Strategy

The Republican convention of 1964 quickly became dominated by far-right Goldwater Republicans that favored what became known as the "Southern strategy." Northeastern Republicans led by Nelson Rockefeller, however, condemned the strategy as immoral, racist, and exclusive in character. In the words of Rockefeller,

"Completely incredible as it is to me, it is now being seriously proposed to the Republican Party that as a strategy for victory in 1964, that it write off the Negro and other minority groups, that it deliberately write off the great industrial states of the North (representing nearly 50 percent of the country's population), that it write off the big cities, and that it direct its appeal primarily to the electoral votes of the South, plus the West and a scattering of other states. The transparent purpose behind this plan is to erect political

power on the outlawed and immoral base of segregation and to transform the
Republican Party from a national party of all the people to a sectional party
for some of the people" (Quoted in Novak, 1965, 209-210).

What Rockefeller saw in the Goldwater supporters clearly contained
elements of truth, but the white South, motivated by bigotry, would begin to
abandon the Democratic Party in 1964 even though Goldwater would
eventually be a landslide election loser. The landslide victory for Democratic
candidate Lyndon Johnson over Goldwater, however, owed more perhaps to
the complex emotional reactions of the public to the Kennedy assassination
than to any coherent grand strategy by the opposition. Goldwater won only
39% of the vote nationally, but won five states in the Deep South in addition
to his home State of Arizona. In essence, the groundwork for the future
success of the conservative Republicans had been laid even if the immediate
battle had ended in miserable failure (Miles, 1980, 290-291).

Johnson's Great Society

For the short term, the election of 1964 not only resulted in Democratic
control of the Presidency, but the Democrats also gained 38 seats in the
House and two in the Senate, giving them almost a two-to-one majority in
both chambers. The death of John F. Kennedy provided moral impetus for
the Democratic program, and this, combined with their strong majorities in
both Houses, allowed the Democrats to pass the Civil Rights Act of 1964 and
initiate some of Lyndon Johnson's "War on Poverty" programs prior to the
election. When the new Congress convened in 1965, the Democrats ushered
through a plethora of programs including the Voting Rights Act of 1965,
Medicare, federal aid to education, federal housing programs, and new
spending on infrastructure (Califano, 1991, 55-59).

The increased governmental activity of Johnson's "Great Society" (as he
called it), was the largest increase in the scope of federal government activity
since the New Deal; consequently, Johnson's program was complete
anathema to both conservative Goldwater Republicans and conservative
Southern Democrats. Furthermore, there was no concurrent crisis of the
magnitude of the Great Depression or WWII that could help Johnson and the
Democrats "justify" or sustain widespread support for their new programs as
they had during the New Deal era. For certain, none of the Democrats'
ambitious new programs could be expected to work without problems;
hence, "flaws" in the Democrats' achievements would very quickly provide
conservatives with assistance in regaining the political upper hand (Califano,
1991, 55-59).

Vietnam and Political Unrest

Lyndon Johnson also aided the conservatives' cause in the coming years by expanding the national headache known as the Vietnam War. Johnson had campaigned in 1964 as the peace candidate, painted Barry Goldwater as a dangerous warmonger, and argued that,

> "we are not going to send American boys nine or ten thousand miles around the world to do what Asian boys ought to be doing for themselves" (Jones, 1996, 591).

Republicans supported Goldwater with the slogan, "In your heart, you know he's right," but the Democrats countered with the more effective, "In your heart, you know he might," suggesting that Goldwater would be reckless with atomic weapons (Jones, 1996, 591).

After the election, however, Johnson displayed his conservative Texan militarism and anti-communist roots when he quickly escalated the American presence in Vietnam. Johnson authorized a massive bombing campaign aimed at destroying the communist enemy's supply lines in spite of the fact that he was warned by Undersecretary of State George Ball that such tactics would be ineffective at anything except for uniting all Vietnam against the American intruders (Jones, 1996, 591).

In February, 1965, Johnson began a troop escalation at the request of General Westmoreland that led eventually to a commitment of over 500,000 troops by 1968. Johnson then failed to impose taxation either for the war or his Great Society, arguing that Americans could have both "guns and butter." Johnson's deficit spending ultimately unleashed an escalation of price inflation that would burden the economy for years to come (Califano, 1991, 122-148).

Beginning in 1965, war protests broke out across the United States coterminous with Johnson's war escalation. Simultaneously, civil rights had not brought peace to race relations and America's urban centers. Instead, Johnson's second term was filled with race riots in America's major urban centers. In the "Watts" riot in Los Angeles in 1965, 34 black Americans were killed by National Guard troops that had to be called in to restore order. In Detroit in 1967, 43 were killed in race riots, and in Newark, 25 persons were killed in another riot the same year. In 1968, the assassinations of Martin Luther King and Robert Kennedy further contributed to the public perception that law and order had been sacrificed under the Democrats' watch, thus further playing into the hands of Republican conservatives (Brinkley, 2003, 836-840).

Republican Resurgence

Positioned to take advantage of the political opening was Richard Nixon, whose "comeback" had essentially begun with the 1964 Goldwater campaign. Nixon campaigned diligently for Goldwater while Republican moderates kept their distance so as to prevent association with Goldwater from tainting their own reelection chances. In doing so, Nixon won the gratitude of the Republican right. Nixon considered the Goldwater campaign and his work on the campaign to be a learning experience that shaped his strategy for 1968. Nixon had lost the California governorship to Edmund Brown in 1962 after Nixon had repudiated the John Birch Society and the extreme right during the campaign. Nixon later stated his lessons thusly,

> "Barry Goldwater found out you can't win an important election with only the right wing behind you...But I found out in 1962 that you can't win an election without the right wing" (Buckley, 1971, 9).

As a consequence, Nixon would take measures to ensure that he could lure the support of the Goldwater right in 1968, and winning Republican Presidential candidates have ensured that they gave the proper respect to the Goldwater right ever since (Miles, 1980, 303).

Meanwhile, in the mid-terms in 1966, with the Vietnam War dragging on and domestic unrest heating up, the Republicans gained 47 House seats and three Senate seats, their best showing since 1946. Republicans also won eight more governorships, including Ronald Reagan in California, who had inspired the conservative wing of the Republican Party with his nationally televised address during the 1964 Presidential campaign. Suddenly, in spite of the disaster of 1964, the window was open for Nixon's return and a Republican victory in 1968 (Miles, 1980, 303).

Ronald Reagan, the new conservative star on the horizon, suddenly became a threat to Nixon's candidacy in 1968 when Governor Reagan suddenly entered the race for the Republican Presidential nomination. Nixon moved to thwart the challenge by meeting with Republican State chairmen and stressing his essentially segregationist views on race, along with his preference for a strong military. For his efforts, Nixon received, among others, the support of Senator Strom Thurmond of South Carolina, the epitome of Southern conservatism. As a result of this "Southern Strategy," which was as "Western" as it was "Southern," Nixon was nominated at the Republican convention in 1968 on the first ballot. Nixon's candidacy was aided greatly by disarray within the Democratic Party after Lyndon Johnson decided not to seek reelection on March 31, 1968 due to a turn for the worse in Vietnam (Califano, 1991, 250-257).

1968 and the Democratic Demise

In Lyndon Johnson's State of the Union Address in January, 1968, Johnson had announced to the nation that the War in Vietnam was in the process of winding down. Two weeks later, and only a week after North Korean forces seized the U.S. ship *Pueblo* in the Sea of Japan and imprisoned 82 American sailors, the Viet Cong in South Vietnam launched a massive offensive (known as Tet) against the cities and provinces of South Vietnam. Americans were shocked to see televised coverage of enemy troops overrunning the U.S. Embassy in Saigon after being informed two weeks prior that the enemy in Vietnam was almost vanquished. Although Johnson described the offensive as a "last gasp," the images demonstrated in the minds of many Americans that the war was not near over and the U.S. was not near victory. As a consequence, public sentiment turned both against the Johnson administration and the war (Herring, 2001, 286).

Realizing that he would lose any attempt at reelection due to the War's unpopularity, Johnson refused to send any more troops, ceased much of the bombing in Vietnam, and announced on March 31 that he would neither seek nor accept the nomination of his Party for the Presidency (Jones, 1996, 604-609). This left the Democratic nomination wide open for the young and energetic Robert F. Kennedy, who subsequently won the California Democratic primary. Tragically, that same night, Kennedy was assassinated in the ballroom of a Los Angeles Hotel, leaving the Democratic nomination to Vice President Hubert H. Humphrey. To make matters worse, the Democratic Convention in Chicago was tainted with demonstrations and clashes between anti-war protesters and those that supported Johnson's war policies. The tension spilled over into the streets of Chicago and a bloody riot erupted where hundreds were injured as police attempted to disperse the crowds with tear gas and clubs. Once again, the violence was proof to conservatives that law and order had broken down under the Democrats' rule (Farber, 1988, 227).

Nixon took advantage of the domestic disarray and Vietnam debacle to essentially ride the Democratic failures to victory. Nixon refused to detail a Vietnam strategy on the convenient basis that it would undermine the war effort and undercut Peace negotiations in Paris. Nixon also campaigned on law and order and claimed to speak for the "silent center, the millions of people in the middle of the political spectrum who do not demonstrate, who do not picket or protest loudly." Furthermore, Nixon campaigned with standard conservative anti-tax rhetoric against what he termed as the "ever-higher piling of Federal tax on State tax on local tax" (Gould, 2003, 376).

In spite of the Democratic disarray, Nixon almost lost the Presidential election of 1968 anyway due to a strong showing in the race from segregationist Alabama Governor and Third Party candidate, George Wallace. Nixon won 43.4% of the vote while Humphrey won 42.7%, but Wallace won 13.5% of the vote and five Southern States. Nixon's strength in the South turned out to be in the upper South, rather than the "deep" South, essentially the reverse of Goldwater's success in 1964. Nixon won only one "deep" South state, South Carolina, while the other five all went to the Alabama Governor and the segregationist American Independence Party. Wallace's supporters, however, were overwhelmingly white conservatives, so when Wallace's votes are added to Nixon's, the conservatives won an overwhelming 57% majority, and the deciding factors were the negative conservative reaction to the domestic unrest surrounding the civil rights struggle and the Vietnam War (Phillips, 1969, 216). Nevertheless, George Wallace had effectively broken the Democrats' New Deal coalition in the South and it has yet to be repaired.

George Wallace

George Wallace was a former liberal Democratic Governor of Alabama who remade himself under a conservative preservationist ideology that well-reflected Southern Traditional Conservative ideology. Wallace spoke in favor of law and order, against government intervention in social problems (i.e. segregation), and against the "acceleration of change." Wallace directed his campaign against federally imposed integration, civil unrest, and the growth in central government power during the Johnson administration, all policy directions that were anathema to Traditional Conservatives (Sherrill, 1968, 266).

Earlier in his political career, Wallace had avoided the race issue until he lost the 1958 Alabama governor's race to John Patterson, a candidate backed by the KKK. Wallace later was quoted as saying "they out-niggered me that time but they'll never do it again" (Quoted in Sherrill, 1968, 267). Wallace then adopted a staunch segregationist stance and won the Alabama Governor's seat in the next election. Wallace subsequently made a national political name for himself as the South's champion for segregation. Wallace displayed his impeccable segregationist credentials when he dispatched the Alabama State police to put down civil rights demonstrations led by Martin Luther King in Birmingham, and sent State police to close a Tuskegee high school in order to prevent it from submitting to federal court integration orders. Then when the University of Alabama was ordered by a federal court to admit two black students, Wallace personally stood in the school's doorway before television cameras to place his body between the federalized Alabama National Guard that had been sent to enforce the court order, and the schoolhouse door. After the cameras stopped rolling, Wallace dutifully removed himself from the doorway and allowed the National Guard to escort the students to class, but his status as the hero of segregation had been solidified (Lipset and Raab, 1970, 343).

Wallace did not, however, champion ideological racism and instead cloaked his segregation arguments in "State's rights" terms. In the words of Wallace,

"a racist is one who despises someone because of his color, and an Alabama segregationist is one who conscientiously believes that it is in the best interest of the Negro and white to have separate educational and social order" (*U.S. News and World Report*, April 20, 1964, 120).

On exactly why segregation was in the best interest of both white and "Negro," Wallace did not much elaborate. Similarly, when asked whether his movement was a backlash against blacks, Wallace replied with his standard States' rights rhetoric;

"I think there is a backlash against the theoreticians and bureaucrats in the national government who are trying to solve problems that ought to be solved at the local level" (Quoted in Synon, 1970, 83).

Despite Wallace's personal claims to be something besides a racist, Wallace's support was certainly galvanized by the race issue. According to a Harris poll, 73% of all Wallace supporters wanted progress for blacks to be halted (*Boston Globe*, September 29, 1968, 4A). Wallace was also strongly supported by the more extreme right-wing groups, including the John Birch Society and the KKK, groups rarely associated with progress and equality for African Americans. In fact, at Wallace's initial Presidential campaign meeting in November, 1965, present were Ned Touchstone, the editor of the *Councilor*, a leading right-wing publication and dispenser of Illuminati and anti-Semitic conspiracy theories, and Richard Cotton, a right-wing radio commentator who saw a "Zionist-Jewish conspiracy behind most of the troubles in the country" (Cleghorn, 1968, 153). Wallace's campaign manager in South Texas, Vance Beaudreau, had been active in the American Nazi Party in Dallas in the 1960s, as had his Napa County, California Party Chairman, Leonard Holstein (Lipset and Raab, 1970, 352-353).

For his part, Wallace did not repudiate support from his far right-wing allies. In the words of Wallace, "At least a Klansman will fight for his country. He doesn't tear up his draft card" (Quoted in Wicker, 1967, 44). Similarly, concerning the John Birch Society, Wallace stated, "I am glad to have their support. I have no quarrel with the Birch Society." In another instance, Wallace proclaimed "I wouldn't know a Bircher if I saw one. I'm concerned about the communists and anarchists in our country, not the

Birchers" (Quoted in Lipset and Raab, 1970, 352). In contrast, Wallace
frequently referred to civil rights and Vietnam War protesters as the "scum
of the earth" and "trash" (Lipset and Raab, 1970, 357)

In addition to playing on racism, Wallace portrayed himself as a
champion of the common man in conservative populist terms. Wallace
presented himself as both anti-elitist and anti-intellectual and often even
deliberately mispronounced words and claimed not to understand certain
terms used by intellectual elites. Wallace's slogan was "Nobody is for
Wallace but the People." In the words of Wallace,

> "We are going to show them in November that the average American is sick
> and tired of all those over-educated ivory-tower folks with pointed heads
> looking down their noses at us" (Quoted in the *New York Times*, September 3,
> 1968, 38).

Similarly, on the subject of judges that "protect the rights of criminals and
protesters," Wallace stated,

> "Of course, if I did what I'd like to do I'd pick up something and smash one
> of these federal judges in the head and then burn the courthouse down. But
> I'm too genteel. What we need in this country is some Governors that used to
> work up here at Birmingham in the steel mills with about a tenth-grade
> education. A Governor like that wouldn't be so genteel. He'd put out his
> orders and he'd say, 'The first man who throws a brick is a dead man. The
> first man who loots something what doesn't belong to him is a dead man. My
> orders are to shot to kill.' That's the way to keep law and order. If you'd
> killed about three that way at Watts, the other forty wouldn't be dead today"
> (Quoted in Lipset and Raab, 1970, 356-357).

Wallace's solution for the civil unrest that beset the country in 1968 was
essentially to create a police state with Federal troops or police on every
corner if necessary in order to ensure that there would not be any riots. In the
words of Wallace, "that's right, we gonna have a police state for folks who
burn the cities down. They aren't gonna burn any more cities (*Newsweek*,
September 16, 1968, 27).

In spite of this right-wing extremism, Harris polls in September, 1968
revealed that close to one-third of the electorate tended to view Wallace and
the things he stood for positively. This was especially true among the less
educated, rural, small town, and working-class population. The support,
however, was not limited to the South. Wallace also had disproportionate
support among residents of small towns and rural areas in the north. Finally,
Wallace's support was disproportionately strong among Christian
fundamentalists (Lipset and Raab, 1970, 357-358). In short, Wallace's

political base was strikingly similar to the political base that George W. Bush would ride to power over three decades later.

The Nixon Presidency

Unlike George Wallace, Richard Nixon was not driven by Southern racism and State's rights rhetoric, and therefore was more open to compromises with his Democratic opposition. Furthermore, the Democrats controlled both Houses of Congress throughout his Presidency; consequently, both his staff and his policies became a mixed assortment of Traditional Conservatism, Classic Liberalism, and Reform Liberalism (Miles, 1980, 309).

In Nixon's Inaugural speech, he called for Americans to "go forward together," which was a reflection of Nixon's desire to unite the divided American people. Nixon attempted to "reach across the aisle" of American politics to the Democrats and invited Democratic Senator Henry Jackson of Washington to be his Secretary of Defense, and 1968 electoral opponent Hubert Humphrey was invited to be the Ambassador to the U.N. Both men declined Nixon's offer, but the attempt at bipartisanship had been made none the less. In this, Nixon would be a great contrast with the conservatism of the future in the George W. Bush administration of the next millennium (Miles, 1980, 310).

Nixon also ignored the anti-elitism of George Wallace and the hard right and instead named Harvard professor Daniel Patrick Moynihan to his staff in the White House. Similarly, Henry Kissinger, a foreign-born "Rockefeller-Republican" was named National Security Adviser. In the spirit of bipartisanship and an attempt to achieve an unwritten truce with his Democratic opposition, Nixon also avoided purging the bureaucracy of Democrats (Buchanan, 1973, 7).

Nixon's economic policies were also decidedly activist in the tradition of the New Deal Keynesian model, a political-economic approach that had been anathema to conservatives for four decades. In his 1971 State of the Union Address, Nixon introduced what he termed as a "full employment budget" as one of his goals, meaning that Nixon intended to deficit-spend to create jobs if the economy were not at full employment (which it was not). In a televised interview on January 4, Nixon even stated, "I am now a Keynesian in economics" (Evans and Novak, 1972, 372). Nixon also increased federal regulation of business through greater federal protection of the environment and the creation of the Environmental Protection Agency (Evans and Novak, 1972, 372).

On welfare, another traditional conservative anathema, Nixon's Family Assistance Plan replaced social services with cash payments, thus reducing bureaucracy as conservatives would favor, but the plan actually put more people on the government payroll in violation of the Traditional Conservative and Classic Liberal ideologies that drove the Republican Party (Miles, 1980, 311).

In 1971, with inflation reaching double digits due to Vietnam War deficit spending, Nixon imposed a 90 day wage and price freeze, whereby no wages or prices in America could increase for 90 days, and after the 90 days, the increases would be subject to governmental limits. Such vast and direct control of the free market was unprecedented even in the depths of the Great Depression under FDR and the New Deal. Together, Nixon termed his programs as the "New American Revolution," but Nixon's "Revolution" bore a striking similarity to FDR's Keynesian New Deal liberalism (Miles, 1980, 312).

Nixon's Keynesianism, however, had its own decidedly conservative bent in that it also catered to States' rights rhetoric with the introduction of "Revenue Sharing," a program whereby federal block grants and categorical grants to States would be reduced in favor of the return of $5 billion to States that could be used at the discretion of the states for any purpose (Prewitt, 1991, 60-62). The impact of Revenue Sharing was that States had more control over federal money that was transferred to them and spent within their States. With this program, "returning authority to the States" was much more than rhetoric, but became actual policy, something few conservatives before or since could actually claim.

Mixed with this Keynesian progressivism and States' rights fiscal policy, however, Nixon included scattered doses of right-wing retrenchment. Nixon favored school desegregation, but opposed the forced busing of children outside their home neighborhoods in pursuit of integration. Instead, Nixon favored a "freedom of choice" plan that was palatable to Southerners, but rendered moot by the U.S. Supreme Court, who had already ruled that "Freedom of Choice" was an inadequate solution to school integration (Miles, 1980, 319).

Nixon also exhibited his conservative "State's rights" and anti-minority colors in attempting to slow the process of school desegregation by relying strictly on individual lawsuits to bring about integration on a case by case basis. Furthermore, Nixon's Attorney General and former law partner, John Mitchell, recommended that the Voting Rights Act of 1965 not be renewed in 1970 in spite of the fact that black voter registration in the South had increased from 29% to 52% since its passage (The Act was renewed anyway without Nixon's support). Nixon also attempted to appoint two Southern segregation-leaning judges to the Supreme Court, but the Senate failed to confirm both. Nixon argued that the judges were not rejected by the Senate because they were racists, but because they, like him, favored "strict construction" of the U.S. Constitution (Miles, 1980, 320). Finally, in March, 1972 as the Presidential primaries heated up, Nixon proposed legislation that would put a moratorium on forced bussing, a program that was particularly unpopular with conservatives both North and South (Miles, 1980, 334).

Nixon's Bigotry

While Nixon's policies were certainly consistent with his strategy to gain support from white Southern voters, they may also have been motivated in part by racial bigotry. Although Nixon was perhaps more anti-Semitic than anti-black, he did make private statements concerning blacks that reveal an underlying racial prejudice. For example, on the subject of blacks in government, Nixon once privately argued that

"with blacks you can usually settle for an incompetent, because there are just not enough competent ones, and so you put incompetents in and get along with them, because the symbolism is vitally important. You have to show you care" (Quoted in Farquhar, 2003, 227).

Similarly, Nixon once mentioned that the problem with "Mexicans" was in "finding a Mexican that is honest." Nixon then added, "And Italians have somewhat the same problem" (Quoted in Farquhar, 2003, 227). While these statements suggest that there was a deep-seated bigotry underneath Nixon's public persona, they are inconsequential in comparison to his concerns about Jews and Jewish plots against him. Nixon evidently believed that Jews were in control of almost everything in America from politics, to the economy, to the bureaucracy, to the media. Nixon also evidently believed that Jews as a group were immoral and evil people involved in plots against America. In Nixon's words, "The Jews are an irreligious, atheistic, immoral bunch of bastards" and "most Jews are disloyal, you can't trust the bastards. They turn on you" (Quoted in Farquhar, 2003, 228). Nixon even envisioned that his own Justice Department ("Listen, the lawyers in government are damn Jews") and the IRS that he intended to use to go after his enemies, were controlled by Jews. In Nixon's words, "The IRS is full of Jews...Go after them like a son of a bitch. The Jews, you know, are stealing in every direction" (Quoted in Farquhar, 2003, 228). On the subject of the media, Nixon again saw a Jewish conspiracy and once stated that,

"Newsweek is totally—it's all run by Jews and dominated by them in their editorial pages. The *New York Times*, the *Washington Post*, totally Jewish, too" (Quoted in Farquhar, 2003, 228).

Finally, Nixon even blamed the Jews for the movement to legalize marijuana. According to Nixon,

> "You know, it's a funny thing. Every one of the bastards that are out for legalizing marijuana is Jewish. What the Christ is the matter with the Jews...What is the matter with them? I suppose because most of them are psychiatrists" (Quoted in Farquhar, 2003, 222-227).

In addition to his anti-Semitism, Nixon also quietly subscribed to the Traditional Conservative view of homosexuality as a sinful and decadent practice that leads to the erosion and destruction of society. Nixon evidently believed that the fall of the Greek and Roman Empires was the result of homosexuality. In the words of Nixon, "Do you know what happened to the Romans? The last six Roman emperors were fags," and, "you know what happened to the Greeks. Homosexuality destroyed them. Aristotle was a homo, we all know that. So was Socrates." Nixon also blamed the decline of the Catholic Church on homosexuality, arguing, "When the Catholic Church went to hell in—I don't know, three or four centuries ago—it was homosexual" (Quoted in Farquhar, 2003, 224-226).

Political Warfare

Given his apparent underlying bigotry, it is perhaps surprising that Nixon made the concerted effort at bipartisanship that he did early in his Presidency. In exchange for his bipartisan approach in domestic policies, however, Nixon expected Democratic Party support for his foreign policies, including the Vietnam War. Eight months into his Presidency in October, 1969, however, Nixon considered his political truce with the Democratic opposition to be over when the country erupted in massive Vietnam War protests. Like Johnson before him, Nixon viewed the anti-war movement as a threat to his policies and his Presidency. Nixon became incensed at what he viewed as a liberal media conspiracy against his Presidency and his Vietnam War policies. Nixon therefore changed his approach toward the liberal opposition after the October, 1969 protests, and gave his famous "Silent Majority" speech of November 3, 1969, where he claimed that there was a "silent majority" in America that opposed the protesters and instead favored his policies and law and order. After Nixon's "Silent Majority" speech, his approval rating soared to 68% (Buchanan, 1973, 312).

Vice President Spiro Agnew quickly became Nixon's attack dog against the protesting opposition and what Agnew termed as "radicalism." At the end of October, 1969, Agnew gave a speech in Harrisburg, Pennsylvania where he denounced what he termed as "small cadres of professional protesters" that were allowed to jeopardize the peace efforts of the United States. Agnew added that "if in challenging (the protesters), we polarize the American people, I say it is time for a positive polarization." In subsequent speeches Agnew attacked the television networks, the *Washington Post*, and the *New York Times* for their critical analysis of Nixon's policies (Coyne, 1972, 258-259).

On May 1, 1970, Nixon publicly referred to the Vietnam War protesters as "bums." Three days later, students at Kent State University in Ohio organized a protest against Nixon's announcement that he had ordered American military intervention against Vietnamese Communist units in Cambodia. Four students were shot and killed by the Ohio National Guard during the protest, one while simply walking to class. In New York City, Mayor John V. Lindsay ordered the flag to be flown at half-mast as a memorial to the fallen students in Ohio. On May 8, student protesters marched on New York's City Hall, but they were intercepted and beaten by construction workers, who then raised the flag to full staff. On May 9, during a protest at Jackson State, Mississippi, two more students were shot to death by government authorities. On May 11, two thousand construction workers in New York City responded with a march in New York's financial district in support of Nixon and his policies. Nixon subsequently displayed his disdain for the student protesters and his support for the construction workers by accepting a white hardhat with the words "Commander-in-Chief" printed on the front from the International Longshoremen's Association (Coyne, 1972, 259-260).

Nixon's War

Richard Nixon campaigned for President in 1968 on a platform of "Peace with Honor," however, Nixon did not unveil his strategy for achieving those goals, ostensibly because he did not want to undermine the American efforts in Vietnam that were underway during Johnson's administration. Privately, Nixon actually wanted to end the Vietnam War by winning it, but once elected, "winning" the war proved to be elusive. With no military victory in sight, Nixon implemented a 3-pronged strategy of Peace talks, a strategy of gradual withdrawal and turning the war over to the South Vietnamese government, known as "Vietnamezation," and increased bombing, in an attempt to win the war from the air while the U.S. gradually withdrew on the ground (Jones, 1996, 617-632).

Peace talks opened in Paris during the final year of Johnson's Presidency in 1968, but the talks immediately went nowhere. The U.S. called for a communist withdrawal of the South, and the communists called for an American withdrawal and communist control of the South. There was little common ground since communist control of the South was precisely what the United States ostensibly entered the war to prevent. The communists also called for an end to all bombing before talks could proceed. Nixon believed that the bombing was his best leverage in the peace negotiations, so the bombing continued (Herring, 2001, 256).

Under Nixon's second prong, Vietnamezation, Nixon planned to increase training and aid to the South Vietnamese military and then gradually withdraw and turn the actual fighting over to the South Vietnamese. In furtherance of this strategy, Nixon announced a gradual withdrawal, beginning with the withdrawal of 25,000 U.S. troops in the summer of 1969. Vietnamezation was part of what became known as the "Nixon Doctrine." Under this doctrine, Nixon essentially asserted that foreign countries were responsible for their own defense (Herring, 2001, 257). This was a break with the Truman and Eisenhower Doctrines that had committed the U.S. to intervene when foreign countries were threatened by communist invasions or insurgencies. Nixon's staunch conservative anti-communist ideological stance of the 1950s had obviously softened when faced with political and military realities. The Nixon Doctrine was essentially a far "softer" position against communism than that of Truman, who twenty years prior had suffered relentless attacks from conservatives for being too "soft" on communism.

The Vietnamezation plan, however, was obviously doomed from the start. Since the South Vietnamese had been unable to subdue the communists in five years of heavy fighting *with* the aid of the U.S. army, how could anyone expect that they were going to be able to defeat the communists *without* the U.S. army? Secondly, Sam Adams of the CIA estimated that one in five South Vietnamese army regulars were Vietcong (VC) (Adams, 1975, 29). With this type of infiltration, the communists knew their enemy's every move and the South Vietnamese army was certain to fail.

While he was engaging in peace talks and Vietnamezation, Nixon increased the bombing campaign and tried to win the war from the air as he simultaneously pulled out on the ground. In furtherance of his objectives, more bombs were dropped on the communists in Vietnam than on Nazi Germany during WWII. During the massive bombing campaign, in April, 1970, Nixon announced that 150,000 troops would come home within one year (Herring, 2001, 260).

The bombing was somewhat ineffective, however, since the communists' supply lines largely ran through Cambodia and Laos. In essence, the largest impact of the bombing then may have been to unite all of the Vienamese people against the "fire from the sky" that indiscriminately killed civilians, just as Undersecretary of State George Ball had warned Lyndon Johnson would be the result. Nixon might have desired to expand his ground war to

Cambodia and Laos to destroy the communist's supply lines, but Congress prohibited the deployment of troops to Cambodia and Laos in January 1971. Congress did not, however, specifically prohibit the use of planes over Cambodia and Laos; consequently, Nixon ordered bombing of Cambodia and Laos to support South Vietnamese army invasions of those countries, with the goals of destroying communist supply lines and sanctuaries. In support of the South Vietnamese Army invasion, the American Air Force dropped four times as many bombs on Cambodia as on Japan during WWII. The massive U.S. bombing campaign in Cambodia was extralegal, however, since it had begun without Congressional knowledge (Herring, 2001, 270).

In October of 1970, Nixon called for a cease-fire, but Hanoi rejected his offer, demanding a total U.S. withdrawal. Nixon retaliated with bombings of Hanoi and Haiphong in North Vietnam, but the communists remained determined (Herring, 2001, 272). In March, 1972, the North Vietnamese launched the "Easter Offensive," involving 200,000 North Vietnamese troops. Nixon Retaliated with "Linebacker I," a massive bombing campaign on North Vietnam, the mining of the port of Haiphong, and a naval blockade of North Vietnam. Nixon then offered the communists a deal whereby the U.S. would withdraw from Vietnam within four months if the communists would accept a cease-fire (Herring, 2001, 276).

In spite of Nixon's offer of a U.S. withdrawal, talks remained stalled, so in the fall of 1972, with the U.S. Presidential election looming, the U.S. dropped its demand for a communist withdrawal from Vietnam at the Paris Peace talks. October 26th, less than two weeks prior to the 1972 Presidential election, Nixon announced that "Peace was at hand" (Herring, 2001, 278).

South Vietnamese President Thieu, for obvious reasons, rejected the U.S. position that would allow the North Vietnamese troops to remain in South Vietnam. The North Vietnamese called for Thieu's resignation, and Peace talks broke off on December 16, 1972. Consequently, two days later, Nixon launched the "Christmas bombing" of Hanoi and Haiphong. In two weeks, U.S. planes dropped more bombs on Vietnam than they had dropped in the three years from 1969-1971, and 2000 Vietnamese civilians were killed. The destruction came at a cost, however, as the U.S. lost 30 planes and over 100 Americans were taken captive. Despite the heavy damage inflicted on the American bombers, the North Vietnamese were suddenly in a difficult position since they were out of surface to air missiles and were low on food; thus, the communists were suddenly ready to negotiate. Consequently, with both sides having incentive to end the carnage, peace talks resumed shortly thereafter. North Vietnam and the U.S. then signed a peace agreement ending the war January 27, 1973 (Herring, 2001, 381).

Paris Agreement

In the Paris Peace agreement that ended the American military involvement in Vietnam, the communists were allowed to keep their troops in forward placement in South Vietnam. Although Nixon termed the agreement "Peace with honor," it is difficult to term this provision anything but a loss and "dishonor" for the Americans since the U.S. had been unable to satisfy its objective of a communist-free South Vietnam (Herring, 2001, 381). In this sense, "Peace with honor," turned out to more resemble "Peace at any price," as the U.S. essentially capitulated to the communists' demands. That Nixon was able to do so and yet remain popular is in part a testimony to the war-weariness of the American nation in 1972 and in part a tribute to Nixon's staunch anti-communist reputation from the 1950s that allowed him to retain conservative support while capitulating to the communists. Still, in the end it was a conservative Republican administration, not liberal Democrats, that made the final decision that "lost" Vietnam to communism. It would be difficult to imagine a Democratic administration doing the same thing in the previous decades and not being denounced as treasonous "pinkos" by McCarthyist conservatives and even Nixon himself. The costs of containment of communism everywhere on the globe turned out to be greater than the American people, including many conservatives, could support.

In the Paris Agreement, the U.S. agreed to pull its military out of Vietnam and the last American combat troops left Vietnam on March 29, 1973. The North Vietnamese agreed to release U.S. POWs and did so March 29, the same day the last American combat troops departed. The U.S. also agreed to pay Hanoi $4.75 billion in "reconstruction assistance" (Herring, 2001, 387). "Reconstruction Assistance" appeared to be vividly similar to the "reparations" that the losers of wars were traditionally forced to pay at the end of military conflicts prior to WWII. By almost every measure, the communists got everything they wanted, and the only thing the U.S. got was out (Herring, 2001, 387). Essentially, "Peace with honor" for the United States was only achieved if one can stretch the imagination so as to term "cutting and running" as honorable. Franklin Roosevelt's concessions to the Soviets at Yalta, so maligned by conservatives ever since, must be considered tremendous American "victories" by any objective comparison.

Nguyen Van Thieu of South Vietnam was understandably unhappy with the terms of the Paris Agreement, since they left his more powerful enemy and the primary threat to his regime in forward positions in South Vietnam where they could easily over-run his government at any time. Thieu protested and only agreed to the accords because the U.S. left him no choice by threatening to cut off all aid if he did not. Nixon also made a secret pledge to Thieu that the U.S. would militarily aid South Vietnam if the North Vietnamese violated the Cease-fire (Jones, 1996, 632). Little did Thieu know that Nixon would not be around for another four years to make good on the promise even if he had been able to do so, which is debatable given the anti-war sentiments of the American public at the time.

Henry Kissinger and Le Duc Tho of North Vietnam won the Nobel Peace Prize (perhaps proving that the Norwegians have a sense of humor), but Le Duc Tho rejected the prize because he said that the war was not over. The only change was that the U.S. had gone home (Jones, 1996, 633). Even so, Nixon had eliminated what appeared to the greatest threat to his Presidency and the greatest issue dividing the American people at the outset of his second term as President. The prospects for "bringing America together" under Nixon's administration were perhaps better than they had been since Nixon took office. Unfortunately for Nixon, the Watergate scandal that was bubbling up from underneath would undermine any consensus he might have built.

Abuse of Power

The Watergate scandal itself was the final manifestation of a whole host of abuses initiated by Nixon due to his own personal paranoia and contempt for his political opposition. The seeds for what eventually became Watergate and Nixon's undoing were sown several years earlier as Nixon began waging a personal war against his political opposition by using all of the powers of the Presidency at his disposal and ignoring whatever legal restrictions on his power he found inconvenient.

On June 5th, 1970, Nixon met with leaders of the FBI, CIA, the Defense Intelligence Agency, and the National Security Agency, for the purpose of finding a way to deal with the Vietnam War and Civil Rights protesters. An Ad Hoc Interagency Committee on Intelligence was assembled and the Committee issued a report on June 25th recommending relaxation of restrictions on mail openings and "surreptitious entries." A week later, Nixon approved of the Committee's recommendations, but was persuaded to rescind his approval five days later by Attorney General John Mitchell. The CIA, however, already had been active in investigating members of the protest movements since 1967 and eventually developed files on 7200 persons and a general index name list of 300,000. The CIA also opened an estimated 250,000 letters between 1953 and 1973 (Miles, 1980, 324).

Nixon then began an effort to use the powers of the IRS to destroy his political enemies. Nixon pressured the IRS to form a "Special Services Staff" to do tax investigations of political protesters. The IRS acquiesced, and by

1973, the IRS Special Services Staff had files on 11,000 individuals and organizations (Miles, 1980, 324-326). When the time came to appoint a new IRS Director, Nixon sought out a Director that would use the IRS to harass Nixon's political enemies. In the words of Nixon,

> "I want to be sure he (the IRS Director) is a ruthless son of a bitch. That he'll do what he's told, that every income tax return I want to see, I see. That he'll go after our enemies, not our friends...Now, it's as simple as that. If he isn't, he doesn't get the job" (Quoted in Farquhar, 2003, 225).

Pentagon Papers

On June 13, 1971, another development occurred that produced another round of reactionary paranoia from the Nixon administration. The *New York Times* began to print a group of documents known as the "Pentagon Papers," which contained official records of America's involvement in the Vietnam War during the Kennedy and Johnson administrations. In spite of the fact that the "Pentagon Papers" contained information that would be politically damaging to the Johnson and Kennedy administrations, since they revealed that they too did not keep Congress "fully and faithfully informed" as to American involvement in Vietnam, Henry Kissinger persuaded Nixon that the publication of the papers would jeopardize Nixon's negotiations with China and the North Vietnamese, so Nixon ordered his administration to get a court injunction to stop their publication. Two weeks later, the Supreme Court ruled that there could be no prior restraint on the documents since they did not threaten national security. When it became known that Nixon aide Daniel Ellsberg had leaked the "Pentagon Papers" information to the press, Nixon had his aides set up a Special Investigations Unit within the White House to plug such leaks known at the "plumbers." The "plumbers" included David Young, an assistant to Henry Kissinger, Egil Krogh, an assistant to John Ehrlichman, Walter Minnick of the Cabinet Committee on International Narcotics Control, White House consultant E. Howard Hunt, and G. Gordon Liddy, Assistant to the Secretary of the Treasury (Dean, 1976, 26).

The plumbers came up with plans to discredit Ellsberg, and through discrediting Ellsberg, it was hoped that they could also discredit other important members of the political opposition as well, including Lesli Gelb, Director of the Vietnam History Task Force that produced the Pentagon Papers, Paul Warnke, who had served as an Assistant Secretary of Defense, Morton Halperin, who had been Warnke's deputy, and Clark Clifford, the former Secretary of Defense in the Johnson Administration. Collectively, the men were viewed as the "doves" of the Johnson administration that opposed and undermined Nixon's Vietnam War strategy (Dean, 1976, 45-47).

The plan to disrupt the Democratic opposition included a plan to harass and burglarize the Brookings Institution, a liberal-leaning Washington Think Tank. The plumbers also came up with a plan for "hush money" to prevent Nixon aides from providing evidence to federal investigators (Dean, 1976, 47).

A separate plan to discredit the liberal opposition was submitted to Attorney General John Mitchell by G. Gordon Liddy. The Liddy plan included infiltration of the Democratic Party leadership with spies and electronic surveillance, "demonstration squads" or "streetfighting teams" that could break up Vietnam war protests, "kidnapping teams" that could kidnap members of the demonstrating opposition, and prostitutes trained to extract information from the Democratic Party leadership via sexual relationships (Dean, 1976, 79-87).

The office of Ellsberg's psychiatrist was burglarized and vandalized by a group led personally by Liddy, although the burglars were unable to find any evidence of value against Ellsberg in their raid. Eventually, three White House aides were convicted of crimes as a result of the break–in, and top Nixon Aide John Ehrlichman was convicted of violating the civil rights of Ellsberg's psychiatrist, Lewis Fielding, and of lying to a grand jury. Ellsberg, however, had to defend himself against indictment for theft of government property and unauthorized possession of documents related to the national defense, as a result of his role in procuring the Pentagon Papers (Dean, 1976, 256-257).

The attacks initiated by Nixon against his political detractors were calculated to gain advantage for his administration and the Republican Party. Nixon correctly perceived that if he could create political division between the anti-war movement and the counterculture, and mainstream conservative America, that he would have the majority on his side (Dean, 1976, 257).

In the spring of 1969, the *New York Times* reported that the Nixon administration had secretly bombed communist sanctuaries in Cambodia, a neutral country in the Vietnam conflict that Nixon had no Congressional authorization to attack. The unauthorized bombings therefore exceeded Nixon's Constitutional powers as commander-in-chief, since the President may only perform his commander-in-chief powers at the pleasure of Congress. The bombings also violated the President's Constitutional authority to keep Congress "fully and faithfully" informed (Miles, 1980, 317).

Nixon was infuriated at the "leaks" that led to the *New York Times* article and viewed the story as part of the liberal media conspiracy against his administration. Nixon also viewed the article as proof that there were those within his administration that were not only disloyal, but co-conspirators bent on destroying his administration and undermining his authority.

Consequently, Nixon fought back in a paranoid rage and asked the FBI for seventeen wiretaps of newsmen and strategically placed White House staff, particularly members of Henry Kissinger's National Security Council Staff. Nixon decided that power must be centralized in the White House so as to fend off those in the bureaucracy that were plotting against him. In the words of Nixon,

> "We have no discipline in this bureaucracy...We never fire anybody. We never reprimand anybody. We never demote anybody. We always promote the sons of bitches that kick us in the ass. That's true in the State Department. It's true in HEW. It's true in OMB, and true for ourselves, and it's just got to stop" (Quoted in Farquhar, 2003, 224).

On another occasion, Nixon essentially denounced his entire Cabinet and staff due to what he viewed as their ineptitude and disloyalty. Nixon stated,

> "I'm sick of the whole bunch. The others are a bunch of god-damned cowards. The staff, except for Haldeman and Ehrlichman, screw them. The cabinet, except for Connolly, the hell with them" (Quoted in Farquhar, 2003, 227).

Displaying excessive vindictiveness and paranoia, Nixon demanded the resignation of all noncareer officials the day after his reelection victory in 1972 (Miles, 1980, 318).

Détente

Criticism of the Nixon administration, however, was not limited to the Democrats and left-leaning protesters. Nixon relaxed restrictions on trade and travel with the People's Republic of China, and visited China himself on a diplomatic mission in February 1972. Nixon then visited the Soviet Union in May 1972, beginning what he termed as détente or a relaxing of the strained relations with the Soviet Union. Nixon viewed détente as part of an overall strategy that would allow the U.S. to exit Vietnam with honor. The idea was that if the United States could come to a diplomatic agreement with the Chinese and the Soviets that they would not attempt to spread communist revolution, then the U.S. would not have to "contain" the spread of Soviet or Chinese communism in Vietnam (Jones, 1996, 634). Nixon eventually signed seven agreements with the Soviets in space exploration, medical research, trade, the environment, maritime laws, technology, and strategic weapons, with the Strategic Arms Limitation Treaty (SALT) being the most noteworthy.

Nixon's efforts (perhaps predictably) were criticized by *National Review* and other conservatives as "soft" on communism and the *National Review* suspended its support of the Nixon administration. In response, H.R. Haldeman told Barbara Walters that criticism of Nixon's Vietnam peace efforts by U.S. Senators should be considered "consciously aiding and abetting the enemy" (in other words, treasonous) (Miles, 1980, 333-334).

Watergate and Paranoia

The paranoia that is evident in Nixon's tirades against Jews, homosexuals, the media, etc. was the driving force behind the events that would eventually bring down Nixon's Presidency. Nixon believed that Congress, the bureaucracy, the Justice Department, the Jews, the media, and liberal Democrats in general, had robbed him of the Presidency in 1960 and continued to plot against him. Out of this paranoid "plot mentality" was hatched Nixon's plan to fight back against the "plots" by using all of the powers of the Executive that were at his disposal, and where necessary, by using extralegal means.

Nixon's paranoia and bigotry began to permeate the White House as Nixon perceived himself to be under attack from all sectors. For example, Nixon told H.R. Haldeman in September 1971 to,

"Please get me the names of the Jews, you know, the big Jewish contributors of the Democrats...All right. Could we please investigate some of the cocksuckers?" (Quoted in Kutler, 1997, 31).

Nixon didn't even trust his own Republican Party by re-election time of 1972 and essentially ran his re-election campaign separate from the Republican Party. In the words of Kansas Senator Bob Dole,

"The Republican Party was not only not involved in Watergate, but it wasn't involved in the nomination, the convention, the campaign, the election or the inauguration" (Quoted, in Small, 1999, 250).

Election of 1972

The Democrats did Nixon a favor in 1972, however, by selecting the intellectual and anti-war liberal Senator from South Dakota, George McGovern. McGovern favored negotiations with the North Vietnamese as a means to end the Vietnam War, a tactic that Nixon eventually followed himself, but the prescription opened McGovern to the criticism that he was soft on communism. That McGovern was also an intellectual who held a Ph.D. was an added hindrance to his ability to pick up votes from working class conservatives. Nixon won every State except Massachusetts and the District of Columbia, including McGovern's home state of South Dakota. Nixon won 60.7% of the vote and it appeared that his "silent majority" had spoken. The victory, however, was a personal one for Nixon rather than a sweeping Republican victory, as the Republicans actually lost one seat in the U.S. Senate (Gould, 2003, 387-389).

Unraveling of Watergate

Nevertheless, Nixon felt that he needed political intelligence on his opponents, and to that end, assigned G.Gordon Liddy the job of Director of Political Intelligence for the Committee to Re-elect the President. During spring and summer 1972, Liddy's political intelligence operatives made four attempts, only one successful, to burglarize the offices of the Democratic National Committee and install a wiretap. On their fourth attempt on June 17, 1972, five burglars were caught and arrested by Washington D.C. police. Reflecting their own plot mentality and paranoia, Liddy and E. Howard Hunt had ordered their intelligence burglars to search for evidence of ties to Communist Cuba and other left-wing organizations within the U.S (Miles, 1980, 337).

The FBI began investigating the source of funding for the burglary that had been routed through Mexico by the Committee to Re-elect the President. A week later on June 23, 1972, Nixon approved a plan to have the CIA intervene into the FBI Mexico investigation. The CIA was to provide the FBI with information that would throw them off-track so as to conceal the relationship of the Watergate burglars to the Committee to Re-elect the President. In furtherance of this plan, Deputy Director of the CIA Vernon Walters told FBI Director L.Patrick Gray that the FBI investigation into Mexico jeopardized CIA operations. Eventually, the taped recording of Nixon's involvement in this ploy to cover up the connection would become the "smoking gun" that the House of Representatives would use to construct an "Obstruction of Justice" case against the President (Miles, 1980, 338).

Early in 1973, Republican leaders including Barry Goldwater, George H.W. Bush, and Ronald Reagan, defended Richard Nixon. Bush stated that "Nixon has said repeatedly he wasn't involved in the sordid Watergate affairs. I believe him." Similarly, Ronald Reagan referred to those pressing the case against Nixon as a "lynch mob" (Quoted in Gould, 2003, 390).

By spring 1973, Nixon's cover-up of the Watergate burglary began to unravel through a combination of the U.S. Senate investigation into the case and reporting by *Washington Post* correspondents Bob Woodward and Carl Bernstein based on their un-named source in the case, "deep throat." On March 19, 1973, a major break in the case occurred when convicted

Watergate burglar and former CIA Agent James McCord handed a letter to Judge John J. Sirica asserting that there had been political pressure applied on the defendants to plead guilty and remain silent, and that perjury had occurred during the trial. Furthermore, McCord charged that there were others involved in the Watergate operation that had not been identified during the trial. Finally, McCord exclaimed that the Watergate burglary was not a CIA operation as had been alleged. Judge Sirica, hoping to elicit previously withheld information from the defendants, reacted by handing down harsh "provisional sentences" to the other defendants with the provision that they were to be reexamined in 90 days (McCord, 1974, 211).

The Watergate Tapes

Shortly thereafter, White House aide John Dean, seeing the writing on the wall, retained a lawyer and began negotiating with prosecutors for immunity. On April 30, Dean was formally fired by Richard Nixon, but the cover-up continued to unravel. Dean, who was a direct point of contact with the President himself, became the chief witness for the prosecution in implicating Nixon in the Watergate cover-up. Haldeman and Ehrlichman resigned, and then on July 16, White House aide Alexander Butterfield revealed the existence of a tape recording system in the Oval Office that could verify the allegations of Watergate witnesses. Special Prosecutor Archibald Cox subpoenaed several of the tapes, thus making them evidence in the case, and their destruction then became illegal (Woodward and Bernstein, 1976, 199).

Nixon refused to turn over the tapes, claiming Executive Privilege, and ordered his Attorney-General, Elliot Richardson, to fire Special Prosecutor Cox. Richardson refused, and Nixon then accepted his resignation. Nixon then turned to Richardson's deputy, William Ruckleshaus and ordered him to fire Cox, but Ruckleshaus also refused and resigned. Finally, Nixon turned to Solicitor General Robert Bork, who dutifully fired Cox in what became known as the "Saturday Night Massacre" (Woodward and Bernstein, 1976, 69-71).

Public opinion began to turn against the President, and consequently, so did the Republicans in Congress. Republican Senator Howard Baker of Tennessee asked the famous question, "What did the President know and when did he know it?" (Quoted in Kutler, 1990, 451). Later, Republican Senator James Buckley of New York publicly called for Nixon's resignation, and Republican Hugh Scott of Pennsylvania referred to Nixon's White House tapes as "disgusting and immoral" (Quoted in Kutler, 1990, 454). "Mr. Conservative," Barry Goldwater, who had once labeled Nixon a "two-fisted, four-square liar," likened Watergate to the Teapot Dome scandal of

the 1920s and argued, "I mean, there's a smell to it. Let's get rid of the
smell." (Gould, 2003, 390). On the House Judiciary Committee, four
Republicans and a number of Southern Democrats voted with the liberal
Democrats in recommending impeachment of the President, and Nixon's
public approval rating dropped to 27% (Gould, 2003, 391).

Nixon's Vice President, Spiro Agnew, had already resigned from office
after pleading no contest to tax evasion in a case in which he was accused of
taking kickbacks from Maryland contractors (Woodward and Bernstein,
1976, 61-62). Backed into a political and legal corner, Nixon finally handed
over the Oval Office tapes to new Special Prosecutor Leon Jaworski. The
public was shocked to learn that the President was exceedingly coarse and
profane in private, and the tapes revealed to the satisfaction of the House
Judiciary Committee that Nixon was indeed involved in the Watergate cover-
up. On July 27, 1974, the House Judiciary Committee voted 27-11 in favor
of impeaching the President on obstruction of justice concerning the
Watergate break-in. In subsequent days, the Committee voted 28-10 in favor
of a second Article of Impeachment concerning abuse of power and 21-17
for a third Article concerning defiance of federal subpoenas (Woodward and
Bernstein, 1976, 293-297).

Nixon's Resignation

Nixon realized that he was about to be impeached, and after being
advised that he only had 15 votes in the Senate, (meaning that he would
almost surely also be convicted and removed from office), Nixon resigned
from office on August 9, 1974, and announced his resignation to the nation
in a teary-eyed television address (Woodward and Bernstein, 1976, 451).

Nixon never admitted any criminal wrongdoing in the Watergate affair,
instead arguing essentially that when national security is threatened,
Presidents may operate above the law (Miles, 1980, 342-343). The Supreme
Court had visited that argument and rejected it after the Civil War in *Ex
Parte Milligan* (1866). If such emergency powers were rejected by the Court
during the Civil War, obviously, it is a bit of a stretch to argue that "national
security" had been so threatened by the Democratic National Committee that
it justified emergency powers of the Executive outside the powers granted in
the Constitution, and thus justified the President's aides in ordering a
burglary of DNC headquarters. The fact that Nixon (and those that aided him
in his attempts to thwart his political enemies) appears to have viewed it this
way is a testimony to his paranoia and his subscription to the "plot
mentality" that has been endemic to Traditional Conservative ideology in
America since the witch hunts at Salem Village. The conservative argument,
however, that the President may essentially ignore the Constitution in the

interest of National Security or emergency would be thwarted in this case, only to be resurrected at the turn of the next century by another Republican administration under George W. Bush.

In the end, Nixon's downfall had perhaps more to do with his paranoia and the plot mentality of his ideology than anything else. Had Nixon not felt the need to illegally keep tabs on his political opposition due to his paranoia, there might not have been a Watergate break-in in the first place. Furthermore, if Nixon had trusted the entire sordid operation to his security apparatus, he would have been free to deny explicit authorization of the actions and most likely would not have had to resign. Nixon, however, was suspicious of the FBI and CIA, believing that they had a globalist liberal bias; therefore he felt the need to create his own intelligence capabilities in the Committee to Re-elect the President. Nixon, it appears, was therefore brought down primarily by his own political paranoia endemic to his ideology.

Chapter Thirteen

Conservatism and the Reagan Revolution

Nixon's successor to the White House, Gerald R. Ford, had been the Republican minority leader in the House and had been appointed Vice President by Nixon upon the resignation of Spiro Agnew. Nixon had chosen Ford at least partially because he believed that Ford offered an insurance policy against his own impeachment, given that Congress surely would not want to risk replacing Nixon with such an unproven commodity as Ford. Unfortunately for Nixon, Ford also had a reputation for honesty; consequently, the prospects of a Ford Presidency, regardless of any other shortcomings, appeared refreshing to many members of Congress, both Republican and Democrat, after the revelations of Watergate (Gould, 2003, 391).

Americans in general and conservatives in particular were devastated to learn that the President of the United States and his associates had been guilty of a conscious attempt to use unconstitutional means to destroy their political enemies and deceive the nation. Religious conservatives in particular were shocked at the immorality of the entire affair, as well as at Nixon's bigotry and coarse language that were revealed on the Watergate tapes. James Dunn of the Christian Life Commission, the social action agency for the Texas Southern Baptists, perhaps spoke for the entire nation when he called for "repentance and revival and a commitment to honesty and integrity and fair dealing in the political realm" (Quoted in Martin, 1996, 148). Perhaps few could have filled the need for a time of honesty and healing in politics more than Democratic Georgia Governor, Jimmy Carter.

Jimmy Carter

Jimmy Carter was a Southern Baptist from Plains, Georgia, who was the epitome of the conservative family values espoused by the emerging Christian right. Carter, however, did not overstress his religious faith and believed in church-state separation as well; consequently, he was palatable to the secular left as well as the Christian right and quickly emerged as a serious challenger to now incumbent Republican Gerald Ford for the Presidency.

Carter also echoed a number of other Traditional Conservative and Classic Liberal ideological preferences on several important issues. Carter expressed his disdain for the welfare system, always a conservative whipping post, and argued that the system needed to be reformed so that it "encourages work and encourages family life" (Quoted in Martin, 1996, 155). Carter also promised to reform the tax system in a way that would help families stay together, encourage a program of family planning that would prevent the need for abortion, and require that federal programs all present "family impact statements" that show their impact on American families. Carter also favored federal aid to parochial schools, a position that was embraced both by conservative fundamentalist Protestants and by conservative Catholics (Martin, 1996, 155).

Gerald Ford, for his part, did Jimmy Carter and the Democrats a major favor one month into his Presidency when he pardoned Richard Nixon for any and all crimes connected with Watergate. Ford believed that losing the Presidency and the public disgrace associated with it were enough punishment for Nixon and he also viewed the pardon as necessary for political healing. To a large segment of the American public, however, the pardon appeared to reflect a corrupt bargain between Ford and Nixon whereby Nixon appointed Ford Vice President (and later President) with the understanding that Ford would pardon Nixon of all crimes if and when the time came. Though there is no record of such a bargain between Ford and Nixon, Ford's approval rating nevertheless dropped from 71% to 50% inside of a week after the pardon, and his own Press Secretary, who had advised against the pardon, resigned in disgust. Ford would never regain the popularity he lost with the pardon, and voters would punish Ford at the polls two years later in the general election (Greene, 1995, 120-121).

To make matters worse for Ford and the Republicans, the double-digit inflation and high unemployment that Ford had inherited from the Nixon administration continued unabated. Kennedy, Johnson, and Nixon, had spent a decade deficit-spending to support the Vietnam War and Johnson's Great Society welfare programs, oil prices remained high, and the manufacturing sector experienced major problems due to international free market competition. The economic problems were decades in the making and simply too large for any President to solve in such a short period of time, but the electorate, both right and left, would not be so patient. Ford also alienated the right wing of the Republican Party with his nomination of their old nemesis, Nelson Rockefeller, for Vice President (Gould, 2003, 403).

Finally, Ford had public relations problems that were related to his rather vanilla personality and an inaccurate public perception of his intellectual capabilities. Though a graduate of Yale law school, Ford was also an ex-collegiate football player from the University of Michigan and not a dynamic speaker; consequently, Ford somehow became portrayed in the media as an ex-athlete who was a bit dull-minded. The fact that he stumbled to the ground on occasion in front of the TV cameras only contributed to this reputation, in spite of the fact that the link between sure-footedness and intellect is a dubious one at best. Ex-President Lyndon Johnson perhaps exemplified the inaccurate general consensus with his assessment that Ford "can't fart and chew gum at the same time" (Hayward, 2001, 399). Regardless of its fairness, Ford would be unable to ever completely shake the "dumb" label with which he became associated.

Challenge from Ronald Reagan

Ironically, among those that thought Ford lacked the intellectual prowess to be President was Ronald Reagan. This is in spite of the fact that Reagan himself was not an intellectual, was not known to be an avid reader, had much less impressive academic and governmental credentials than Ford, and was also not known as a deep thinker. Instead, Reagan was a Hollywood actor that previously had been a Democrat, and had supported both Franklin Roosevelt and Hubert Humphrey in the 1940s. Reagan was also formerly the head of a labor union, the Screen Actors' Guild, an organization that traditionally had not been known for its conservatism (although it certainly turned conservative with Reagan at the helm). Reagan's political views, however, would undergo a metamorphosis in the 1950s as a result of his personal reaction to a punitive graduated tax structure that punished wealthy actors like himself, his staunch anti-communist beliefs that were endemic to the time of the 1950s, and a personal opposition to Civil Rights for blacks. Reagan would eventually capitulate to his ideological leanings and join the Republican Party in 1962 (Gould, 2003, 404-407).

Reagan's Ideological Conservatism

Reagan's disdain for the tax structure is simple enough to decipher since the top federal tax bracket for wealthy individuals (like him) at the time was a punitive 70%. In this sense, Reagan's political shift surely can be viewed as driven as much by a sense of personal economic well-being as by ideological predispositions. Reagan's distaste for communism, however, was clearly a function of his Classic Liberal free-market ideology that had become the hallmark of contemporary conservatism.

According to his daughter, Pattti Davis, Reagan's anti-communist sentiments were so strong as to border on paranoia. Reagan, according to Davis, apparently saw communists and communist plots everywhere, and viewed communism as the driving force behind everything with which he disagreed. Davis (1992, 30), in her autobiography, explains how her father viewed Medicare as "socialized Medicine that would destroy America," and "socialism," of course, as "the first step to communism." As head of the Screen Actors' Guild in the 1950s, Davis relates how Reagan took pride in helping to "ferret out the communists" that were "infiltrating Hollywood." Furthermore, according to Davis, when she became involved in the anti-nuclear movement in the 1980s (while her father was engaging in a massive nuclear weapons buildup), her father informed her that the entire anti-nuclear movement was created by the Communist Party and the KGB. When Davis handed her father a copy of Reagan's own Defense Department report that concluded that the U.S. had basic nuclear parity with the Soviets in military strength (thus suggesting that his nuclear arms buildup was unnecessary), Reagan's response was, "that's a forgery." Clearly, Reagan was a "don't confuse me with the facts, my mind is made up" type of ideologue (Davis, 1992, 260).

Reagan also took the traditional conservative position on the issue of States' rights; therefore, like Goldwater, had opposed the Civil Rights Act of 1964 and the Voting Rights Act of 1965 as unconstitutional expansions of federal power. Reagan also espoused the long-standing conservative position in opposition to the general "largeness" of the federal government and believed that the federal government was full of waste and fraud (O'Reilly, 1995, 112).

On the subjects of law and order in the 1960s, Reagan concurred with Richard Nixon, taking the traditional conservative Burkeian position in opposition to the Civil Rights and Vietnam War protests as unpatriotic threats to security. Typifying Reagan's approach, Reagan blamed the student protesters for their own deaths in the Kent State tragedy because they had hurled bottles and rocks at the Ohio National Guard. In taking such a position, Reagan evidently viewed such non-lethal actions as justifying the National Guard's use of lethal force, a violation of two hundred years of American common law principles (Davis, 1992, 126).

According to Davis, Reagan's political leanings had to be driven largely by ideology since Reagan had little knowledge of the substance of policy or the day-to-day workings of government. Reagan then exacerbated the effects of his own ideological and non-analytical approach to politics by surrounding himself with individuals that were likeminded, so that "groupthink" prevailed and opposing points of view were not considered (Davis, 1992, 258). With his limited education and limited political experience, Reagan essentially thought simplistically and spoke simplistically to the American public in an anecdotal language they found compelling. Reagan used stories, some fictional and some not, about welfare queens and wrong-sized file cabinets, in place of real policy analysis, but his stories sold well with the American public at large, whose political knowledge is often suspect at best (Stockman, 1987).

Reagan's simplistic, unread, and ideological, thought process is conveyed vividly by his daughter, who recounts in her autobiography a discussion she once had with her father about the Bible and her cohabitational living arrangement at the time. In the words of Davis (192, 175-176)

> "'This is just immoral, what you're doing,' my father continued. 'Living together without the benefit of marriage is a sin in the eyes of God. He tells us this in the Bible.' 'He does? It's in the Bible that you shouldn't live together?' I figured I must have missed that. 'Yes,' my father said emphatically. 'God wrote that men and women should get married.' 'But God didn't write the Bible. The disciples wrote the Bible,' I pointed out. 'No, they didn't. God wrote it.' This is the most aggravating aspect of discussing anything with my father. He has this ability to make statements that are so far outside the parameters of logic that they leave you speechless. You sit there with you're your mouth open, thinking, 'This is ridiculous.'"

Election of 1976

Again, if there is irony here, it is that Reagan personally thought that Gerald Ford lacked the mental capacity necessary for the Oval Office. Nevertheless, Ford would win the Republican nomination, but only after the Reagan challenge produced deep divisions within the Republican Party. In order to placate the conservative Reagan faction, Ford was compelled to dump Nelson Rockefeller as his running mate and replace him with the more conservative Kansas Senator, Bob Dole, and Ford's victory was secured only after Ronald Reagan lost the Florida primary when senior citizens reacted negatively to his plan to invest the Social Security Trust Fund in the Stock Market (Greene, 2000, 162). Ford was also forced to make major concessions to the right at the 1976 Republican convention, adding an anti-abortion plank and essentially abandoning Nixon's détente in foreign policy (Gould, 2003, 410).

Unfortunately for Ford, the bloody fight for the nomination with Reagan had weakened the Republican Party, and the economic malaise he had inherited from the Nixon administration continued. The Democrats gained mileage from the economic "misery index," that combined an inflation rate of over 6% with an unemployment rate of 8%. Ford then fumbled the second of his Presidential debates with Carter when he inexplicably asserted that the Soviet Union did not dominate Eastern Europe and stated that, "I don't believe that the Poles consider themselves dominated by the Soviet Union" (Quoted in Frankel, 1999, 229). The episode reinforced for the American public that Ford was a bit slow-minded, and this combined with the economic malaise, the bloodletting within the Republican Party, and the inability of the public to disassociate Ford from his pardon of Richard Nixon, created the situation where the inexperienced Jimmy Carter would win a close election with 49.9% of the vote to 47.9% for Ford.

Carter and the Republican Resurgence

Jimmy Carter had won the Presidency with the backing of Southern Christian fundamentalists due to his own Baptist religious beliefs and the moral outrage of Americans over the Watergate affair, coupled with Ford's pardon of Nixon. Carter also played the "regular guy" well to the American people, with his humble origins as a peanut farmer from the small town of Plains, Georgia. Carter held town meetings and call-in talk sessions and asked callers in good Southern fashion if they were kin to someone of the same name that he knew in Georgia. Carter wore a cardigan sweater while in front of the television cameras in the White House, mended his own clothes in front of reporters on an airplane, and carried his own luggage, thus proving to many Americans, conservative and liberal alike, that he was "just like them" (Martin, 1996, 159).

Carter, ERA, and Protestant Fundamentalists

Carter would alienate his conservative Christian fundamentalist constituency, however, by supporting the pro-choice position on abortion, opposing discrimination against gays, and favoring the Equal Rights Amendment (ERA) that would prohibit the denial of equal rights on the basis of sex. The Equal Rights Amendment had been originally introduced in the 1960s with Republican support, and it passed both houses of Congress in 1972 under the Nixon administration. Conservatives, however, led by social conservative activist Phyllis Schlafly, would turn against ERA after its passage in Congress, and oppose its ratification (Martin, 1996, 159).

ERA was allotted seven years to achieve ratification by ¾ of the States and 22 States ratified the Amendment the first year. Early on, it appeared that the Amendment would sail easily through the ratification process. Phyllis Schlafly, however, began to oppose the Amendment in 1972 and in 1975, Schlafly quickly organized and founded the Eagle Forum, a conservative women's organization opposed to the ratification of ERA. Schlafly and her followers used the tried and true conservative methods of employing outrageous scare tactics to deter ERA supporters, depicting the Amendment as leading to unisex toilets, homosexual marriages, women in combat, and the release of males from their responsibility to support their children. (*Time*. April 25, 1977, 89-90). Schlafly and the Eagle Forum were also able to successfully confuse ERA with homosexuality and gay rights (never the intention of the Amendment's sponsors), thus ensuring that the Amendment would not be supported by the religious right, and therefore ensuring that the Amendment would not be ratified in the Protestant fundamentalist-dominated Southern States or Mormon-influenced Utah and Idaho. Consequently, the window for ERA's ratification would expire and the Amendment would not be resurrected (Martin, 1996, 160).

Abortion

In 1973, the U.S. Supreme Court issued its decision in *Roe v. Wade* that essentially struck down State regulation of abortions in the first trimester. At the time, protestant fundamentalists were essentially unconcerned with the abortion issue, and in 1971, the Southern Baptist convention even voted in support of a resolution affirming a woman's right to have an abortion if the health of the mother were threatened (Martin, 1996, 156). In fact, evangelist Jerry Falwell, who later became the leader of the Protestant fundamentalist political group, Moral Majority, did not preach his first sermon against abortion until 1978, five years after the *Roe v. Wade* decision. Instead, it was Catholics who took the early lead in opposing legal abortions and *Roe v. Wade* due to the long-standing Catholic Church prohibition against any form of birth control (Martin, 1996, 193).

In 1975, however, fundamentalist Protestant evangelists Billy Graham and Francis Schaeffer, along with *Christianity Today* editor Harold O.J. Brown and pediatrician C. Everett Koop, formed the Christian Action Council that lobbied Congress for measures to curb abortions. Koop and Schaeffer produced a five-segment film and companion book entitled, *Whatever Happened to the Human Race?,* that taught that abortion was both a cause and the result of the loss of appreciation for human life in American society and that acceptance of abortion would eventually lead to acceptance of infanticide and euthanasia (Martin, 1996, 156, 194). That same year, Jerry Falwell, along with Paul Weyrich of the Heritage Foundation, started their conservative political organization known as the Moral Majority, and made opposition to abortion a focus, with the goal of luring Catholic voters away from the Democratic Party (D'Souza1984, 109-112).

Rise of the Religious Right

Falwell's Moral Majority would quickly catapult the religious right to a position of major importance in American politics in support of the Republican Party and ideologically conservative politics. Falwell himself characterized the Moral Majority as "pro-life, pro-family, pro-moral, pro-

American, pro-Israel, and against abortion, divorce, and secular humanism" (Falwell, 1980, 257). Falwell argued that the Moral Majority's goals would be to,

> "exert a significant influence on the spiritual and moral direction of the nation by: (a) mobilizing the grassroots of moral Americans in one clear and effective voice; (b) informing the moral majority what is going on behind their backs in Washington and in state legislatures across the country; (c) lobbying intensively in Congress to defeat left-wing, social-welfare bills that will further erode our precious freedom; (d) pushing for positive legislation such as that to establish the Family Protection Agency, which will ensure a strong, enduring America; and (e) helping the moral majority in local communities to fight pornography, homosexuality, the advocacy of immorality in school textbooks, and other issues facing each and every one of us" (Falwell, 1980, 257-263).

Falwell's exhortation to the religious right to become involved in politics was a reversal of his position in the 1960s when Falwell urged Christians to stay out of the Civil Rights movement (Martin, 1996, 202). By 1979, however, religious fundamentalists that had supported Jimmy Carter in 1976 due to Carter's religious faith were becoming disenchanted with President Carter due to his failure to adopt anything resembling the Moral Majority's platform. As Bill Godsey, a member of Jerry Falwell's Thomas Road Baptist Church put it, "Carter practiced a version of Christianity that, if you used the term 'liberal,' you would probably be close to what he was, and that was not popular with evangelicals and fundamentalists" (Quoted in Martin, 1996, 207). Similarly, editorial columnist Bob Novak stated in 1979 that he knew that Carter was going to lose in 1980 because,

> "Minister after minister stood up and said, 'I was part of Carter's team in 1976. I delivered my congregation for Carter. I urged them all to vote for Carter because I thought he was a moral individual. I found out otherwise and I'm angry'" (Quoted in Martin, 1996, 207).

Falwell and his followers were drawn into politics due to what they viewed as attacks on the family and moral social issues, but they quickly adopted conservative positions on non-values issues as well. Both the Moral Majority and the Christian Voice (another Christian political organization) opposed, for example, American economic sanctions against Rhodesia for the human rights abuses by Idi Amin, abrogation of the U.S. military treaty with Taiwan, and the "giving away" of the Panama Canal (Martin, 1996, 207-208).

In the Panama Canal case, President Carter and the two-thirds of the Senators that ratified the Treaty recognized that the Canal no longer had the strategic or commercial importance that it once had. Commercially, the most important ships, the oil supertankers, could not use the Canal because they were simply too large. Strategically, the Canal had been reduced in importance since the largest and most important military surface ships, the latest aircraft carriers, were also too large for the Canal. The Canal was also useless to American nuclear submarines since use of the Canal would reveal their positions (which were kept secret as much as possible as a check on the Soviet Union). Given these factors, Carter and the Senators calculated that the advantage in good will with Latin America gained by the Canal Treaty would outweigh any strategic or commercial negatives associated with the return of the canal to Panama. The Christian Right simply ignored such analysis and viewed the Treaty as an agreement that sold out American interests and weakened America (Jones, 1996, 654-658).

The religious right also favored a hard line against the Soviet Union and an increase in defense spending; hence, religious conservatives opposed the Strategic Arms Limitation Treaty (SALT II) that called for limits on nuclear arsenals (Martin, 1996, 207). Reverend Falwell argued in his book, *Listen America* (1980, 98), that the United States had fallen behind the Soviet Union in nuclear capabilities so far that, in the words of Falwell,

"the sad fact is that in an exchange of missiles today the Soviet Union would kill 135 million to 160 million Americans, and the United States would kill only three to five percent of the Soviets because of their antiballistic missiles and their civil defense" (Falwell, 1980, 98).

Regardless of the suspect nature of Falwell's nuclear mathematics, the argument was consistent with the positions of the Republican candidate for the Presidency at the time, Ronald Reagan, who blamed President Carter for America's "weakness" vis-à-vis the Soviet Union and therefore called for a nuclear arms buildup. In spite of the dubious connection between defense spending and Christianity, Falwell made the support of defense-spending a Christian cause and even condemned members of Congress who voted against the B-1 bomber (Martin, 1996, 211).

Religious Right and Homosexuality

The Christian right in the 1970s (as well as ever since) was decidedly anti-gay, and, as previously mentioned, the linkage of gay rights to ERA was most certainly a contributor to the demise of ERA; however, the religious right did not limit their opposition to homosexuality exclusively to the battle over ERA. According to Reverend Falwell, homosexuality was an evil sin in the same category with rape, adultery, and incest (Falwell, 1980, 181-186).

Consequently, when San Francisco Mayor George Moscone and City Supervisor Harvey Milk, the city's first openly gay elected official, were assassinated, Falwell stated that the murders, which were committed by a fundamentalist Christian who admitted that his belief in God had prompted his action, were a judgment from God (Strober and Tomczak, 1979, 198).

Christian fundamentalist opposition to homosexuality would broadside an effort by Jimmy Carter in 1980 to cater to the Protestant fundamentalists that had supported him in 1976. In 1980, Jimmy Carter organized a National White House Conference on the Family with the intention of showing his pro-family colors. Fundamentalist Christians, however, ended up storming out of the Family Conference in protest when the definition of "family" at the Conference was not limited to one married couple consisting of one man and one woman and their biological children. In particular, the religious right objected to any definition of family that might include unmarried partners, unwed mothers and their children, and most particularly, homosexual couples. In the words of Beverly LaHaye, wife of best selling Christian fundamentalist author Tim LaHaye, "we were determined to hold onto the real true meaning of the genuine family, as God intended it to be" (*New York Times*, June 7, 1980).

Falwell and his associates used typical "alarm the masses" scare tactics, replete with hyperbole and liberties with the facts, in order to get their anti-gay messages across. In February, 1979, for example, evangelist James Robison contended on his Christian TV show that gays recruit children to participate in homosexual activity (Martin, 1996, 198). Similarly, in August, 1980, the Moral Majority sent out a fundraising letter warning their followers that the "Grand Old Flag is going down the drain" and "we are losing the war against homosexuals." As proof, the reader was informed that gays were given permission to lay a wreath on the Tomb of the Unknown Soldier in honor of any "sexual deviants" that served in the military. According to the letter, "the gays were allowed to turn our Tomb of the Unknown soldier into: THE TOMB OF THE UNKNOWN SODOMITE!" (Martin, 1996, 205).

Falwell and his associates were so vehemently anti-gay that when they were unable to get their point across by taking liberties with the truth, they resorted to out and out fabrications. For example, at a Moral Majority rally in Alaska, Falwell told his audience that he had been at the White House and asked President Carter, "Sir, why do you have homosexuals on your senior staff at the White House?" As Falwell told it, Carter's supposed reply was that since he wanted "to represent everyone, he had to hire some homosexuals." Unfortunately for Falwell, the conversation that he actually had with Carter had been taped, and there was no record of Carter ever saying such a thing. Falwell then attempted to sidestep allegations that he had fabricated the story by characterizing his statements as a "parable" or "allegory" (Martin, 1996, 211). In spite of the fact that Falwell had been caught in a bold-faced fabrication, Carter's status as a "pro-family" Democrat was damaged by Falwell's allegations since Falwell's followers had a tendency to believe him regardless of the evidence. In the words of Nancy Godsey, one of the members of Falwell's Church,

> "Somebody had to take a stand. I think Dr. Falwell was the one to do it because he gets his wisdom and knowledge from God. That's why we're for him a hundred percent. It's not just his point of view. He goes back to God's word. None of us is perfect, and we don't worship Dr. Falwell, but we love him because he preaches the Bible. And right off the top of my head, I can't think of anything that he's ever tried to teach us that was wrong, because he is inspired of God, and we just trust him" (Quoted in Martin, 1996, 202-203).

Ronald Reagan and the Religious Right

Given the nature of the political arguments coming from the religious right, Ronald Reagan may have been as unlikely a hero for their cause as could be imagined. Reagan was a former Democrat and Hollywood actor whose life reflected "Hollywood California liberal" values. Reagan had been divorced, and had been rumored to have had extramarital affairs when married to his first wife, Jane Wyman. Furthermore, one of the women with whom Reagan had had a relationship was rumored to have had an abortion (*Time*, October 19, 1987). Furthermore, Patti Davis, the oldest child born to Ronald and Nancy Reagan, was born seven months after the couple were married (Davis, 1992, 14). Reagan had signed liberal abortion bills as Governor of California and had opposed legislation that would have barred gays from teaching in the public schools. Reagan's 1979 tax return revealed that he had contributed less than 1% of his income to charitable causes; furthermore, he did not attend church regularly and was therefore unfamiliar and uncomfortable with common fundamentalist religious terms such as "born again" (Martin, 1996, 208).

Reagan's wife Nancy, who would eventually lead a "Just Say No" campaign against drugs, spent a good portion of her adult lifetime addicted to tranquilizers (Davis, 1992, 38). Nancy was also a believer in astrology, which is generally viewed by the religious right as "Satanic," and coordinated her entire schedule and that of her husband with her horoscope and the advice of astrologers. In the words of her daughter Patti,

> "I'd heard my parents read their horoscopes aloud at the breakfast table, but that seemed pretty innocuous to me. Occasionally, I read mine, too—usually so I can do the exact opposite of what it says. But my parents have done what

the stars suggested—altered schedules, changed travel plans, stayed home, cancelled appearances" (Davis, 1992, 97).

Corroborating Davis' contention that her parents directed their lives by the stars was Reagan's own Chief of Staff in his second term, Donald Regan. According to Regan (1988, 3-4),

> "Virtually every major move and decision the Reagans made during my time as White House Chief of Staff was cleared in advance with a woman in San Francisco who drew up horoscopes to make certain that the planets were in a favorable alignment for the enterprise. Nancy Reagan seemed to have absolute faith in the clairvoyant powers of this woman…Although I never met this seer—Mrs. Reagan passed along her prognostications to me after conferring with her on the telephone—she had become such a factor in my work, and in the highest affairs of the nation, that at one point I kept a color-coded calendar on my desk (numerals highlighted in green ink for 'good' days, red for 'bad' days, yellow for 'iffy' days) as an aid to remembering when it was propitious to move the President from one place to another, or schedule him to speak in public, or commence negotiations with a foreign power."

Reagan also had distant relationships with his children and the Reagans did little together as an entire family according to their daughter Patti (Davis, 1992, Regan, 1988).

In spite of the incongruity of his personal life with much of what the religious right espouse, candidate Ronald Reagan in the 1980 campaign quickly began spouting the family values themes so highly valued by the religious right, and gave lip service to the religious right's agenda. For example, Reagan was invited to an event in Dallas in August, 1980 called the National Affairs Briefing, sponsored by the Religious Roundtable and led by evangelist James Robison. The idea behind the event was to allow the Presidential candidates, Reagan, Carter, and independent candidate John Anderson, to articulate their views before a gathering of conservative Christian pastors and laypersons. Evidently sensing that the deck was stacked against them at the event, Carter and Anderson declined their invitations, but Reagan accepted and made the most of his opportunity (Martin, 1996, 217).

In a pre-speech press conference for the event, Reagan suggested that the Biblical creation story should be taught in public schools, endorsed tuition tax credit for families that send their children to parochial schools, and condemned the Supreme Court for having "expelled God from the classroom." Reagan also observed that "everybody in favor of abortion had already been born" and asserted that if he were shipwrecked and could only choose one book to read for the rest of his life, he would choose the Bible. Reagan also asserted that "all the complex questions facing us at home and abroad could have their answer in that single book" (Quoted in Martin, 1996, 217-218).

Though the Conference was certainly a victory for Reagan with the Christian right, the Conference achieved some major notoriety when Dr. Bailey Smith, president of the Southern Baptist Convention, stated,

"It is interesting at great political rallies how you have a Protestant to pray, a Catholic to pray, and then you have a Jew to pray. With all due respect to those dear people, my friends, God Almighty does not hear the prayer of a Jew" (Shriver, 1981, 29-30).

Obviously, under most circumstances it would behoove a politician to distance himself from this type of support, but Reagan was able to effectively court the religious right without seriously alienating the political middle, a feat accomplished largely by giving lip-service to the religious fundamentalists during his campaign, and then ignoring their program for change throughout his Presidency.

Nevertheless, Reagan's courtship of the Christian right continued into the Republican convention of 1980. For instance, Reagan ended his acceptance speech at the 1980 Republican Convention with a moment of silent prayer. Reagan then ended the moment of silence with the statement, "God bless America" effectively wrapping patriotism in religious overtones. The Republican platform at the 1980 Convention also reflected the religious right influence in its stated opposition to ERA, support for a Constitutional Amendment to outlaw abortion, and a recommendation that all appointees to the federal judiciary be pro-life. The Republicans also called for tax cuts and reductions in federal spending, free trade, and an increase in defense spending. Somehow, however, the Republicans included a plank in favor of a balanced budget amid their proposals for tax cuts and defense increases (*Time*. July 28, 1980).

Vice Presidential Candidate George H.W. Bush

For his running mate, after a brief flirtation with former President Gerald Ford, who indicated that he would decline any such invitation, Reagan chose George H.W. Bush, who had been his strongest challenger for the nomination in the Republican Primaries. In spite of Bush's resume as a Republican Congressional leader, Ambassador to China, Ambassador to the UN, and Director of the CIA, there were reservations in some Republican corners concerning Bush. In specific, Bush had vocally criticized the central feature of Reagan's "supply-side" economic plan as "voodoo economics," correctly arguing that the tax cuts and proposed defense spending increases espoused by candidate Reagan could only produce massive deficits. Furthermore, Bush had been a supporter of ERA and had a history of a pro-choice stance on abortion. In fact, Bush had been such an ardent supporter of population control in the 1960s that he had earned the nickname "Rubbers" in Congress (Germond and Witcover, 1981, 170).

Election of 1980

There was little chance that Jimmy Carter could achieve an electoral victory in 1980 due to a combination of economic malaise and foreign policy crises that Carter had been unable to solve. Oil and gasoline prices soared in 1979 to unprecedented highs, contributing to another round of double-digit inflation. Iranian militants had taken Americans hostage at the U.S. Embassy in Tehran in 1979, and 52 Americans had been held in Iran for over a year when the 1980 November election was held. Furthermore, the Soviet Union had invaded Afghanistan in what most Americans interpreted as an expansionist attempt by the Soviet Union to spread communism, and Carter's diplomatic efforts and economic sanctions had been unable to dissuade the Soviet "aggression." Conservatives argued that Carter had been to "soft" on the Soviet Union as well as Iran, and candidate Reagan promised a harder line against both. In the end, the harder line carried the American electorate as Reagan won 44 states and 489 electoral votes in a landslide election that also put control of the U.S. Senate in Republican hands. The Democrats still controlled the House, but when Southern Democrats were added to the Republicans, the House approximated a conservative majority. Importantly, numerous white conservative Democratic politicians in the South switched parties along with the conservative white Southern voters so that the South, which had been solid Democrat since the Civil War, henceforth would be solid Republican (Mayer, 2002, 168).

The Reagan Administration

Ronald Reagan's Presidency is perhaps one of the most important in American history, if for no other reason than that he presided over one of the great realignments of American politics, as ideological Traditional Conservatives in the American South completed the shift that had been brewing for decades and abandoned the Democratic Party permanently for the Republicans. Essentially, Ronald Reagan succeeded where Goldwater and Nixon had failed in putting together a conservative governing coalition. Reagan also presided over the largest peacetime increase in defense spending in American history and renewed the intensification of the Cold War with the Soviet Union. In fact, the Soviet's attempt to keep up with Reagan's defense spending is a major factor that led to their demise a few short years after Reagan left office. Conservatives would later consider it to be the "genius" of Reagan's policy that he was able to "bankrupt" the Soviet Union, but there is little evidence that Reagan had formulated such a calculated plan (Mayer, 2002, 168-169).

Importantly, Ronald Reagan also presided over a shift in the Republican Party toward politics based on ideological prescriptions rather than pragmatic policy analysis. Reagan essentially prided himself on his own ideological convictions, frequently substituted ideology in place of rational analysis, and then imputed it to himself as wisdom. In Reagan's words,

"I say there are simple answers to many of our problems—simple but hard...It's the complicated answer that's easy because it avoids facing the hard moral issues" (Quoted in *Economist*, June 12, 2004, 24).

In keeping with what he stated, Reagan simplistically viewed foreign policy as a simple clash between the "good" United States and the "Evil Empire" Soviet Union, viewed the free market as the solution to all economic problems, and believed in lower taxes and less government without any in-depth analysis of their ramifications. In essence, Reagan was the expression of the conservative ideological movement and the first "movement" conservative to occupy the Presidency. Reagan was also the first President to measure his success and failure in terms of his ability to stick to the movement's core principles (Mickelthwait and Wooldridge, 2005, 90).

In Ronald Reagan's inaugural address, Reagan proclaimed that "government is not the solution to our problems; government is the problem" (Quoted in Gould, 2003, 420). Consequently, Reagan intended to reduce the size of government, reduce government regulation, and allow the free market to correct America's economic ills, consistent with his conservative ideology. Unfortunately for Reagan, his ideological rhetoric turned out to be ineffective at quickly solving the nation's economic problems. The nation experienced a sharp recession in 1981-82 with 8.4% unemployment and double digit inflation. The prime lending rate in February 1982 stood at an astonishing 16.75%, and the gross national product was shrinking at an annual rate of 0.1% (Regan, 1988, 173). Reagan instituted his promised tax cut in 1981, but with the promised defense increases and without accompanying spending cuts, the national debt would triple during Reagan's eight years in office. In August, 1982, Reagan was forced to push Congress for a tax increase to address the burgeoning deficits, the first of six tax increases that would be passed during his Presidency (Stockman, 1987, 397-398).

Supply-Side Economics and Ideology

Ronald Reagan's first objective in domestic policy in 1981 was to institute a massive tax cut. Reagan's perception was that a restructuring of the tax code was needed and that the tax structure should be much flatter, with the highest tax rates greatly reduced. When Reagan became acquainted with the supply-side economic theory of Professor Arthur Laffer, who essentially argued that a tax cut would produce such great economic growth that the government would actually have more money after instituting a cut, Reagan quickly adopted the idea as his own. Reagan, however, was never much for attention to detail, and he conveniently ignored the fact that Laffer's theory required adherence to the gold standard and a zero inflation economy in order for it to work properly (Stockman, 1987, 10). The U.S., of course, had not been on the gold standard since the Great Depression and inflation was in double-digits when Reagan implemented his first round of tax cuts.

Reagan's budget director, David Stockman, was essentially the architect of Reagan's supply-side plan and Stockman fully understood that massive tax cuts unaccompanied by spending cuts would lead to deficits. Stockman was unable, however, to convey this message to President Reagan in a manner so that he and his top aides could understand it. Stockman (1987, 50), stated that Reagan "only had the foggiest idea of what supply side was all about" and that "no one close to him had any more idea." Stockman contended that Reagan's top aides knew nothing about fiscal policy and refused to learn, preferring to follow ideological solutions instead of any rational policy analysis. In Stockman's words, "They never read anything. They lived off the tube. They understood nothing about the serious ideas underlying the Reagan Revolution" (Stockman, 1987, 7). Reagan's Treasury Secretary at the time, Donald Regan, (himself a supply-sider) corroborates Stockman's assessment of the situation. In the words of Regan,

> "Stockman had the trust and confidence of Meese, who had become the Counselor to the President, and of James Baker III, the Chief of Staff. Stockman understood the budget; they didn't. As a result, they tended to give him his head...Reagan didn't understand the budget either, and his aides were bringing Stockman in to explain it to him" (Quoted in Regan, 198, 153).

Nevertheless, Stockman designed a massive tax cut plan that eventually became the Economic Recovery Tax Act of 1981, the largest single tax reduction bill in U.S. history. The legislation cut the tax rate for individuals with the lowest incomes from 14% to 11% percent, and lowered the rate for individuals with the highest incomes from 70% to 50%. Tax cuts were also instituted for corporations, and taxes were lowered on capital gains, gifts, and inheritances (Roark et al., 2005, 1121).

In order to prevent such massive tax cuts from producing deficits, Stockman planned to institute massive spending cuts. What Stockman didn't understand, however, was that Republicans in Congress in actuality were just as attached to federal spending in their home districts as were the Democrats, regardless of their "less government" rhetoric; consequently, the kind of meaningful spending cuts necessary to offset the tax cuts would be extremely difficult. In his book, *The Triumph of Politics*, Stockman (1987) describes his repeated proposals for domestic spending cuts that were one by one eliminated by Republican members of Congress—the same Republican members of Congress that in rhetoric supposedly favored spending cuts. Evidently, however, the Congressional Republicans' love of federal spending cuts did not extend to reducing money going into their home districts. In the words of Regan (1988, 155), "The fatal flaw in Stockman's approach was a practical, not a theoretical, one. The budget is not controlled by the Executive Branch but by Congress." To compound matters further, Stockman made an error in calculation when figuring the increase in the military budget. In a meeting with Defense Secretary Casper Weinberger, Stockman scribbled a proposed defense budget for Weinberger on a napkin. Weinberger quickly accepted the figures as gospel and they were released to the public, but Stockman had made a calculation error, and the increase in the defense budget was to be double that which Reagan had promised in his campaign budget plan (Stockman, 1987, 118-119).

When it became obvious to Stockman that not even the most unrealistically optimistic economic forecasts could produce a balanced budget, Stockman says that he created what he termed as the "magic asterisk," which he described as a "bookkeeping invention" that would balance the budget with a footnote that said "Future savings to be identified" (Stockman, 1987, 135). Stockman justified his magic asterisk to himself because he believed that the Republicans would cut Social Security, but his battles with Republicans in Congress quickly proved to him that there would be no significant cuts in Social Security or any other Entitlement programs (Stockman, 1987, 195).

Stockman attempted to explain the problems to Reagan and his top advisers, but they essentially dismissed Stockman's arguments because they believed that their tax cuts would somehow create more government revenue. Treasury Secretary Donald Regan explained his perspective on supply-side economics thusly,

"I suggested that we ought not to be talking about spending in isolation from management of the process. Nor should we be speaking in visionary terms about deep cuts in spending. As a practical matter, though waste should and could be reduced, federal spending would continue to increase. The key to the situation was to hold the increase within bounds, controlling it in such a way that it grew at a slower rate than revenues. The increase in revenues should be financed not by new and higher taxes, but by lower tax rates that would produce more money for the government by stimulating higher earnings by corporations and workers in an atmosphere of ready capital" (Quoted in Regan, 1988, 155).

Stockman tried to explain to Regan and his top aides that there would be deficits even with robust economic growth created by the tax cuts, but Reagan's response was that it must just be because of the "mess" they had inherited from Carter, and Stockman was instructed to "make the numbers prove all this." In Stockman's words, "Well, you couldn't, No known method of accounting could" because the fiscal disaster was due primarily to the policies constructed by the Reagan Administration rather than Carter (Stockman, 1987, 388-389). Stockman was befuddled by the impenetrable ideology of the President and his advisers and their inability to engage in sound analysis. Stockman asked, "What do you do when your President ignores all the palpable, relevant facts and wanders in circles" (Stockman, 1987, 435). As a consequence, Stockman stated that "what started out as an idea-based Reagan Revolution, ended up as an unintended exercise in free lunch economics" (Stockman, 1987, 8).

Ideology and Ignorance in the White House

Stockman, however, was not the only one to notice that the President was generally ignorant of any real policy details. Donald Regan, who was White House Chief of Staff in Reagan's second term, lamented that Reagan would often have to,

"apologize for asking a basic—sometimes even a startling basic—question about an arcane subject, I would joke that the President of the United States was not supposed to know everything: if he did, he'd be editor of the Encyclopedia Britannica" (Quoted in Regan, 1988, 189).

Regan (1988, 266-167) relates another story where he created a Policy Paper for Reagan upon becoming Reagan's new Chief of Staff in his second term. Regan says that the President returned the paper to him without spoken or written comment. When Regan asked the President what he thought of it, Reagan replied, "It's good. It's really good, Don" and then said nothing more, and had "no questions, no objections, and no instructions." In the words of Regan,

"By now I understood that the President did not share my love of detail and my enthusiasm for planning...Another President would almost certainly have had his own ideas on the mechanics of policy, but Reagan did not trouble himself with such minutiae" (Quoted in Regan, 1988, 267).

Instead of becoming involved in the policy details, Regan's assessment was that the President chose his aides and then followed their advice almost without question. In the words of Regan (1988, 143), "The President himself had very little to do with the invention and the implementation of the policies...He was content to exercise the symbolic powers of his office." Regan also went on record as stating that Reagan never actually issued a direct order, suggesting that it was his advisers that were the real architects of policy (Regan, 1988, 268).

That Reagan essentially had to leave the policy details to his advisers was only partially because his own base of policy knowledge was extremely limited, however. In general, Reagan compounded his ignorance with a lax work ethic and a lack of interest in in-depth information. According to Regan, the President was not known to be a rigorous worker, beginning his day promptly at 9:00AM every morning by feeding acorns to squirrels outside his office (Regan, 1988, 49). Reagan's relatively late (9:00AM) arrival at work every day, however, was not typically due to any regimen of late night work and study. According to Regan, (1988, 271), he could tell that Reagan was not a heavy reader because "he rarely spoke of anything that he had read the night before." Regan states that Reagan did, however, read the *Los Angeles Times* and whatever he did read there, he tended to believe as gospel; hence, those who wanted Reagan to become aware of anything in particular would plant stories in the *Los Angeles Times* (Regan, 1988, 57).

White House Chief of Staff James Baker supported Regan's conclusions concerning President Reagan's focus and reading habits with a story of an economic summit in Williamsburg, Virginia in 1983. According to Baker, he provided Reagan with a thick briefing book on the afternoon before the summit intending for Reagan to read it that evening. When Baker saw Reagan the next day, he noticed that the briefing book remained unopened. Baker asked the President why he hadn't done his homework, and Reagan replied, "Well, Jim, 'The Sound of Music' was on last night'" (*Economist*, June 12, 2004, 24).

Due to Reagan's general ignorance, in a manner similar to the political handlers for Warren Harding and William McKinley, his advisers, if possible, attempted to keep him from making any off-the-cuff remarks so as to prevent embarrassment. In the words of Regan (1988, 248),

"His position was always chosen with the idea of keeping him as far away as possible from the reporters who hovered at the edge of these events with the intention of shouting questions. Every moment of every public appearance was scheduled, every word was scripted, every place where Reagan was expected to stand was chalked with toe marks. The President was always being prepared for a performance, and this had the inevitable effect of preserving him from confrontation and the genuine interplay of opinion, question, and argument that form the basis of decision."

Other measures were also taken to prevent Reagan from making embarrassing, unscripted remarks. When Reagan landed in the Presidential helicopter, the pilot was instructed to keep the rotors turning while the President disembarked so that he would be unable to hear and reply to any questions that might be shouted out impromptu (Lineberry, Edwards, and Wattenberg, 1993, 472).

In a policy sense, it was therefore imperative then that Reagan's advisers, such as Treasury Secretary Donald Regan, Attorney General Ed Meese, Deputy Chief of Staff Michael Deaver, and White House Chief of Staff James Baker, were policy experts, especially since Reagan was introducing radical changes in fiscal policy. According to Stockman (1987, 12), however, Deaver and Baker were persons who understood the politics of public opinion, but neither were strong in understanding fiscal policy. Donald Regan concurs with Stockman's assessment, stating of Deaver that,

"When fiscal and monetary policy were discussed, Deaver's eyes visibly glazed over. There was, of course, no reason for him to be interested in the substance of policy. His job was to sell the product once it was invented and ready to be marketed. Deaver was in charge of the Reagans' public image" (Quoted in Regan, 1988, 225).

To make matters worse, Stockman essentially viewed Meese and Regan as individuals who not only did not understand fiscal policy, but didn't understand much of anything else either. Consequently, Stockman argued that none of Reagan's top advisers had a full grasp of the implications of the major overhaul in American fiscal policy that Stockman had designed and the reasons for the massive debt that resulted. Stockman, however, quickly realized his mistakes and calculated that the national debt would have been approximately half of what it had ended up being if Reagan had simply followed the fiscal policies that were set in place under Jimmy Carter (Stockman, 1987, 388-389).

Something clearly had to be done quickly and early in the Reagan Administration in an attempt to correct the impending fiscal disaster caused by the Administration's tax cuts. Consequently, in 1982, Republican Senate

Finance committee chairman Bob Dole argued publicly that new taxes were unavoidable due to the burgeoning deficits. Treasury Secretary Donald Regan, consistent with his supply-side ideology, opposed the taxes, arguing that "I never have believed, and never will believe, that increasing taxes is a cure for recession" (Quoted in Regan, 1988, 174). Regan argued that the debt in the short run did not matter if the economy could generate long-run growth. In other words, Regan ignored the record $128 billion deficit reality in favor of his supply-side ideology that taught him that the government would eventually have more money with tax cuts. In spite of the Treasury Secretary's objections, the Reagan Administration in January 1982 proposed a tax increase of $86.6 billion (Regan, 1988, 175-177).

Deregulation

President Reagan pushed for deregulation of the nation's economy based on the Classic Liberal ideological premise that the free market is most efficient without government intervention. Pursuant to their ideological goals, the Reagan administration declined to enforce the Sherman Antitrust Act against an unprecedented number of business mergers and takeovers. Reagan also moved to loosen health, safety, and environmental concerns on business (Roark et al., 2005, 1121).

In furtherance of his deregulatory environmental goals, Reagan outraged environmentalists with the appointment of James Watt as Secretary of the Interior. Watt had been a leader of what was known as the "Sagebrush Rebellion" in the Western States where citizens protested against government environmental regulations as interferences with their property rights. With the Department of the Interior under his tutelage, Watt declared that "We will mine more, drill more, and cut more timber." Watt then released federal lands to private companies for harvesting of natural resources (Roark et al., 2005, 1131). Meanwhile, Reagan's Environmental Protection Agency eased enforcement of air and water pollution measures and relaxed automobile safety requirements. In specific, a requirement by the National Highway Transportation and Safety Administration that all cars would have driver's side airbags was suspended. Reagan's other appointees in the EPA and Department of Interior and other federal regulatory agencies tended to be individuals with close ties to the business interests they were supposed to be in charge of regulating. In essence, Reagan placed the "foxes" in charge of guarding the "henhouses" (Cannon, 1991, 141).

Reagan's personal attitude toward the environment is perhaps best exemplified by a story related by his daughter, Patti Davis. Davis (1992, 219) states that,

"I drove up to my parents' Santa Barbara ranch one weekend and found my father throwing magazines and colored newsprint into the fireplace, something which is not environmentally responsible because of the dyes used. 'You shouldn't be burning colored paper like that,' I told my father. 'The dyes are very harmful when they're burned.' 'What's the difference?' 'He said. It just goes up in the air.'"

Reagan also favored efforts to weaken organized labor. When the Professional Air Traffic Controllers Organization (PATCO) went on strike in 1981, Reagan followed the path of his favorite President, Calvin Coolidge (who proclaimed in the Boston policemen's strike in 1919 that "there is no right of public employees to strike, anytime, anywhere"), and fired the air traffic controllers (Roark et al., 2005, 1121).

Ideology and the Banking Crisis

While there may be some truth to Reagan's premise that the free market is most efficient without government interference, the free market also has a tendency to be extremely disorderly and subject to harsh dislocations; hence, deregulation of the free market may be expected to contribute to some calamity of its own. Evidently not learning anything from the bank crises of the 1930s that Reagan lived through, as President, Reagan initiated deregulation of the nation's financial sector, consistent with his laissez-faire ideology. Perhaps predictably, deregulation of the banking and savings and loan industries in the 1980s was followed by a series of loan institution failures not seen in America since the Great Depression. By the end of 1985, 120 banks had failed, and 184 had failed by 1987 (O'Sullivan and Keuchel, 1989, 262).

Savings and Loans and other thrift institutions were even worse off. In 1985, a federal survey showed that the assets of more than 400 Savings and Loans barely exceeded their liabilities. Furthermore, it was estimated that up to 1/3 of the federally insured Savings and Loans would be gone by 1990. The Chairman of the Federal Home Loan Bank Board announced that it would cost the taxpayers $17.4 billion to resolve the financial difficulties of what he termed as 259 "grossly insolvent" thrifts (O'Sullivan and Keuchel, 1989, 264).

In Ohio in 1985, a bank crisis caused the first bank holiday in the United States since the Great Depression. Home State Savings Bank of Ohio had loaned money to E.S.M., a small Florida firm that showed a loss of $300 million when it collapsed due to questionable securities practices and abuses by its Board members. One E.S.M. official had a purchased a $1.65 million house, $1 million worth of polo ponies, a $1.35 million yacht, a $150,000 sports car, and a 5600 acre bird hunting farm, all in the midst of the firm's collapse. When news of E.S.M.'s failure and its impact on Home State Savings Bank reached Ohio, a run started on the bank. The State of Ohio's State Deposit Insurance fund was inadequate to cover Home State Savings Bank's $175 million loss, leaving depositors without their money that they had believed was safe and insured. The failure of the Ohio thrifts then led to a run on thrifts in Maryland. In order to prevent a complete collapse, the Maryland Governor imposed an FDR-style $1000 a month limit on withdrawals from Maryland's state-insured thrifts (O'Sullivan and Keuchel, 1989, 264).

Election of 1984

By 1984, the economy had made a comeback that would continue throughout the decade in spite of Reagan's deficit spending. The Democrats then did the Republicans a favor by nominating the unexciting Walter Mondale of Minnesota and his female running mate Geraldine Ferraro, who brought little to the ticket besides her status as the first woman to be nominated as Vice President by either major party. Mondale then promised an unpopular tax increase for the purpose of addressing the burgeoning deficit, and the Democratic challenge was doomed. The Democrats would not even win Ferraro's home state of New York. Confident of victory, the Republicans essentially ran an issueless "It's Morning in America" campaign that bypassed policy substance altogether (Darman, 1996, 141). On Election Day, Reagan won every state except Mondale's home state of Minnesota and the District of Columbia.

Reagan Presidency and the Religious Right

Evangelist Pat Robertson echoed the sentiments of perhaps millions of fundamentalist Protestants when he declared,

> "It was no coincidence that Ronald Reagan was elected President. It was the direct act of God…The Republican takeover and reversal of direction in this country is no coincidence" (Quoted in Blumenthal, 1990, 103).

From the beginning of his Presidency through to the end, Ronald Reagan remained a darling of the religious right and his status with religious conservatives has not diminished over time. This "saintly" status is perhaps surprising not only since (as mentioned previously) Reagan's personal life was generally incongruent with the values espoused by the religious right, but his overtures to the religious right during his entire career as a politician were generally much more lip-service than substance. In the words of John Conlan,

> "The core group around Reagan—the Mike Deavers of the world and the others—were not at all interested either in appointing evangelical Christians into the administration or in concentrating on their values, because they didn't understand. Their hearts were not with the middle-class, upper working-class, or even the poor classes that were oriented to church and moral values. There was no money to be extracted from those people, there were no titles, no fancy dinners, no private concerts at the Corcoran Art Gallery or anything else, so they were not interested" (Quoted in Martin, 1996, 220).

Reflecting this attitude, shortly after the 1980 election, both Reagan and Republican Senate Majority Leader Howard Baker announced that serious consideration of the social agenda of the religious right would have to wait at least a year while the new administration focused on the economy (Cromartie, 1993, 53). Reagan's top aides, Michael Deaver and James Baker in particular, felt that it was in the President's interest to downplay the values issues, and they viewed visits with leaders of the "family values" crowd to be wastes of the President's time (Cannon, 1991, 53).

On the abortion issue, Reagan essentially did nothing. Meanwhile, conservative North Carolina Senator Jesse Helms and Illinois Congressman Henry Hyde introduced a bill that declared that "human life shall be deemed to exist from conception." Passage of the bill was intended to allow States to define abortion as murder, and thus provide a way for States to end all abortions. Reagan's White House offered no assistance on the Helms-Hyde bill, and the bill did not pass. When the opportunity arose for Reagan to appoint a Supreme Court Justice, Reagan appointed Sandra Day O'Connor, who had no religious affiliation, had been a supporter of ERA, and had once fought for the legalization of abortions in the Arizona State Senate. To prevent uproar over the O'Connor nomination from the religious community, Reagan personally called Jerry Falwell and asked him not to oppose O'Connor's nomination, which he did not. In the words of Falwell, "I do not believe (Reagan) would intentionally appoint someone who supports abortion" (Quoted in Martin, 1996, 227-228). Reagan did, however, appoint the evangelical anti-abortion advocate, C. Everett Koop, to the position of Surgeon General.

On the school prayer issue, another issue important to religious conservatives, Reagan adopted the religious conservatives' position, and in 1982 supported a Prayer Amendment in Congress that would allow individual and group prayers in public schools, but the bill failed to gain the 2/3 majority support in the Senate necessary for its passage (*Conservative Digest*, May, 1982, 13).

Scandals of the Religious Right

The last two years of Reagan's Presidency were difficult ones for the religious right since a number of their popular and very public leaders became embroiled in scandals and embarrassing situations. Unfortunately for the religious right, it would be difficult to argue any position other than that the scandals hindered the influence of the religious right with the Reagan administration in Washington.

The first incident that tainted the reputation of the religious right was instigated by evangelist Oral Roberts in the spring of 1987 when he announced that God was going to "call him home" if he were unable to raise eight million dollars needed for his ministry. In spite of his dubious claim, the money was eventually raised, but the episode was viewed as folly by most Americans (Shepard, 1989, 275).

Shortly after Roberts' shenanigans, a more explosive scandal erupted involving one of America's best known televangelists, Jim Bakker of PTL. In March, 1987, the *Charlotte Observer* revealed that Bakker had engaged in an extramarital affair with Jessica Hahn, a former church secretary, and had paid Hahn $250,000 in hush money. The Jessica Hahn revelation was followed by revelations of gross deception, exploitation of trusting supporters for money, mismanagement and misuse of funds, exorbitant salaries, luxuries, and the drug dependency of Bakker's cosmetic-covered wife, Tammy Faye (Shepard, 1989, 275). Hahn would eventually pose in Playboy Magazine to further taint the sordid affair. Bakker handed his ministry over to Jerry Falwell, but Falwell's management was unable to save the ministry from bankruptcy. Before he gave up, however, Falwell was able to subject the ministry to further ridicule when he went down a waterslide at PTL's amusement park fully clothed in a business suit. The IRS eventually revoked PTL's nonprofit status and sued the ministry for $56 million in back taxes, and Bakker was sentenced to 45 years in prison for defrauding his supporters of $158 million (Shepard, 1989, 275-276).

As if that were not enough, in 1988, televangelist Pat Robertson made his own contribution to the evangelicals' embarrassment when he decided to run for President, but his campaign based on Christian morality began inauspiciously when it was revealed that Robertson's oldest son was conceived out of wedlock. Robertson subsequently further damaged his already-tainted image when he claimed to have been a "combat veteran" of the Korean War, but his assertion was exposed as fraudulent when Congressman Pete McCloskey revealed that he had been on the same troop ship bound for Korea as Robertson when Robertson's Congressman father had used his influence to get young Pat pulled off the ship. Finally,

Robertson claimed on his CBN network that he knew the location of American hostages in Lebanon, but then had to back down and admit that he only knew the names of the hostages, and not their location (Martin, 1996, 284).

To top off the evangelical scandal-go-round, later that same year it was revealed that televangelist Jimmy Swaggart had been photographed taking a prostitute into a motel room on the outskirts of New Orleans. Swaggart denied having sexual intercourse with the prostitute, instead tearily stating before his congregation that he had merely masturbated while the prostitute performed "pornographic acts," but the scandal was damaging to the religious right in general and to Pat Robertson's Presidential bid all the same (Martin, 1996, 289).

AIDS and the Reagan Administration

In 1981, Reagan's first year in office, AIDS arrived in the United States, bringing with it an obvious public need for education about AIDS to the American people. The Surgeon General of the United States is mandated by Congress to inform the American people about the prevention of disease and the promotion of health, but Surgeon General C. Everett Koop was instructed not to make any statements about AIDS because any federal AIDS education plan was likely to alienate Reagan's support from the religious right. Consequently, the media were told at Reagan's press conferences by Reagan officials that AIDS questions were not on the agenda (Koop, 1991, 194-195).

Republican Congressman Newt Gingrich and many members of the religious right viewed AIDS both as God's judgment for the sin of homosexuality and as a means for political gain. At a conference on "How to Win an Election," sponsored by Tim LaHaye's American Coalition for Traditional Values, Gingrich stated that,

"AIDS will do more to direct America back to the cost of violating traditional values, and to make America aware of the danger of certain behavior than anything we've seen...For us it is a great rallying cry" (Quoted in *The Freedom Writer*, February 1995, 1).

Some members of the religious right called for quarantines of HIV positive persons. Jerry Falwell, who termed AIDS as "the wrath of God," argued that quarantines of people with AIDS were no more unreasonable than quarantining cows with brucellosis. Similarly, Reverend Donald Wildmon of the American Family Association called for a quarantine of "all homosexual establishments" (Altman, 1986, 67). In Nevada, a newspaper ran a full page "AIDS Alert" advertisement posted by a fundamentalist minister who stated, "I think we should do what the Bible says and cut their throats" (Quoted in Altman, 1986, 68). In 1988, a *Los Angeles Times* poll revealed that 57% of religious fundamentalists favored a quarantine of people with AIDS (*Los Angeles Times*, July 20, 1988). *National Review* Editor William F. Buckley added his contribution to the paranoia when he suggested that those afflicted with AIDS should be given an identifiable tattoo so that others could recognize them and thus avoid contact (*New York Times*, March 18, 1986, A7).

Congress, as the official representative of the people in the United States, was not immune to the hysteria. California Republican Congressman William Dannemeyer stated that if it were possible to identify every HIV positive person in the country, he would "wipe them off the face of the earth" if he were able to do so (Quoted in Koop, 1991, 208). The response of the Reagan administration reflected similar thinking. Dr. James O. Mason, Director of the Center for Disease Control, acknowledged that a quarantine was being considered as an option as late as 1985 (Martin, 1996, 243).

With the AIDS hysteria in full swing, Surgeon General C. Everett Koop in July, 1985, told his superiors that he could no longer remain silent about AIDS. Koop was then given the permission to say whatever he felt was necessary about AIDS, along with the authority to appoint a task force to study the problem. In February 1986, President Reagan asked Koop to prepare a special report on AIDS, and the Report was finally released in October the same year (Koop, 1991, 204).

Koop's Report detailed the ways in which AIDS could be transmitted from person to person, and therefore recommended against sex outside monogamous relationships and against the use of illegal drugs. For those that were determined to have sex outside of monogamous relationships, however, Koop recommended the use of condoms. Koop also recommended sex and AIDS education in the public schools, beginning as early as third grade (Koop, 1991, 205).

Koop's recommendation of condoms and sex education provoked a predictable firestorm from the religious right and conservatives in general. Richard Viguerie of *Conservative Digest* accused Koop of,

"proposing instruction in buggery for schoolchildren as young as the third grade on the spurious grounds that the problem is one of ignorance and not morality" (Quoted in Martin, 1996, 250).

Similarly, William F. Buckley's *National Review* declared Koop to be guilty of "criminal negligence" for recommending the use of condoms (Martin, 1996, 250). Not to be outdone, Phyllis Schlafly stated in a television interview that she would "rather see her children become infected with sexually transmitted diseases than for them to know there was such a thing as condoms" (Quoted in Koop, 1991, 218).

The reaction of the Reagan Administration to the public backlash against Koop's report was to have the President's adviser regarding family policy, Gary Bauer, ask Koop to remove the references in the report to condoms. Bauer explained the reasoning behind such a change to Koop with a story of a Bauer family Christmas dinner at which members of Bauer's family had mentioned they understood that Koop wanted to give condoms to children in the third grade. Koop dismissed Bauer's recommendation to remove condoms from the report as "ridiculous," but concluded that, in the words of Koop, "the Reagan White House, including the President himself at times, reasoned anecdotally instead of examining the evidence and drawing conclusions" (Koop, 1991, 220-221).

Robert Bork Appointment

In June of 1987, Justice Lewis Powell resigned his position on the Supreme Court, leaving President Reagan the task of appointing a successor. Reagan chose Yale law professor and U.S. Court of Appeals judge Robert Bork, a staunch conservative who had opposed the 1964 Civil Rights Act for "intruding on the rights of citizens." Bork also disagreed with the Supreme Court's "Judicial Activism" and the "creation of new rights" such as the Right to Privacy that had been the basis of the *Roe v.Wade* decision. Provoking further anger from the left, Bork had been the Solicitor General in the Watergate "Saturday Night Massacre" that had fired Special Prosecutor Archibald Cox at the behest of Richard Nixon (Bronner, 1989, 180). As a result, therefore, of what Democrats viewed as his extreme conservative views, coupled with his actions in the Watergate affair, Bork was voted down in the Senate by a vote of 58-42.

Reagan followed up the Bork appointment with the nomination of Douglas Ginsburg, a Harvard Law professor, but the Ginsburg nomination unraveled when it was revealed that Ginsburg had used marijuana while working as a professor at Harvard. Finally, Reagan appointed Appeals Court Justice Anthony Kennedy, who was confirmed unanimously by the Senate in 1988 (Bronner, 1989, 186).

The Bork affair, however, had long term consequences. Republicans correctly charged that the Democrats had voted down Bork for his political views rather than for his legal qualifications. After the Bork affair, Senate confirmation of judicial appointees became highly politicized, and a series of similar affairs would rage on in cases of appointees to lower courts for the next decade and a half. Those who would fail to be confirmed were often said to be "Borked" (Gould, 2003, 432-433).

The reasons for the political firestorm over Bork were ideologically based and reflected the political realities of the new ideological bitterness that had developed in American politics in the late Twentieth Century. Members of the opposing Parties in Congress tended to socialize with each other less than they had in the past due to the increased emphasis on social, cultural, and moral issues that forced a premium on ideological consistency with Parties and constituents. Demonization of the political opposition became more common and tended to produce more campaign contributions and political support for the "Demonizers." Southern conservatives had largely exited the Democratic Party, leaving the Democrats more liberal by subtraction. The loss of their conservative faction rendered the Democratic Party more ideological and less flexible in dealing with their Republican counterparts. Simultaneously, religiosity in the United States had not become more intense, but the makeup of American religion had shifted away from the more liberal, old-line Protestant Churches, and toward religious fundamentalist sects. Although members of religious fundamentalist Protestant Churches were only approximately a fourth of the American population, fundamentalist Protestants had become a majority of the Republican Party (*Economist*, June 24, 2005). Both Parties recognized the negatives of the development of ideological polarization, but religious conservatives that now had power in the Republican Party were not open to compromise, and neither Party was able to make any headway in the reducing partisan and ideological strife that would continue into the Twenty-First century (Gould, 2003, 434).

The Great Crash

On October 19, 1987, known as "Black Monday," the New York Stock Exchange dropped 22.6%, almost double the record 12.8% drop of the 1929 crash that had signaled the dawning of the Great Depression of the 1930s. Although the market rallied to recoup 40% of its losses by the end of the week, economic prognosticators and the general public feared that another Great Depression might follow, thus causing a drop in consumer confidence and further depressing the economy. Many economic observers blamed the crash on the reckless deficit spending by the Reagan administration. Chrysler chairman Lee Iacocca summed up the views of many when he stated, "I don't know what they're on down in Washington. It's wacko time" (Quoted in O'Sullivan and Keuchel, 1989). The stock market would eventually recover, but the crash and fears that ensued suggested to many that "deregulation" of the financial markets might not be quite so wise after all, thus allowing a political opening for the Democrats in 1988.

Economic Inequality

As perhaps could have been expected with the move toward a more free market-oriented economy during the Reagan years, economic inequality increased significantly during the 1980s. In 1979, the poorest 40% of Americans held 18% of the total income in America and the wealthiest 5% held 15.6% of the total income. After eight years of Reaganomics, however, the wealthiest 5% of Americans produced 21% of all income and the poorest 40% of Americans earned only 14% of all income. Unfortunately for America's working class and poor, Adam Smith's "rising tide" did not lift all boats equally. Personal income for the wealthiest 20% of Americans increased, while it actually decreased 9.8% for the poorest 20% of Americans. No longer could all Americans expect, as they had in the previous decades following World War II, that their children would live better than they had. Similarly, between 1980 and 1988, the number of individuals living below the poverty line increased from 11.7% of the population to 13.5%, the highest poverty rate among industrialized democracies of the world (Roark, 2005, 1123).

Reagan and Foreign Policy

At a time that America seemed impotent in foreign policy to many (largely due to the Iranian hostage crisis and the Soviet invasion of Afghanistan), Ronald Reagan had campaigned against Jimmy Carter in 1980 promising to "make America strong again" and arguing for a foreign policy of "Peace through strength." Reagan talked of a "missile gap" between the United States and the Soviet Union, and argued that the Soviet "Evil Empire" was the basis of all of the world's unrest, and therefore had to be contained. Reagan also termed the Vietnam War as a "noble cause" to prevent the spread of communism. Reagan essentially reversed Nixon's Détente by referring to the USSR as the "focus of evil in the modern world" and Reagan was not only anti-Soviet, but determined to fight communism anywhere and everywhere in the world, through military means if necessary (Jones, 1996, 677-678).

George Kennan, the original architect of the containment doctrine, was unimpressed with Reagan's new cold warrior attitude and termed the President's views as "intellectual primitivism," but they played well with the American public, just as they had for Kennedy in 1960. In 1981, Reagan began a defense buildup that amounted to a 40% defense spending increase in the first three years of his Presidency. The defense spending increases were so immense that Reagan's defense budget exceeded Vietnam War spending as a percentage of the economy (Jones, 1996, 677-678).

Adding to his massive buildup, in 1983, Reagan introduced the Strategic Defense Initiative (SDI) in his State of the Union Address. Without first consulting scientists, Reagan proposed to spend $24 billion on a space laser system designed to shoot down Soviet ICBMs. Despite almost unanimous proclamations from the scientific community that such a system was infeasible, Congress appropriated the funding for the program. By 2004, over $60 billion had been spent on the program with essentially no results (Roark et al., 2005, 1131). Reagan also installed new cruise missiles in Europe and doubled the size of the American nuclear arsenal in an attempt to gain "parity" with the Soviet Union. Reagan's claims, however, that the U.S. had fallen behind in the nuclear race, were true only if one merely counted land based missiles, but ignored the fact that the U.S. had a 2-1 advantage over the Soviets in submarine launched missiles in 1982 that counterbalanced the disadvantage in land based systems (Jones, 1996, 681-682).

Reagan and the Middle East

In 1982, a civil war broke out in Lebanon between Maronite Christians, several groups of Lebanese Muslims, and the Palestinian Liberation Organization (PLO). In an attempt to remedy the chaos on their border due to the bloody Lebanese civil war, Syria invaded Lebanon with a "Peacekeeping force." Israel retaliated against the Syrian invasion with an invasion of their own, and the Israeli "peacekeeping force" then pushed Syrian and PLO forces all the way to Beirut. Israel then shelled the City of Beirut, and the U.S. sent Ambassador Philip Habib to negotiate a cease-fire. The next year, the combatants signed an agreement to allow U.S., French, and Italian troops to supervise the PLO withdrawal of Beirut, and Syrian and Israeli withdrawals of Lebanon. American troops were deployed to Lebanon pursuant to the agreement, but on October 23, 1983, an Islamic Suicide Bomber working for the Iranian terrorist organization Hizbollah drove a truck full of explosives into the U.S. marine headquarters at the Beirut airport and killed 241 U.S. marines. Congress failed to pass a resolution authorizing the placement of American troops in a combat zone as required by the War Powers Act of 1973, so President Reagan was forced to redeploy the marines to ships off shore in the Mediterranean (Jones, 1996, 701).

Liberals in the press criticized the Reagan administration for recklessly placing American troops in harm's way, but two days later, Reagan diverted attention from the Lebanon disaster by ordering a U.S. invasion of Grenada, a small island in the Caribbean that had been taken over by a Marxist group. Almost 6,000 American troops were involved in the operation, which quickly overwhelmed the Grenadan leftists and Cuban construction workers; however, 18 Americans were killed and 134 were wounded in the fighting.

396 Grenadans and Cubans were also killed, but the invasion had the desired effect for the Reagan administration since the focus of the American media and the public shifted from the tragedy and defeat of Lebanon to the "victory" in Greanada. Furthermore, Reagan could boast that he had ended the "communist threat" on the tiny Caribbean Island (Jones, 1996, 692-693).

Bombing of Qadaffi

In October, 1985, four Arab terrorists seized control of the Italian Cruise ship Achille Lauro in the Mediterranean and killed an elderly Jewish-American tourist, tossing his body overboard. The terrorists surrendered to Egyptian authorities on the condition that they would be flown safely to Libya, and Egypt complied. President Reagan had Navy fighter jets intercept the terrorist jet and force it to land in Italy, where the terrorists were apprehended. Other Arab terrorists in support of their captured comrades retaliated with bombings of nightclubs in France, Germany, and Italy that were next to U.S. military bases and frequented by U.S. servicemen (Jones, 1996, 704).

"Hawks" within the Reagan administration, headed by Oliver North and Under Secretary of State for political affairs Richard Armitage, wanted to launch retaliatory strikes against the terrorists, but the whereabouts of the Palestinian terrorists was unknown, and the Iranians and Syrians had state-of-the-art anti-aircraft weapons that made air strikes against them risky. Libyan dictator Moamar Qadaffi was chosen as a target because of his accessibility, support of terrorism throughout the Middle East, and his known desire to develop nuclear weapons. Additionally, the U.S. had already had confrontations with Qadaffi during the Reagan Presidency. In August, 1981, Reagan had authorized a series of naval war games in the Libyan Gulf of Sidra in an effort to bait the Libyans into a confrontation, and the U.S. Navy jets ended up shooting down two Libyan planes 60 miles off the Libyan coast (Hersh, 1987, 18-19).

In order to whip up public sentiments against Qadaffi, the CIA (according to Undersecretary of State William Clark) gave false information to the American media alleging that Libyan hit teams had arrived in the United States to assassinate President Reagan (Hersh, 1987, 17). Reagan's aides informed him that Qadaffi was behind the nightclub bombings, and as proof, offered evidence of a telephone call from someone purported to be Qadaffi ordering the bombings via telephone (in Arabic). Based on that information, Reagan then ordered a bombing mission against Libya with the intention to assassinate Qadaffi (Hersh, 1987, 17-28).

French, British, Italian, and German intelligence, however, concluded that the bombings were not Libyan, but backed by Iranians, Syrians and

Palestinians. The bombings were ordered supposedly via telephone, but the European intelligence community concluded that the voice patterns weren't Qadaffi's, and such a phone call would be very unusual for Qadaffi since he had previously always worked through couriers. France therefore refused to allow the U.S. to fly over its air space for such a mission, and the U.S. was forced to fly around France from England to Libya. The U.S. first claimed that it had targeted only terrorist training bases, but Qadaffi's personal residence was destroyed miles from any terrorist training ground, suggesting that the American bombing was a clear assassination attempt by the U.S. One of Qadaffi's daughters died in the bombings, which were generally condemned in the European press. Qadaffi survived because he had been behind his house in his tent rather than inside, but .Reagan's popularity in the U.S. soared to an all time high (Hersh, 1987-28).

Reagan and the Iran-Iraq War

The Iranian Shiite Islamic Revolution in 1979 quickly spilled over into Iraq and created a revolutionary fervor among Iraq's Shiite population. Ayatollah Khomeini of Iran appealed to Iraq's Shiities to overthrow the "apostate" Iraqi regime led by Sunni Muslims. Simultaneously, Saddam Hussein became chairman of Iraq's Revolutionary Command Council and forced President Bakr of Iraq to step down. Hussein then took control of the government and immediately set out to quell the Shiite unrest. In November 1979, the Carter administration encouraged Hussein to attack Iran, who at that time was still holding Americans hostage. Confident that he had full U.S. support, Saddam Hussein ordered an Iraqi invasion of Iran, a country three times as large and four times more populous than Iraq, on September 22, 1980. Supported with U.S. aid, Hussein expected his army to overthrow the regime in Tehran within a month, but instead the war would rage in a bloody stalemate for eight years (Hiro, 2002, 28-29).

The ascension of Ronald Reagan to the Presidency in 1981 essentially continued the American policy of support for Iraq in the ongoing war. After four years of stalemate, in February 1985, the war began to tilt toward Iran when the Iranians captured Iraq's oil rich Manjoon Islands in Iraq's southern marshes. Iraq responded to the loss of the Manjoon Islands with attacks on Iranian oil tankers using French-made Exocet cruise missiles. Iran then retaliated against the missile attacks on its tankers with attacks on oil tankers of American allies, Kuwait and Saudi Arabia, who had been financing Iraq and providing intelligence (Miller and Mylroie, 1990, 128-129).

In 1986, Saudi Arabia and Kuwait responded to the attacks on their tankers by flooding the market with excess oil in an attempt to drive down oil prices and thus bankrupt the Iranians and end the war. As a result, oil prices dropped below $10 per barrel. In July 1986, the Reagan administration attempted to tilt the war back in favor of Iraq by secretly sending Air Force officers to work with the Iraqi Air Force in selection of targets, strategy, and training. The U.S. also sent 60 ships to the gulf to protect Saudi and Kuwaiti oil tankers. The oil tankers were reflagged with American flags, thus making attacks on the tankers attacks on the United States, and thus allowing the U.S. to retaliate against Iran militarily (Jones, 1996, 703).

Direct U.S. military action against the Iranians came in October 1987, when the U.S. navy, claiming that Iran had fired on a US patrol helicopter, sank three Iranian patrol boats. An Iranian missile hit an US-flagged Kuwaiti supertanker the next day, and the U.S. retaliated by ordering American warships to destroy two Iranian offshore oil platforms (Hiro, 2002, 29). Although it was undeclared, the U.S. was essentially conducting joint military operations with Iraq against Iran.

In 1988, Iraq began firing SCUD missiles on Tehran, a tactic that would be labeled by the Bush administration as "terrorist tactics" just three years later. In April, Iraq recaptured the Fao Peninsula using chemical weapons while US warships blew up two Iranian oilrigs, destroyed one Iranian frigate, damaged another, and sank an Iranian missile boat. Iraq recaptured the Manjoon Islands the next month, again using chemical weapons. Before the war was over, Iraq fired 110,000 chemical munitions. In one case at the town of Halabja in March 1988, Saddam Hussein ordered the gassing of up to 5,000 of his own civilians in an attempt to kill the Iranian army that had occupied the town. The U.S. and Britain continued to back Iraq against Iran in spite of the use of chemical weapons on a massive scale (Hiro, 2002, 28-34).

The end of the Iran-Iraq war would come shortly after the American action of July 3, 1988, when a US navy cruiser accidentally shot down an Iranian Airliner carrying 290 Iranian civilians over the Persian Gulf. Though the incident was an "accident" and an error in judgment by U.S. naval personnel (who mistook the jetliner for incoming Iranian military aircraft on their radar screens), Iran believed that full-scale war with the U.S. was imminent and subsequently accepted UN Resolution 598 that called for a cease-fire the same week (Hiro, 2002, 29-32).

Up to 250,000 Iraqis and 500,000 Iranians died in the war (the figures are in question due to inadequate "accounting" by the governments involved), and Iraq owed $98 billion to the US, USSR, Japan, Saudi Arabia, and Kuwait. In addition to the loans, from 1985-1990, Iraq received $500 million in direct U.S. aid—most of it technological equipment for their military. Saddam Hussein of Iraq had firm reasons to believe that the U.S. was a "friend" in the gulf that he could count on in the future (Hiro, 2002, 29-32).

Reagan Doctrine

In his December, 1985, State of the Union Address, Reagan announced what became known as the "Reagan Doctrine," proclaiming his administration's support for anti-Communist "freedom fighters" as part of American "self-defense." The announcement was essentially a reversal of the policies of Nixon and Carter, where foreign countries would be responsible for their own defense against communism. Instead, the Reagan Doctrine represented a return to the Cold War Truman and Eisenhower Doctrines that had been largely discredited since they had led to the disastrous war in Vietnam. Reagan's critics argued that the U.S. had been extracted from Vietnam for barely over a decade, but evidently the "lessons" of Vietnam already had been forgotten. In furtherance of the Reagan Doctrine, Reagan armed the Contra rebels against the communist government of the Sandinistas in Nicaragua at a cost of $19 million. Reagan also mined the harbors of Nicaragua, an act of War under international law. In a separate application of the Reagan Doctrine in Central America, Reagan armed the government of the unpopular right-wing dictator, Jose Napoleon Duarte, against leftist rebels in El Salvador. Aid to El Salvador was $6 million under Carter, and $82 million in Reagan's first budget. Critics charged that American aid to Duarte's government was partially to blame escalation of the Salvadoran conflict and for the fact that 53,000 El Salvadorans were killed in the Civil War (Jones, 1996, 695).

Iran-Contra Scandal

On Election Day 1986, the Iran-Contra scandal, the most serious threat to the Reagan Presidency, became known to the American public. Reagan had termed the Contra rebels in Nicaragua as "freedom fighters" without seriously investigating what kind of group they were. After all, since they were opposed to the communist Sandinista government of Nicaragaua, that was all the President needed to know, since in Reagan's view, any group that was anti-communist was worthy of support. In 1984, however, Congress cut off Contra Aid because the Sandinista government had been elected democratically in 1984, and many felt that it was questionable whether or not the Contras, regardless of their anti-communism, were "good guys" (Jones, 201, 465-467).

Between 1984 and 1986, however, Reagan's National Security Council kept aid to the Contras flowing secretly against the Congressional ban, and in doing so violated a whole host of federal laws, as well as Reagan's Oath of Office where he pledged to "faithfully execute the laws of Congress," rather than circumvent them. The covert Contra Aid was secretly funded through a scheme developed by Lt. Colonel Oliver North, who ran the operation out of the White House basement. According to the Congressional Report that was eventually compiled about the operation, North was running his operation openly within the Reagan administration and it would have been difficult for Reagan and his senior aides not to have known what was going on. North developed a scheme whereby by profits from arms sales to Iran were diverted to the Contra rebels in Nicaragua.

The arms sales to Iran violated a Congressional Embargo on Iran, who not only had held Americans hostage for 444 days during the Carter administration, but was heavily engaged in an effort to spread Shiite Islamic revolution throughout the globe and was involved in the 1983 truck bombing of the U.S. marine compound in Lebanon. Partially as a result of this attempt to spread Iranian-style revolution, during the entire Reagan era, Iran was also embroiled in a war with Saddam Hussein's Iraq (previously discussed), who in turn was receiving U.S. aid for the Iraqi war effort against Iran. As a result, the Reagan administration was obviously undermining its own policy of support for Iraq by selling arms to Iran. In return for the Arms from the United States, the Iranians released American hostages held in Iran, though Reagan had previously stated that the U.S. would not make deals with terrorists (*Harper's*, February 1988, 46-56).

The Iran-Contra operation also made use of planes owned by South American drug lords, who flew cocaine into the U.S. with their planes under CIA protection, and flew arms to the Contras for the American government. South American cocaine trafficker George Morales admitted that he donated $3 million in cash and some aircraft, as well as his top pilots, at the request of the CIA. Also involved in aiding the arms-to-the-Contras scheme with planes was Panamanian President Manuel Noriega, who would later be indicted in Florida for drug trafficking during the same arms-to-Contras covert operation (*Harper's*, February 1988, 46-56).

Mercenaries to help the Contra operation were recruited in the United States, trained in Central America, and then sent to the Contra camps to fight. Americans were involved in running two of the training camps, using Miami Cubans as Contras, thus also violating the Neutrality Act (*Harper's* February 1988, 50-51). All told, the list of laws broken and the scope of the illegal activity by the Reagan administration during the Iran-Contra scandal may have far exceeded the illegal activities of the Nixon administration that led to the resignation of the American President.

Since Congress would not fund the Contra operation, the Reagan administration also solicited private funds to support the Contra rebels, and were successful in gaining support from American right-wing groups and individuals. The largest single private donor among these was Pat Robertson's Christian Broadcast Network (CBN), that contributed between three and seven million dollars in Contra aid (Martin, 1996, 284).

Between November 21 and 25, 1987, Attorney General Ed Meese launched an inquiry into the Iran-Contra scandal at the request of the President. Meese then informed senior White House officials a day in advance of the impending document review, and immediately thereafter, Oliver North and his subordinates shredded most of the documents connected to the Iran-Contra affair. As a consequence of the head start given to those involved by the Attorney General, the full scope of the scandal could never be completely known. North's actions (and Meese's) were essentially acts of Obstruction of Justice, one of the same charges that led to Richard Nixon's resignation in the previous decade (*Harper's,* February 1988, 56).

Reagan first admitted on November 13, 1987, that he had ordered the covert Iran-Contra operation under John Poindexter and LT. Colonel Oliver North, though he denied that the U.S. had sold arms to Iran in exchange for hostages. Furthermore, on May 15, 1988, Reagan stated that the arms-to-the-Contras covert scheme was "my idea to begin with" (*Harper's,* February, 1988, 48). Reagan later changed his story, however, and said that he couldn't remember whether he had known about the operation or not. This was despite the possession by Congress of taped phone conversations of Reagan asking Poindexter if the arms did in fact get to the Contras (*Harper's,* 1988, 48).

Upon reading the Congressional Report on the Iran-Contra scandal, CBS and National Public Radio correspondent Daniel Schorr stated,

> "What really emerges from this report is a picture of a President who doesn't want to know all the details of the things that he has ordered. He sits there and dreams. He dreams about freedom fighters. He dreams that in Nicaragua— and in Angola and in Afghanistan—there are these people, anti-communist freedom fighters. Boy, you could make a really great movie about these guerillas who selflessly fight for freedom against the Soviet horror. And he says, 'I think Congress is wrong to say we can't arm them. I want them kept alive'" (Quoted in *Harper's,* 1988, 49).

The Congressional Committee that was constructed to investigate the Iran-Contra scandal, however, included 26 persons, 17 of whom had favored Contra aid and were considered loyal to the President. As a consequence, the Committee essentially ignored the damning evidence against Reagan and chose to do nothing. By that time, Reagan was near the end of his term anyway, so the idea of impeachment and removal was in a sense pointless (*Harper's* 1988, 56). Oliver North and John Poindexter were later pardoned for their parts in the scandal by President George H.W. Bush, and a greater Constitutional breach than Watergate was essentially swept under the rug. In subsequent decades, the wrongdoing in the scandal would essentially be ignored or forgotten by America's conservatives, Oliver North would gain status as a patriotic American "hero" in conservative circles, and Ronald

Reagan's status would grow to near deification, and the President that had tripled the National debt, traded arms for hostages, and circumvented Congressional arms embargoes against both Iran and the Contras, became a symbol of all that is right with conservatism.

Chapter Fourteen

Conservatism from Bush to Bush

George H.W. Bush

With Ronald Reagan unable to run again in 1988 due to term limits, Vice President George H.W. Bush quickly emerged as the best candidate to continue the Reagan legacy, although he first had to withstand primary election challenges from Senator Bob Dole of Kansas and televangelist Pat Robertson. Bush was visibly irritated at his Republican challengers and there was a general sense in the Bush camp that it was simply "his turn," since he had waited patiently for eight years as a loyal VP to Reagan during Reagan's Presidency. Nevertheless, the Bush camp would be forced to prove their mettle against more formidable Republican opponents than they had hoped. To make matters worse, Bush was not generally viewed as a dynamic personality type, and was even referenced frequently in the media as a "wimp." For most Republicans, however, Bush was essentially viewed as "Reagan without the charm," and Bush was expected to continue the low tax, strong defense policies that Reagan had earlier initiated (Parmet, 1997, 232).

Election of 1988

The Bush campaign got off to a rocky start in the Iowa caucuses where they not only lost to Bob Dole, but also suffered a surprising defeat to Pat Robertson, who had waged an effective Iowa grass-roots campaign. Robertson also came in 1st or second in Hawaii, Nevada, Alaska, Minnesota, and South Dakota, all small population states. Bush, however, had better organization and superior financial backing and won a convincing victory in New Hampshire, and then won every primary on Super Tuesday, thus sealing his nomination (Martin, 1996, 289-290).

Bush needed to consolidate the religious right into his camp, however, a task made more difficult by his campaign's open disdain for Robertson. George Bush's brother Neil further damaged Bush's effort in this regard by referring to Robertson's supporters as "cockroaches issuing out from underneath the baseboard of the South" (Quoted in Martin, 1996, 290).

Compounding Bush's problems with the Christian right, Bush had not taken
a strong stand on abortion; consequently, some of his delegates from Texas,
Bush's home state, were prevented from attending the National Republican
Convention by the religious right wing of the Texas Republican Party that
effectively took over the Texas State Republican convention in 1988
(Maxwell and Crain, 2002, 200).

The Democrats nominated Massachusetts Governor Michael Dukakis, a
political moderate and son of Greek immigrants, who personified the "self-
made man" story that sells so well to the American electorate. Dukakis was a
fresh face with an endearing personality and opinion polls in the spring of
1988 showed Dukakis with a double digit lead over Bush (Gould, 2003,
442). Bush then contributed to his own difficulties that summer by choosing
the semantically error-prone young Senator, Dan Quayle of Indiana, as his
running mate, thus giving the Democrats an easy target for their political
potshots. Bob Dole had run second in the primaries to Bush, but Bush and
Dole did not personally like each other, causing Bush to look elsewhere for
his running mate. Quayle possessed the youth and good looks that Bush
lacked, and it was hoped that Quayle would help Bush with women voters
(Parmet, 1997, 309).

The Quayle selection, however, quickly turned against George Bush.
Democrats criticized Quayle for ducking out of the Vietnam War by serving
in the Indiana National Guard. Quayle further hurt Bush's campaign with
repeated verbal gaffes that essentially became known as "Qualyespeak."
Quayle quickly proved himself to be a less than adept public speaker,
appearing nervous (even frightened) in front of television cameras, often
fumbling his way through prepared speeches, and his extemporaneous
comments frequently defied comprehension. Quayle and his gaffes soon
became the butt of numerous jokes from late-night comedians, and Quayle
was characterized as "stupid" by the public and the media, a label that would
prove impossible for the Republicans to remove once it had been affixed
(Parmet, 1997, 310-311).

Most of Quayle's gaffe's were simply twisted syntax and the inevitable
result of the volume of speech that is required from a Vice Presidential
candidate. One could also argue that Quayle's gaffes were no more "twisted"
than many of the off-the-cuff quotes from Reagan and Bush, but for Quayle,
unlike Reagan, they made headlines and stuck like glue. For example,
Quayle once exclaimed that "It isn't pollution that's harming the
environment. It's the impurities in the air and water that are doing it." Quayle
also stated in a manner most humorous to Democrats that "I am not part of
the problem. I am a Republican." Finally, Quayle defended himself against
the critics of his gaffes by stating that "I stand by all the misstatements that
I've made" (Quoted in *Los Angeles Times*, May 21, 1989).

In spite of his mistake with the selection of Quayle, Bush would gain momentum from the Republican National Convention when he delivered a speech where he effectively wrapped himself in conservative social values and patriotism, two cornerstones of the religious right, and also reinforced his commitment to low taxes, thus catering also to the "country club" Republicans. Bush assailed Dukakis for vetoing a bill requiring school children to recite the Pledge of Allegiance, and ended his speech by reciting the pledge himself. Bush also emphasized the need for private, rather than governmental, efforts to help the less fortunate, and described American volunteerism as "a thousand points of light." Finally, Bush proclaimed his dedication to continued low taxation (in spite of the mounting national debt), with the statement, "read my lips, no new taxes" (Quoted in Parmet, 1997, 342).

Bush's campaign against Dukakis after the Convention was decidedly negative; so negative, in fact, that it was considered by some to be the most negative campaign of the Twentieth Century (Brinkley, 2003, 912). Through his negative propaganda, Bush was successfully able to tie Dukakis to most of the libertine social and cultural stances that conservatives had come to identify with "liberals." Given that Republicans expected their candidate to continue the Reagan legacy, Bush offered no real changes for the future, instead arguing that "We don't need radical new directions" (Quoted in Roark et al., 2005, 1143).

Without any new and exciting program to promote, Bush instead concentrated on attacking Michael Dukakis' record as governor of Massachusetts. In particular, the Republicans made mileage from their criticism of a furlough program for convicted felons in Massachusetts' State prison system. The Massachusetts furlough program that the Republicans so disparaged was actually initiated by Dukakis' Republican predecessor and simply inherited and continued by Dukakis, a fact that the Republicans neglected to mention. Furthermore, Ronald Reagan had favored a similar policy as governor of California in the 1960s'; nevertheless, the Republicans found and used the case of William Horton, an African-American who had been serving a life sentence in Massachusetts for murder, but was released on a weekend furlough, only to assault a couple in Maryland and rape the woman in the process. The Republicans referred to William Horton as "Willie Horton," and pro-Bush groups, not directly affiliated with the Republican Party or the candidate, created commercials featuring Horton's unflattering mug shot that explained how Dukakis favored the furlough program that allowed convicted murderers to be released, only to commit crimes again. Dukakis then did the Republicans a favor with an ill-conceived publicity stunt where he donned a military helmet and rode around in a tank. Dukakis' tank episode backfired since he essentially looked to many like a

Saturday Night Live parody of a military leader in a comedy sketch, and Dukakis dropped in the polls (Parmet, 1997, 336-337).

The Willie Horton affair galvanized racially-motivated Southern voters and retribution-oriented conservatives behind Bush. Evangelicals, who had been reluctant supporters of Bush just months earlier, became the largest single group of Bush voters, with eighty percent of evangelicals voting for Bush (Hertzke, 1993, 160-161). In general, however, the campaign had been essentially lackluster and most Americans appeared to be unexcited about either Bush or Dukakis. Reflecting this apathy, on Election Day, Bush won 54% of the popular vote, but half of the eligible voters stayed home, and Democrats still controlled both Houses of Congress (Roark et al., 2005, 1143).

The Bush Presidency

Early in George H.W. Bush's Presidency, the new Republican Executive quickly revealed that he was not genuinely the flag bearer for the Reagan legacy. Bush quickly embarked on a more activist approach to governing and implemented a much more hands-on management approach than Reagan. For example, billing himself as the "Environmental President," Bush signed the Clean Air Act of 1990, perhaps the strongest, most comprehensive environmental law in history. The Act required power plants to cut sulfur dioxide emissions by more than 50% by the year 2000, and oil companies were required to develop cleaner-burning gasoline (Roark, 2005, 1143). Clearly, the Clean Air Act was hardly consistent with the deregulatory push of the Reagan administration and was instead the same type of federal government regulation of industry that conservatives had been fighting against for decades. Bush also signed the 1991 Americans with Disabilities Act (ADA), which required that public accommodations be made accessible to the handicapped, and prohibited discrimination against the handicapped in employment (Roark, 2005, 1143).

ADA carried with it a further anathema to conservatives in that it constituted a massive unfunded mandate to the States that forced States and local governments to spend billions in order to ensure that public accommodations were handicapped-accessible. The measure was therefore not only a violation of conservative laissez-faire ideology and a reversal of Reagan's "deregulation," but it also eroded State sovereignty by removing State discretion concerning the handicapped, and thus violated the traditional conservative preference for the preservation of States' rights.

Although Bush had well-played the part of the Vice Presidential loyalist during Reagan's tenure in office, Bush demonstrated his private disdain for his Presidential predecessor when he quietly instituted a purge of Reagan loyalists from the federal executive branch. In the words of one close friend of Ronald Reagan, there was a "systematic purge...of anyone with any association with the Reagan-Nixon-Goldwater wing of the Party" (Parmet, 1997, 361).

Bush did not, however, favor a complete abandonment of the conservative "less government" mantra, and he used the veto 36 times during his tenure in office to block Congressional bills that would have lifted abortion restrictions, extended unemployment benefits, raised taxes, mandated family and medical leave for workers, and reformed campaign financing. The veto of such measures was not only consistent with Reaganism, but they were also perhaps to be expected, given "divided government" with Democratic control of Congress and Republican control of the Presidency (Parmet, 1997, 363).

In spite of these commitments to conservatism, Bush would essentially lose the confidence of ideological conservatives in the fall of 1990 when he reneged on his 1988 Convention pledge against raising taxes. Both Bush and the Democrats in Congress (as well as many Republicans) were concerned with the soaring deficits they had inherited from the Regan administration. Reagan had essentially proven that significant spending cuts were politically impossible; consequently, the only method left for dealing with the deficit was a tax increase. In October 1990, Bush and the Democrats in Congress agreed to a compromise plan that raised the highest marginal tax rate. The tax increase was anathema to conservative Republicans, ¾ of whom voted against the measure, and final proof to many Republican voters that Bush was not really a true conservative in the mold of Ronald Reagan (Greene, 2000, 87-88).

Bush and the Religious Right

Economic conservatives, however, were not the only ones in the conservative camp that disapproved of Bush's policies. Social conservatives quickly became disenchanted with Bush since their suggestions for appointees were essentially ignored, and neither Bush nor his advisers appeared to have any enthusiasm for the religious right's agenda. Although Bush, unlike Reagan, generally attended church every Sunday, he did not attend an evangelical church in the Southern mold, and Bush appeared uncomfortable with the evangelical religious right. In the words of Bush aide Douglas Wead,

"There was almost never a time when I took one of these evangelical issues to somebody on the staff when there was a connect. There was never a connect. They didn't understand it" (Quoted in Martin, 1996, 313).

Given these prevailing attitudes and the general disdain from the Bush administration for the religious right's agenda, Bush quickly became viewed with suspicion by many evangelicals. To make matters worse for Bush, he signed a hate crimes bill in April, 1990 that mandated stiff penalties for crimes committed against people primarily because they are members of a specific group. Gay rights groups supported the bill and Bush invited some representatives of the gay rights groups to a signing ceremony at the White House. Immediately, the Bush White House was deluged with criticism from the religious right for contributing to America's moral decay by supporting gay rights. In July of the same year, Bush committed another grievous sin against the religious right when he entertained Christie Hefner, the daughter of *Playboy* publisher Hugh Hefner, as part of a group of major magazine executives at the White House. Finally, less than two weeks later at a ceremony for the signing of ADA, Bush committed another "gay transgression" when it was revealed that members of a well-known gay rights group were in attendance at the ADA event. Bush's entertaining of gays at the White House was condemned by Richard Land, executive director of the Southern Baptist Convention's Christian Life Commission, and Robert Dugan, director of the National Association of Evangelicals (*Washington Times*, August 2, 1990).

Christian Coalition

Disenchantment with the Bush administration was a contributing factor in causing former Presidential candidate Pat Robertson and Ralph Reed, a young, ambitious, leader of a religious conservative organization known as Students for America, to join forces to form a new evangelical political organization known as the Christian Coalition. The Christian Coalition's purpose was to create a grass-roots political organization that could galvanize religious conservatives in support of Republican candidates. The organization quickly made use of the tried and true conservative organizational tactic of outraging its constituency with sensational accounts of isolated offenses against religion, morality, and patriotism, committed by liberals, homosexuals, or the government. The Christian Coalition's first mailing utilized this ploy by attacking the National Endowment for the Arts for subsidizing an art exhibit of Andres Serrano, who had urinated in a glass jar in which he subsequently submerged a crucifix and then photographed his "work." The artwork itself was aptly labeled as "Piss Christ," a name itself that was bound to inflame religious conservatives regardless of the symbolism of a plastic crucifix floating in human urine. The Christian

Coalition's mailing then asked persons to join their efforts against the use of federal tax money to fund such exhibits (Martin, 1996, 303).

The initial Christian Coalition mailer quickly brought in a flood of funding to the organization. The Christian Coalition then used the funding to purchase full page ads in the *New York Times*, *Washington Post*, and *USA Today*, calling on Congress to stop the use of federal funding to underwrite pornography, obscenity, or attacks on religion. Conservative Republicans in Congress contributed to the Christian Coalition's success by debating the controversy on the floor of Congress (Martin, 1996, 303).

With this success providing a springboard, Ralph Reed and the Christian Coalition then followed up their advertisements and mailings with a series of "Leadership Schools" where Reed would show a video presentation entitled "America at the Crossroads," in which Pat Robertson spoke of the need for Christians to become politically involved in order to "stop the nation's slide into hell." The video was circulated in Protestant fundamentalist churches throughout the U.S. (Martin, 1996, 305).

In 1992, with the election approaching, the Christian Coalition expanded its operation to a focus on the distribution of "voter guides" that would instruct potential voters as to which candidate was the moral candidate (conspicuously always Republican), and which was the immoral candidate (conspicuously always a Democrat). Eventually, the Christian Coalition would lose its tax-exempt status over the voter guide distribution since the guides were clearly partisan in character, although the Christian Coalition maintained that they were merely "informative" (Cantor, 1994, 115). Nevertheless, the Christian Coalition would remain important throughout the decade and played a major role in the Republican takeover of the House of Representatives in 1994.

Operation Rescue and Abortion

A more radical Christian group than the Christian Coalition emerged during the Bush Presidency known as Operation Rescue under its leader Randall Terry. The purpose of Operation Rescue was to end abortions, and to accomplish that end, virtually all means considered were fair game, whether conventional or unconventional, legal or illegal. Terry was influenced by Francis Schaeffer's book, *A Christian Manifesto*, where Schaeffer argues that obedience to God's law takes precedent over human laws. As a consequence, Terry urged his followers to violate laws when necessary in their efforts to prevent abortions. Consequently, Operation Rescue's methods included blocking the driveways, sidewalks, and doors of abortion clinics, and physically preventing people from entering the clinics when necessary. Terry's antics even included personally accosting President Bush over the abortion issue on the golf course at Kennebunkport, Maine, and attempting to hand Democratic candidate Bill Clinton a human fetus during the Democratic National Convention in New York (Martin, 1996, 322-325).

Operation Rescue's distribution materials were equally bold and forceful. In one pamphlet, Terry declared that "to vote for Bill Clinton is to sin against God." Terry's home Church in Binghamton, NY went a step further and took out a full page ad in *USA Today* stating that "the Bible warns us to not follow another man in his sin, nor help him promote sin—lest God chasten us," thus inferring that God would punish America if Clinton were reelected. For these actions, Terry's group had their tax-exempt status revoked by the IRS as a partisan, rather than purely information-oriented, organization (Cantor, 1994, 116).

Religious Right and the Election of 1992

The religious right essentially took over the Republican National Convention in 1992 and forced the inclusion of an anti-abortion plank, as well as measures favoring prayer in school, and a parochial school voucher system. The platform also reflected the religious right's influence in the things that they opposed, stating Republicans' opposition to gay marriage, sex education, and the use of public funding for obscene or anti-Christian art. Pat Buchanan, who refused to let any Party officials review his speech beforehand, contributed to the social conservative cause by giving a culture war speech at the Convention, arguing that,

> "There is a religious war going on in this country. It is a cultural war as critical to the kind of nation we shall be as the Cold War itself. This war is for the soul of America. And in that struggle for the soul of America, Clinton and Clinton are on the other side, and George Bush is on our side" (Quoted in Martin, 1996, 325).

The Christian Coalition also helped the Republicans by engaging in voter registration drives in the Churches, with the final result that evangelicals turned out in the polls in the largest numbers that they ever had in a Presidential election. Furthermore, in spite of the religious right's previous disappointment with Bush, Bush would win the evangelical vote by more than a 2-1 margin. Although Bush would lose the election to the more dynamic and camera-friendly Democrat, Bill Clinton, all was not completely gloomy for the Christian Coalition wing of the Republican Party. An estimated 500 candidates supported by the Christian Coalition won State and local elections, mostly in State legislatures and school boards (Martin, 1996, 328).

Clarence Thomas Appointment

Bush continued the Reagan legacy of appointing very conservative individuals to the federal judiciary, and his first appointee to the Supreme Court, David Souter, won easy confirmation in the Senate, although the confirmation was at least partly due to the fact that Souter refused to reveal his positions on controversial issues such as abortion. Without any evidence of where Souter stood on the most divisive issues, the Democrats had no major grounds for objection and voted for confirmation.

In 1991, however, Justice Thurgood Marshall, the only African American on the Supreme Court, retired, thus placing pressure on Bush to appoint another African American judge to his position. This, of course, presented Bush with a problem since conservative African American judges were in exceedingly short supply. After reviewing a very short list of possibilities, Bush nominated Clarence Thomas, a conservative African American appellate court judge who had opposed affirmative action as the head of the Equal Employment Opportunity commission under Ronald Reagan. Unfortunately, Thomas had only been on the bench at the time for 18 months, and therefore could hardly be considered the most qualified judge of African American ethnicity, or any other ethnicity for that matter. To make matters worse for Bush, the National Association for the Advancement of Colored People (NAACP), the leading organization for the championing of African-American causes, opposed Thomas' confirmation. Subsequently, Anita Hill, a law professor at the University of Oklahoma and a former EEOC employee under Clarence Thomas, came forward to accuse Thomas of sexual harassment while she worked at the EEOC. Specifically, Hill alleged that Thomas asked her to view pornographic movies with him. The Senate Judiciary Committee investigated the hearings, but dismissed Hill's charges after three days of nationally televised hearings in which other women who came forward with similar allegations were not allowed to testify (Phelps, 1992, 132).

Bush and Foreign Policy

Panama

Manuel Noriega, head of the Panamanian Military in 1983, became the head of State in Panama in 1984 with American CIA help. Noriega had also cooperated with the CIA against the Sandinistas in Nicaragua in the 1980s and was confident that the U.S. Government was a friend who supported his regime, especially since Bush had been so heavily involved in the Iran-Contra affair. In 1988, however, Noriega was indicted by a Grand Jury in

Miami and Tampa, Florida, for drug trafficking, gun running, and money laundering, some of it associated with his role in the Iran-Contra operation. Noriega's troubles were compounded in November, 1989, when he lost the Panamanian election and then followed the defeat at the polls with a refusal to vacate office. Noriega then had his electoral opponents severely beaten ,and their battered and bloody images were shown on international television. Given this gross violation of the democratic process and human rights, coupled with his status as a wanted fugitive in Florida, the Bush administration denounced the Noriega government and asked him to step down (Jones, 1996, 722-723).

December 15, 1989, Panama's National Assembly named Noriega head of Government and proclaimed that Panama was in a "State of War" with the U.S. The next day, four off-duty US servicemen were beaten by Panamanian police and one was shot and killed. One of the officer's wives was also roughed up by the Panamanian police. That officer and his wife turned out to be personal friends of President George H.W. Bush, who was incensed that the Panamanians had put their hands all over his friend's wife. According to Colin Powell, the attack was very personal to the President, and he believed that retribution against Noriega would be a "just cause" (Powell and Perisco, 1995, 191).

Bush responded with "Operation Just Cause," an American invasion of Panama on December 20, 1989. 12,000 troops landed and 12,000 U.S. troops already present in Panama were also involved in the invasion. Noriega attempted to flee from the invading force and hide in the Vatican Embassy, but surrendered to the U.S. on December 31. The invasion was considered a smashing success, but 23 U.S. Soldiers were killed, as were 4,000 Panamanians, many of whom were civilians. Noriega was taken to Miami where he was imprisoned and convicted on drug charges stemming from his 1989 indictment (Jones, 1996, 722-723).

End of the Cold War/Fall of USSR

In 1989, the Communist regimes that had dominated political life in Eastern Europe since 1945 all collapsed after Gorbachev renounced the right of any nation to interfere with the sovereignty of another in July, 1989, thus essentially letting the Eastern European nations know that if they overthrew their Soviet-imposed communist governments, Gorbachev would not intervene. The Soviet Union was in dire financial straits from seven decades of their inefficient command economy, combined with the excessive Cold War military spending that had essentially bankrupted the country. Consequently, the Soviets no longer had the energy and resources to militarily control Eastern Europe. Without the Soviet tanks to prop up the illegitimate communist governments, the entire Soviet system in Eastern Europe collapsed like a house of cards (Hauss, 1997, 240-243).

In Poland, Solidarity Union forced negotiations with the communists through strikes and demonstrations. The Communists granted free elections in which some seats were reserved for Communists. When the elections were held, Solidarity won an overwhelming majority. Further negotiations between Solidarity and the Communists led to the Communists peacefully giving up power in August, 1989. The other governments of Eastern Europe would quickly follow in the Polish footsteps in a series of bloodless revolutions (although the Romanian Revolution was not "bloodless" as the Romanian rebels assassinated Communist leader Nikolai Ceaucescu). Communists allowed the destruction of the Berlin Wall, one of the Cold War's most vivid symbols, on November 9, 1989, and free elections were held in East Germany in the spring of 1990, with the Democratic opposition winning easily (Hauss, 1997, 241-242).

In the USSR in 1990, new political organizations were forming everywhere after Communist Party General Secretary Mikhail Gorbachev had called for glasnost (openness) and perestroika (restructuring). Nationalist groups emerged in all 14 Republics and street violence erupted all over the USSR. In the summer of 1990, Boris Yeltsin led radical reformers in a split with the Communist Party. Gorbachev reacted by increasingly turning to the communist hard-liners for support. In April, 1991, Lithuania, Estonia, and Latvia all declared independence, and Gorbachev did not put down the revolts militarily. Realizing that the breakup of the USSR was imminent, Soviet military leaders staged a coup against Gorbachev in August of 1991 and placed Gorbachev under arrest. Gorbachev and his wife were held hostage for four days until Boris Yeltsin led the people in the streets to overthrow the coup and free Gorbachev. The main arms of the Soviet Military turned from their military leaders and supported Yeltsin, and communism in Russia was essentially finished (Hauss, 1997, 242-243).

On August 22, Gorbachev returned to power in Moscow, but by December 31, 1991, all 14 of the Soviet Republics had declared their independence. In December, the new leaders of each republic met and agreed to form a new Commonwealth of Independent States. Gorbachev then resigned as the President of the USSR, which ceased to exist on December 31, 1991 (Hauss, 1997, 242-243).

As these monumental events of the Twentieth Century occurred across the waters, George Bush's approach was to adopt what he called a "status quo plus" approach to these developments. Bush used as his road map Secretary of Defense Dick Cheney's "Forward Defense Policy," where the now- defunct Soviet Union was still viewed as a threat that should be contained. Furthermore, Cheney's Forward Defense Policy called for the continuation of a forward American military presence throughout the globe. Bush himself essentially accepted the Cheney view that the Soviet Union should still be viewed as a threat. Instead of immediately assisting the Eastern Europeans in their transition to capitalist democracies, Bush was cautious and hesitant to alter the American approach to Eastern Europe. Reflecting the paranoia that often characterizes conservative ideologues, Bush at first even opposed the reunification of Germany, fearing that a reunited Germany posed another "threat." Bush then only changed his position on German reunification after it became clear that reunification was inevitable. It also became clear very quickly that the old Soviet Union and communist threat were clearly gone, but Cheney's "Forward Defense Policy" premised on containing the Soviet Union would remain in place throughout the Bush Presidency (Jones, 1996, 730).

Tiananmen Square

Coterminous with the communist collapse in Eastern Europe, in May 1989, thousands of Chinese students held pro-democracy demonstrations in Tiananmen Square in Beijing. The visual images of the unarmed students standing up to the communist government roused feelings of patriotism and sympathy in the United States, but Chinese leader Deng Xiao Peng put down the demonstrations with the Chinese military on June 3 in brutal fashion. Bush responded with an embargo on military goods to China and announced that the U.S. would not consider reestablishment of good relations with China until the leadership acknowledged the "validity of the pro-democracy movement." On June 20, Bush then halted all contact with the Chinese government (Jones, 1996, 720-721).

Bush's "get tough with China" stance, however, turned out to be nothing more than show and pandering to the anti-communist American right wing. One month later, Bush secretly directed National Security Adviser Brent Scowcroft to restore relations. Before the end of the year, Bush lifted the ban on weapons sales to China and approved loans to businesses dealing with China. In December, NSA Brent Scowcroft officially visited Beijing, thus restoring relations, and China retained its Most Favored Nation Trade status (Jones, 1996, 721).

Persian Gulf War

In the aftermath of the Iran-Iraq war, where Saudi Arabia and Kuwait had flooded the world market with oil, Kuwait continued to produce oil at a rate of 40% over OPEC quotas, and demanded payment of the $14 billion that Iraq owed to Kuwait. The continued production over the OPEC quotas angered Saddam Hussein of Iraq, who viewed the cheating on OPEC quotas as damaging to Iraq's economy and a hindrance to his ability to pay his international debts of $98 billion. Saddam Hussein was also unenthusiastic about repaying the loans to Kuwait because he believed that his war with Iran had saved Kuwait from imminent takeover by Iranian Shiite revolutionaries. While Kuwait had supported the Iraqi war against Iran with billions in oil money, the Iraqis had paid with their lives, and Saddam Hussein viewed Kuwaiti aid as insufficient (Miller and Mylroie, 1990, 9-10). Kuwait announced another increase in oil production one day after the Iran-Iraq truce, further angering Saddam Hussein. Saddam declared that he considered cheating on OPEC quotas to be "war on Iraq" and threatened retaliation. Saddam revealed that for every dollar that oil declined, Iraq would lose $1 billion annually. Saddam also, probably accurately, accused Kuwait of horizontal drilling near the Kuwait-Iraq border (Hiro, 2002, 33-34).

Iraq had also lost the use of the Shatt al-Arab waterway, its most important access waterway to the Persian Gulf, because of ships sunk in the waterway during the Iran-Iraq war. Kuwait possessed a fine port and coastline on the Gulf that Saddam Hussein coveted. Thus, Saddam Hussein had a number of motives for an invasion and takeover of Kuwait. A takeover of Kuwait would not only solve some of his debt problems, but also gain him better Gulf access and allow him to shut down Kuwaiti overproduction of oil, thus forcing an increase in oil prices (Hiro, 2002, 33-34).

On June 25, 1990, U.S. Ambassador to Iraq April Glaspie assured Saddam Hussein that the U.S. would not get involved in a dispute between two Arab neighbors. Glaspie testified before Congress,

"I told him we would defend our vital interests, support our friends in the Gulf, and defend their sovereignty and integrity. My main mistake was that I did not realize he was stupid" (Quoted in Hiro, 2002, 34).

With what he evidently believed was assurance from Glaspie, Saddam Hussein evidently believed that he could invade his neighbor and the United States would not intervene. August 2, 1990, Saddam Hussein's Iraqi army invaded Kuwait, and the conquest and occupation was completed in only eight hours. The UN Security Council reacted to the Iraqi aggression by condemning the invasion and voting 14-0 to demand withdrawal. The U.S. and the USSR issued a Joint Statement of Condemnation and the UN Security Council Unanimously imposed trade sanctions. Saddam countered with an attempt to gain sympathy from his other Arab neighbors by announcing a peace proposal that involved the withdrawal of Israel from the occupied territories while Saddam withdrew from Kuwait (Jones, 1996, 724).

George Bush denounced Saddam Hussein's peace proposal, arguing that there could be no "linkage" between the Iraqi invasion of Kuwait and the Israeli/Palestinian issue. Meanwhile, Amnesty International published a report portraying widespread arrests, torture, and summary executions in Kuwait (Jones, 1996, 724-725).

America's conservative Republican President, George Bush, viewed Saddam as "another Hitler" who invaded his neighbor intent on domination (Jones, 1996, 725). Bush demanded that Iraq withdraw from Kuwait, and when they did not do so, immediately began "Operation Desert Shield," building U.S. troop strength in Saudi Arabia to 580,000 in preparation for an invasion. Bush, a former Ambassador to the UN, was determined that the U.S. would have international support for any invasion, and on November 29, 1990, UN Resolution 678 gave Saddam Hussein until January 15, 1991 to withdraw or expect to be removed by force. January 12, the Use of Force Resolution in the American Congress passed the House 250-183 and 52-47 in the Senate, largely along partisan lines, but with numerous Democrats breaking ranks and voting with the Republicans in favor of removing Saddam Hussein's army from Kuwait by force (Jones, 1996, 725).

January 16, 1991, the U.S. began a 42-day bombing operation in Iraq and Kuwait. On January 18, Saddam fired 12 SCUD missiles at Israel, and he fired three more on January 22, in an attempt to goad Israel into the war and thereby divide the Arab coalition that had joined the United States against him. Israel denounced the attacks, but realizing that any Israeli action against Iraq could unite all Arab nations against them, stayed out of the war so as not to divide the coalition that Bush had forged (Hiro, 2002, 35).

In an attempt to stave off the imminent destruction of his army, at 12:00 Greenwich mean times (GMT) on February 23, Iraq announced the acceptance of a Soviet peace plan that called for immediate and unconditional withdrawal from Kuwait. In spite of his knowledge of this development, at 18:00 GMT, George Bush ordered General Norman Schwarzkopf to expel the Iraqis from Kuwait. The ground war to expel the Iraqi military from Kuwait followed on February 24th and took 100 hours. At 10:00 GMT February 24, the U.S. launched its ground war. At 21:30 GMT February 24, Saddam ordered a withdrawal from Kuwait. Retreating Iraqis then set 640 Kuwaiti oil wells ablaze in one of the worst environmental disasters in human history. The black petroleum cloud that developed over Kuwait was clearly visible from satellites in outer space. By noon on February 26, the Iraqi troops had withdrawn from Kuwait City and its suburbs, and a long convoy of Iraqi vehicles was on its way to Basra along a six lane Highway. As it approached Mitla ridge, 20 miles north of Kuwait City, the Iraqi convoy was hit in a massive attack by U.S. ground-attack aircraft. U.S. planes would attack the convoy for the next 40 hours until the truce of 08:00 local time on February 28 (Hiro, 2002, 38).

American deaths in what came to be known as the Persian Gulf War were 184, while Iraqi deaths were estimated at 100,000. Most died in the bombings (30,000 in the convoy alone), but some were buried in their bunkers by U.S. bulldozers. Americans generally approved of the attack on the retreating convoy, but many Arabs did not, and the event was reported in the Arab media as "the most terrible harassment of a retreating army from the air in the history of warfare" (Quoted in Hiro, 2002, 38).

Before the Iraqis fled Kuwait, Iraqi soldiers had looted virtually everything of value, even eating most of the animals at the Kuwaiti National Zoo, thus further justifying the war to the American people. Although many conservatives, such as future Undersecretary of State Paul Wolfowitz, argued that the U.S. military should go all the way into Iraq and remove Saddam Hussein from power, Bush would not do so because the UN Resolution did not call for ousting Hussein, and to do so would surely destroy the International coalition. Bush also recognized that an impotent Iraq would make Iran the most powerful military nation in the region without a chief rival; hence, leaving Saddam Hussein in power made sense in the Persian Gulf balance of power (Jones, 1996, 729). Ousting Hussein, as George W. Bush would discover in the next decade, would also mean a costly long-term occupation army with many more potential casualties and "another Vietnam" that the elder Bush was determined not to repeat. Finally, Bush had hoped that Saddam's own military officers would overthrow him, but after the war, Saddam carried out an internal purge on all of his political opposition within Iraq. A gruesome videotape was also circulated throughout Iraq and the Middle East that showed Saddam's executed military officers hanging on meat hooks, thus discouraging others from coup attempts (Hiro, 2002, 40).

Immediately after the war, Saddam Hussein also faced a Shiite uprising in the south that was aided by Iran. Iran sent not only supplies and weapons, but thousands of "volunteers" crossed the border into Iraq. On March 9, 1991 Saddam sent his Republican Guard into the South to put down the Shiite rebellion. The U.S. did not intervene because the Bush administration favored Saddam Hussein to Shiite revolutionaries. After all, the United States had aided Saddam Hussein in his war with Iran in the 1980s specifically to prevent a takeover by Shiite revolutionaries. 30,000 died in Saddam's crushing defeat of the Shiite rebellion, and 70,000 Shiites fled to Iran. The rebellion was over in a week. National Security adviser Brent Scowcroft told ABC News,

"I frankly wish the uprising hadn't happened. I envisioned a post-war government being a military government...It's the colonel with the brigade

patrolling his palace that's going to get Saddam if someone gets him"
(Quoted in Hiro, 2002, 42).

Similarly, Richard Haas, then director for Near East Affairs on the NSC
stated, "Our policy is to get rid of Saddam, not his regime" (Quoted in Hiro,
2002, 42). Obviously, Democracy (or the lack of it) in Iraq in 1992 was not
the highest American priority.

Simultaneous with the Iraqi Shiite rebellion in 1991, Kurdish nationalists
rebelled in northern Iraq as a 100,000-man Kurdish Auxiliary force in
Saddam's army changed sides and turned on Saddam. Turkey feared that an
independent Kurdistan in Iraq might lead Kurds in Turkey to also revolt and
demand that part of Turkey be united with a new Kurdistan. Consequently,
Turkey urged President Bush not to intervene in the Iraqi Kurdish rebellion.
Bush viewed the rebellion as an Iraqi Civil War with potential as another
Vietnam that should be avoided, so the U.S. again remained on the sidelines
while Saddam's army quickly put down the rebellion, with the result that an
estimated 1.5 million Kurds were forced to flee to Turkey (Hiro, 2002, 43).

In 1992, George Bush was voted out as President, and Iraq began
challenging the no-fly zones imposed by the U.S. The lame-duck President
Bush, however, continued his resolve to keep Saddam subdued, and in
December, the U.S. shot down an Iraqi MIG fighter. On January 10, 1993,
Iraq refused to allow UN inspectors to use airspace south of the 32nd parallel
as demanded by the U.S. The US responded on January 13 by bombing 5
Iraqi air bases, and on January 17, the U.S. hit an Iraqi factory with a cruise
missile. The next day, U.S. jets hit 75 Iraqi targets south of the 32nd parallel
of Southern Iraq. On January 21, Baghdad announced acceptance of UN
inspections so that the new American President could "study the no-fly
zone," and thus was the status of the American-Iraqi situation upon the
inauguration of Bill Clinton in January, 1993 (Hiro, 2002, 49).

Election of 1992

After the conclusion of the Persian Gulf War in 1991, President Bush's
approval rating soared to 88% and his prospects for reelection appeared very
good (Roark, 2005, 1149). The next year and a half, however, would see the
country slide into a prolonged economic recession and Bush's own
ideological preference for laissez-faire would make him appear inattentive
and uncaring about the plight of the average American. As unemployment
rose to over 7% in 1992, a large segment of the electorate began to call for
bold action against the recession, but Bush would not deliver. Instead, Bush
clung to his conservative, laissez-faire ideology and repeatedly stated in the
summer and fall of 1992 that the economy was improving and that others

should stop saying that it was not. In his contention that the economy was improving, Bush was actually correct, because when the third quarter economic numbers were released that fall, they did indeed indicate that the economy was on the upswing, but the economic recovery would be too little and too late to save the Bush Presidency (Goldman, 1994, 350-358).

As Bush's popularity slid in the winter of 1991, Bush fired the unpopular White House Chief of Staff John Sununu, thus separating himself from one of his top advisers. To further complicate things for Bush, former RNC chief Lee Atwater had died of a brain tumor earlier in the year. Without these advisers, the Bush campaign was unable to articulate a message for his campaign. In the words of one Bush friend, "If you asked him why he wanted to be reelected, he'd have to look at his note cards. That's the fundamental problem at the core" (Quoted in Goldman et al., 1994, 358).

Before he could take on the Democratic challenger, Bush first had to withstand a primary challenge from hard right candidate Pat Buchanan, who referred to the President as "King George" and denounced what he termed as the President's "moderate" policies that failed to put America first. Buchanan then embarrassed the President by gaining 37% of the vote in the New Hampshire Primary. As a consequence, Bush was forced to move somewhat to the right so as to prevent alienation of the Buchanan voters, but a rightward move would hinder Bush in his effort to pick up Democratic middle voters in the November General election (Goldman et al., 194, 340-349).

Bush also had to face a Third Party challenge from conservative Texas billionaire Ross Perot, who personally disliked Bush, but appealed to the public as an American success story and rags-to-riches self-made billionaire. By late spring, polls suggested that Ross Perot was attractive to middle voters, and was actually the electoral front-runner in terms of his popularity. That summer, however, Perot would effectively destroy his own candidacy by dropping out of the race due to what he viewed as unfair media coverage, only to re-enter again in the fall, but with much less popular support upon his re-entry (Goldman et al., 1994, 675).

In contrast to Bush's lackluster campaign, Democratic candidate and Arkansas governor Bill Clinton articulated a more dynamic campaign and better-defined message. Clinton stole some of the Republican thunder by denouncing welfare and calling for tax cuts to the middle class, as well as advocating the use of the powers of the federal government to combat the recession. A sign at the Clinton campaign headquarters that read, "It's the economy, stupid," reflected Clinton's campaign themes and resonated well with the public (Roark, 2005, 1149). The Bush camp mistakenly did not view Clinton as a serious threat in the spring of 1992, however, because of problems in Clinton's personal life that included marital infidelity. A Bush aide even wrote the President in April, 1992, and told him that "The swing voters have dismissed Bill Clinton as a serious alternative to President Bush" (Quoted in Goldman, 1994, 675).

Clinton would essentially defeat both Bush and Perot in the Presidential debates with his two rivals, thus harming Bush's popularity, and the approval ratings of the President fell even further just five days before the election when it was revealed by Lawrence Walsh, the independent counsel investigating the Iran-Contra affair, that Bush had known as Vice President about the effort to exchange arms for hostages with Iran, an allegation that Bush had long denied. To make matters worse, former Secretary of Defense, Caspar Weinberger was indicted for his role in the affair, further suggesting that Bush was guilty by association (Goldman et al., 1994, 205). Compounding Bush's electoral problems, the economy was still in recession, and in spite of his tax hike, the debt situation inherited from the Reagan administration continued to spiral out of control, producing a crowding out of credit, rising interest rates, and sluggish economic growth. As a consequence, Bush would suffer the worst loss of any sitting President since William Howard Taft in 1912. Bush won only 37% of the popular vote as compared to 43% for Clinton and 18% for Ross Perot. The twelve years of Republican dominance of the White House that had been initiated by Ronald Reagan had come to an abrupt end.

Loathing Clinton

Perhaps no American President (with the possible exception of Clinton's successor, George W. Bush) has ever been loathed as fully and completely by his political opposition as William Jefferson Clinton. Republican Senator Bob Dole announced after the election that the Republican Party would represent the 57% of Americans that did not vote for Clinton, inferring (though incorrectly) that the vast majority of persons that voted Perot would have voted for Bush if Perot had not been in the race. The general mood of the Republican Party and conservative electorate was that Clinton did not win the majority of the popular vote, was not the legitimate President, and was not representative of the "true America" (Gould, 2003, 459-460). In the words of Gould (2003, 460),

> "The animosity against Clinton moved beyond intense political opposition into loathing that sometimes unhinged Republican judgments. Many on the far right of the party depicted the President as a drug addict, cocaine dealer, murderer, and potential dictator with covert plans to perpetuate himself in office and to end democracy in the United States. In the eyes of Republicans, Clinton was alternately a ruthless immoral man and ineffectual bumbler."

As a consequence, the Republicans engaged in an eight year campaign to remove Clinton from the Presidency, by electoral means if possible, but by any and all other means if necessary. For his part, Clinton only contributed to the Republican fervor against him in his first year by endorsing the admission of gays into the military. Former Bush aide Bobbie Kilberg summed up Clinton's impact on galvanizing the right thusly,

> "What better way to galvanize your troops than to have Bill Clinton to fight against? He was a new bad guy. They no longer had the bad guy of communism. The Cold War was over, the Berlin Wall was gone. They had a lot of trouble raising money and organizing in the last two years of the Bush administration, because there was nobody to be angry at, and you don't raise money just by sending out 'feel-good' letters. Now they had this other big bad guy, and the first thing he did was decide to put gays in the military. I don't know where his head was, but what a wonderful issue to galvanize the far right, and they were off and running" (Quoted in Martin, 1996, 328).

Among the more substantive Clinton policies that were anathema to conservatives and served to galvanize the right was the tax increase that Clinton and the Democrats ushered through in the summer of 1993. Not a single Republican in Congress voted for the tax increase, which passed the Senate only after Vice President Al Gore cast the deciding vote. Although the tax bill reduced the budget deficit for 1993 from $255 to $203 billion, consistent with the conservatives' historic preference for a balanced budget, Republicans viewed the measure as an example of "tax and spend liberalism" and condemned the measure as the "largest tax increase in the history of the world" (Gould, 2003, 461). This, of course, was actually false since Ronald Reagan's "whoops" tax increase of 1982 (that became necessary after Republicans realized that their own tax-cutting folly was going to lead to unacceptable deficits) was actually larger in constant dollars (Gould, 2003, 461). Republican Senator Phil Gramm of Texas, the same Phil Gramm that sponsored the Gramm-Rudman balanced budget bill in the 1980s, denounced the tax increase, arguing that "hundres of thousands of Americans will lose their jobs because of this bill" (*New York Times*, June 24, 1993). Instead, 22.8 million jobs would be created over the next eight years under Bill Clinton, the most ever in an eight year period (Begala, 2002, 4-5).

Waco

Clinton further galvanized the right by his handling of the Branch Davidian affair at Waco, Texas, in April, 1993. The Branch Davidians were a fundamentalist Christian separatist group had been under suspicion from federal authorities for possession of illegal weapons. Federal authorities attempted to arrest Branch Davidian leader David Koresh, but Koresh was tipped off by a Branch Davidian member employed by the U.S. postal service, who had noticed federal agents staking out the Branch Davidian compound. Federal agents then attempted to arrest Koresh at the compound itself, the place of residence as well as worship for the Branch Davidians, but federal agents were met with gunfire from the Branch Davidians when they attempted to serve them with a warrant. Four of the Treasury Department's Bureau of Alcohol, Tobacco, and Firearms (ATF) agents were killed and 20 were wounded in a hail of gunfire from inside the compound. The Branch Davidians opened fire before the ATF agents even reached the door. The gunfire continued until the Davidians agreed to a cease-fire, but a standoff between the Branch Davidians and the ATF agents lasted 51 days. Finally, the FBI used tanks to fire tear gas into the compound in an attempt to get the Branch Davidians to surrender, but the entire compound erupted in a fire set by the Branch Davidians, and 74 individuals, including women and children, died in the fire inside (*U.S. Department of Treasury*, 1993).

Conservative gun advocates and anti-government conservatives viewed the Waco tragedy as proof that Clinton and his administration were engaged in a plot to take away firearms from Americans, end religious freedom, and impose a socialist police state. A bogus video tape circulated around America suggesting that the ATF tanks that fired the tear gas were actually flamethrower tanks that started the fire. A group called *Committee for Waco Justice* wrote a paper that was posted on the internet entitled the "Massacre of the Branch Davidians" where they alleged that the ATF was not only responsible for the fire, but that the government "demolition actions" "trapped" the Branch Davidians inside to die in the fire and purposefully destroyed evidence at the scene that would have proven ATF responsibility. *The Committee for Waco* also alleged that it was the ATF, rather than the Banch Davidians, that fired the first shots at the beginning of the crisis (www.firearmsandliberty.com).

Conservatives combined what they viewed as inappropriate government action at Waco with an incident that became known as "Ruby Ridge," in reference to the 1992 FBI siege of a ranch owned by the Randy Weaver family at Ruby Ridge, Idaho. At "Ruby Ridge," FBI agents had gunned down Weaver's wife and his 13 year-old son in a gun battle between FBI agents and the Weaver family. In the ill-fated incident, the FBI was attempting to arrest Weaver for the sale of sawed-off shotguns, but when agents arrived at the family's ranch their position was exposed by the family's barking dog. Using perhaps questionable judgment, the FBI agents then shot the Weavers' family dog. In return, the FBI agents were then met with gunfire from Weaver's 13 year-old son, who was retaliating against the intruders for the death of his dog. FBI agents returned fire, tragically killing the boy. Later, when the agents approached the Weaver household, an FBI agent fatally shot Mrs. Weaver as she walked by the window on the front door carrying her infant child (www.boogieonline.com).

Right-wing gun advocates used the Ruby Ridge incident in conjunction with the Waco tragedy to argue that the federal government was out of control and determined to destroy the rights, especially Second Amendment Rights, of citizens (www.boogieonline.com).

Clinton poured gasoline on his own gun lobby opposition fire when he supported the Brady Bill that placed restrictions on firearms. Later, Clinton issued an Executive Order banning certain types of assault weapons from being imported into the United States after the Republican Congress refused to impose such a ban. Clinton's status as "evil incarnate" to the NRA and other pro-gun groups became etched in stone.

Scandal and Smear Campaign

Negative attacks against Clinton from the conservative propaganda machine had begun during the 1992 campaign and would continue throughout his Presidency in perhaps the most broad-based media smear campaign against a President in American history. Clinton, of course, did his own part to add fuel to the fire by allowing an intern to perform oral sex on him in the oval office and then lying about the affair under oath, but for every mistake in judgment Clinton actually made, there were legions of unsubstantiated allegations of much more from the right-wing smear machine.

The great smear campaign against Clinton had its most important beginning with allegations of marital infidelity in the January 29, 1992 issue of the grocery store tabloid, the *Star*. According to the *Star*, an ex-aide to Clinton alleged that Clinton had engaged in sexual relationships with a former Miss America and "four other beauties" (*Star*, January 29, 1992). One of the "beauties," Susie Whitacre, denied the allegation through her lawyer and eventually got a retraction. Three of the other "beauties" had no comment, but one, Gennifer Flowers, a nightclub singer from Little Rock, Arkansas, gave her story of an alleged twelve year love affair with Bill Clinton to the *Star* for $150,000 (Conason and Lyons, 2000, 22).

Flowers' credibility was suspect from the beginning. On her resume, Flowers listed a Dallas prep school she'd never attended, a University of Arkansas nursing degree she'd never earned, and a membership in a sorority to which there was no record of her ever belonging. Her resume claimed that she had once opened as a nightclub act for comedian Rich Little, but her agent contradicted such a claim. Flowers did appear briefly on the Hee Haw television show, but was fired after she vanished for a couple of weeks with a man she had met in a Las Vegas casino and then concocted a story about having been kidnapped. Her resume also stated that she had been Miss Teenage America, which she had not, and she spoke of a twin sister that did not exist. Concerning Clinton specifically, Flowers claimed to have had numerous trysts with the Arkansas Governor at the Little Rock Excelsior Hotel between 1978 and 1980, but that Hotel was not built until 1983. Flowers produced no photographs, cards, letters, or any other physical evidence of her alleged twelve year affair with Bill Clinton, thus causing the mainstream media to be skeptical of her story and force Flowers to stoop to selling it to the tabloid press (Conason and Lyons, 2000, 26-27).

The Flowers affair and other allegations of marital infidelity sold well with the republican right wing and may have cost Clinton some votes in 1992, but they were still not enough to prevent Clinton from winning the 1992 election. Republicans were not satisfied however, in limiting their personal attacks against Clinton to sex scandals, and the Republicans sought other fields of attack as well. Mimicking the tactics of Richard Nixon before him, President Bush used the power of the White House to attempt to obtain derogatory information about Clinton from federal government agencies. In particular, the Bush administration illegally sought information from Clinton's passport files so as to support their contention that his antiwar activism during the Vietnam conflict had been unpatriotic (Conason and Lyons, 2000, 45). When that too failed to gain the desired results, the Republicans settled on a small, 1978 Arkansas land speculation deal that the Clintons invested in with their partner, James McDougal, in 1978. The failed real estate deal would become known to the American public simply as "Whitewater," and the investigation of "Whitewater" would essentially last throughout the Clinton Presidency.

Other Scandals and Smears

On July 20, 1993, Clinton's deputy White House counsel Vincent Foster shot himself in the mouth with a revolver and committed suicide. The body was found by officers from the U.S. Park Service, who concluded (obviously) that the death was a suicide. Unpersuaded by facts, Republicans in Congress nevertheless launched five separate federal investigations of the Vince Foster death, including two by independent counsels Robert Fiske and Kenneth Starr, in an effort to somehow link Clinton to foul play in the minds of the voting public. All five of the federal investigations concurred that Foster died of suicide caused by clinical depression. Nevertheless, rumors persisted throughout Clinton's eight years in office on the right-wing radio talk show and email networks suggesting that Clinton had somehow had something to do with Foster's death (www.snopes.com).

This, however, was only the tip of the right-wing smear campaign iceberg. When truth wasn't enough to secure for themselves political victory, conservatives adopted the age old, often effective, tactic of lying, and lying repeatedly, evidently under the premise that one can tell the most outlandish lies, but if they are repeated often enough, a certain segment of the population will believe them. The outlandish lies and complete fabrications about Clinton from the right-wing propaganda machine were seemingly unending, and there is space to mention only a few of them here, but some of the more important allegations and fabrications are detailed below.

For starters, in 1994, Jerry Falwell's Liberty Alliance distributed a 30 minute video entitled *Circle of Power*, where evangelists argue that there were "countless people who mysteriously died" after getting in the way of Clinton's political ambitions (Conason and Lyons, 2000, 464). Later that same year, Falwell and Patrick Matriciana released a video (with a book to follow), entitled *The Clinton Chronicles*. The video and book depicted the "Clinton machine" as achieving "absolute control" over the state of Arkansas and misusing government power for sinister purposes. According to Arkansas Judge and right-wing politician Jim Johnson in the *Chronicles*, the evidence of Clinton's "crimes" was "more credible than the evidence of 90 percent of the people who are confined on death row across America" (Matriciana, 1995, 155).

In addition to overstated and unsubstantiated statements such as that of Jim Johnson, *The Clinton Chronicles* was replete with absolutely false information that was easily exposed as such. For example, Matriciana (1995, 170) made the false assertion that Clinton had never balanced the Arkansas budget, even though he had done so every year in office because Arkansas State law forbade deficit spending. Matriciana asserted that Clinton had issued a pardon to a political supporter named Dan Lasater, who was convicted in federal court of giving cocaine to his acquaintances. This too was obviously false because Clinton, as Governor of Arkansas, had no power to pardon anyone for a federal crime. Matriciana asserted that financial records of Clinton's political campaigns had mysteriously vanished, but they were actually all on file with the Arkansas Secretary of State. Matriciana asserted that Don Tyson of Tyson foods donated $700,000 to Clinton's campaign, and in return Tyson received a $10 million loan from the State of Arkansas, but neither Tyson, nor his company actually donated anything to Clinton's campaign and Tyson never obtained a loan from the State of Arkansas. Matriciana absurdly alleged that the Arkansas Development Finance Authority (ADFA) was engaged in helping Clinton and his associates launder billions in drug-smuggling profits, and finance Clinton's trysts with loose women. Furthermore, Webster Hubbell's (Hubbell was a Clinton business associate) father-in-law's company, which actually

Chapter Fourteen

manufactured parking meters, was alleged to manufacture hollow airplane nose cones for stashing and smuggling cocaine (Conason and Lyons, 2000, 142).

The absurdities of the *Clinton Chronicles*, however, did not prevent Jerry Falwell from promoting it on his Christian television programs. In May, 1994, viewers were treated to four weeks of excerpts from *Circle of Power* and *The Clinton Chronicles* along with a half-hour infomercial urging viewers to purchase the videos (Conason and Lyons, 2000, 142).

Emails originating in right-wing camps circulated the homes and workstations of America, suggesting that Clinton had raped a woman named Juanita Broaddrick, a claim that FBI agents working for the Office of the Independent Counsel would eventually conclude to be unsubstantiated (Conason and Lyons, 2000, 64). Vince Foster was rumored to have been having an affair with Hillary Clinton, who was also often somehow rumored to be a lesbian (Conason and Lyons, 2000, 85).

David Hale, a Little Rock business man, accused Clinton of having pressured him into making an illicit $300,000 loan to Clinton's Whitewater partners, James and Susan McDougal in 1986. This allegation too would be proven to be unsubstantiated by the Whitewater investigation (Conason and Lyons, 2000, 85).

The conservative smear and propaganda campaign was backed by a number of important "big money" interests, but perhaps none were more important than Pittsburgh billionaire Richard Mellon Scaife, who spent $2.4 million dollars in conjunction with his right-wing magazine, the *American Spectator*, to gather "intelligence" that he hoped would lead to Clinton's political demise. In an event that eventually became known as "Troopergate," the *American Spectator* ran a story they obtained from Arkansas State Troopers painting Clinton as an avaricious and lascivious sexual deviant. The troopers alleged, among other things, that they had engaged in helping Clinton secure women for his extramarital affairs, and that Hillary Clinton had a disagreeable personality and a foul vocabulary. One particular Trooper, L.D. Brown, absurdly alleged that he had worked for the CIA on a secret contract to deliver arms to the Contras in Honduras and pick up duffel bags full of cocaine to return to the U.S. and market for Bill Clinton (*American Spectator*, July, 1995). In spite of its obvious lack of credibility, the Trooper story sold well with American conservatives.

Rush Limbaugh

The conservative smear campaigns and conservatism in general were undoubtedly helped by the ascendancy of talk radio host Rush Limbaugh, who gained unprecedented popularity in the early 1990s as a political radio commentator and talk show host. Limbaugh gained unprecedented success in his radio show using hyperbole, liberty with the facts, and complete fabrications when necessary, in order to lampoon Democrats and liberals at every opportunity. Although Limbaugh's actual influence is difficult to measure, Republicans and Democrats alike agreed that he was exceedingly influential, and numerous Republican politicians credited Limbaugh with assistance in their own Congressional victories in 1994. Limbaugh referred to the American situation under Clinton as "America held hostage," and denounced Clinton as a drug user and draft dodger, even though Limbaugh himself had evaded the draft for the medical reason of a "periodontal cyst" and later admitted that he himself was addicted to prescription pain medication (Franken, 2003, 227).

Conservatives and Clinton's Health Care Plan

As a Presidential candidate in 1992, Bill Clinton had promised to solve what he termed as a "health care crisis" in the United States. In an attempt to make good on his promise and develop a remedy for America's health care problems, in January, 1993, President Clinton created a National Health Care Reform Task Force chaired by First Lady Hillary Clinton. Included on the Task Force were noted health care experts from around the country who worked for nine months to compose the health care plan that eventually became President Clinton's national health care proposal.

On October 27, 1993, President Clinton delivered to the 103rd Congress the health care plan that he described as "healthcare that is always there." Clinton announced to Congress that the American health care system was "badly broken" and urged that "it is time to fix it" (Quoted in Castro, 1994, 42). President Clinton's Health Care Reform Task Force essentially opted to retain (with modifications) the American "free market" system of health care by the creation of a system with "managed competition." The Clinton Health Care plan had as its primary goal the universal access to health care for all Americans. The central features of the plan were that the third-party payer system of private insurance plus Medicare and Medicaid would be retained, but adequate coverage would be extended so as to become universal. Employers would be forced to provide health care insurance coverage for their employees and health care coverage would become a new right of citizenship. Coverage was to include both emergency care and preventive care, and benefits would be portable, meaning that individuals would not lose health coverage even if they lost their jobs (Castro, 1994, 86-87).

Very quickly, leading Republicans in Congress announced their opposition to the Clinton health care plan. Republican Whip Newt Gingrich promised to oppose the plan and labeled it an example of costly "big-government inefficiency" (*New York Times*, October 3, 1993, E3). Similarly, Representative Dick Armey (R-TX) claimed that the Clinton plan would create 59 new federal programs, expand 20 others, and impose 79 new federal mandates that would mean higher taxes, reduced choice and efficiency, longer waits for care, and bigger government (*Wall Street Journal*, October 13, 1993). The Republican revolt against the Clinton plan spread rapidly and was picked up immediately by conservative political radio hosts who enthusiastically bashed the Clinton plan as "socialized medicine" in spite of the fact that nothing was being "socialized" (Egan, 1995). Quickly, writings in opposition to the Clinton plan began appearing in more mainstream media publications such as *Readers Digest* (Bennett, 1994).

In February, 1994, the Christian Coalition announced a $1.4 million grass-roots campaign to oppose the Clinton plan, in spite of the fact that any connection between Christianity and health care reform is tenuous at best (Toner, 1994, A11). The Christian Coalition was joined by small and mid-sized insurance companies, who stood to lose out in the "managed competition" plan proposed by Clinton. All told, it is estimated that over $100 million was spent in lobby efforts either in support of, or against the Clinton health care plan (Center for Public Integrity, 1994, 1). In the end, the conservatives' anti-reform lobby efforts proved to be successful. Although the majority of Americans had supported the principles of Clinton's health care plan when it was announced, by the summer of 1994, polls were showing that the majority of the public had turned against the plan. The conservative propaganda machine had proven to be effective not only at smearing Clinton, but at shaping public opinion on a major policy issue.

Gingrich Revolution

In late 1993, Republican House leader Bob Michel of Illinois announced that he would not run for reelection in 1994, thus opening the door for Republican Whip Newt Gingrich of Georgia. Gingrich sought to reform the Party to be more in tune with voters so as to take over the House of Representatives from the Democrats in the 1994 elections. Gingrich conducted extensive polling along with focus group research to determine which issues resonated with voters, and the data were then combined into a proposed "Contract With America" that Gingrich pledged to push through Congress. Even though Gingrich had opposed Clinton's tax hike, the purpose of which was to address the burgeoning government budget deficits, Gingrich's "Contract" called for a balanced budget amendment. Reflecting Reagan's supply-side economics influence, however, the "Contract," also called for tax cuts. Exactly how the budget could be balanced while simultaneously cutting taxes, however, was not realistically explained.

Nevertheless, tax cuts had become an inviolate part of the Republican Party ideology regardless of their consequences that might undermine fiscal responsibility (*Washington Monthly*, September, 1995, 29-32).

The "Contract" also called for term limits for members of Congress, cuts in crime prevention programs, the relaxing of federal regulations in numerous areas, increasing defense spending, and repealing a means tax that had been placed on affluent Social Security recipients. The Republicans also countered Clinton's health care plan with a Republican version of Health Care reform. The "Contract" called for cutting Medicaid and transforming it into a block grant program with greater State control, and cutting Medicare by over $200 billion. On education, the "Contract" attacked what were viewed as traditionally "Democrat" programs, calling for the cutting of $137 million from the Head Start program (which offered preschool education and health care to impoverished children) and eliminating the Americorps program, through which people could earn money for college in exchange for performance of community service. On the issue of gun control, Gingrich's "Contact" called for eliminating Clinton's Executive Order banning certain assault weapons (*Washington Monthly*, September, 1995, 29-32).

Perhaps the cornerstone of the "Contract," however, was welfare reform, in this case, the proposed replacement of AFDC with a new program (which eventually became Temporary Assistance for Needy Families or TANF). TANF was expected to return welfare authority to the States, force welfare recipients to work, and limit the time that individuals could receive aid over their life span. The reformers also sought to deny welfare benefits to unmarried teenagers and children born out of wedlock to mothers who were receiving welfare (*Washington Monthly*, September, 1995, 29-32).

With the gun lobby, health care industry, insurance industry, Christian Coalition, and "angry white males" solidly behind them, the Republicans rode Gingrich's "Contract with America" to Congressional election victory in 1994. The Republicans gained 52 seats in the House to regain control for the first time in 40 years, and also won back the Senate, which they controlled 53-47. Newt Gingrich became Speaker of the House and Bob Dole of Kansas became the Republican Senate Majority Leader (Gould, 2003, 465).

Gingrich's Republican Revolution would be representative of a different kind of conservatism than the Reagan conservatives of 1980 in that it had a much stronger Southern fundamentalist flavor and the leaders tended to be uncompromising hard-line conservatives. All of the Republican Congressional leaders were Southerners, including Strom Thurmond of South Carolina as president pro tem of the Senate, Trent Lott of Mississippi as Senate Majority leader, Newt Gingrich of Georgia as Speaker of the

House, Dick Armey of Texas as House majority leader and Tom Delay of Texas as House majority whip. All of the Republican leaders except Armey were Southern Baptists (Phillips, 2004, 83). DeLay was a former pest exterminator who opposed environmental regulations, referred to the EPA as the "Gestapo," and urged its abolition. DeLay also referred to the Palestinian territories occupied by Israel since 1967 by the Biblical names, "Judaea and Samaria," and argued that the territories rightfully belonged to Israel. Not to be completely outdone, Armey, in his 1995 book *The Freedom Revolution*, compared Franklin Roosevelt to Joseph Stalin and Mao Ze Dong (Phillips, 2004, 116-117, 230).

The New Republican Congressional leaders not only set out to pass the items in their "Contract," but they also followed the Jacksonian path of consolidating their power and rewarding their supporters. New Republican majority whip Tom Delay of Sugarland, Texas, pressured lobbyists not to contribute to Democratic candidates. Simultaneously, Delay worked with Congressional leaders to direct federal appropriations away from Democratic Congressional districts and toward the districts composed of affluent supporters of the Republican Party. In the words of Dick Armey, "To the victor belong the spoils" (Quoted in Drew, 1996, 56).

The Republican leaders also revealed the "free market" and "anti-government" ideological bent of the new regime with numerous clearly ideological proclamations by members. Dick Armey, for example, reflected the stance of most conservatives when he stated that "the market is rational and the government is dumb" (Quoted in Gould, 2003, 466).

Problems with the Contract

The Republicans had soundly won the Congressional elections riding populist ideological rhetoric, but ideology is often inconsistent with political realities; hence, Republican policy initiatives would face greater difficulties than their electoral candidates. Gingrich's proposed balanced budget amendment was voted down in the Senate, and a Constitutional Amendment to impose term limits on members of Congress was also voted down. President Clinton used his veto against a number of Republican measures, and the Republicans lacked the 2/3 majority needed to overturn them. Instead of a "Contract with America," as promised in the campaign, the result appeared to more closely resemble governmental gridlock (Drew, 1996, 321).

Of perhaps greatest importance, Gingrich and the Republicans dueled with the President over the budget in a struggle that would eventually be their undoing. In spite of a dozen years of unprecedented deficit spending under Republican Presidents Reagan and Bush, Gingrich and his allies suddenly demanded a balanced budget and demanded that it be achieved within seven years. President Clinton expressed his own preference for a balanced budget as well, but argued that the budget cuts necessary to achieve balance in seven years would cause too much hardship and calamity, both in and outside of government. Instead, Clinton pushed for a plan that would balance the budget within ten years. Determined to have it their way, Gingrich and his allies decided that failure to reach a compromise on the budget with Clinton would be to their political advantage in that it would cause a shut down of government agencies for lack of funds, and therefore cause Clinton to appear foolish. Unfortunately for the Republicans, when the government was twice shut down due to their impasse with the President in November and December, 1996, the public largely blamed the Republican Congress, rather than President Clinton, for the government shut-down (Drew, 1996, 321-375).

After the embarrassing disaster of the government shut-down, the Republicans decided to push for welfare reform, another major piece of the Contract for which they believed they had broad-based support, but learning from their mistakes, they also decided that it was better to compromise with Clinton when necessary in order to ensure that they were able to deliver something to the American people, especially before the election of 1996.

Welfare Battle

Despite the public support for welfare reform and the Republican majority in both houses, passage of the Republican welfare reform would not be easy, as numerous groups benefited from the system that was in place. The battle for the passage of the welfare reform bill would reveal not only the strength of stakeholder groups and the Democratic Party, but the diversity within the Republican Party and the difficulty that diversity would present to the Party in formulating and passing legislation.

The Republican Agricultural Committee in the House provided the first major stumbling block to welfare reform when Members rejected the idea of relinquishing control of Food Stamps to the States through block grants. In the words of one Congressional Staff Member:

"Agriculture needs an urban base . . . . Farming makes up such a small portion of agriculture spending today, and that of our constituency, that without urban spending, agriculture would be lost. And you need to remember . . . . welfare is big business, not so much in the amount we spend for benefits, but who carries out the programs. In agriculture, grocery stores are big beneficiaries of food stamps, as are those in the computer industry who are developing 'debit card' type spending mechanisms, and those who are constantly investigating

fraud. Food stamps is big business and agriculture had to hang on to them"
(Dobelstein, 1999, 7).

Despite the roadblocks and setbacks, on Wednesday afternoon, March
22, 1995, a roll call vote was announced in the U.S. House of
Representatives concerning House Resolution 119 on Welfare. Andrew
Dobelstein records the following conversation between two Republican
House Members in the hall on the way to the House floor: "What is it?"
asked one member, meaning what is it that we are voting on? "House
Resolution 119 on Welfare" replied the other member. "What's Dick Armey
(Republican House Majority leader) say," says one Congressman to the
other. "Yes," replies his colleague, meaning that the Majority Leader wants
all Republicans to vote for the bill. "What about the Christian Coalition?" the
first Member asked his colleague. "Leadership says we just eat it Frank.
That's it. Period!" Both legislators then made their way to their places on the
floor of the House (Dobelstein, 1999, 3).

House Resolution 119 passed the House, 217-211, largely along Party
lines. Three Democrats voted for the bill, but fifteen Republicans broke with
their Party and voted against the bill. Most of the Republicans who voted
against the bill did so because of pressure brought upon them by anti-
abortion groups. The welfare reform legislation would deny cash assistance
to teenage mothers and reward States for reducing out of wedlock births.
Some Anti-abortion groups, such as the National Right to Life Committee
and the U.S. Catholic Conference, feared that these provisions could induce
some women into having abortions when they otherwise would not. In
contrast, some other anti-abortion groups, such as the Family Research
Council and the Christian Coalition, supported the provisions of the bill as a
means of taking a stand against teen pregnancies and births out of wedlock.
Consequently, Republicans were deeply divided over the "abortion"
provision of the welfare reform bill, and bickering over the wording of the
bill delayed its passage for weeks, so much so that some observers believed
that welfare reform would not pass during that session of Congress
(Dobelstein, 1999, 3-4).

Finally, an exasperated Republican House majority leader, Dick Armey
(R-TX) approached House Speaker Newt Gingrich for a "rule" on the
proposed welfare reform bill that would require the bill to include
Amendments that the House had already approved, yet no separate vote on
these Amendments would be allowed. Furthermore, no additional
Amendments could be added to the bill. In other words, the House would
have to accept the entire bill as is, or not at all. All such rules in the House
would have to be approved by the House Rules Committee, but Armey was
in hopes that the Speaker could persuade the Rules Committee to adopt his

proposed rule on the welfare bill, since Speaker Gingrich was known to be influential with the Rules Committee even though his formal authority over it is quite incomplete (Dobelstein, 1999, 4-5).

Originally, Gigngrich told Armey to go to the Rules Committee and ask for the rule himself. Armey was reluctant to do so since the Chair of the Rules Committee, Congressman Solomon, had strong anti-abortion views, and Solomon was known to be opposed to the welfare reform bill in its present form because of his position on abortion. Gingrich relented on his position and spoke with Solomon on Armey's behalf in an effort to get some form of the welfare reform bill moving again (Dobelstein, 1999, 4-5).

When the roll was called on House Resolution 119, the vote was expected to be close, with Democrats and staunch anti-abortion Republicans opposed to the bill. When all the votes were counted in the House, the measure passed by a narrow, eight vote victory, 217-211. Though the measure had passed, closer inspection reveals that the margin of victory may not even have been achieved if eight democrats had not missed the vote because they were attending a White House briefing. Furthermore, the bill still had to clear the Senate, and avoid a Presidential veto if it were to become law. Clearly, with a victory margin of six votes, the House would be unlikely to over-ride a Presidential Veto (Dobelstein, 1999, 3).

Welfare reform also passed in the U.S. Senate, but in a different form, thus requiring the convening of a conference committee, which eventually reconciled differences in the bill. President Clinton vetoed the proposal in January, 1996, the second welfare reform veto of his Presidency. Both Houses went back to work and hammered out a new resolution, which became eventually the Personal Responsibility and Work Opportunity Act of 1996. Democrats opposed the bill's provisions, which again included the denial of welfare benefits to aliens and unwed mothers; consequently, liberal Democrats urged the President to again veto the bill. President Clinton feared that if he vetoed the welfare reform bill this time, so close to the election in November, he could lose important "middle" voters who had blamed the Republicans for gridlock, but were not necessarily in favor of welfare. Indeed, Republican campaign commercials attacked Clinton for "giving welfare benefits to illegal immigrants." Consequently, Clinton reluctantly signed the bill into law amid protests from liberal Democrats in August of 1996 (Koon, 1997, 156-157). The welfare reform battle made clear, however, that Republican control of Congress was far from complete.

Election of 1996

No less than eight Republicans announced their candidacy for the Presidency in 1996, including Phil Gramm, Pat Buchanan, Bob Dole, publishing magnate Steve Forbes, California Governor Pete Wilson, and Lamar Alexander of Tennessee. Dole was the big money favorite, but his campaign essentially stumbled out of the gate in the 1996 primary season. Forbes stole some of Dole's thunder with a proposal to eliminate the graduated tax structure and replace it with a flat tax, and Pat Buchanan, a perpetual darling of the far right, defeated Dole in the New Hampshire primary. Dole regrouped, and in spite of the presence of Southerners Gramm and Alexander, did well in the Southern primaries and essentially locked up the Republican nomination prior to the convention. At the Republican Convention in July, Dole abandoned his history of support for fiscal responsibility and announced his support for tax cuts and reform of the tax code to produce a "fairer, flatter tax." Democrats charged that Dole's tax cuts would create massive deficits, but Dole, echoing Ronald Reagan, promised that he would offset the tax cuts with unnamed spending cuts (Morris, 1997, 311-312). Dole then tabbed supply-side enthusiast Senator Jack Kemp of New York as his running mate.

Ross Perot once again ran as a Third Party candidate, but Perot met with much less success this time around as his previous run had developed for himself a reputation as an eccentric that he could not overcome. Furthermore, Perot offered little that voters could latch on to as a real difference between the conservative platform of Dole and Kemp. The Democrats, however, were able to paint Dole as a "mean spirited" man, and voters were generally turned off by Dole's age at 72. Clinton had helped himself by following a more moderate path since the failure of his health care proposal, and the Republicans had hurt themselves with the gridlock and shutdown of the government. Clinton led the race from beginning to end, and won 50% of the popular vote to Dole's 41%. Clinton also won the largest gender gap in history, with 54% of American women casting votes for Clinton and only 38% for Bob Dole (Roark et al., 2005, 1153).

Clinton's Second Term

Clinton began his second term in the midst of a booming economy and soaring stock market that increased federal tax revenues. The tax windfall from the economic good fortune allowed Clinton and the Republicans to compromise on a budget in 1997 that actually balanced or the first time in three decades. It was difficult to conclude anything other than the fact that Clinton's 1993 tax increase, which the Republicans had fought against, had produced long-term benefits for the fiscal health of the nation. Republican attempts to claim responsibility for the balanced budget success rang hollow after Bob Dole's irresponsible Presidential campaign based on tax cuts. Clinton's strong position was aided by Republican infighting in the House as a rebellious group of Republicans, unhappy with the Republican failures in the government shutdown and the 1996 election, attempted to oust Newt Gingrich as Speaker in the summer of 1997. Gingrich survived the attempted coup, but the Republicans were left in disarray (Steely, 2000, 347-353).

Whitewater

Whitewater was a reference to property in which the Clintons invested during the 1980s in a small, failed, Arkansas real estate venture. The Clintons' total investment in the Whitewater property in the Ozark Mountains together with their partner was only $200,000. If the deal had worked as well as they had anticipated, their total profit would have been $45,000 (Conason and Lyons, 2000, 30). The Clintons' partner in the Watergate venture, James McDougal, however, turned out to be less than honest in his business dealings and less than mentally stable in his personal life. McDougal was indicted in 1990 for fraud in a check-kiting scheme, but the FBI and the United States Attorney concluded that there was insufficient evidence to suggest that the Clintons had knowledge of McDougal's illegal activity (Conason and Lyons, 2000, 43).

Nevertheless, Republicans in Congress demanded an Independent Counsel investigation, in spite of the fact that Republican Senate Majority Leader Bob Dole had previously criticized the Independent Counsel Law because he opposed "political" indictments (Conason and Lyons, 2000, 118). Republicans, however, had no legal method for the appointment of an Independent Counsel except for appointment by the Attorney General. Under political pressure for the Whitewater affair and certain that he would be exonerated, Clinton asked Attorney General Janet Reno to name a Whitewater Special Counsel. Reno then appointed Robert B. Fiske of New York to head the investigation, that unknown to Clinton at the time, would continue throughout his Presidency. Fiske would later be replaced by right wing Christian fundamentalist, Kenneth Starr (Conason and Lyons, 2000, 118).

When the Republicans gained control of Congress in 1995, House Speaker Newt Gingrich, who had stated during the 1994 election campaign that he would use "subpoena power" to wage political war with the White House, pressed forward anew with investigations of Whitewater in particular and the White House in general. Gingrich referred to Clinton as "the enemy of normal Americans" and stated that he envisioned as many as "twenty Congressional committees simultaneously investigating the White House." Thus, the House Banking Committee under James Leach of Iowa and the Senate Banking Committee under new chairman Alfonse D'Amato revived the Whitewater probe with renewed vigor. Other probes were launched investigating the White House for firing of White House Travel Office employees, alleged misuse of FBI files, and, of course, the failed Madison Guaranty Savings and Loan in Arkansas that was connected to Whitewater. Representative Leach was perhaps motivated by his constituents back home since the Iowa Republican Party was under the control of the Christian Coalition in 42 of 46 precincts and decidedly anti-Clinton. Leach's energetic work on the Clinton witch hunt would therefore purchase for him political capital in his home district (Conason and Lyons, 2000, 175).

In the case of D'Amato and the Senate Banking Committee's investigation, there was an added twist of irony. D'Amato had previously been linked to organized crime figures and had once appeared as a character witness for a crime-syndicate-connected New York nightclub owner that contributed to his campaign. He had also twice asked U.S. Attorney for Manhattan, Rudolph Giuliani (later Mayor of NYC) for leniency for organized crime figures represented by Roy Cohn, Joseph McCarthy's attack dog attorney in the 1950's communist witch hunts, who had been close friends of D'Amato. D'Amato himself also had been the subject of a lengthy and still-secret investigation by the Senate Ethics committee in 1991 for illicit fund raising and allowing his lobbyist brother, Armandm to misuse his Senate office. Armand D'Amato had been indicted and convicted of fraud and conspiracy in a related matter involving a defense contractor. The Senate reprimanded D'Amato in the matter, but D'Amato refused to unseal his testimony before the Ethics Committee, which could not be unsealed under Senate rules without his approval. Nevertheless, D'Amato would call for "full disclosure" from the White House in the Whitewater affair. By the time D'Amato and his Banking Committee were through with their hearings, they had been at it for seventy days, exceeding the days of hearings allocated to either Watergate or Iran-contra (Conason and Lyons, 2000, 210).

The Republican investigations were decidedly biased from the beginning. The Republicans leveled unsubstantiated broad allegations of corruption against the Clintons and their friends and associates. The media would then carry out their job of reporting by simply repeating the accusations, essentially suggesting, intentionally or unintentionally, that where there is smoke, there is fire, and raising public suspicions about misdeeds in the White House. Subsequent testimony would fail to support the allegations, but the seeds of suspicion would have been planted in the minds of the public. Democratic Senator Christopher Dodd described the proceedings thusly,

> "If you get a witness who says, 'Oh, I don't recall,' the immediate accusation is 'You're being disingenuous.' If you have witnesses with conflicting testimony, the allegation is 'Someone's lying.' And if you have witnesses that have consistent statements, 'It's a conspiracy'" (Quoted in Conason and Lyons, 2000, 189).

Politically motivated witnesses attempted to tie the Clintons to the Savings and Loan scandals of the previous decade by alleging that a loan from Madison Guaranty Savings of Arkansas to the Whitewater investment group led to the demise of the Savings and Loan. Witnesses that could dispute accusations against the Clintons were not allowed to testify, and exculpatory evidence was repeatedly ignored. On June 26, 1995, the *Wall Street Journal* published details of a report prepared for the Resolution Trust Corporation (RTC) by the San Francisco Law firm of Pillsbury, Madison, and Sutro, concerning the Whitewater affair. The report showed that the Clintons were passive investors in Whitewater, weren't involved in its financial transactions until 1986, and therefore could not have played a role in the collapse of the Madison Guaranty Savings and Loan that transferred $43,000 to Whitewater prior to 1986. Furthermore, the report concluded that the Clinton's Partner, James McDougal, had without their knowledge taken money from their investment and transferred money between entities he owned (essentially a check kiting scheme), including Whitewater.

After ten weeks of hearings, some of it even occurring during the government shutdown, the Senate Banking Committee finally concluded without proving any of the Republicans' initial accusations. In spite of all of the allegations of perjury and obstruction of justice, not a single witness was ever charged with any offense (Conason and Lyons, 2000, 211). Meanwhile, however, numerous Repbublicans had become entangled in shady dealings of their own. Bob Dole's finance vice-chairman was sentenced to prison for laundering millions into the Dole campaign and it was revealed that Republican Party Chairman, Haley Barbour, had illegally siphoned $2 million into the Republican campaign though a loan scheme with a Hong Kong investor (Conason and Lyons, 2000, 256).

As Whitewater dragged on and on, even some of the most rabid Republicans began to give up on it. In February, 1997, Independent Counsel Kenneth Starr, with essentially no more leads and all of his roads toward anything substantial exhausted, temporarily resigned his post as Independent Counsel in the Whitewater case in favor of a position as Dean of the Law School at Pepperdine University. In April, 1997, even Senator Alfonse D'Amato confessed that the entire affair needed to end. In the words of D'Amato,

"I don't have too much faith in the whole thing…People come up to me and say, 'Why are we still doing this?' It goes on and on and on…It's become very politicized. People don't have any great confidence in it" (*New York Post*, April 29, 1997).

Clinton Impeachment

On May 27, 1997, the Republicans were handed a break in the case, however, when the U.S. Supreme Court ruled that Paula Jones' sexual harassment civil suit against the President should go forward while he remained in office. Paula Jones had been a clerical employee of the Arkansas Industrial Development Commission in 1991, and had helped staff a state-sponsored "quality management" conference at Little Rock's Excelsior Hotel. Jones claimed that Clinton had invited her to a room at the hotel, made sexually aggressive advances, asked her for "a type of sex," and exposed himself to her in the hotel room (Conason and Lyons, 2000, 270).

Jones' claims appeared dubious, however, since she claimed that she met Clinton on the Afternoon of May 8, 1991, at 2:30 in the afternoon, but Clinton had given a breakfast speech at the hotel that morning and left the hotel not long afterward. That afternoon, a function at the governor's mansion precluded any secret return by Clinton to the Excelsior unless he was also so talented that he could be in two places at once. Jones later changed her story and claimed that Clinton had ducked out of the reception at the governor's mansion and "walked three blocks" back to the Excelsior to meet with Jones, but the governor's mansion and the Excelsior are at opposite ends of downtown Little Rock, over a mile apart, and separated by a six lane freeway (Conason and Lyons, 2000, 270).

Fuel was added to the sex-scandal fire later that year when Kathleen Willey, a financially strapped widow and former White House worker, claimed that Clinton had groped her in the Oval Office in 1993. Ironically, Willey's story was unraveled by Monica Lewinsky confidant Linda Tripp, who testified before a grand jury that there was "no harassment whatsoever" in the Willey case, and that instead of Clinton chasing Willey, Willey had been chasing Clinton, because her husband had died, and she was in dire financial straits (Consaon and Lyons, 2000, 290).

By the fall of 1997, Ken Starr and his prosecutors in the Office of the Independent Council were at a series of dead ends. Although he had not announced as such, Starr had essentially given up on prosecuting Bill and Hillary Clinton for any wrongdoing involving the White House Travel Office, the FBI files, or the Madison Guaranty Savings and Loan. In fact, Starr himself admitted to Larry King in December of 1997 that he in fact had nothing, stating that "We didn't think that the evidence was there" (Quoted in Conason and Lyons, 2000, 318).

In January, 1998, however, the Republicans received another break when Linda Tripp, a friend of former Presidential intern Monica Lewinsky, brought evidence of an extramarital affair between Lewinsky and Clinton to the attention of the Independent Counsel. Tripp had secretly taped conversations between herself and Lewinsky where Lewinsky discussed details of the affair, including her possession of a dress with stains left by the President's semen. Starr investigated the Lewinsky affair in conjunction with the Paula Jones case (a loose connection at best). The Jones case, of course, Starr had been investigating due to its connection to Whitewater (another very loose connection at best). Nevertheless, the President, unaware that Lewinsky had kept the stained dress, would lie under oath to cover up his affair with Lewinsky and commit perjury, thus giving the Republicans the "crime" they needed to commence with impeachment (Conason and Lyons, 2000).

While it was clear that the President was guilty of perjury, opinion polls suggested that Clinton's approval had increased to over 50%, and it was clear that the majority of Americans did not want Clinton to be impeached or removed from office. Furthermore, the Republicans had nowhere near the 67 votes in the Senate needed to convict Clinton of anything; consequently, the fact that Clinton would remain in office was a foregone conclusion. The Republican constituents in House Members' home districts, however, were overwhelmingly in favor or removing Clinton. This, combined with their own loathing of Clinton and the fact that Clinton most certainly did commit perjury, pushed the Republicans to ignore the will of the majority and pander to the preference of their local constituents and press for impeachment (Baker, 2001, 15-42).

On August 17, 1998, President Clinton gave a televised speech to the nation where he admitted to "inappropriate" conduct with Monica Lewinsky. The Republicans then released the report of the Independent Counsel, Kenneth Starr, which made the case for impeachment and contained graphic details of the sexual interludes between Clinton and Lewinsky, including a bizarre episode where Clinton evidently inserted a cigar into Lewinsky's vagina. The Republicans expected that the Starr report would shock the nation into supporting impeachment and help the Republicans win the Congressional elections in November. Instead, the Democrats gained five seats in the House. The unexpected electoral loss led to a coup in the House, Newt Gingrich stepped down as speaker, and then resigned his House seat amid suspicion that he would not be reelected as Speaker by the House Republicans. (Schaller and Rising, 2002, 143-145). Gingrich's heir apparent to the Speaker's position was Robert Livingston of Louisiana, but Livingston was quickly forced to remove himself from consideration when it was revealed that he too had had extramarital sexual relationships. The Republicans finally chose Dennis Hastert of Illinois (Steely, 2000, 389-394).

In spite of the fact that they had lost the mid-term elections, a clear message from the public that they had grown weary of the Republican witch-hunting, the Republicans decided to press on with impeachment. The House

Judiciary Committee, led by Henry Hyde, drafted four articles of impeachment, which were passed in his committee by a vote of 21-16, strictly along partisan lines. Hyde pressed for the impeachment even though it was revealed publicly that he himself had had an extramarital affair in 1986. Hyde dismissed the reports of his own infidelity as a "youthful indiscretion," although it had occurred at a time that Hyde was approximately Clinton's age. The House then passed two of the four articles of impeachment, one for perjury, and one for obstruction of justice (Baker, 2001, 245).

In the Senate, however, the Republicans were not only unable to garner the Democratic votes necessary for a two-thirds majority necessary to convict, but they were unable to foster a majority on either count, and Clinton was effectively acquitted on both counts. The Republican attempted coup through smear, investigation, and impeachment, had failed (Baker, 2001).

George W. Bush

By mid-1999, George W. Bush, the Texas Governor and son of former President George H.W. Bush, was the early frontrunner for the Republican nomination as voters set aside their dissatisfaction with the Presidential performance of the elder Bush. Unfortunately for the Republicans, a strong economy and a bull market in stocks would tend to boost the incumbent Democrats. Without leverage of the economy to work with, the Republicans plotted a strategy based on the nation's moral revulsion at President Clinton's sexual indiscretions (Phillips, 2004, 84). George W. Bush quickly picked up on the theme and hearkened back to how his grandfather, Senator Prescott Bush, had condemned Nelson Rockefeller for his scandalous divorce. Bush also catered to the Christian right by naming Jesus as the political philosopher with whom he most identified (Phillips, 2004, 88-89).

As governor of Texas, George W. Bush had catered to right-wing constituencies and conservative ideology in pushing for tax cuts, relaxation of environmental standards, and the legalization of the right to carry concealed weapons. Bush was also a strong proponent of the Death Penalty and gained notoriety for allowing the execution of women and the mentally handicapped in Texas. Reflecting Bush's conservatism, in 2000 Texas ranked 49th of the fifty States in State taxes and fiftieth in per capita State spending (Phillips, 2004, 113-114). In spite of this hard line conservative record as the Texas Governor, Bush espoused a more moderate theme for his campaign that he labeled as "Compassionate Conservatism," as he launched his Presidential bid. In rhetoric at least, "Compassionate Conservatism" clearly represented a move to the left for Bush and an attempt to appeal to the swing voters in the middle.

True to his conservative "less government" ideology, Bush took a page from the Reagan campaign manual and made tax cuts a central theme of his campaign. Clinton's federal budget was now not only balanced, but in the black to the tune of over $160 billion, and Bush told Americans that as President, he would give the people back "their money." Democrats, in contrast, argued that the surplus should be used to "save social security" (Gould, 2003, 474).

Bush quickly proved himself an adept fund raiser, with over $100 million (an all-time record) collected for the Republican primaries. In fact, Bush was so successful as a fund raiser that he did not accept federal matching funds. In refusing the matching funds, Bush's campaign was able to avoid any federally imposed spending limits (Gould, 2003, 474).

Bush, however, was not a perfect candidate. Bush was not a good speaker and his campaign was full of twisted syntax and speaking gaffes for which Bush would eventually become famous. Bush's campaign speeches were replete with statements such as "I will have a foreign-handed foreign policy" and "Families is where our nation finds hope, where wings take dream" (Quoted in Miller, 2002, 6). Bush was also certainly not an avid reader, and appeared to some to be slow-minded, if not almost illiterate. Bush contributed to this public perception by answering a South Carolina schoolchild's question about what he liked to read as a child with "I can't remember any specific books." Bush then changed his story a few weeks later to say that his favorite children's book was *The Very Hungry Caterpillar*, which was published in 1969 when Bush was 23 years old (Miller, 2002, 12). Finally, Bush admitted in *Vanity Fair* that the only thing he had read as a child were baseball cards (Sheehy, 2000, 168).

Bush also had a history of alcohol abuse, and admitted himself that he had been a heavy drinker until age 40. There were also unconfirmed rumors of cocaine use and erratic behavior, such as running over the family mailbox while drunk and challenging his father to a fist fight. Bush was also rumored to have been charged with a crime in 1972 for which he was forced to work with minority children in an organization called Professionals United for Leadership League (PULL) that was chaired by his father. J.H. Hatfield (2000, 303-310) argues that Bush was actually arrested for cocaine possession, the record of which was expunged by the court after Bush completed six months of community service with PULL. Hatfield's allegations were never substantiated, but they were also never comprehensively refuted by Bush himself. Instead of denying that he had ever used drugs, Bush merely stated that he had not done so since 1974 (Phillips, 2004, 45, 89). Further suspicions of Bush's alleged criminal activity were raised when it became public that he had been issued a new driver's license in Texas by his newly-appointed head of the Texas Department of Public Safety two months after he became Governor. Critics alleged that the new license was issued to Bush so as to eliminate some record of past infractions collected under Texas law as an informational attachment to driver's licenses. When the new license was issued, portions of the record were deleted (Phillips, 2004, 89).

Bush also had to answer questions about where he was during the Vietnam War. For eight years, Republicans had gained political mileage by labeling President Clinton as a "draft dodger" for spending the Vietnam War years studying in England rather than serving his country in Vietnam. Bush, however, had also avoided Vietnam and instead joined the Texas Air National Guard, where his service record appeared to have some gaps (Ivins and Dubose, 2002, 3-10). To make matters worse, the probable Democratic candidate, Vice President Al Gore, had actually served in Vietnam. With such baggage, one could only expect the November election to be an uphill battle.

Election of 2000

Before Bush could defeat Vice President Al Gore, he faced a challenge for the Republican nomination from the enigmatic Arizona Senator John McCain, a Vietnam War veteran and former POW. McCain defeated Bush in the New Hampshire primary, but McCain's campaign was short on cash, and after Bush defeated McCain in South Carolina, McCain was forced to abandon the fight due to lack of funding (Gould, 2003, 475).

With McCain out of the way after his loss in South Carolina, Bush was able to return to his attacks on the Democratic program. In addition to his tax cut theme, Bush argued in favor of privatization of Social Security and attacked the Clinton Administration for its internationalism and the overextension of the American military overseas. In fact, the foreign policy Bush favored in his campaign appeared to be the complete opposite of that which he would espouse as President. In the words of Bush,

> "I'm worried about an opponent who uses nation building and the military in the same sentence. See, our view of the military is for our military to be properly prepared to fight and win a war and, therefore prevent war from happening in the first place" (*Washington Post*, February 26, 2003).

To that, Bush added in his debate with Al Gore, "I'm not so sure the role of the United States is to go around the world and say, 'This is the way it's got to be'" (Quoted in Gould, 2003, 478). Bush's position would be much different once he occupied the Oval Office.

Election Farce

The fact that George W. Bush was elected at all, as it turns out, was perhaps Bush's biggest coup of all. Al Gore won the popular vote by 540,000 votes, but the antiquated American Electoral College system still allows the popular vote winner to lose an election, thus providing Bush with his opportunity. The election was too close to call on election night due to a dispute in Florida, where fortunately for Bush, his brother was governor, and one of his campaign workers and allies, Katherine Harris, was Secretary of State. Without Florida, Gore had won 266 electoral votes and Bush had won 246, but Florida's 25 electoral votes would give either candidate the 271 needed to win. Exit polls suggested that Al Gore would carry the State, but a confusing butterfly ballot in West Palm Beach, Florida caused several thousand voters in a county with a large Jewish population to accidentally vote for Pat Buchanan (a person with a fuzzy recollection of the Holocaust) when they believed they were voting for Al Gore (Brinkley, 2003, 924) . Six thousand ballots in West Palm Beach County were double-punched for both Gore and Pat Buchanan and another 3,000 were double-punched for Gore and Socialist candidate David McReynolds. In all, Gore's name was included in 46,000 such "over-votes" while Bush's name was included in only 17,000 (Phillips, 2004, 101-103). This unfortunate confusion, along with the 90,000 far-left votes in Florida that were siphoned from the Democrats by Ralph Nader, would essentially give Bush the Presidency, but there were other unsavory elements that surfaced as well.

In the summer of 1999, Florida Republican Secretary of State Katherine Harris, who was also Bush's campaign cochairwoman, arranged for the State of Florida to pay $4 million to a company called Database Technologies to go through Florida's voter rolls and remove any felons from the approved voter lists. Unfortunately, thousands of eligible voters with similar names to convicted felons, mostly minorities who typically vote Democrat, were also purged from the voter lists. Among the 181,000 citizens that were purged from the voter lists were 8,000 individuals on a list supplied by the State of Texas (where candidate Bush was governor at the time) of suspected felons from Texas that had moved to Florida (Getter, 2001, Phillips, 2004, 102).

On election night, one network declared Al Gore the winner of the election and then retracted it. Another network, Fox News, whose election coverage was overseen by Bush's cousin, John Ellis, declared Bush the winner. In the first count, Bush was declared the winner by 537 votes, but Florida law called for a recount in an election so close, and the Democrats asked for a hand recount since machine errors had left hundreds of votes unrecorded in several heavily Democratic counties. The Bush team then sued to stop the recount in spite of the fact that Bush himself had signed a similar law in Texas in 1997 that required hand recounts in such cases and required that election officials accept various degrees of punching or indentation that "show a clearly ascertainable intent of the voter to vote" (Phillips, 2004, 100). After 36 days, the Republican-dominated U.S. Supreme Court ordered the recount stopped, thus violating the Republican preference for "States' rights" in elections. After the Supreme Court decision, there was little else Al Gore could do but concede the election to Bush. For the first time since 1888, a candidate who lost the popular vote won the Presidential election (Roark et al., 2005, 1168-1169). Janet Rehnquist, the daughter of Chief Justice William Rehnquist, was then appointed Inspector General of the Department of Health and Human Services. Eugene Scalia, son of Supreme Court Justice Antonin Scalia, was subsequently appointed solicitor of the Department of Labor (Phillips, 2004, 16).

Chapter Fifteen

Conservatism and George W. Bush

The ascension of George W. Bush to the Presidency in 2001 brought to the United States (and the world) a new direction in conservatism largely centered on the ideological leanings of President Bush himself, but grounded in the long American heritage of Traditional Conservatism and Classic Liberalism. Like Reagan, Bush should be considered a "movement" conservative who was catapulted into office through conservative populism. Although his victory margin was nothing near the Reagan landslide over Jimmy Carter in 1980, Bush became the clear leader of American conservatives after the terror attacks of 9/11/01, with approval ratings spiking briefly at 90%, thus providing him with a higher spike of approval than those achieved by either Reagan or his Father. Partly as a consequence of that spike in public opinion, and partly due to his staunch adherence to conservative principles, his influence on both American politics and the politics of the entire world perhaps cannot be understated.

George W. Bush: Traditional Conservative Ideologue

Bush's Presidency, like that of Ronald Reagan, has been driven by largely by his conservative ideological predispositions as opposed to rational or scientific analysis as will be demonstrated in the pages to follow. To argue differently is essentially to argue against statements from Bush himself that fundamentally state the same. For example, in an appearance at Crawford Elementary School in Crawford, Texas two weeks before the 9/11 terrorist attacks, a student asked President Bush if it was hard to make decisions as President. Bush's response was, "Not really. If you know what you believe, decisions come pretty easy" (Quoted in Miller, 2002, 298). Clearly, Bush's emphasis in this exchange is on the concept of "belief" rather than rational analysis of facts. Similarly, in Genoa, Italy in July the previous month, the President stated,

> "I know what I believe. I will continue to articulate what I believe and what I believe—I believe what I believe is right" (Quoted in Miller, 2002, 298).

These statements are in some respects a summation of the Presidency of George W. Bush, but they also provide insight into his convictions and decision processes and how they are shaped by his ideology.

Although it certainly may be a good thing to have convictions, depending on what they might be, it obviously is not so good to have a mind that is so ideologically driven that it is closed to all contradictory ideas. After all, Hitler had his anti-Semitic principles, Osama Bin Laden has his anti-infidel principles, Saddam Hussein had his "I will not step aside" principles, and so forth. Bush, of course, is not completely closed-minded, but Bush himself admitted that he has a tendency to disregard conflicting information. For example, Bush once stated that, "I'm the kind of person that when I make up my mind, I'm not going to change it" (Quoted in Miller, 2002, 299). Unfortunately, if this statement may be taken literally, it might also mean that Bush could be expected to stay the course after he has made a decision, regardless of any and all evidence that might suggest his decision to be the wrong one. The history of this kind of ideological thinking is fraught with pitfalls, as evidenced by the eerily similar statements of Adolph Hitler in the 1930s when he declared, "I developed my political views at an early age and I never came across any reason to change them" (Quoted in Spielvogel, 2004, 72). This represents quite a contrast with Franklin Roosevelt's "Try Something" approach in the 1930s.

The contrast between the approaches of Bush and Hitler to that of Roosevelt perhaps reflects differences in the way the men thought about policy, namely, Bush and Hitler, in their own words revealed their penchant for ideologically-driven politics as opposed to the construction of policy based on pragmatism and experimentation as pursued by Roosevelt. Whereas Roosevelt freely admitted that he did not have all the answers, Hitler and Bush confidently believed that they did, because their ideologies had conveniently prescribed them.

Bush's Ideological Socialization

There are some important factors that have perhaps predisposed Bush more toward ideological thinking instead of rational analysis. First of all, since Bush's father, George H.W. Bush, once stated, "I will never apologize for the United States of America—I don't care what the facts are" (Quoted in Miller, 2002, 81), one possibility is that Bush's "don't confuse me with the facts, my mind's made up" ideological thought processes were transferred to him from his father through the socialization process. After all, the two President Bush's also appeared to share the same modest study habits and similar short reading lists. In the words of the elder Bush,

"I had to read War and Peace when I was like 16 or 17. Don't give me a quiz on the thousands of characters in it, but I guess it had an influence because it was a discipline. It was more that than remembering anything in it. And of course, we had to read Shakespeare in school. It was required" (*New York Times*, 1988).

Ignorance and Inexperience

Lack of study (and therefore knowledge) and socialization aside, another part of the reason for the younger Bush's reliance on ideology may stem from the fact that Bush lacked experience in Washington and foreign affairs prior to becoming President; consequently, without knowledge and experience, ideology all too often becomes the trusted guide, if not the only guide.

It must be noted, however, that Bush's lack of experience before his election is hardly a novelty since his predecessor, Bill Clinton, like Bush, had ascended to the Presidency from his position as a State governor with no prior experience in the federal government. Similarly, former Presidents Jimmy Carter and Ronald Reagan had become President in the 1970s and 1980s with resumes that included State governorships, but no federal governmental experience. Clinton and Carter attempted to compensate for their lack of experience through intense study and rigorous work schedules (Brinkley, 2003, Clarke, 2004). Reagan compensated for his lack of experience through delegation of authority, but his administration, like Bush's, was also widely criticized for being ideologically motivated rather than driven by sound rational analysis of facts (Skidmore, 1994, Stockman, 1987).

Unlike Reagan, however, Bush appears to more directly assume control of policy on a grand scale, often guided only by his "instincts," or, as stated by Molly Ivins and Lou Dubose, "his gut." In the words of Ivins and Dubose (2002, xxxix),

"When Bush feels he is right "in my gut," no amount of evidence will sway him. His thinking process is very much swayed by what he sees as higher moral claims, so he is not prone to rethink his stands on anything other than limited straight political issues. On larger ideological issues, evidence is irrelevant, for example, his repeated pushes for even more tax cuts in the face of increasing deficits."

Ivins and Dubose, however, are merely political observers and are not insiders in Bush's White House. Furthermore, their work has been widely criticized by conservatives for their "liberal" slant. Therefore, their analysis

could be discounted if it were inconsistent with the views of those who have
been close to the President. Instead, however, more and more individuals that
have worked closely in the White House with Bush are providing similar
observations. For example, John J. DiIulio, who was in charge of Bush's
Faith-based Initiative, described Bush and his policy apparatus, or lack of
one, thusly:

> "Every modern Presidency moves on the fly, but on social policy and related
> issues, the lack of even basic policy knowledge, and the only casual interest in
> knowing more, was somewhat breathtaking: discussions by fairly senior
> people who meant Medicaid but were talking Medicare; near-instant shifts
> from discussing any actual policy pros and cons to discussing political
> communications, media strategy, et cetera. Even quite junior staff would
> sometimes hear quite senior staff pooh-pooh any need to dig deeper for
> pertinent information on a given issue" (Quoted in Suskind, 2004, 172).

Once again, if DiIulio were unique, then perhaps his comments should be
disregarded; however, DiIulio is not the only Bush administration insider
who holds a view of Bush, and the administration in general, as ideologically
driven. Richard Perle, a fellow at the American Enterprise Institute and
former Assistant Secretary of Defense under Ronald Reagan, sized up Bush
thusly:

> "The first time I met Bush, I knew he was different. Two things became clear.
> One, he didn't know very much. The other was he had the confidence to ask
> questions that revealed he didn't know very much. Most people are reluctant
> to say when they don't know something, a word or a term they haven't heard
> before. Not him. You'd raise a point, and he'd say, 'I didn't realize that. Can
> you explain that?'" (Quoted in Suskind, 2004, 80).

Perle's observation that Bush's knowledge is lacking is shared by many,
including even many of Bush's own supporters (Brinkley, 2003, 925).
Among those is Bush's first Treasury Secretary, Paul O'Neill, who has
offered views strikingly similar to those of Perle. For example, O'Neill (as
presented by Suskind, 2004) described both Bush and his administration as
ignorant and ideologically-driven individuals that ignore facts and analysis in
favor of predetermined ideological answers. O'Neill presents a picture of a
President that has read little and is greatly ignorant of the issues, but has the
confidence to make decisions on any issue due to his internal ideological
guide. O'Neill states that he kept his memos to the President shortened to
three pages "designed for the President's study habits" (quoted in Suskind,
2004, 231), suggesting the President is not only ignorant, but employs study
habits that are likely to keep him that way. O'Neill also questioned the

President's native intellectual capacity. According to O'Neill's wife, Nancy, the Treasury Secretary would often,

> "leave meetings with the President and shake his head. It was like, I'm not sure if this guy's got what it takes to pull this off" (Quoted in Suskind, 2004, 188).

Similarly, O'Neill brings into question the President's critical thinking ability, adding that he personally,

> "had never heard the President analyze a complex issue, parse opposing positions, and settle on a judicious path. In fact, no one—inside or outside the government, here or across the globe—had heard him do that to any significant degree" (Quoted in Suskind, 2004, 114).

Finally, O'Neill essentially argues that Bush does not have to think because his guiding ideology provides all of his predetermined answers for him. In the words of O'Neill,

> "Ideology is a lot easier, because you don't have to know anything or search for anything. You already know the answer to everything. It's not penetrable by facts" (Quoted in Suskind, 2004, 292).

Even Bush himself admitted to O'Neill that his knowledge was limited, but Bush essentially told O'Neill that it was not a cause for concern because he had "good instincts." Unfortunately, since humans in reality have actually very few real instincts, when knowledge is lacking, there is little left to guide one besides flawed ideologies. On another occasion, Bush stated that "If I have any genius or smarts, it's the ability to recognize talent" (Pfiffner, 2005, 95). Once again, most Europeans and approximately half of the American population (if the last election is any indicator) would beg to differ, as liberal Americans and progressive Europeans generally tend to view Bush appointees Donald Rumsfeld, John Ashcroft, and Paul Wolfowitz, along with Federal Emergency Management Agency (FEMA) head Michael Brown (among others) to be some of the worst Presidential appointees in recent memory. Brown, for example, received much of the blame for the inadequate federal response to Hurricane Katrina in New Orleans in 2005. Prior to being appointed by Bush to head FEMA, Brown was evidently fired from his position as head of the International Arabian Horse Association, an organization not normally associated with management of public emergencies (www.time.com/time/nation/article/0,8599,1103003,00.html).

Nevertheless, critics might argue that former Treasury Secretary O'Neill's assessment of Bush as a conservative ideologue lacks objectivity since O'Neill's own resignation was forced by President Bush, and O'Neill therefore is merely an opportunist with a case of sour grapes, and profiting off of his time in the Bush administration through book sales. In other words, critics of O'Neill charge that his account of Bush's ideological direction is no more than O'Neill sounding off against his former boss as a disgruntled employee who was asked to resign. The policies of the George W. Bush administration, however, reflect that there may be more to O'Neill's comments than merely sour grapes. Bush himself essentially admitted in an interview with Tucker Carlson in *Talk* magazine in September, 1999 that he has little knowledge of policy. When Carlson asked Bush to name something he isn't good at, Bush replied, "Sitting down and reading a 500-page book on public policy or philosophy or something" (*Talk*, 1999). Given that Bush is admittedly without the knowledge that comes from reading books about policy, Bush is left with little to guide him besides ideology and the desires of his political constituents, the most important of whom may be the religious right, a group whom Bush has embraced like no President ever before.

Bush and the Religious Right

There are multiple reasons for the marriage between the religious right and the George W. Bush administration, but the faith of the President himself appears to be an important factor. In other words, one reason Bush may cater to the religious right is that the President and fundamentalist Protestants appear to share the same beliefs and values. For example, Anthony Evans of Dallas, a fundamentalist minister and confidant of George W. Bush, explained to a British journalist in 2003 that one of the impetuses for Bush's consideration of running for President in 2000 was Biblical teaching and direction from God. In the words of Evans, Bush "feels God is talking to him" (*London Observer*, 2003). Similarly, journalist Bob Woodward wrote (based on his interviews with Bush) that "the president was casting his vision and that of the country in the grand vision of God's master plan" (Woodward, 2002, 67). Likewise, presidential adviser David Gergen told the *New York Times* (2003) that Bush "has made it clear he feels that Providence intervened to save his life, and now he is somehow an instrument of Providence." Finally, Bush as much as admitted that he viewed his role as part of a Divine plan at the National Prayer Breakfast on February 6, 2003, when Bush stated,

> "We can be confident in the ways of Providence…Behind all of life and all of history, there's a dedication and purpose set by the hand of a just and faithful God" (Quoted in Phillips, 2004, 239).

While the old Puritans Cotton and Increase Mather must surely be pleased with what has arisen to the Presidency in the Twenty-First Century from their Seventeenth Century roots, with this type of mindset, one may expect that Bush would support the politics of the religious right simply because it appears that he shares similar beliefs. In Bush's case, however, the incentive is perhaps even greater since Bush owed his ascendancy to the White House perhaps as much to the Religious right as to any other group. In each religious category in the 2000 election, whether evangelical, mainline Protestant, Catholic, or even Muslim, the higher the religiosity of the person, the more likely it was that they supported George W. Bush. For example, eighty-four per cent of high-commitment evangelicals supported Bush. Similarly, Catholics, formerly a strongly Democratic demographic, supported Bush by approximately 60 percent (Phillips, 2004, 223).

As President, Bush would act accordingly and remember those who put him in the White House by placing religious right conservatives in numerous key positions throughout the federal government. Bush appointed Kay Coles James, formerly dean of the Robertson School of Government at Pat Robertson's Regent University, as head of the Office of Personnel Management. David Caprara, a former director of the American Family Coalition, an affiliate of Sun Myung Moon's Unification Church, was appointed the head of AmericCorps VISTA. Moon himself, a Bush supporter who controls the conservative pro-Bush newspaper the *Washington Times*, sponsored an Inaugural Prayer Luncheon for Bush on January 19, 2001, where propaganda on the Unification Church was distributed. This partiality to Reverend Moon is in spite of the fact that Moon is often condemned by other evangelical Protestants for asserting that he wants to take over the world, abolish all religions except the Unification Church, abolish all languages except Korean, and abolish all governments except his own, one-world, theocracy (Phillips, 2004, 235).

Although Moon simply sponsored a Prayer Luncheon and was not appointed by Bush to a position in government, Bush did nominate J. Robert Brame III, a former board member of American Vision, a group that favored putting the United States under Biblical law and opposed women's rights, to the National Labor Relations Board. Additionally, to chair the Food and Drug Administration's Reproductive Health Drugs Advisory Committee, Bush appointed W. David Hager, a person who recommended specific scriptural readings and prayers for headaches and premenstrual syndrome. Finally and most famously, Bush appointed John Ashcroft, a devout Pentecostal Christian who had his own head anointed with Crisco cooking oil before being sworn in, as Attorney General (Phillips, 2004, 226-227).

Faith-Based Initiative

Less than two weeks into his Presidency on January 29, 2001, President Bush created the White House Office of Faith-Based and Community Initiatives by Executive Order. The purpose of the new organization was to assist faith-based institutions or religious organizations in applying for federal social service grants so as to help meet America's social-welfare needs. In short, Bush was attempting to provide social services through religious organizations. Bush followed up his faith-based initiative with an Executive Order in December 2002 that required equal protection under law for faith-based organizations. The Executive Orders appear to be symbolic as much as anything else since the percentage of the federal social welfare system that has involved faith-based institutions since 2001 has been negligible, but the symbolism itself is very important to many members of the religious right. Bush also pushed for a school voucher program favored by the religious right that would provide essentially a tax rebate in the form of a voucher that individuals could use to send their children to parochial schools instead of the secular public schools. The Republicans in Congress were evidently less impressed with the idea and passed a version of Bush's education plan without the vouchers in the fall of 2001, but Bush had done his part and made his good will gesture to the religions right (Pfiffner, 2004, 4).

In November 2003, Bush also used religious language when calling for a ban on cloning, by stating that "Life is a creation, not a commodity," a position that resonated well with a large number of evangelicals. The same month, Bush signed a bill banning partial-birth abortions (another measure popular with America's religious conservatives), calling it an end to "a terrible form of violence" (Pfiffner, 2004, 5).

Bush was not alone among Republicans, however, in catering to the religious right. Other leading Republicans during the Bush years have tended to make statements favorable to the Christian right and support the policies they champion. Republican House majority leader Tom DeLay, for instance, exhibited his own consistency with religious right thinking when he assured a Texas Baptist audience that God had elevated Bush to the presidency in order to "promote a Biblical world-view." DeLay also refers to the Israeli-occupied territories in Palestine by their Biblical names of Samaria and Judea and argues that they rightly belong to Israel (Phillips, 2004, 230).

In the spring of 2005, in one of the more celebrated cases of the American blend of fundamentalist Protestantism and politics, it was the Republican House Majority leader, Tom DeLay, and Republican Senate Majority Leader, Bill Frist, that led the Republicans in Congress in their effort to save the life of Terry Schiavo. Schiavo was a severely brain-damaged woman in Florida who had been kept on life support for fifteen years in spite of no measurable brain activity, but her husband had won a decision in Florida courts to have her feeding tube removed, thus effectively ending her life. DeLay, Frist, and other Republicans in Congress intervened (unsuccessfully) under the premise that decisions of life and death are the domain of God, not men. Senate majority leader Bill Frist, a physician by trade, declared from watching videotape of Schiavo that he was sure there was brain activity, but a later autopsy showed that Ms. Schiavo's brain had so severely atrophied that it was approximately half the size of a normal brain.

The views of Frist and DeLay's would clearly be viewed as an aberration in more secular Europe, but they are not so in conservative evangelical America, nor does DeLay represent a serious departure from his predecessor, the previous Republican U.S. House majority leader, Dick Armey. Armey was a Texas Baptist who once displayed his social conservative leanings by referring to Barney Frank, an openly gay Congressman from Massachusetts, as "Barney Fag" on a radio show (Micklethwait and Wooldridge, 2004, 116). While such a statement might have doomed Armey's political career in some parts of the United States, Armey experienced little difficulty in gaining re-election to the U.S. House of Representatives from his Protestant fundamentalist dominated district in Texas.

Meanwhile, the leaders of the Christian right itself would spend the years of Bush's first term flailing from one controversial issue to another. For instance, Franklin Graham inflamed Muslims by referring to Islam as "evil," while the Reverend Jerry Falwell referred to the prophet Mohammed as a terrorist, and Dr. Jerry Vines, Pastor of the First Baptist Church in Jacksonville, Florida, declared that Mohammed was a "demon-possessed pedophile" (www.warriorsfortruth.com). Not to be outdone, Reverend Pat Robertson referenced Mohammed as a "wild-eyed fanatic, a robber, and a brigand." Another group, known as the "Cattlemen of the Apocalypse," spent their time shipping cattle to the Holy Land in an attempt to breed the red heifer that would signal Israelis to rebuild the Temple and thus usher in the "end times" (Phillips, 2004, 230). Exhibiting a different Israel-centered view, John Hagee, a well-known Protestant fundamentalist minister and televangelist in San Antonio, announced that his congregation would give over $1 million to Israel for the resettlement of Jews from the former Soviet Union to the West Bank and Jerusalem in the Israeli-occupied territories of Palestine (Phillips, 2004, 230). Simultaneously, still another religious right group raised money to hire lawyers to defend Israelis who were arrested for planning to blow up Jerusalem's Al-Aqsa Mosque" (Phillips, 2004, 230-231). Obviously, if the Bush administration is to cater to the American religious right, it will find itself more in step with the witch-hunters of Seventeenth Century Massachusetts than it will be with the governments of the rest of the developed industrial world.

George W. Bush and Environmental Policy

From the opening weeks of his Presidency, George W. Bush and his administration exemplified the Classic Liberal and Libertarian attitudes concerning environmental regulation of business. Eric Pooley in *Time* magazine perhaps captured the essence of Bush's environmental views when he wrote,

"Bush let industry write an anti-pollution measure, and believes voluntary plans, not regulation, can clean up air and water. No wonder Texas has a world-class pollution problem" (*Time*, February 21, 2000).

Though he campaigned as a moderate, and in his campaign debates with Al Gore even argued for reductions in greenhouse gases (Begala, 2002, Miller, 2002, Corn, 2003), perhaps no Presidential administration in history has proven to be more ideologically opposed to governmental environmental regulations than that of George W. Bush, and that ideology has been transposed into policy action. In the words of former EPA Directory of Regulatory Enforcement Erick Schaeffer,

"In a matter of weeks, the Bush administration was able to undo the environmental progress we had worked years to secure. Millions of tons of unnecessary pollution continue to pour from these power plants each year as a result. Adding insult to injury, the White House sought to slash the EPA's enforcement budget, making it harder for us to pursue cases we'd already launched against other polluters that had run afoul of the law, from auto manufacturers to refineries, large industrial hog feedlots, and paper companies. It became clear that Bush had little regard for the environment— and even less for enforcing laws to protect it" (Schaeffer, 2002).

In furtherance of Bush's Classic Liberal ideological goal of freeing business from costly environmental restrictions, the Environmental Protection Agency's budget was sliced by $500 million (Moore, 2001, 33). As a result, the pace of the cleanup of Superfund sites under the Bush administration was cut approximately in half from what it was in the Clinton years. Eighty Superfund sights were cleaned up in each year of the Clinton administration, but only 47 were cleaned up in Bush's first year, and 40 in each of the next two years (*New York Times*, 2002).

In March 2001, just Bush's second full month in office, the Bush administration began their assault on environmental rules that had been issued under the Clinton administration. Funding for research into renewable energy sources was cut by 50% and funding for research into cleaner, more efficient motor vehicles was cut by 28%. Also in March 2001, the Bush administration announced that several Clinton administration initiatives that imposed environmental restrictions on the mining industry would be suspended. Included among those was a rule that allowed the Federal government to prohibit mining projects that caused "substantial, irreparable harm" to the environment (*New York Times*, February 4, 2002).

These relaxations of Federal regulations are representative of the Classic Liberal and Libertarian positions against greater government spending and regulation, but they also, suspiciously, are friendly to the petroleum and mineral extraction industries where both President George W. Bush and Vice President Dick Cheney have strong ties. In these cases, critics have argued that the policies could be driven by interest group connections as much as ideology. Further fuel to the "favoritism" fire was added when Haliburton, an oil field service company for whom Dick Cheney was formerly CEO, won contracts for Iraqi reconstruction without competing bids.

Bush and Clean Water Regulations

On the day of Bush's inauguration, Bush's Chief of Staff, Andrew Card, issued a memo to all Federal agencies ordering a 60-day freeze on new rules that had been finalized by the Clinton administration at the end of Clinton's term. This freeze covered a number of environmental standards, including rules issued under the Clinton administration that were designed to limit the discharge of raw sewage into the surface water and requiring public notice when sewage does overflow (*Natural Resource Defense Council*, 2002). Simultaneously, a rule that strengthened the power of the federal government to deny contracts to companies that violate federal environmental laws was also revoked (Moore, 2001, 32). These are obviously the type of policies that one can expect to produce unfavorable press and a political backlash from environmentalists, but the Bush administration pursued the policies anyway, consistent with the President's ideological leanings against federal government regulations of business.

As if raw sewage in the water were not controversial enough, also in March, 2001, Bush's EPA director, Christine Todd Whitman, announced that the EPA was overturning a rule issued during the Clinton administration that lowered the allowable level of arsenic in drinking water from 50 parts per billion (ppb) to ten (*Boston Globe,* 2001). Whitman conceded that most scientists agreed that the 50 ppb standard was not safe, but Bush argued that the 10ppb standard had been rushed through by the Clinton administration and required further study (Corn, 2003, 74). In fact, however, Congress had directed the EPA to establish a new standard and appropriated $2.5 million for the study of the problem between 1997 and 2000. The EPA concluded from its study that a 3 ppb standard was justified by scientific evidence, but they recommended the 10ppb standard due to exorbitant costs of implementing a 3ppb standard. Furthermore, a separate study by the National Academy of Sciences (NAS) concluded that a 50ppb standard could easily result in a one per hundred-person cancer risk. The NAS then recommended the lowering of acceptable levels of arsenic in drinking water as quickly as possible (Corn, 2003, 75). As could be expected, a plan to increase the allowable levels of arsenic in drinking water received unfavorable press and was met with opposition from environmental groups, but it was only after enormous public outcry when the results of the NAS study were leaked to the press that the Bush EPA determined that it was best to keep the more stringent 10 ppb arsenic standard (Corn, 2003, 75).

The Bush administration continued to push, however, for a loosening of federal standards on water pollution in a manner consistent with their Classic Liberal and Libertarian ideological positions against government regulations. For example, on August 7, 2002, the Bush EPA eroded the Clean Water Act with a new rule designed to effectively discard the Act's primary program for cleaning up 20,000 polluted lakes in the United States. Three days later, Bush's White House moved to lift environmental review provisions that applied to oceanic waters and regulated waste-dumping by the oil and gas construction industry. The next week on August 19, 2002, Congress forced the EPA to withdraw a new penalty calculation scheme for fines levied against clean water, air, pesticide, and waste management violations after Congress determined that the new scheme would result in a smaller increase in penalties than is provided by law (Ivins and Dubose, 2002, xxxii).

Bush and Clean Air Regulations

Bush's position on clean air regulations, like his policies on clean water standards, has proven to be ideologically opposed to government regulations of business. Before the end of March 2001, President Bush had written a letter to Republican Senator Chuck Hagel, where he informed Hagel that he had decided to renege on his 2000 campaign promise to regulate carbon dioxide emissions (a leading global warming gas) from power plants, after encountering strong resistance from the coal and oil industries (*Washington Post*, 2001). Bush also declared that he was opposed to the Kyoto Protocol, the 1997 international accord on global warming. The Treaty called for the reduction of greenhouse gases to 1990 levels by 2012. This Treaty was signed by President Clinton, but never ratified by the U.S. Senate, so all Bush had to do was abandon the fight for Senate ratification and the Treaty was dead. Bush's abandonment of the Kyoto Protocol is in spite of the fact that in February 2001, Bush's own EPA director Christine Todd Whitman argued that global warming is real and warned of possibly catastrophic consequences. In the words of Whitman, "There's no question but that global warming is a real phenomenon that is occurring." Furthermore, Whitman added, "while scientists can't predict where the droughts will occur, where the flooding will occur precisely, or when, we know those things will occur" (Quoted in Suskind, 2004, 98-99). Obviously, these statements not only indicate that Bush's own EPA director viewed global warming as real, but that her perspective reflects that of the scientific consensus. Her statements were also made four years before Hurricane Katrina would ravage the city of New Orleans and the Gulf coast of the U.S. and focus renewed attention on Global warming.

Bush, however, was evidently unpersuaded by scientific consensus and strictly adhered to the Classic Liberal/Libertarian ideological position against government regulation of business in his decision to withdraw from the Kyoto Treaty. Bush claimed that the Kyoto Treaty would be too costly for the U.S. and that it was also unfair to the U.S. because it called for developed nations to reduce their greenhouse gas emissions prior to the implementation of reductions by lesser-developed countries. Bush suggested that the Treaty should be altered so that lesser developed countries would instead be forced to reduce their emissions first (in spite of the fact that 25% of greenhouse gases worldwide are released by the U.S.). Bush also claimed that the science behind Global warming was uncertain, thus contradicting the opinion of his own expert, EPA director Christine Todd Whitman; consequently, Bush called for more study, including a report from the National Academy of Sciences (Corn, 2003, 110).

In June 2001, the National Academy of Sciences released their report on global warming as Bush had requested. The opening lines of the report stated,

"Greenhouse gases are accumulating in Earth's atmosphere as a result of human activities, causing surface air temperatures and subsurface ocean temperatures to rise. Temperatures are, in fact, rising. The changes observed over the last several decades are likely mostly due to human activities, but we cannot rule out that some significant part of these changes are also a reflection of natural variability. Human-induced warming and associated sea level rises are expected to continue through the 21st Century" (Quoted in Corn, 2003, 110-111).

The last paragraph of the first page of this same NAS document states that the NAS agrees with the conclusions of the International Panel on Climate Change (an international body of scientists that issued a report stating that the increase in global temperatures is at least in part due to human activities) (Corn, 2003, 111). After receiving the study from the NAS,

Bush's Press Secretary at the time, Arie Fleischer, stated that the report "concludes that the earth is warming, but it is inconclusive on why—whether it's man-made causes or whether it's natural causes" (Quoted in Corn, 2003, 111). Obviously, since the report from the NAS attributes global warming to human causes no less than three times on the very first page, it is difficult to conclude anything other than that Fleischer and the Bush administration decided to ignore the consensus of their own experts and scientific policy analysis in favor of their own pre-determined anti-regulatory ideology. It is also possible, however, that the decision was influenced by energy industry lobbyists, since according to former Treasury Secretary Paul O'Neill, compliance with the Treaty would have also meant a decline in U.S. energy consumption by over 30% by 2012 (Suskind, 2004, 104). The fact that President Bush and Vice President Dick Cheney were heavily involved in the energy industry as private citizens before their tenure in the Executive branch, not to mention their clear preference for Halliburton as a government contractor, has caused their critics to suspect that they were unduly influenced by the energy industry in their Kyoto decision-making.

Bush and the Electric Power Shortage

Later in the summer of 2001, Dick Cheney provided more fuel to the environmental critics when he suggested that California's electric power shortage (which resulted in rolling blackouts in California and was therefore a hotly debated issue that summer), was caused by too many government environmental regulations that had slowed the building of new electrical power facilities. Cheney then called for the reduction of those governmental regulations (Suskind, 2004, 104). Cheney's position on the issue, whether correct or incorrect, was again consistent with the Classic Liberal and Libertarian ideological positions against governmental regulations of business. Given that Cheney offered no facts to support his claims, however, the appearance is that Cheney's position was again based on ideology or interest group pressure rather than sound analysis.

Liberals such as Michael Moore (2001) countered Cheney's statement with the argument that the California electrical power problem was caused by deregulation policies favored by conservatives that went into effect in 1996. Moore (2001, 139) illuminated the fact that Los Angeles and other areas where the public still owns the energy did not experience electrical power shortages. Furthermore, Moore states that under the new electrical power "deregulation," electricity prices were frozen for four years at above-market prices. Additionally, competition under the new "deregulation" was limited. In effect, Moore argues that "deregulation" created a prohibition against the building of new power plants, so California had to grow more dependent on out-of-State power that was sold to them at daily spot market prices that tended to be higher (Moore, 2001, 139). Furthermore, Moore argues that the California energy crisis was not due to a lack of electrical power. Moore states that California has access to enough power for summertime peak demand, but that power companies held back as much as 13,000 megawatts of power. Moore's arguments are buttressed by the generally conservative *Wall Street Journal,* who stated that in August of 2000, 461 percent more electrical capacity was being held back "off-line" than in the previous year, thus increasing electrical power prices. Given this evidence, it appears that Dick Cheney's ideological assertion that that the California electrical power crisis was created by "too much government regulation" does not hold up to sound analysis, but it is not immediately apparent that Cheney studied any facts on the matter since he offered none to support his claim. Ideology, of course, does not require study since it provides the answers without any such effort.

Bush and Protected Lands

Finally, perhaps the most controversial Bush administration environmental policy was Bush's proposal for drilling for oil in National Monuments and Wildlife refuges. In his first year in office, Bush approved plans to auction off areas close to Florida's eastern shore for oil and gas development and announced plans to allow oil drilling in Montana's Lewis and Clark National Forest (Moore, 2001, 34). The policy making the most headlines and stirring the greatest controversy, however, was Bush's proposal to drill for oil in the Alaskan Arctic National Wildlife Refuge (ANWR) (*Denver Post*, 2001). Vice President Dick Cheney pushed the plan to the public for the Bush administration, arguing that the ANWR covered 19 million acres, but the amount of land affected by oil production would only be 2,000 of those acres. In coming up with this 2,000 acre estimate, Cheney only counted the space of the oilfield and pipeline equipment actually touching the ground. Even road widths were left out of Cheney's estimate. According to the U.S. Geological Survey, however, the main collections of oil in the ANWR lay in over 30 deposits spread over 1.5 million acres (Corn, 2003, 100). In the final analysis, Bush's plan to drill for oil in the ANWR was inconsistent with his campaign pledges to protect the environment, but his policy in the ANWR was consistent with the Classic Liberal and Libertarian positions against federal government regulation of business and the interests of the oil industry. Bush's goal of developing the oil potential of the ANWR failed, but his ideology has otherwise resulted in perhaps the greatest reversal in environmental policies in the last forty years.

Bush and Civil Rights

While in the area of the environment, Bush has exhibited his disposition toward Classic Liberal and Libertarian solutions and opposed larger government and interference with free enterprise, in the area of Civil Rights, Bush has reflected his Traditional Conservative, if not Conservative Extremist, side in increasing government power, and limiting rights and dissent, ostensibly in the interest of national security. The argument is essentially that the age of terrorism has brought with it unprecedented threats to security, thus meriting unprecedented government measures to combat it in response. Although it is clear that the threats posed by terrorism are indeed unique challenges to national security, it is less clear that the threat of terrorism has merited the Bush response. It is also true that Bush is not the only President to be faced with the problem of how to balance civil liberties and national security.

In 1798 during the Quasi-War with France, John Adams and the Federalists prosecuted their political opposition under the Alien and Sedition Acts. During the Civil War, while Abraham Lincoln was freeing the slaves and preserving the Union, he was also suspending Habeas Corpus and trying civilians by military tribunals. In 1917, Woodrow Wilson asked Congress for a Declaration of War against Germany to "Make the world safe for Democracy," but civil liberties were seriously curtailed at home. Similarly, in 1941, Franklin Roosevelt called for war against the Axis for the purpose of creating a world of four fundamental freedoms: freedom of speech, religion, freedom from want, and freedom from fear (*Economist*, November 1, 2003). While securing those fundamental freedoms abroad, Roosevelt proceeded to intern Japanese Americans at home.

Following in the footsteps of his Presidential predecessors, George W. Bush in 2001 also launched war for the purpose of "making the world safe for Democracy" and securing "freedom from fear." In the process, however, buoyed by the terrorist attacks of 9/11/01, freedom of speech, freedom of religion, and freedom from want, as well as American criminal rights, have again suffered significant erosion. The narrowing of individual rights under the Bush Administration is consistent with the Traditional Conservative ideological preference for order over freedom, but certainly inconsistent with most scholarly conceptions of the Democracy and Freedom for which Bush's administration is supposedly fighting.

Most notorious among Bush's Civil Rights innovations is a controversial piece of Congressional legislation entitled the "Uniting and Strengthening America by Providing Appropriate Tools Required to Intercept and Obstruct Terrorism Act," better known by acronym as the "USA Patriot Act." The Act broadened the definition of who might be considered a terrorist and gave

Attorney General John Ashroft (the same individual that had his head anointed with Crisco upon taking the job) the power to detain certain foreigners indefinitely if he determined there were "reasonable grounds to believe" they might be terrorists (Pfiffner, 2004, 7). The Act also granted the Federal government the authority to develop a project to promote "total information awareness," a program that allows the Federal government the authority to obtain all sorts of information on American citizens without probable cause. This includes the authority of the Federal government to monitor religious and political institutions and organizations, perhaps violating First Amendment Free Exercise and Assembly Rights as well as criminal due process protections (Ivins and Dubose, 2002, xxxi). The Government's new authority under the USA PATRIOT Act includes the powers to impose roving wire taps and the authority to spy on email (Pfiffner, 2004, 8).

The Act also alters the relationship between the Executive branch and Congress in that it allows the Justice Department to "defer" submittal of reports to Congress on intelligence, thus perhaps violating the Constitutional requirements that the President keep Congress fully and faithfully informed. As written, the USA PATRIOT Act would allow the FBI, CIA, and Defense Department to compile lists and engage in electronic surveillance of their political enemies, including anti-administration journalists and college professors (Bolton, 2005, 93). Evidently, the purpose behind the Act is to allow the Federal government the authority to eavesdrop on Mosques and other Islamic organizations in order to snoop for terrorist activity. The result, however, violates long-standing legal traditions protecting Americans against government infringement on their personal lives without probable cause.

Civil Rights Infringements

As could be expected with such a vague and hastily written law, numerous violations of the rights of ordinary Americans with no connections to terrorism quickly occurred. In one instance, 20 peace activists, including nuns and high school students, were detained as security risks for saying that they were traveling to a rally to protest against U.S. military aid to Colombia. Furthermore, the entire High School wrestling team from Juneau, Alaska was held up at airports seven times because one member was the son of a retired Coast Guard officer on an FBI watch list (Koh, 2003, 25). The day after the 9/11 terrorist attacks, Dr. Al Bader al Hamzi, a radiologist from Saudi Arabia practicing in San Antonio, was arrested and held for twelve days before he was permitted to answer questions given him by federal authorities. He was released after twelve days in custody and no charges were filed against him (Fisher, 2005, 111). Similarly, Hady Hassan Omar, an Egyptian living in

Fort Smith, Arkansas with his American wife and daughter, was held for 73 days, some of it in solitary confinement, but no charges were filed against him (Fisher, 2005, 111). In another case in May 2002, Jose Padilla, an alleged al Qaeda recruit, but U.S. citizen, was suspected of plotting to detonate a radioactive bomb on U.S. soil. Padilla was classified as an "enemy combatant" in spite of his American citizenship, and imprisoned in a military brig without access to a lawyer (Bolton, 2005, 46).

The FBI under the Justice Department oversight of John Ashcroft dramatically changed standard operating procedures from that of only arresting those suspected of a crime, to arresting people based on neighbors' suspicions and then refusing to release any information about those detained or allow them access to lawyers. The American tradition of assumption of innocence in such cases has been effectively reversed. In the words of Ashcroft, due to the War on Terrorism, the priorities of the FBI and the Justice Department changed "from prosecution to prevention." Ashcroft went on to say that

> "If there's a question between protecting a source and protecting the American people, we burn the source and we protect the American people. That's just the way it has to be" (Quoted in Bolton, 2005, 138).

With "prevention" as a premise, in June, 2002, Ashcroft announced his intention to fingerprint and photograph more than 100,000 visa holders that the Justice Department had determined to pose national security concerns. Immigrant groups immediately criticized the policy as "racial and ethnic profiling" of hundreds of thousands of Middle Eastern students, workers, and tourists (*Washington Post*, June 6, 2002).

Immigration and Guantanamo Bay

The USA PATRIOT Act also made life difficult for immigration to the U.S. and for political refugees. The number of political refugees coming to the United States declined 70% between 2001 and 2003 due to tighter immigration restrictions. To make matters worse, at this writing, an estimated 600 persons from 42 countries are still being held in prison at the U.S. naval base at Guantanamo Bay, Cuba, without being formally charged of anything. Of those detained, three are children, the youngest age 13, several are over 70, and one claims to be over 100. The detainees have been denied the rights of Habeas Corpus, the Rights to Speedy and Public Trials, the Rights to Counsel, and perhaps, Protections against Cruel and Unusual Punishment. The Justice Department even suppressed the names of the detainees, essentially creating a "secret arrest" situation that would normally be considered odious to a democratic society. To make matters worse, evidently, the same types of tortures that were endured by Iraqi POWs in Abu Ghraib prison in Iraq were evidently also applied in Guantanamo Bay, including sleep deprivation and stress positions (Koh, 2003, 25). Additionally, the religious rights and sensibilities of prisoners at Guantanamo Bay apparently also have been compromised since prisoners were prevented from wearing their traditional head coverings during prayer (Bolton, 2005, 67). In 2005, allegations have arisen that interrogators at Guantanamo Bay also desecrated the Koran in front of prisoners as part of the interrogation process, although the extent of such activity has been greatly contested by the Bush administration.

The Bush administration has declared that the detainees are not POWs, and therefore do not receive the protections of the Geneva Convention under International Law, but the Bush administration also claims that the detainees are outside of the jurisdiction of any American civil or criminal court, being in Guantanamo Bay, Cuba. Essentially, the Bush Administration has created a new designation outside of the protections of any law, and those designated as "detainees" are at the complete mercy of the Bush Administration. As a consequence, legal scholars, such as Yale International Law Professor Harold Hongju Koh, have condemned the Bush administration for creating an international law double standard where there is essentially one set of rules for the U.S., and another separate set of rules for the rest of the world (Koh, 2003, 25). In the words of Koh (2003, 25),

"The emerging doctrine has placed startling pressure upon the structure of human rights and international law that the U.S. itself designed and supported since 1948. In a remarkably short time, the United States moved from being the principal supporter of that system to its most visible outlier."

This is perhaps most important to note since the Bush administration cited Iraq's violations of International Law as reason sufficient for invasion, yet the same administration has tossed International Law aside when it comes to the rights of international prisoners. Koh (2003, 25) further argues that the shift in American policy away from International Law and human rights is not due to a shift in American National culture, but instead is a result of "short-sided decisions made by a particularly extreme American administration." In other words, Bush's assault on liberties reflects the Traditional Conservative, if not Conservative Extremist, ideological preference of his administration for order over freedom; however, American attitudes toward civil liberties have not experienced an identical shift to the right, although Americans will clearly tolerate more government infringement on their liberties since 9/11/01, such as passenger searches at the nation's airports, if that is what is necessary in order to ensure against another terrorist attack.

The Secrecy of the Bush Administration

The Bush administration has also attempted to limit civil liberties through its preference for secrecy and the withholding of information from Congress, a practice endemic in the Bush administration as explained by John Dean (2003, ix-xvii). For example, in an unprecedented fashion in October, 2001, President Bush sent an Executive memo to federal agencies instructing them to limit the disclosure of classified and sensitive law enforcement information. Disclosure of such information was to be limited to eight members of Congress, including only the House Speaker, House Minority Leader, the Senate Majority and Minority Leaders, and the chairs and ranking members of Congressional Intelligence Committees (Fischer, 2005, 102). Immediately, there was fallout in Congress, even from members of Bush's own Republican Party. Senator Chuck Hagel of Nebraska expressed his objection to the memo as an affront to Congressional integrity. In the words of Hagel,

> "To put out a public document telling the world he doesn't trust the Congress and we leak everything, I'm not sure that helps develop unanimity and comradeship" (Quoted in Fisher, 2005, 102).

Other members pointed out that Congress is charged in the Constitution with oversight and that classified briefings are necessary if Congress is to perform its Constitutionally-mandated oversight role, and that members of numerous committees, including Foreign Relations, Armed Services, Judiciary, and Appropriations Committees, could not function properly without access to classified materials. In the words of Constitutional Law scholar Louis Fisher,

> "Anyone familiar with executive-legislative relations should have recognized the memo's absurdity. It read like something drafted late at night without enough alert, experienced people to stop it before it went out" (Quoted in Fisher, 2005, 102).

In the face of bipartisan revolt in Congress, Bush retreated from the position of his memo, but his attempt to withhold information from the public and other entities within government continued. One week after Bush's memo announcing the withholding of information from Congress, Attorney General John Ashcroft issued a guideline to the heads of federal agencies instructing them of the need to consider "sensitive business data and personal privacy" as well as "national security and law" before releasing documents to the public. Furthermore, Ashcroft promised Justice Department backing of Executive decisions to withhold records (Fisher, 2005, 104). To put it more succinctly, Ashcroft encouraged federal agencies to limit public access to government documents. Republicans in Congress, however, again proved to be on a different page than the Bush administration and issued a statement in their "Citizen's Guide" on the Freedom of Information Act that contradicted Ashcroft's position. Specifically, it was stated in the "Citizen's Guide,"

"contrary to the instructions issued by the Department of Justice on October 12, 2001, the standard should not be to allow the withholding of information whenever there is merely a 'sound legal basis' for doing so" (quoted in Fisher, 2005, 104).

Consistent with the efforts of the Justice Department to suppress public information, Bush's original head of Homeland Security, Tom Ridge, on March 4, 2002, refused to testify before Congress on the $38 billion budget for his agency on the basis that he was a Presidential adviser and not a Senate-confirmed head of an agency (Fisher, 2005, 104). Bush's Immigration and Naturalization Service also became more secret after 9/11 and began closing deportation proceedings to the public in spite of rulings from the Sixth Circuit Court of Appeals that there is a First Amendment right of access by the press and the public to deportation proceedings (Fisher, 2005, 112).

The Bush administration has also limited civil rights by attempting to infringe on the freedom of speech and freedom of the press. Not only has the Bush administration arrested protesters at their campaign stops and prohibited the media from showing photos of caskets draped with American flags, but Defense Secretary Donald Rumsfeld announced in February, 2002, that the Department of Defense would prosecute persons that leak classified information. Rumsfeld's Defense Department also created a new agency under its oversight, the Office of Strategic Influence (OSI), with a $10 billion supplemental appropriation from Congress, the purpose of which was to produce propaganda for the Department of Defense. When news of the disinformation campaign was embarrassingly leaked to the press, the Bush administration announced that they would use the agency as an office of global diplomacy to spread a positive image of the U.S. around the world and combat "anti-Americanism" (Bolton, 2005, 103).

The Bush administration has been aided in part in its efforts to quell free speech by Republican leaders in Congress, such as Trent Lott, who criticized Democratic Senate leader Tom Daschle for his denigration of the Bush administration's War on Terror. In the words of Lott, "How dare Senator

Daschle criticize President Bush while we are fighting our war on terrorism, especially when we have troops in the field?" (Bolton, 2005, 62, 69)

The potential impact on the free flow of information in such an atmosphere is obviously chilling and undemocratic. If the people must simply acquiesce to governmental policies without holding it accountable, then one cannot say that the government is run by the people and it therefore cannot qualify as democracy. Conversely, the failure of the people in a democratic society to hold their government accountable can only be termed as dereliction of duty by the people in a democratic polity. Other than Daschle's miniscule outburst and a scattered few others, the Democrats had few questions and offered little criticism of the Bush administration in the early months of the War on Terror. Such behavior may simply reflect a lack of political backbone, but it may also reflect the fact that the center of debate in the U.S. during the Bush years moved significantly to the right and the American left is comparably further to the right than left-wing parties in most other developed democracies.

At any rate, Bush's disregard for civil rights predictably encouraged similar behavior by foreign governments abroad. In Indonesia, for example, the army cited America's Guantanamo detention center as a model for a proposal to build an offshore prison camp on Nasi Island, where "detainees" can be held without charges indefinitely. In China, the founder of a pro-democracy magazine was imprisoned for life on the charge of "terrorism." In Egypt, the government extended for three years its Emergency Law that allows it to detain suspected terrorists indefinitely (Koh, 2003, 25). Obviously, the message that other countries received from Bush's approach to civil liberties and international law at Guantanamo Bay is that if international law is irrelevant to the U.S., it is irrelevant to others as well.

The erosion of civil liberties by the Bush administration does not stop with international law and the rights of international terror suspects, however. The USA PATRIOT Act also erodes American Fourth Amendment protections against unreasonable searches and seizures for U.S. citizens by expanding federal authority on computer surveillance, as well as giving the Federal government the authority to seize citizens' papers and effects without probable cause if it is in conjunction with a terror investigation (Pfiffner, 2004, 7). The Federal government even has the authority to review which books one checks out at the library, and under the threat of incarceration, librarians are prohibited from informing individuals of federal inquiries into to their personal reading lists. The USA PATRIOT Act also infringes on the right to counsel by granting the federal government the authority to monitor federal prison conversations between attorneys and clients and deny the right to counsel completely to those accused of terrorism activities (Ivins and Dubose, 2002, xxxi).

The compromising of individual liberties during the tenure of the Bush administration is obviously not without precedent since (as previously discussed) former Presidents also infringed on individual rights during times of war or emergency, but the infringement on liberties during the Bush administration may be different than its predecessors in that there is danger that it may become permanent. Whereas the Civil War, the World Wars, and even the Cold War could be expected to some day come to an end, the War on Terror that spurred Bush's attack on individual liberties appears to be indefinite in nature. That being the case, it is unclear at what point, if ever, the U.S. can restore the constitutional protections of individual liberties (Conley, 2005, 10). The Bush administration argues that these invasions of liberty are necessary in order to ensure safety against terrorism. Adolph Hitler, of course, made similar arguments when he ordered detainment of the Jews. The dangers of such thinking should be obvious to all, but were perhaps best summed up by Benjamin Franklin in 1759, who argued, "They that can give up essential liberty to obtain a little temporary safety deserve neither" (Quoted in Koh, 2003, 25).

Bush and Gay Rights

The twenty-first century brought with it a continuation of the gay rights debate, and gay marriage became a major focus of the 2004 Presidential campaign on February 24, 2004, when Republican George W. Bush asked Americans, "Do you want a Constitutional ban on gay marriage?" Bush asked this question despite the fact that at a speech to the Republican Governor's Association just twelve hours earlier he had argued that,

> "voters face a stark choice between two visions of government: one (Bush's) that encourages individual freedom, the other (the Democrats') that takes your money and makes your choices" (*Economist*, 2004).

Obviously, Bush's Constitutional ban on gay marriage would limit choice for gay Americans, thus not encouraging individual freedom, and instead "making their choices" for them. Just as obvious, Bush's Traditional Conservative ideology that favors the use of government to "correct human weaknesses," as in his opposition to gay rights, conflicts with his own Libertarian and Classic Liberal ideologies that place premiums on personal freedoms and oppose the expansion of government to correct societal "weaknesses." Of course, Bush's Constitutional ban also violates his own "States' rights" conservative ideology, and Bush himself even argued that "some activist judges and local officials will permit gay marriage in one place," thus necessitating federal intervention (*Economist*, 2004). This is in spite of the fact that "permitting gay marriage in one place" would be consistent with the conservative mantra of "returning authority to the States." It is also worth noting that Bush has criticized "activist judges" on the gay marriage issue, but Bush certainly did not criticize the "activist judges" on the U.S. Supreme Court that intervened into State affairs in the 2000 Florida election, and stopped the recount mandated by Florida law so that he could gain the Presidency in the first place.

Bush and Fiscal Policy

When George W. Bush became President in 2001, he inherited an estimated federal budget surplus for that year of $281 billion, the largest annual surplus in American history. Furthermore, the Congressional Budget Office estimated that the ten-year surplus would be $5.6 Trillion and the national debt would be eliminated by 2009 (Congressional Budget Office, 2001). The surplus was certainly as much a result of a robust economy and runaway stock market as it was the result of fiscal restraint by the Republican Congress or President Clinton either one, but after three decades of annual deficits, both the Republican Congress and President Clinton could boast of "responsible" fiscal policies.

Tax Cuts and Debt

In the election of 2000, however, a major tax cut was the centerpiece of George W. Bush's campaign strategy and he made implementing that cut his top priority (Suskind, 2004, 57-58). Bush argued, consistent with Ronald Reagan's supply-side economics ideology, that his tax cuts would not produce deficits. Instead, Bush argued during a radio address in early 2001 that his budget proposal, even with his tax cuts and his promise not to dip into the Social Security Surplus, would still leave "almost a trillion dollars...for additional needs." Bush went on to say, "My plan reduces the national debt...so fast, in fact, that economists worry that we are going to run out of debt to retire (Quoted in Corn, 2003, 87).

If Bush did indeed believe that his budget, complete with its tax cuts, could possibly eliminate the national debt, it reflects that he is either severely mathematically challenged, ignorant of the history of such policies during the Reagan years that produced massive deficits, was catering to wealthy constituents who would benefit from tax cuts, or could only be living in a world of extreme ideological guidance. Bush's first Treasury Secretary, Paul O'Neill, argues for the latter.

From the early days of his administration, Bush was told repeatedly by his Treasury Secretary Paul O'Neill that his tax cut plan would not provide much of an economic stimulus and he was certainly not informed by his Treasury Secretary that his tax cuts would eliminate the National debt (Suskind, 2004, 57). Instead, O'Neill and Federal Reserve Chairman Alan Greenspan feared that the cuts would produce a return to deficits, and O'Neill argued for the inclusion of safety measures in the tax cut bills that would eliminate the cuts if deficits returned (Suskind, 2004, 57). Former Federal Reserve Chairman Paul Volcker also came out publicly against the President's tax cut plan as "fiscally unsound" (Suskind, 2004, 131). O'Neill stated that Bush ignored his personal warnings (and those of other experts) about deficits, and instead adhered to his ideological "supply-side" position on tax cuts. In the words of O'Neill, the idea was that "tax cuts were always good, the deeper the better," furthermore, O'Neill adds that the faith in "deep tax cuts" proved to be an ideology that was "impenetrable by facts" in the Bush administration (Quoted in Suskind, 2004, 280, 307). In spite of these warnings of deficits by his top economic advisers (as well as by other experts such as Volcker), Bush argued in a speech at Western Michigan University in March 2001, "we can proceed with tax relief without fear of budget deficits even if the economy softens" (Quoted in Begala, 2002, 21).

The facts in the matter appear to fly in the face of the Bush administration's tax-cutting confidence, and vindicate the predictions of O'Neill, Greenspan, and Volcker, since Bush's first budget ended in a deficit of $165 billion, the largest one-year reversal in projected budgets since 1982, the last time a conservative President (Ronald Reagan) was able to persuade Congress to implement sweeping tax cuts while simultaneously increasing military spending (Begala, 2002, 17-18).

While it is true that economic downturn and a stock market malaise were partially to blame for the deficit (though Bush had stated that a softening of the economy wouldn't matter), the Congressional Budget Office concluded that Bush's tax cuts were the largest single factor in creating the budget deficit (Begala, 2002, 18). In fact, by 2004, Bush's tax cuts accounted for over half of the federal deficit despite the fact that the U.S. was still funding over 130,000 occupation forces in Iraq and spending more on the military ($400 billion annually) than potential enemies Russia, China, Iraq, Syria, Iran, North Korea, Libya, and Cuba combined. In fact, American military spending under Bush was so large that it was more than double that of all of the nations of NATO combined (Phillips, 2004, 272). As a percentage of the American economy, Bush's defense spending even outstripped the average defense budgets during the Vietnam War (Bolton, 2005, 98). What's more, the deficits would only get worse in subsequent years of the Bush administration as spending on the war in Iraq combined with more tax cuts to push the annual deficit to over $500 billion and over 4.2% of GDP by 2004 (Shapiro and Friedman, 2004).

Bush's tax cuts did, however, drop federal revenues in 2004 to the lowest level as a percentage of GNP (15.8%) since 1950 (Shapiro and Friedman, 2004). In this sense, Bush has succeeded in implementing the conservatives' ideological position in favor of less government. Unfortunately, it is estimated that the debt that will result from the tax cuts will increase interest payments on the debt by $1.1 Trillion between 2005 and 2014, thus negating the impact of the tax cuts by creating another huge Federal government obligation (Shapiro and Friedman, 2004). In the final analysis then, Bush's tax cuts betray the conservative ideological position in favor of less government by creating greater federal government obligations in the future.

Tax Cuts and Economic Growth

Bush's tax cuts have also failed to create the kind of economic growth that was predicted by the Bush administration. For example, the Bush administration predicted that with the passage of their tax cuts, 5.5 million jobs would be created from June 2003 to December 2004. In the first nine months of this time period, only 689,000 jobs were created, just 13% of the administration's projections (Shapiro and Friedman, 2004). Although a GDP growth rate of 3.6% occurred during the period of "economic recovery" since the implementation of the tax cuts, the growth rate lags behind the growth rate in seven of the previous eight economic recoveries since WWII. Even the Bush Administration's own *Economic Report of the President* in February, 2004 stated that: "The performance of employment in this recovery has lagged that in the typical recovery and even that in the 'jobless recovery' of 1990-1991" (Quoted in Shapiro and Friedman, 2004, 9). Similarly, the International Monetary Fund concluded in a January, 2004 report,

> "the recent emphasis on cutting taxes, boosting defense and security outlays, and spurring an economic recovery may come at the eventual cost of upward pressure on interest rates, a crowding out of private investment, and an erosion of longer-term U.S. productivity growth" (Quoted in Shapiro and Friedman, 2004, 11).

In other words, money is just a commodity like everything else bought and sold and Bush's governmental borrowing increases the demand for money, thus producing a crowding out of credit. Private entities that need to borrow will have difficulty finding money to borrow in the future because the federal government will have borrowed too much of that which is available. The likely result is higher interest rates followed by a long-term slowing down of the economy. In the words of Bush's first Treasury Secretary Paul O'Neill, "one of the most significant things Ronald Reagan had proved is that deficits do matter" (Quoted in Suskind, 2004, 292), but in Bush's ideology, tax cuts, mattered more, regardless of contrary analysis by economic experts or historical analysis of the failed fiscal policies of Ronald Reagan that suggest otherwise.

Tax Cuts for the Wealthy

The money from the Bush tax cuts went disproportionately to the wealthiest Americans, much as Bush's Democratic opponent Al Gore and other critics had argued it would during the campaign of 2000 and afterwards. Gore further argued that if Bush lopped off the top one percent that he was giving in tax relief, he could pay for the cost of every other program. When asked about Gore's statement on Larry King Live, Bush replied,

"Oh, I don't—you know, I hadn't—I'm not so sure. I'm not quick in my mind at math, but I don't believe in trying to pick and choose winners when it comes to tax relief" (Quoted in Miller, 2002, 215).

For Bush, evidently, such analysis is not necessary because in his supply-side ideology, tax cuts for the rich will "trickle-down" to the poor and thus benefit all. Actual analysis of such things is therefore unnecessary.

Those who do study fiscal policies, however, are fairly adept at being able to pick and choose "winners and losers" when it comes to "tax relief." According to the Urban-Brookings Tax Policy Center, 24.2% of Bush's cuts from 2001-2004 went to the top 1% of Americans in income. Tax cuts for millionaires, just 0.2% of American households, accounted for 15.3% of the tax cut revenue (Shapiro and Friedman, 2004). Furthermore, almost a third of the poorest households with children received no tax cuts at all (Begala, 2002, 20). This is in spite of the fact that Bush claimed in his radio address on February 3, 2001, that his plan "reduces taxes for everyone who pays taxes" (Quoted in Corn, 2003, 80). Two days later, Bush asserted at a White House event that "the bottom end of the economic ladder receives the biggest percentage cuts" from his tax package (Quoted in Corn, 2003, 80). Obviously, Bush's statements were in conflict with reality, but ideology is very often in conflict with reality, and Bush's is no exception.

Tax Cuts and Economic Performance

Bush's fiscal policy is clearly a repeat of Ronald Reagan's "trickle-down" economics of the 1980s, an ideologically-based economic policy that has not proven itself with economic performance. The theory behind "trickle-down" economics is that tax cuts for the rich will allow the rich to accumulate capital. The accumulation of capital, as every student of Adam Smith knows, will then allow the rich to consume and invest, thus creating employment and wages for the common people. The tax cuts will then "trickle down" to the poor and working classes through the investment and consumption of the rich. The operative word here in practice, unfortunately, has been "trickle." In the two decades following the implementation of Reagan's trickle-down economics in the 1980s, the income gap between the rich and poor grew, the rich got richer, and the poor got poorer, as measured by income adjusted for inflation. Furthermore, the greater inequality appears to correlate with slower economic growth (*Economist*, 1994).

The trends that had surfaced during the trickle-down years of Ronald Reagan have repeated themselves in the George W. Bush years. In the first two years of Bush's Presidency, the number of poor increased by 3 million people to 34.6 million, the poverty rate rose from 11.7% to 12.1%, and the median household income fell by $500 or 1.1%. Furthermore, the average amount by which the incomes of those who are poor fall below the poverty line was greater in 2002 than in any other year on record. Unemployment was 5.8% in 2002, up from 4.0% in 2000. The number of long-term unemployed, those out of work for more than six months, increased from 650,000 in 2000, to 1.55 million in 2002 and 1.89 million in 2003. Once again, it appears that the operative word in "trickle down economics" is certainly "trickle," unless, it appears, one is discussing unemployment, and then the operative word should perhaps be "flood" (Center on Budget and Policy Priorities, 2003).

Bush Stays the Course

Given these kinds of numbers, one would think that Bush and the supply-siders would have learned from their folly, but this does not seem to be the case. If ideology is a blinder that is immune to facts, as argued by Paul O'Neill, then it perhaps made perfect sense to Bush to stay on his tax-cutting course in spite of all of the bad news concerning federal deficits. Instead of recognizing that his tax cuts had been a fiscal disaster, Bush claimed in November 2002 that without his tax cuts, the deficit would be worse. In the words of Bush:

> "We have a deficit because tax revenues are down. Make no mistake about it, the tax relief package that we passed...has helped the economy, and...the deficit would have been bigger without the tax relief package" (Quoted in Corn, 2003, 251).

Two months later in January 2003, Bush introduced a new tax-cuts proposal and again argued that his tax cuts would lead to "higher revenues for the government" (Quoted in Corn, 2003, 251). Unfortunately, that is not what the 2003 *Economic Report of the President* released by Bush's own Council of Economic Advisers indicated. Instead, Bush's Economic Advisers stated in the Report,

> "The modest effect of government debt on interest rates does not mean that tax cuts pay for themselves with higher output. Although the economy grows in response to tax reductions, it is unlikely to grow so much that lost tax revenue is completely recovered by the higher level of economic activity" (Quoted in Corn, 2003, 251).

The fact that Bush does not follow the *Report* from his own Council on Economic Advisers is an indicator of the extent to which he is captive to ideology (or, perhaps to wealthy constituents that benefit from tax cuts). Once again, ideology has no need of experts, because ideology provides all of the correct answers without study. As a consequence, the United States drifts toward unparalleled fiscal disaster under Bush's leadership. Meanwhile, in March 2003, the Congressional Budget Office (CBO) issued a report that noted that without Bush's tax and spending plan, the Federal government would have run almost a $900 billion surplus over ten years. The CBO also stated that Bush's tax cut plans were unlikely to improve the economy (Quoted in Corn, 2003, 254-256). In spite of their own negative analysis, however, Congress passed another $320 billion tax cut package in May 2003. The *Financial Times* reacted to the most recent tax-cutting folly with the following:

> "The long-run costs of financing huge U.S. fiscal deficits, which stretch far into the future, will weigh heavily on future generations. With little of the tax cut having an immediate effect, the necessary short-run economic stimulus will be negligible...The lunatics are now in charge of the asylum. Including sunsetting provisions to cut the ten year cost of the tax measures is an insult to the intelligence of the U.S. people...In response to this onslaught, there is not much the rational majority can do: reason cuts no ice; economic theory is dismissed; and contrary evidence is ignored" (Quoted in Corn, 2003, 260).

Tax Cuts and Employment

Bush's 2001 tax cut was the largest in history, and his 2003 cut was the third largest. That being the case, is should be obvious to even the "lunatics" that tax cuts essentially can be expected to produce marginal growth at best, but large deficits most likely. If there is anything else that is certain, it is that they do not seem to create jobs. The American economy lost 236,000 jobs in the first half of 2003, and the unemployment rate stood at 6.4% in June, the highest level in nine years (Corn, 2003, 261). Consequently, to conclude that Bush's tax cuts were beneficial to employment perhaps requires the heaviest of supply-side ideological blinders.

Bush and Social Welfare

George W. Bush and the Republican Congress have reflected the conservative ideological opposition to social welfare programs, with the reauthorization of TANF and the inclusion in that reauthorization of a provision known as "Superwaiver." The Superwaiver provision would give sweeping authority to the governor of any state to override most federal laws or rules governing social welfare programs, including the Food Stamp Program and public housing programs. Under Superwaiver, governors could alter how federal funds are used for these programs, alter the target population for benefits, and alter the types and amount of benefits provided. Furthermore, governors could use Superwaivers to shift Federal resources to low-income programs previously funded exclusively with State funds and thus free up those State funds for unrelated purposes, thereby reducing overall funding for low-income programs (Fremstad and Parrott, 2004). These Superwaivers would have no requirement that they have any research objective or even be subject to an independent evaluation; hence, Superwaivers could be used by individual governors to essentially overturn Congressional social welfare decisions in any given State (Fremstad and Parrott, 2004). Superwaiver is obviously not only anti-social welfare, and thus consistent with individualist conservative "personal responsibility" ideology, but also consistent with the conservatives' ideological preference to "return authority to the states."

Exactly how Superwaivers square with the National Supremacy Clause of the U.S. Constitution, however, is a bit unclear. The impact of Superwaivers is potentially the equivalent of John C. Calhoun's "Doctrine of Nullification" from the 1830s under which South Carolina claimed the right to "nullify" federal laws within its borders. Even States' rights advocate Andrew Jackson in the 1830s correctly perceived that if States had the authority to nullify federal laws, it would destroy the federal system and essentially return the U.S. to the unworkable Confederation that was abolished by the Constitution in 1789. Consequently, Jackson threatened to send 200,000 Federal troops to South Carolina unless they renounced their nullification law (Brinkley, 2003, 243). Unfortunately, the ideologically-driven Bush Administration is evidently unable to draw such lessons from history. Bush's conservative ideology teaches that "States' Rights" is the correct path and ignores the historical truth that a primary purpose of the writing of the Constitution in the first place was to create national supremacy since the State supremacy approach under the Articles of Confederation had not worked. This principle is explained in virtually every Freshman history and government, text, but either Bush has not read it, or his ideology filters out the information since it is inconsistent with his ideology.

Bush's assault on the social welfare system also includes a provision introduced in his Budget in 2003 that would reduce social welfare by reducing the number of children that would receive child care assistance by 300,000 children by the year 2009 (Mezey et al., 2004). Between 2002 and 2003, the number of children receiving child care assistance had already dropped by 100,000 due to cutbacks by the Bush administration (Mezey et al., 2004).

While it is true that this measure does reduce social welfare, a major goal of conservatives, what is less clear is whether or not it furthers the conservatives' insistence that low-income people find and hold employment. Instead, the reduction in child care assistance has occurred in spite of studies that have concluded that child care assistance programs in the last half of the 1990s increased employment and full-time work among TANF recipients (Fremstad, 2004). Given this information, it is difficult to conclude anything other than that Bush's policies reducing child care assistance are in conflict with his administration's stated policies that favor employment for low-income individuals; hence conservative ideology in this case is again in conflict with itself.

Bush and Health Care

As a principle, George W. Bush once stated, "Every low-income, working family in America must have access to basic health insurance—for themselves and their children" (Quoted in Corn, 2003, 44). When faced with what to do about the 43.6 million Americans without health insurance, Bush predictably relied on his "supply-side" ideology to provide him with a cure. For Bush, his standard ideological response to any problem (or at least those that do not require military action) is to implement a tax cut. Health Care is no different in this respect, so Bush's solution was a tax credit for families making under $30,000 a year that would pay up to $2000 toward the cost of a health insurance policy.

Unfortunately, rising health care costs have made it impossible for one to get adequate health coverage in the United States for a family of four for the $2000 a year provided under his plan. Instead, adequate family health insurance coverage is likely to cost approximately $5000 when deductibles and copays are included in the mix (Corn, 2003, 45). Furthermore, according to the *USA Today*, it is estimated that Bush's plan would expand coverage to less than 10% of the uninsured Americans, thus leaving most of the health coverage problem unsolved (Quoted in Corn, 2003, 45). In health care, as in other policy areas, Bush's ideology again evidently led him to believe that tax cuts and the free market correct all problems, but actual data suggest otherwise.

Medicare Expansion

In an obvious contradiction with Bush's anti-government and anti-entitlement ideology, however, in December 2003, President George W. Bush signed into law an expansion of the Medicare program to include prescription drug coverage. Bush announced that the plan would cost approximately $400 billion over the next decade, but subsequent analysis at the Department of Health and Social Security now estimates the cost at over $550 billion. The Department of Health and Social Security had passed that information on to the White House and Office of Management and Budget prior to passage, but Bush announced the lower estimate anyway. Evidently, the information was not passed on to Congress prior to passage because the Chief Administrator of Medicare, a Bush appointee, threatened to fire his Chief analyst if he told Congress of the higher estimates (*Economist*, April 3, 2004).

Deception aside, this expansion of Medicare is now expected to cost over $550 billion in the next decade and over $1 Trillion for the decade after that (Park et al., 2003). Obviously, this expansion of a federal government entitlement program is in conflict with Bush's tax cuts that deny the government the revenue to fund expansion of massive redistribution programs; therefore, the passage of the program can only exacerbate the country's budget problem created by the Bush tax cuts. The legislation does, however, reflect conservative laissez-faire ideology in that it includes no provisions aimed at controlling the spiraling costs of medical drugs.

Bush's Medicare program also reflects the Classic Liberal/Libertarian ideological preference for private, rather than governmental, provision of services in that it allows beneficiaries to elect to receive all of their Medicare benefits from private managed care plans (primarily HMOs). The federal government will then provide $14 billion a year in subsidies to the HMOs, thus creating an uneven playing field in favor of the subsidized HMOs at taxpayer expense.

Bush's plan also reflects his "supply-side" ideology, however, in that it provides for Health Savings Accounts. The proposed accounts would be tax-advantaged savings accounts established to pay out-of-pocket medical expenses. Holders of these accounts would be able to make tax-deductible deposits in them, watch the earnings compound tax-free, and pay no taxes on the funds upon withdrawal as long as they are used for medical expenses (Park et al., 2003).

Regardless of whether such a tax break has utility or not, it is clear that this tax break, along with Bush's other tax breaks, will certainly contribute to the national debt, in violation of what once was standard conservative "balanced budget" ideology. This is partially due to the fact that Bush's Health Savings Accounts are different than 401(k)s and traditional IRAs, since withdrawals from those accounts are taxed as ordinary income. Under the Health Savings Accounts, however, not only are deposits to be tax deductible and earnings then compounded on a tax-free basis, but withdrawals are also tax-free if used for a medical purpose; hence, the money in the Health Savings Account is *never* taxed if it is used for its intended purpose.

As a final note on Medicare, it should be mentioned that it is expected that Medicare obligations will exceed Medicare revenue over the next 75 years by over $8 Trillion. Similarly, Social Security obligations will exceed Social Security revenue over the same time period by over $3.5 Trillion. The cost of making Bush's tax cuts permanent over the same 75 years is estimated at $11 Trillion, or almost equal to the estimated cost of the Medicare and Social Security shortfalls (Greenstein and Orszag, 2004).

Bush and Social Security

As a Presidential candidate in 2000, Bush stated, "Social security is…a test of Presidential candidates—a measure of seriousness and resolve" (Quoted in Corn, 2003, 44). Like his approaches to other social programs, Bush's "resolve" concerning Social Security has reflected his conservative anti-government and anti-redistribution ideology. In Bush's own words, "They want the Federal government controlling Social Security like its some kind of Federal Program" (Quoted in *USA Today*, 2000).

To begin with, Bush's "resolve" has not been to ensure that Social Security will receive adequate funding (it would be difficult to do so and still maintain his tax cuts). In March, 2001, Bush pledged that Social Security funds would only be spent on Social Security, yet one year later, the Congressional Budget Office released a report revealing that Bush's budget would use $1.8 trillion in Social Security surpluses to pay for other government programs (Begala, 2002, 34). In other words, the long-term fiscal viability of Social Security was sacrificed in the interest of covering for Bush's ideologically-driven tax cuts. Bush himself acknowledged his awareness of the impending doom of Social Security in 2001 while visiting a senior center when he stated, "if we do nothing to reform the system, the year 2037 will be the moment of financial collapse" (Quoted in Corn, 2003, 42). One would think, therefore, since Bush believed that the Social Security trust fund would be bankrupt in 35 years, that he would not be raiding that same trust fund to support his tax cuts. That the tax cuts therefore had a long term detrimental effect on the viability of Social Security should be obvious. Ideology, however, evidently has the power to obscure the obvious. On the other hand, it may just be that Social Security, an income redistribution program, is in conflict with Bush's conservative ideological bent against "welfare" and his policies are well-calculated with the eventual destruction of the "statist" program as a goal.

To address what to do with Social Security, Bush put together a Presidential Commission on Social Security to study the matter. Bush ensured that the Commission would not make any recommendation that might threaten his tax cuts by admittedly stacking the Commission with like-minded conservative ideologues; hence, Bush's Press Secretary Arie Fleischer announced,

> "The commission that the President will announce will, of course, be comprised of people who share the President's view that personal retirement accounts are the way to save Social Security" (Quoted in Begala, 2002, 36).

In other words, the outcome of the Commission's "study" of Social Security had been predetermined by stacking the Commission with conservative privatization ideologues. In such an environment, all sides of an issue are unlikely to be weighed, dissenting voices are likely to be absent, and real critical thinking is necessarily compromised. Not surprisingly, in November 2001, the Commission released their recommendations with an outline of three possible plans, all of which were purposed to privatize Social Security (Corn, 2003, 43).

Bush's Commission correctly underlined the fact that the stock market growth over the previous 40 years had well outpaced the "return" on the tax money that people get from Social Security. Specifically, the Commission pointed out that over the long term, the stock market had averaged a 6% return, but the real return that people received from contributing to Social Security was only 2% (Corn, 2003, 43). Bush's Commission ignored, however, the fact that minimum wage workers could work all their life and contribute their Social Security taxes to an individual retirement account the entire time, but still end up destitute if they live for several decades beyond retirement age. In the United States at present, a 65 year-old man has an average life expectancy of 16 years, and an 18% chance of living to age 90. Life expectancy for women at 65 is 20 years, and a 65 year-old American woman has a 31% chance of living to age 90. In such cases of extended life span, it is reasonable to expect that a government redistribution plan would have to be retained to fill the gap for former low-wage earners that outlive their trust funds (*Economist*, March 27, 2004). Bush also conveniently ignored the fact that Social Security's "return" included disability and survivor's benefits, which account for approximately a third of Social Security payments. Consequently, the potential "gains" from shifting to a privatization plan were somewhat exaggerated (Corn, 2003, 43).

Bush planned to make the transition to a privatized Social Security system by taking 16% of employee contributions and diverting them from the current trust fund to be invested in private retirement accounts. Obviously, this would have caused a shortfall in the Trust Fund's capability to pay Social Security beneficiaries that are drawing Social Security in the present. Such a diversion would have caused the Trust Fund to be bankrupt in 2023, rather than 2037, unless Social Security benefits were reduced accordingly (Corn, 2003, 43). Consequently, Bush also planned to reduce the costs of Social Security by cutting benefits. Bush's administration essentially planned to do this by indexing Social Security benefits to inflation rather than to growth in wages. Since growth in wages has surpassed the inflation rate in recent decades, the shift would actually result in a reduction of Social Security benefits if the trend continued as expected. Bush also proposed increasing the age of Social Security eligibility (which has already been raised to age 67 beginning in 2009) and thus reducing federal obligations (Begala, 2002, 38-39). Even Bush's chief economic adviser at the time, Larry Lindsay, admitted in *Newsweek*, "Reductions in the guaranteed amounts of benefits that will go to plan participants are absolutely obvious, so I will say it" (Quoted in Corn, 2003, 43). These measures, if implemented, most certainly therefore would have reduced Social Security Benefits, and therefore government in general, in a manner consistent with conservative "less government" and "anti-socialism" ideology.

Enron Scandal

Whether or not Bush's Social Security proposals were in the interest of the common good, however, became moot by the end of 2002 due to what simply became known as "the Enron scandal." Enron was a corporate giant in the energy industry with close connections to the White House. As such, Enron contributed over $1.3 million to Bush and the Republican Party during the Presidential campaign of 2000. Furthermore, Enron CEO Ken Lay served on Bush's transition team and interviewed candidates for the Federal Energy Regulatory Commission (Begala, 2002, 100, 107). Enron was apparently viewed by the White House as a "model" company in the American capitalist model and Ken Lay was obviously respected by Bush as an honest and capable manager when the story broke in 2001 that Enron had over-reported its earnings and was, in fact, bankrupt. Thousands of Enron employees lost their life savings in worthless Enron stock that had been provided by the company as the corporate contribution to their employee retirement accounts. One of the most outrageous misdeeds in the Enron scandal was that the company prevented employees from selling the Enron stock in their retirement portfolios while the firm was in the process of becoming insolvent, but the Company's top executives simultaneously dumped over $1 billion worth of their own shares. During this same time period, Enron CEO Ken Lay even advised employees to purchase more Enron stock, while he sold approximately $50 million worth of his own Enron stock (Corn, 2003, 176). The Enron scandal proved once again that market investments are not always secure. In the aftermath of the Enron disaster, support in Congress for privatization of Social Security eroded and the Bush plan to privatize Social Security has not yet been realized.

Bush and Education

Education is an area of public policy that traditionally has been primarily a State concern, so one might expect a laissez-faire conservative President that favors privatization and "State's Rights" to do nothing with education policy except for to allow the States to run their own programs without interference. This may be especially true with Bush since his own educational experience was finished at the private schools, Andover Academy, Yale, and Harvard. Like other conservative Presidents before him over the last three decades, however, Bush continued and even expanded federal involvement in public education. The centerpiece of Bush's Federal education program is called the No Child Left Behind Act. When Bush signed the Act, Bush stated,

> "The new role of the federal government...is to set high standards, provide resources, hold people accountable, and liberate school districts to meet the standards...We're going to spend more on our schools, and we're going to spend it wisely" (Quoted in Begala, 2002, 48).

A month after President Bush signed the bill into law, however, Bush cut the funding for the program; hence, instead of "spending more on education" as Bush had promised, Bush's federal education budget proposal for 2003 was the smallest increase in education funding in seven years (2.8%) and barely enough to keep up with inflation (Begala, 2002, 48). Bush would follow those cuts with further cuts to education in his proposed budget of 2005 (*Amarillo Globe News*, June 7, 2005).

Bush's budget proposal also froze or reduced funding for a number of important federal education programs. Included was a freeze on funding for the Teacher Quality initiative, a program that helps States reduce class sizes and do a better job of training teachers, and the Twenty-First Century Community Learning Centers program, a program that provides safe, healthy places for children to learn after school. Funding was also cut 14% for the Safe and Drug-Free Schools Act, a program designed to build safe schools by reducing drugs and violence. Bush's budget provided less than half the funding allowed for the Individuals with Disabilities Education Act (IDEA) that provides funding to States to help with the education of special needs children, and Bush also proposed cutting $122 million from federal technology education programs. Similarly, Pell Grants were frozen at the previous year's maximum level of $4000.

The freeze on Pell Grants continued the trend during the conservative-dominated era since 1980 concerning federal education grants. In 1976, a Pell Grant covered 84% of the cost of attending a public University, but in 2003 it was only 40% (Begala, 2002, 49-53). These cuts followed Bush's 2001 proposal for a 19% reduction in spending on libraries at the same time that his wife, former school librarian Laura Bush, was engaging in a campaign to boost America's libraries, calling them "community treasure chests, loaded with a wealth of information available to everyone, equally" (Quoted in Moore, 2002, 104).

Bush and Foreign Policy

Perhaps nowhere has a policy area been more driven by conservative ideological abstraction than the foreign policy area of the George W. Bush Administration. Unfortunately, there is also perhaps no policy area where the results have been more controversial as well as deadly. Furthermore, the ramifications of the policies that the Bush administration has set in motion may take generations to reverse should the American people decide to pursue different directions.

Neoconservatism and the PNAC

Since Bush had no previous foreign policy experience, and his education in foreign affairs must be considered quite limited, foreign policy is an area where Bush must rely both on his famous "instincts" and his trusted foreign policy advisers. The majority of Bush's most important foreign policy advisers, with the exception of Secretary of State in his first term, Colin Powell, have proven to be largely a group of ideologues that subscribe to an ideology termed as "neoconservatism" espoused and formulated by a conservative Washington Think Tank known as the Project for the New American Century (PNAC).

"Neoconservatism," definitionally, is essentially conservatism that resists the most recent changes and calls for a return to the directions of a previous era. That being the case, the neoconservatives of the present are somewhat different than the neoconservatives of the past. In the 1980s, for instance, neoconservatives such as Jean Kirkpatrick, Daniel Bell, and Seymour Lipset were reformed liberals who had experienced a change of heart and desired to return to the policies that had been in vogue before the liberal "revolution" of the 1960s. The neoconservatives of the early Twenty-First century espouse similar goals, i.e., reversing the folly created by runaway "liberalism," but specifically oppose the "namby-pamby" multilateralism and preference for "soft power" pursued by the Clinton Administration in foreign policy. The most important group of neoconservatives with this ideological bent that are associated with the Bush administration and the PNAC includes Vice President Dick Cheney, Defense Secretary Donald Rumsfeld, and former Undersecretary of Defense Paul Wolfowitz, as well as former Vice President Dan Quayle, publishing magnate and former Presidential candidate Steve Forbes, and the President's own brother and Florida Governor, Jeb Bush.

According to the PNAC in their own "Statement of Principles" (PNAC, 1997), American foreign policy under the Clinton Administration had been "adrift" and had abandoned the "sound" principles of Ronald Reagan. PNAC argues for increases in military spending and an active role for the U.S. in promoting its interests abroad. Importantly, however, PNAC argues that the

> "history of the 20th Century should have taught us that it is important to shape circumstances before crises emerge and to meet the threats before they become dire" (www.newamericancentury.org, 1997).

Translated, what this means is that the PNAC believes that the great errors of the Twentieth Century are that fascism, Nazism, and communism were allowed to exist and grow unchecked until they wreaked havoc on the world and grew to such proportions that they could only be eliminated by tremendous and costly effort. The "lesson" that should be learned in the eyes of the PNAC is that tyrants cannot be "appeased," as the Allies attempted to do with Adolph Hitler in 1938, but must be thwarted at the outset.

In furtherance of this thinking, the PNAC argues that the U.S. must "challenge regimes hostile to our interests and values" (www.newamericancentury.org, 1997). In other words, the PNAC argues for Bush's policy that became known as "preemption," or the idea that the U.S. should take the initiative in overthrowing unfriendly and undemocratic governments, militarily if necessary, and replacing them with pro-U.S., capitalist, and democratic regimes. The "anti-American" and "undemocratic" rogue State of Iraq under Saddam Hussein would be a perfect example of the kind of regime the PNAC argues that the U.S. should militarily overthrow and replace. To fail to do so would be to repeat the error of 1938 and "appease" a tyrant, most probably leading to disastrous consequences.

That President Bush was persuaded by the arguments of these "neocons" is obvious since he launched what he himself termed as a preemptive war to oust Saddam Hussein from Iraq in March, 2003, and bring "freedom and democracy" to the Iraqi people. That the ideology has a few problems is also obvious since things in Iraq clearly have not gone according to the well-laid plans of the "neocons," Iraq (arguably) does not appear much closer to "freedom and democracy" than they were under Saddam Hussein, security in Iraq appears to be more fragile than it was prior to the invasion, and there is no evidence to suggest that the U.S. is safer from terrorism after the war than it was before it. Instead, the U.S. army is subject to daily terror attacks by Iraqi insurgents, and over 1800 Americans and 2200 coalition troops total have died in the fighting at this writing. Evidently, reality has again proven to be more complex than ideologically driven policies created by a conservative Washington Think Tank.

Protestant Fundamentalism and Bush's Foreign Policy

Besides the neocons, another major foreign policy influence on the Bush administration has been the influence of fundamentalist Protestant Christianity. Undoubtedly, Bush's war on terror is also a war of religion whether or not that was Bush's intention. Essentially, Bush's adversary that sparked the war on terror, Osama bin Laden, made the conflict a war of religion by asserting that "these events have divided the world into two camps, the camp of the faithful and the camp of the infidels" (Quoted in Phillips, 2004, 236). Bush himself confirmed at least part of bin Laden's assertion ("these events have divided the world into two camps") by proclaiming that "Every nation has a choice to make in this conflict...There is no neutral ground" and then later terming the war on terror as a "crusade" (Quoted in Phillips, 2004, 236).

Bush's religious right supporters tend to see the conflict in similar terms and many even view the conflict as part of the so-called "end times" cataclysmic struggle between Jesus and the anti-Christ. According to a 1999 Newsweek poll, 71% of evangelical Protestants believe in Armageddon, and 75%-80% of those believers in Armageddon supported George W. Bush (Phillips, 2004, 242). These same dispensationalist Protestants are decidedly pro-Israel in their views of Middle Eastern politics based on the premise that Israel plays a crucial role in the Divine plan for the end of the world

(Phillips, 2004, 243). Perhaps not coincidentally, Bush's Middle East policy has been decidedly pro-Israel, resulting in a significant rise in anti-American sentiments in the Muslim world. For example, a 2002 Pew Survey revealed that 83% of Indonesians, the world's most populous Muslim country, had negative attitudes toward the United States, up from just 36% the year previous. While perhaps coincidental, another element not lost on Muslim observers is the fact that some major neoconservatives, including Paul Wolfowitz and publisher William Kristol, are also Jewish. Finally, the rise in anti-Americanism appears to be linked specifically to Bush and his policies. In all but four of the nations polled in the spring of 2003, respondents said that the problem was "mostly Bush" rather than "Americans in general" (Phillips, 2004, 236).

Ideology and Bush's Foreign Policy Failures

Ever since the tragedies of the 9/11/01 terrorist attacks on the United States, Americans have been forced to ask the question; what went wrong? For conservative ideologues, of course, the answers are simple and easily conjured by ideology without investigation. The problem is that the Clinton administration did not pay any attention to terrorism, was "asleep at the wheel," did not vigilantly pursue Osama Bin Laden, and left President Bush without the necessary information to prevent the attacks. In short, the 9/11/01 terrorist attacks are directly the result of what Clinton either did or did not do, and no blame could be placed on the Bush administration, which had not even been in office a full eight months. This perspective, however, does not hold up to sound analysis. There is much blame to spread around for the 9/11/01 terrorist attacks, but at least part of the blame should be directed to the ideological constraints within the Bush administration.

Condoleeza Rice and the Focus on Great Power Conflict

First of all, one of Bush's most trusted foreign policy advisers is National Security Adviser Condoleezza Rice. Dr. Condoleeza Rice holds a Ph.D. in political science and is well read in international relations theory. Among the international relations theories with which Rice is obviously familiar is the systemic theory of international relations that became in vogue in political science during the 1980s. The systemic approach to international relations during the 1980s was exemplified by the work of Kenneth Waltz (1978), in his *Theory of Interantional Politics*. Waltz (1978, 97) argued that "students of international relations make distinctions between international political systems only according to the number of their great powers." In Waltz's view, only the great powers in international relations are important and smaller powers, such as Iraq, or nonstate actors, such as al Qaeda, may be ignored. A decade later, international relations scholars Robert Keohane and Joseph Nye (1989) essentially challenged Waltz's contentions that only great powers were of particular importance, arguing that nonstate actors were becoming increasingly important in international relations and could not be ignored. Similarly, Samuel Huntington (1993) argued that the greatest cause of international conflict in the world in the coming decades would be culture clash between developed democracies and traditional societies in developing countries.

Either Rice did not keep up with the more current readings among international relations scholars, or she discarded the newer theories as lacking merit, because in an article she wrote in *Foreign Affairs* (2000), Rice argued in Waltzian fashion that a foreign policy was required that "separates the important from the trivial," and she then chastised the Clinton administration for their failure to do that. China and Russia, Rice asserted, were what were really important and Clinton had "frittered away" American power and prestige by devoting too much time to what she viewed as "second or third-tier" concerns. In Rices' view, terrorism needed attention only insofar as it was used by rogue States to advance their interests. That Rice was captivated by neoconservative ideology in her arguments is blatantly obvious. Unfortunately, Rice's ideology allowed her to filter out information that was inconsistent with her ideological predispositions, with disastrous results.

According to Daniel Benjamin and Steven Simon, Director and Senior Director for counterterrorism on Clinton's National Security Council, Clinton's National Security adviser Sandy Berger explicitly told Rice when they handed her the files on al Qaeda that, "You're going to spend more time during your four years on terrorism generally and al-Qaeda specifically than any other issue" (Benjamin and Simon, 2002, 328). Rice, however, was not persuaded. Instead, Rice dismissed the Clinton administration's focus on terrorism as "empty rhetoric that made us look feckless" (*Washington Post.* January 20, 2002).

Richard Clarke (2004), who was known as the counter-terrorism "Tsar" and National Coordinator for Security, Infrastructure Protection, essentially concurs with Benjamin and Simon's overview of Rice's priorities. Clarke explains,

"As I briefed Rice on al Qaeda, her facial expression gave me the impression that she had never heard the term before…Rice looked skeptical…I realized that Rice, and her deputy, Steve Hadley, were still operating with the old Cold War paradigm" (Clark, 2004, 229-230).

Bush's Foreign Policy Directions Prior to 9/11/01

Instead of carefully analyzing the data handed to them by the Clinton administration personnel and focusing on al Qaeda, the Bush administration came into office with a belief that China posed an immediate and long-term threat to the U.S. Bush himself criticized the Clinton Administration for viewing China as a "strategic partner" instead of a "strategic competitor." As a consequence, Bush's top priority, and the security issue he had spoken of most frequently, was the construction of a national missile defense system that would have nothing to do with defense against terrorism (Benjamin and Simon, 2002, 329). Instead, in furtherance of Bush's goal of providing a check on China's power, Bush approved a multibillion dollar weapons sale to Taiwan (Benjamin and Simon, 2002, 330).

Concerning Iran, a country that has sponsored terrorism since the Islamic Revolution of 1979 and has had a hand in numerous terrorist attacks on the U.S., including the Khobar Towers bombing in Saudi Arabia in 1996 and the truck bombing of the marine compound in Lebanon in 1983 that killed 241 Americans, Bush was committed to normalizing trade relations (Benjamin and Simon, 2002, 330). This clearly indicates that Bush was not so concerned about terrorism. In fact, Bush even said so himself in an interview with Bob Woodward before he evidently realized that such candor could have serious negative political fallout (Woodward, 2002). It was only after the terror attacks of 9/11 that Bush would change his posture toward Iran to describe them as a part of the "Axis of Evil."

Bush's inattention to terrorism was reflected in numerous other policies pursued by his administration in the eight months leading up to 9/11/01 as well. In the area of finance for terrorist groups, the Clinton administration had pursued policies through the G-7 multilateral Financial Action Task Force and the Organization for Economic Cooperation and Development that would encourage countries with loose banking regulations into tightening their laws to make them more difficult for money launderers. The Bush administration, however, opposed such measures as "coercive" and unnecessary regulations of business that were contrary to American interests (*Time*, 2001, 73). The Clinton Administration had also pushed for, and at least on paper achieved, the creation of a National Terrorist Asset Tracking Center, but no funding for the Center was provided under the Bush Administration (Wechsler, 2001). The idea that the Bush Administration did not give tracking money for terrorism a high priority is reinforced by Richard Clarke (2004), who stated,

"When the Bush administration came into office, I wanted to raise the profile of our efforts to combat terrorist financing, but found little interest. The

President's economic adviser, Larry Lindsey, had long argued for weakening U.S. anti-money laundering laws in a way that would undercut international standards" (Clarke, 2004, 196).

According to Clark (2004, 196), the Bush administration distrusted everything from the Clinton Administration and anything multilateral in nature. The distrust of the Clinton Administration is surely related to Bush's Traditional Conservative ideology that divides the world into good and evil, black and white, and with us, or against us, but the opposition to multilateralism also reflects the influence of neoconservatism. It should be noted that Clinton defeated Bush's father for the Presidency in 1992; hence, in Bush's conception, Clinton himself may qualify as an evil enemy. Multilateralism, of course, was vehemently denounced by the neoconservatives in the PNAC think tank. In the neoconservative's ideology, multilateralism erodes America's sovereignty and therefore leads to a weak America. This argument can be traced back at least as far as the opposition to the Versailles Treaty and the League of Nations after WWI. In the words of Senator Albert Beverage in 1919, "The League of Nations is the work of amiable old grannies...who would emasculate America's manhood" (Quoted in Jones, 1996, 254). Finally, the proposed regulations on banking interfered with the free market and introduced greater governmental regulation of capitalism in violation of the tenets of the Reaganesque Classic Liberalism to which Bush subscribes. In the final analysis, since Bush's neoconservative ideology taught him that nonstate actors are not a real threat, such interference into the free market could not be justified.

Attorney General John Ashcroft showed that the Justice Department was expecting no terrorist attacks when he proposed cutting $65 million from Clinton's Federal grant program to local governments that assisted communities in buying equipment such as decontamination suits and radios that might be needed for dealing with response to a terrorist attack. Ashcroft also declined to support the FBI's request for $58 million that would have provided for the hiring of 400 counterterrorism agents, analysts, and translators (*New York Times*, February 28, 2002).

Terrorism Warnings

All in Bush's administration, however, were not so oblivious to the terror threats. Between May and August 2001, the FBI three times notified 18,000 State and local law enforcement agencies, and the FAA contacted every airline and airport with "credible, but not specific" terrorism threats (Benjamin and Simon, 2002, 342). In July, 2001, Egyptian President Hosni Mubarak informed the U.S. that his intelligence service had received information that al-Qaeda planned to attack President Bush at the annual G-7 meeting held that month in Genoa, Italy. The Italians mounted antiaircraft guns at the Genoa airport and the air space around the city was closed, and the G-7 meeting passed without incident, but Bush had been given another warning (Benjamin and Simon, 2002, 342).

Bush's reaction to that warning, as well as his reaction to the memo from Richard Clarke to Condoleezza Rice entitled "Bin Laden Plans Attacks on the United States" was to depart on August 4, 2001, for a vacation at Crawford Ranch. How Bush could nonchalantly go on vacation after receiving such threats is illustrative of the fact that his ideology taught him that al Qaeda was not a threat; consequently, he was unable to grasp the gravity of the danger in spite of the facts. Bush's ideological information filter is therefore perhaps as much to blame for the 9/11/01 terrorist attacks as any other government failure.

9/11 Attacks and Bush's Initial Response

In spite of the famous Clarke memo to Rice, the terrorist attacks of 9/11/01 clearly came as a shock to President Bush and his administration. At the time of the attacks, Bush was famously reading with children in a Florida school classroom. Bush's political adviser, Karl Rove, whispered in the President's ear evidently the news that the first plane had hit the Twin Towers. Bush continued reading with the schoolchildren, appearing as confused as a deer in the headlights of an oncoming car. Approximately thirty minutes later, Chief of Staff Andrew Card whispered the message in the President's ear that a second plane had hit the second tower, thus confirming for certain that America was under attack. Thirty minutes later, Bush appeared before television cameras and delivered a shaky statement describing what had happened as "an apparent terrorist" and declaring that he would chase down "those folks who committed this act" (Quoted in Bolton, 2005, 129).

Bush's first official response was to shut down all air travel in the United States at 9:50AM EDT, while he himself flew around the country from place to place, returning to Washington only at 7:00PM after all was clear. Bush's second Presidential directive was to accede to Vice President Cheney's recommendation to order American fighter planes to shoot down a passenger jetliner over Pennsylvania, at that time only sixty miles from Washington, D.C. (Bolton, 2005, 132). Perhaps most fortunate for Bush's political career, the shooting down of that passenger plane by an American military jet did not become necessary, but Bush's shaky response to the attack and frantic flight around the country did little to calm the panic that gripped the nation.

Bush and the War on Terror

Three days after the terrorist attacks of 9/11/01 Bush revealed his ideological approach to terrorism in a speech at the National Cathedral in Washington, D.C. when he argued that, "our responsibility to history is already clear: to answer these attacks and rid the world of evil" (Quoted in Bolton, 2005, 123). Bush's phrasing of the conflict with terrorists in good and evil terms reflected his Traditional Conservative ideological roots reminiscent of Seventeenth Century Puritanism. The terrorist attacks of 9/11/01 permanently altered Bush's presidency, but they did not alter his view of the world as a place populated by dangerous, threatening demons that must be confronted and vanquished. Sudenly, the events of 9/11/01 allowed Bush's already-present Traditional Conservative ideology, combined with neoconservatism, to become the driving forces behind American policy on virtually everything from civil liberties, to fiscal policy, to foreign policy. That Bush is a religious Protestant moralist somewhat after the Puritan American tradition is well documented, but the terror attacks of 9/11 evidently confirmed for him what he had always believed, that God had chosen him for a purpose, and then showed him what that purpose was (*New York Times*, March 23, 2002). Later, Bush again revealed his religious Protestant roots (and his own ignorance of the negative connotation of the word "crusade" among Muslims) when he referred to the war on terrorism as a "crusade," thus fostering fear and resentment in the Islamic world that Bush's War on Terror was in essence another Western attempt to stamp out Islam (Bolton, 2005, 134).

Bush's good versus evil worldview is not new in American political thought, but is consistent with the worldview of the Puritans, Woodrow Wilson during WWI, and the McCarthyists during the Cold War. Like Wilson during WWI, the evidence suggests that Bush views the American role in the War on Terror as one of the world's "good" crusaders who are called upon to thwart evil and tyranny worldwide. Rightly or wrongly, Americans and American leaders for the last hundred years have often viewed themselves as the only nation with the moral character and the material resources to confront such tyranny and evil in the world. In this, Bush's war on terror is consistent with McKinley's invasion of Cuba to save the Cuban people from Spanish "atrocities," Wilson's war "to make the world safe for Democracy," the global struggle against Nazism and Japanese militarism during WWII, and the long Cold War struggle against communism (Bolton, 2005, 145).

Congress, dominated by conservative Republicans, allowed Bush to put his ideology into action when they passed a resolution giving President Bush broad discretion in his direction of the military response to the 9/11 terrorist attacks. Section 2 (a) of the resolution states that,

> "The President is authorized to use all necessary and appropriate force against those nations, organizations, or persons he determines planned, authorized, committed, or aided the terrorist attacks that occurred on September 11, 2001, or harbored such organizations or persons, in order to prevent any future acts of international terrorism against the United States by such nations, organizations, or persons" (Pfiffner, 2004, 6).

Obviously, the resolution is extremely broad and leaves the war on terror largely to the discretion of the President, including the authority to take action to "prevent any future acts," thus providing Bush the authority to invade any nation (such as Iraq) if in his subjective judgment he determined that they might engage in "future acts" of terrorism against the U.S. Much like Lyndon Johnson considered the Gulf of Tonkin Resolution to be his "blank check" in Vietnam, this resolution of Congress is so broad that it is in essence a similar "blank check" that Bush has used at his discretion.

The Democrats in Congress offered little resistance to Bush's foreign policy directions. Instead, as Bush's approval rating soared to the 90% range, Democratic Senate Majority Leader Tom Daschle and House Minority Leader Dick Gephardt pledged bipartisan support for the President's leadership in the War on terror. Democratic Senator Robert Byrd of West Virginia even announced that he was praying for President Bush and told the President directly of the floor of Congress that, "Mighty forces will come to your aid." Evidently, however, "mighty forces" did not include Byrd himself since Byrd would later oppose Bush's invasion of Iraq (Bolton, 2005, 88).

Bush and the Invasion of Afghanistan

Bush initially used his "blank check" to pursue and destroy the terrorists that attacked the United States on 9/11/01. Informed by CIA director George Tenet that the culprits were most likely al Qaeda and their leader was Osama bin Laden, who was harbored by the Taliban in Afghanistan, Bush ignored the advice of neocons such as Paul Wolfowitz, who argued for an invasion of Iraq, and launched a war in Afghanistan against the Taliban and al Qaeda in 2002.

Several Middle Eastern States made requests to the Bush administration to see the evidence held by the Bush administration tying the 9/11 attacks to Bin Laden, but Bush refused on the basis that doing so would compromise American intelligence sources. Whether accurate or not, international critics of the Bush administration quickly concluded that Bush was without evidence, otherwise he would not object to sharing the intelligence (Bolton, 2005, 19).

For his part, Bush did not seem to care much what the rest of the world thought about the American War on Terror. For example, in his 2002 State of the Union Address, Bush referred to Iran, Iraq, and North Korea as an "Axis of Evil," a statement denounced by the French, British, and Russians as "simplistic" and denounced by South Korea as counter to their foreign policy goals. Bush also announced to the world his black and white view of the War on Terror when he proclaimed to the rest of the world that they are either "with us or against us" and announced that the U.S. would get the terrorists "dead or alive" with Texas swagger and bravado (Bolton, 2005, 64).

Although Bush had previously derided nation-building as a goal, after the Taliban government was ousted by American and Afghan rebel forces, Bush allocated resources to prop up a new American-backed government in Afghanistan that he hoped would grow into a friendly democracy (Pfiffner, 2004, 8). At this writing, significant numbers of American forces remain in Afghanistan on that same nation-building mission.

The success of the American mission in Afghanistan, however, was almost immediately in doubt. By June 2002, the *New York Times* ran a story that leaked out of the CIA concerning FBI and CIA studies of the War on terror. The FBI and CIA evidently concluded that the U.S.-led war in Afghanistan had "failed to diminish the threat to the United States," thus suggesting that the "war" part of the Afghan mission is in part a failure. Instead, the FBI and CIA conclusions were that the War had dispersed the loose coalition of radical Islamic terror groups over a larger geographic area and therefore made the War on terror more difficult (*New York Times*, June 16, 2002). As for the nation-building part of the mission, the creation of a healthy, American-friendly, Democracy appears to be long into the future.

In spite of these conclusions from Bush's own intelligence agencies, and even though the U.S. had not found the main target in the Afghan war, Osama bin Laden, by mid 2002, Bush began to turn his attention away from Afghanistan. In a speech at West Point in June, Bush declared that the growing threat to the U.S. from terrorism and rogue States made it necessary to consider preemptive military strikes in defense of the United States, thus laying the groundwork for an invasion of Iraq (Pfiffner, 2004, 9).

The End of Deterrence

Shortly following the terror attacks of 9/11, the Defense Department under Donald Rumsfeld began revising American nuclear strategy, which had been predicated on the concepts of deterrence and mutual assured destruction (MAD) since the 1960s. The Defense Department released a "nuclear posture review" that identified seven countries against which the

United States might use nuclear weapons under certain scenarios, including China, Russia, Iraq, Iran, North Korea, Libya, and Syria. The "nuclear posture review" directed the military to prepare contingency plans to use nuclear weapons against these seven countries and to build smaller nuclear weapons for use in battlefield situations. Exactly how this new strategy could be useful in stopping terrorism was unexplained, since the al Qaeda terrorists against whom Bush had declared war had no counties and knew no borders (Bolton, 2005, 104).

Bush and Iraq

Besides being distracted by the neoconservative focus on Great Power competition prior to 9/11/01, Bush and important neoconservative actors within his administration were also distracted from al Qaeda both before and after 9/11 by what can only be described as an obsession with Iraq. Unremembered by most Americans, Saddam Hussein sent a hit team into Kuwait in March, 1993 in an attempt to assassinate George H.W. Bush, who was in Kuwait on a speaking engagement two months after his term had ended in the White House (Hiro, 2002, 63). Bush's obsession with Iraq therefore might possibly be best explained as a personal vendetta instead of an ideological tangent. Only George W. Bush knows his true motive, and he is unlikely to publicly admit to such pettiness, but the motives of his subordinates, who are unlikely to be so strongly driven by any such revenge factor, appear to be driven by the neoconservative "preemption" ideology of the PNAC think tank.

In support of the notion that it is the neoconservative "preemption ideology" that drove Bush's Iraq policy, Richard Clarke (2004, 231-232) discusses an April, 2001 Deputies Committee meeting on terrorism, where he stressed the threat of al Qaeda to the other Deputies. According to Clarke,

"Paul Wolfowitz, Donald Rumsfeld's deputy at Defense, fidgeted and scowled. (Stephen) Hadley asked him if he was all right. "Well I just don't understand why we are beginning by talking about this one man Bin Laden," Wolfowitz responded."

When Clarke responded that al Qaeda posed an immediate and serious threat to the U.S., Wolfowitz replied, "Well, there are others that do that as well, at least as much. Iraqi terrorism for example" (Quoted in Clarke, 2004, 231). Clarke then responded that he knew of no Iraqi terrorism directed at the United States since 1993 (the Bush assassination attempt being the last), to which Wolfowitz replied that "Just because the FBI and CIA have failed to find the linkages does not mean they don't exist" (Quoted in Clarke, 2004,

231). Wolfowitz then announced that he resented any comparison between the Holocaust and "this little terrorist in Afghanistan."

In this exchange with Clarke, Wolfowitz clearly takes the ideological, "don't confuse me with the facts, path." The fact that Iraq was not behind al Qaeda terrorist attacks on the U.S. was inconsistent with Wolfowitz' PNAC goal of using the U.S. military to launch "preemptive strikes" against rogue States and replacing their despotic leaders with democratic regimes favorable to the U.S. The focus on al Qaeda was also inconsistent with the ideology of Condoleeza Rice, an ideology that Wolfowitz may have shared, that stresses the importance of focusing on great powers only and ignores non-state actors such as al Qaeda.

The exchange between Clarke and Wolfowitz was virtually repeated by Clarke and Secretary of Defense Donald Rumsfeld at a Principals Committee meeting on al Qaeda on September 4, 2001, that Clarke had "urgently"called for eight months prior. Merely the fact that it took eight months for the "terrorism Tsar" to get his meeting with the Principals demonstrates the low priority for terrorism in the Bush administration prior to 9/11. At any rate, according to Clarke, he, CIA director George Tenet, and Secretary of State Colin Powell, used the Principals meeting to lay out an aggressive strategy against al Qaeda, which Clarke explained as the primary terrorism threat. In the words of Clarke (2004, 238), however,

> "Rumsfeld, who looked distracted throughout the session, took the Wolfowitz line that there were other terrorist concerns, like Iraq, and whatever we did on this al Qaeda business, we had to deal with the other sources of terrorism."

Rumsfeld, like Wolfowitz, obviously had been reading his PNAC "preemption Bible" and evidently did not want to be confused with any facts. His plan, from the beginning, apparently had been to invade Iraq. According to former Treasury Secretary Paul O'Neill, on January 30, 2001, ten days in to Bush's administration, Bush met with the Principals of his National Security Council for the first time. In this meeting, during a discussion of the problems between Israel and the Palestinians, Bush turned to Condoleezza Rice and asked her what was next on the agenda. Rice's response was, "How Iraq is destabilizing the region." In what O'Neill then describes as a "scripted exchange," Rice had CIA director George Tenet unveil a photograph of a possible chemical or biological weapons factory in Iraq. Tenet did mention, however, that there was "no confirming intelligence as to the materials being produced" (Quoted in Suskind, 2004, 73). By the end of the meeting, O'Neill explains that Bush directed Colin Powell to draw up a new sanctions regime, and Donald Rumsfeld and Hugh Shelton were to examine military options and explain how it might look to use U.S. ground forces in Iraq in support of insurgents to topple Saddam Hussein. CIA director George Tenet was charged with investigating how the U.S. could use intelligence on Iraq (Suskind, 2004, 75).

One would assume after the 9/11/01 terrorist attacks, however, that Rumsfeld's obsession and focus on Iraq would have abated and been replaced with an obsession with al Qaeda; however, it appears that the Defense Secretary retained his obsession with Iraq even after the 9/11/01 terrorist attacks. According to O'Neill, Rumsfeld raised the question of invading Iraq just two days after the attacks on September 13, even though he knew that al Qaeda, not Saddam Hussein, was behind the attacks (Suskind, 2004, 184). This is in spite of the fact that, according to O'Neill, it was clear from NSC meetings that any connection between Saddam and al Qaeda was unlikely. In O'Neill's words,

"Saddam Hussein had been slaughtering Islamic fundamentalists for years—al Qaeda hated him as much as they did the United States. Saddam was no fool—he'd been tamping down fundamentalists in his country for two decades; the last thing he'd do was arm them, if he had any arms to give" (Quoted in Suskind, 2004, 279).

Rumsfeld had to be well-aware of these conclusions, but they were evidently ignored due to the over-riding ideology of preemption. Rumsfeld himself publicly admitted that he recalled saying to Bush that whenever the U.S. was attacked or threatened, the Clinton administration had followed a pattern of "reflexive pullback." In contrast, Rumsfeld argued that he believed that U.S. power was needed to help discipline the world (Quoted in Bolton, 2005, 136).

.Richard Clarke (2004) states that Bush asked him privately to investigate any links between al Qaeda and Iraq. When Clarke replied that it had already been investigated thoroughly and that no links existed, Bush urged him to look again and search hard for a link. Obviously, Bush and Rumsfeld were clearly aware that there was no link between Iraq and al Qaeda, but, their ideology had little use for contradictory information. O'Neill argues, therefore, that instead of rational thinking and sound analysis of facts, Bush's decision to invade Iraq was based on the ideology of preemption, and "the ideology was not subject to penetration by facts." Unfortunately, O'Neill concluded that the ideology itself is on a "collision course with reality" (Quoted in Suskind, 2004, 280, 305, 307) and O'Neill added, "trust me, they haven't thought this through" when discussing Bush's decision to invade Iraq (Suskind, 2004, 328). O'Neill is most certainly correct, since all ideologies are on a collision course with reality and ideology by nature does not "think things through," or it would not be considered ideology in the first place.

Warnings Against an Invasion of Iraq

Bush and his administration were also warned not to invade Iraq, not only by their own terrorism expert, but by others both within and without their administration. During the summer of 2002, a number of senior U.S. military officers, top generals, and members of the Joint Chiefs of Staff argued for a cautious approach to Iraq. Essentially, they argued that Iraq was not connected to the terrorist attacks of 9/11/01, containment of Saddam was working, and a U.S. military occupation of Iraq would be lengthy and problematic. Bush, however, simply brushed off the warnings of his military advisers by saying that "there's a lot of nervous nellies at the Pentagon" (Quoted in Pfiffner, 2005, 91). Bush's dismissal of these expert opinions once again displays his preference for ideology over analysis, and the fact that it was the preemption ideology of the neoconservatives that he found most persuasive, not facts.

The warnings to Bush not to invade Iraq were not limited, however, to the "nervous nellies" in the Pentagon. Brent Scowcroft, George H.W. Bush's National Security Adviser and mentor to Condoleeza Rice, wrote an opinion piece imploring Bush not to invade Iraq since there was little connection between Saddam Hussein and terrorism, even less to the 9/11 attacks, and an invasion ran the risk of alienating the U.S. in the international community. Similary, James Baker, Secretary of State for George H.W. Bush, argued that the costs of occupation of Iraq made the invasion unwise. Finally, James Webb, Assistant Secretary of Defense under Ronald Reagan, argued that there was no vital interest in Iraq that should lead to a policy change away from deterrence to a unilateral war and long-term occupation of Iraq. (Pfiffner, 2005, 91).

Adding to these civilian opinions were the warnings of retired high ranking, military leaders. Leading the chorus was retired General Anthony Zinni, Senior Adviser to Secretary of State Colin Powell and former Chief of the U.S. Central Command, who argued that the invasion would make enemies of people that did not need to be enemies. Zinni was not alone, however, as former Generals Wesley Clark and Norman Schwartzkopf expressed similar reservations. On August 5, 2002, even Bush's own Secretary of State, former Chairman of the Joint Chiefs, Colin Powell, evidently spent two hours with the President arguing that an invasion of Iraq would destabilize the Middle East, be viewed as hostile by the Muslim World, and should not be done unilaterally (Pfiffner, 2005, 91-92).

International leaders in the Middle East also warned the Bush administration against an invasion of Iraq. Jordan's King Abdullah publicly warned Dick Cheney, who was on a Middle East trip to explain U.S. policy in Iraq, that "U.S. military action against Iraq could undermine stability in the entire region" (Quoted in Bolton, 2005, 37). Hosni Mubarak of Egypt reiterated King Abdullah's position when Cheney arrived in Egypt on the same trip (Bolton, 2005, 37). Similarly, the Saudi Arabians, American allies in the first Gulf War, echoed the same message to Cheney when he visited the Kingdom on his Middle-Eastern tour. Crown Prince Abdullah, who essentially controlled politics in Saudi Arabia, told Cheney, "I do not believe it is in the U.S. interest, or the interest of the region, or the world's interest" for the U.S. to get involved in Iraq (Quoted in Bolton, 2005, 38).

Bush, for his part, heeded the advice of his Secretary of State only in that he made an attempt to gain multilateral support for his invasion. Not only did Bush send Dick Cheney on his tour of the Middle East in a futile attempt to gain multilateral Arab support, but he also attempted to work through the UN, calling for a UN resolution to oust Saddam if he did not disarm. At Bush's prodding, the UN Security Council issued Resolution 1441 that gave Iraq one week to promise to comply with U.N. orders to disarm, and if he did not, there would be widespread international support for military action against Iraq (Pfiffner, 2005, 93).

Onward To War

Meanwhile, Saddam Hussein in Iraq attempted to head off the impending American attack by announcing that he would respect Kuwait's borders and allow the return of U.N. weapons inspectors, moves that Prince Abdullah of Saudi Arabia announced that he accepted on "face value" (Bolton, 2005, 41). UN weapons inspectors quickly returned to Iraq, but were unable to find Iraq's weapons of mass destruction. The Bush administration, certain that the UN was covering for Saddam Hussein, ordered a CIA investigation of Chief UN weapons inspector Hans Blix (Bolton, 2005, 108).

The Bush administration then began a media blitz to sell the war to the American people and the world, warning that bridges, nuclear power plants, and shopping malls could be threatened. News was revealed about possible al Qaeda plots to deliver biological or chemical agents via crop dusters, and anthrax-laced letters that were conspicuously sent only to Democrats on Capitol Hill, were somehow traced by Bush administration officials to Iraq (Bolton, 2005, 42-43).

UN inspectors searched Iraq, but by late January, 2003 had still not found the dangerous weapons stockpiles referenced by the Bush administration. Bush, however, did not wait for a verdict from UN inspectors and instead began a troop buildup in the Middle East in preparation for war. When head UN weapons inspector Hans Blix pleaded for more time, the Bush administration denounced Iraq for noncompliance. Bush himself stated,

"This business about, you know, more time—you know, how much time do we need to see clearly that he's not disarming? This looks like a rerun of a bad movie and I'm not interested in watching it" (Washington Post, January 22, 3003).

In his State of the Union Address on January 28, 2003, Bush stated that the UN had given Saddam Hussein his "final chance to disarm," but "he has shown instead utter contempt for the United Nations and for the opinion of the world," a statement that sounds eerily like editorials in the European press about Bush himself. In the speech, Bush added allegations that Iraq had recently sought significant quantities of uranium from Africa, an allegation that would be refuted by Joseph Wilson, who investigated the matter in Niger and found the allegations to be groundless (Pfiffner, 2005, 94).

Nevertheless, the United States ordered the UN inspectors to leave, subsequently invaded Iraq in March, 2003, quickly overwhelmed the Iraqi army, and seized control of the country. On May 1, 2003, Bush landed on aircraft carrier in a fighter jet in a full flight suit in front of a huge banner that said "Mission Accomplished," and the neoconservative dream had finally come to full fruition. Bush declared the war to be over, but he evidently did not understand that a war is only over if both sides agree to cease fighting. Immediately, insurgents in Iraq began guerrilla attacks against the Americans that have continued through the present.

Bush said he ordered the invasion of Iraq to eliminate the Iraqi's "weapons of mass destruction" and liberate the Iraqi people from the "murderous" regime of Saddam Hussein, although Bush did also argue that the U.S. had to strike rogue States before they had the chance to strike the United States. This "preemption" assertion, of course, was straight from the PNAC's ideological Think Tank. Bush planned to then install a pro-American democratic regime in Iraq as advocated by the neocons in the PNAC.

The result of Bush's ideologically-driven folly is that Iraq is obviously less stable and more dangerous than it was before the U.S. invasion, terror attacks on the U.S. are no less likely, Iraq is not anywhere near approaching democracy, and a military dictatorship (America's) is still killing Iraqi people. Iraq's new Defense minister, installed by the United States, recently stated that he would send Saddam Hussein's resurrected army into Iraq's insurgency hot spots, conduct house-to-house searches, and personally "cut off the heads and hands" of insurgents (*Economist*, June 27, 4004). Somehow, this sounds more like the regime of Saddam Hussein than it does "freedom and Democracy." To make matters worse, at a press conference in the Rose Garden with Canada's new Prime Minister, Paul Martin, in May 2004, Bush asserted, "gone are Saddam Hussein's torture chambers and rape rooms"

(*Economist*, May 8, 2004, 34). Since picture proof hit the American media the previous week in April, 2004 demonstrating that those "torture chambers and rape rooms" were still in use, and they were still being employed for use as torture chambers by the U.S. army at Abu Ghraib prison, critics contended that the only change was that the torture chambers were no longer Saddam Hussein's, but George W. Bush's. In fact, to many Iraqis, the biggest difference in Iraq in general after over a year of American occupation appears to be that the military dictator oppressing, torturing, and killing Iraqi people is no longer named Saddam Hussein, but George W. Bush. If there is anywhere that the PNAC and the neoconservatives have proven to be correct, it is that it is folly to repeat the mistakes of the Twentieth Century and allow ideology to run amuck. Unfortunately, in the case of Iraq and the "war on terror," the ideology that appears to have run amuck is their own.

Concluding Remarks

In spite of an ongoing quagmire in Iraq, George W. Bush was re-elected President of the United States in November 2004, over the non-charismatic Democratic Senator from Massachusetts, John Kerry. Bush won by large margins in the traditionally conservative rural areas and areas of Protestant fundamentalist strength, while Kerry won in the more secular urban centers of the coasts. Fifty-one percent of Americans voted for George W. Bush, suggesting that his conservative ideologically-driven Presidency is consistent with the views of the majority of Americans.

Simultaneously, there was a collective groan of bewilderment issued from Europe, where Bush had generally been disparaged in the press for four years as the "Toxic Texan." For example, the Headline in the *London Daily Mirror* read, "How can 59,054,087 People be so dumb?" At the top of the publication was printed in the style of cartoon character Homer Simpson, the statement, "DOH, 4 More Years of DUBYA." As if that did not drive the point home far enough, inside the magazine, several pages of election coverage bore the heading, "U.S. Election Disaster." Similarly, in Germany, the printed-in-English headline on the German publication *Tageszeitung* read, "Ooops—they did it again." Sharing similar sentiments, in Switzerland, the cover of the Swiss newsmagazine *Facts* proclaimed, "Europe's Nightmare," while another Swiss weekly, *L'Hebdo* disparagingly asked, "Victory for the Hothead: How far will he go?" (msnbc.msn.com)

The European dismay over Bush's re-election could be discounted if it were merely limited to a few publications in the left-wing European media; however, this does not appear to be the case; rather, it instead appears that such sentiments were representative of a general consensus in European public opinion. For example, in fifteen countries surveyed in June 2003 (two and a half years into Bush's Presidency), favorable opinions of America were between fifteen and twenty points lower than they had been prior to Bush's 2000 election. Almost two thirds of Europeans, including 81% of Germans and 82% of French, disapproved of George W. Bush's handling of foreign policy. In Britain, widely viewed as America's closest ally in the world, 60% polled in November, 2003 labeled Bush a threat to world peace, 37% labeled Bush as stupid, and 33% considered Bush to be incoherent. Conversely, only 10% of respondents indicated that they believed Bush to be intelligent and only 7% responded that they considered him a good world leader. If the "Toxic Texan" were facing reelection in Europe, it appears that his prospects would have been grim (Micklethwait and Wooldridge, 2004, 293-294).

Meanwhile, however, in the United States Americans exhibited very different attitudes. Bush's defeat of Democratic challenger John Kerry suggests that a far greater percentage of Americans than 7% (as the polls indicated in Britain) considered Bush to be a good world leader. Instead of rejecting Bush along with their European counterparts, the election revealed that the so-called "Toxic Texan" was the choice of the majority of the American electorate and that Americans thought very differently than their European counterparts. This glaring difference in political views between Europeans and Americans is simply the latest version of "American exceptionalism" based on the Burkeian conservatism that has permeated American history and been perpetuated by its history, geography, and demographics. In the final analysis, the 2004 Presidential election results demonstrate that the United States has remained politically in the first decade of the new millennium, an "exceptional" country in comparison to Europe, dominated by conservatives who control the Presidency, U.S. Supreme Court, and both Houses of Congress. George W. Bush, who is viewed as disparagingly exceptional in Europe, is now representative of the political views of the majority of American voters, (much to the chagrin of the Europeans). Whether the Bush administration is the last hurrah for American Burkeian conservatism in the ever-smaller and more interconnected world remains to be seen, but the resilience and consistency of American conservative "exceptionalism" since the landing of the Pilgrims at Plymouth suggests that Europeans may be holding their collective noses for some time to come.

Bibliography

Aaron, Henry, and William B. Schwartz. 1984. *The Painful Prescription: Rationing Hospital Care*. Boston, Beacon Press.

Adams, Samuel Hopkins. 1970. *Incredible Era: the Life and times of Warren Gamaliel Harding 1865-1920*. Columbus, OH: Ohio State University Press.

Adams, Sam. 1975. "Vietnam Cover-up: Playing War with Numbers." *Harper's*. May.

Adelson, Joseph, and Robert O'Neil. 1970. "Growth of Political Ideas in Adolescence: The Sense of of Community." In Roberta S. Sigel Ed. *Learning About Politics: A Reader in Political Socialization*. New York: Random House.

Aiken, Henry D. 1956. *The Age of Ideology: The Nineteenth Century Philosophers*. New York: Mentor.

Alexander, Charles C. 1965. *The Ku Klux Klan in the Southwest*. Lexington, KY: University of Kentucky Press.

Alexander, Edward. 1938. *A Revolutionary Conservative, James Duane of New York*. New York: Columbia University Press.

Altman, Dennis. 1986. *AIDS in the Mind of America*. New York: Anchor Books.

Ambrose, Steven. *Eisenhower: the President*. New York: Simon and Schuster, 1984.

American Civil Liberties Union. 1996. "ACLU Submits Statement Before House Anti-Gay Marriage Hearing." Washington D.C.: *ACLU*, May 22.

_____. 1996. "ACLU Says that Clinton Panders to Bigotry With Announcement That He Will Sign Ban on Same-Sex Marriage." Washington, D.C.: *ACLU*, May 22.

_____. 1996. "ACLU Criticizes Allies for Jumping Ship on Gay Marriage." Washington, D.C.: *ACLU*, July ll.

_____. 1996. "Testimony Regarding S. 1740-Defense of Marriage Act." Washington, D.C.: *ACLU*, July 11.

444 Bibliography

_____. 1996. "ACLU Condemns House Passage of Anti-Gay Marriage Bill, Says Measure is Unconstitutional and Bad Public Policy." Washington, D.C.: *ACLU*, July 12.

_____. 1996. "ACLU Background Briefing: Congress Considers Anti-Gay Marriage Bill and Employment Non-Discrimination Act." Washington, D.C.: *ACLU*, August 6.

_____. 1996. "ACLU Blasts Senate Passage of Anti-Gay Marriage Ban." Washington, D.C.: *ACLU*, September 10.

_____. "Statewide Anti-Gay Marriage Law." Washington, D.C.: *ACLU*, January, 6, 1998.

American Monthly Review of Reviews. 1908. Volume 38.

American Spectator. 1995. July.

Anderson, Ronald, and John F. Newman. 1990. "Societal and Individual Determinants of Medical Care Utilization in the United States." In S.J. Williams, Ed. *Issues in Health Services*. New York: Wiley and Sons.

Andrews, Pat. 1993. *Voices of Diversity*. Guilford, CT: Dushkin.

Attarian, John. 1996. "The Entitlement Time Bomb." *The World and I*. November.

Bacon, Kenneth H. 1989. "AARP Now Championing Health Care for All, Scrambles to Prove it's More than a Paper Tiger." *Wall Street Journal*. December 27.

Baer, Robert. 2002. *See No Evil*. New York: Three Rivers Press.

_____. 2003. *Sleeping With the Devil*. New York: Crown Publishers.

Baker, Peter. 2001. *The Breach: Inside the Impeachment and Trial of William Jefferson Clinton*. East Rutherford, NJ: Berkley Trade.

Bane, M.J., and D. Ellwood. 1994. *Welfare Realities: From Rhetoric to Reform*. Cambridge, MA: Harvard University Press.

Bardach, Eugene, and Robert Kagan. 1982. *Going by the Book: The Problem of Regulatory Unreasonableness*. Philadelphia: Temple University Press.

Bassett, John, ed. 1989. *The Writings of Colonel William Byrd of Westover in Virginia Esq*. New York: Doubleday.

Bayer, Ronald, and Daniel Callahan. 1985. "Medicare Reform: Social and Ethical Perspectives." *Journal of Health Politics, Policy, and Law*. 10 (3).

Beck, Allen. 1995. "Survey of State Prison Inmates." Washington, D.C.: U.S. Department of Justice, Bureau of Justice Statistics, March.

Becker, Carl L. 1909. *The History of Political Parties in the Province of New York, 1760-1776*. Madison, WI: University of Wisconsin.

Begala, Paul. 2002. *It's Still the Economy Stupid*. New York, Simon and Schuster.

Bell, Daniel. 1960. *The End of Ideology: On the Exhaustion of Political Ideas in the Fifties*. New York: Free Press.

Bell, P.M.H. 1986. *The Origins of the Second World War in Europe*. London and New York: Longman.

Bellah, Robert, Richard Madsen, William Sullivan, Ann Swidler, and Steven M. Tipton. 1985. *Habits of the Heart: Individualism and Commitment in American Political Life*. Berkley, CA: University of California Press.

Bennett, Ralph Kinney. 1994. "Tour Risk Under the Clinton Health Plan." *Reader's Digest*. March.

Benjamin, Daniel, and Steven Simon. 2002. *The Age of Sacred Terror*. New York: Random House.

Benson, Lee. 1961. *The Concept of Jeffersonian Democracy: New York: A Test Case*. Princeton: Princeton University Press.

Berlet, Chip. 1998. "Dances with Devils." *Political Research Associates*. www.publiceye.org.

Bernays, Edward. 2004. *Propaganda*. Brooklyn, NY: IG Publishing.

Bernstein, R. B. 2003. *Thomas Jefferson*. New York, Oxford: Oxford University Press.

Billig, Michael. 1979. *Fascists: A Social Psychological View*. New York: Academic Press.

Billington, Ray Allen. 1938. *The Protestant Crusade 1800-1860*. New York: Rinehart.

Bishop, George 2003. *New England Judged by the Spirit of the Lord*. Whitefish, MT: Kessinger Publishing.

Blumstein, Alfred. 1995. "Prisons." In James Q. Wilson and Joan Petersilia Eds., *Crime*. San Francisco: Institute for Contemporary Studies.

Blumenthal, Sydney. 1990. *Our Long National Daydream. A Political Pageant of the Reagan Era*. New York: HarperCollins.

Bolles, Blair. 1951. *Tyrant from Illinois: Uncle Joe Cannon's Experiment with Personal Power*. New York: W.W. Norton.

Bolton, Kent. 2005. U.S. *Foreign Policy and International Politics: Geogre W. Bush, 9/11, and the Global-Terrorist Hydra*. Englewood Cliffs, NJ: Pearson Prentice-Hall.

Bosso, Christopher J. 2000. "Environmental Groups and the New Political Landsdcape." In Kraft and Vig eds. *Environmental Policy*. Fourth Edition. Washington, D.C.: Congressional Quarterly Press.

Boston Globe. 2001. March 21.

_____. 1968. September 29, 4A.

Boucher, Jonathan. 1967. *Reminiscences of an American Loyalist, 1738-1789*. Port Washington, NY. Kennikat Press.

_____. 1967. *Views of the Causes and Consequences of the American Revolution*. New York: Russell and Russell.

Bradford, William. 1856, 1981. *Of Plymouth Plantation 1620-1647*. New York: Random House.

Branch, Taylor. 1989. *Parting the Waters: America in the King Years 1954-1963*. New York: Simon and Schuster.

Breckenridge, Adam C. 2002. "The History of the Constitution of the United States." In Bruce Stinebricker Ed. *Annual Editions: American Government 02/03*. Guilford, CT: Dushkin/McGraw-Hill.

Brinkley, Alan. 2003. *American History: A Survey*. 11th Edition. Boston, MA: McGraw-Hill.

Bronner, Ethan. 1989. *Battle for Justice*. New York: W.W. Norton.

Brookhiser, Richard. 2003. *Rules of Civility: 110 Precepts that Guided Our First President in War and Peace*. Charlottesville, VA: University of Virginia Press.

Broun, Heywood, and Margaret Leech. 1927. *Anthony Comstock: Roundsman of the Lord*. New York: Albert and Charles Boni.

Brown, Lawrence D. 1985. "The Managerial Imperative and Organizational Innovation in Health Services." In Eli K. Ginzberg, Ed. *The U.S. Health Care System: A Look to the 1990s*. Totowa, NJ: Rowman and Allenheld.

Broyles, J. Allen. 1964. *The John Birch Society: Anatomy of a Protest*. Boston: Beacon Press.

Bryce, James. 1888, 2004. *The American Commonwealth*. Kila, MT: Kessinger.

Buchanan, Patrick J. 1973. *The New Majority: President Nixon at Mid-Passage*. Philadelphia: Girard Bank.

Buckley, William F. 1951. *God and Man at Yale: The Superstitions of Academic Freedom*. Washington, D.C.: Regnery Gateway.

_____. 1971. "Say It Isn't So, Mr. President." *New York Times Magazine*.

Buckley, William, and Brent Bozell. 1954. *McCarthy and His Enemies: The Record and Its Meaning*. Chicago: Regnery.

Burner, David 1979. *Herbert Hoover: A Public Life*. New York: Knopf.

Butts, R. Freeman. 1950. *The American Tradition in Religion and Education*. Boston: Beacon Press.

Butz, Arthur R. *The Hoax of the Twentieth Century: The Case Against the Presumed Extermination of European Jewry*. 2003. Chicago: Theses and Dissertations Press.

Califano, Joseph. 1991. *The Triumph and Tragedy of Lyndon Johnson: The White House Years*. New York: Simon and Schuster.

Callahan, Daniel 1987. *Setting Limits: Medical Goals in an Aging Society*. New York: Simon and Schuster.

Calvert, Robert A., Arnoldo De Leon, and Gregg Cantrell. 2002. *The History of Texas*. Third Edition. Wheeling, Illinois: Harlan Davidson.

Campbell, Robert. 2003. *Gone to Texas*. New York: Oxford University Press.

Campbell, Angus, Philip E. Converse, Warren E. Miller, and Donald E. Stokes. 1960. *The American Voter*. New York: John Wiley and Sons.

Cannon, Lou. 1991. *President Reagan: The Role of a Lifetime*. New York: Simon and Schuster.

Cantor, David. 1994. *The Religious Right: The Assault on Tolerance and Pluralism in America*. New York: Anti-Defammation League.

Carson, Gerald H. 1997. "Who Put the Borax in Dr. Wiley's Butter." In Kenneth G. Alfers, C. Larry Pool, and William Mugleston eds. *Perspectives On America, Volume 2: Readings in United States History Since 1877*. New York: Forbes Custom Publishing.

Carter, Landon. 1965. *The Diary of Colonel Landon Carter*. Charlottesville, VA: University of Virginia Press.

Cash, W. J. 1941. *The Mind of the South*. New York: Knopf.

Cassels, Alan. 1968. *Fascist Italy*. Wheeling, IL: Harlan Davidson.

Castro, Janice. 1994. *The American Way of Health: How Medicine is Changing and What it Means to You*. Boston: Little, Brown.

Center for Budget and Policy Priorities. 2003. "Number of Americans Without Helath Insurance Rose in 2002." October 8.

_____. 2003. "Poverty Increases and Median Income Declines for Second Consecutive Year." September 29.

Chalmers, David M. 1965. *Hooded Americanism: The History of the Ku Klux Klan*. New York: Doubleday.

Chamberlin, William Henry. 1950, 1962. *America's Second Crusade*. Chicago: Ralph Myles Publishing.

Chernow, Ron. *Alexander Hamilton*. 2004. New York: Penguin-Putnam.

Chinard, Gilbert Ed. 1934. *A Huguenot Exile in Virginia: Or Voyages of a Frenchman Exiled for His Religion with a Description of Virginia and Maryland*. New York: The Press of the Pioneers.

Chodorov, Frank. 1954. *Income Tax: The Root of All Evil*. New York: Devin-Adair.

Clarke, Richard. 2004. *Against All Enemies: Inside America's War on Terror*. New York: Free Press.

Clear, Todd, and George F. Cole. 1990. *American Corrections*. Second Edition. Pacific Grove, CA: Brooks/Cole.

Cleghorn, Reese. 1968. *Radicalism: Southern Style*. Atlanta: Southern Regional Council.

Colden, Cadwallader. 1973. *The Letters and Papers of Cadwallader Colden*. New York: AMS Press.

Cole, Wayne S. 1953, 1971. *America First: The Battle Against Intervention 1940-1941*. Madison, WI: Octogon Books.

Conason, Joe, and Gene Lyons. 2000. *The Hunting of the President: The Ten Year Campaign to Destroy Bill and Hillary Clinton.* New York: Bedford/St. Martin's.

Congressional Budget Office. 2001. "Budget and Economic Outlook: Fiscal Years 2002-2011." January 1.

Congressional Quarterly Weekly Report. 1983. "Administration of Justice Escapes Deep Spending Cuts in New Reagan Budget Plan." February 13.

Congressional Record. 1954. 82nd Congress, 1st Session, 4515, 1956.

_____. 83rd Congress, Second Session, 16001.

Conley, Richard S. 2005. "Introduction," in Richard S. Conley ed., *Transforming the American Polity: The Presidency of George W. Bush and the War on Terrorism.* Upper Saddle River, NJ: Pearson Education.

Conservative Digest. 1982, May.

Contosta, David R., and Robert Muccigrosso. 1988. *America in the Twentieth Century: Coming of Age.* New York: Addison-Wesley.

Corn, David. *The Lies of George W. Bush.* 2003. New York: Crown.

Cousins, Norman. *In God We Trust.* 1958. New York: Harper and Brothers.

Cox, Patrick L. 2002. *Ralph W. Yarborough: The People's Senator.* Austin, TX: University of Texas Press.

Coyne, John R. 1972. *The Impudent Snobs: Agnew vs. The Intellectual Establishment.* New Rochelle, NY: Arlington House.

Craven, Avery. 1942. *The Coming of the Civil War.* New York: Scribner.

Cram, Ralph Adams. 1937. *The End of Democracy.* Boston: Marshall Jones.

Cremin, Lawrence A. 1970. *American Education: The Colonial Experience 1607-1783.* New York: HarperCollins.

Crispino, Ralph J. 1996. "The EPA Dilemma." In Theodore and Theodore Eds. *Major Environmental Issues Facing the 21st Century.* Upper Saddle River, NJ: Prentice-Hall.

Cromartie, Michael. 1993. *No Longer Exiles: The Religious New Right in American Politics.* Washington, DC: Ethics and Public Policy Center.

Croly, Herbert. 1997. *Progressive Democracy.* Somerset, NJ: Transaction Publishers.

Cross, Barbara M., ed. 1961. *The Autobiography of Lyman Beecher.* Cambridge, MA: Harvard University Press.

Cross, Whitney R. 1950. *The Burned-over District.* Ithaca, NY: Cornell University Press.

Csikszentmihalyi, Mihaly, and Reed Larson. 1984. *Being Adolescent: Conflict and Growth in Teenage Years.* New York: Basic Books.

Cummings, Homer, and Carl McFarland. 1937. *Federal Justice.* New York: Macmillan.

Current, Richard N. *Daniel Webster and the Rise of National Conservatism.* Boston, Little, Brown, 1955.

Dahl, Robert. 2003. *How Democratic is the American Constitution?* New Haven, CT: Yale University Press.

Darman, Richard. 1996. *Who's in Control: Polar Politics and the Sensible Center.* New York: Simon and Schuster.

Davis, David Brian. "Some Themes of Counter-Subversion: An Analysis of Anti-Masonic, Anti-Catholic and Anti-Mormon Literature." *Mississippi Valley Historical Review.* XLVII, 1960.

Davis, Patti. 1992. *The Way I See It.* New York: Jove Books.

Dean, John. 1976. *Blind Ambition: The White House Years.* New York: Simon and Schuster.

Dean, John. 2003. *Worse than Watergate: The Secret Presidency of George W. Bush.* New York: Little, Brown.

Denver Post. 2001. March 15.

Desmond, Humphrey J. 1912. *The APA Movement: A Sketch.* Washington, D.C.: New Century Press.

De Toqueville, Alexis. 1835, 2001. *Democracy in America.* New York: HarperCollins.

DiIulio, John. 1995. "The Federal Role in Crime Control." In James Q. Wilson and Joan Petersilia Eds. *Crime.* San Francisco: Institute for Contemporary Studies.

Dinnerstein, Leonard. 1968. *The Leo Frank Case.* New York: Columbia University Press.

Dobelstein, Andrew. 1999. *Moral Authority, Ideology, and the Future of American Social Welfare.* Boulder, CO: Westview Press.

Donald, David. 1961. *Lincoln Reconsidered.* New York: Vintage.

Drew, Elizabeth. 1996. *Showdown: The Struggle Between the Gingrich Congress and the Clinton White House.* New York: Simon and Schuster.

D'Souza, Dinesh. 1984. *Falwell, Before the Millennium.* Chicago: Regnery Gateway.

Dunn, Charles W., and J.David Woodard. 1991. *American Conservatism from Burke to Bush: An Introduction.* Lanham, MD.: Madison Books.

Eatwell, Roger. 1989. "The Nature of the Right, 2: The Right as a Variety of Styles of Thought." In Roger Eatwell and Noel O'Sullivan Editors, *The Nature of the Right.* Boston, MA: Twayne.

Ebenstein, William, and Alan O. Ebenstein. 1992. *Introduction to Political Thinkers.* Fort Worth, TX: Harcourt Brace.

Economist. 1994. "Inequality: For Richer, For Poorer." November 5, 19-21.

_____. 2003. "Honor Laws." June 21.

_____. 2003. November 1.

_____. 2004. "New Fuel for the Culture Wars." March 5.

_____. 2004. "Forever Young." March 27.

_____. 2004. "A Matter of Trust." April 3.

_____. 2004. April 10.

_____. 2004. "Lexington: A House Divided." May 8.

_____. 2004. "Special Report: The Reagan Legacy." June 12.

_____. 2004. June 26.

_____. 2005. June 25.

Edwards, Lee. 1995. *Goldwater: The Man Who Made a Revolution.* Washington, Regnery.

Egan, Timothy. 1995. "Triumph Leaves No Targets for Conservative Talk Shows." *New York Times.* January 1.

Ellerbe, Helen. 1995. *The Dark Side of Christian History.* Orlando, FL: Morninstar and Lark.

Ellis, Joseph J. 2004. *His Excellency: George Washington.* New York: Random House.

Emery, Edwin. 1999. *The Press and America: An Interpretive History of the Mass Media.* Ninth Edition. Englewood Cliffs, NJ: Pearson.

Erikson, Kai. 1966. *Wayward Puritans: A Study in the Sociology of Deviance.* Boston: Allyn and Bacon.

Etzioni, Amitai. 1994. "Has the ACLU Lost Its Mind?" *Washington Monthly.* October, 9-11.

Evans, Rowland, and Robert Novak. *Nixon in the White House: The Frustration of Power*: New York: Random House, 1972.

Falwell, Jerry. 1980. *Listen, America!* New York: Doubleday-Galilee.

Farber, David. 1988. *Chicago 68.* Chicago: University of Chicago Press.

Farmer, Brian R. 2003. *American Domestic Policy: Substance and Process.* Lanham, MD: University Press of America.

Farquhar, Michael. 2003. *Great American Scandals.* New York, London: Penguin.

Ferguson, E. 1961. James. *Power of the Purse: A History of American Public Finance.* Chapel Hill, NC: University of North Carolina Press.

Ferrell, Robert H. 1998. *The Presidency of Calvin Coolidge.* Lawrence, KS: University of Kansas Press.

Ferry, Barbara. 1997. "New Mexico Congressman Linked to 'Wise Use' Movement." *States News Service.* June 5.

Fingerhut, Lois, and Joel C. Kleinman. 1990. "International and Interstate Comparisons of Homicide Among Young Males." *Journal of the American Medical Association.* 263 (24) June.

Finke, Roger, and Rodney Stark. 1993. *The Churching of America 1776-1990. Winners and Losers in Our Religious Economy.* Camden, New Jersey: Rutgers University Press.

Fischer, David Hackett. 1975. *The Revolution of American Conservatism.* Chicago, IL: University of Chicago Press.

Fisher, Louis. 2005. "Challenges to Civil Liberties in a Time of War," In Richard S. Conley, ed., *Transforming the American Polity: The Presidency of George W. Bush and the War on Terrorism.* Upper Saddle River, NJ: Pearson/Prentice-Hall.

Flower, Milton. 1983. *John Dickinson: Conservative Revolutionary.* Charlottesville, VA: University of Virginia Press.

Flynn, John T. 1955. The *Decline of the American Republic and How to Rebuild It.* New York: Devin-Adair Publishers.

Fowler, Robert Booth, and Jeffrey R. Orenstein. 1993. *An Introduction to Political Theory.* New York: HarperCollins.

Fox, Dixon Ryan. 1965. *The Decline of Aristocracy in the Politics of New York 1801-1840.* New York: Harper Torchbooks.

Frankel, Max. 1999. *The Times of My Life and My Life with the Times.* New York: Random House.

Franken, Al. 1999. *Rush Limbaugh is a Big Fat Idiot: And Other Observations.* New York: Dell.

_____. 2003. *Lies and the Lying Liars Who Tell Them: A Fair and Balanced Look at the Right.* New York: E.P. Dutton.

Franklin, Daniel. 1995. "Act Now—There's Still Time to Stop the Revolution." *The Washington Monthly.* September.

Freeden, Michael. 2003. *Ideology: A Very Short Introduction.* Oxford and New York: Oxford University Press.

Freedom Writer. 1995. February.

Freehling, William H. 1992. *Prelude to Civil War. The Nullification Controversy in South Carolina 1816-1836.* New York: Oxford University Press.

Freeman, Douglas S. 1996. *Washington.* New York: Simon and Schuster.

Freidel, Frank. 1964. *The New Deal and the American People.* Englewood Cliffs, NJ: Prentice-Hall.

Fremstad, Shawn. 2004. "Recent Welfare Reform Research Findings: Implications for TANF Reauthorization and State TANF Policies." *Center on Budget and Policy Priorities.* January 30.

Fremstad, Shawn, and Sharon Parrott. 2004. "Superwaiver Provision in House TANF Reauthorization Bill Could Significantly Weaken Public Housing, Food Stamps, and Other Low-Income Programs." *Center on Budget and Policy Priorities.* March 23.

Friedman, Milton. 1962. *Capitalism and Freedom.* Chicago: University of Chicago Press.

Friedman, Milton, and Anna J. Schwartz. 1966. *The Great Contraction, 1929-1933.* Boston: Houghton Mifflin.

Forst, Brian. 1995. "Prosecution and Sentencing." In James Q. Wilson and Joan Petersilia Eds. *Crime*. San Francisco: Institute for Contemporary Studies.

Forst, Brian, and Kathleen Brosi. 1977. "A Theoretical and Empirical Analysis of the Prosecutor." *Journal of Legal Studies*. 6.

Furniss, Norman. 1963. *The Fundamentalist Controversy, 1918-1931*. Hamden, CT: Archon Books.

Gaer, Joseph, and Ben Siegel. 1964. *The Puritan Heritage: America's Roots in the Bible*. New York: Mentor Books.

Garraty, John A. 1991. The *American Nation: A History of the United States Since 1865*. Seventh Edition. New York: HarperCollins.

Garraty, John A., and Robert McCaughey 1987. The *American Nation: A History of the United States Since 1865*. Sixth Edition. New York: HarperCollins.

Germond, Jack W. and Jules Witcover. 1981. *Blue Smoke and Mirrors: How Reagan Won and Why Carter Lost the Election of 1980*. New York: The Viking Press.

Getter, Lisa. 2001. "Florida Net Too Wide in Purge of Voter Rolls." *Los Angeles Times*. May 21.

Gilliard, Darrell K. 2003. "Prisoners in 2002." Washington, D.C.: Bureau of Justice Statistics. May.

Glamour, 2000. June.

Goldman, Peter, Mark Miller, Andrew Murr, Tom Mathews, and Thomas DeFrank. 1994. *Quest for the Presidency 1992*. College Station, TX: Texas A&M University Press.

Goldwater, Barry. 1990. *The Conscience of a Conservative*. Washington, DC: Regnery.

Goodman, John C. 1980. *The Regulation of Medical Care: Is the Price Too High?* Washington, D.C.: Cato Institute.

Goodman, Walter. 1969. *The Committee: The Extraordinary Career of the House Committee on UnAmerican Affairs*. Baltimore, MD: Farrar, Straus, and Giroux.

Goodwin, Doris Kearns. 1995. *No Ordinary Time: Franklin and Eleanor Roosevelt: The Home Front During World War II*. New York: Touchstone.

Gordon, Robert Aaron. 1974. *Economic Instability and Growth: the American Record*. New York: Harper and Row.

Gould, Lewis L. 1973. *Progressives and Prohibitionists: Texas Democrats in the Wilson Era*. Austin: University of Texas Press.

_____. 2003. *Grand Old Party: A History of Republicans*. New York: Random House.

Grant, Madison. 1970. *The Passing of the Great Race, or, the Racial Basis of European History*: Manchester, NH: Ayer.

Greene, John Robert. 1995. *The Presidency of Gerald R. Ford*. Lawrence: University of Kansas Press.

_____. 2000. *The Presidency of George Bush*. Lawrence, KS: University Press of Kansas.

Greenstein, Robert. 2004. "What the Trustees' Report Indicates About the Financial Status of Social Security. *Center on Budget and Policy Priorities*. March 31.

Greenstein, Robert, and Edwin Park. 2003. "Health Savings Accounts in Final Medicare Conference Agreement Pose Threats Both to Long-Term Fiscal Policy and to the Employer-Based Health Insurance System." *Center on Budget and Policy Priorities*. December 1.

Greenstein, Robert, and Peter Orszag. 2004. "Misleading Claims About New Social Security and Medicare Projections." *Center on Budget and Policy Priorities*. April 2.

Griffith, Robert. 1970, 1987. *The Politics of Fear: Joseph McCarthy and the Senate*. Boston: University of Massachusetts Press.

Grunhut, M. *Penal Reform*. 1948. London: Oxford University Press.

Haas, Ben. 1963. *KKK: The Hooded Face of Vengeance*. Evanston, IL: Regency.

Hamby, Alonso. 1973. *Beyond the New Deal*. New York: St. Martin's Press.

Hardball with Chris Matthews. 1998. August 11.

Harper's. 1988. "Hearing Nothing, Saying Nothing." February, 46-56.

Harris, James F. 2005. *The Survivor: Clinton in the White House*. New York: Random House.

Harwood, Richard. 1974. *Did Six Million Really Die? The Truth at Last*. Uckfield, East Sussex, U.K.: Historical Review Press.

Hasenfeld, Y., and J. Rafferty. 1989. "The Determinants of Public Attitudes Toward the Welfare State." *Social Forces*. 67.

Hatfield, J.H. *Fortunate Son*. 2000. New York: Soft Skull Press.

Hauss, Charles. 1997. *Comparative Politics: Domestic Responses to Global Challenges*. Second Edition. St. Paul, MN: West Publishing.

Hayek, Friedrich Von.1944. *The Road to Serfdom*. Chicago: University of Chicago Press.

Hayward, Steven F. 2001. *The Age of Reagan: The Fall of the Old Liberal Order, 1964-1980*. Roseville, CA: Primus.

Heclo, Hugh. 1994. "Poverty in Politics." In S. Danziger, G.D. Sandefur, and D. Weinberg Eds. *Confronting Poverty: Prescriptions for Change*. Cambridge, MA: Harvard University Press.

Henly, Julia R., and Sandra K. Danziger. 1996. "Confronting Welfare Stereotypes: Characteristics of General Assistance Recipients and Postassistance Employment." *Social Work Research*. December 20.

Herrnstein, Richard J. and Charles Murray. 1996. *The Bell Curve: Intelligence and Class Structure in American Life*. New York: Touchstone.

Herring, George C. 2001. *America's Longest War: The United States and Vietnam 1950-1975*. Fourth Edition. Boston: McGraw-Hill.

Hersh. Seymour M. 1987. "Target Qaddafi." *New York Times Magazine*. February 22.

Hertzke, Allen. 1993. *Echoes of Discontent: Jesse Jackson, Pat Robertson, and the Resurgence of Populism*. Washington, DC: CQ Press.

Hess, Karl. *Community Technology*. New York: Harper and Row, 1979.

Higham, John. *Strangers in the Land*. New Brunswick, NJ: Rutgers University Press, 1955.

Hiro, Dilip. *Iraq: In the Eye of the Storm*. New York: Nation Books, 2002.

Hoffman, Bruce. "Holy Terror: The Implications of Terrorism Motivated by a Religious Imperative." *Studies in Conflict and Terrorism*. 18: 271-284, 1995.

Hoffman, Peter, and Barbara Stone-Meierhoefer. "Post-Release Arrest Experiences of Federal Prisoners: A Six Year Follow-Up." *Journal of Criminal Justice*. 7, 1979.

Hofstadter, Richard. The *Paranoid Style in American Politics*. New York: Alfred A. Knopf, 1965.

_____. *Anti-Intellectualism in American Life*. New York: Vintage, 1962.

Hoover, Herbert. *Addresses from the American Road*. New York: American Libraries Press, 1941, 1972.

Hoover, Kenneth. *Ideology and Political Life*. Second Edition. Belmont, CA: Wadsworth, 1994.

Howe, Daniel Walker. 1979. *The Political Culture of the American Whigs*. Chicago, IL: University of Chicago Press.

Hull, Robert R. 1932. "Regarding Klan Agitators," in Michael Williams ed., *The Shadow of the Pope*. New York: McGraw-Hill, 1932.

Huntington, Samuel. 1957. "Conservatism as an Ideology." *American Political Science Review*. Volume 51, 454-473.

Hyman, Herbert H. *Political Socialization*. 1959. Glencoe: The Free Press.

Ingersoll, David E., Richard K. Matthews and Andrew Davison. 2001. *The Philosophic Roots of Modern Ideology*. Upper Saddle River, New Jersey: Prentice-Hall.

Interpol. *International Crime Statistics*. 2001. March.

Irons, Peter. 2000. *A People's History of the Supreme Court*. New York: Penguin.

Ives, Joseph Moss. 1969. *The Beginnings of Civil and Religious Liberties in America.* Lanham, MD: Rowman and Littlefield.

Ivins, Molly, and Lou Dubose. 2002. *Shrub: The Short but Happy Political Life of George W. Bush.* New York: Vintage.

Jackson, Kenneth T. 1967. The *Ku Klux Klan in the City, 1915-1930.* New York: Oxford University Press.

Jacoby, Susan. 2004. *Freethinkers: A History of American Secularism.* New York: Henry Holt.

James, Clayton. 1975. *The Years of MacArthur 1941-1945.* Boston: Houghton Mifflin.

Janda, Kenneth, Jeffrey M. Berry, and Jerry Goldman. 1992. *The Challenge of Democracy: Government in America.* Third Edition. Boston, Houghton Mifflin.

Janowitz, Morris. 1951. "Black Legions on the March," in Daniel Aaron, ed., *America in Crisis.* New York: Knopf.

Johnstone, Ronald L. 1992. *Religion in Society: A Sociology of Religion.* Fourth Edition. Englewood Cliffs, NJ: Prentice Hall.

Jones, Howard. 1996. *Quest for Security: A History of U.S. Foreign Relations.* New York: McGraw-Hil.

_____. 2001. *Crucible of Power: A History of American Foreign Relations from 1897.* Wilmington, Delaware: SR Books.

Justice Assistance News. 1981. Washington, D.C.: U.S. Department of Justice, November 2.

Karger, Jacob, and David Stoesz. 1998. *American Social Welfare Policy.* New York: Longman.

Katz, M. *The Underserving Poor.* 1989. New York: Pantheon.

Keller, Morton. 1977. *Affairs of State: Public Life in Late Nineteenth Century America.* New York: Lawbook Exchange.

Kellstedt, Lyman A., and Corwin E. Smidt. 1993. "Doctrinal Beliefs and Political Behavior: Views of the Bible." In David C. Leege and Lyman A. Kellstedt Eds. *Rediscovering the Religious Factor in American Politics.* Armonk, NY: M.E. Sharpe.

Kellstedt, Lyman A., and John C. Green. 1993. "Knowing God's Many People: Denominational Preference and Political Behavior." In David C. Leege and Lyman A. Kellstedt eds. *Rediscovering the Religious Factor in American Politics.* Armonk, NY: M.E. Sharpe.

Kemmerer, Donald L. 1940. *Path to Freedom: The Struggle for Self-Government in Colonial New Jersey, 1703-1776.* Princeton: Princeton University Press.

Kemper, Vicki, and Viveca Novak. 1992. *Common Cause Magazine.* January-March.

Keohane, Robert, and Joseph S. Nye. 1989. *Power and Interdependence.* Cambridge, MA: Harper-Collins.

Kinsey, Alfred. 1948, 1998. *Sexual Behavior in the Human Male.* Bloomington, IN: Indiana University Press.

Kinzer, Donald L. 1964. *An Episode in Anti-Catholicism.* Seattle: University of Washington Press.

Kirk, Russell. 1982. "Libertarians: Chirping Sectaries." *The Heritage Lectures: Proclaiming a Patrimony.* Washington, D.C.: The Heritage Foundation.

Kneese, Allen V., and Charles L. Schultze. 1975. *Pollution, Prices, and Public Policy.* Washington, D.C.: Brookings Institution.

Koch, G. Adolf. 1933. *Republican Religion: The American Revolution and the Cult of Reason.* New York: Henry Holt.

Koh, Harold Hongju. 2003. "Rights to Remember." *The Economist.* November 1.

Kohlberg, Alfred. 1948. "China Via Stilwell Road." *The China Monthly.* October.

Koon, Richard L. 1997. *Welfare Reform: Helping the Least Fortunate Become Less Dependent.* New York: Garland.

Koop, C. Everett. 1991. *Koop: The Memoirs of America's Family Doctor.* New York: Random House.

Kosterlitz, Julie. 1994. "Itching for a Fight?" *National Journal.* January 15.

Kraft, Michael E., and Norman J. Vig. 2000. "Environmental Policy from the 1970s to 2000: An Overview." In Kraft and Vig, Eds. *Environmental Policy.* 4th Edition. Washington, D.C.: Congressional Quarterly Press.

Kramer, Heinrich, and James Sprenger. 1971. *The Malleus Maleficarum.* New York: Dover Publications.

Kristol, Irving. *Two Cheers for Capitalism.* 1983. New York: New American Library.

Kupperman, Karen, Ed. 1988. *Captain John Smith. A Selected Edition of His Writings.* Chapel Hill, NC: University of North Carolina Press.

Kutler, Stanley. 1997. *Abuse of Power: The New Nixon Tapes.* New York: Free Press.

_____. 1990. *The Wars of Watergate: The Last Crisis of Richard Nixon.* New York: Alfred A. Knopf.

Labaree, Leonard Woods. 1948. *Conservatism in Early American History.* Ithaca, NY: Great Seal Books.

_____. 1935. *Royal Instructions to British Colonial Governors, 1670-1776.* New York: D. Appleton-Century.

LaHaye, Tim. 1980. *The Battle for the Mind.* Old Tappan, NJ: Fleming H. Revell Co.

Lane, Robert E. 1959. *Political Life.* Glencoe, New York: The Free Press.

Lasswell, Harold. 1958. *Politics: Who Gets What, When, How.* New York: Meridian Books.

Lav, I.J., E. Lazere, R. Greenstein, and S. Gold. 1992. "The States and the Poor: How Budget Decisions Affected Low Income People in 1992." Washington, D.C.: Center on Budget and Policy Priorities.

Lence, Ross M., ed. 1995. *Union and Liberty: The Political Philosophy of John C. Calhoun.* Indianapolis, IN: Liberty Fund.

Levine, Lawrence W. 1965, 1987. *Defender of the Faith: William Jennings Bryan. The Last Decade, 1915-1925.* Cambridge, MA: Harvard University Press.

Levington, John. 1870. *Origin of the Masonic Conspiracy.* Dayton, OH: United Brethren Publishing.

Levy, Leonard. 1993. "The Framers and Original Intent." In George M. McKenna and Stanley Feingold eds. *Taking Sides:Clashing Views on Controversial Political Issues.* Eighth Edition. Guilford, CT: Dushkin.

Lincoln, Charles Henry. 1968. *The Revolutionary Movement in Pennsylvania, 1770-1776.* Philadelphia: University of Pennsylvania.

Lindorff, David, 2004. *This Can't Be Happening!: Resisting the Disintegration of American Democracy.* Monroe, ME: Common Courage Press.

Lindsay, James. 2003. "Apathy and Interest: The American Public Rediscovers Foreign Policy After September 11th." In James M. Lindsay Ed., *American Politics After September 11th.* Cincinnati, OH: Atomic Dog.

Lindsay, James. 2003. "Chronology of America's War on Terrorism." In James M. Lindsay Ed., *American Politics After September 11th.* Cincinnati, OH: Atomic Dog.

Linebery, Robert L., George C.C. Edwards, and Martin P. Wattenberg. 1993. *Government in America. People, Politics, and Policy.* Sixth Edition. Englewood Cliffs, NJ: Prentice-Hall.

Lippman, Walter. 1937, 2004. *The Good Society.* Piscataway, NJ: Transaction Publishers.

Lipset, Seymour Martin. 1967. *Political Man.* Garden City, NY: Doubleday.
_____. 1967. *The First New Nation.* Garden City, NY: Doubleday.

Lipset, Seymour Martin, and Earl Raab. 1970. *The Politics of Unreason: Right-Wing Extremism in America, 1790-1970.* New York: Harper and Row, 1970.

Lippy, Charles H. 1981. *Seasonable Revolutionary: The Mind of Charles Chauncy.* Chicago: Nelson-Hall.

Loconte, Joe. 1998. "I'll Stand Bayou." *Policy Review.* May/June.

London Observer. 2003. January 26.

Los Angeles Times. 1988. July 20.

_____. 1989, May 21.

Loucks, Emerson. 1936. *The Ku Klux Klan in Pennsylvania.* Harrisburg: Telegraph Press.

Lynch, James. 1995. "Crime in International Perspective." In James Q. Wilson and Joan Petersilia Eds. *Crime.* San Francisco: Institute for Contemporary Studies.

MacArthur, Douglas. 1964, 1985. *Reminiscences.* New York: Perseus.

Machan, Tibor. 1974. *The Libertarian Alternative.* Chicago: Nelson Hall.

Madison, James. "The Federalist No. 51." In Edward Mead Earle, ed., *The Federalist.* New York: Modern Library College Editions, 1987.

Manchester, William. 1983. *The Last Lion: Winston Spencer Churchill.* Boston: Little, Brown.

Manning, D.J. *Liberalism.* 1976. New York: St. Martin's.

Mark, Irving. 1940. *Agrarian Conflicts in Colonial New York, 1711-1715.* New York: Columbia University Press.

Martin, William. 1996. *With God on Our Side: The Rise of the Religious Right in America.* New York: Broadway Books.

Martinson, Robert. 1974. "What Works? Questions and Answers about Prison Reform." *Public Interest.* 35 Spring.

Marx, Karl. 1992. *Capital: A Critique of Political Economy.* New York: Penquin.

Mather, Cotton. 1999. *Wonders of the Invisible World.* Temecula, CA: Reprint Services.

Matriciana, Patrick. 1995. *The Clinton Chronicles.* Hemet, CA: Jeremiah Films.

Maxwell, William, and Ernest Crain. 1995. *Texas Politics Today.* Seventh Edition. Belmont, CA: West Publishing.

_____. 2003. *Texas Politics Today.* Tenth Edition. Belmont, CA: Wadsworth.

_____. 2003. *Texas Politics Today.* Eleventh Edition. Belmont, CA: Wadsworth.

Mayer, George H. 1967. *The Republican Party 1854-1966.* New York: Oxford University Press.

_____. 1973. "The Republican Party, 1932-1952." In Arthur M. Schlesinger, Jr. ed., *History of U.S. Political Parties.* Volume 4.

Mayer, Jeremy D. 2002. *Running on Ralce: Racial Politics in Presidential Campaigns, 1960-2000.* New York: Random House.

McCollough, David. 2001. *John Adams.* New York: Simon and Schuster.

McCord, James. 1974. *A Piece of Tape. The Watergate Story: Fact and Fiction.* Rockville, MD: McCord Publications.

McCoy, Donald R. 1990. *Calvin Coolidge: The Quiet President.* Lawrence, KS: University of Kansas Press.

McKee, Thomas, ed. 2004. *The National Platform of All Political Parties*. Washington, D.C.: Library Reprints.

McKinlay, John B., and Sonja M. McKinlay. 1980. "The Questionable Contribution of Medical Measures to the Decline of Mortality in the United States in the Twentieth Century." In Stephen J. Williams Ed. *Issues in Health Services*. New York: Wiley and Sons.

McLoughlin, William G. *Billy Sunday Was His Real Name*. 1955. Chicago: University of Chicago Press.

McQueen, Michel. 1991. "Voters, Sick of Current Health-Care System, Want Federal Government to Prescribe Remedy." *Wall Street Journal*. June 28.

Mecklin, John M. 1924. *The Ku Klux Klan: A Study of the American Mind*. New York: Harcourt Brace.

Mencken, H.L. 1996. *A Carnival of Buncombe*. New York: John Hopkins University Press.

Mezey, Jennifer. 2004. Sharon Parrott, Mark Greenberg, and Shawn Fremstad. "Reversing Direction on Welfare Reform: President's Budget Cuts Child Care for More than 300,000 Children." *Center on Budget and Policy Priorities*. February 10.

Micklethwait, John, and Adrian Wooldridge. 2004. *The Right Nation: Conservative Power in America*. New York: Penguin Press.

Miles, Michael. 1980. *The Odyssey of the American Right*. New York, Oxford: Oxford University Press.

Miller, Mark Crispin. 2000. *The Bush Dyslexicon: Observations on a National Disorder*. New York: Norton.

Miller, Perry, and Thomas H. Johnson, Eds. 1968. *The Puritans: A Sourcebook of their Writings Volume II*. New York: Harper.

Miller, Judith, and Laurie Mylroie, 1990. *Saddam Hussein and the Crisis in the Gulf*. New York: Times Books.

Miller, Mark Crispin. *The Bush Dyslexicon: Observations on a National Disorder*. New York: Norton, 2000.

Miner, Brad. *The Concise Conservative Encyclopedia*. 1996. New York: Simon and Schuster.

Mitchell, Robert. 1979. *Calvin's and the Puritans' View of the Protestant Ethic*. Lanham, MD: University Press of America.

Moore, Michael. 2001. *Stupid White Men*. New York: HarperCollins.

_____. 2004. *Dude, Where's My Country*. New York: Warner Books.

Morgan, H. Wayne. 1969. *From Hayes to McKinley: National Party Politics, 1877-1896*. Syracuse, NY: Syracuse University Press.

Morgenstern, George. 1947, 1987. *Pearl Harbor: The Story of the Secret War*. New York: Institute for Historical Review.

460   Bibliography

Morris, Dick. 1997. *Behind the Oval Office: Winning the Presidency in the Nineties.* New York: Random House.

Morris, Edmund. 2001. *Theodore Rex.* New York: Random House.

Mosse, George. 1964. *The Crisis of German Ideology: Intellectual Origins of the Third Reich.* New York: Grosset and Dunlap.

Muccigrosso, Robert. 2001. *Basic History of Conservatism.* Melbourne, FL: Krieger.

Muller, Jerry Z. 1987. *The Other God that Failed: Hans Freyer and the Deradicalization of German Conservatism.* Princeton, NJ: Princeton University Press.

Muller, Jerry Z. 1997. *Conservatism: An Anthology of Social and Political Thought from David Hume to the present.* Princeton, NJ: Princeton University Press.

Murphy, Francis. 1981. "Introduction." In Bradford, William, *Of Plymouth Plantation 1620-1647.* New York: Random House.

Murray, Charles. 1986. *Losing Ground.* New York: Basic Books.

Murray, Robert. 1955. *Red Scare: A Study in National Hysteria, 1919-1920.* Minneapolis, MN: University of Minnesota Press.

Murrin, John M. 1990. "Religion and Politics in America from the First Settlements to the Civil War," in Mark A. Noll, ed., *Religion and American Politics: From the Colonial Period to the 1980s.* New York: Oxford University Press.

Murrin, John R., Paul E. Johnson, James M. McPherson, Gary Gerstle, Emily S. Rosenberg, and Norman L. Rosenberg. 1996. *Liberty, Equality, Power: A History of the American People.* Fort Worth: Harcourt Brace.

Mussolini, Benito. 1963. "The Doctrine of Fascism," in John Somerville and Ronald E. Santoni, eds. *Social and Political Philosophy.* Garden City, NY: Doubleday.

Nagle, Robert. 1988. *American Conservatism: An Illustrated History.* New York: Allied Books.

Nakane, Chie. 1986. *Japanese Society.* Berkeley, CA: University of California Press.

Nash, Gary B., 1998. Julie Roy Jeffrey, John R. Howe, Peter J. Frederick, Allen F. Davis, and Allan M. Winkler. *The American People: Creating a Nation and a Society.* Fourth Edition. New York: Longman.

_____. 2004. *The American People: Creating a Nation and a Society.* Sixth Edition. New York: Longman.

National Women's Political Caucus. 1987. May 26.

Natural Resource Defense Council. 2002. "Rewriting the Rules: The Bush Administration's Assault on the Environment." April 22.

New York Post. 1990. March 17.

New York Times. 1941. August 6.

_____. 1953. August 6.

_____. 1968. September 3, 38.

_____. 1986. "Identify All the Carriers." March 18, A7.

_____. 1993. June 24.

_____. 1993. "Clinton Plan Alive Upon Arrival." October 3, 1993.

_____. 2002. February 4.

_____. 2002. February 24.

_____. 2002. February 28.

_____. 2002. March 22.

_____. 2003. February 9.

_____. 2003. June 16.

Newsweek. 1968. September 16, 27.

Nichols. Roy F. 1962. *The Disruption of American Democracy.* New York: Collier.

Nietzsche, Friedrich. 1969. *Thus Spake Zarathustra.* New York: Penguin.

Nixon, Richard. 1979. *RN: The Memoirs.* New York: Warner Books.

Nock, Albert J. 1931. *The Theory of Education in the United States.* New York, Arno Press.

_____, *Our Enemy the State.* 1936, 1972. New York: Arno Press.

Noggle, Burl. 1962. *Teapot Dome: Oil and Politics in the 1920s.* New York: Norton.

Northwest Arkansas Times. 1998. "Human Dignity Resolution Fails." November 4.

Novak, Robert. 1965. *The Agony of the G.O.P. 1964.* New York: Macmillan.

Nozick, Robert. 1974. *Anarchy, State, and Utopia.* New York: Basic Books.

NYPost.com/millenium/mill. 2003.

Observer. 1987. September 29.

O'Reilly, Kenneth. 1995. *Nixon's Piano: Presidents and Racial Politics from Washington to Clinton.* New York: Free Press.

O'Sullivan, John, and Edward F. Keuchel. 1989. *American Economic History: From Abundance to Constraint.* New York: Markus Wiener.

Pach, Chester J., and Elmo Richardson. 1991. *The Presidency of Dwight D. Eisenhower.* Lawrence: University Press of Kansas.

Packer, H. 1968. *The Limits of Criminal Sanction.* Palo Alto, CA: Stanford University Press.

Palmer, Robert. 1964. *The Age of the Democratic Revolution: The Struggle.* Princeton, NJ: Princeton University Press.

Palumbo, Dennis J. 1994. *Public Policy in America: Government in Action.* Second Edition. Fort Worth: Harcourt Brace.

Paine, Thomas. 1776, 1997. *Common Sense.* Dover, DE: Dover Publications.

Paniccia, Domonic. 1996. "The Environmental Movement." In Theodore and
    Theodore Eds. *Major Environmental Issues Facing the 21ˢᵗ Century.*
    Upper Saddle River, NJ: Prentice-Hall.
Park, Edwin, and Robert Greenstein. 2003. "The AARP Ads and the New
    Medicare Prescription Drug Law." *Center on Budget and Policy
    Priorities.* December 11.
Park, Edwin, Melanie Nathanson, Robert Greenstein, and John Springer.
    2003. "The Troubling Medicare Legislation." *Center on Budget and
    Policy Priorities.* December 8.
Parmet, Herbert S. 1997. *George Bush: The Life of a Lone Star Yankee.* New
    York: Scribner.
People For the American Way Foundation. 2000. "Anti-Gay Politics and the
    Religious Right." Washington, D.C.: *People for the American Way.*
Perdue, Theda, and Michael Green. 2005. *The Cherokee Removal: A Brief
    History with Documents.* Second Edition. Boston: Bedford/St. Martin's
Perlstein, Rick. 2001. *Before the Storm: Barry Goldwater and the Unmaking
    of the American Consensus.* New York: Hill and Wang.
Petersilia, Joan, Susan Turner, James Kahan, and Joyce Peterson. 1985.
    Granting Felons Probation: Public Risks and Alternatives. Santa
    Monica Ca: Rand Corporation.
Pfiffner, James P. 2004. "Assessing the Bush Presidency" in Gregg, Gary,
    and Mark J. Rozell. *Considering the Bush Presidency.* New York:
    Oxford University Press.
_____. 2005. "National Security Policymaking and the Bush War Cabinet,"
    in Richard S. Conley ed., *Transforming the American Polity: The
    Presidency of George W. Bush and the War on Terrorism.* Upper Saddle
    River, NJ: Pearson Education.
Phelps, Timothy M. 1992. *Capitol Games: Clarence Thomas, Anita Hill, and
    the Behind-the-Scenes Story of a Supreme Court Nomination.* New
    York: Hyperion.
Phillips, Kevin. 1969. *The Emerging Republican Majority.* New Rochelle,
    NY: Arlington House.
_____. 2004. *American Dynasty. Aristocracy, Fortune, and the Politics of
    Deceit in the House of Bush.* New York: Viking Penguin.
Poliakov, Leon. 1974. *The Aryan Myth.* New York: New American Library.
Pollack, Andrew. 1991. "Medical Technology Arms Race Adds Billions to
    the Nation's Bill. *New York Times.* April 29.
Porter, Kirk H. and Donald Bruce Johnson, eds. 1972. *National Party
    Platforms 1840-1968.* Urbana, IL: University of Illinois Press.
Powell, Colin, and Joseph E. Perisco. 1995. *My American Journey.* New
    York: Random House.

Preston, William. 1963. *Aliens and Dissenters: Federal Suppression of Radicals, 1903-1933*. Cambridge: Harvard University Press.

Quinton, Anthony. 1978. *The Politics of Imperfection: The Religious and Secular Traditions of Conservative Thought in England from Hooker to Oakeshott*. London: Routledge.

Rand, Ayn. 1961. *The Virtue of Selfishness*. New York: New American Library.

_____. 1962. *Conservatism: an Obituary*.

_____. 1966. *Capitalism: The Unknown Ideal*. New York: Signet Books.

Randel, William Pierce. 1965. *The Ku Klux Klan*. Philadelphia, PA: Chilton.

Rankin, Robert, and David Hess. 1994. "Reinventing Welfare." *Wisconsin State Journal*.

Reagan, Michael. 1992. *Curing the Crisis: Options for America's Health Care*. Boulder, CO: Westview Press.

Regan, Donald. 1988. *For the Record: From Wall Street to Washington*. San Diego: Harcourt Brace Jovanovich.

Reinhardt, Uwe. 1989. "Book Review of Rosemary Stevens, *In Sickness and in Wealth*." *New York Times*. August 20.

Rhodes, Steven. 1980. *Valuing Life: Public Policy Dilemmas*. Boulder, CO: Westview Press.

Rice, Arnold. 1962. *The Ku Klux Klan in American Politics*. Washington, D.C.: Public Affairs Press.

Rice, Condoleeza. 2000. "Promoting the National Interest." *Foreign Affairs*. January-February.

Roark, James L., Michael P. Johnson, Patricia Cline Cohen, Sarah Stage, Alan Lawson, and Susan M. Hartmann. 2005. *The American Promise: A History of the United States Volume II*. Third Edition. Bedford/St. Martin's.

Rokeach, Milton. 1972. *The Open and Closed Mind: Investigations into the Nature of Belief Systems and Personality Systems*. New York: Basic Books.

Roosevelt, Theodore. 1904, 1954. "Letter to George Otto Trevelyan, " in Elting E. Morison, ed., *The Letters of Theodore Roosevelt*. Cambridge, MA: Harvard Univeristy Press.

Rosenman, Samuel I. ed. 1938. The *Public Papers and Addresses of Franklin D. Roosevelt*. New York: Random House.

Rosengren, William R. 1980. *Sociology of Medicine: Diversity, Conflict and Change*. New York: Harper and Row.

Rosenthal, Elisabeth. 1994. "Health Problems of Inner City Poor Reach Crisis Point." *New York Times*. December 24.

Rossiter, Clinton. 1982. *Conservatism in America.* Second Edition. Cambridge, MA: Harvard University Press.

Roy, Ralph. 1953. *Aposteles of Discord*. Boston: Beacon Press, 1953.

Rothbard, Murray. 1975. *America's Great Depression*. New York: New York University Press.

Rutland, Robert Allen. 1983. *The Ordeal of the Constitution: The Anti-Federalists and the Ratification Struggle*. Boston, MA: Northeastern University Press.

Sale, K. *The Green Revolution*. 1993. New York: Hill and Wang.

Sanders, Bernard. 1997. "What's Really Going on with the Economy." *USA Today Magazine*. March.

Sargent, Lyman Tower, 1993. *Contemporary Political Ideologies: A Comparative Analysis*, Ninth edition. Belmont, CA: Wadsworth.

Saunders, William L. Ed. 1999. *The Colonial Records of North Carolina*. Temecula CA: Reprint Services Corporation.

Schaeffer, Eric. 2002. "Clearing the Air: Why I Quit Bush's EPA." *Washington Monthly*. July/August.

Schaeffer, Francis, and C. Everett Koop. 1979. *Whatever Happened to the Human Race?* Grand Rapids, MI: Baker Publishing.

Schaller, Michael, and George Rising. 2002. *Republican Ascendancy: The Republican Party in Power Since the 1960s*. Wheeling, IL: Harlan Davidson.

Schlesinger, Arthur M. Sr. 1993. *The Colonial Merchants and the American Revolution, 1763-1776*. Temecula, CA: Reprint Services Corporation.

Schneider, Carol, and Herbert C. Schneider Ed. 2002. *Samuel Johnson: His Career and Writings, 1929 Edition*. Bristol, UK: Thoemmes Press.

Schudson, Michael. 2000. "America's Ignorant Voters." *The Wilson Quarterly*. Spring, 16-22.

Schumaker, Paul, Dwight C. Kiel, and Thomas Heilke. 1996. *Great Ideas/Grand Scheme*. New York: McGraw-Hill.

_____. 1997. *Ideological Voices: An Anthology in Modern Political Ideas*. New York: McGraw-Hill.

Schwartz, William B. 1992. "Do Advancing Medical Technologies Drive Up the Cost of Health Care?" *Priorities*, Fall, 26-28.

Serafini, Marilyn Werber. 2000. "Welfare Reform, Act 2." *National Journal*. June.

Shabecroff, Philip. 1993. *A Fierce Green Fire*. New York: Hill and Wang.

Shapiro, Isaac, and Joel Friedman. 2004. "Tax Returns: A Comprehensive Assessment of the Bush Administration's Record on Cutting Taxes." *Center on Budget and Policy Priorities*. April 23.

Sheehy, Gail. 2000. "The Accidental Candidate." *Vanity Fair*, October.

Shepard, Charles. 1989. *Forgiven: The Rise and Fall of Jim Bakker and the PTL Ministry*. Boston: Atlantic Monthly Press.

Sherrill, Robert. 1968. *Gothic Politics in the Deep South*. New York: Grossman.

Shriver, Peggy. *The Bible Vote*. 1981. New York: Pilgrim Press.

Siegel, Larry J. 1989. *Criminology*. Third Edition. St. Paul, MN: West Publishing.

Silbey, Joel H. 1977. *A Respectable Minority: The Democratic Party in the Civil War Era*. New York: W. W. Norton.

Sinclair, Upton. 1906, 2003. *The Jungle*. New York: See Sharp Press.

Singer, J.L., and D. G. Singer. 1981. *Television, Imagination and Aggression: A Study of Preschoolers*. Hillsdale, NJ: Erlbaum.

Sizer, Mona D. 2002. *Texas Politicians: Good 'n' Bad*. Plano, TX: Republic of Texas Press.

Skidmore, Max. 1993. *Ideologies: Politics in Action*. Second Edition. Fort Worth, TX: Harcourt Brace.

Skocpol, Theda. 1992. *Protecting Soldiers and Mothers*. Cambridge, MA: Harvard Univeristy Press.

Sloan, John Henry. 1998. "Handgun Regulations, Crime, Assaults, and Homicide." *The New England Journal of Medicine*. November 10.

Sloan, William David, James G. Stovall and James Startt. 1993. *The Media in America: A History*. Upper Saddle River, NJ: Gorsuch Scarisbrick.

Small, Melvin. 1999. *The Presidency of Richard Nixon*. Lawrence, KS: Univeristy Press of Kansas.

Smith, Adam. 1776, 1991. *Wealth of Nations*. Amherst, NY: Prometheus Books.

Smith, B.D. and J.J. Vetter. 1982. *Theoretical Approaches to Personality*. Englewood Cliffs, NJ: Prentice-Hall.

Smith, James M. 1966. *The Alien and Sedition Laws and American Civil Liberties*. New York: Cornell University Press.

Somerville, John, and Ronald Santoni. 1963. *Social and Political Philosophy: Readings from Plato to Gandhi*. New York: Anchor.

Sorel, G. 1969. *Reflexions on Violence*. Glencoe, IL: Free Press.

Specter, Michael. 1991. "Unhealthy Care for the Poor." *Washington Post National Weekly Edition*. July 15-21.

Spencer, Herbert. 1851. "The Survival of the Fittest," in *Social Statics*. New York: D. Appleton.

Spielvogel, Jackson J. 2004. *Hitler and Nazi Germany: A History*. Upper Saddle River, NJ: Pearson Prentice-Hall.

Squire, Peverill, James M. Lindsay, Cary R. Covington, and Eric R.A.N. Smith. 2001. *Dynamics of Democracy*. Third Edition. Cincinnati, OH: Atomic Dog.

Stanard, William G. and Mary N. Stanard. 1902. *The Colonial Virginia Register*. Albany, NY: Joel Munsell's Sons.

Stanfield, Rochelle. 1995. "The New Federalism." *National Journal*. January 28.

Star. 1992. January 29.

Starkey, Marion L. 1955. *A Little Rebellion*. New York: Alfred A. Knopf.

Steely, Mel. 2000. *The Gentleman from Georgia: The Biography of Newt Gingrich*. Macon, GA: Mercer University Press.

Steinbruner, John. 1974. *The Cybernetic Theory of Decision*. Princeton, NJ: Princeton University Press.

Sterling, Bryan B., ed. 1997. *The Best of Will Rogers*. New York: MJF Books.

Stillman, Richard J. 1991. *Preface to Public Administration: A Search for Themes and Direction*. New York: St. Martin's Press.

Stockman, David. 1987. *The Triumph of Politics*. New York: Random House.

Storey, John W. 1986. *Texas Baptist Leadership and Social Christianity, 1900-1980*. College Station, TX: Texas A&M University Press.

Strober, Jerry, and Ruth Tomczak. 1979. *Jerry Falwell: Aflame for God*. Nashville, TN: Thomas Nelson Publishing.

Suskind, Ron. 2004. *The Price of Loyalty: George W. Bush, the White House, and the Education of Paul O'Neill*. New York: Simon and Schuster.

Swoboda, Frank. 1990. "Major Firms, Unions Join National Health Insurance Bid." *Washington Post*. March 14.

Synon, John. 1970. *George Wallace: Profile of a Presidential Candidate*. Kilmarnock, VA: MS Inc.

Taft, Robert A. 1941. "The Future of the Republican Party." *The Nation*. December 13.

Taft, William H. 1916. *Our Chief Magistrate and His Powers*. New York: Columbia University Press.

Talk. 1999. September.

Territo, Leonard, James Halstead, and Max Bromley. 1989. *Crime and Justice in America*. St. Paul, MN: West Publishing.

Thomas, Benjamin Platt. 1952. *Abraham Lincoln: A Biography*. New York: Knopf, 1960.

Thompson, Frank J. 1981. *Health Policy and the Bureaucracy: Politics and Implementation*. Cambridge, MA: MIT Press.

Thompson, James J. Jr. 1982. *Tried as by Fire: Southern Baptists and the Religious Controversies of the 1920s*. Macon, GA: Mercer University Press.

Time. 1977. April 25, 89-90.

_____. 1987. October 19.

_____. 1980. July 28.

_____. 2000. February 21.

_____. 2001. October 22.

Tindall, George, and David Shi. 2000. *America: A Narrative History*. Brief Fifth Edition.

Tinder, Glen. 1989. *The Political Meaning of Christianity*. Baton Rouge, LA: Louisiana State University Press.

Toner, Robin. 1994. "Gold Rush Fever Grips Capital as Health Care Struggle Begins." *New York Times*. March 13.

Tracy, Joseph. 1997. *The Great Awakening. A History of the Revival of Religion in the Time of Edwards and Whitefield*. Carlisle, PA: Banner of Truth.

Tsai, Mark. 1948. "Now It Can Be Told." *The China Monthly*. September.

Tsou, Tang. 1967. *America's Failure in China*. Chicago: University of Chicago Press.

Tucille, Jerome. 1970. *Radical Libertarianism: A Right Wing Alternative*. New York: MacMillan.

Tull, Charles J. 1965. *Father Coughlin and the New Deal*. Syracuse: Syracuse University Press.

Tyrrell, R. Emmett. 1996. *Boy Clinton*. Chicago: Regnery.

Tweedie, Jack. 1998. "When Welfare Ends." *State Legislatures*. October/November.

United Nations. *Human Development Report 2003*. 2003. New York and Oxford: Oxford University Press.

United States Census Bureau. 1998. "The Official Statistics." U.S. Government Printing Office. Washington, D.C.: September 9.

United States Department of Energy. 1996. "OEPA Environmental Law Summary: Clean Air Act." *Office of Environmental Policy and Assistance*. Washington, D.C.: January 25.

United Stated Department of Health, Education, and Welfare. 1976. *Health in America 1776-1976*. Washington, D.C.: Government Printing Office.

United States Department of Justice. 2003. "Crime and Victims Statistics." Washington, D.C.: *Bureau of Justice Statistics*.

United Stated Department of Labor, 2005. Washington, D.C. *Bureau of Labor Statistics*.

United States General Accounting Office. 1983. "Waste Water Dischargers are Not Complying with EPA Pollution Control Permits." Washington, D.C.: *General Accounting Office*.

_____. 1996. "Water Pollution: Many Violators have not Received Appropriate Federal Attention." Washington, D.C.: *General Accounting Office*.

United States Office of Management and Budget. 1976. "Budget of the United States Government." Washington, D.C.: Government Printing Office.
_____. 1986. "Budget of the United States Government." Washington, D.C.: Government Printing Office.
_____. 1999. "Budget of the United States Government." Washington, D.C.: Government Printing Office.
USA Today. 2000. November 3.
U.S. News and World Report. 1964. April 20, 120.
Vachss, A.H., and Y.Bakal. 1979. *The Life-Style Violent Juvenile*. Lexington, MA: Lexington Press.
Von Hoffman, Nicholas. 1988. *Citizen Cohn*. New York: Bantam Dell.
Wall Street Journal. 1993. October 13.
_____. 1995. June 26,
Waltz, Kenneth. 1978. *Theory of International Politics*. New York: Random House.
Waltzman, Nancy. 1991. "Socialized Medicine Now-Without the Wait." *The Washington Monthly*. 23, 10 October.
Washington Monthly. 1995. September, 29-32.
Washington Post. 194. February 28.
_____. 2001. March 14.
_____. 2002. January 2002.
_____. 2002. June 6.
_____. 2003. February 26.
Washington Times. 1990. August 2.
Watts, John. 1928. *Letter Book of John Watts: Merchant and Councillor of New York*. New York: New York Historical Society.
Webb, George E. 1994. *The Evolution Controversy in America*. Lexington, KY: University Press of Kentucky.
Wechsler, William F. 2001. "Follow the Money." *Foreign Affairs*. July-August.
Weisberg, Jacob, 1996. *In Defense of Government: The Fall and Rise of Public Trust*. New York: Scribner.
Weisman, Steven R. 2002. *The Great Tax Wars*. New York: Simon and Schuster.
Welch, Michael R., David C. Leege, Kenneth D. Wald, and Lyman A. Kellstedt. 1993. "Are the Sheep Hearing the Shepherds? Cue Perceptions, Congregational Responses, and Political Communication Processes." In David C. Leege and Lyman A. Kellstedt Eds. *Rediscovering the Religious Factor in American Politics*. Armonk, NY: M.E. Sharpe.

Wells, Donald. 1996. *Environmental Policy*. Upper Saddle River, NJ: Prentice-Hall.

Westerfield, Bradford H. 1955. *Foreign Policy and Party Politics*. New Haven, CT: Yale University Press.

Wheeler, James O. and Peter O. Muller. 1986. *Economic Geography*. New York: John Wiley and Sons.

Wheless, Joseph. 1997. *Is it God's Word?* Kila MT: Kessinger.

White, Jonathan. 2001. *Terrorism: An Introduction*. Belmont, CA: Wadsworth.

White, Morton. 1956. *The Age of Analysis: The Twentieth Century Philosophers*. New York: Mentor.

White, William S. 1954. *The Taft Story*. New York: Harper and Row.

Wicker, Tom. 1967. "George Wallace: A Gross and Simple Heart. *Harper's*. April.

Widenor, William C. 1980. *Henry Cabot Lodge and the Search for an American Foreign Policy*. Berkeley, CA: University of California Press.

Williams, Michael. 1932. *The Shadow of the Pope*. New York: McGraw-Hill.

Wilson, James Q. 1983. *Thinking About Crime: A Policy Guide*. Second Edition. New York: Basic Books.

_____. 1995. "Crime and Public Policy." In James Q. Wilson and Joan Petersilia Eds. *Crime*. San Francisco: Institute for Contemporary Studies.

Wilson, James Q., and John DiIulio. 1995. *American Government*. 6th Edition. Lexington, MA: D.C. Heath.

Wincek, Henry. 2003. *Imperfect God: George Washington, His Slaves, and the Creation of America*. Baltimore, MD: Farrar, Strauss, and Giroux.

Wolfskill, George. 1974. *Revolt of the Conservatives*. Cambridge, MA: Greenwood.

Woods, Roger. 1989. "The Radical Right: The Conservative Revolutionaries in Germany." In Roger Eatwell and Noel O'Sullivan Editors, *The Nature of the Right*. Boston, MA: Twayne.

Woodward, Bob. 2002. *Bush at War*. New York: Simon and Schuster.

_____. 2004. *Plan of Attack*. New York: Simon and Schuster.

Woodward, Bob, and Carl Bernstein. 1976. *The Final Days*. New York: Simon and Schuster.

Woodward, C. Vann. 1963. *Tom Watson: Agrarian Rebel*. New York: Oxford University Press.

World Bank. 1998. *World Development Indicators*. Washington, D.C.: World Bank.

Wright, Louis B. 1970. *The First Gentlemen of Virginia: Intellectual Qualities of the Early Colonial Ruling Class*. Charlottesville, VA: University of Virginia Press.

www.boogieonline.com, 2005.

www.cviog.uga.edu/Projects/gainfo/manifesto.htm. 2005.

www.epa.gov/globalwarming/climate/index.html, 2005.

www.firearmsandliberty.com, 2005.

www.newamericancentury.org, 1997. January 3.

www.time.com/time/nation/article/0,8599,1103003,00.html

Yazawa, Melvin, ed. 1998. *Diary and Life of Samuel Sewall*. New York: St. Martin's Press.

Zastrow, Charles. 1996. *Social Work and Social Welfare*. Sixth Edition. Pacific Grove, CA: Brooks/Cole.